Honduras & the Bay Islands

Greg Benchwick

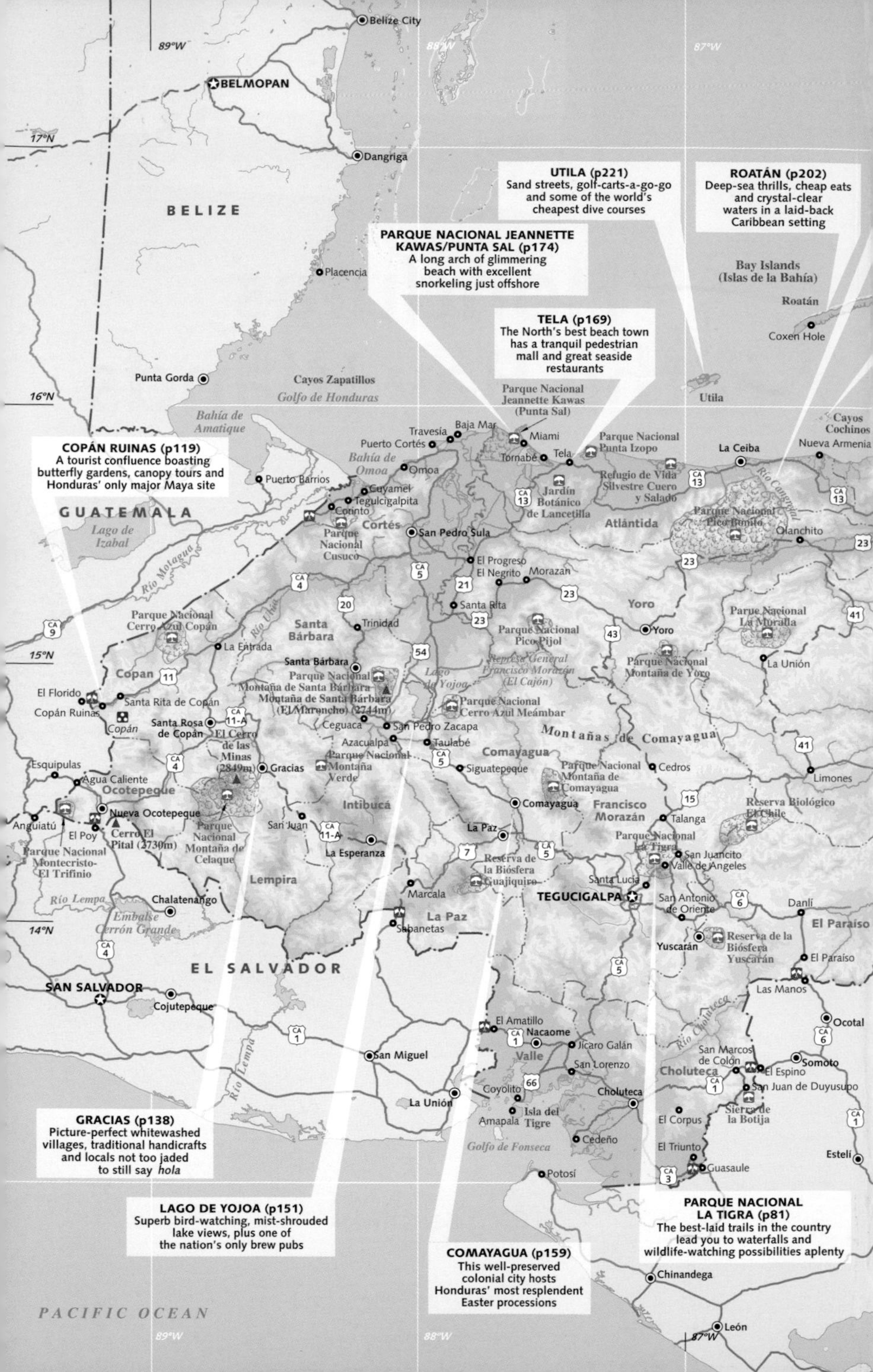

UTILA (p221)
Sand streets, golf-carts-a-go-go and some of the world's cheapest dive courses
ROATÁN (p202)
Deep-sea thrills, cheap eats and crystal-clear waters in a laid-back Caribbean setting
PARQUE NACIONAL JEANNETTE KAWAS/PUNTA SAL (p174)
A long arch of glimmering beach with excellent snorkeling just offshore
TELA (p169)
The North's best beach town has a tranquil pedestrian mall and great seaside restaurants
COPÁN RUINAS (p119)
A tourist confluence boasting butterfly gardens, canopy tours and Honduras' only major Maya site
GRACIAS (p138)
Picture-perfect whitewashed villages, traditional handicrafts and locals not too jaded to still say *hola*
LAGO DE YOJOA (p151)
Superb bird-watching, mist-shrouded lake views, plus one of the nation's only brew pubs
COMAYAGUA (p159)
This well-preserved colonial city hosts Honduras' most resplendent Easter processions
PARQUE NACIONAL LA TIGRA (p81)
The best-laid trails in the country lead you to waterfalls and wildlife-watching possibilities aplenty
BELIZE
GUATEMALA
EL SALVADOR
PACIFIC OCEAN
Belize City
BELMOPAN
Dangriga
Placencia
Punta Gorda
Cayos Zapatillos
Golfo de Honduras
Bahía de Amatique
Puerto Barrios
Lago de Izabal
Bay Islands (Islas de la Bahía)
Roatán
Coxen Hole
Utila
Cayos Cochinos
Nueva Armenia
La Ceiba
Parque Nacional Jeannette Kawas (Punta Sal)
Travesía
Baja Mar
Puerto Cortés
Miami
Tornabé
Tela
Parque Nacional Punta Izopo
Refugio de Vida Silvestre Cuero y Salado
Jardín Botánico de Lancetilla
Atlántida
Parque Nacional Pico Bonito
Olanchito
Bahía de Omoa
Omoa
Cuyamel
Tegulcigalpita
Corinto
Cortés
Parque Nacional Cusuco
San Pedro Sula
El Progreso
El Negrito
Morazán
Santa Rita
Yoro
Parque Nacional La Muralla
La Unión
Parque Nacional Pico Pijol
Represa General Francisco Morazán (El Cajón)
Parque Nacional Montaña de Yoro
Río Motagua
Río Ulúa
Río Cangrejal
Parque Nacional Cerro Azul Copán
La Entrada
Santa Bárbara
Trinidad
Parque Nacional Montaña de Santa Bárbara
Montaña de Santa Bárbara (El Marancho) (2744m)
Lago de Yojoa
Parque Nacional Cerro Azul Meámbar
Copan
El Florido
Santa Rita de Copán
Copán Ruinas
Copán
Santa Rosa de Copán
El Cerro de las Minas (2849m)
Ceguaca
San Pedro Zacapa
Azacualpa
Taulabé
Comayagua
Montañas de Comayagua
Cedros
Limones
Esquipulas
Agua Caliente
Ocotepeque
Gracias
Parque Nacional Montaña Verde
Siguatepeque
Parque Nacional Montaña de Comayagua
Reserva Biológico El Chile
Nueva Ocotepeque
Anguiatú
El Poy
Cerro El Pital (2730m)
Parque Nacional Montecristo-El Trifinio
Parque Nacional Montaña de Celaque
Intibucá
San Juan
La Esperanza
La Paz
Francisco Morazán
Talanga
Parque Nacional La Tigra
San Juancito
Valle de Ángeles
Reserva de la Biósfera Guajiquiro
Santa Lucía
TEGUCIGALPA
San Antonio de Oriente
Danlí
El Paraíso
Río Lempa
Chalatenango
Embalse Cerrón Grande
Lempira
Marcala
Sabanetas
Yuscarán
Reserva de la Biósfera Yuscarán
Las Manos
SAN SALVADOR
Cojutepeque
Ocotal
El Amatillo
Nacaome
Jícaro Galán
Valle
San Lorenzo
San Miguel
La Unión
Coyolito
Amapala
Isla del Tigre
Choluteca
Cedeño
Golfo de Fonseca
Río Choluteca
San Marcos de Colón
El Espino
Somoto
San Juan de Duyusupo
Sierra de la Botija
El Corpus
El Triunfo
Guasaule
Estelí
Potosí
Chinandega
León
89°W
88°W
87°W
17°N
16°N
15°N
14°N

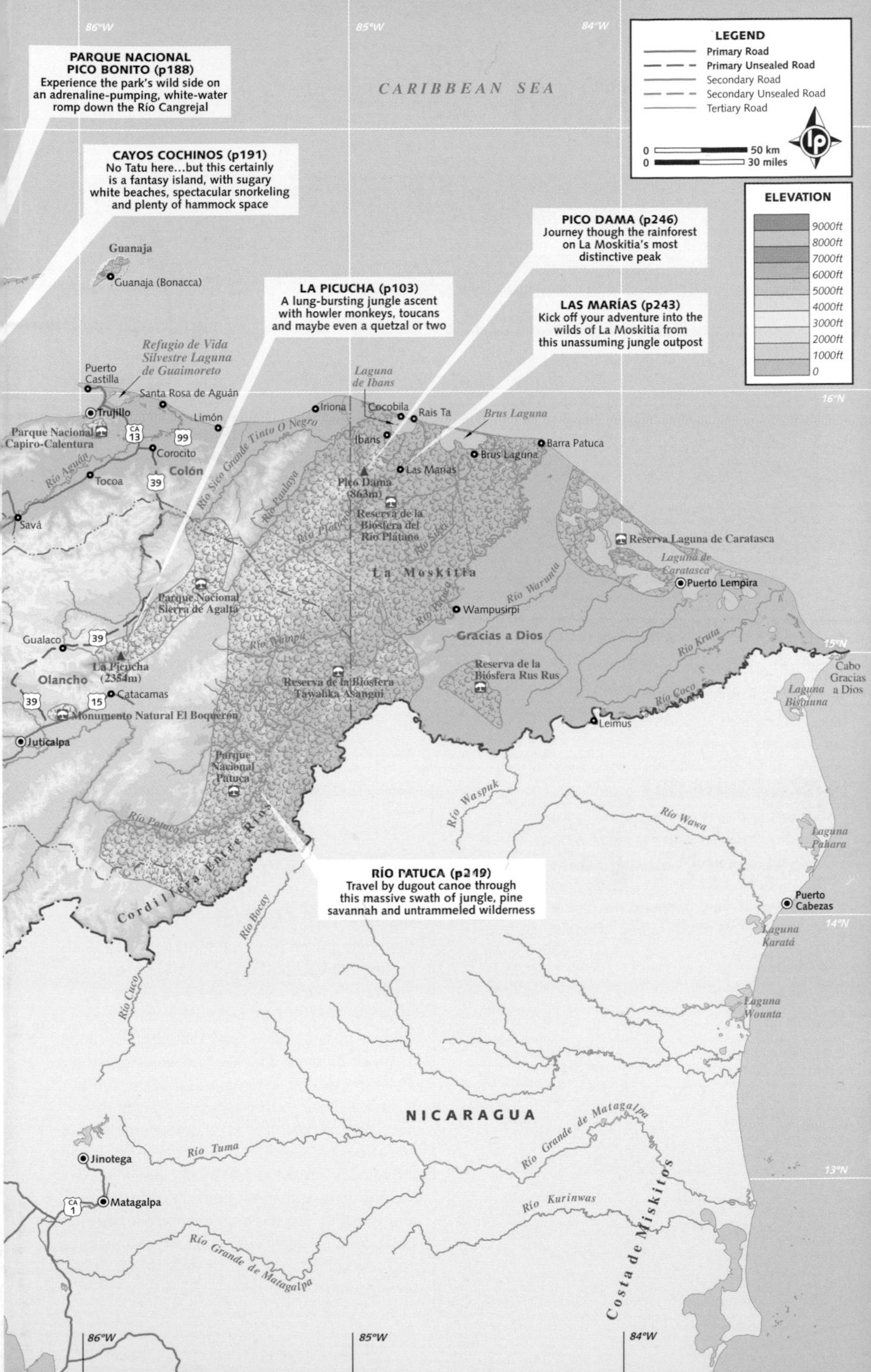

PARQUE NACIONAL PICO BONITO (p188)
Experience the park's wild side on an adrenaline-pumping, white-water romp down the Río Cangrejal
CAYOS COCHINOS (p191)
No Tatu here…but this certainly is a fantasy island, with sugary white beaches, spectacular snorkeling and plenty of hammock space
LA PICUCHA (p103)
A lung-bursting jungle ascent with howler monkeys, toucans and maybe even a quetzal or two
PICO DAMA (p246)
Journey though the rainforest on La Moskitia's most distinctive peak
LAS MARÍAS (p243)
Kick off your adventure into the wilds of La Moskitia from this unassuming jungle outpost
RÍO PATUCA (p249)
Travel by dugout canoe through this massive swath of jungle, pine savannah and untrammeled wilderness
LEGEND
Primary Road
Primary Unsealed Road
Secondary Road
Secondary Unsealed Road
Tertiary Road
0 50 km
0 30 miles
ELEVATION
9000ft
8000ft
7000ft
6000ft
5000ft
4000ft
3000ft
2000ft
1000ft
0
CARIBBEAN SEA
NICARAGUA
La Moskitia
Guanaja
Guanaja (Bonacca)
Refugio de Vida Silvestre Laguna de Guaimoreto
Puerto Castilla
Trujillo
Santa Rosa de Aguán
Limón
Iriona
Laguna de Ibans
Cocobila
Rais Ta
Ibans
Brus Laguna
Barra Patuca
Las Marías
Pico Dama (863m)
Reserva de la Biósfera del Río Plátano
Reserva Laguna de Caratasca
Laguna de Caratasca
Puerto Lempira
Wampusirpi
Gracias a Dios
Reserva de la Biósfera Rus Rus
Cabo Gracias a Dios
Laguna Bismuna
Leimus
Parque Nacional Capiro-Calentura
Corocito
Colón
Tocoa
Savá
Parque Nacional Sierra de Agalta
Gualaco
La Picucha (2354m)
Olancho
Catacamas
Monumento Natural El Boquerón
Juticalpa
Reserva de la Biósfera Tawahka Asangni
Parque Nacional Patuca
Cordillera Entre Ríos
Río Aguán
Río Sico Grande Tinto O Negro
Río Paulaya
Río Plátano
Río Sikre
Río Warunta
Río Patuca
Río Wampú
Río Kruta
Río Coco
Río Waspuk
Río Wawa
Laguna Pahara
Puerto Cabezas
Laguna Karatá
Laguna Wounta
Río Bocay
Río Cuco
Río Tuma
Río Grande de Matagalpa
Río Kurinwas
Costa de Miskitos
Jinotega
Matagalpa
86°W
85°W
84°W
16°N
15°N
14°N
13°N

On the Road

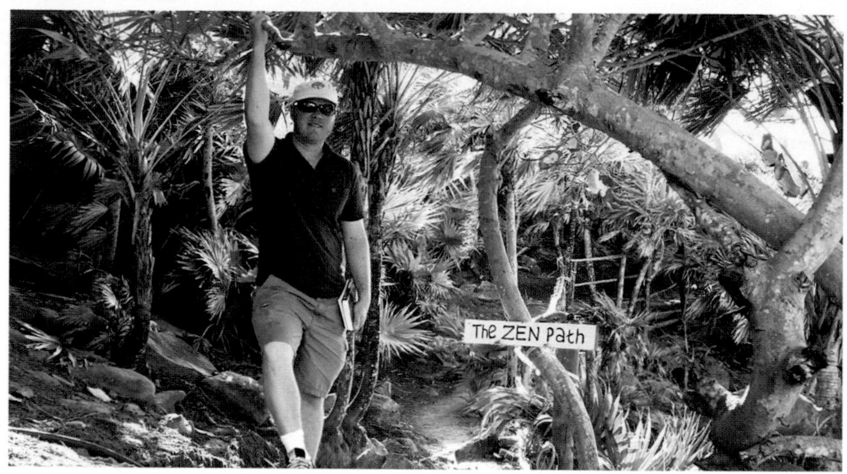

GREG BENCHWICK Author

On the Zen Path as always (after all, even Buddha had a little belly!) on a secret trail outside Paya Bay (p220) on Roatán. The trail leads to the island's only nude beach. I wore my clothes (tsk, tsk, not very Zenlike), taking the time to go for a quick swim on the pitch-perfect beach with my lovely wife.

MY FAVORITE TRIP

I start the day at 6am, crossing La Moskitia's Laguna de Ibans with my guide Alberto. We're looking for a new way to get to Las Marías (p243) and Alberto says he can take me there. The only catch: we'll need to spend the next eight hours in *lodo* (mud) up to our knees. After arriving in Las Marías, I can either head out for another three days of jungle trekking to Pico Dama (p246) or take it easy with a day hike to nearby petroglyphs (p247). After a few days in Las Marías, I head back by dugout canoe to my little jungle lodge in Rais Ta (p242).

ABOUT THE AUTHOR

Greg first passed through Honduras in 1995 on his first big backpacking adventure: a magical-mystery chicken bus journey from Costa Rica to Belize. For this trip, he traveled the entire country, making his way by foot, dugout canoe, a 10-person plane that seemed like it might not make the takeoff, catamaran, ferry, chicken bus, tuk-tuk and car to the extreme edges of the nation. Greg now lives in Colorado with his wife and their three-legged Turkish street-dog, spending his days studying sustainable practices, writing and speaking about travel in Latin America, and heading into the high-country for skiing and backpacking adventures. You can read his blog and see videos from his research in Honduras at www.soundtraveler.com.

Honduras Highlights

This is Central America's forgotten land, a rippling firmament of pine mountains, cloud-shrouded jungle, sinuously seductive rivers and a few Caribbean islands whose perfect beaches and waters will make your heart skip a beat. It's a place where you can dive, hike, raft and bike all in one day. There's so much to do, in fact, that you might want to dedicate your travels to a specific area or pursuit: rafting in La Moskitia for the adventurous, diving and drinking in the Bay Islands for the dedicated escapist, exploring ruins and traditional villages in the west for the cultural inquisitor, or just taking a day off to dip your toe into the diaphanous waters of the Caribbean for the romantic in all of us.

MICHAEL LAWRENCE

1 GLIDE INTO NEPTUNE'S REALM

Dive certification courses in the Bay Islands (p201) are inexpensive yet professional, and the underwater scenery is diverse and spectacular. On a night dive, I encountered an electric-blue octopus. It was surreal watching this otherworldly creature chilling in the lookout of a wrecked ship. Whale sharks are also a common sight. We would often finish our dives with a stop at one of the small villages on the outer cays to order a fresh fish burger.

Mary Polizzotti, Lonely Planet Staff

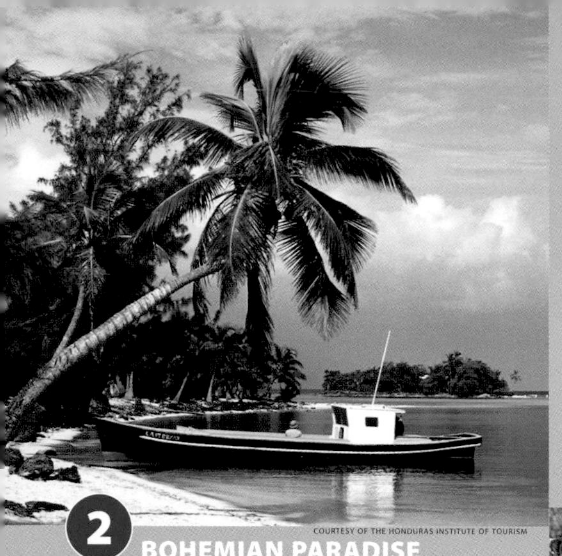

COURTESY OF THE HONDURAS INSTITUTE OF TOURISM

2 BOHEMIAN PARADISE

Utila (p221) is often overlooked for its bigger, better-known neighbor Roatán, but this is one of the very reasons that you should visit. The compact island has a low-key, slightly bohemian feel, the pace of life is slow and if you stick around for a few days (which you definitely will), you'll soon get to know some of the people who call Utila home.

Heather Carswell, Lonely Planet Staff

4 GET DIRTY! REAL DIRTY!

After the first few hundred meters, you'll finally give up your futile effort to keep your shoes clean, slopping into the muddy slopes on your way up to the remote jungle town of Las Marías (p243). Seven to 15 hours later you'll arrive at your destination, sopping wet, tired as hell, hungry and ready to chuck it all in for a night at the Holiday Inn. But don't give up just yet, you still have two or three more days of jungle trekking ahead as you explore the remarkable ecosystem of the vast Moskitia wilderness.

Greg Benchwick, Lonely Planet Author

TORRIONE STEFANO / HEMIS.FR/ALAMY

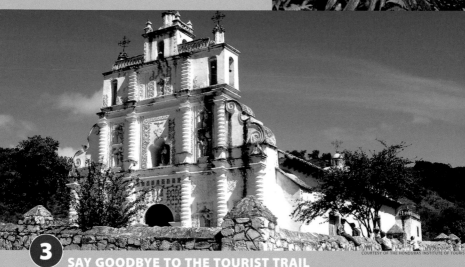

COURTESY OF THE HONDURAS INSTITUTE OF TOURISM

3 SAY GOODBYE TO THE TOURIST TRAIL

Explore Lenca territory, hitching rides on pickups as you wind your way from the coffee town of Marcala (p149) to remote San Juan (p146) via slow-paced La Esperanza (p147). Then head to Gracias (p138), Central America's former colonial capital, for some R&R, Honduran style. Stroll into the surrounding forests, soak your weary body in the town's hot springs, sniff out indigenous handicrafts and don't forget to try some original organic Lencan dishes and learn about this age-old culture.

Annelies Mertens, Lonely Planet Staff

WHISPERS OF THE MAYA

Just outside the charming town of Copán Ruinas, massive blocks of ancient stone peak through the jungle from the awesome Mayan ruins of Copán (p126). We moved through the temples, traveling up and down stairs built thousands of years ago that always stopped at spots with the most amazing views of the valley. We found a beautiful carved statue at the center of what was once a city. Our jaws dropped when we discovered that it once functioned as an instrument of sacrifice – unlucky people would have their heads removed there and the blood would flow down the sculpted sides to appease the gods! The ruins are full of surprises like that – equally as exciting as finishing the day on a 2km-long zipline over the treetops (p125).

Ken Miller, Traveler, USA

5

SEAN CAFFREY

CALL OF THE WILD

Forget Costa Rica! Honduras has some remarkable national parks. Along the coast you have sparkling beaches and terrific snorkeling at Parque Nacional Jeannette Kawas (p174), canoeing at the Cuero y Salado Wildlife Refuge (p187) and jungle treks up to the heights of Parque Nacional Capiro-Calentura (p198). Intrepid explorers shouldn't miss the multi-day trek to the top of Pico La Picucha (p105) in Central Honduras or the 10-day river romp through several remote reserves in La Moskitia (p103).

Greg Benchwick, Lonely Planet Author

6

COURTESY OF THE HONDURAS INSTITUTE OF TOURISM

7

COURTESY OF THE HONDURAS INSTITUTE OF TOURISM

FEEL THE RUSH

Let the adrenaline fill you from tip to toe as you drop into some of Central America's best white-water along the Río Cangrejal (p181), saving some energy for sunset *cervezas* in your little ecolodge down by the river (p184). The next day, you can hike it or bike it along the trails that feather out from these affordable retreats.

Greg Benchwick, Lonely Planet Author

COURTESY OF THE HONDURAS INSTITUTE OF TOURISM

8 RHYTHM IS A DANCER

It certainly is a soul's companion, especially when you are two days deep into the Garífuna Festival at the traditional seaside village of Baja Mar (p166). Island hoppers may want to swing out to Roatán's Punta Gorda (p219) for the five-day festival commemorating the arrival of the Garífuna in Honduras. Into saintly pleasures? Check out the La Feria de San Isidro in La Ceiba (p180) and the Feria Juniana in San Pedro Sula (p112). For dancing and decadence, make your way to Utila's Water Cay for the annual Sun Jam (p229).

Greg Benchwick, Lonely Planet Author

9 CHASING THE DAWN

Set your clock early for a predawn departure into the wilderness surrounding Lago de Yojoa (p151). There are over 350 bird species to be spotted in the parks and preserves that are transforming this into one of the mainland's premier destinations. Start at the small Los Naranjos ecopark (p152), saving time for an afternoon jaunt through the large, and unappreciated, Parque Nacional Cerro Azul Meámbar (p154).

Greg Benchwick, Lonely Planet Author

COURTESY OF THE HONDURAS INSTITUTE OF TOURIS

COURTESY OF THE HONDURAS INSTITUTE OF TOURISM

10 SOMETHING TO BRING HOME

Loll away the afternoon wandering the cobblestone streets of Valle de Ángeles (p80) in search of that perfect piece of Lenca pottery or handcrafted textile. You'll have plenty of time to check out the trails and waterfalls of nearby Parque Nacional La Tigra (p81) the next day.

Greg Benchwick, Lonely Planet Author

Contents

Regional Map Contents

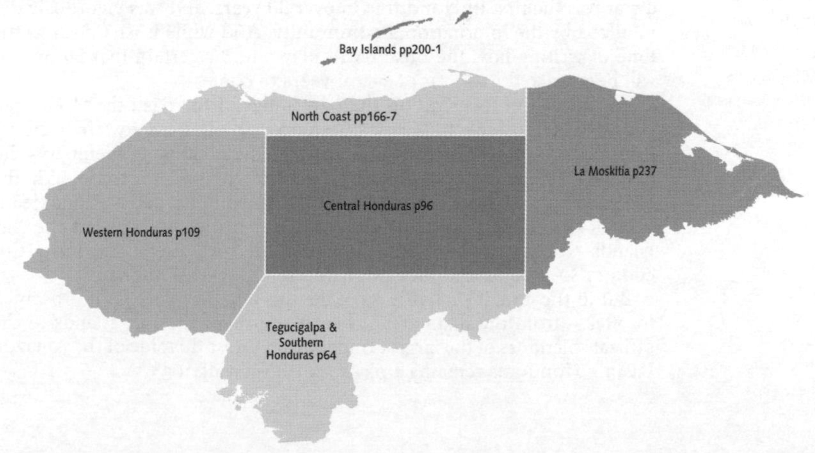

Destination Honduras

The face of a nation changed forever on June 28, 2009, when a military coup removed Honduran President Manuel Zelaya from power. But the Honduran people are strong.

There's plenty going on in this rough and rugged country to complain about – coups, widespread corruption, deforestation, pollution, landlessness, a growing wealth gap, gangs, drugs, AIDS, constitutional changes, and the rebirth of old-school, extra-jurisdictional intimidation and murder – but you won't hear many complaints. It's not that Hondurans are eternal optimists – in fact, quite the opposite appears to be true – it's that they've decided to submit themselves to the passage of time. And like the pine-encrusted hillsides of the west, the verdant savannah and jungle of La Moskitia, the lolling Caribbean waters of the Bay Islands and the stifling hot alleyways of the frenetic city centers, the people of Honduras will abide.

FAST FACTS

Population: 7.79 million

Life expectancy: 67.8 (men), 71 (women)

Population growth: 1.956%

Type of government: Democratic Constitutional Republic

Dominant religions: Roman Catholic (97%), Protestant (3%)

Literacy rate: 80%

GDP per person: US$4400 (US$46,000 per person in the US)

Urbanization 2.9% annual growth (48% currently live in cities)

People living with HIV/AIDS: 28,000

Arable land: 9.53% (18.01% in the US, 13.22% in Guatemala)

With the global economic meltdown hitting full-tilt, money was on everyone's mind at the beginning of 2009. The left-leaning government, led by President Zelaya, pushed through legislation in the early part of the year to raise the minimum monthly wage by 11% to L$5500 (around US$290). Good news for factory workers, bad news for business owners. And while there certainly was much hemming and hawing on both sides of the debate, it seemed perfectly clear that the new wage, combined with the unstoppable tides of the global economy, were going to cause more Hondurans to lose their jobs – bad news for a country with an unemployment rate estimated at 28%.

Honduras' societal problems mirror those of many of its neighbors in Latin America – a legacy of landlessness, government greed and corruption, gangs, guns and narco-trafficking – and stem largely from a history of avarice and inequality. President Zelaya claimed to be trying to combat these problems – being so bold as to push for a referendum that would have rewritten the Honduran constitution – but the average Honduran, rich or poor, didn't seem to support the idea, and the Supreme Court ordered the military to arrest Zelaya and send him into exile. The coup d'etat was the first in Honduras in over 30 years, and was vigorously denounced by the international community. And while it isn't clear at the time of writing how the ouster will play out, it's certain that Honduras will be a scarred nation for several years to come.

But instead of focusing on the bad things of the past, the Honduran people seem to look forward, hoping for small steps toward a better future: more protection from the estimated 20,000 gang members who have made this one of the world's murder capitals; protection for the beautiful natural areas such as Lago de Yojoa and Parque Nacional Jeannette Kawas (Punta Sal) that may one day bring tourists past the Bay Islands–Copan–La Ceiba trail and into the rural areas that make this country so unique; and they hope and fight for land reform.

But in the end, it's a battle to make this a better place. With so much to offer – from the mainstream beach resorts of the Bay Islands to the offbeat splendors of the largest tract of rain forest this side of the Amazon Basin – Honduras remains a place worth fighting for.

Getting Started

Honduras is just beginning to develop its tourism potential, and there is truly something for everyone here. There are high-end resorts and world-class food in the major resort areas of the Bay Islands, and to a lesser degree in the bigger tourist towns of the mainland such as Copán Ruinas, Tela, San Pedro Sula, Tegucigalpa, the area around Lago de Yojoa and La Ceiba. Once you venture beyond this tourist trail expect back-to-basics lodging, less tourist infrastructure and adventure opportunities aplenty. While getting to Honduras is a snap, with many direct flights to San Pedro, Tegucigalpa and Roatán, prepare yourself for the inevitable headaches and ear-to-ear smiles of traveling in the developing world. Buses arrive late, the water in your hotel may go out for a day or two, and congestion, noise and pollution are part and parcel of everyday life.

Much of the country is a malaria zone, and international health organizations recommend taking malaria pills (if you decide to take them, you'll need to start your course one or two weeks before you arrive in Honduras). And like most of Latin America, you can't drink the tap water. Instead of bottled water, consider bringing a filter to help reduce landfill waste. See the Health chapter (p275) for more on staying healthy in Honduras.

WHEN TO GO

Like most tropical countries, Honduras experiences a rainy season and a dry season, known locally as *invierno* (winter) and *verano* (summer) respectively. In the interior, especially the west and south, the rainy season runs from about May to November. Rains usually come in the afternoon and last an hour or so. On the north coast and Bay Islands, the rainy season is later, from around September to December, with *nortes* ('northerners', cool storms from the north) possible into February. Hurricane season runs from June to the end of November. Hurricanes are most likely from September to October, though they rarely hit Honduras directly. However, even a far-off hurricane can send heavy rain Honduras' way and can cause flooding or minor mudslides.

See Climate Charts (p259) for more information.

Travel is easier during the dry season, especially for scuba diving and trips to La Moskitia. Then again, the forests and countryside are more lush during the rainy season. February and March are good months to visit because the weather is fairly stable across the country; the trails and roads are drying out but the trees and underbrush are still full and green.

You won't need much advance planning traveling to and around Honduras unless you come during the Easter week, or over Christmas.

COSTS & MONEY

Honduras is an inexpensive country overall, but a trip here can be pricey simply because of the activities you're likely to do, namely diving. US dollars and euros are widely accepted in the Bay Islands, but you'll need local currency (lempiras) for the rest of the country. It's becoming more and more difficult to exchange traveler's checks, and most travelers are now opting to use ATMs for their cash needs instead. Most cities have ATMs. See p263 for more on money matters.

Besides diving, accommodation will likely be your biggest expense. Hotel prices run the gamut in Honduras, the majority being high-budget or low-midrange, around L$300 (US$16) to L$500 (US$26) per night. Bare-bones budget travelers can often arrange homestays in the more

DON'T LEAVE HOME WITHOUT...

- Passport and US cash – universal travel essentials
- Sunscreen – very expensive in Honduras
- Bug repellent – expensive and can be hard to find
- Toiletries – you'll appreciate having your preferred brands of tampons, pads, condoms, deodorant, etc
- Travel alarm clock – it's rare to find one in hotels, even high-end ones
- Copies of important documents – having a copy of your passport and plane tickets will make replacing them, if necessary, much easier
- A flashlight (torch) – you never know when the lights will go out...or when there will be no lights at all
- Diver certification card and logbook – bring them if you've got them; you don't want to repeat the Open Water course, do you?
- Extra eyeglasses or contacts – expensive and difficult to replace
- Rain gear and plastic bags – handy for travel in the rainy season, or anytime in La Moskitia

remote parts of the country, and can probably find lodging for around L$200 (US$10), though the cheapest hotels can be pretty grim.

Eating out will cost from around L$60 (US$3) to L$200 (US$10) per person per meal, once drinks, taxes, and tip are added in. You can save money by eating at street food vendors and no-name eateries, and by getting lunch or breakfast items at a grocery store instead of a restaurant.

The big-ticket item for most travelers is diving, plus the higher cost of hotels and restaurants on the Bay Islands. An Open Water course will cost L$5000 (US$264) to L$6000 (US$317). Fun dives cost from L$665 (US$35, one tank) to L$1050 (US$55, two tanks), but you can save some cash by booking a multi-dive package. Lodging and food tend to be more expensive on Roatán than Utila. Most dive shops on Utila have basic dorms, and offer students either two to four free nights or two free fun dives. A trip to La Moskitia can also be pricey, whether by tour or on your own.

HOW MUCH?

Moto-taxi ride L$20 (US$1)

Bottle of Salva Vida beer L$20 (US$1)

Open Water dive certification L$5000-6000 (US$264-317)

Plato típico L$40 (US$2)

Rafting trip on the Río Cangrejal L$760 (US$40)

Buses are a bargain, especially considering how big the country is. There are three classes of service: *ordinario* or *parando* (literally, stopping) is the classic 'chicken bus' that stops frequently to pick up and drop off passengers. *Directos* are generally safer, make fewer stops and cost only slightly more – for most travelers this is the way to go. Some popular routes are covered by the luxury or deluxe lines Hedman Alas, King Quality or Saenz Clase Primera. Prices are double or triple, but it can be a worthwhile splurge.

Taxis are safe and affordable, with fares typically charged per person. Expect to pay L$10 to L$20 (US$0.50 to US$1) per person within town, and from L$30 (US$1.50) for destinations out of town or at night.

Rental cars cost from L$567 (US$30) to L$1134 (US$60) per day, including taxes and insurance; internet access costs around L$20 (US$1) per hour; and laundry is around L$70 (US$3.70) per load.

TRAVELING RESPONSIBLY

Sustainable travel is all about respect. Respect the environment, respect the culture, respect the economy and respect the rules. There are some easy steps you can take to lower your impact, including offsetting your travel, hiring local guides, buying responsibly and staying the night in small villages rather than just visiting them on day trips. This encourages locals to preserve their culture and traditions, and mitigates the rampant urban migration that is affecting the cultural makeup of this diverse country.

Most travelers are quite conscientious about minimizing their physical impact: not littering, not disturbing flora and fauna (above water or below it), not buying food or gifts that are made from protected species. In Honduras, especially on the Bay Islands, limit your water use – take short showers! – and try reusing bottles and plastic bags to cut down on trash.

Controlling your 'cultural impact' is a bit more tricky. Taking photos is such an integral part of traveling – if you didn't get a photo, were you really there? – but it's vital that travelers exercise restraint in taking pictures, especially of local people, and doubly so if those people happen to be indigenous. Travelers may not realize how intrusive other habits are, like talking loudly or dressing sloppily, especially in a church or government office.

It's also a great idea to put your guidebook down for the day (or even a week), leaving the tourist trail behind in search of your own adventures. This book has a GreenDex (p302) to get you started.

One last tip: even if you don't speak Spanish, do learn how to use the formal tense, addressing individuals you don't know with the formal *usted* instead of the *familiartu* or *vos*. It goes a long way in showing respect.

TRAVEL LITERATURE

While topics such as Copán archaeological site, the banana industry and the Contra War have been well studied and written about, others, such as non-Maya indigenous communities and environmental issues, have not. Gangs are a hot topic and have received extensive newspaper and magazine coverage; full-length books are still rare, though several are in the works.

TOP TIPS FOR STAYING SAFE

Let's not sugarcoat it: Honduras is a dangerous country, and with the 2009 coup (p34), things were looking even more unstable when this book went to press. It's well worth your time to check out the country's political situation before you go. Here are some more details on Honduras' security situation: there were 101 kidnappings in 2008 and 62 US citizens have been murdered here since 1995. Then again, the US and other parts of the developed world also have high murder rates and occasional kidnappings. So while you'll need to keep your wits about you while traveling here, there's no reason this should ruin your trip. We discuss specifics for staying safe within the regional chapters, but here are a few general tips.

- Take cabs at night. It's super cheap, and whether you are going two blocks or two miles, it's definitely worth it. You can skip the cab on the Bay Islands and Copán Ruinas, where the streets are tightly patrolled. A general rule: if there are a lot of people out, especially women and children, you are probably safe.
- Avoid municipal buses. City buses are regularly attacked by street gangs. Just take a cab.
- Leave the camera and MP3 player at home. We get numerous complaints about expensive cameras and MP3 players being stolen. In a country with a minimum wage of around L$5500 (US$300) per month, these luxury items (and conspicuous jewelry) are attractive targets.
- Skip the moonlight beach walk. Most of the country's beaches are safe by day, but you should avoid them at night.
- Don't walk down dark alleys. Heading down a dark alley to buy a dime bag is never safe.
- Don't fight back. If you get robbed, just let them have the stuff. It's all replaceable.
- Relax and have fun! The majority of visitors to Honduras have absolutely zero problems on their journey.

Honduras: A Country Guide (1991), by Tom Barry and Kent Norsworthy, and *Honduras: A Country Study* (1990), by the US Federal Research Division, are oldish but have concise historical information. *Working Hard, Drinking Hard: On Violence and Survival in Honduras* (2008), by Adrienne Pine, is a sociological study that uses violence and the export manufacturing (*maquiladora*) industry as a backdrop.

Enrique's Journey (2007), by Pulitzer Prize–winning reporter Sonia Nazario, chronicles a 17-year-old Honduran boy's attempt to reunite with his mother, who left the family when the boy was just five to find work in the US.

The United States, Honduras, and the Crisis in Central America (1994), by Donald E Schultz and Deborah Sundloff Schulz, discusses the role of the US in Central America during the region's tumultuous civil wars.

Don't be Afraid, Gringo (1987) is the intriguing firsthand story of peasant Elvia Alvarado's reluctant rise as a labor leader, and of the Honduran labor movement, flaws and all.

Bitter Fruit, by Stephen C Schlesinger, is mostly about the United Fruit Company in Guatemala, but provides insight into the banana giant's impact on Honduras as well. *The Banana Men: American Mercenaries and Entrepreneurs in Central America, 1880-1930* (1995) and *The Banana Wars: United States Intervention in the Caribbean, 1898-1934* (2002), both by Lester D Langley, are incisive accounts of the banana companies' political and economic influence in Central America and the Caribbean.

Alison Acker's *Honduras: The Making of a Banana Republic* (1989) lacks the detail and analysis of more recent studies, but is a worthy read.

Copán is one of the most extensively studied archaeological sites in the Maya world; many studies are highly technical but several have been written with a more general readership in mind. *Copán: The History of an Ancient Kingdom* (2005), by William L Fash and E Wyllys Andrews, is an excellent overview, while *Scribes Warriors and Kings* (2001), also by Fash, is a fine on-site companion and is often sold at the Copán ruins' bookstore.

Los Barcos (The Ships; 1992), *El Humano y La Diosa* (The Human and the Goddess; 1996) and *The Big Banana* (1999) are all by Roberto Quesada, one of Honduras' best-known living novelists. *Gringos in Honduras: The Good, the Bad, and the Ugly* (1995) and *Velasquez: The Man and His Art* are two of many books by Guillermo Yuscarán, aka William Lewis, an American writer and painter living in Honduras.

INTERNET RESOURCES

A growing number of sites provide reliable up-to-date information on Honduras. Many are maintained by expats and are in English.

About Utila (www.aboututila.com) General info and news about Utila.

Honduran Tourism Ministry (www.letsgohonduras.com) Website of the Honduran Tourism Ministry.

Honduras This Week (www.hondurasthisweek.com) Official site of *Honduras This Week*, Honduras' only English-language newspaper.

Honduras Tips (www.hondurastips.honduras.com) The website of the free tourist magazine.

La Ruta Moskitia (www.larutamoskitia.com) Good info on travel to La Moskitia.

Latin American Network Information Center (http://lanic.utexas.edu/la/ca/honduras/) Extensive list of links to articles and websites on everything from politics to sports to tourism.

Lonely Planet (www.lonelyplanet.com/honduras) The source of updated Lonely Planet coverage.

Roatán Online (www.roatanonline.com) A charmless but comprehensive guide to all things Roatán.

Travel-to-Honduras.com (www.travel-to-honduras.com) Links to various services, including volunteer organizations.

TOP PICKS

Guatemala
HONDURAS
Tegucigalpa
El Salvador

SMALL TOWNS

Small towns are one of the joys of Honduras, where a bit of Spanish and a friendly manner can earn you plenty of lunchtime conversations and interesting insights.

- Cocobila – a quiet Miskito village on a thin strip of sand with trees between the Caribbean and a huge island lagoon (p241)
- San Manuel de Colohete – about as far down the road as it gets, this traditional Lenca village sees very few foreign visitors (p145)
- Las Marías – a Miskito-Pech village in the heart of the Reserva de la Biósfera del Río Plátano, and a perfect base for excursions in the area (p243)
- Jewel and Pigeon Cay – off the western tip of Utila, these sun-bleached islets are even smaller and mellower than Utila itself, and no less picturesque (p229)
- Valle de Ángeles – a quaint colonial village in the mountains (p80)
- Chachauate – a traditional Garífuna village on a picture-perfect Caribbean cay (p191)
- Yuscarán – on the way to Honduras' cigar country, this colonial town has winding cobblestone streets and several aguardiente breweries (p85)
- Miami – a cluster of thatched-roof homes on a rustic beach at the end of a long, sandy road near Jeannette Kawas National Park (p176)
- San Marcos de Colón – a cool, colonial refuge in the otherwise sweltering southern region, with a seldom-visited wildlife reserve nearby (p91)
- Travesía – a Garífuna village with an excellent beach and good accommodation options (p166)

FESTIVALS & PARTIES

Whether a local celebration or a national holiday, festivals and parties offer a unique window into the culture, history and lore of this nation.

- Copán Ruinas (Valle de Copán), every night is Saturday night in this backpacker hotspot (p119)
- Feria de la Virgen de Suyapa (Suyapa), February (p261)
- Festival Nacional de Maíz (Danlí), August (p86)
- Garífuna Festival (Baja Mar), July (p166)
- Feria de San Isidro (La Ceiba), May (p180)
- Guancasco (La Ruta Lenca), mostly December & January; dates vary by town (p140)
- Noche de Fumadores (Santa Rosa de Copán), August (p135)
- Semana Santa (Comayagua), the week before Easter (p160)
- Semana Santa (Tela), the week before Easter (p171)
- Sun Jam (Utila), August (p229)

WAYS TO GET WET & WILD

- Diving off Utila – some of the cheapest diving certification courses on the planet (p223)
- Rafting the Cangrejal – charge down Central America's best white water (p181)
- Paddling a dugout canoe – it's hard work, but the monkeys won't hear you coming (p246)
- Stargazing from a hot spring – but keep your swimsuit on…please (p139)
- Snorkeling off Punta Sal – some of the best shore snorkeling on the coast (p174)
- Finding your own beach – go ahead, head down that unmarked road. A lost beach paradise may just be waiting for you.
- Ascending La Picucha – you pass through seven microclimates on the way to the summit; we're sure you'll get wet in one of them (p103)

Itineraries

CLASSIC ROUTES

THE WHOLE COUNTRY (ALMOST) — Three to Four Weeks

Start your journey from **San Pedro Sula** (p109), heading overland to **La Ceiba** (p177) where there's something for everyone. Had your fill? Take the ferry over to **Roatán** (p202) or **Utila** (p221), spending at least three days diving, snorkeling and wearing flip-flops. Next, hop over to **Tela** (p169) for a day at the beach, the **Jardín Botánico Lancetilla** (p174) or **Parque Nacional Jeannette Kawas** (p174). Afterwards, head to **Copán Ruinas** (p119), where you can visit Honduras' only major archaeological site. If you like colonial towns, make your next stop **Santa Rosa de Copán** (p134), otherwise head straight to **Gracias** (p138), gateway to **Parque Nacional Montaña de Celaque** (p141). Continue down through the southern half of the **Ruta Lenca** (p133) to **Comayagua** (p159) and back toward **Tegucigalpa** (p65), where you can head out to **Parque Nacional La Tigra** (p81) for hiking, or to **Valle de Ángeles** (p80) for craft shopping. From here, head westward to **Lago de Yojoa** (p151) for bird-watching in the morning, then to **Pulhapanzak Falls** (p151) in the afternoon.

Here's Honduras from top to bottom: from the highest peak to 30m underwater. It includes national parks, Maya ruins and offbeat colonial villages.

INTO THE WILD — Two to Three Weeks

Fly into **Tegucigalpa** (p65) where, appropriately enough, your tour begins with Honduras' first national park, **Parque Nacional La Tigra** (p81). Plan to stay the night at one of the two entrances and make an all-day loop hike. From La Tigra, head north to **Parque Nacional Cerro Azul Meámbar** (p154) with its well-marked trails, easy-to-follow signs and excellent campgrounds. Continue north to **Tela** (p169) and the beautiful **Parque Nacional Jeannette Kawas** (p174). Take it easy on a guided day trip, or rough it by hiking in from the tiny village of **Miami** and camping on the beach. Next head east of **La Ceiba** to the tiny Garífuna village of **Sambo Creek** (p190), a jumping off point for **Parque Nacional Marino Cayos Cochinos** (p191). Crystalline water and pristine coral reefs make this a divers' and snorkelers' paradise, not to mention one of the most photographed spots in Honduras. Back on the mainland, take a bus from San Pedro Sula to Gracias, where **Parque Nacional Montaña de Celaque** (p141), and Honduras' highest peak, Cerro de las Minas, awaits. If your time and energy permit, head straight to **Parque Nacional Sierra de Agalta** (p102) to climb La Picucha mountain, one of Honduras' most challenging ascents, doable from either **Gualaco** (p105) or **Catacamas** (p100). Otherwise, return to Tegucigalpa for your flight home.

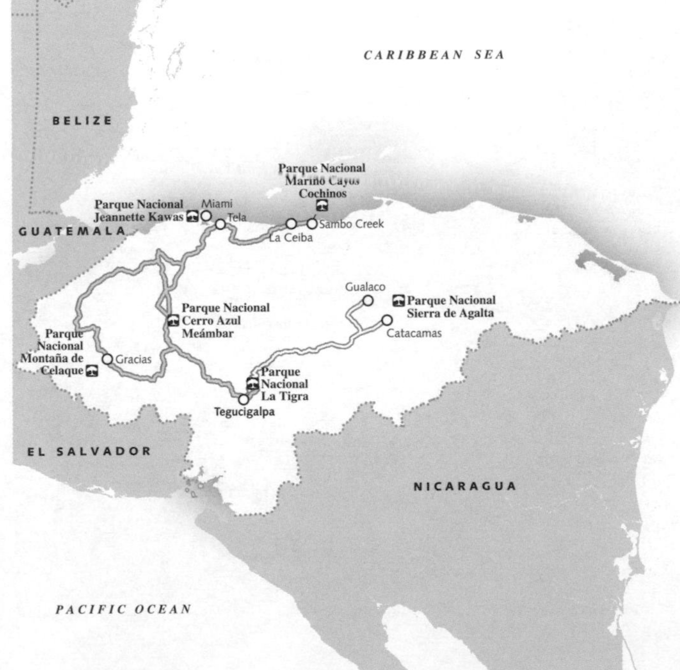

This trip takes you to Honduras' best national parks, from the rugged Parque Nacional Sierra de Agalta to coral-fringed Parque Nacional Marino Cayos Cochinos.

ROADS LESS TRAVELED

A WORLD APART: THE MOSQUITO COAST

Depending on your time, budget and tolerance for long land journeys, fly into La Moskitia or go overland – either way, make your way to **Belén** (p241) or **Rais Ta** (p241), neighboring towns on Laguna de Ibans. Take a day to get your bearings straight and check out the peaceful towns of **Plaplaya** (p240) and **Cocobila** (p241). Early the next morning, settle in for the five- to six-hour boat ride or one- or two-day hike to **Las Marías** (p243). There, arrange a mellow day trip to the petroglyphs or a more challenging three-day rain-forest hike to **Pico Dama** (p246). Back in Belén and Rais Ta, arrange a morning boat ride or flight to **Brus Laguna** (p247) for a night or two in the savannah cabañas. Afterwards, head back to Brus Laguna town, stock up on supplies and fly to **Wampusirpi** (p251) where – knock on wood – you'll be able to hitch or hire a boat ride into the **Reserva de la Biósfera Tawahka Asangni** (p251). Boat back to Wampusirpi and fly to **Puerto Lempira** (p252). Time permitting, bike to **Mistruk** (p254) or **Kaukira** (p254) for the day; otherwise fly from Puerto Lempira back to **La Ceiba** (p177).

An organized tour can be a good option for exploring this part of the country, visiting many of the places in this itinerary but saving you the time and hassle of arranging transport and other details. In fact, one of the best ways to see La Moskitia is on a seven- to 10-day rafting trip, starting in Olancho (see p238). The trip takes you down the lush Río Patuca and through the Tawahka region...an incredible journey.

This itinerary includes the Río Plátano and Tawahka Biosphere Reserves, and small Miskitu and Garífuna villages along the coast. A full tour takes two weeks, but you can hit the highlights in seven to 10 days. A five-day visit will feel rushed.

COBBLESTONES & CATHEDRALS

From **Tegucigalpa** (p65), head straight to **Santa Lucía** (p79), a pretty hilltop village that is often overlooked for better-known Valle de Ángeles. Loop around to **Yuscarán** (p85), a charming colonial town on the way to nowhere. Back in Tegucigalpa, head north to **Comayagua** (p159) with its soaring cathedral, broad Parque Central and traditional religious festivals. Next, go up and around to **Copán Ruinas** (p119), which in addition to its archaeological riches, is a picturesque and lively town, popular with backpackers. From here it's a short drive or bus ride to **Santa Rosa de Copán** (p134) and its recently restored city center and a boho bar scene. Continue south to **Gracias** (p138), a cool mountain redoubt with clay tile–roofed houses, cobblestone streets and great hiking nearby. This is part of the Ruta Lenca (Lenca Route), a string of small indigenous villages that eventually leads back to the main highway, and on to Tegucigalpa. An intrepid traveler could hike their way from village to village, stopping for a day in **La Campa** (p143), **San Manuel de Colohete** (p145) and **San Marcos de Caiquín** (p144), even extending the trip with backwoods romps to **San Sebastián** (p145) and **Belén Gualcho** (p137). Time permitting, continue your colonial exploration by zipping out to **San Marcos de Colón** (p91), an underappreciated colonial gem near the Nicaraguan border that serves as a gateway to a nature reserve brimming with monkeys.

This tour visits the places many travelers skip en route to bigger, better-known destinations. You'll appreciate having a car for part of this itinerary – buses to some of these towns are few and far between. Allow two to three weeks.

TAILORED TRIPS

BENEATH THE SURFACE

This Caribbean romp takes you to the best beaches, dive spots and snorkeling and maritime adventures the nation has to offer. From the US you can take a non-stop flight to **Roatán** (p202), thus avoiding San Pedro Sula or La Ceiba. In Roatán, look for a hotel and independent dive shop in **West End** (p207), or stay at a resort with its own dive shop in **Sandy Bay** (p215) or **West Bay** (p213). For more isolation, look for resorts further afield, at **Palmetto Bay** (p218) or **Paya Bay** (p220). Some of Roatán's most memorable dive spots include Hole in the Wall, West End Wall and Mary's Place. For snorkeling, West Bay is good (though showing increasing damage).

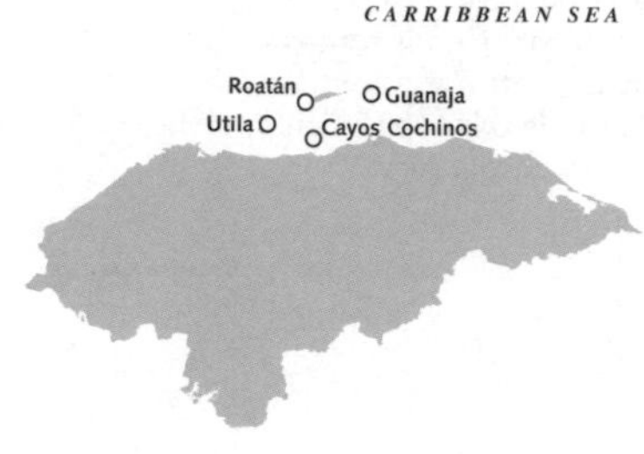

From Roatán, head across to **Utila** (p221) aboard Captain Vern's 'almost seaworthy' **catamaran** (p203) – we love the duct-taped windows. Laid-back Utila caters mostly to backpackers and independent travelers, with just a few upscale resorts on the western end. Utila's best diving is on the north shore, though the sea mounds on the south side are gorgeous. For snorkeling, try Airport Reef, the Utila Cays and Blue Bayou beach.

Take the ferry back to La Ceiba and get onto a plane for **Guanaja** (p230). Instead of staying in Bonacca, the main town, head to one of the resorts around the island, all of which offer diving and snorkeling. The Pinnacle, Lee's Pleasure, Jim's Silver Lode and the Jado Trader are all favorite spots.

Fly back to La Ceiba for one last stop – **Cayos Cochinos** (p191). You can arrange a one-day snorkel or dive trip through Palma Real hotel or arrange an independent trip –snorkeling only – from one of the boatmen in Sambo Creek (p190). Plantation Beach Resort is the only hotel in Cayos Cochinos offering daily and weekly dive-and-lodging packages.

GIVING BACK & KEEPING IT GREEN

This sustainable adventure takes you to some of the nation's wildest areas and most remote towns. Begin in **San Pedro Sula** (p109), where you may be able to arrange volunteer opportunities through local NGOs, before heading on to La Moskitia. Forget the airplane, instead travel by 'chicken boat,' dugout canoe and foot to the **Laguna de Ibans** (p239) and on to **Las Marías** (p243). The grassroots tourist infrastructure here is bare-bones basic, but your money goes a long way toward developing school programs, keeping kids healthy and protecting an already-at-risk environment. From here, it's back to the mainland, where you can skip the mainstay attractions, opting instead to ascend **La Picucha** (p102) with a local guide, volunteer at a school near **Valle de Ángeles** (p81) or **Copán Ruinas** (p120), or help protect the wildlife of Parque Nacional Pico Bonito as a volunteer for **Guaruma Servicios** (p190). Along the way, check if your tour operator, hotelier and restaurant owner are able to do anything to help protect the environment and give back to the local community.

History

The history of Honduras is one of haves and have-nots. It's a story of avarice and occasional altruism. And while many of Honduras' seminal events mirror those of neighboring countries, the regional history remains a fascinating testament to what the nation was, and what it will become.

PRE-COLUMBIAN HISTORY

The oldest known evidence of human presence in present-day Honduras are some stone knives, scrapers and other tools uncovered by archaeologists in 1962 near La Esperanza, Intibucá, and thought to be 6000 to 8000 years old. Central America's earliest occupants almost certainly were Paleo-Indians from the north, but linguistic and other evidence suggests that many indigenous people present in Honduras today (Pech, Tawahka and probably Lenca) are descended from later migrations of people from rainforest regions of South America, especially present-day Colombia.

The Maya arrived in Honduras by way of Guatemala and Mexico, and settled in the fertile Sula, Copán and Comayagua valleys. Over centuries, they came to dominate the area, as they did much of Mesoamerica. Copán was a heavily settled, agriculturally rich trading zone and eventually became one of the great Maya city-states of the Classic Period (AD 300 to AD 900). The Classic Period ended with the rapid and mysterious collapse of most Maya centers, including Copán, where the last dated hieroglyph is from AD 800. To learn more about the history of Copán see p126.

The Maya population declined precipitously, but did not disappear, of course. They were just one of many indigenous groups that made up Honduras' native population when European explorers began their conquest of the American mainland. Copán has since returned to prominence as an archaeological mother lode, having more hieroglyphic inscriptions and stone monuments than any other Maya ruin. Copán was the first site visited by John Lloyd Stephens and Frederick Catherwood on their groundbreaking exploration of Mesoamerica in 1839. It was also the first site to be studied by Alfred Mausley (in 1885), whose compendium of Maya stone monuments remains a classic in the field, and whose work prompted the preeminent Harvard Peabody Museum to enter into Maya investigation (and which in turn selected Copán as its inaugural excavation). It was also the first stop for Sylvanus Morley and the Carnegie Institute in the 1920s. More recently, research has focused on Copán's outlying areas; the site has provided important insight into the lives of ordinary Classic-era Mayas. For more on Maya history, see p128.

See www.mostlymaya.com for a list of over 100 Maya-related websites, including Maya calendar translators, virtual ruins tours (including Copán), and scientific and general interest websites.

The 2008 documentary, *Breaking the Maya Code*, reveals the Promethean steps taken to crack the Maya hieroglyphic script.

Scribes, Warriors and Kings (2001), by William L Fash and Barbara W Fash, is a detailed and sometimes technical account of ongoing research and excavation at Copán by the authors, leading experts on the site.

TIMELINE

6000–4000 BC

The first traces of humans in Honduras date back to the arrival of Paleo-Indians from the north. Later migrations from South America will come together to create Pech, Tawahka and possibly Lenca ethnic groups.

3114 BC

Our current universe is created, at least according to Maya mythology. Archaeologists have been able to pin down the specific date of creation: August 13, 3114 BC

1400 BC

Non-Maya peoples are living in the Valle de Copán. There's clear archaeological evidence that these early people had trade with El Salvador, Guatemala and even far-away Mexico.

CONQUEST & COLONIZATION

Now in its 7th edition, Michael Coe's book *The Maya* (2005) is a definitive, though somewhat dry, look at Maya history and culture.

On his fourth and final voyage, Admiral Christopher Columbus made landfall near present-day Trujillo. The date was August 14, 1502, and it was the first time any European explorer had set foot on the American mainland. Columbus named the area Honduras, or 'depths,' for the deep waters there. Before the historic landing, Columbus had also had his (and Europe's) first encounter with mainland indigenous people: the crew of a large canoe he had spotted near the Bay Islands. Columbus commandeered the canoe, which was laden with trade goods, and forced its captain (probably a Maya merchant) to serve as his guide. The expedition continued east around Cabo Gracias a Díos (another of Columbus' placenames) all the way to present-day Panama, where the admiral dropped his unlucky captive, before returning to Spain.

Around 5000 pirates lived on the Bay Islands in the early 1600s.

Having been the site of such an historic landing, the Honduran Caribbean coast was all but ignored by explorers for the next 20 years; they focused instead on Mexico, Panama and the Caribbean islands. Hernán Cortés' expedition into the Aztec heartland, however, revived interest in Central America. Exploration of the region was marked by feuding among would-be conquistadores: Gil González Davila 'discovered' the Golfo de Fonseca and tried claiming it as his own, only to be captured by rival Spaniard Cristóbal de Olid, who had similar designs. González Davila turned the tables, however, by luring Olid's men to his side, then capturing and beheading Olid. Hernán Cortéz and others tried to quell the feuding, but to no avail.

The term 'Banana Republic' was coined by American writer O Henry in reference to Honduras.

The discovery of gold and silver in the 1530s drew more Spanish settlers and, more importantly, increased the demand for indigenous slave labor. Native Hondurans had long resisted Spanish invasion and enslavement and, in 1537, a young Lenca chief named Lempira led an indigenous uprising against the Spanish (see opposite). Inspired by Lempira's example, revolt swept the western region, and the Spanish were very nearly expelled. But Lempira was assassinated at peace talks arranged with the Spanish in 1538, and the native resistance was soon quelled. A cycle of smaller revolts and brutal repression followed, decimating the native population. African slaves were introduced in the 1540s to fill the growing labor shortage.

Mining sustained the colony for the remainder of the century, but a collapse of silver prices (and the constant challenges of excavating such rugged terrain) devastated the Honduran economy. Cattle and tobacco enterprises gained some traction, and a change in the Spanish throne in the early 1700s reduced corruption and helped revive the mining industry. However, another upheaval in Spanish rule in 1808 – when Napoleon Bonaparte installed one of his own on the Spanish throne – sparked revolts on both sides of the Atlantic, which irreparably damaged Spanish colonial rule.

2000 BC–AD 250

The Pre-Classic period. Early Maya villages begin to form in Southern Mexico and Guatemala. The Maya become adept farmers and astronomers, but development in Copán is slow going.

AD 250–800

The Classic period. Grand times are marked by the invasion of Teotihuacán in Mexico, the rise of great ceremonial centers in Honduras and Belize, and the ascendancy and eventual demise of the Maya in Copán.

426

King 'Great Sun First Quetzal Macaw' comes to Copán, ruling until AD 435 and giving rise to the Classic Period of Copán. Later kings revere him as the semi-divine founder of the city.

LEMPIRA: MAN OF THE MOUNTAIN

The Spanish conquest was never kind to indigenous people, and the early 1500s saw native Hondurans enslaved and forced to perform difficult and dangerous work in colonial gold and silver mines. In 1537 a young Lenca chief named Lempira ('Man of the Mountain' in Lenca) gathered a large and disparate band of indigenous fighters – some reports say his army had 30,000 men from dozens of tribes – to oppose Spanish repression. Lempira directed a series of surprise attacks on Spanish stations, which in turn inspired indigenous revolts in other regions, including Comayagua and Trujillo. A Spanish force tracked Lempira to a fortified mountain redoubt called Peñol de Cerquín, near present-day Erandique. There, Lempira repelled all attacks, holding off better-armed and better-equipped Spanish soldiers for more than six months. In 1538 the Spanish finally resorted to treachery. Though there is disagreement about the exact circumstances, what is known is that Lempira was lured to peace talks and then murdered; resistance collapsed after his death. Lempira is now seen as a hero – the national currency is named after him, as are numerous towns and the state where he led his famous revolt.

BIRTH OF A NATION

On September 15, 1821, Honduras, Guatemala, El Salvador, Costa Rica and Nicaragua declared independence from Spain, and shortly after joined the newly formed Mexican Empire. The relationship didn't last long and in 1823 the same countries declared independence from Mexico and formed the Federal Republic of Central America. Though Honduras was the poorest and least-populated of the countries, it produced some of the federation's most important leaders. Chief among them was the liberal hero General Francisco Morazán, commonly dubbed the 'George Washington of Central America,' who led the federation from 1830 to 1838. But bitter conflicts between liberals and conservatives proved too divisive for the nascent union, and in May 1838 the Central American Congress freed its members to form independent states – Honduras did so on November 15 of that year.

Gringos in Honduras, by Guillermo Yuscarán, is an informative book (despite the flippant title), containing short biographies of seven Americans who have impacted Honduras, from William Walker to naturalist/humorist Archie Carr.

The liberal and conservative factions continued to wrestle for power in Honduras after independence. Conservatives favored a pro-church, aristocratic style of government, while liberals supported free-market development of the kind taking place in the US and parts of Western Europe. Power alternated between the two factions, and Honduras was ruled by a succession of civilian governments and military regimes. (The country's constitution would be rewritten 17 times between 1821 and 1982.) Government has officially been by popular election, but Honduras has experienced hundreds of coups, rebellions, power seizures, electoral 'irregularities,' foreign invasion and meddling since achieving independence from Spain.

Operated by the nonprofit United Fruit Company Historical Society, www.unitedfruit.org offers detailed and independent information on the United Fruit Company's role in Central America.

Fighting between liberals and conservatives was briefly suspended in the 1880s when an American adventurer named William Walker (see p193) launched a bizarre and ill-fated attempt to conquer Central America. He

800–1200

While the Maya are in decline, pre-Hispanic populations are reaching their peak in present-day La Moskitia. The first inhabitants of the Bay Islands are also setting down roots.

800–1500

Post-Classic period. Copán and other great Maya city-states begin a rapid decline. Deforestation, overpopulation and flooding may be to blame. By 1200, farmers have departed Copán, and the royal city is reclaimed by the jungle.

1502

Christopher Columbus lands near Trujillo – the first European contact with mainland America – but the country draws less conquistador action than Mexico or Panama.

succeeded in gaining control of Nicaragua in 1856, but a joint Central American military effort forced Walker back to the US within a year. He returned in 1860, landing near Trujillo. He was captured by British agents and turned over to Honduran authorities, who promptly executed him. He is buried in Trujillo.

THE BANANA YEARS

Where William Walker failed, US free enterprise succeeded. In the 1880s the New York and Honduras Rosario Mining Company (NYHRMC) revived Honduras' promising but underdeveloped mining industry. The company enjoyed almost unfettered (and untaxed) access to the ore-rich mountains near the town of El Rosario, east of Tegucigalpa. In 74 years of operation – the area was turned into a national park in 1954 – the NYHRMC extracted an estimated US$100 million of gold, silver, copper and zinc; however, little of that money or product remained in Honduras.

But it was the banana that would most entangle Honduras with foreign interests and governments. In 1899 the Boston Fruit Company merged with the Snyder Fruit Company to form the United Fruit Company. The new company imported most of its fruit from Panama and Costa Rica, but soon acquired seven small banana operations in Honduras. That same year, three Italian brothers named Luca, Felix, and Joseph Vaccaro founded Vaccaro Brothers & Co – the predecessor of Standard Fruit Company – and began exporting bananas from the La Ceiba region to their base in New Orleans. In 1902 Russian émigré Samuel Zemurray established the Hubbard-Zemurray company, which would eventually become the Cuyamel Fruit Company. United purchased Cuyamel in 1929 and made Zemurray company president in 1933. United and Standard – which are today known as Chiquita and Dole fruit companies – have been battling for control of the Honduran (and world) banana market ever since.

Bananas accounted for 11% of Honduras' exports in 1892, 42% in 1903, 66% in 1913, and 80% in 1929. The spectacular economic success of the banana industry made the banana companies extremely powerful within Honduras, with the rival companies allying themselves with competing political parties. Political, environmental, labor and bribery scandals have marred the industry throughout its existence, including Zemurray's support of a 1908 coup attempt against a Vaccaro-friendly president; Chiquita's 1975 and 1976 bribery of the Honduran minister of economy; and in 1998, allegations of repressive labor practices and use of toxic pesticides in Honduras and Colombia. A two-month strike in 1954 – in which as many as 25,000 banana workers and thousands of sympathizers in textile, mining and other trades participated – remains a seminal moment in Honduran labor history. For more on the banana companies, see p195.

Elvia: The Fight for Land and Liberty (1988) is a half-hour PBS documentary about Elvia Alvarado and her path from rural girlhood to national peasant organizer.

1530s

The discovery of gold and silver in the 1530s draws more Spanish settlers and, more importantly, increases the demand for indigenous slave labor.

1536

San Pedro Sula – originally called San Pedro de Puerto Caballos – is founded by Pedro de Alvarado. It becomes an important commercial center and is eventually sacked by pirates in the 17th century.

1537

Lenca chief Lempira leads an indigenous uprising across Western Honduras; he nearly succeeds in expelling the Europeans. Lured into peace negotiations, he is assassinated in 1538.

BRITISH INFLUENCE IN HONDURAS

British influence in Central America is often thought to extend no further than Belize, which was a colony of the UK until 1981 and where English is still the official language. However, British merchants – and pirates – played an important role in colonial Honduras, and their influence is still very evident today.

Spain colonized and exploited Central America with little competition for almost a century. However, all those New World riches eventually caught the attention of rival countries. By the turn of the 17th century, British pirates (and some Dutch and French) frequently attacked Spanish fleets; in 1643, they destroyed the city of Trujillo, which was then Honduras' main shipping port. British merchants also began to establish timber operations along the coast, extending from Cabo Gracias a Díos to present-day Belize. For labor, the British brought black slaves from their colonies in Jamaica and elsewhere. The British also armed indigenous groups to help contest Spanish rule; in fact, the Miskitu people of the so-called Mosquito Coast actually derive their name not from 'mosquito,' but from 'musket,' a weapon they were given by British pirates and settlers, and used with notorious effect against the Spanish. Spain slowly regained the upper hand through the 18th century, and in 1786 Britain recognized Spanish sovereignty over the Honduran Caribbean coast. But just over a half-century later, Britain retook the Bay Islands during the chaotic years of the Central American federation, remaining there until 1859. Even as the UK ceded military control, British bankers hatched a sham railroad deal in the 1860s that left Honduras with less than 100km of usable track and some £6 million in debt, which ballooned to US$125 million over the next half-century. In 1925 Honduras managed to negotiate a substantial forbearance, but many point to British loans as the beginning of Honduras' long struggle with foreign debt. Finally, the British also played an important role in the creation of the Garífuna ethnic group, one of Honduras' most well known. In 1797, following a deadly uprising on the island of Saint Vincent, British colonizers loaded several thousand slaves onto boats and shipped them to the island of Roatán. Over 1000 died en-route, but those who survived prospered and multiplied, mixing with indigenous people. Today Garífuna villages dot the Caribbean Coast as far as Guatemala and Belize.

British influence in Honduras is still evident today. English is the principle language on the Bay Islands, and almost 30% of the Miskitu vocabulary is English, including the days of the week, and words such as 'landing' (for pier). Many Hondurans from those areas feel a sentimental kinship with the UK; for some, it even exceeds their affinity for Spain or Honduras itself.

RISE OF THE STRONGMEN

The Spanish-American war in 1898 laid the groundwork for increased US involvement in the region. The US averted and mediated a number of conflicts in Central America, including Nicaragua's 1907 invasion of Honduras and a border dispute between Guatemala and Honduras in 1917. Of course, American involvement in those and other disputes had everything to do with protecting American business interests, especially

1538–50

Small-scale revolts are met with even harder oppression. Nearly 95% of the indigenous population in Central and Western Honduras will be wiped out in the first 50 years of the conquest. Most die from disease.

1540–45

Mining is sustaining the backwater colony, and 2000 enslaved Africans are brought to Honduras to work in gold and silver mines. The big problem: the natives are dead, with just 8000 under Spanish control.

1643

British pirates destroy Trujillo, Honduras' main shipping port, and establish timber operations along the North Coast. They bring more slaves from their colonies in the Caribbean and begin arming indigenous groups.

its banana companies, by force if necessary. When workers struck against Standard Fruit Company in 1920, the US sent advisors – and a warship.

In 1932 General Tiburcio Carías Andino was elected president amid a deep worldwide depression. Carías strengthened the armed forces, then gained favor with banana companies by opposing strikes, and with foreign governments by strictly adhering to debt payments. He also consolidated his own power, outlawing the Honduran communist party and restricting the press. The Honduran constitution did not allow re-election so Carías had it amended, extending the presidential term from four to six years. He served as a virtual dictator, and did not step down until 1949, and then only under pressure from the US.

And the Sea Shall Hide Them (2005), by William Jackson, is the true story of the murder of 10 crew members and passengers aboard the *Olympia* as it sailed from Utila to Roatán in 1905.

In 1956 a power grab by the country's vice president prompted a military coup, the first (but not the last) in Honduran history. The military soon stepped aside for civilian elections, but a new constitution ratified in 1957 made the head of the armed forces – not the president – the country's top military authority. In 1963, 10 days before the next presidential election, the military again seized power. Colonel López Arellano suspended elections for two years, then ran himself (and won). He served the full six-year term, and was notable for his authoritarian excess and disregard for bureaucratic process. He stepped aside for civilian elections in 1971, only to be reinstalled a year later following another military coup.

In 1839 American explorer John Lloyd Stephens purchased Copán ruins for US$50 from the landowner, who considered the land useless – too rocky, it seems.

A succession of military leaders, each as corrupt and ineffective as the last, ruled the country from 1972 to 1981. Arellano was removed following allegations he had accepted a US$1.25 million bribe from United Brands Company (formerly United Fruit Company); for his part, United Brands chief Eli Black committed suicide by jumping from his New York City office window when the accusations surfaced. Arellano was succeeded by General Juan Alberto Melgar Castro, who succumbed to a scandal implicating members of the military with murder and drug trafficking and was replaced by General Policarpo Paz García. Paz García was the only one to follow through with a long-standing promise to return Honduras to civilian rule. In 1980, voters elected a congress, and in 1981, a president. Honduras' era of military rule was over.

Between 1920 and 1923, there were 17 uprisings or coup attempts in Honduras.

LATE 20TH CENTURY

The 1980s

During the 1980s, Honduras found itself surrounded on all sides by political upheaval and popular uprisings. In Nicaragua, the Somoza dictatorship was overthrown by Sandinista rebels in 1979, its guardsmen fleeing across the border into Honduras. The following year, full-scale war broke out in El Salvador as the government cranked up its repression of opposition leaders (Archbishop Óscar Romero was assassinated in March 1980) and

1700s

Silver prices rise and fall, bringing more ranching and tobacco farming to the country. By 1786, the Spanish win control of the coast from the Brits, but the ethnic make-up will be changed forever.

1797

After a slave uprising on the island of Saint Vincent, the British dump some 2000 black Caribes on Roatán, who establish a village at Punta Gorda, giving rise to a new ethnic group, the Garífuna.

1821

Spanish colonial rule is severely weakened by revolts and political gaffes. Honduras, Guatemala, El Salvador, Costa Rica and Nicaragua declare independence from Spain. Honduran José Cecilio del Valle writes the Declaration of Independence.

THE SOCCER WAR

There's little love lost between most Hondurans and Salvadorans, who seem to despise each other with equal vigor to this day. Much of the enmity can be traced to a brief but embittered war the two countries fought in 1969, known commonly as the Guerra de Fútbol – the Soccer War.

During the '50s and '60s, El Salvador's flagging economy and severe overpopulation had led as many as 300,000 Salvadorans to cross illegally into Honduras in search of work and arable land. The Honduran economy declined in the same period, and Hondurans began to blame Salvadoran immigrants for stealing jobs and depressing wages. In June 1969 Honduras announced it would begin expelling illegal Salvadoran immigrants; hundreds were deported, and many thousands left on their own accord. Honduran media continued the blame-game, while Salvadoran reports alleged abuse by Honduran police and immigration officers.

That same month, by chance, the two countries were competing against each other in a World Cup qualifying match. At the game, which was played in San Salvador, Salvadoran fans attacked Hondurans, destroyed the Honduran flag and ridiculed the anthem. Back in Honduras, angry Hondurans assaulted Salvadorans on the streets.

Tensions soared and on July 14, El Salvador invaded its neighbor. Salvadoran troops penetrated several kilometers into Honduran territory and captured the western town of Nueva Ocotepeque. Honduras responded with air strikes, destroying military installations and oil and gas storage tanks.

The Soccer War lasted just four days; around 2000 people died, mostly Honduran civilians, and as many as 100,000 Salvadorans fled or were expelled. Relations between the countries took years to mend, and in many ways never have. (The official peace treaty wasn't ratified until 1980.) Relations between the two countries were tested again not long thereafter, when El Salvador erupted into civil war, bringing fresh waves of refugees across the border into Honduras.

the new Nicaraguan government provided insurgents with a fresh supply of weapons. Meanwhile, the civil war in Guatemala continued unabated.

Although Honduras experienced some unrest, the country never broke into out-and-out civil war, a fact that is puzzling to many observers. Certainly the conditions for civil unrest were there: military rule, a repressed (but organized) working class, a history of foreign meddling and exploitation, especially by the US, not to mention the example set by its neighbors.

Historians and political scientists point to a variety of factors to explain Honduras' emergence from the 1980s revolution-free. The long-standing domination of the banana companies seems to have prevented the development of a native-born economic and political elite. Honduras did not have the Somozas, whose excesses of wealth and power in Nicaragua were legendary, or the '14 families' of El Salvador whose control of the coffee industry and connections with the military turned the country into an agricultural oligarchy.

The Digital National Security Archive (http://nsarchive.chadwyck.com) contains every officially released document related to the Iran-Contra affair and subsequent congressional investigation; registration required for access.

1822–38

Central America joins the Mexican Empire. A year later, with the overthrow of Mexican emperor Agustine Inturbide, it forms an independent Central American Federation. Honduran Francisco Morazán leads the new federation from 1830 to 1838.

1838

Conflicts between liberals and conservatives rip the Central American Federation apart. Honduras declares independence on November 15, but infighting continues.

1856

With the idea of conquering Central America, William Walker invades Nicaragua, but is expelled a year later. In 1860 he returns to the Honduran Coast, but is captured and executed in Trujillo.

This in turn opened political space for genuine agrarian reform, the lack of which had heightened working-class frustration and militancy in other countries. Honduras has long had one of Central America's most effective and organized labor movements. Despite the overwhelming power of banana interests, Honduran *campesinos* (peasants) and other workers have consistently managed to wrest concessions (and accept compromises) without resorting to violence. Notably, labor disputes in Honduras have rarely included a call for upending the government, but rather for the enforcement of existing laws. The Honduran military, more democratic and less beholden to the nation's elite than in other countries, played a more stabilizing, rather than repressive, role.

US military aid to Honduras jumped from US$3.3 million in 1980 to US$31.3 million in 1982.

Of course, the US had a powerful interest in keeping Honduras stable. With Marxist revolutions erupting on all sides (and Cuban and Soviet influence plain to see) the US viewed Honduras as a crucial battleground in its effort to halt the so-called 'domino effect' and the spread of communism in the Americas. Economic aid poured into Honduras, quickly making it one of the top-10 recipients of US military and economic aid. In return, the US used Honduras as a staging ground for counterinsurgency efforts throughout the region. Nicaraguan refugee camps in Honduras were used as bases for a US-sponsored undeclared covert war against the Sandinista government, which became known as the Contra War. At the same time the US was training the Salvadoran military at Salvadoran refugee camps inside Honduras.

The two-lempira bank note features the town of Amapala on Isla del Tigre.

Economic aid slowed local opposition, but it wasn't long before Hondurans began agitating against US militarization in their country. Demonstrations drew 60,000 demonstrators in Tegucigalpa and 40,000 in San Pedro Sula, and a few nascent revolutionary groups appeared. In reply, military commanders ordered the kidnapping and killing of hundreds of opposition and student leaders – a first for Honduras. The tactic backfired, swelling the ranks of demonstrators and alienating many in the military establishment, who were themselves growing uneasy about the army's complicity with increasingly brutal US-sponsored conflicts in the region. In March 1984 the military's pro-American commander was toppled in a bloodless coup by his fellow officers. General Walter López Reyes was appointed the successor, and the Honduran government promptly announced it would re-examine US military presence in the country. In August 1984 it suspended US training of Salvadoran military within its borders.

Left-leaning website www.mayispeakfreely.org has detailed information of human rights issues in Honduras and other countries, including an up-to-date 'News in Brief' section.

In 1986 Washington was rocked with revelations that the Reagan administration had secretly and illegally used money from the sale of arms to Iran to support anti-Sandinista Contras operating out of Honduras. The scandal rekindled demonstrations in Honduras; in November 1988, the Honduran government refused to sign a new military agreement with the US, and then-president José Azcona Hoyo said the Contras would have to leave Honduras. With the election of Violeta Chamorro as president

1860–80

In 1860, the British finally cede the Bay Islands to Honduras. On the mainland, the Honduran government moves the capital from Comayagua to Tegucigalpa in 1880. US investment revives the Honduran mining industry.

1899

Birth of the Banana Republic. The Vaccaro Brothers found a banana export company that will eventually become Standard Fruit Company. The banana industry will dominate the Honduran economy and politics for the next 100 years.

1898–1925

The Spanish-American war establishes precedent for increased US activity in the region. Honduras endures a prolonged period of severe instability. There are 17 coup attempts or documented uprisings between 1920 and 1923 alone.

THE LEGACY OF HURRICANE MITCH

With new shopping malls, cruise docks and bridges going up, Honduras is finally starting to recover from Hurricane Mitch.

The slow-moving storm made landfall east of La Ceiba on October 29, 1998 and then simply sat there – for four days. Honduran officials had had time to evacuate some 100,000 people from the coastal areas, including 45,000 from the Bay Islands, but at least 6000 people were killed by the storm, which dropped its heaviest loads in the middle of the country.

The property damage was equally staggering. In Honduras, the destruction included the decimation of 70% of roads and virtually every bridge in the country. Thirty-three thousand homes were destroyed and another 55,000 damaged, leaving 20% of the population without shelter. At least 25 villages were wiped from the map. Fifty thousand cows and 70% of the nation's crops were lost. In all, Honduras suffered an estimated US$2.5 billion in damages.

The international community responded with a massive relief effort, but as in so many other natural disasters, funds dried up as the initial emergency subsided. While the storm's physical effects are slowly disappearing, the social and emotional blows are yet to heal. A decade on, many Hondurans still point to El Mitch as the root of the country's (and their own) current woes.

of Nicaragua in 1990, the Contra war ended and the Contras were finally out of Honduras.

The 1990s

Elections in 1989 ushered in Rafael Leonardo Callejas Romero of the National Party – who had lost in 1985 – to the presidency in Honduras; he won 51% of the votes and assumed office in January 1990. Early that year, the new administration instituted a severe economic-austerity program, which provoked widespread alarm, unrest and protest. Callejas had promised to keep the lempira stable; instead during his tenure the lempira's value jumped from around two lempiras to eight against the US dollar. Prices rose dramatically to keep pace with the US dollar, but salaries lagged behind. Hondurans grew poorer and poorer, a trend that continues today.

In the elections of November 1993, Callejas was convincingly beaten by Carlos Roberto Reina Idiaquez of the center-left Liberal Party, who campaigned on a platform of moral reform, promising to attack government corruption and reform state institutions, including the judicial system and the military. Reina had inherited an economically depressed country and a currency that seemed to be in an unstoppable slide. By 1996 it had fallen past 12 lempiras to the US dollar and was heading for 13; at the time of writing, it is at nearly 20.

On January 27, 1998, Carlos Roberto Flores Facusse took office as Honduras' fifth democratically elected president. A member of the Liberal Party, like his predecessors, he was elected with a 10% margin over his nearest

The five stars on the flag represent the members of the former Federal Republic of Central America (ie Costa Rica, El Salvador, Guatemala, Honduras and Nicaragua).

Enrique's Journey (2006), by Sonia Nazario, is the book version of a Pulitzer Prize–winning *Los Angeles Times* series about a Honduran boy who travels from Tegucigalpa to North Carolina in search of his mother.

1920–50

Moravian missionaries arrive in La Moskitia, setting up schools, clinics and churches. With the formation of indigenous rights organizations in the 1950s, the Honduran government begins taking up some civic duties in the region.

1932–49

The great depression affects the world economy. Although elected fairly, Tiburcio Carías Andino rules as a virtual dictator, repeatedly revising the constitution to extend his term.

1954

The banana companies control huge amounts of Honduran land. The idea of land reform begins to creep into the national consciousness, and some 25,000 banana workers strike for better working conditions.

GANGS IN HONDURAS

Mara Salvatrucha (MS-13) is considered by some to be the most dangerous criminal gang in the Americas. It emerged in the 1980s from the poor, tough streets of Los Angeles, and its earliest members were Salvadoran children of refugees fleeing a US-sponsored civil war. M-18, a rival *mara* (gang), formed at the same time.

The gangs jumped to Central America in the 1990s, as new immigration laws had alien criminals deported rather than tried in US courts. The gangs quickly took root, with easier access to weapons, less-effective policing, and a virtually bottomless pool of poor, disaffected youth. Today, MS-13 and M-18 have around 100,000 members between them, mostly in El Salvador, Honduras, Guatemala, Nicaragua, Mexico and the US. In Honduras around 30,000 young people are thought to be gang members.

Mara members are known for their extensive tattooing and the gruesomeness of their attacks (machetes are popular weapons). Most attacks are on opposing gang members, but a few incidents – such as a 2004 assault on a public bus outside San Pedro Sula that killed 28 people, including four children – gained international attention.

Honduras' former president Ricardo Maduro was the first Central American leader to adopt harsh anti-gang policies known as Mano Dura (Hard Hand). The policies made tattoos, hand signals and writing graffiti crimes of 'illicit association,' punishable by long jail terms. Mano Dura slowed gang recruitment and activity, but prisons quickly swelled beyond capacity and abuse allegations mounted. In 2003 a fire at a Honduran prison killed 68 suspected gang members, but an investigation found at least 59 had in fact been shot by the guards. A year later, another prison fire killed 104 suspected gang members as guards stood by doing nothing.

Off-duty officers and private security guards have also allegedly formed vigilante groups, reminiscent of military 'death squads' of the not-so-distant past. More than 2000 children and young adults have been killed in Honduras between 1998 and 2004; researchers say 15% to 20% of the killings were conducted by the police or with tacit police approval. In 2002 President Maduro took the unusual step of acknowledging extrajudicial killings but said a government study had found police involvement in only 23 cases in the previous five years. For now most Hondurans, unnerved by images of gang brutality, seem willing to overlook human-rights issues if they continue to stem the violence.

rival, National Party nominee Nora de Melgar, in elections that were considered fair and clean. He instigated a program of reform and modernization of the economy. The arrival of Hurricane Mitch (see boxed text, p31) on October 1998, at that time the strongest Atlantic hurricane on record, dashed those plans. In fact, President Flores would later say the storm had erased 50 years of progress in Honduras.

Land struggles and occupations continue in Honduras. There are reports of indigenous leaders being detained in order to obstruct their efforts to reclaim indigenous land.

THE 21ST CENTURY

Honduras' tourist industry was just recovering from Hurricane Mitch when the September 11, 2001, terror attacks slashed the number of travelers once

1962–69

President Ramón Villeda signs the country's first agrarian reform in 1962, but very little 'reforming' actually happens. Some 300,000 Salvadorans seek reprieve from poverty in Honduras, eventually kicking off the four-day 'Soccer War' in 1969.

1980–89

The US aids (or straight out wages) covert wars in Nicaragua and El Salvador. Bases are established in Honduras to fund the war in Nicaragua. US involvement eventually leads to the Iran-Contra scandal.

1998

Hurricane Mitch causes more than 6000 deaths and US$2.5 billion in damage in Honduras alone. The hurricane destroys 70% of the nation's roads and leaves 20% of the population without shelter.

more, especially the all-important American scuba-diver market. Later that year Hondurans elected Ricardo Maduro as their president, on promises to promote tourism and, more importantly, to reduce crime.

Gang violence (see opposite) and narco-trafficking was then the prevailing preoccupation of average Hondurans (as it is today). Rival gangs *(maras)* had spread to Honduras from El Salvador, where gang members deported from the US, especially Los Angeles, had taken root. (Central American countries have long called on the US to stop deporting known gang members but to no avail – some 20,000 felons were sent to Central America between 2000 and 2004.)

On December 23, 2012, the Maya long-count calendar reaches completion, signaling the end of this universe – hopefully we'll do a better job next time.

Maduro's own son was kidnapped and murdered in 1997, and Maduro promised a get-tough approach to gangs. He proposed legislation called 'Mano Dura' (Hard Hand), which dramatically increased penalties for gang-related crimes, and broadened the definition of 'illicit association.' The country's murder rate remains one of the highest in the world. Disturbing allegations are also surfacing that the government may be using 'death squads' to cope with the problem.

Journalist Dina Meza won the 2007 Amnesty International Special Award for Human Rights Journalism Under Threat for her coverage of alleged abuses by private security companies at her Spanish-language site www.revistazo.com.

Maduro was succeeded in the November 2005 elections by Manuel Zelaya, a cowboy hat–wearing rancher from Olancho, who was later removed from office in a military-backed coup d'etat on June 28, 2009. For details on the events leading up to the coup, see p34. While Zelaya lost the reigns of power by the end of his term, his presidency was not without its successes and controversies.

Zelaya's early administration was smudged by widespread allegations of corruption – in the first year of his presidency alone, as many as 11 ministers resigned amid corruption charges. And despite campaign promises to alleviate the violence associated with gangs and narco-trafficking, the nation's murder and kidnapping rates continued to rise.

During his tenure, Zelaya aligned himself closely with other Latin American left-wing leaders such as Venezuela's Hugo Chavez – a sea change for a nation that had long been Central America's strongest US ally. Zelaya also succeeded in raising the national minimum wage by 11%, a controversial move that may have played a part in his eventual ouster.

A massive 7.1 magnitude earthquake hit northern Honduras in May 2009. Luckily, only one bridge collapsed after the quake, and human casualties were limited.

Despite a leftward tilt in Honduran politics, the nation was one of the first signatories of the controversial Central America and Dominican Republic Free Trade Agreement (CAFTA DR). The trade deal, signed into law in 2005 by US President George W Bush after a bitter congressional fight, and ratified in Honduras on April 1, 2006, ended tariffs on as much as US$33 billion in goods and services when it went into full effect on January 1, 2009. The pact covers the US, El Salvador, Honduras, Guatemala, Nicaragua, Costa Rica and the Dominican Republic, and remains highly controversial. Advocates say it will open markets to US businesses, especially farmers and ranchers, while providing manufacturing jobs for Central Americans that

1998

On January 27, Carlos Roberto Flores Facusse takes office as Honduras' fifth democratically elected president. He instigates a program of reform and modernization of the economy.

2004

Gang members kill 28 people, including four children, on a public bus in San Pedro Sula, epitomizing growing gang violence in Central America.

2005

Some 1500 Maya-Chortí take over the Copán archaeological site, demanding land reform. The occupation lasts five days. With little agrarian reform to date, there continues to be land occupations throughout the nation to this day.

MARCHING ORDERS: THE MAKING OF A COUP D'ETAT

On the morning of June 28, 2009, soldiers stormed Honduras' presidential palace. It was the beginning of the first coup d'etat the nation had seen since 1978. The soldiers arrested President Manuel Zelaya in his pajamas and flew him into exile.

The military was acting on orders of the Supreme Court, which said Zelaya was breaking the law with his proposed constitutional referendum, which many opponents said was a thin-veiled ruse to extend his presidential term – much like the constitutional reforms enacted by Venezuelan President Hugo Chavez. The referendum was pre-empted when the Supreme Court declared Zelaya's maneuverings unconstitutional and ordered his arrest. According to Associated Press reports, it was the military that decided to fly Zelaya to Costa Rica rather than have him face charges at home.

In the days following the coup, massive protests rocked the capital and other parts of the country, and the Supreme Court installed Roberto Micheletti, president of the National Congress, as the interim president. Micheletti vowed to move forward with free presidential elections in November 2009, but international organizations continued to press the new government to re-instate the ousted president.

Zelaya attempted to re-enter Honduras on July 5, 2009, but the Honduran military blocked the runways in Tegucigalpa amid popular protests to allow his return. It was a country divided. Opponents of the coup – every nation in the Western Hemisphere, including the US and Venezuela (odd bedfellows indeed) – said the coup was unconstitutional, and that Zelaya should be allowed to return to power. The US went as far as to threaten new sanctions if a peace deal could not be bartered through talks being led by Costa Rican President Oscar Arias. Those in favor of the ouster said the Supreme Court was merely trying to uphold the constitution and protect Honduras' democratic tradition.

As of press time, it remained unclear where this situation would lead. Talks appeared to be breaking down, with neither side seeming willing to give an inch. Zelaya was making plans to return to Honduras again – by land, sea or sky – and words like 'civil war' and 'alternative government' were floating through the mainstream press.

Battle lines are being drawn over the Patuca Hydroelectric Dam project, which will flood 72 sq miles. According to the Minority Rights Group International, two activists fighting the project were killed in 2006.

would otherwise go to Asia. American labor unions fought the plan, saying it would take jobs from Americans and did not provide enough protections for Central American workers. In Central America, opposition came from the left which predicted the plan, like NAFTA before it, would lead to increased disenfranchisement of small farmers and business owners.

But it was Zelaya's plan to hold a referendum to re-write Honduras' Constitution – which has been around since way back when (1982) – that got him into hot water with the Supreme Court and eventually led to his ouster (see above). At the time this book went to press, it remained unclear how the coup would play out. Only time will tell the future of this little nation.

2006

A leftward shift continues in Latin America when Manuel 'Mel' Zelaya becomes president. Despite liberal tendencies, he implements the Central America and Dominican Republic Free Trade Agreement (CAFTA-DR).

2006–09

Liberal reforms continue, with a raise in the national minimum wage and plans to hold a national referendum to re-write the constitution. The referendum is declared illegal by the Supreme Court.

2009

On June 28 Zelaya is removed from power in a military-backed coup d'etat. The international community condemns the coup, Zelaya is removed to Costa Rica, and peace talks continue.

The Culture

THE NATIONAL PSYCHE

Hondurans don't seem to smile much – especially when confronted by foreigners. It's not that they are an unhappy people, but they are a people that at times seem resigned to follow a pre-destined path, to maintain the status quo and to avoid shaking the boat at all costs. But in a country with as much ethnic diversity as this – there are subsistence Tawahka farmers in Moskitia, radical students in Tegucigalpa, and well-heeled aristocrats with legacies dating back to colonial days nearly everywhere in between – there's truly no national consciousness or way of doing things. But one or two commonalities do run across the well-drawn lines of race and class. Family comes first and foremost. You follow that by ties to your church, class and ethnicity and, finally, to your nation. And while this may seem a disparate social make-up, one only need hear the deafening roar of 'goal!' when the national team scores to understand that, beyond the strictures of race and class, a strong national pride does exist.

Hondurans' are extremely passionate about *fútbol*, but the national soccer team has qualified to play in the World Cup only once, in 1982.

While, on the surface, Hondurans share many common traits with fellow Latinos – machismo, church, family, love of life, music and dance – it's safe to say that the attitude of most Hondurans is subdued when compared with that of their neighbors. Guatemala, El Salvador and Nicaragua all fought fierce civil wars in the 1980s – how is it possible that Honduras, which had many of the same economic and social conditions, did not also erupt into class warfare? There are many answers to that question, starting with a very simple one: the USA didn't let it happen. But there is also a prevailing go-with-the-flow attitude among Hondurans that surely played a role. It is unlike most Hondurans to raise their voices or complain too loudly, whether for having to wait in another seemingly endless line, or for having been born poor with little means of changing one's circumstances.

Hondurans endearingly refer to themselves as Catrachos, which is purportedly derived from General Florencio Xatruch, who led Honduran forces against William Walker (see p193)

Which is not to say Hondurans are accepting of injustice, or will turn a blind eye toward poor or unfair treatment, at least within the range of their own sphere. Honduras has long been a deeply unionized country, and Hondurans have used collective action with great success to exact land reforms or force changes in pay or working conditions. There is a rich tradition of organizing, especially among the poor and the landless. Demands tend to be modest, but are pursued with unwavering conviction.

Understanding the nexus of those two tendencies – mellow and accepting on one hand, committed to justice and collective action on the other – is the key to understanding the Honduran national psyche. In one sense, Hondurans simply have a higher level of tolerance. Whereas Salvadorans and Guatemalans are quick to decry a perceived wrong, Hondurans are more likely to take a wait-and-see approach. You might compare Hondurans to, say, an especially large stone. It takes much more pushing to get it moving but, once going, its momentum is almost impossible to oppose.

Check out www.honduras.com/catracho-forum, a Honduran chat room with forums on politics, religion, food, current events, sports and women's issues. It's a good intro to national culture.

LIFESTYLE

Honduras is a deeply stratified country, where the rich are super rich, the poor are desperately poor, and lifestyle is largely determined by the accident of one's birth. For the very wealthy, Honduras offers virtually all the luxuries that wealth commands in more developed countries, whether it's import cars or regular trips to beachside resorts in Roatán, New Orleans or Miami. The country's elite is divided between Tegucigalpa, where government and Honduras' nascent entertainment industry are based, and San Pedro Sula,

HOMOSEXUALITY IN HONDURAS

With the emergence of AIDS in the mid-1980s, homosexuals in Honduras suddenly faced a dual challenge. The disease raged through the gay community, quickly making Honduras the 'AIDS capital of Central America' (a distinction it still holds). But almost of equal importance was the change in attitudes toward gays by the general population. Though homosexuality was never widely accepted, it was generally tolerated. With AIDS came a dramatic increase in anti-homosexual rhetoric and fear-mongering – and, before long, physical assaults. In fact, the government began a campaign of harassment and marginalization that continues today.

In 2000 Amnesty International issued a scathing report of government-sponsored human-rights abuses. The group pointed to more than 200 murders of gay and transsexual sex workers in the previous 10 years that had received only perfunctory police investigation, or none at all. Amnesty International also accused the government of hampering gay organizations by blocking their registration as nonprofits. In May 2002, then-President Ricardo Maduro signed the 'Social and Co-Existence Law,' which ostensibly targeted gangs and organized crime but in effect gave police the authority to wantonly arrest gays and lesbians (usually for the purpose of preventing 'amoral behavior'). In 2004 the mayor of San Pedro Sula – which has Honduras' most visible and outspoken gay population – ordered the raiding of a gay club, resulting in multiple arrests. In early 2005 a constitutional amendment was unanimously ratified, prohibiting gay marriage and adoption by same-sex couples. In 2008 several killings and attacks were reported that were allegedly connected with the sexual orientation of the victims, including the murder of two transgender sex workers in Comayaguëla.

The gay community has responded to anti-gay sentiment with activism of its own. Several advocacy organizations have been founded to help homosexuals to protect their civil rights. As early as 1988, an organization called Las Hijas del Maíz (Daughters of the Corn) was active in supporting gays and lesbians, and promoting tolerance. At least three organizations are presently active in Tegucigalpa and San Pedro Sula; see p262 for contact information. Despite this activism (or perhaps because of it) there has been a series of violent attacks on gay-rights activists.

where private business executives tend to live. There is a small group of merchants and tradesmen that makes up the middle class. These people may be college educated and have some disposable income for luxuries like owning a car, but are still tied to the economic necessities of life like their lower-class brethren.

For the destitute, life can be very difficult. The official minimum monthly wage went up by 11% at the beginning of 2009 to L$5500 (around US$291) per month, though people working on the fringes of the economy earn even less. The urban poor are crowded into decaying neighborhoods – often rife with gang violence – and shantytowns built on unused hillsides and river banks, vulnerable to flooding and mudslides. The rural and coastal poor seem somehow less desperate, since, in the end, the land and the ocean provide at least minimal sustenance. But life in those areas poses its own set of challenges: Garífuna communities are in the fight of their lives to hang on to their traditional lands, which developers have long eyed for beach resorts. Likewise, farmers struggle to hold onto their modest plots against the expansion of logging and commercial farming.

Daylight saving time was adopted for the first time in Honduras in 1994, but abandoned the same year.

Family life in Honduras is similar to that of much of Central America, where strong Catholic and other religious traditions butt up against the practical concerns of life in a developing country. Family is deeply important, and ideally children grow up, marry, start a family and settle down near their parents (and their grandparents before them). However, the reality is that many families, especially rural and small-town ones, are scattered by the need to find work; countless families have husbands, mother, brothers or sisters working in San Pedro Sula, Tegucigalpa, the

To learn more about Garífuna culture, history and contemporaneous issues, head to www.stanford.edu/group/arts/honduras.

Bay Islands (where there's a major construction boom), or in El Salvador or the United States.

The same goes for sex and marriage: traditional beliefs run deep, but frequently bend under the pressure of young people living without one or both or their parents, or spouses separated for long periods. Divorce, sex before marriage, children out of wedlock: though frowned upon, they are a relatively common and tolerated aspect of modern Honduran life. Only abortion and homosexuality (especially in the age of AIDS) remain deeply taboo.

ECONOMY

Honduras is one of the poorest countries in the Western Hemisphere, along with Haiti, Nicaragua, Guyana and Bolivia. Nearly two-thirds of Hondurans live in poverty – and 45% in extreme poverty – and the unemployment rate hovers at 28%. Honduras' GDP is US$13.78 billion; with a population of seven million, its per capita GDP is around US$4400.

Like many developing countries, Honduras is saddled with enormous foreign debt (around US$3.6 billion). It was one of only seven countries outside of sub-Saharan Africa to qualify for the Heavily Indebted Poor Countries (HIPC) Initiative, which went into effect for Honduras in July 2006. Yet the HIPC relief amounts to only US$1.3 billion.

The Honduran economy was for many years almost entirely dependent on coffee and banana exports, and controlled by Standard and United Fruit Companies. Those companies – now Dole and Chiquita, respectively – still exert powerful economic and political leverage, but the economy as a whole has significantly diversified in the last two decades. Honduras has also expanded its non-traditional exports, such as shrimp and melons, and promoted tourism. *Maquila*s (export-only factories), which import US yarn and fabric and turn them into clothing for export, now employ well over 100,000 Hondurans, mostly around San Pedro Sula and Puerto Cortes. Remittances from abroad represent over a quarter of GDP. And while the world economy was flagging in mid-2009, the government was still hoping for around 4% growth.

Walker (1987), directed by Alex Cox and starring Ed Harris, is a somewhat hallucinogenic portrayal of William Walker and his misadventures in 1850s Central America; it includes a mute lover and anachronisms like helicopters and Zippo lighters.

The controversial Central America and Dominican Republic Free Trade Agreement (CAFTA-DR) came into effect in Honduras in April 2006. The agreement lowered tariffs and trade barriers for scores of goods, services, agricultural products and investments. The effects of CAFTA have yet to play out. Supporters say it will stimulate the economies of Central American countries while critics say multinational corporations will squeeze out small businesses. CAFTA also includes safeguards for labor rights and environmental protection – it remains to be seen if it will help to end illegal pine and mahogany logging in Honduras (see p57) or accelerate it, as some predict.

POPULATION

Approximately 10% of the population – 700,000 Hondurans – live and work abroad.

Honduras is experiencing the most rapid urbanization in Central America: the urban population was 44% in 1990 and around 48% in 2008, with a predicted annual growth rate of 2.9%. Around 85% to 90% of Hondurans are ladino, a mixture of Spanish and *indígena* (indigenous people). The rest are part of 10 different ethnic minorities: some indigenous, some immigrants, others a mixture of the two.

The Tolupanes (also called Jicaque or Xicaque) live in small villages dotting the departments of Yoro and Francisco Morazán (see p97). They are thought to be one of the oldest indigenous communities in Honduras, having retained certain ancient traditions like making clothing from pounded tree bark (though this is fast disappearing). They are reclusive and widely

LOST LANGUAGES

Ethnic minorities make up nearly 15% of the Honduran population, yet only 1% speak an indigenous or minority language. Two of Honduras' major ethnic groups – the Lenca and Maya-Chortí – have lost their ancestral language altogether (though related languages are spoken by Lenca and Maya groups in Guatemala and El Salvador). The Tolupanes, Pech and Tawahka communities are so small – in the case of the Tawahka, less than 1000 members – that their language is in danger of disappearing as well.

Bilingual education has been proposed to reclaim and reinforce these languages. But that is much easier said than done: all of Honduras' indigenous languages are fundamentally oral, and a full-scale 'language rescue' program would require establishing a standardized orthography, writing and producing grammar books and dictionaries, and recruiting and training teachers who can teach in both languages. The Honduran government, for one, seems unwilling to make the investment. International efforts have focused more on post-Conquest language groups, especially Miskitu and Garífuna, which pose most of the same challenges but have many more active speakers. Those groups also have a more established and active leadership, which is able to mobilize community support and garner international attention.

scattered; there are seven Tolupán communities that were not identified as such until the late 1980s.

The Maya-Chortí people live near the Guatemalan border, in the department of Copán. They are embroiled in a bitter land dispute with the government, which has promised to redistribute traditional lands but has found a thousand reasons to delay the process.

The Lenca live in southwestern Honduras in several colonial towns along the namesake Ruta Lenca (see p133). More than other groups, the Lenca have preserved their traditional clothing, easily spotted for their brilliant colors and designs, similar to those seen in Guatemala. The Maya-Chortí live near the Guatemalan border, in the department of Copán (see p118).

Almas de Media Noche (Souls at Midnight; 2002) is Honduras' first commercial feature film, written and directed by Juan Carlos Franconi. It's a mystery-fantasy about six journalism students investigating a Lenca legend near Lago de Yojoa.

The Miskitu (see p244) live in La Moskitia, on the northeastern coast and along the Río Coco, which forms the border between Honduras and Nicaragua. Miskitus are more involved with tourism than other groups, serving as guides and boatmen for the growing influx of visitors to the Mosquito Coast.

The Pech live in the interior river regions of La Moskitia. Though generally less outgoing than the Miskitu, they are also involved in tourism to the Moskitia, mainly up the Río Plátano in Las Marías and beyond.

The Tawahka (see p40) also live in the interior of La Moskitia in the area around the Río Patuca designated as the Tawahka Asangni Biosphere Reserve. The Tawahka number less than 1000, though their language has been preserved.

The Garífuna live on Honduras' north coast, from La Moskitia all the way across to Belize. Other Black Caribs – descendants of immigrants from the Cayman Islands and other Caribbean islands, who came to work on the banana plantations – live on the north coast as well as the Bay Islands (see p197).

SPORTS

As in most Latin American countries, *fútbol* (soccer) is the number one spectator sport in Honduras. The country's soccer league, **La Liga Mayor de Fútbol Francisco Morazán** (Francisco Morazán Major League Soccer; www.hondurasfutbol.com), is made up of 10 teams from around the country. The league has two seasons – one from February to June, the other August to October; games are played around the country, although there are only three stadiums – in Tegucigalpa, San Pedro Sula and La Ceiba.

Baseball is a distant second in popularity with a semi-professional league, La Liga Mayor de Beísbol Francisco Morazán (Francisco Morazán Major League Baseball). It is made up of five teams from around the country, and is particularly popular on the Bay Islands and the North Coast, where people keep track of the US major leagues.

Outfielder Gerald Young is the only Honduran to have played in Major League Baseball. He played for the Astros (1987–92), the Rockies (1993) and the Cardinals (1994).

MULTICULTURALISM

Honduras is surely one of Central America's most diverse nations, with 10 distinctive ethnic groups – five indigenous, and five that emerged from post-Conquest mixing and immigration. The groups vary in history, size, language and appearance, but together form part of Honduras' fascinating ethnic milieu.

The largest group are ladinos (or mestizos), who make up what can be called 'mainstream' Honduras. Spanish-speaking, they are descended from intermixing among European explorers and the indigenous people they encountered. Today ladinos, who range from very fair skinned to fairly dark, dominate most aspects of Honduran politics and economy.

Honduras' largest indigenous group is the Lenca, concentrated in southwestern Honduras – hence La Ruta Lenca (Lenca Route). The Lenca are believed to have descended from Chibcha-speaking Amerindians of present-day Colombia and Venezuela who immigrated to Honduras around 3000 years ago. The Lenca were a large enough group to develop regional subgroups, mostly lowland versus highland, and internecine rivalries and even warfare were common. To minimize fighting, the Lenca developed peace treaties that were reaffirmed every year in elaborate ceremonies known as *guancascos,* which are still practiced in many communities today. The Lenca language has been lost, and what few non-Spanish words remain in the common vernacular are mostly Nahuatl, evidence of the strong Aztec and Central Mexican influence on Lenca society that took place before and just after the conquest. For more details on the Lenca, see p140.

Pre-Hispanic *guancascos* (peace ceremonies) are still practiced in some remote villages along the Ruta Lenca.

The Maya-Chortí are the next largest of Honduras' indigenous groups. Concentrated in the Copán Valley, they are descended from the builders of the great Copán temples. Today, Chortí communities are desperately poor, riven by drugs and alcohol, land loss and unemployment. Their circumstances are accentuated by the thriving tourism industry in Copán village. But if Chortí were once resigned to their circumstances, they are no longer; since the early 1990s, indigenous activists have led a bitter fight to recover their traditional farmland, much of it acquired by private landowners during government-sanctioned land-grabs in the 1950s. Chortí protesters have occupied the Copán archaeological site several times to draw attention to their fight, and have paid dearly for their newfound outspokenness: dozens have been murdered or jailed for their political work (p118).

You'll find links to schools, Spanish language programs, and cultural centers in Honduras at www.worldwide.edu/ci/honduras.

The Pech and Tawahka indigenous groups are both found deep in the interior of La Moskitia, and though ethnically distinct, share a common history. Both groups are descended from the Chibcha-speaking migration from South America around 1000 BC, which also gave rise to the Lenca. Both groups lived over a large area in pre-Conquest times, but receded into the rainforest in the face of Spanish incursion (and Miskitu collusion). Today both groups live mostly by subsistence farming; the Pech are increasingly involved with ecotourism (mostly as guides in Las Marías; see p244). In 1999 the Tawahka (the smallest of the Honduran indigenous groups) won the establishment of the Tawahka Asangni Biosphere Reserve, protecting their ancestral lands; for more see p40.

Ghosts, or *duppies*, as they are known in the Bay Islands, are alive and well. They are said to live in the forests, and are charged with protecting lost pirate treasure.

The Tolupanes are the fifth and last indigenous group of Honduras. While some ethnologists believe they, like the other groups, emerged from the Chibcha migration around 3000 years ago, others believe the Tolupanes arrived from the north at least 5000 years ago. It is known that the Tolupanes once ranged over virtually all of present-day Honduras, but retreated into the mountains around today's Yoro rather than face the enslavement and disease brought by the Spanish. They are a deeply reclusive group, and only a few pockets still speak the Tolupan tongue. For more info see p97.

Two of Honduras' best-known ethnic groups are not truly indigenous, though they are often portrayed that way. Like mainstream ladinos, the Miskito and Garífuna people are the result of interracial mixing. In the case of the Miskito, it was between an unknown indigenous group in La Moskitia and African slaves, who most likely escaped slave ships and swam ashore. The Miskito also have English blood, from English pirates who used lagoons in La Moskitia as a hideaway. In fact British pirates befriended and armed the Miskito as a way to undermine Spanish control and to ward off other native groups. Today the Miskito are the dominant ethnic group in La Moskitia, and make up the majority of guides, boatmen, and guesthouse operators that travelers are likely to encounter.

UNDERSTANDING HONDURAS' SMALLEST ETHNIC GROUP: THE TAWAHKA

Honduras' smallest ethnic group is the Tawahka. By most accounts there are less than 1000 Tawahka people in Honduras (another 8000 or so live in Nicaragua). They are also the most isolated of Honduran ethnic groups, living in a handful of communities along the Patuca and Wampú rivers, including Krausirpe (the largest), Krautara, Yapawas, Kamakasna and Parwas. They were the last of Honduras' indigenous groups to be contacted by European explorers, and also the last to be converted to Christianity.

The Tawahka live much as they have for centuries, through fishing and subsistence farming, growing mostly plantains, rice, beans and yucca. European colonizers introduced them to panning for gold, which remains a source of extra income for some. They are also adept hunters, using trained dogs – only a quarter of households own a gun of any sort – to capture armadillos, peccaries and tapirs. But the Tawahka are perhaps best known for their production of enormous dugout canoes. Made from a single mahogany log, the canoes can measure a remarkable 10m in length. The Tawahka rarely use their impressive creations, though – most are sold downriver.

The Tawahka language – called *twanka* – is still widely spoken. However, it has been deeply infiltrated with Miskitu and subsequently English (since almost a third of Miskitu words come from English). More alarming is the illiteracy rate: a study of one typical community found 96% of men and 100% of the women could not read. Few children attend school beyond the third grade.

Accustomed to isolation, the Tawahka have seen their ancestral lands severely reduced by the encroachment of mainstream farmers, ranchers and timber harvesters in the Río Patuca area. In 1999 – after much foot dragging – the Honduran government approved the creation of the Reserva de la Biósfera Tawahka Asangni (Tawahka Asangni Biosphere Reserve), setting aside 250,000 hectares of traditional Tawahka territory. A victory for the Tawahka people was a victory for the environment as well. The reserve accounts for just 2% of Honduras' landmass, but contains a whopping 90% of its mammal species. It borders three other protected areas – the Reserva de la Biósfera del Río Plátano to the north, the Río Patuca National Park to the south, and the Bosawas National Park in Nicaragua to the east – and together they form a key nexus in the Mesoamerican Biological Corridor, spanning all seven Central American countries.

The Tawahka were for many years referred to as Sumo, a term you still read and hear occasionally. It was the name Miskitu used when describing their upriver neighbors to European explorers. But it was almost certainly pejorative – the Miskitu and Tawahka have historically been rivals, and some say the name was Miskitu for 'inferior.' True or not, today it is considered very un-PC.

DON'T MESS WITH DISNEY!

In May 2005 the National Garífuna Council of Belize sent a letter to the Walt Disney Company, which was preparing to film sequels to its hit film *Pirates of the Caribbean*. The council objected to the scripts' portrayal of Carib islanders as cannibals, arguing that there is no evidence that Caribs regularly ate humans (though roasting a prisoner or two probably did figure into certain warrior rituals). Disney demurred, saying cannibalism was too integral to the plot to change.

The Garífuna are also of mixed race; in their case, freed African slaves with Carib and Arawak native people who had migrated to the Caribbean islands, including St Vincent, many millennia prior. After being literally dumped by British ships on the island of Roatán in 1787, the Garífuna have since spread all along the north coast and into Guatemala and Belize. Unemployment, especially among men, is a longtime issue for the Garífuna; many men have left Honduras to seek jobs in the USA. In fact, as many Garífuna live outside Honduras (around 100,000) as inside it.

Other ethnic groups in Honduras include white islanders and non-Garífuna black islanders. The former are descended from British pirates, the latter from slaves or free blacks from British-controlled Cayman Islands. Both primarily speak English, with a familiar Jamaican lilt. Finally, Chinese immigrants number relatively few, but are very visible in many communities, typically running Chinese restaurants.

El Espíritu de Mi Mamá (My Mother's Spirit; 2003),directed by Alí Allié, focuses on a Garífuna housekeeper in Los Angeles who returns to Honduras to lay her mother's spirit to rest.

MEDIA

Freedom of the press is protected under Honduran law, and most advocates say there is a reasonable amount of autonomy and integrity in the nation's media, which is controlled by a small group of elite business-owners. However, there were limited reports of 'government intimidation of journalists, government takeovers of TV transmission frequencies and journalistic self-censorship,' according to a 2008 US State Department Human Rights Report. During his time in office, President Zelaya heavily regulated the media, which he said propagated a 'culture of death.'

Honduras Tips (www.hondurastips.honduras.com) is a bilingual (English and Spanish) and biannual magazine-directory that makes a handy supplement to any guidebook. Most useful is the bus information in the front, with a guide to which lines go where, and select departure and contact information. It also has information on things to see and do, and places to stay and eat, with maps and photos of most tourist destinations. Theoretically the info is no more than six months old, but do take some listings with a grain of salt.

The weekly English-language newspaper *Honduras This Week* (www.hondurasthisweek.com) is published in Tegucigalpa. The paper makes for interesting reading, covering serious issues of the day – including immigration, the economy, environment, crime – along with a fair amount of fluff. The newspaper comes out every Saturday and can be found in major hotels and English-language bookshops in Tegucigalpa, San Pedro Sula, La Ceiba, Roatán and Utila.

Los Barcos (1992), written by Roberto Quesada, is a roundabout love story about a young man in La Ceiba, who aspires to be a writer but must work as a fruit picker to support himself.

The *Bay Islands Voice* (www.bayislandsvoice.com) is published twice monthly and includes a wide range of articles about issues facing both locals and expats in the Bay Islands. It's mostly in English, and has a searchable archive online. *Utila East Wind* (www.aboututila.com) is a monthly newspaper focused on Utila (Bay Islands). On the Travel-to-Honduras (www.travel-to-honduras.com) website, follow the 'articles & news' link for a number of useful pieces, including 'miniguides' to Tegucigalpa, San Pedro Sula and Santa Rosa de Copán.

THE MORAVIAN CHURCH

The Moravian Church, a Christian sect formed in the present-day Czech Republic during the 1400s, has played an influential role in the Moskitia since its arrival in 1928. At that time, and well into the 1950s, the Honduran government paid little attention to conditions in the remote Moskitia province. Early Moravian missionaries found communities with no clinics, no schools, and no prospects for either. Poverty levels in the Moskitia were then some of the highest in the Americas, and although still high today, they have been significantly alleviated by Moravian efforts and programs.

The church opened the Moskitia's first health clinic in 1946 in Ahuas, and it remains the best medical center in the region. Other clinics followed in Kaukira and Ocotales. Moravian-run schools in Brus Laguna and Ahuas offer kids a chance to study beyond elementary school – a rarity in this part of the country, where children rarely attend school beyond the third grade and illiteracy is sky-high. In the process, the Moravians have converted many thousands of Miskitus. The church began with a single congregation in Brus Laguna and today boasts nearly 100 congregations and over 22,000 members.

The Moravian Church in the Moskitia experienced a bitter split in 1999 when one of its ministers undertook a 40-day fast that resulted in spontaneous dancing and speaking in tongues. Believing he'd had a revelation, the minister introduced fasting to members of his congregation, which brought harsh disapproval from traditionalists in the church. 'Reformed' and 'traditional' factions formed, and disagreement soon spread to other matters. Most notably, the reformists condemned the use of pre-Christian rites, which had long been accepted in the traditional church. The conflict resulted in an official split in the church, and many communities now have two Moravian congregations.

Honduras has five daily Spanish-language newspapers. *El Heraldo* (www.elheraldo.hn) and *La Tribuna* (www.latribunahon.com) are published in Tegucigalpa, *La Prensa* (www.laprensahn.com), *El Tiempo* (www.tiempo.hn) and *El Nuevo Día* in San Pedro Sula. Like many media outlets in Latin America, Honduran newspapers are prone to sensationalism, often running large photos of auto accidents or gang killings on the front page. Fortunately, coverage of other subjects, whether politics, the economy or world affairs, is often much more sober than the bloody front page might otherwise suggest.

Honduran Cardinal Óscar Andrés Rodríguez was a candidate for pope in the papal conclave of 2005.

RELIGION

The Roman Catholic church has been a powerful institution in Honduras since the colonial era, and a vast majority of Hondurans consider themselves Catholic. The constitution calls for the separation of church and state (and guarantees religious freedom) but the archdiocese receives government subsidies, and Catholic instruction is part of the public school curriculum.

In the 1960s and '70s, the concept of 'liberation theology' was adopted by many Honduran priests (and foreign priests working there) who took up vocal positions against abuse by the Honduran military and the exploitation of the poor. As in El Salvador and elsewhere, priests became targets for right-wing attacks, including a notorious incident in 1975 when 10 peasants, two students and two priests were murdered by landowners in Olancho. Around that time, the government also began arresting and deporting foreign priests who were seen as rabble-rousers, and community groups that had been linked to the church were shut down.

More than half the population of Honduras (around 4 million) is registered to vote.

Although the Moravians had been present since the late 1920s in La Moskitia (above), the 1980s saw a major growth in mainstream evangelical Protestant denominations around the country. Methodists, the Church of God, Seventh Day Adventists and the Assemblies of God began promoting their religions, primarily through much-needed social services, and membership in poor communities rocketed. Today it is estimated that over 100,000 Hondurans are Protestants.

WOMEN IN HONDURAS

Honduran women enjoy the same legal rights and status as men – they can vote, own property, and are represented in government. They have the right to education, but are often relegated to household duties as part of a male-dominated cultural paradigm, though that too is changing, as more women seek education. But the majority are afforded a distinctly lower social and economic status, mainly because of institutional barriers and age-old prejudice. The rate of domestic violence and femicide are on the rise. There were more than 8000 reports of domestic violence in 2007, and in the first 11 months of 2008, there were 171 women reported murdered. The Center of Women's Rights says that 90% of those deaths went unpunished. Trafficking of women and children for sexual exploitation is also prevalent (p174). Professional and wage-earning women receive less pay for performing the same jobs as men, if they are allowed equal access to those occupations in the first place. In rural Honduras, women are the driving economic force, producing an estimated 60% to 80% of agricultural products consumed in Honduras, not to mention their contribution in the form of domestic work and *artesanía* (handicraft) production. And yet, Honduran women in general live in greater poverty than men and have a higher mortality rate. Breast, ovarian and cervical cancers are leading killers, and nearly 22% of deaths in women between ages 18 and 44 are associated with childbirth, mostly due to poor access to healthcare.

There are a few good signs; in 2005, more women were elected to congress than ever before – 32 of the 128 seats were occupied by women – and there are nine female justices on the 17-member Supreme Court, including the chief justice. Many hope that with the growing numbers of women in positions of legislative power, circumstances for all women in Honduras will change for the better.

Of the 1000 women from 150 countries selected for the '1000 Women for the Nobel Peace Prize 2005', (www.1000peacewomen.org), six were from Honduras.

The Land that Never Was: Sir Gregor MacGregor and the Most Audacious Fraud in History (2004) chronicles the life and times of the Scottish charlatan who conned some 250 settlers into moving to La Moskitia.

ARTS

Honduras is not as renowned for its arts and crafts as nearby Guatemala and El Salvador, but it does have some interesting art forms.

Artesanía

Travelers are most likely to encounter – and are inclined to buy – folk art produced in the country's rural or ethnic-minority areas. Lenca 'negativo' pottery is recognizable for its black-and-white design, usually buffed to

LA VIRGEN DE SUYAPA

In 1747 a farmer named Alejandro Colindres was returning home to Suyapa when he stopped to camp for the night. Settling down, he felt a hard object under his back, which he removed and threw into the brush. When he lay back, the lump was still there; he again pried it out but this time placed it in his knapsack. The object turned out to be a 6cm wooden statue of the Virgin Mary, which Colindres' neighbors came to worship for its healing powers. The statue's fame spread; when it cured a wealthy landowner of his kidney stones in 1768 he built a temple in its honor, where it remains today. (The massive Basílica de Suyapa was built nearby in 1954 after the icon was declared Honduras' patron saint; it is moved there for holidays only.) The statue has been stolen twice, most notoriously in September 1986, when it turned up several hours later, wrapped in newspaper, in the men's room of La Terraza de Don Pepe, a popular downtown restaurant. The Feria de la Virgen de Suyapa is celebrated every year on February 3.

a high shine. Excellent replicas of Maya masks and glyphs can be bought fairly cheaply in Copán Ruinas. Miskitu children in Las Marías are sure to find newly arrived travelers and break out a large collection of balsa-wood animals and miniature *pipantes* (flat-bottomed boats). Also produced in the Moskitia, though easier to find in *artesanía* shops elsewhere, are *cuadros de tunu (*designs made from tree bark pounded into a thick paper). Shops specializing in Garífuna folk art often carry 'naïf' style paintings, as well as handmade tambores, and souvenir-size *rayadores (*wood planks embedded with hundreds of tiny sharp stones and used for grating yucca). Other popular arts include basketry, embroidery and leather crafting.

Cabbage and Kings (1904), O Henry's first book, is a collection of humorous interconnected vignettes based in 'Coralio', a fictional village fashioned after Trujillo, where the famous author spent a year avoiding embezzlement charges in Texas.

Literature

Lucila Gamero de Medina (1873–1964) was born in Danlí and is considered one of the first Central American female writers, publishing stories as early as 1894. Her novel *Blanco Olmeda* (1903) was the first novel published by a Honduran writer, male or female. That, and other favorites she wrote, including *Amalia Montiel* and *Adriana y Margarita,* are still widely read today.

José Trinidad Reyes (1797–1855) was a poet and playwright who founded the National University of Honduras and introduced the printing press to Honduras. José Cecilio del Valle, known as *El Sabio* (the Wise) was another important writer and philosopher, born in the southern Honduran city of Choluteca (for more on del Valle, see p89).

In modern times, important writers include Ramón Amaya-Amador (1916–1966), a one-time banana fieldworker turned prolific journalist who fled Honduras because of political persecution in 1944. He wrote over 30 books, among them *Prisión Verde* (1945), *Los Brujos de Ilamatepeque* (1958) and *Operación Gorila* (1965).

The Mosquito Coast (1982), by Paul Theroux, is a gripping novel about a brilliant inventor who, fed up with American society, takes his family to a remote Honduran village and goes mad in the process.

Roberto Quesada, one of Honduras' top living authors, has written *Los Barcos* (The Ships; 1992), *El Humano y La Diosa* (The Human & the Goddess; 1996) and *The Big Banana* (1999).

Visual Arts

Honduras' most characteristic style of painting is known as 'naïf' and was popularized by José Antonio Velásquez (1906–83), one of Honduras' most enduring visual artists. His paintings depict scenes of typical mountain villages, especially his adopted hometown of San Antonio de Oriente, with cobblestone lanes winding among houses with white adobe walls and red tile roofs. Velásquez reached an international audience thanks in large part to the patronage of Wilson Popenoe, the American agronomist who founded

PUNTA DANCE: BET YOUR HIPS DON'T MOVE LIKE THAT

Sometimes called *bangidy, punta* is one of the most recognizable Garífuna dances in Honduras. It is typically performed by a pair of dancers, swinging their hips and moving their arms to a throbbing, haunting sound made by two large drums, maracas, a conch and a turtle-shell xylophone. As they move, the dancers chant words like a litany, to which the audience responds. Although the meaning of the dance is debated, most agree that it was originally performed to mourn the death of a relative; a means to usher the deceased to a restful place so that they could be in peace.

Today, a new sound – punta-rock – has been created using the same beats mixed with an electric guitar. Although this new music is all the rage, traditional *punta* dance is still very much alive. Travelers can see it performed in any number of Garífuna festivals held on the north coast. The most famous of them is the Baja Mar Garífuna Festival (p166), during which an all-night dance competition is held among the 36 Garífuna communities that come together for the event.

the Jardín Botánico Lancetilla and later the Zamorano agricultural school. The Zamorano school has a large collection of Velasquez's work.

Arturo López Rodezno (1906–75) was another influential early painter. A muralist, López Rodezno founded the National School of Arts and Crafts in Comayaguëla, where a number of his pieces can be viewed.

Other important Honduran painters include Miguel Ángel Ruíz Matute, Arturo Luna and Roque Zalaya, among many others. A 'virtual museum' can be viewed at www.honduras.com/museum/museo.html.

Music

Most of the music heard in Honduras is a combination of outside influences: Mexican ballads and *rancheras,* Caribbean merengue and salsa, Latin and English-language rock, as well as hip hop, regguetón (hip hop with a blend of Jamaican and Latin American influences), and even a bit of country thrown in for good measure.

Music created within Honduras is limited but still interesting: Aurelio Martínez has taken off as one of the stars of the new punta-rock rage, a fusion of traditional Garífuna *punta* with an electric sound. He has produced three albums, *Songs of the Garífuna, Garífuna Soul* and *Inocencia.*

Karla Lara, a folksy singer-songwriter, produced a popular album in 2004, *Dónde Andar,* and collaborated on the album *Mujer Canción, Canción Mujer* with Guillermo Anderson.

In the early 1980s, the hard-rock band Khaos was the first Honduran group to make a splash in the emerging *rock en español* scene. The band produced only one album – *Forjado en Rocka* – before breaking up in 1985, but songs like 'Roleando' and 'En las Garras del Diablo' are still popular in Honduras and throughout Central America.

Dance

Dance is another popular art form, as most indigenous and ethnic groups have traditional dances. Most notable are the Garífunas of the North Coast, known for their distinctive music and dance, including *punta* (see opposite) and *wanaragua* (masked warrior dancing; see p220). It's worth checking out a performance by the Ballet Nacional Folklórico Garífuna if you're lucky enough to be in the country when they are.

Food & Drink

Honduran food is remarkably uniform. The menu at a *comedor* (basic eatery) or midrange restaurant in Choluteca would be virtually identical to one in Trujillo. Both would include some combination of fried and baked fish, fried and baked chicken, grilled steak, pork chops, and maybe sandwiches and pasta dishes, usually served with a small side salad (iceberg lettuce, sliced cucumber, tomato), rice and beans; which doesn't make the food bad, but travelers spending an extended period here (especially those who've come from Guatemala or Mexico) may tire of the sameness of it.

Traditional Honduran healing utilizes 'hot' or 'cold' foods as remedies. 'Hot' medicines may include oranges and beef, 'cold' ones salt and seafood.

Most travelers will get sick at some point during their culinary exploration of the country. See p278 for tips on staying healthy.

STAPLES & SPECIALITIES

Somehow, despite its ethnic diversity and many cultural influences, Honduras never developed a distinctive local cuisine. The best variety is on the North Coast, where the seafood is fresh and varied, especially fish, shrimp, conch and lobster.

For breakfast, the *plato típico* reigns supreme. From deep in La Moskitia to the heart of San Pedro Sula, the 'typical plate' means eggs, beans, fried plantains, cheese, cream, a piece of sausage or bacon, served with tortillas or bread and coffee.

Reviviendo la Cocina Hondureña (Reviving Honduran Cuisine; 1987), by Dolores Prats de Avila, is a Spanish-language cookbook with step-by-step instructions on preparing a variety of Honduran dishes.

A lunchtime *plato típico* includes a piece of meat – *bistec* (beef), *chuleta* (pork chop) or *pollo* (chicken) – served with beans, rice and a side salad and tortillas or bread. This is not much different from a standard dinner plate, though that would rarely be called a *plato típico*. And whereas lunch meats are usually just grilled or fried, dinner dishes might also include a somewhat more involved preparation, like *encebollada* (covered in grilled onions) or *entomatada* (covered in tomato sauce). If fish is one of the options, it can usually be prepared *frito* (fried) or *al ajillo* (with garlic).

With dinner or drinks, you may be served *anafre* – runny, refried beans served with tortilla chips in a clay pot with a small chamber in the bottom for hot coals, which keeps the beans bubbly. It's a sort of Honduran fondue.

On the North Coast, it's hard to go wrong by ordering fish – for the freshest piece, ask the server which of the dishes is prepared with fish caught that same day. Also be sure to try *ceviche de pescado* (fish ceviche, where the fish is marinated in lime juice, garlic and seasonings). *Sopa de caracol* (conch soup) is a Bay Islands' specialty made with potatoes and coconut milk. But with reports of widespread illegal conch harvesting, local environmentalists recommend against sampling the soup. Another meal to avoid is iguana – they are an endangered species.

An online bilingual cookbook of Honduran dishes can be found at www.honduras.net/foods

Garífuna communities on the North Coast are famous for *pan de coco,* a dense sweet bread made with fresh coconut. It's often sold on the street by women and children, and is good for long bus rides. A staple of the Garífuna diet is *casabe,* a crispy waferlike bread made from yucca roots in a long and time-consuming process. Eaten alone, *casabe* (also spelled *cazabe*) is rather bland, at least to most Western palates. More appealing is *tapado de casabe* (casabe stew) in which the wafers are boiled until soft, and mixed with broth, cabbage, salted pork, vinegar, salt and pepper.

On the Bay Islands, another traditional – and delicious – food is *bando,* a seafood stew made from pretty much whatever is handy (including fish, crab, mussels, potatoes, yucca and coconut milk) boiled over a fire.

DRINKS

Nonalcoholic Drinks

One of Honduras' most popular drinks among locals and foreigners alike are *licuados* (smoothies), which are made of fruit, ice, and several tablespoons of sugar blended with either water or milk. Though they can be made with just about any fruit, popular varieties include *piña* (pineapple), *guineo* (banana), *sandía* (watermelon), *fresa* (strawberry) and papaya. Granola, oatmeal and corn flakes are typical extras that can be added to turn a simple *licuado* into a hearty drink.

Yucca, the base of Garífuna *casabe* bread, is a poisonous root containing cyanide.

Jugos (juices) are typically made fresh right in front of you and are a great pick-me-up on a hot day. Popular flavors include *naranja* (orange), *piña*, and *zanahoria* (carrot). Very similar are *aguas*, fruit drinks made with water and a fruit or grain – the equivalent of an '-ade' in English. Favorites are *melón* (cantaloupe), *sandía* (watermelon), *mora* (blueberry), *tamarindo* (tamarind), *horchata* (sweet rice milk) and of course *limonada* (lemonade). Locals also recommend a juice derived from the noni plant for ailments of all stripes.

Coffee is popular in Honduras, and often perfectly good, even in modest eateries. It is served *negro* (black) or *con leche* (with milk), the latter usually costing a bit more.

In 2006 there were over 90 million coffee bushes in cultivation in Honduras.

Alcoholic Drinks

Honduras has two well-known beers – Port Royal and Salva Vida; neither will impress serious beer drinkers, but they're decent enough (or cheap enough) to be popular here and in several neighboring countries. Rum, mostly Bacardi and Flor de Caña, is popular as well. *Aguardiente* is a cheap, generic liquor that happens to be a national favorite, especially Yuscarán which is made in the town of the same name. *Chicha* is a traditional drink made from fermented pineapple skins. If you stay in a Garífuna village ask to try some *guifiti*, a potent elixir of rum, herbs and spices.

Pupusas (stuffed cornmeal patties), which are sold throughout Honduras, originated in long-time rival El Salvador.

WHERE TO EAT & DRINK

Restaurante generally refers to restaurants on the slightly fancier side, often with tablecloths and a set menu. Informal eateries are usually called *comedores;* they are typically less expensive, with daily specials and a basic menu. Both are usually open daily from 7am to 9pm. Reservations are rarely needed (or taken, for that matter) even in upscale places. There are very few places in the country where only tourists go, though certainly some cater more to foreigners and their prices prove it. Most of the restaurants in this book are popular with locals and tourists…or sometimes, just the locals.

Quick Eats

No matter where you travel, eating on the street can be a great way to feel like you're connecting with local people and experiences; it's also a good way to get sick if you're not careful. *Baleadas* are the ultimate Honduran quick-eat: a flour tortilla smeared with beans, a drizzle of cream and sometimes fresh cheese. Look for a stand where they're made and sold fresh; the pre-prepared ones sold from baskets are usually okay, but may be past their prime. *Pinchos* (kebabs cooked on small streetside grills) are tasty and fairly reliable, especially if you can see they've been cooked thoroughly and haven't been sitting around. Corn on the cob, either grilled or boiled, is also popular and you may see tamales and *atole* (a thick drink made of corn or wheat) as well. With all street eating, pick a place that is relatively busy – locals aren't immune to spoiled food and will patronize stands they trust.

VEGETARIANS & VEGANS

Vegetarianism is not widely practiced in Honduras, and beyond the major cities and well-touristed towns like Copán Ruinas and Utila, vegetarians don't have many options. Rice, beans and tortillas are staples and can be ordered just about anywhere. Bean dishes, however, are often made with lard – better ask first to be sure. Fast food restaurants, which are ubiquitous in Honduras, often have pizza or fries – not the healthiest of options but at least it gives you a couple more choices. Of course, for those 'vegetarians' who make an exception for seafood, there are many more options, making traveling in Honduras much more interesting and enjoyable from a culinary perspective. There is at least one vegetarian restaurant in Honduras – a place called Fuente de Salud y Juventud in San Pedro Sula – but nearly all the restaurants listed in this book have at least some non-meat alternatives.

Cooking the Central American Way (2005), by Alison Behnkeet et al, is a cookbook containing a general overview of Central American recipes including Honduran favorites, vegetarian fare and low-fat options.

EATING WITH KIDS

Children are very welcome in Honduran restaurants, where dining is traditionally a family affair. In fact, as in many Latin American countries, children are simultaneously *more* welcome at restaurants (and weddings, gatherings etc) than they are in other countries, but *less* likely to be the center of all the adults' attention. Children learn early to play among themselves when grown-ups are talking, and parents spend considerably less time responding to their children's every need.

Honduran food has very few hidden surprises – no extra-spicy sauces or unusual flavors. Most foods will be familiar to Western travelers and should satisfy even picky eaters. Juices figure prominently, including 'regular' ones like orange, lime, apple and pineapple. Large grocery stores in Honduras carry a variety of baby foods and formulas, many of the same brands as found in the US and Canada.

Da Núbebe: Un Compendio de Comidas Garífunas (Da Núbebe: A Collection of Garífuna Dishes; 1997), by Salvador Suazo, is a cookbook containing traditional Garífuna recipes.

HABITS & CUSTOMS

Dining habits and customs in Honduras are similar to those elsewhere in the region, and in the home countries of most Western travelers. As in many Latin American countries, the waiter won't bring you the bill until you ask for it. A 10% tip is customary and in some tourist areas servers will include the tip with the meal price.

EAT YOUR WORDS

Although hand signals can get you a long way when it comes to food, knowing a few key Spanish words and phrases and their pronunciations will definitely enhance your dining experience, even if it's at a street cart. For pronunciation guidelines see p281.

TOP FIVE BEST EATS

- Mavis and Dixie's (p212) – We love the coconut-stung wahoo and the arching ocean views.
- Baleada Express (p114) – The best *baleadas* west of the Río Plátano.
- Expatriates Bar & Grill (p185) – Popular with locals and travelers alike, this La Ceiba restaurant has delicious salads – greatly appreciated after a month of rice, beans and no greens.
- NoBu (p76) – Pan-Asian cuisine in an upmarket environment with delicious city views.
- D&D Bed & Breakfast and Microbrewery (p153) – Yep, it's a brewery, but the blueberry pancakes can't be beaten.

TRAVEL YOUR TASTEBUDS

During Semana Santa, the traditional dish is *sopa de pescado* (fish soup) made with fish and egg patties, dunked in a broth made from garlic and fish heads. It is tradition that the father of the house and one of the sons beat the eggs used to make the fish patties and, later, the traditional desserts like *pan de yema* (egg yolk bread) and *torrijas de piñol* (a type of cornbread French toast).

Useful Phrases

I'd like to see a menu.
Quisiera ver la carta. kee·*sye*·ra ver la *kar*·ta
Do you have a menu in English?
¿Tienen una carta en inglés? *tye*·nen *oo*·na *kar*·ta en een·*gles*
What is today's special?
¿Cuál es el plato del día? kwal es el *pla*·to del *dee*·a
What do you recommend?
¿Qué me recomienda? ke me re·ko·*myen*·da
How's this dish prepared?
¿Cómo preparan ese plato? *ko*·mo pre·*pa*·ran *e*·se *pla*·to
Can I have a (beer) please?
Una (cerveza) por favor. *oo*·na (ser·*ve*·sa) por fa·*vor*
Is service included in the bill?
¿La cuenta incluye el servicio? la *kwen*·ta een·*kloo*·ye el ser·*vee*·syo
Thank you, that was delicious.
Muchas gracias, estuvo delicioso. *moo*·chas *gra*·syas es·*too*·vo de·lee·*syo*·so
The bill, please.
La cuenta, por favor. la *kwen*·ta por fa·*vor*
I'm a vegetarian.
Soy vegetariano/a. (m/f) soy ve·khe·ta·*rya*·no/a
Do you have any vegetarian dishes?
¿Tienen algún plato vegetariano? *tye*·nen al·*goon* *pla*·to ve·khe·ta·*rya*·no
Are you open?
¿Está abierto? es·*ta* a·*byer*·to
When are you open?
¿Cuando está abierto? *kwan*·do es·*ta* a·*byer*·to
Are you now serving breakfast/lunch/dinner?
¿Ahora, está sirviendo desayuno/ la comida/la cena? a·*o*·ra es·*ta* seer·*vyen*·do de·sa·*yoo*·no/ la ko·*mee*·da/la *se*·na
I'd like mineral water/natural bottled water.
Quiero agua mineral/ agua purificada. *kye*·ro *a*·gwa mee·ne·*ral*/ *a*·gwa poo·ree·fee·*ka*·da
Is it spicy?
¿Es picante? es pee·*kan*·te

Jungle meat such as tapir, which tastes like incredibly chewy, oversalted pork, is often consumed in La Moskitia.

A coffee-lovers forum, www.ineedcoffee.com includes information on Honduran bean varieties.

Food Glossary

arroz	*a*·ros	rice
azúcar	a·*soo*·kar	sugar
caldo	*kal*·*do*	broth, often meat-based
coco	*ko*·ko	coconut
frijoles	free·*kho*·les	black beans
huevos fritos/revueltos	*we*·vos *free*·tos/re·*vwel*·tos	fried/scrambled eggs
miel	myel	honey
milanesa	mee·la·*ne*·sa	crumbed, breaded meat
pan	pan	bread

picante	pee·*kan*·te	any hot/spicy sauce
plato típico	*pla*·to *tee*·pee·ko	standard breakfast or lunch dish
postre	*pos*·tre	dessert
tapado	ta·*pa*·do	any kind of stew (beef, seafood etc)

SNACKS

anafre	a·*na*·fre	refried beans served fondue style
baleada	ba·le·*a*·da	flour tortilla with beans or other filling
golosinas	go·lo·*see*·nas	snacks (many varieties)
hamburguesa	am·boor·*ge*·sa	hamburger
helado	e·*la*·do	ice cream
pastel	pas·*tel*	cake
pupusa	poo·*poo*·sa	stuffed cornmeal patty; Salvadoran
quesadilla	ke·sa·*dee*·ya	flour tortilla with melted cheese
tajadas	ta·*kha*·do	fried banana chips
tamal	ta·*mal*	stuffed, steamed corn-dough patty
tostada	tos·*ta*·da	flat, crisp tortilla

MEAT & SEAFOOD

bistec	*bees*·tek	beefsteak
camarones	ka·ma·*ro*·nes	shrimp
caracol	ka·ra·*kol*	conch
carne	*kar*·ne	meat
carne asada	*kar*·ne a·*sa*·da	tough but tasty grilled beef
ceviche	se·*vee*·che	raw fish/conch marinated in lime juice
chicharrón	chee·cha·*ron*	pork crackling
chuletas (de puerco)	choo·*le*·tas (de *pwer*·ko)	(pork) chops
churrasco	choo·*ras*·ko	slab of grilled meat
filete de pescado	fee·*le*·te de pes·*ka*·do	fish fillet
langosta	lan·*go*·sta	lobster
mariscos	ma·*rees*·kos	seafood
mondongo	mon·*don*·go	tripe stew
nacatamales	na·ka·ta·*ma*·les	boiled pork tamales
pescado (al ajillo)	pes·*ka*·do (al a·*khee*·yo)	fish (fried in butter and garlic)
pincho	*peen*·cho	shish kebob
pollo (asado/frito)	*po*·yo (a·*sa*·do/*free*·to)	(grilled/fried) chicken
puerco	*pwer*·ko	pork
puyaso	poo·*ya*·so	a choice cut of steak
salchicha	sal·*chee*·cha	sausage

FRUIT & VEGETABLES

aguacate	a·gwa·*ka*·te	avocado
ajo	*a*·kho	garlic
guineo	gee·*ne*·o	banana
cebolla	se·*bo*·ya	onion
fresas	*fre*·sas	strawberries
fruta	*froo*·ta	fruit
lechuga	le·*choo*·ga	lettuce
limón	lee·*mon*	lime or lemon
naranja	na·*ran*·kha	orange
papa	*pa*·pa	potato
papaya	pa·*pa*·ya	papaya
piña	*pee*·nya	pineapple
plátano	*pla*·ta·no	plantain, usually served fried
tomate	to·*ma*·te	tomato

verduras	ver·*doo*·ras	green vegetables
zanahoria	sa·na·*o*·rya	carrot

DRINKS

agua	*a*·gwa	water
café (negro/con leche)	ka·*fe* (*ne*·gro/kon *le*·che)	coffee (black/with milk)
cerveza	ser·*ve*·sa	beer
leche	*le*·che	milk
licuado	lee·*kwa*·do	fruit smoothie made with milk or water
limonada	lee·mo·*na*·da	lemonade
(natural/con gas)	(na·too·*ral*/kon gas)	(natural/carbonated water)
naranjada	na·ran·*kha*·da	a fizzy drink made from orange juice

Environment

Honduras' topography and ecology is as diverse as it gets. Here you'll find large swaths of rainforest inhabited by a riot of jungle critters from macaws to howler monkeys. There are pine-encrusted mountain ranges and flat savannah country, and of course, just offshore along the Caribbean coast you have coral-reef wonderworlds inhabited by whale sharks, dolphins, Hawksbill turtles and a motley crew of fantastically festooned fish and underwater fauna. From sky to sea, there's much to be explored in Honduras' wild places, but ecological threats – from logging to pollution – are putting many of these delicate ecosystems at risk.

THE LAND

The Bay Islands sit on the Meso-American Barrier Reef, the second longest in the world after the Great Barrier Reef in Australia.

Honduras is the second-largest country in Central America, with an area of 112,090 sq km. Over 75% of Honduras is made up of rugged mountains, a geologic jumble caused by the collision of three tectonic plates. Among the jumble are several discernable mountain ranges, including the massive Sierra Nombre de Dios along the North Coast, the eastern Sierra de Agalta and Sierra del Río Tinto, which divide La Moskitia from the rest of the country, and the Sierra del Celaque and Sierra del Merendón in the west along the Salvadoran and Guatemalan borders. The western ranges are home to the country's highest peak Cerro de las Minas (2849m) in Parque Nacional Montaña de Celaque. With all these mountains, Honduras has precious little arable land – just 9.53%. Compare that to 18.01% in the US and 13.22% in Guatemala, and you'll see why land ownership is such a big issue in this country.

Throughout the mountains there are a number of high valleys, which make ranching and agriculture somewhat more viable, especially in the interior. Many towns and cities, including Tegucigalpa, grew up in such highland valleys. Despite its rugged terrain, Honduras has no volcanoes and relatively little seismic activity when compared to neighboring Nicaragua, El Salvador and Guatemala, though there was a massive 7.1 quake off the Caribbean coast in May 2009 that killed at least six people and injured 40 more.

Calling itself the 'global journal of practical eco-tourism,' www.planeta.com has a number of links and articles about Honduras in its Central America section.

Honduras has 644km of Caribbean coast and 124km of Pacific coast, along the Golfo de Fonseca. Both coastal areas are low-lying alluvial plains. Along the Golfo de Fonseca, the lowlands form a strip just 25km wide; it is flat, hot and swampy near the shore – not exactly a welcoming environment for people, but ideal for mangroves and numerous wetland and shallow-water creatures, especially shrimp, shellfish and birdlife.

The north coastal plain has long been the most intensely developed and exploited region in Honduras, enriched by several major rivers and by soils washed down from the Nombre de Dios mountain range. In the northwestern corner of Honduras, the Ulúa and Chamelcón rivers form the huge Valle de Sula, which contains Puerto de Cortés and San Pedro Sula and extends nearly to Lago de Yojoa and Copán Ruinas. This fertile region has supported human settlement for millennia. The central portion of the Caribbean coast has been utilized primarily for large-scale plantations, especially bananas, African palm, and (most recently) pineapples.

Of the 225 mammal species found in Honduras, almost half are *murciélagos* (bats).

La Moskitia is, geologically speaking, part of the northern coastal plain. However, the Río Aguán and Río Tinto (aka Río Sico and Río Negro) form natural barriers, as do the Sierra Río Tinto and Sierra de Agalta mountain ranges. La Moskitia is Central America's largest intact rainforest and the largest north of the Amazon; it contains two of the country's longest rivers,

THE BIRDS OF PARADISE

Honduras is a birder's paradise; its variety of ecosystems – cloud forests, pine forests, savannahs, lagoons, mangroves, freshwater lakes and oceans – attracts and hosts an impressive number of birds; 725 species to be exact, in over 58 families, and birders are still counting. For a wealth of information on birds and birding in Honduras, check out www.birdinghonduras.com. Here are some of our favorite birding spots:

- Lago de Yojoa (p151) – where it is often related that a birder spotted 37 species in one tree without leaving the front porch of his hotel room.
- Parque Nacional La Tigra (p81) and Parque Nacional Montaña de Celaque (p141) – both have cloud forests that are home to brilliantly marked and elusive quetzals (the best time to see them is during the mating season, from March to May).
- Parque Nacional Pico Bonito (p188) – where hawks, parrots and swallows can be spotted alongside keel-billed toucans, blue-crowned motmot and white-collared manakins.
- Reserva de la Biósfera del Río Plátano (p243) – located within the largest rainforest north of the Amazon, with finds like scarlet macaws, yellow-eared toucanets and jabirus.
- Parque Nacional Jeannette Kawas (p174) & Refugio de Vida Silvestre Cuero y Salado (p187) – where the coastal wetlands boast ibis, egrets, roseate spoonbills and other water fowl.

the Río Coco and Río Patuca. The far eastern stretches of La Moskitia are classified as pine savannah.

WILDLIFE

There are plenty of animals to see in Honduras. Unfortunately, some of the most interesting species are becoming endangered, primarily due to loss of habitat. The national bird, the *guara roja* or scarlet macaw, is on the endangered species' list, as are some species of *loro* (parrot). Manatees and jaguars, among many others, also make it on to Honduras' endangered list. The best place for spotting wildlife is in the country's national parks, wildlife reserves and other protected areas. As more areas become protected, populations of depleted species might be saved from early extinction.

In 2005 two new species of poisonous snakes were discovered in Olancho.

Animals

Talk about biological diversity: Honduras is home to more than 200 species of mammals, nearly 300 species of reptiles and amphibians, and more than 700 species of birds. While an exhaustive review is impractical, a few creatures may be of special interest to travelers.

Whale sharks, which are seen year-round off Utila, can live to be 150 years old.

Monkeys are plentiful in Honduras, and are always a crowd favorite. Honduras has three species – *mono cara blanca* (white-faced monkey), *mono araña* (spider monkey) and *mono aullador* (howler monkey) – which are easiest to spot in La Moskitia, Parque Nacional Cuero y Salado, Parque Nacional Jeannette Kawas, Parque Nacional Sierra de Agalta and in the Refugio de Vida Silvestre Ojochal. Even if you don't see howler monkeys, you may hear them; they get their name from their otherworldly howl, often heard at dawn or dusk.

Everyone wants to see a jaguar, though very few people actually do. La Moskitia is the best place to spot one, though they are known to exist in the Pico Bonito and Sierra de Agalta regions. Honduras has four other species of wild cat, all smaller than the jaguar: puma, jaguarondi, ocelot and tigrillo.

Divers and snorkelers see the most wildlife of any visitor to Honduras, and few animals evoke a more enthusiastic reaction than sea turtles. Hawksbill and olive ridley turtles are most common, but huge leatherbacks and loggerheads also visit, nesting on beaches in La Moskitia (see p240).

NATIONAL PARKS & PROTECTED AREAS

Honduras has over 80 protected wildlife areas, including 20 national parks, two biosphere reserves, plus another dozen or so semi-protected regions. For travelers, certain national parks, wildlife reserves and protected areas are especially important:

Jardín Botánico Lancetilla (p174) This botanical garden has more than 700 plant species and 365 species of bird. It's the second-largest botanical garden in the world, and has the largest collection of Asiatic fruit trees in the western hemisphere.

Parque Nacional Cusuco (p112) A cloud forest with a large population of quetzals, this national park has interpretive trails and a visitors center. The highest peak is Cerro Jilinco (2242m). The park can be reached all year round with a 4x4. The visitors center is 20km west of San Pedro Sula.

Parque Nacional Jeannette Kawas (Punta Sal) (p174) This park has various habitats, including mangrove forests and swamps, a small tropical forest, offshore reefs and several coves. It also has a large number of migratory and coastal birds. The easiest access is on a tour from Tela.

Parque Nacional La Tigra (p81) Honduras' first national park, established in 1980, is located just 22km from Tegucigalpa. This cloud forest is set in former mining country and has interpretive trails and visitors centers at two entrances. Dormitories and camping are available.

Parque Nacional Marino Cayos Cochinos (p191) Known also as the Hog Islands, Cayos Cochinos form a national marine park. Thirteen cays – two of them large – with beautiful coral reefs, well-preserved forests and fishing villages make up the reserve. Access is by motorized boat from Sambo Creek or Nueva Armenia, just east of La Ceiba.

Parque Nacional Montaña de Celaque (p141) This cloud forest has four peaks over 2800m above sea level, including the highest peak in Honduras at 2849m. There are hundreds of different animal and plant species, many of which are visible along the park's four main trails. Access to the park is easy: there's a ranger station 6.5km southwest of Gracias and another entrance near Belén Gualcho.

Amphibians of Honduras (2002), by James R McCranie and Larry David Wilson, is an extremely detailed account of the 116 amphibian species in Honduras, with an insightful discussion of the country's environmental crisis as well.

Whale sharks (see p223) are another marine creature prevalent in Honduras, particularly around Utila. Seeing one is a true thrill and not a little intimidating – they measure up to 16m and can weigh 15,000kg.

While it looks a lot like underwater rock, coral is actually a living microscopic marine mammal pulled together into colonies that create fantastic formations. The Bay Islands' reef system 'is one of the last remaining healthy reefs,' according to James Foley, director of the Roatán Marine Park. 'But it's at a tipping point…. After a bleaching event in '98 [with Hurricane Mitch], the reef is becoming more algal.' Before the hurricane, 34% of the reef was living coral. Now it's just 17%.

ENDANGERED SPECIES

The West Indian manatee, also known as the American manatee, was once plentiful in many parts of Honduras and the Caribbean. But a combination of overhunting, and encroachment by people and motorboats (which can maim or kill manatees grazing on the surface) has reduced manatee numbers severely. They are known to exist in the Refugio de Vida Silvestre Cuero y Salado, and in less trafficked lagoons in La Moskitia.

Approximately 96% of all marine life found in the Caribbean has been spotted in the waters around Roatán.

On Utila, the spiny-tailed iguana is endemic to the island but endangered from overhunting – for both their meat and eggs – and habitat loss due to development. Also known as a 'swamper' or 'wishiwilli' the iguana has been the focus of a concerted conservation effort since 1994, when it was first identified as being in danger. See p222 for more information.

Other threatened animals in Honduras include the Central American tapir (a large wallowing creature that looks half hippo, half pig), the giant anteater, the Roatán Agouti (a small rodent endemic to the island) and two species of bats.

Parque Nacional Pico Bonito (p188) The diversity of this park ranges from pine-oak forest to cloud forest, and includes numerous rivers and waterfalls. Most of the park is closed to development of any kind, including building and maintaining trails. Two short hikes on opposite ends of the park are about all you can do in the park proper. A number of outings, however, include hikes in the park's buffer zone.

Refugio de Vida Silvestre Cuero y Salado (p187) This is the largest manatee refuge in Central America, although that doesn't mean you'll necessarily spot one! Fortunately, it's also teeming with birds and monkeys. The park is 30km west of La Ceiba. Access is easy, either by tour or on your own.

Refugio de Vida Silvestre Laguna de Guaimoreto (p198) Just 5km east of Trujillo, this mangrove forest has an incredible coastal biodiversity, which visitors can explore by boat.

Refugio de Vida Silvestre Punta Izopo (p175) One of the most recently established national parks, Punta Izopo is made up of tropical wet forest, mangrove forest and wetlands. It has many migratory and coastal birds, a beautiful rocky point and attractive white-sand beaches. It's accessible by boat.

Reserva de la Biósfera del Río Plátano (p243) A World Heritage site and the first biosphere reserve in Central America, the Río Plátano is 5251 sq km of lowland tropical rainforest with remarkable natural, archaeological and cultural resources. Access is through Las Marías, or by a multi-day raft-ride down the river from Dulce Nombre de Culmí.

Reserva de la Biósfera Tawahka Asangni (p40) This tropical rainforest is on the ancestral lands of the Tawahka people, one of the most threatened indigenous groups in Honduras. Access is by plane to Ahuas or Wampusirpi then by boat upstream to Krausirpe and Krautara, or by a multi-day rafting trip down the Río Patuca from Juticalpa.

Reserva Marina Turtle Harbour (p224) On the northwestern side of Utila in the Bay Islands, Turtle Harbour is a marine reserve and proposed national marine park visited frequently by divers.

Sandy Bay & West End Marine Park (p205) On the western end of Roatán, this area has coral reefs that are easily accessible by divers.

Plants

Despite rampant deforestation, Honduras' forests still cover a larger total area and represents a larger percentage of its total land mass than any other country in Central America. Honduran forest falls into four general categories: pine forest, cloud forest, rainforest and mangrove.

In 1980 Unesco recognized the Reserva de la Biósfera del Río Plátano as the first biosphere reserve in Central America.

It is a testament to Honduras' mountainous terrain that the pine is the national tree. In fact, Honduras has seven different species of pines, primarily the Caribbean pine and the ocote pine. They tend to occur at higher elevations, but the former extends well down the hillsides to the northern coastal plains.

Honduras has more than 36 distinct protected cloud-forest areas, containing a plethora of plant species including bromeliads and ferns as well as mosses and aggressive vines. There are over 600 species of orchids, though the number of orchids in bloom and within sight of the trail you happen to be hiking on is pot luck at best. The butterfly and orchid enclosures in Copán Ruinas (p125) and on Roatán (p205) are a good place to admire these fascinating flowers up close and personal, without having to risk wandering off the trail.

Honduras' national flower was originally the rose, but was changed to the orchid in 1969. Turns out roses are not actually native to Honduras.

Mangroves are no less impressive, though their preference for a hot, humid climate and brackish water certainly makes them less accessible to human exploration. That said, gliding through tangled mangrove forests in a kayak in the early morning is surely one of the more sublime natural experiences available in the country. Mangroves come in three general varieties – red, black and white – and provide a habitat for innumerable species, including shrimp, fish and birds, all of which can hide from predators in the mangroves' tangled root system (see boxed text, p189).

Another notable member of Honduras' rich range of flora is the ceiba tree, a massive solitary tree found in rainforests and costal regions. It was sacred to the early Maya, who believed it represented a link between the godly realm, the present realm and Xibalba, the underworld. The city of La Ceiba derived its name from this tree, a particularly large specimen of which grew by the pier where fishermen and merchants gathered, and a township eventually formed.

The Bay Islands of Honduras (2003), by Honduran-born journalist Jacqueline Laffite Bloch, is a beautiful coffee-table book with photos and text (Spanish and English). Proceeds go to a Garífuna clinic in Roatán.

Hiking in a rainforest, you're sure to spot a tree with smooth, red bark known as *indio desnudo* (naked Indian) or *palo de turista* (tourist tree). The bark is constantly peeling – like a sunburned traveler – an ingenious defense against the innumerable bromeliads and strangling vines, which can never quite gain purchase on the tree's trunk.

Mahogany, known locally as *caoba*, is one reason so much of Honduras' forest has been cut down; it is prized for its durable and richly colored wood. This slow-growing tree takes decades to reach its full height. Other valuable hardwoods in Honduras' forests include Spanish cedar, rosewood and ironwood.

ENVIRONMENTAL ISSUES

Environmentalism is a touchy subject in Honduras. In one of the poorest country's in the hemisphere, there's a strong need to develop and exploit natural resources in order to ensure economic well-being. There is also pressure, both internal and external, to protect the vast swaths of wildland found here. Those defending environmental causes are often victims of government-sponsored intimidation and detention, according to US State Department Human Rights Reports, and killings of vocal advocates are not unheard of. Deforestation (see boxed text, opposite) is without question the number one environmental issue facing the nation. But other issues of conservation and habitat protection remain critical.

Think before you drink! Around 2.7 million tons of plastic are used to bottle water each year. Stay green by asking your hotelier to provide water coolers or by carrying your own water filter.

In September 1999, oil experts hired by the Honduran government confirmed that the country is sitting on top of four to five billion tons of untapped oil reserves. However, the bulk of these lies along La Moskitia, one of the most environmentally sensitive regions in the country, and indeed Central America. The oil field stretches as far west as Tela, raising the prospect of oil rigs just off the coast of places such as Parque Nacional Jeannette Kawas and Refugio de Vida Silvestre Cuero y Salado, not to mention the Bay Islands. In late 2008, the Honduran government hired a Norwegian company to begin petroleum exploration off the coast, but large-scale drilling would take around US$250 million in initial outlay, which Honduras does not have, so it still sits in the relatively distant future. According to environmental reports, mining activity is polluting the Lago de Yojoa (the largest source of fresh water in the country) with heavy metals.

Hawksbill turtles are known as *carey* in the Bay Islands. While the species are critically endangered, some locals still sell jewelry made from their shells.

Overfishing is another longstanding environmental concern in Honduras. Large fishing boats are not permitted to drop their nets within 5km of the low-tide mark, but the rule is often ignored, even in heavily trafficked areas near Tela and La Ceiba. For small-time fishermen, especially Garífuna, illegal net fishing means fewer fish can be caught from shore or canoes, and those that are caught tend to be smaller. The shallows are also a breeding ground for fish, shrimp, lobster, even dolphins and manatees, and overfishing can skew the delicate ecological balance found there. Only four boats in Honduras are allowed to harvest conch, but much illegal fishing is reputed to take place in Caribbean waters. As always, it's a balance of conservation and survival. People need food and money to live, and until a conch is worth more alive than dead, overfishing will continue. Perhaps the arrival of more tourists will help alleviate this problem. Then again, with a new cruise-ship

CUTTING DOWN THE FORESTS

The health of Honduras' forests hangs in the balance. Over the past two decades, over 37% of the country's forests have disappeared (the highest rate of deforestation in Central America), but many say that cutting down the forest – to raise cattle, collect firewood, and plant subsistence crops – is necessary for survival in this extremely impoverished nation.

And while subsistence farming and fuelwood collection – around 65% of the country's energy comes from wood – may seem an unavoidable evil, the rampant illegal logging that plagues the nation could surely be avoided, according to many environmentalists.

According to an October 2005 report by the Environmental Investigation Agency and the Center for International Policy, 85% of Honduras' timber production is illegal. The numbers alone are staggering: in 2004, the Honduran Ministry of Agriculture estimated the country was losing 1000 sq km of forest every year – nearly 2% of the country's total forest cover, or four times the combined landmass of the Bay Islands. According to the report, deforestation contributes to soil erosion, reduced water retention and a greater incidence of forest fires. There were 500 forest fires in the first four months of 2005, including one in April that blanketed the county in smoke and forced all four major airports to be closed. Most observers say deforestation significantly worsened the flooding and mudslides that killed thousands during Hurricane Mitch.

Pine trees account for 96% of Honduras' timber harvest; half are extracted illegally. Mahogany accounts for a fraction of the total harvest, but is one of the most valuable and sought-after hardwoods, fetching US$1300 per cubic meter on the world market. As much as 80% of the mahogany harvest is illegal; in 2003-04, an estimated two million board feet (one board foot equals a board 1ft long, 1ft wide and 1in thick) were illegally extracted from the Reserva de la Biósfera del Río Plátano, representing a tax loss of US$3 million, not to mention the much higher value of the wood itself and untold costs associated with environmental degradation. One auditor estimated Honduras' total losses due to illegal logging between 1998 and 2003 at US$6.5 billion.

Popular opposition to logging companies has been strong, rallied by groups such as Movimiento Ambiental de Olancho (MAO; Environmental Movement of Olancho). MAO is led by Father José Andrés Tamayo, a fearless Catholic priest who received the 2005 Goldman Environmental Award – as well as numerous death threats – for his efforts. The group has organized marches and negotiations. A number of environmental activists have been threatened or killed in Honduras. Though reports are thin, at least five activists have been killed since 1996. On July 1, 2008, 'a court convicted four policemen of the 2006 killings of Heraldo Zuniga and Roger Murillo, two environmentalists working to protect the forest in Olancho Province,' according to a 2008 US State Department Human Rights Report. The policemen faced prison sentences of up to 30 years, but managed to escape from prison later that month.

Of course, much stronger leverage could be applied by the US, which receives 38% of Honduran wood exports, far more than any other country. The US has pledged under CAFTA (the Central America and Dominican Republic Free Trade Agreement) and other agreements to help halt illegal logging – steps which could include closing verification loopholes and advocating for the addition of more species to the protected trees list.

dock going into Roatán's Mahogany Bay and reports of sewage problems in West Bay, who knows whether increased tourist traffic is hurting or helping. More divers certainly will not help reef ecology. See p214 for details on diving responsibly.

Finally, more than 10 years after Hurricane Mitch (see boxed text, p31), the country continues to recover. The hurricane destroyed vital mangrove forests on Guanaja, Roatán and the mainland, devastating the North Coast's shrimp industry. The recovery has heightened awareness of the vital role mangroves play in any coastal environment: as habitat for juvenile creatures, as a natural filter for waste and contaminants in the estuary, and as a source of both above-water and below-water biomass that feeds the ecosystem's food chain.

To learn more about deforestation in Honduras, head over to www.mongabay.com.

Honduras Outdoors

There are enough outdoor activities in Honduras to keep an intrepid explorer busy for several months. The country has a well-deserved reputation as one of the best (and cheapest) places to learn to dive or complete your divemaster training. It has the perfect combination of warm water, spectacular reefs and lively island communities. Just as travelers go to Guatemala for the culture and Costa Rica for the wildlife, they go to Honduras for the diving.

The three highest peaks in Honduras are Montaña de Celaque/Cerro de las Minas (2849m), Montaña de Santa Bárbara (2744m) and Pico Bonito (2436m).

But what most people don't realize is how much more Honduras has to offer beyond snorkeling and diving. Did you know, for example, that it is home to the largest tropical rainforest north of the Amazon? La Moskitia (aka the Mosquito Coast) is one of the few truly pristine ecosystems left in Central America, and can be visited by plane, dugout canoe or on an unforgettable week-long rafting trip that starts deep in the Honduran heartland.

There are no places to rent kiteboards or windsurf rigs anywhere in Honduras, but if you take your own gear you could definitely pioneer some sweet spots.

Other sporting opportunities in Honduras include hiking in one of the many national parks, mountain biking along the North Coast, bird-watching around the country's largest freshwater lake, kayaking through mangrove forests and world-class sport-fishing. Enjoy!

'The Glowing Skulls of Talgua' were discovered in 1994 by an amateur group of spelunkers, who instantly 'burrowed' themselves into the history books…sorry we couldn't resist.

CANOPY TOURS

Canopy tours – in which you don a harness, helmet and leather gloves, and slide from treetop to treetop on fixed cables – are the latest craze in Honduras. Jungle River Tours in La Ceiba (p181) had the first one, starting with a cable extended over the rushing Río Cangrejal. There are several more now, one east of La Ceiba (see p181), two on Roatán (p219 and p213), one near Copán Ruinas (p125) and another by Sambo Creek (p190).

CAVING

Cavers should head to Central Honduras, where caving opportunities await in the Cuevas de Susmay (p105) and the Cuevas de Talgua (p101). As always,

TOP FIVE OUTDOOR ACTIVITIES

There's so much to do in Honduras, you might want to focus your efforts on a single activity or region.

- Learning to dive in Utila (p223) – It's one of the cheapest spots on the planet to get certified. Plus, you'll be learning to dive on the world's second-longest barrier reef.
- Rafting the Río Cangrejal (p181) – Believe it or not, you can actually raft down a waterfall. Better still, you're rafting through one of the country's best national parks.
- Jungle tromping in La Moskitia (p246) – Get up early – real early – for the best wildlife-watching possibilities as you trek near the remote jungle town of Las Marías.
- Getting high along the Ruta Lenca (p141) – Take on Honduras' highest peak in Parque Nacional Montaña de Celaque.
- Leaving this book behind – The best adventures are had by the seat of your pants. Close this book for a day or a week and see where your spirit takes you. Just remember, it's easy to get lost in the Honduran wilderness, so you'll probably want to take a friend with local knowledge.

you should have a guide or be an experienced spelunker to venture into one of the area caves.

DIVING & SNORKELING

If you're in Honduras, or are thinking of going, snorkeling or scuba diving is probably high on your list of things to do. And with good reason: Honduras boasts world-class diving at famously affordable prices. Shops are almost uniformly top-rate, with experienced instructors and solid safety records. All this set on idyllic Caribbean islands – what more could you ask?

Honduras is rightly known as a great place to learn to dive. Shops focus heavily on the basic Open Water courses – Utila Dive Centre (p224) is regularly among the top shops *in the world* in terms of the number of PADI Open Water certificates it issues annually. But plenty of experienced divers come here too. Shops also offer all the advanced-level courses, from Advanced Open Water to Instructor. It is an especially popular place to come for multi-week divemaster courses, partly because life on the islands is as enjoyable as the diving. Even if you're only fun diving, the Bay Islands do not disappoint.

Website of the official PADI Society magazine, www.sportdiver.com has frequent articles on the Bay Islands.

Roatán (p202) and Utila (p221) attract the majority of divers, and everyone faces the same decision: which island to go to? The diving is comparable on both islands. Utila has incredible walls and sea mounds, while Roatán has somewhat healthier reefs and a larger reef. Different people have favorites, but for novice divers especially, the difference is negligible. Utila has many more whale-shark sightings, especially in season. Utila's dive day starts at 7am, while on Roatán it starts at 9am – with surface interval back on shore – which is no small consideration if you're not a morning person!

External pressure on a diver's body doubles in the first 10m of a dive.

More often the decision comes down to budget and style. Utila is known to be more geared toward backpackers and budget travelers, and tends to attract a younger crowd. The courses there often include free lodging. On Roatán you'll probably need to pay for lodging (though a few all-inclusive courses do exist). Dive prices are about the same for both, though you'll probably save a few lemps by going to Utila.

Excellent laminated dive maps of Roatán are available at www.mantamaps.com

HIKING & TREKKING

Honduras has excellent hiking, particularly on the country's many mountains. Well-marked and maintained trail systems are rare, however, and in most cases hikers will need to hire a guide.

Parque Nacional La Tigra (p81) has the country's best trail system, with easy-to-follow trails of various lengths and difficulties. The park can be visited as a day trip from Tegucigalpa, but has camping and rustic accommodation, plus a highly recommended guesthouse at the El Rosario entrance. Parque Nacional Montaña de Celaque (p141) is another great do-it-yourself spot, with a challenging day-climb (taking between one and three days) through cloud forest to the top of Honduras' highest mountain. Other areas with good do-it-yourself hiking include Parque Nacional Cerro Azul Meámbar (p154), Monumento Natural El Boquerón (p99), and on the beach from Miami to Parque Nacional Jeannette Kawas (Punta Sal) near Tela (p174).

A number of other terrific hikes require guides, mainly for safety (see also p260 for information on hiking hazards). In Olancho, climbing La Picucha (p103) in the Sierra de Agalta National Park is certainly one of the more adventurous and rewarding hikes in the country, doable from either Catacamas or, more commonly, Gualaco. Parque Nacional de Santa Bárbara (p155) has the second-highest mountain in the country and tremendous views from the summit. There are several routes to the top, all involving lots of bushwhacking.

DIVING RESPONSIBLY

Honduras' reefs are at risk, as over-diving takes its toll. Here are a few tips that will help preserve these beautiful ecosystems for future generations.

- Never use anchors on the reef, and take care not to ground boats on coral.
- Avoid touching or standing on living marine organisms or dragging equipment across the reef. Polyps can be damaged by even the gentlest contact. If you must hold on to the reef, only touch exposed rock or dead coral.
- Be conscious of your fins. Even without contact, the surge from fin strokes near the reef can damage delicate organisms. Take care not to kick up clouds of sand, which can smother organisms.
- Practice and maintain proper buoyancy control. Major damage can be done by divers descending too fast and colliding with the reef.
- Take great care in underwater caves. Spend as little time within them as possible as your air bubbles may be caught within the roof and thereby leave organisms high and dry. Take turns to inspect the interior of a small cave.
- Resist the temptation to collect or buy corals or shells or to loot marine archaeological sites (including shipwrecks).
- Ensure that you take home all your rubbish and any litter you may find as well. Plastics in particular are a serious threat to marine life.
- Do not feed fish.
- Minimize your disturbance of marine animals. Never ride on the backs of turtles.

Of course La Moskitia offers unforgettable hiking as well; see p246 for more info. From Las Marías, two- and three-day hikes up Pico Dama and Cerro Baltimore take you through pristine rainforest, teeming with monkeys, birds and other wildlife.

MOUNTAIN BIKING

Honduras has the potential to be a great mountain-biking destination, with myriad dirt roads winding through stunning mountain terrain. Travelers with their own bikes can certainly grab a map and start exploring, while those without gear have fewer options. Definitely plan to ride in the dry season – mud forms fast and thick even after a short rain.

The best guided mountain-bike trips are in La Ceiba (p181). At least two different tour outfits offer day trips or multi-day excursions for riders of all levels. Most rides are in the Río Cangrejal area, on the edges of Pico Bonito National Park, where the same tour operators also have jungle lodges – a free night's stay is included in all trips. You can also rent bicycles by the hour or the day for exploring on you own.

In Tela, Jardín Botánico Lancetilla (p174) is a popular biking destination, and there are a couple of places in town to rent bikes.

Experienced riders with their own bikes have many more options, of course. Western Honduras, especially the Ruta Lenca (p133), has relatively little traffic and challenging, topsy-turvy terrain. For those looking for some serious up-and-down, the 50km road between Gracias and San Sebastian will have you sucking air in no time. The road is well-maintained and goes through several picturesque villages.

La Esperanza (p149) also has excellent riding nearby in the Valle de Azacualpa, a broad, rolling valley circled by a well-maintained dirt road and dotted with small villages, churches and other sights along the way. The vast central interior has even better biking possibilities, but is quite remote and known for roadside hold-ups, especially in Olancho department.

Finally, Isla del Tigre (p92) is hardly a top destination but a visit there would be much nicer if you had a bike. An 18km paved road circles the island, with no major climbs, very little traffic and plenty of places to stop and enjoy the view or go down to the water.

RAFTING & KAYAKING

Honduras has some of the best rafting and kayaking in Central America, dealing up solid Class II to Class IV whitewater (even Class V during high water) while paddling through beautiful gorges and river valleys. If there's a drawback to the rafting here, it is that trips are either half-day or week-plus, and not much middle ground.

Honduras & Belize: White Star Guides Diving (2005), by Roberto Rinaldi, describes some of the top dive sites in Honduras.

Honduras' best rafting outfits are in La Ceiba (see p181) offering half-day trips on the Río Cangrejal, east of town. The river tumbles down the coastal mountains toward the bottom, which form the border of the massive Pico Bonito National Park. Rafting trips generally include short excursions into the national park, such as hiking to nearby waterfalls. The two outfits that do most of the Río Cangrejal business, Jungle River Tours (p182) and Omega Tours (p182) also have jungle lodges near the take-out, and all trips include a free night's stay.

The Coral Reef Alliance (www.coral.org) is dedicated to preserving coral reefs through local conservation, education and sustainable tourism programs worldwide, including on Roatán.

For an experience of a whole different category, the same rafting companies offer multi-day expeditions down the Río Plátano or Río Patuca into La Moskitia (see p103). Trips start in Olancho – Dulce Nombre de Culmí for the Río Plátano and Juticalpa for the Río Patuca – and last a week to 10 days. Both trips go through the heart of Honduras' most pristine natural habitat, the largest rainforest north of the Amazon. It includes stretches of four or five days during which you'll see no sign of human settlement, but plenty of wildlife. The Río Plátano trip also includes Class III rapids, and passes through Las Marías, a popular destination in La Moskitia where a number of additional trips are possible. The Río Patuca winds

TIPS FOR TREKKING SAFELY & RESPONSIBLY

A few simple guidelines will make any wilderness foray not only better, but safer for you and for the plants and animals you may encounter on the way.

- Ask permission – Always ask permission when passing through farm land, especially in indigenous areas, or if you want to camp nearby. Same goes for taking photos of people.
- Buying souvenirs – Do not buy souvenirs or other gifts that are made from protected or endangered animals, whether black coral, sea turtles, animal pelts or feathers.
- Do not approach animals – An animal that feels cornered or threatened can be very dangerous.
- Going to the toilet – Dig a hole at least 40m from the nearest water and cover well when finished.
- Pack out what you pack in – Never leave trash in the wilderness, even organic products.
- Speak quietly – You're more likely to see animals if they don't hear you from 1km away.
- Stay on the trail – You're less likely to get lost, and will do less damage to the environment.
- Hire a guide – Trails are often overgrown and hard to follow. A local guide will help you keep from getting lost, can show you many plants and animals you might not have seen, and provide an invaluable liaison with locals who can sometimes be distrustful of foreigners. Plus, hiring a local brings a much-needed cash infusion into the local economy, meaning that finally a live tapir might be worth more than a dead one.

through the Tawahka Asangni Biosphere Reserve, home to the reclusive Tawahka indigenous group, and emerges at the town of Ahuas, where you can catch a flight back to La Ceiba or elsewhere in La Moskitia. Trips include camping on the beach and short excursions into the rainforest to see caves and waterfalls.

One of the largest tarpon caught in Brus Laguna weighed 210 pounds and took six hours to land.

Kayakers can descend the Río Cangrejal along the same route as rafters. Omega Tours (p182) has kayak tours and offers kayak instruction and rental. For flat-water excursions, try boating at Cuero y Salado Wildlife Refuge (see p187) near La Ceiba or Punta Izopo National Park near Tela. Both are good places to spot birds and other wildlife.

SPORT FISHING

Honduras has terrific sport fishing, both deep-sea and flat-water. The Bay Islands are a logical place for ocean fishing, of course. Roatán has several outfits, most at West End. Trips can be arranged through most of the larger hotels, for slightly higher prices. Fishing is not cheap, typically costing upwards of L$11,340 (US$600) for an all-day trip for up to eight people. You may be able to save some money by hiring a local fisherman, but of course you are less certain your guide will know what he's doing.

The Insituto Geográfico Nacional in Tegucigalpa has a wide selection of topographic and political maps.

Anglers can choose the type of fishing – and fish – they're interested in. Trolling is popular for hooking trophy fish, including dorado, barracuda, tuna, wahoo and even marlin in season. Deep-sea fishing produces grouper and snapper, which are the most common fish served at restaurants and are sometimes called 'dinner fish.' Flat fishing targets bone fish that live in the shallow, flat water of lagoons and estuaries, and are typically catch-and-release.

But for truly spectacular flat-water fishing, head straight to Brus Laguna in La Moskitia. The huge shallow lagoon teems with snook, grouper, snapper and – get this – tarpon weighing 200 pounds or more. Now that's a wild ride! Anglers tell tales of four-, five- and six-hour battles to land one of those monsters.

Honduras has over 80 ecologically protected areas, home to more than 200 different species of mammal, 700 bird species and around 300 reptiles and amphibians.

Finally, Lago de Yojoa (p151) is famous for its fine lake-fishing, especially for bass. Ask at your hotel for a guide.

WILDLIFE WATCHING

As well as the amazing aquatic flora and fauna in the Bay Islands, there's plenty of terrafirma wildlife to be seen in Honduras. Your best bet is to head into one of the numerous national parks and preserves around the country. If you really want to see wildlife, you'll need to get up early (leave just before sunrise) when the animals are their most active. The North Coast and La Moskitia both offer excellent bird-watching, where you can log numerous maritime and migratory species. Inland, your best bet is in the wild areas surrounding Lago de Yojoa (p151).

See Environment (p52) for more details on the country's flora and fauna.

Tegucigalpa & Southern Honduras

It's not the prettiest place around – there are bigger peaks in Western Honduras, broader wild areas in La Moskitia, better city settings in the colonial villages along La Ruta Lenca, and brighter beaches just about anywhere in the Bay Islands – but southern Honduras is the bleeding, gritty, raw heart of a nation.

The capital city of Tegucigalpa can be slightly intimidating – this is one of the more dangerous metropolitan areas in Central America – but a good attitude and a bit of common sense will help you appreciate the hillside neighborhoods (that rival anything you'd see in Rio de Janeiro), the decent selection of museums, and the hustle, buzz and cacophonous roar that only a developing-world capital can create.

Outside the city there's a number of small towns and bigger-than-life parks worth visiting. The twin colonial cities of Valle de Ángeles and Santa Lucía offer some of the best crafts shopping in the country, and a pastoral mountain setting that'll have you extending your stay for a few more days. Nearby, Parque Nacional La Tigra was the nation's first national park, and remains an excellent (and easily accessible) entry into the wilds of Honduras. Along the sweltering Pacific Coast, there are unbeatable sunsets and decent beach haunts on Isla del Tigre. And everywhere in between you'll find something even more valuable: a hard-drawn isolation and quiet stillness not easily won in this modern day.

HIGHLIGHTS

- Test your metal as you explore the twisted and tormented urban core of **Tegucigalpa** (p65) for a chance to see how most of the world lives
- Get up early for a birding expedition in Honduras' oldest national park at **Parque Nacional La Tigra** (p81)
- Strike out on your own from the white-washed colonial village of **Yuscarán** (p85) to the seldom-visited **Reserva Biológica Yuscarán** (p86), right on your doorstep
- Spend an afternoon drinking in the sun and refined air of **Valle de Ángeles (p80)** before heading over to nearby **Santa Lucía** (**p79**), which offers the same colonial charm but only a fraction of the tourist traffic
- Spend your vacation with the locals at the down-and-dirty seaside haunts of **Isla del Tigre** (**p92**)

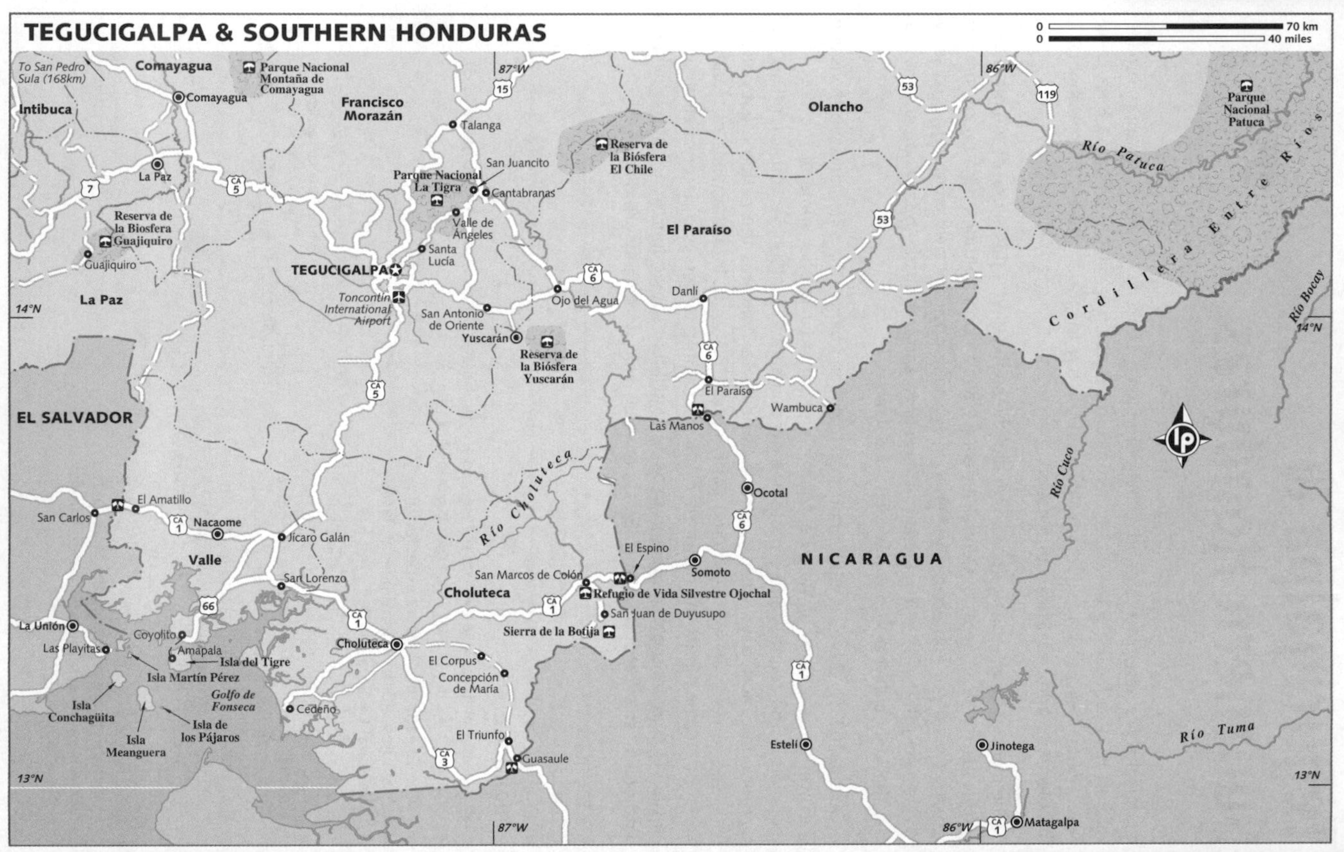
TEGUCIGALPA & SOUTHERN HONDURAS
0 70 km
0 40 miles
To San Pedro Sula (168km)
Comayagua
Parque Nacional Montaña de Comayagua
Comayagua
Intibuca
Francisco Morazán
Talanga
Olancho
Parque Nacional Patuca
Río Patuca
Cordillera Entre Ríos
La Paz
Reserva de la Biósfera El Chile
San Juancito
Parque Nacional La Tigra
Cantabranas
Valle de Ángeles
Reserva de la Biosfera Guajiquiro
Guajiquiro
Santa Lucía
El Paraíso
TEGUCIGALPA
Toncontín International Airport
Ojo del Agua
Danlí
La Paz
14°N
San Antonio de Oriente
Yuscarán
Reserva de la Biósfera Yuscarán
Río Bocay
El Paraíso
Wambuca
Las Manos
EL SALVADOR
Río Cuco
Río Choluteca
Ocotal
El Amatillo
San Carlos
Nacaome
Jícaro Galán
El Espino
Valle
San Marcos de Colón
Somoto
NICARAGUA
San Lorenzo
Choluteca
Refugio de Vida Silvestre Ojochal
San Juan de Duyusupo
La Unión
Sierra de la Botija
Coyolito
Choluteca
Las Playitas
Amapala
Isla del Tigre
El Corpus
Isla Martín Pérez
Concepción de María
Golfo de Fonseca
Isla Conchagüita
Cedeño
Isla de los Pájaros
Isla Meanguera
El Triunfo
Guasaule
Estelí
Jinotega
Río Tuma
13°N
87°W
86°W
Matagalpa

TEGUCIGALPA

pop 1.08 million

This is the intellectual and cultural crossroads of a nation. Here politicians and street-thugs share the crowded sidewalk with wandering travelers, university radicals and starched-shirt businessmen. Despite its mean-streets reputation – this is a dangerous town, don't get us wrong, but so are New York and Jerusalem – a visit to this sprawling metropolis may be worth your time, especially if you've never visited a developing-world capital before. There's a smattering of decent museums in the colonial core but, more than that, there's the chaos and clutter, the honks and shouts and putrid smells, and gritty realness that make a city a city.

And with its unique topography – the city is lovingly situated in a massive bowl-shaped valley – this is one capital that can appeal to the inner esthete in all of us (though it's best to behold it through rose-tinted glasses).

HISTORY

The name Tegucigalpa (Teh-goos-ee-*gal*-pa) is a mouthful, and not just for newcomers to the city or the language. Hondurans themselves commonly shorten it to Tegus (*teh*-goos) or simply *la capital* (the capital). The modern name, which dates from the 16th century, is undoubtedly derived from the name of the original indigenous village here, and is most commonly translated as 'silver hill.' The problem with that story, of course, is that the original residents did not mine silver and probably didn't even have a word for the material before Spanish colonizers appeared on the scene. More recently, linguists have suggested the name means, roughly, 'place of painted stones' (which you can imagine being twisted into 'silver hill' by colonizers seeking to legitimize their presence). Tegucigalpa became the capital of Honduras in 1880, when the government seat was moved from Comayagua, 82km to the northwest. In 1938 Comayagüela, on the opposite side of the river from Tegucigalpa, became part of the city.

ORIENTATION

The city is divided by the Río Choluteca. On the east side of the river is Tegucigalpa, with the city center and the more affluent districts. Plaza Morazán, also known simply as Parque Central, with its imposing cathedral, is at the heart of the city. On the west side of Parque Central, Av Miguel Paz Barahona serves as a pedestrian shopping district, extending four blocks from the plaza to Calle El Telégrafo; this section has been renamed Calle Peatonal (Pedestrian Street), and it's a busy thoroughfare with many shops, restaurants and banks.

Across the river from Tegucigalpa is Comayagüela, which is generally poorer and dirtier than the east side of the river, with a sprawling market area, lots of long-distance bus stations, cheap hotels and *comedores* (cheap eateries). The two areas are connected by a number of bridges. The Anillo Periférico encircles the southern half of the city.

INFORMATION

Bookstores

Librería Guaymuras (Map p71; ☎ 222-4140; libreguay@cablecolor.hn; Av Miguel de Cervantes, near Calle Salvador Corleto; 🕑 8:30am-6:30pm Mon-Fri, to 12:30pm Sat) Spanish-language books on the history, people and culture of Honduras.

Metromedia Av San Carlos (Map p74; metromedia2@mulitvisionhn.net; Av San Carlos; ☎ 221-0770; 🕑 10am-8pm Mon-Sat, noon-6pm Sun); Multiplaza Mall (off Map pp66-7; ☎ 231-2410; Av Juan Pablo; 🕑 8am-8pm) Sells an excellent and wide selection of English-language books and periodicals.

Cultural Centers

Mujeres En Las Artes (Map p71; ☎ 222-3015; www.muaartes.org.hn; Av Miguel de Cervantes) Hosts art exhibits and performances by female artists; workshops and lecture series are offered occasionally. It's near the bridge to Col Palmira.

Emergency

Ambulance (Red Cross; ☎ 195; 🕑 24hr)

Police (Map p71; ☎ 199, 222-8736; 5a Av; 🕑 24hr)

Immigration

Immigration Office (off Map pp66-7; ☎ 238-5613; Anillo Periférico near the Universidad Tecnológica de Honduras; 🕑 8:30am-4:30pm Mon-Fri) Extends visas and handles other immigration matters.

Internet Access

Cíber Planet (Map p71; ☎ 237-0200; cnr Av Máximo Jérez & Calle Finlay; internet per hr L$20; 🕑 8:30am-10pm Mon-Sat, 10am-10pm Sun) Also offers cheap international calling.

Downtown Hondutel office (Map p71; ☎ 222-1120; Av Cristóbal Colón at Calle El Telégrafo; per hr

TEGUCIGALPA

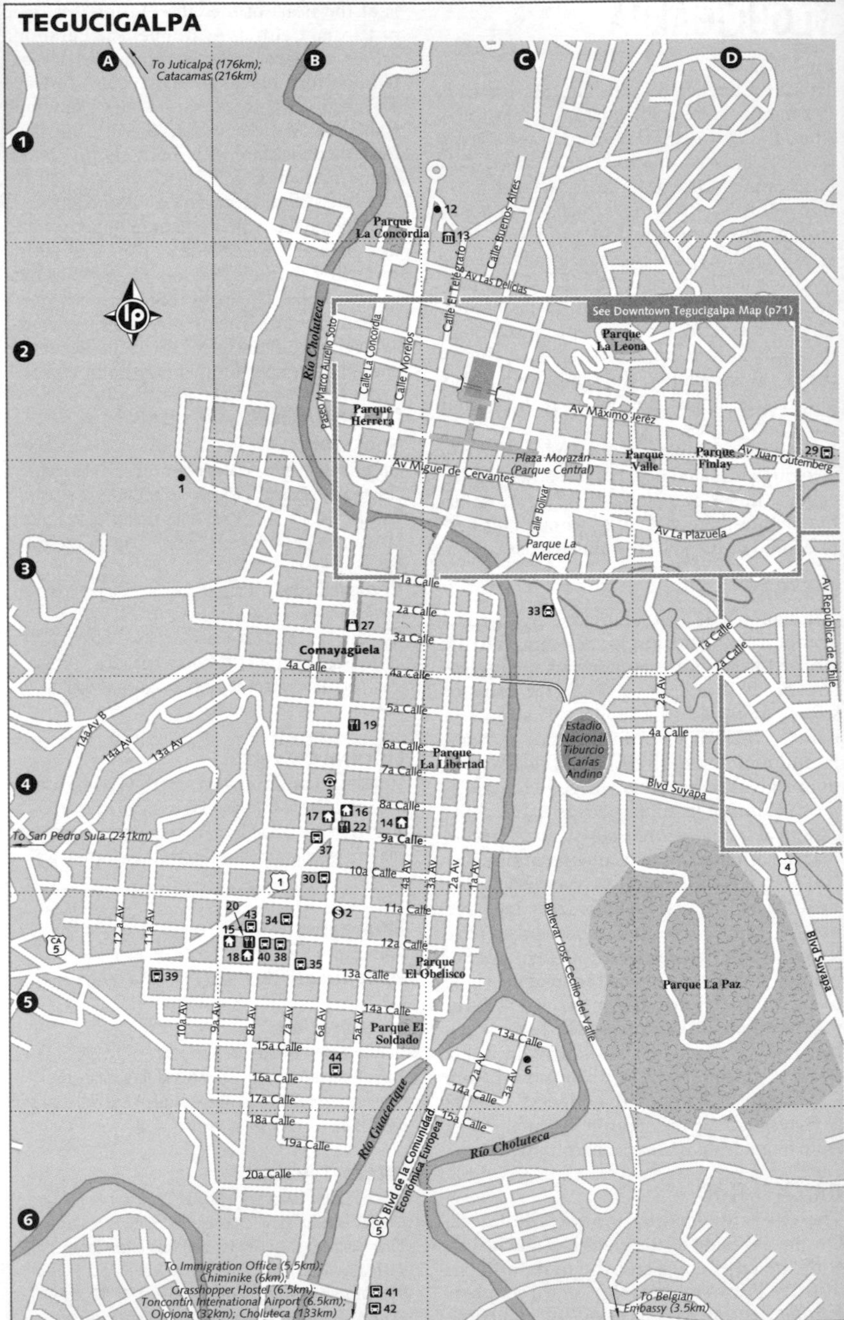

0 800 m
0 0.5 miles
E
F
G
H
1
2
3
4
5
6
To Parque Naciones Unidas El Picacho & Zoo (3.5km)
INFORMATION
Administración Forestal del Estado - COHDEFOR....1 A3
Banco Atlántida....2 B5
Comayagüela Hondutel Office....3 B4
Comayagüela Post Office....(see 3)
Finnish Embassy....4 H3
Honduras Medical Center....5 F4
Instituto Geográfico Nacional....6 C5
Italian Embassy....7 F2
Nicaraguan Embassy....8 E5
Spanish Embassy....9 F3
Super Jet....10 E3
Swedish Embassy....11 G4
SIGHTS & ACTIVITIES
Honduran Institute of Anthropology and History....12 C1
Museo Nacional de Historia y Antropología Villa Roy....13 C1
SLEEPING
Hotel Hedman Alas....14 B4
Hotel Palace....15 B5
Hotel Plaza Real....16 B4
Hotel San Pedro....17 B4
Hotel Unión....18 B5
Subida Casamata
Río Chiquito
2a Av
3a Av
4a Av
5a Av
6a Av
7a Av
Monumento a Simón Bolivar
Hospital San Felipe
Av de los Próceres
Av La Paz
Av Ramón Ernesto Cruz
Av República Dominicana
Colonia Palmira
Blvd Morazán
To Norwegian Embassy (1 block); Danish Embassy (1.5 blocks); Swiss Embassy (1.5 blocks); Santa Lucía (14km); Valle de Ángeles (22km)
4a Av
See Colonia Palmira & Boulevard Morazán Map (p74)
8a Calle
2a Av
Quebrada Las Lomas
To Salvadoran Embassy (0.5km); Avis (2km); Dutch Embassy (4km); Mercado Jacaleapa (5km); Buses to Danlí & Nicaragua border (5km); Museo de Historia Natural & UNAH (6.5km); Basílica & Iglesia de Suyapa (7km); Danlí (92km)
To Costa Rican Embassy (1km); Mexican Embassy, Taiwanese Embassy, InterContinental, Jaguar (1.5km); Casa De Puros, Multiplaza Mall & Cinemark (1.5km); Guatemalan Embassy (1.7km); Canadian Embassy (2km)
To German Embassy (5km)
EATING
Centro Comercial Jerusalem....19 B4
Delia Comidas....20 B5
Delitortas....(see 19)
Supermercado Más x Menos....21 E3
Todo de Pollo....22 B4
ENTERTAINMENT
Bamboo....23 H3
La Grotta....24 G4
Over Time....25 H3
Rió....26 G3
SHOPPING
Mercado San Isidro....27 B3
TRANSPORT
Air France....28 F3
Bus to Juticalpa & Parque Nacional La Tigra....29 D2
Buses to El Amatillo & El Salvador border....30 B4
Buses to San Juancito & El Rosario....31 F2
Buses to Valle de Ángeles & Santa Lucía....32 G3
Colectivo Taxis to UNAH & Suyapa/Contraibal....33 C3
Contraibal....34 B5
Discovery....35 B5
Econo Rent-a-Car....36 H4
El Rey de Oro....37 B4
El Rey Express....38 B5
Hedman Alas....39 A5
Kamaldy....40 B5
King Quality....41 B6
Mi Esperanza....42 B6
Saenz....(see 37)
Sultana de Occidente....43 B5
Tica Bus....44 B5

L$20; 7:30am-9pm Mon-Sat) Air-conditioning and sleek black Dells with flat screens.
Multinet (Map p74; Plaza Criolla; internet per hr L$30, international calls per min from L$1)

Laundry

Lavandería Maya (Map p74; 4a Calle; per 10lb L$140; 7am-6pm Mon-Fri, 8am-4pm Sat)
Super Jet (Map pp66-7; Av Juan Gutemberg; per 10lb $140; 8am-6pm Mon-Sat)

Libraries

Biblioteca Nacional (Map p71; 220-1746; Av Miguel de Cervantes near Calle Salvador Corleto; 7:30am-noon & 12:30pm-3:30pm Mon-Fri) Houses a good collection of Honduran history books. On-site use only; leave your passport as a deposit.

Medical Services

Farma City (Map p74; 232-4415; Blvd Morazán near Plaza Criolla; 9am-9pm Mon-Sat, to 7pm Sun)
Farmacia Divel (Map p71; 237-4064; Av Cristóbal Colón at Calle Los Dolores; 8am-6pm Mon-Fri, 9am-1pm Sun)
Honduras Medical Center (Map pp66-7; 216-1201; Av Juan Lindo; 24hr) Considered one of the best hospitals in the country.

Money

In addition to the places listed here, there is a Unibanc ATM at Tegucigalpa airport, and cash machines of all major banks at the malls.
BAC (Map p74; Blvd Morazán at Av Ramón Ernesto Cruz; 9am-5pm Mon-Fri, 9am-noon Sat) Changes traveler's checks and has a 24-hour ATM.
Banco Atlántida (9am-4pm Mon-Fri, 8:30-11:30am Sat) 6a Av at 11a Calle **(Map pp66-7)**; Downtown Tegucigalpa (Map p71; Parque Central) Also has 24-hour ATMs and will change traveler's checks.
HSBC (Map p74; Blvd Morazán; 9am-5pm Mon-Fri, 9am-noon Sat) Changes traveler's check; has a 24-hour ATM.

Post

Comayagüela post office (Map pp66-7; 6a Av btwn Calles 7a & 8a; 7:30am-5pm Mon-Fri, 8am-1pm Sat) In the same building as Hondutel.
Downtown post office (Map p71; Av Miguel Paz Barahona at Calle El Telégrafo; 7:30am-6pm Mon-Fri, 8am-1pm Sat)
Mailboxes, Etc. (Map p74; 232-3184; Blvd Morazán; 8am-6pm Mon-Fri, 9am-1pm Sat) More reliable international shipping.

Telephone

Most internet cafes (see p65) also offer domestic and international calling.
Comayagüela Hondutel office (Map pp66-7; 220-0707; 6a Av btwn Calles 7a & 8a; 7am-8:30pm Mon-Fri) In same building as the post office.
Downtown Hondutel office (Map p71; 222-1120; Av Cristóbal Colón at Calle El Telégrafo; 7:30am-9pm Mon-Sat) Call center and internet cafe.

Tourist Information

Administración Forestal del Estado – Corporación Hondureña de Desarrollo Forestal (COHDEFOR; Map pp66-7; 223-4346; Colonia El Carrizal; 8am-4pm Mon-Fri) Headquarters, offering information on Honduras' national parks, wildlife refuges and other protected areas. It's near the Cemeterio General.
Amitigra (Fundación Amigos de la Tigra; Map p74; 238-6269; www.amitigra.org; 5a Av Edificio Italia, 4th fl, office No 6; 8am-12:30pm & 1-5pm Mon-Fri) Offers information about, and manages overnight visits to, Parque Nacional La Tigra.
Honduras Tips A free guidebook with good bus and sights information. Pick it up at most hotels and at the Instituto Hondureño de Turismo, or visit www.hondurastips.honduras.com.
Instituto Geográfico Nacional (Map pp66-7; 225-0752; 3a Av Barrio La Bolsa; 7:30am-noon & 12:30-3:30pm Mon-Fri) Sells large detailed maps of Honduras, its regions and several of its cities. Also sells road and topographical maps.
Instituto Hondureño de Turismo (Map p74; 220-1600; www.letsgohonduras.com in English, www.visitehonduras.com in Spanish; Edificio Europa, 2nd fl, Av Ramón Ernesto Cruz at Calle República de México; 7:30am-4:30pm Mon-Fri) Offers brochures and basic information on the country's sights. Staff speak English.

Travel Agencies

There are several reliable travel agencies near the Hotel Honduras Maya; others are downtown on Calle Peatonal near Parque Central. Be aware that some agencies charge just for the *cotización* (trip quote).
Mundirama Travel (Map p74; 232-3909; fax 232-0072; Edificio CIICSA, Avs República de Panamá & República de Chile; 8am-5pm Mon-Fri, to noon Sat) American Express office.

DANGERS & ANNOYANCES

Crime is on everyone's mind in Tegucigalpa – the Honduran Congress recently abbreviated its sessions because too many representatives were getting held up on their way home. But, by using a bit of common sense, you can enjoy

Tegus while minimizing the risk of experiencing any crime, much less violent crime, during your stay.

Criminals aren't stupid: they will watch a potential target to see if they're carrying anything valuable. Cameras and jewelry (real or faux) are sure to be seen, and make easy targets – don't walk around with them. Try doing without a daypack or purse; even if there's nothing valuable in it, a potential thief won't know that. Carry the money you need for the day and a copy of your passport, but avoid flashing it around. Dress modestly: shorts and sandals may seem fine to you but they stick out like a sore thumb in most Latin American cities, Tegus included. Try wearing pants and sneakers instead. And remember, the point isn't to 'fit in' – you won't, no matter how hard you try – but rather to avoid being the one person in 1000 who gets targeted for crime. If you do happen to be that one person, cooperate and do not resist.

The downtown area is fine during the day, as are Colonia Palmira and Blvd Morazán. Comayagüela can be dodgy, especially around San Isidro Market, and a trip to Parque La Paz is not recommended. Avoid walking around Comayagüela after sunset – there's not much to do, anyway. You should also avoid walking anywhere in the city – even a few blocks – after 9pm. Instead, take a cab. Same goes if you're going to or from a bus terminal with bags. When waiting for a bus, go inside the terminal, or at least near the ticket booth, and keep a hand on your bags at all times.

Local public buses occasionally get held up. In the end, it's just safer and easier – and not that much more expensive – to cab it.

And one last thing: relax. The chances of anything happening to any one person at any one time are exceedingly low, even in a 'crime-ridden' place like Tegucigalpa.

SIGHTS

Though none compare to the amazing museums and galleries, and soaring churches and plazas that make other Latin American cities special, Tegucigalpa has a number of interesting sights that are well worth a short visit.

Museums

The **Museo Nacional de Historia y Antropología Villa Roy** (Map pp66-7; ☎ 222-0079; Calle el Telegrafo; admission L$60; 🕑 8am-4pm Mon-Sat) is housed in the former home of ex-president Julio Lozano (near Calle Morelos), an opulent two-story mansion overlooking the city. Fascinating, if somewhat intense, the museum traces a chronological path through Honduran history, from independence, through the Liberal reform period, to modern-day Honduras. Displays are long and detailed (and in Spanish only). The section on the Vaccaro brothers and the rise of Standard and United Fruit companies will be interesting even to casual visitors, as few events have more deeply shaped Honduras' past and present. The **Honduran Institute of Anthropology & History** (IHAH; Map pp66-7; ☎ 222-0079; Calle el Telegrafo; 🕑 8am-4pm Mon-Fri) operates the museum and has its headquarters and research library near the museum entrance.

Located in what was once a 17th-century convent, the **Galería Nacional de Arte** (Map p71; ☎ 237-9884; fundarte@usa.net; Parque La Merced; admission L$60; 🕑 9am-4pm Mon-Sat, to 1pm Sun) is well worth a visit. Seven exhibition rooms house modern artwork, colonial-era paintings and religious artifacts. There is also a small exhibit of pictographs found in Honduras – all replicas – but interesting nonetheless. Most signage is in English and Spanish.

The **Museo del Hombre Hondureño** (Map p71; ☎ 220-1678; Av Miguel de Cervantes btwn Calles Salvador Corleto & Las Damas) displays Honduran art, mostly contemporary work. Admission price and hours vary: it is often closed, opening mainly for special events or private parties.

Tegucigalpa's newest museum is the ambitious **Museo para la Identidad Nacional** (MIN; Map p71; ☎ 222-2299; www.min-honduras.org; Av Miguel Paz Barahona btwn Calles Morelos & El Telégrafo), which is intended to encapsulate the whole of Honduran history, from pre-Colombian civilization to the present day. It still hasn't achieved that to great end. Admission costs and hours vary.

The **Centro de Documentación Historica** (Map p71; ☎ 237-0268; Paseo Marco Aurelio Soto at Calle Salvador Mendieta; admission L$60, last Thu of month free; 🕑 8:30am-noon & 1-4pm Wed-Sun) is another museum tracing the history of Honduras from independence to the present. The displays are interesting enough, but other museums cover the same ground just as well (sometimes better). The building housing them is the real gem, having served as the Casa Presidencial (Presidential Palace) from 1920 until 1992.

Just down the hill from the Basilica de Suyapa (7km south of the city center) is the **Universidad Nacional Autónoma de Honduras** (UNAH, Ciudad Universitaria), which houses the **Museo de Historia Natural**. Despite the upbeat listing in Honduras Tips, its sadly deteriorating collection of stuffed birds and animals is not worth visiting. Also not worth your time is the **Museo Histórico Militar** (Map p71; ☎ 237-9729; Parque Valle), which was closed when we visited but, when open, could barely rustle up a few uniforms and rusty weapons.

Churches & Plazas

The most important church in Tegucigalpa, and therefore in Honduras, is the Gothic **Basílica de Suyapa** (off Map pp66–7), about 7km south of the city center in the suburb of Suyapa, near UNAH, the national university. La Virgen de Suyapa is the patron saint of Honduras; in 1982 a papal decree made her the patron saint of all Central America. Construction of the basilica, which is famous for its large stained-glass windows, began in 1954; finishing touches were still being added when we visited.

La Virgen de Suyapa (see p43) is a 6cm wooden statue. Many believe she has performed hundreds of miracles. She is brought to the large basilica on holidays, especially for the annual Feria de la Virgen de Suyapa (p72); the celebrations attract pilgrims from all over Central America. Most of the time, however, the little statue is kept in the very simple **Iglesia de Suyapa** (if you squint, you'll see her on the main altar). Built in the late 18th and early 19th centuries, and renovated multiple times, the *iglesia* (church) stands a few hundred meters behind the impressive basilica.

Buses for Suyapa (L$5, 20 minutes) leave from the gas station at 6a Av and 9 Calle in Comayagüela; get off at the university and walk the short distance from there. *Colectivo* (shared) taxis leave from a stop a short distance south of Parque La Merced.

At the center of the city is the fine **cathedral** (Map p71) and, in front of it, the **Plaza Morazán**, often just called Parque Central. The domed 18th-century cathedral (built between 1765 and 1782) has an intricate baroque altar of gold and silver. Parque Central, with its statue of Morazán on horseback, is the hub of the city.

Three blocks east of the cathedral is the **Parque Valle**, with the **Iglesia de San Francisco** (Map p71), the first church in Tegucigalpa, founded in 1592 by the Franciscans.

Iglesia Los Dolores (1732; Map p71), northwest of the cathedral, is worth a visit, with a plaza out front and religious art inside. On the front of Los Dolores are figures representing the Passion of Christ – his unseamed cloak, the cock that crowed three times – all crowned by the more indigenous symbol of the sun. Further west is **Parque Herrera**, which seems to attract a somewhat less savory crowd, but the 18th-century **Iglesia El Calvario** (Map p71) is worth a peek, as is the Teatro Nacional Manuel Bonilla, if it happens to be open when you pass by.

Another 18th-century church, **Iglesia La Merced** (Map p71), located next to the Galería Nacional de Arte, faces **Parque La Merced**. In 1847, the convent of La Merced was converted to house Honduras' first university; the national gallery was established there in 1996. The well-restored building is itself a work of art, and is as impressive as the paintings inside. The unusual modern building on stilts next door is the **Palacio Legislativo** (Map p71), where Congress meets.

A couple of blocks west of the Museo Nacional de Historia y Antropología Villa Roy is **Parque La Concordia** (Map pp66–7), a mellow park full of reproductions of the Maya ruins at Copán (p119), including a pyramid and many stone carvings.

ACTIVITIES

The **Hotel Honduras Maya** (Map p74; ☎ 220-5000; www.hondurasmaya.hn; Av Segunda, Colonia Palmira) has a swimming pool, gym, spa and sauna that are open to nonguests for L$200 per day (L$100 for children).

Parks

On the north side of Tegucigalpa is **Parque Naciones Unidas El Picacho** (United Nations Park El Picacho; off Map pp66-7; adult/child L$20/10; 8am-5pm), established to commemorate the UN's 40th anniversary. Besides excellent views of the city, there's a soccer field where games are held on Sunday, and a somewhat decrepit **zoo** (adult/child L$5/2; 9am-4:30pm Wed-Sun).

The park is located about 6km from the center of town, up a winding road past some of the capital's most exclusive real estate (the US Ambassador's residence, for one). On Sundays, buses leave from behind Iglesia Los Dolores and take you all the way to the park gates. Otherwise, take an El Hatillo bus (L$7, every 25 minutes 5am to 10pm, last return bus at 9pm) from Av Juan Gutemberg or Parque Herrera and get off at the junction. It takes

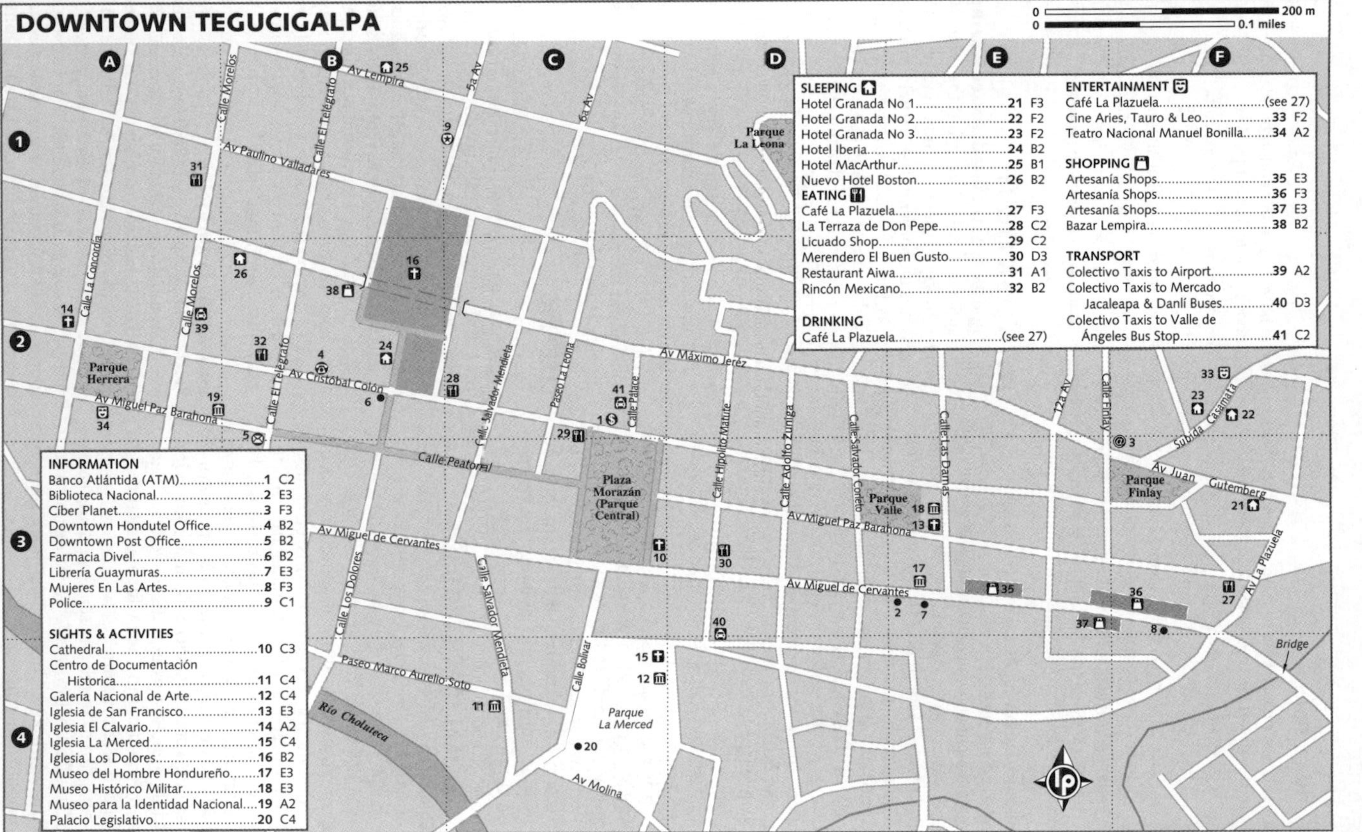
DOWNTOWN TEGUCIGALPA
0 200 m
0 0.1 miles
SLEEPING
Hotel Granada No 1 21 F3
Hotel Granada No 2 22 F2
Hotel Granada No 3 23 F2
Hotel Iberia 24 B2
Hotel MacArthur 25 B1
Nuevo Hotel Boston 26 B2
EATING
Café La Plazuela 27 F3
La Terraza de Don Pepe 28 C2
Licuado Shop 29 C2
Merendero El Buen Gusto 30 D3
Restaurant Aiwa 31 A1
Rincón Mexicano 32 B2
DRINKING
Café La Plazuela (see 27)
ENTERTAINMENT
Café La Plazuela (see 27)
Cine Aries, Tauro & Leo 33 F2
Teatro Nacional Manuel Bonilla 34 A2
SHOPPING
Artesanía Shops 35 E3
Artesanía Shops 36 F3
Artesanía Shops 37 E3
Bazar Lempira 38 B2
TRANSPORT
Colectivo Taxis to Airport 39 A2
Colectivo Taxis to Mercado Jacaleapa & Danlí Buses 40 D3
Colectivo Taxis to Valle de Ángeles Bus Stop 41 C2
INFORMATION
Banco Atlántida (ATM) 1 C2
Biblioteca Nacional 2 E3
Cíber Planet 3 F3
Downtown Hondutel Office 4 B2
Downtown Post Office 5 B2
Farmacia Divel 6 B2
Librería Guaymuras 7 E3
Mujeres En Las Artes 8 F3
Police 9 C1
SIGHTS & ACTIVITIES
Cathedral 10 C3
Centro de Documentación Historica 11 C4
Galería Nacional de Arte 12 C4
Iglesia de San Francisco 13 E3
Iglesia El Calvario 14 A2
Iglesia La Merced 15 C4
Iglesia Los Dolores 16 B2
Museo del Hombre Hondureño 17 E3
Museo Histórico Militar 18 E3
Museo para la Identidad Nacional 19 A2
Palacio Legislativo 20 C4
Av Lempira
Calle Morelos
Calle El Telégrafo
5a Av
6a Av
Av Paulino Valladares
Calle La Concordia
Parque Herrera
Av Cristóbal Colón
Av Miguel Paz Barahona
Calle Peatonal
Calle Salvador Mendieta
Paseo La Leona
Parque La Leona
Calle Palace
Av Máximo Jeréz
Calle Hipolito Matute
Calle Adolfo Zuniga
Calle Salvador Corleto
Calle Las Damas
12a Av
Calle Finlay
Subida Casamata
Av Juan Gutemberg
Parque Finlay
Av La Plazuela
Plaza Morazán (Parque Central)
Parque Valle
Av Miguel de Cervantes
Calle Los Dolores
Paseo Marco Aurelio Soto
Calle Bolívar
Parque La Merced
Av Molina
Río Choluteca
Bridge

QUICK TRIPS

You don't have to pack up your bags and check out of the hotel to see something besides Tegus proper. Here are a couple of day trips that will have you back in time for happy-hour.

- Parque Nacional La Tigra (p81) – the park offers hikes of various lengths and difficulties, through cloud forest and past old-growth trees. The Jutiapa entrance is just 22km away.
- Valle de Ángeles (p80) & Santa Lucía (p79) – just a half hour from the capital, these small, arty towns have colonial buildings, cobblestone streets and crisp, clean mountain air.
- El Paraíso (p85) – no, it's not exactly paradise, but a trip to El Paraíso Department's capital at Yuscarán, a pleasant white-washed city just 66km from Tegus, is well worth the trip.

about 20 minutes. A taxi from the center costs around L$100.

If you don't want to make the trip all the way to Parque Naciones Unidas, **Parque La Leona** (Map pp66–7) also offers quiet respite from the bustle of downtown and almost-as-good views over the city. It's one of Tegucigalpa's most pleasant (and undervisited) parks, though there could be more shade for the benches. You can walk there, but it's further – and a lot steeper – than it appears on the map. Take Paseo La Leona from the central park and follow it up, up, up. A few small stands sell sodas and chips.

It is not recommended you visit **Parque La Paz** (Map pp66–7), a wooded hill and park south of the Estadio Nacional. Though the views are impressive, it is a notorious hangout of delinquent kids, many hooked on glue sniffing, and assaults on visitors are common.

TEGUCIGALPA FOR CHILDREN

Chiminike (off Map pp66-7; ☎ 291-0339; www.chiminike.com; Blvd Fuerzas Amadas de Honduras; admission L$50; ⏰ 9am-noon & 2-5pm Tue-Fri, 10am-1pm & 2-5pm Sat & Sun) is Tegucigalpa's excellent children's museum. Situated about 7km south of downtown, it caters to kids of all ages, from a peaceful infant/nursing area to adolescent-level displays on Maya history. It's refreshingly frank: the area about the human body has exhibits on the hows and whys of farting, vomiting, sneezing and body odor, while a crawl-through digestive tract starts at the mouth and ends with a slide through an oversized rectum.

It's fun to watch the semi-pro **soccer games** at the field below the 4a Av bridge between downtown and Comaygüela. They seem to play most afternoons.

FESTIVALS & EVENTS

Tegucigalpa is virtually deserted during Semana Santa (Holy Week), but the celebration is slowly growing in popularity, with processions and *alfombras* – 'carpets' made of brightly colored sawdust like those in Antigua, Guatemala. Comayagua (p160), just up the highway, has a larger and better celebration.

The Feria de la Virgen de Suyapa is a celebration of a tiny cedar statue of the Virgin Mary (see p43) that is one of the most revered Catholic icons in Honduras and Central America. The actual saint's day is February 3, but the whole celebration lasts a week – masses and processions are held around the city (and the country, for that matter) but especially at the Basílica de Suyapa, Honduras' largest cathedral.

SLEEPING

The city's cheapest lodging is in Comayagüela, which is also where most of the bus terminals are, but the area can be dodgy during the day and downright dangerous at night. Downtown is slightly more expensive, safe during the day (but not at night) and near most of the sights. If you can afford it, Colonia Palmira offers the best quality and safest surroundings, day and night. And those looking for a bit of quiet may consider staying in Valle de Ángeles (p81) or Santa Lucía (p79), two easy-going colonial towns just 30 minutes away.

Downtown Tegucigalpa

Hotel Iberia (Map p71; ☎ 237-9267; Calle Los Dolores near Av Cristóbal Colón; s/d with shared bathroom L$150/220; d L$240) Half a block south of Iglesia Los Dolores and somewhat hidden by the market stalls out front, the Iberia is an excellent budget deal, and has some of the cleanest shared bathrooms in town. Upstairs rooms have private bathrooms that open onto a pleasant, sunny sitting area. Watch your pockets in the market when you exit.

Nuevo Hotel Boston (Map p71; ☎ 237-9411; Av Máximo Jérez 321; s/d/tr L$270/360/675) The 'New Boston' is slightly better on the inside than the outside, with well-kept rooms, high ceilings and squeaky-clean bathrooms. Two large and airy common rooms have couches, rocking chairs and TVs for guests to use. Free coffee and cookies are always available too. The one drawback: the soft beds will probably leave a lasting crick in your back.

Hotel Granada No 2 (Map p71; ☎ 238-4438; Subida Casamata 1326; s/d L$350/400; P) Comfortable but plain, this is the best of a group of three large, 1970s-style hotels; most of the 48 rooms have nicely renovated bathrooms, TV and in-room telephone.

Hotel Granada No 3 (Map p71; ☎ 237-8066; Subida Casamata 1325; s/d L$350/400) This is across the street from No 2 and has identical prices, but the rooms are somewhat neglected and gloomy.

Hotel Granada No 1 (Map p71; ☎ 237-2381; Av Juan Gutemberg 1401; s/d L$370/488) A block south of its sister establishments, this place is very clean with small bathrooms and comfy beds – a good choice if every lempira counts.

Hotel MacArthur (Map p71; ☎ 237-9839; homacart@datum.hn; Av Lempira near Calle El Telégrafo; s/d with fan L$665/760, s/d with air-con L$855/950; P) A spectacularly modern entrance with gleaming floors and high ceilings greets you at this nice downtown spot. Wander down the lobby a bit and you'll bump into a glorious pool with crystal-clear water, lounge chairs and shaded tables. Then go up to your room. It's as if it were in a completely different hotel; very clean but somewhat worn and dated – a letdown for sure. Another letdown is the hotel's downtown location.

Colonia Palmira

Hotel Guadalupe 2 (Map p74; ☎ 238-5001; 1a Calle; s/d L$390/440, tr L$530-660; P) If it weren't for the safe and scenic location, we'd probably not list this hotel here. The service was rude when we visited and the rooms are simple. But it's clean and, well, it's impossible to find a cheaper alternative in this *colonia* (neighborhood within a city).

our pick **Hotel Linda Vista** (Map p74; ☎ 238-2099; www.lindavistahotel.net; Calle Las Acacias 1438; s/d/tr incl breakfast L$950/1240/1580; P) This cozy, well-run B&B is small – just six rooms – which means it can be hard to get a reservation, though definitely worth trying. The foyer and common area have colonial-style wooden chairs and potted plants, and a grassy backyard and patio offer a truly *linda vista* (pretty view). Rooms have firm beds and ceramic floors, with decorative touches like throw pillows, large wooden headboards and framed paintings. We only wish they supplied a big water jug to help cut down on plastic waste.

Casal B&B (Map p74; ☎ 235-8891; casabedbreakfast@yahoo.com; Av República de Perú; s/d/tr incl breakfast L$1079/1322/1542) A B&B that feels more like a hotel with free breakfast. The rooms are fine and clean – with in-room phones, water coolers and cable TV – but are relatively charmless. It's in a good location, however, which means a lot in this town. You're better off staying at the Linda Vista for the price, but this is a good second option.

Leslie's Place (Map p74; ☎ 220-7494; www.dormir.com; Calzada San Martín; s/d incl breakfast L$1672/1995) This is a charming B&B, where the little details up the rate: luxurious linens, matching furniture sets, quality *artesanía* (handicraft) on the walls, wireless internet, and a garden dining area where complimentary breakfast is served. The 20 rooms are quite cute – though some can feel cramped. Ask for a room with a private terrace.

Hotel Honduras Maya (Map p74; ☎ 280-5000; www.hotelhondurasmaya.hn; Av Segunda; s/d incl buffet breakfast L$2204/2424; P) This is the nicest hotel in Palmira. The lobby is amazing in a 'world-weary business traveler getting wasted at the hotel bar' sort of way, as are the giant pool and nice grounds. But the rooms (some with stained bedspreads and carpets) could use some work. Nonetheless, it's a good deal, especially for those looking for a larger, business-style hotel.

Hotel Portal del Ángel (Map p74; ☎ 236-9588; www.portaldelangel.com; Av República de Perú; s/d incl breakfast L$2424/2755; P) One of the few 'boutique' hotels in the country, the Portal del Ángel is upscale and classy. Rooms can get a bit dowdy, with gold accents everywhere, and the bathrooms are in bad need of renovation. But the rooms have all the modern conveniences you'd expect – silent air conditioners, heavy desks and large flat-screen TVs. Some even feature locally crafted *artesanía*. There is a pool in the center of the hotel, with a garden patio and a gourmet restaurant running along two

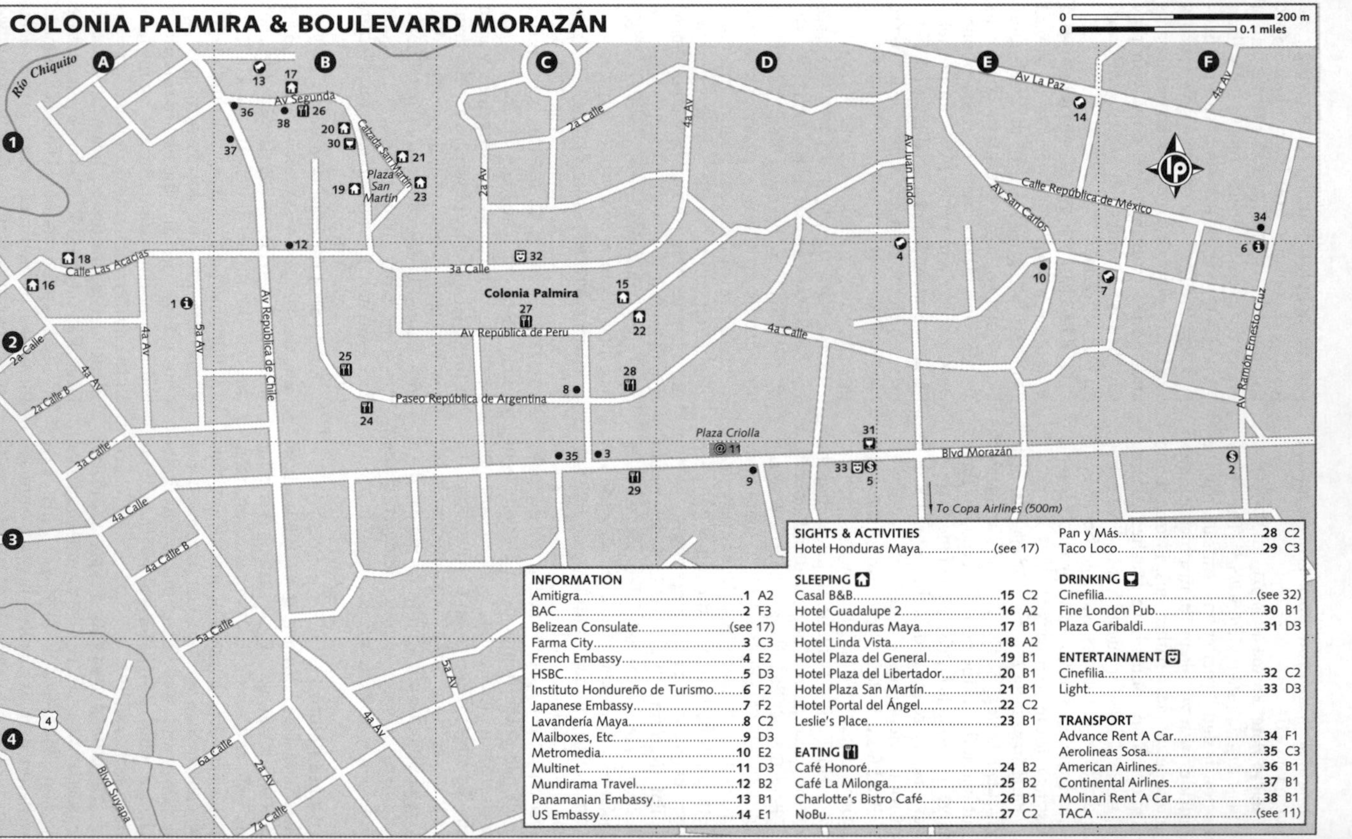
COLONIA PALMIRA & BOULEVARD MORAZÁN
0 200 m
0 0.1 miles
Río Chiquito
Av Segunda
Calzada San Martín
Plaza San Martín
2a Calle
2a Av
4a Av
Av Juan Lindo
Av La Paz
Calle República de México
Av San Carlos
Av Ramón Ernesto Cruz
Calle Las Acacias
3a Calle
Colonia Palmira
Av República de Peru
Av República de Chile
5a Av
4a Calle
Paseo República de Argentina
2a Calle B
3a Calle
Plaza Criolla
Blvd Morazán
To Copa Airlines (500m)
4a Calle
4a Calle B
5a Calle
6a Calle
2a Av
7a Calle
Blvd Suyapa
SIGHTS & ACTIVITIES
Hotel Honduras Maya (see 17)
INFORMATION
Amitigra 1 A2
BAC 2 F3
Belizean Consulate (see 17)
Farma City 3 C3
French Embassy 4 E2
HSBC 5 D3
Instituto Hondureño de Turismo 6 F2
Japanese Embassy 7 F2
Lavandería Maya 8 C2
Mailboxes, Etc. 9 D3
Metromedia 10 E2
Multinet 11 D3
Mundirama Travel 12 B2
Panamanian Embassy 13 B1
US Embassy 14 E1
SLEEPING
Casal B&B 15 C2
Hotel Guadalupe 2 16 A2
Hotel Honduras Maya 17 B1
Hotel Linda Vista 18 A2
Hotel Plaza del General 19 B1
Hotel Plaza del Libertador 20 B1
Hotel Plaza San Martín 21 B1
Hotel Portal del Ángel 22 C2
Leslie's Place 23 B1
EATING
Café Honoré 24 B2
Café La Milonga 25 B2
Charlotte's Bistro Café 26 B1
NoBu 27 C2
Pan y Más 28 C2
Taco Loco 29 C3
DRINKING
Cinefilia (see 32)
Fine London Pub 30 B1
Plaza Garibaldi 31 D3
ENTERTAINMENT
Cinefilia 32 C2
Light 33 D3
TRANSPORT
Advance Rent A Car 34 F1
Aerolineas Sosa 35 C3
American Airlines 36 B1
Continental Airlines 37 B1
Molinari Rent A Car 38 B1
TACA (see 11)

sides. Best of all, you get free shuttle service to and from the airport.

Hotel Plaza del Libertador (Map p74; ☎ 220-4141; www.dhpsm.com; Plaza San Martín, s/d L$2424/2865; P ✱ ☐) Our favorite of the three sister hotels clustered at the top of a small hill in Colonia Palmira is the Libertador. This classy hotel has rooms with a cozy chalet–like look; junior suites have king-size beds and better bathrooms. All rooms have a great little terrace; definitely ask for one with a city view.

These hotels are just across the way from Plaza del Libertador:

Hotel Plaza San Martín (Map p74; ☎ 238-4500; www.dhpsm.com; s/d L$2181/2530) Slightly cheaper than the Libertador, but not worth the price of admission.

Hotel Plaza del General (Map p74; ☎ 220-7272; www.dhpsm.com; s/d L$2394/2850) Pricey, but worth it.

Comayagüela

Hotel Plaza Real (Map pp66-7; ☎ 237-0084; 6a Av near 8a Calle; s/d with shared bathroom L$200/230, s/d L$250/290) The rooms smell a bit funky and the beds slope down at odd angles, but it at least feels secure. The shared bathrooms are clean and there's always hot water. All the rooms open onto a leafy courtyard, which is fitted out with tables and chairs, plus there's also a *pila* (laundry station) for guests to handwash their clothes.

Hotel San Pedro (Map pp66-7; ☎ 222-8987; 6a Av btwn Calles 8a & 9a; s/d with shared bathroom L$100/280, s L$170) Despite saggy beds and brusque service, the San Pedro remains popular with budget travelers – though with locks that barely lock, security may be an issue here. Rooms are relatively clean despite the dirt-cheap prices. The small on-site cafeteria is a nice convenience.

Hotel Unión (Map pp66-7; ☎ 238-0573; 8a Av btwn Calles 12a & 13a; s/d L$200/300; ☐) Opened in 2005, the Hotel Unión offers cramped but clean rooms with gleaming tile floors, pine wood furnishings and cable TV. All have private bathrooms, though only some have hot water. Service is friendly and there's always free purified water and coffee for guests.

Hotel Hedman Alas (Map pp66-7; ☎ 237-9333; www.hedmanalas.com; 4 Av btwn Calles 8a & 9a; s/d L348/456) Not as nice as the bus line, this is nonetheless one of your better options in the area. We love the security here, and the smallish rooms are well scrubbed. It's a little pricey for the area, though reasonable for what you get.

Hotel Palace (Map pp66-7; ☎ 237-6660; 12a Calle btwn Avs 8a & 9a; s/d/tr L$450/800/1000; P ✱) This is the Fort Knox of Comayagüela: guests have to greet a shotgun-toting security guard, get through two secured doors and shout to the receptionist through a thick plexi-glass window to get into the place. Rooms are distributed over five floors, and although somewhat small, are comfortable, with firm beds and private hot-water bathrooms. It's a decent place, although for the price, you might as well stay in a nicer neighborhood – they have shotgun-toting security guards there too.

Other Neighborhoods

our pick Grasshopper Hostel (off Map pp66-7; ☎ 234-2002; Colonia 15 de Septiembre Bloque 1, No 39; dm L$250, r L$600; ☐) Run by a super-friendly English-speaking family, this brand new hostel has four spacious rooms with bunks and Guatemalan bedspreads, clean shared bathrooms, large lockers, common room with cable TV and internet access, laundry service, luggage storage, book exchange, free coffee and tea, and no curfew. But here's the catch: the hostel is about two grasshopper leaps from the airport, which is great for coming or going, but well away from the center. It's about 7km south of Downtown Tegus. Buses and taxis (*colectivo* and private) pass within steps of the hostel, so getting back and forth is easy enough, but it's not the same as having everything within walking distance.

InterContinental (off Map pp66-7; ☎ 231-2727; www.intercontinental.com; Av Roble at Blvd Juan Pablo II; r from L$2400; P ⊠ ✱ ☐ ☐) Next to Multiplaza Mall, the InterContinental is Tegucigalpa's top hotel and popular with upscale tourists, businesspeople, visiting diplomats and politicians. The huge air-cooled lobby is a study of marble and muted tones. Standard rooms feature marble bathrooms, firm beds and the expected amenities: safe, mini-bar, iron, hairdryer, etc. Executive rooms have higher ceilings, and extras including free breakfast, free in-room internet and quick checkout.

EATING

Like any large city, Tegucigalpa runs the gamut in eating options, from street food to five-star gourmet. Self-caters should check out **Supermercado Más x Menos** (Map pp66-7; Av La Paz at 4a Av; ⏲ 8am-8pm) or the street markets in Comaygüela.

Downtown Tegucigalpa

Merendero El Buen Gusto (Map p71; ☎ 238-7767; Calle Hipolito Matute; dishes L$40-60; breakfast & lunch Mon-Sat) A true Honduran greasy spoon behind the Cathedral, packed with workers of all stripes. Counter-seating only, with quick unceremonious service; food ranges from fried chicken to beef stew and not much further.

Café La Plazuela (Map p71; ☎ 237-0501; Av Miguel Paz Barahona 1349; dishes L$40-80; breakfast, lunch & dinner Mon-Sat) This casual modern eatery has soups and light meals, and a happy-hour from 5pm to 7pm.

Rincón Mexicano (Map p71; ☎ 222-8368; Av Cristóbal Colón at Calle El Telégrafo; mains L$50-80; breakfast, lunch & dinner) This 'Mexican corner' is indeed a quiet little place where you can escape the noise and exhaust of Av Colón traffic. The menu has all the usual suspects: tacos, mole, tortas (even 'drowned tortas,' a specialty of Guadalajara), plus American variations including fajitas and burritos.

La Terraza de Don Pepe (Map p71; ☎ 237-1084; Av Cristóbal Colón 2062; dishes L$30-100; 8:30am-10pm) A popular 2nd-floor eatery, La Terraza has good *platos del día* (daily specials) and live crooning most evenings. Tables on the small terrace, or just inside, overlook the busy street and catch nice natural light.

Restaurant Aiwa (Map p71; Calle Morelos btwn Avs Máximo Jerez & Paulin Vallardes; mains L$80-140; lunch & dinner) A huge marquee-like sign and swinging glass doors make it easy to mistake Aiwa for a movie theater; inside, the air-cooled dining room has gleaming tables and floors, and waiters zipping around with huge plates of chop suey, chow mein and more. Portions are enormous – a regular plate serves two, a family plate serves four or more.

There's an awesome **licuado shop** (Map p71; 8am-6pm Mon-Fri, 8:30am-4pm Sat, 10am-4pm Sun) at the northwest corner of Parque Central. At lunch, the **food stands** (Map p71; mains L$10-20) in front of Iglesia Los Dolores fill the air with the smoke, sounds and smells of sizzling meats, and people ordering, eating and talking.

Colonia Palmira

Pan y Más (Map p74; ☎ 232-4064; Bakery Center, Paseo República de Argentina; 7:30am-7:30pm) This small 1st-floor shop has fresh cookies, bread, good bagels, plus light sandwiches.

Taco Loco (Map p74; ☎ 239-7131; Blvd Morazán; mains L$40-80; lunch & dinner) A cheap option in a high-price neighborhood, this crazy little taco shop (it has a hot-dog logo but tacos on the menu) offers up flour or corn tortillas, and a choice of beef, pork or chicken filling. An order of *cebollas lloronas* (grilled, literally 'cry baby,' onions) is worth the extra few lemps.

Café Honoré (Map p74; ☎ 239-7566; Paseo República de Argentina 1941; mains L$70-160) More than L$100 is a lot for a sandwich, but this may be the only place in Honduras to get the real deal instead of processed ham and Wonder bread. Sandwiches come with combinations of salami, roast beef, prosciutto, roast peppers, mozzarella cheese and more.

Café La Milonga (Map p74; ☎ 232-2654; Paseo República de Argentina 1802; mains L$80-160; lunch & dinner Mon-Fri, lunch until 6:30pm Sat) This terrific Argentinean grill has much more than just meat – and is much more than just a restaurant, for that matter. The extensive lunch and dinner menu includes sandwiches (several veggie options available), thick wedges of quiche (spinach, eggplant, broccoli, Lorraine), empanadas (chicken, beef or spinach) and of course excellent cuts of meat, in 8oz or 12oz portions that are melt-in-your-mouth tender. Judging from the name (*la milonga* is an Argentinean dance) it's no surprise that music and dance also figure prominently: this is where folk singer Karla Lara got her start, and Guillermo Anderson has played here too. Friday night is for tango, including a short class for beginners. Movies are played Wednesday at 7:30pm.

Charlotte's Bistro Café (Map p74; ☎ 238-1803; Av Segunda; mains L$200-400; noon-10pm Mon-Sat) Charlotte blends Asian, French and a few Honduran faves to create a unique global fusion. There's inside seating, but it's nicer to sit in the outside garden. You'll feel miles away from the din and detritus of Tegucigalpa.

our pick **NoBu** (Map p74; ☎ 232-5348; Av República de Peru; mains L$195-300; noon-3pm & 6-11pm Mon-Sat, noon-8pm Sun) A slice of Eastern Zen in the heart of western Tegucigalpa, this place is certainly an indulgence for most. But the authentic sushi, Thai and mixed-Asian cuisine is well worth it. The best spots are in the back garden, where open-air views reveal a city of light and quiet.

Comayagüela

Centro Comercial Jerusalem (Map pp66-7; 6a Av btwn Calles 5a & 6a; 8am-6pm Mon-Sat, 8am-noon Sun) This small shopping center has a handful of cheap but clean eateries, most offering *típica*,

ASK A LOCAL: BEST PARTY SPOTS IN TEGUS

- **La Grotta** (Map pp66-7; Blvd Morazán in Plaza Savanah) This is a nightclub for a young crowd
- **Río** (Map pp66-7; Plaza los Próceres) A good nightclub with a cover
- **Cinefilia** (below) This nice cafe is a chill-out spot that serves beer and has movies
- **Casa de Puros** (off Map pp66-7) A martini and cigar bar, where preppy people go to chill. It's in front of the Casa Presidencial by the InterContinental Hotel.
- **Jaguar** (Blvd Juan Pablo II) One of the few backpacker-ish places in town. It's a nightclub that plays rave music.

Nadia & Nicole Sabat, Missi Love & Carolina Jackson: owners, patrons and beautiful people we met at NoBu

sandwiches and snacks. Delitortas on the 3rd floor (mains L$20 to L$40) is known for its good daily specials, but be sure to check out the other options.

Delia Comidas (Map pp66-7; 8a Av btwn Calles 12a & 13a; mains L$30-60; breakfast, lunch & dinner) A simple buffet-style eatery that also doubles as a *pulpería* (mini-mart), internet cafe and call center.

Todo de Pollo (Map pp66-7; 6a Av near 8a Calle; mains L$40-70; breakfast, lunch & dinner) *Todo de Pollo* (Everything Made of Chicken) is right. This colorful eatery serves up chicken in 'every which way but goose.'

DRINKING

Café La Plazuela (Map p71; ☎ 237-0501; Av Miguel Paz Barahona 1349; 9am-11pm Mon-Sat) The place to go for football and occasional live music performances. It's also a great spot to get your swerve on.

Plaza Garibaldi (Map p74; ☎ 232-0017; Blvd Morazán at Av Juan Lindo; 24hr) Great for your karaoke and '80s music fix.

Fine London Pub (Map p74; Av Segunda, Colonia Palmira; 11am-2pm & 5:30pm-11:30pm) This pricy bar and grill is popular with business men. It serves up a decent pint.

ENTERTAINMENT

Nightclubs

Most of Tegucigalpa's nightlife is found on Blvd Morazán, and is usually open from Wednesday to Saturday.

Light (Map p74; ☎ 235-3437; Blvd Morazán; cover L$100-200; 7pm-2am Wed-Sat) Situated close to Colonia Palmira hotels, this sleek modern bar and club sees a mixed crowd of foreigners and locals.

Bamboo (Map pp66-7; ☎ 236-5391; Blvd Morazán; cover L$120-200; 9pm-2am Wed-Sat) Dress up for this nightclub.

Over Time (Map pp66-7; ☎ 963-6703; Blvd Morazán; admission free; 2pm-midnight) In case you can't get into Bamboo – it happens – you can always nurse your ego at the large bar next door.

Cinemas

Cinemark (off Map pp66-7; ☎ 231-2044; www.cinemarkca.com; Multiplaza Mall, Av Juan Pablo II; tickets L$50) Large mall movie theater showing mostly Hollywood movies; call or check the paper for show times.

Cine Aries, Tauro & Leo (Map p71; Subida Casamata near Juan Gutemberg; tickets L$5) Screening Hollywood and Latin-American films at 7pm and 9pm daily.

Cinefilia (Map p74; 3a Calle, Colonia Palmira) Shows movies in a bar setting.

Theater

Teatro Nacional Manuel Bonilla (Map p71; ☎ 222-4366; Av Miguel Paz Barahona) Hosts a variety of performing-arts shows, including plays, dance and music. Built in 1912, the theater's interior was inspired by the Athens Theatre of Paris, making it a very enjoyable place to attend a performance.

Live Music

No one would call Tegucigalpa a live-music mecca, but there are a few places to see shows now and again.

Café La Milonga (opposite) has tango classes on Friday evening, sometimes with live music accompanying. Café La Plazuela (opposite) has occasional shows by local cover bands and singer/songwriters.

Sport

The **Estadio Nacional Tiburcio Carías Andino** (Map pp66-7; 9a Calle at Blvd Suyapa) is across the river from Comayagüela and hosts soccer games and other sporting matches. Tickets are sold the day of the event.

SHOPPING

There is a string of **artesanía shops** (Map p71) on Av Miguel de Cervantes a couple of blocks past the bridge that separates downtown from Colonia Palmira. Browsing them, you'll find the capital's largest selection of Honduran folk art, from Lenca pottery to homemade paper products from La Moskitia.

Bazar Lempira (Map p71; ☎ 237-9436; Av Máximo Meréz, near Iglesia Los Dolores; 🕑 8am-5:30pm Mon-Fri, 9am-5pm Sat) Although mostly kitsch, this small, over-stuffed shop has a few good buys.

Mercado San Isidro (Map pp66-7; 🕑 6am-5pm) You can find just about anything for sale, excellent *artesanía* included, in this chaotic market in Comayagüela. However, there's a catch-22: pickpocketing and snatch-and-run theft are common, and the market is the last place you want to carry anything valuable, especially a wad of money.

Multiplaza Mall (off Map pp66-7; Blvd Juan Pablo II; 8am-10pm) Tegucigalpa has a number of large modern malls. This one, a couple of kilometers southwest of Colonia Palmira, is the best of the bunch, a sprawling complex with department stores, some 20 banks and ATMs, bookstores, internet cafes and a movie theater.

GETTING THERE & AWAY

Air

Tocontín International Airport in Tegucigalpa is decidedly down-scale compared to the modern airport in San Pedro Sula.

Aerolineas Sosa (Map p74; ☎ 233-4351; www.aerolineasosa.com; Blvd Morazán; 🕑 8am-noon & 1-4pm Mon-Fri, 8am-noon Sat)

Air France (Map pp66-7; ☎ 236-0029; www.airfrance.com; Av La Paz at Av Juan Lindo; 🕑 8am-5pm Mon-Fri, to noon Sat)

American Airlines (Map p74; ☎ 216-4800; Edif Palmira; 🕑 8am-6pm Mon-Fri, to noon Sat) Across from Hotel Honduras Maya.

Continental Airlines (Map p74; ☎ 220-0999, at airport 233-3676; www.continental.com; Av República de Chile; 🕑 8am-5pm Mon-Fri, to 2pm Sat)

Copa Airlines (off Map p74; ☎ 235-5610, at airport 291-0099; Hotel Clarion, Av República de Chile; 8am-6pm Mon-Fri, to 2pm Sun)

TACA (Map p74; ☎ 236-8778; www.taca.com; Blvd Morazán; 🕑 8am-5pm Mon-Fri, 9am-5pm Sat, 9am-2pm Sun)

Bus

Excellent bus service connects Tegucigalpa with other parts of Honduras. Unfortunately, each bus line has its own separate terminal. Most terminals are clustered in Comayagüela (Map pp66–7), where you should keep a close eye on your bags and belongings while waiting for the bus. The free magazine *Honduras Tips* has a helpful section on bus routes and schedules.

INTERNATIONAL BUSES

Tica Bus (Map pp66-7; ☎ 220-0579; www.ticabus.com; 16a Calle btwn Avs 5a & 6a, Comayagüela) and **King Quality** (Map pp66-7; ☎ 225-5415; Blvd Commanded Economical European near 6a Av) offer international service to El Salvador (L$500), Guatemala (L$500), and Nicaragua (L$600), with a connecting service to Costa Rica (L$1000) and Panama (L$1653).

GETTING AROUND

To/From the Airport

Colectivo taxis (Map p71) leave from their designated spot downtown every 15 minutes or so, passing right in front of the airport (L$10). The airport is easy to miss – ask the driver to tell you where to get off; it's across from a huge Burger King.

Taking a private taxi (L$160) to or from the airport is recommended from late afternoon onwards. As usual, it's much cheaper to catch a cab on the main street rather than from the terminal.

Bus

It is not recommended you use local public buses. Petty crime is common, and gang members have taken to boarding public buses and 'collecting' from everyone on board. This happens mainly in outlying neighborhoods (and almost never on intercity buses) but most travelers won't know when an area has turned from good to bad.

Car & Motorcycle

Rental car rates average L$950 per day, more for a 4x4 vehicle, less for an economy car or for longer-term rentals. If your credit card offers rental insurance, you may be able to save around L$200 per day by declining the insur-

LONG-DISTANCE BUSES FROM TEGUCIGALPA

Destination	Bus line	Phone	Fare	Frequency	Duration
Catacamas*	Discovery	222-4256	L$108	hourly 6:15am-5pm	3½hr
Choluteca	Mi Esperanza	no phone	L$58	hourly 6am-5:30pm	3½hr
Comayagua	El Rey de Oro	237-6609	L$50	hourly 3am-6pm	2hr
El Amatillo	various buses	no phone	L$50		3½hr
Juticalpa	Discovery	222-4256	L$86	hourly 6:15am-4:15pm	2½hr
La Ceiba**	Hedman Alas	237-7143	L$450	5:45am, 10am, 1:30pm	5½hr
La Ceiba	Kamaldy	220-0117	L$180	6:30am & 1:30pm	5½hr
La Ceiba	Contraibal	237-1666	L$182	7 departures 6:15am-3:30pm	7hr
Lago de Yojoa (La Guama)	El Rey de Oro	237-6609	L$80	hourly 3am-6pm	3hr
San Pedro Sula*	El Rey Express	237-8561	L$140	hourly 5:30am-6:30pm	3½hr
San Pedro Sula	El Rey de Oro	237-6609	L$120	hourly 3am-6pm	4hr
San Pedro Sula**	Hedman Alas	237-7143	L$323	4 departures 5:45am-4:30pm	3½hr
San Pedro Sula**	Saenz	233-4229	L$323	6-7 departures 6am-6pm	4hr
Santa Rosa de Copán	Sultana	237-8101	L$300	hourly 6am-1:30pm	7hr
Tela	Kamaldy	220-0117	L$217	7 departures 6:15am-3:30pm	5hr
Trujillo	Contraibal	237-1666	L$280	7:30am	9hr

*Direct service
**1st-class/luxury service

ance provided by the rental agency. Not all agencies allow this, but it's worth trying. Be sure to ask about the deductible, as it can be as high as US$1600. Airport desks are open daily, but renting there usually costs 10% to 15% more than in town. Your best buys are generally found on a new place called the internet.

Advance Rent A Car (Map p74; ☎ 235-9531, at airport 233-3927; www.advancerentacar.com; Calle República de México; 🕑 8am-6pm)

Avis (off Map pp66-7; ☎ 239-5712; at airport 232-0088; www.avis.com; Blvd Suyapa, Edif Marina; 🕑 8am-6pm)

Budget (☎ 235-9528, 265-8000; www.budget.com; airport only)

Econo Rent-a-Car (Map pp66-7; ☎ 235-8582, at airport 291-0107; off Calzada San Martín; 🕑 8am-6pm)

Molinari Rent A Car (Map p74; ☎ 237-5335; molinarirentacar@yahoo.com; Centro Comercio Villa Real, off Calzada San Martín; 🕑 8am-noon & 2-6pm Mon-Fri, 8am-noon Sat)

Taxi

Private taxis cruise all over town, giving a honk to advertise when they are available. A ride in town costs from L$60 to L$130. There is also a system of *colectivo* taxis (see Map p71 & Map pp66–7 for locations), which operate essentially like a bus, following a fixed route and carrying multiple passengers. Convenient routes include those to the airport, Suyapa and the bus stops for Valle de Ángeles and for Danlí. The fare is around L$11.

AROUND TEGUCIGALPA

You can easily explore the pastoral areas around Tegucigalpa in two to four days. There's great shopping in the quaint colonial villages of Santa Lucía and Valle de Ángeles, and excellent bird-watching and nature hikes in the Yuscarán and La Tigra reserves.

SANTA LUCÍA

pop 9300

Santa Lucía is a charming old Spanish mining town built on a hilltop. Cobblestone lanes and walkways wind around the hillside, leading to small colonial-style homes and businesses. The main plaza, with its fountain and landscaped garden, is a nice place to nurse a licuado. On most weekends, Santa Lucía's restaurants, *artesanía* shops and *viveros* (plant nurseries) fill up with day-trippers from the capital. Come on a weekday to avoid the crowds.

Information

The **police station** (☎ 779-0476; 🕑 24hr) is located at the entrance to town. Phone calls can be made at **Hondutel** (🕑 8am-8pm Mon-Sat, 10am-4pm Sun), which is a block from the *iglesia*.

Sights & Activities

Santa Lucía has great views of pine-covered hills and Tegucigalpa in the valley. The 18th-century **iglesia** perched on a hillside is especially beautiful; inside are old Spanish paintings and the Christ of Las Mercedes, given to Santa Lucía by King Felipe II in 1572. If the doors of the *iglesia* are closed, walk around to the office at the rear and ask to have them opened.

Sleeping

There are two hotels just outside Santa Lucía, on the road that leads up to town from the highway.

Hotel Santa Lucía Resort (☎ 779-0540; Calle a Santa Lucía; r/cabin L$639/1372; P) While the rooms are a bit run-down with old furniture and a musty smell, the setting couldn't be more perfect. Surrounded by pines, it's a few hundred meters off the road (and 1km from the town) and the feeling is one of peaceful isolation. The rooms range from full-on suites complete with kitchens and living areas to small chambers. The decor seems haphazard in places, but not unpleasantly so. The restaurant (mains L$100 to L$200, open 8:30am to 8:30pm) has indoor and outdoor seating, a full bar and a menu of mostly meat and seafood dishes.

Hotel Brisas de Santa Lucía Casa de Huéspedes (☎ 779-0597, 779-0238; www.honduristica.com; Calle a Santa Lucía; s/d incl continental breakfast L$650/900; P) While this pleasant converted home offers a more intimate setting than the rambling Hotel Santa Lucía, for the price you are still better off there. Rooms here feel like bedrooms more than hotel units, and open onto a large sitting area. While it's closer to town than the Hotel Santa Lucía, it's also right on the road.

Eating

Restaurante Miluska (☎ 231-3905; mains L$60-160; 10am-8pm Tue-Sun) A favorite, with tables indoors and outdoors on a pleasant covered patio, this is a 'European corner in the heart of Honduras,' serving German and Czech dishes in addition to typical Honduran fare. Look for the signs.

Lely's (mains L$75-180; 11am-8pm) Lely has got her fingers wrapped around the town with two restaurants centered on the main plaza. One is a grill, and is a better bet for dinner, while the other serves snacks such as *pupusas* and *baleadas*.

Getting There & Away

Santa Lucía is 14km northeast of Tegucigalpa, about 2km off the road leading to Valle de Ángeles and San Juancito. Buses leave Tegus every 45 to 60 minutes from 7:30am to 8pm (L$8.50, 30 minutes). Return buses leave Santa Lucía from 7:30am to 8pm. Alternatively, take an *ordinario* (slow) bus headed to Valle de Ángeles from Tegus (see opposite), get off at the crossroads to town, and walk or hitch the 2km or so into town (all uphill).

VALLE DE ÁNGELES

pop 14,300

Eight kilometers past Santa Lucía, Valle de Ángeles is another beautiful, historic Spanish mining town. Much of the town center has been restored to its original 16th-century appearance. In front of the old *iglesia* is an attractive shady plaza, which has a pretty fountain that is lit up at night. Some of the surrounding streets have been closed to cars and are now pedestrian walkways. The annual fair takes place on October 4.

Artesanía souvenir shops line the streets, selling excellent Honduran crafts for less than they cost in Tegucigalpa.

Most people come to Valle de Ángeles as a day trip from Tegucigalpa, but it is an excellent (and quieter) alternative to staying in the city.

Information

There are two ATMs on Parque Central.

Aroma del Café (Parque Central) Has ice cream, coffee, international calling and internet (L$20 per hour).

Banco de Occidente (Parque Central; 8:30am-12:30pm & 1-4pm Mon-Fri) Exchanges US dollars. No ATM.

CESAMO (7am-4pm Mon-Fri) Basic health clinic with a pharmacy. Located on the road to San Juancito, just past the island triangle.

Police (☎ 766-5121; Parque Central; 24hr)

Tourist Office (☎ 9996-4477; 8am-5pm Mon-Fri, 9am-6pm Sat & Sun) Located in the back of a gift shop half a block from Parque Central.

Sights & Activities

Right on Parque Central, **La Casa de la Cultura** hosts occasional art exhibits and is a good spot to go for some free info. At the entrance to town from Tegucigalpa, the **Museo Santa María de los Ángeles** (admission L$20; 8am-5pm) has an interesting collection of historic photos from around the country.

BUYING LOCAL HANDICRAFTS

Valle de los Ángeles has more T-shirt shops than residents, but there is some decent stuff here if you can dive past the kitsch. Handcrafted leather is made mostly in town but you'll see items from all over Honduras: *junco* (straw weavings) from Santa Bárbara, drums from Garífuna villages, clay pottery from La Ruta Lenca, and *cuadro de tunu* (tree-bark art) from La Moskitia. For a sampling of what the town – and country – has to offer, head to **Pabellones Artesanales** (9am-5pm), a warehouse-sized *artesanía* market one block east of Parque Central.

There's a pleasant and mildly challenging hike from Valle de Ángeles to **Los Golondrinas waterfall**. The hike is mostly uphill on the way there – allow two hours up and an hour to return. There's no need for a guide, as the trail is well marked; if you're ever in doubt, ask any passerby for *la cascada* (the waterfall). The trailhead is almost impossible to miss: on the left side over 1km from town on the road toward San Juancito.

At the entrance to town from the Tegucigalpa side are a couple of **recreational parks**, with restaurants, swimming pools, soccer fields and volleyball courts; there are also ultra-mellow horseback rides.

Courses

Escuela de Español Koinonia (www.escuelavalledeangeles.org) Offers Spanish classes (L$3040 per week, plus a one-time L$950 registration fee), as well as homestays (L$1805 per week). The proceeds benefit a children's home; there may be volunteer opportunities here as well.

Sleeping & Eating

Posada del Ángel (766-2420; www.posadadelangelhotel.com; s/d L$475/950; P) The only hotel option in the town's center, this budget place has simple, clean rooms. All open onto a large rectangular pool, which is a big plus on hot days. Service is a bit lacking, however. Located two blocks north of Parque Central.

Villas del Valle (766-2534; www.villasdelvalle.com; Carr a San Juancito; r/ste L$600/928, apt with kitchen L$1300; P) You are probably better off in town at the Posada, but if that's full, this countryside 'villa' is a good alternative. The 'resort' offers several brick bungalows on an ample, green property. The sheets are bit scratchy, but everything seems to be spotlessly clean. An above-ground pool is particularly popular with kids. It's on the same road as Posada del Ángel, heading out of town.

Parque central is the hub of restaurant life in Valle de los Ángeles. Catering to *capitalinos* (residents of the capital) with cash, most of the restaurants are hip and attractive, with menus that show off their clients' discerning palates. Some of the favorites on Parque Central include **Restaurante Jalapeño** (mains L$60-120; lunch & dinner Tue-Sun) with good veggie options, **El Anafre** (766-2942; mains L$100-240; lunch & dinner) serving up Italian specialties and **El Asado Don Juan** (mains L$90-140; lunch & dinner Tue-Sun), a meat-lover's paradise.

Getting There & Away

Two bus lines provide service between Valle de Ángeles and Tegucigalpa. In Tegucigalpa, *ordinario* buses (L$14, 45 minutes to one hour, hourly) come and go from a stop on the corner of Av de los Próceres and Av República Dominicana (Map pp66–7). *Rapiditos* (microbuses) depart more frequently and drop passengers a block from the cathedral in Tegus (L$17, 30 minutes, every 30 minutes). From Tegucigalpa, both lines have service from 5:30am to 8pm on weekdays, until 7pm on weekends. In Valle de Ángeles, both lines depart from the large paved square east of the central park. The last return bus departs Valle de Valle de Ángeles at 6pm.

PARQUE NACIONAL LA TIGRA

Covering 238 sq km of rugged forest, **Parque Nacional La Tigra** (231-3641; www.amitigra.org; adult/child L$190/95; 8am-5pm Tue-Sun, no entry after 2pm) is a short distance northeast of the capital. The park includes cloud forest and dry pine forest, numerous rivers and waterfalls, and a large and varied (but exceedingly shy) population of mammals, including pumas, peccaries, armadillos and agoutis (rabbit-sized rodents). Somewhat easier to spy are the park's numerous birds – 350 species in all – making La Tigra the country's best bird-watching spot after Lago de Yojoa. If you're lucky, you may even spot a quetzal, a distinctive aqua-colored bird with long tail feathers. Impossible to miss is the park's exuberant flora: lush trees, vines, lichens, large ferns, colorful mushrooms, bromeliads and a million orchids (so it seems).

THE SLIGHTLY TAINTED HISTORY OF HONDURAS' FIRST NATIONAL PARK

For all its natural beauty, La Tigra bears many scars too: for more than 70 years it was the site of intense mining and logging by the American-owned Rosario Mining Company. Most of the forest along the trails is actually secondary growth. On the upside, abandoned mines and buildings – even the ruins of a US consulate – dot the area. Although you should never enter one without a guide, they make for interesting sights: some are filled with water, others are being slowly reclaimed by the forest. Upwards of US$100 million in gold, silver, copper and zinc was extracted from the mountains between 1880 and 1954, mostly by thousands of exploited Hondurans. The mining company finally pulled out after the Honduran government began talk of instituting corporate taxes and miners began to lobby for better wages. The park was set aside as a forest reserve in 1952 and declared a national park – Honduras' first – in 1980. Today, besides being a major tourist destination, the park provides fresh water for 33 communities around its periphery, and almost a third of Tegucigalpa's water.

Ready access and a series of well-maintained trails of varying difficulty make La Tigra a popular destination for day trippers. A campground, simple ecolodges and a mountain retreat (Cabaña Mirador El Rosario, opposite) make staying the night a good option too.

The temperature in La Tigra can fluctuate unexpectedly – wear suitable shoes and bring an extra layer of clothing. Long pants and long sleeves are good protection from mosquitoes, which are annoyingly abundant.

Information & Orientation

The park's closest entrance is in Jutiapa, just 22km from Tegucigalpa. There's another entrance at El Rosario. The road to Jutiapa is dull compared to the one to San Juancito and El Rosario, but the Jutiapa side of the park is less deforested. Both entrances have a visitors center. If you enter through El Rosario, consider stopping at the Cabaña Mirador El Rosario (opposite) for more hiking info.

Amitigra (Fundación Amigos de la Tigra; Map p74; ☎ 231-3641; www.amitigra.org; Edificio Italia, 4th fl, office No 6; 🕒 8am-12:30pm & 1-5pm Mon-Fri) has friendly staff and complete information about getting to, hiking in, and staying at the national park. You can pay park/lodging fees here or at the park entrance.

You don't really need one, but guides are available at either entrance to point out features of the forest and (if you're lucky) its wildlife. Guides are typically used for large groups, and charge L$100 to L$400 per group. Couples or solo travelers should negotiate a price.

Dangers & Annoyances

La Tigra is a rugged, mountainous area – wear suitable shoes and know that damp ground can give way unexpectedly. Dense forest and unmarked mine shafts are a good reason to stay *on* the beaten path. It should go without saying – but we will anyway – that you should *never* enter a mine alone or without an experienced guide.

Hiking

Eight trails form a series of intersecting loops through the forest. All are well maintained and relatively easy to follow – be alert for signs.

SENDERO PRINCIPAL

The main trail is in fact the old road that connected Tegucigalpa with the area's mining operations. It is the most direct route through the park, extending 6km from Jutiapa to El Rosario. From Jutiapa, the first 2km is dirt road, still used occasionally by park maintenance crews, arriving at Rancho Quemado (Burned Ranch), the highest point of the park trail system. From there, the road becomes more trail-like, descending 4km past abandoned mines, small rivers and a few fine views of the San Juancito valley before reaching El Rosario. This is the busiest trail in the park and, though attractive, it's not the most memorable. It is a good way to 'close the loop' on the longer hikes, like Los Plancitos or La Mina/La Cascada.

SENDERO LA CASCADA

A more appealing trail is to 'the waterfall,' a 40m no-name falls that is impressive in the winter (October to February) but which can dry up considerably in the summer. Coming from Jutiapa, follow the Sendero Principal over 1km to the Sendero La Cascada cut-off, located at a sharp bend in the trail. Descend the steep stone steps and continue another 2km past smaller falls and abandoned mines to a T-intersection: go straight to reach the falls (10 to 20 minutes), or left to reach El Rosario via Sendero La Mina.

SENDERO LA MINA

The 'Mine Trail' is the one to take to reach the waterfall from El Rosario. The trail begins at El Mirador (the overlook), a short distance along the Sendero Principal from the Rosario visitors center. After 1km of level hiking you will pass a cluster of abandoned mining buildings and a cement dynamite bunker; a side trail leads up a stone ramp and over a footbridge to the mine. Back at the main trail, continue for more than 1km, past earthen scars caused by landslides during Hurricane Mitch, to a T-intersection; go left to the falls (10 to 20 minutes) or right onto Sendero La Cascada, toward Jutiapa.

SENDERO LOS PLANCITOS

The park's longest and least-trafficked trail forms a rambling 8km half-loop from Jutiapa to an intersection on the Sendero Principal about 25 minutes west of El Rosario. The trail takes hikers through pine forest, past the park's lowest point and along the foot of Mt Estrella. You can use Sendero Principal to make it a loop; from either entrance, it's about 15km, with plenty of up and down.

OTHER TRAILS

The park's remaining four trails all start from the Jutiapa visitors center and, combined with each other or the Sendero Principal, make for relatively easy loop-hikes. Sendero Bosque Nublado (Cloud Forest Trail; 1km) was the park's first trail and probably the most rewarding of these four for its thick, dripping vegetation. La Esperanza (2km) has the park's best stretch of primary forest, including some impressive ancient trees; a good shortish loop from the Jutiapa side would be out on Bosque Nublado and back on La Esperanza. Sendero Jucuara (2km) has a camping area (below) and forms the first part of Sendero Los Plancitos, while Las Granadillas (600m) is designed for children, seniors and those with limited mobility.

Sleeping & Eating

Jucuara campground (per person L$100) Located 1km from the Jutiapa visitors center, with latrine toilets, unpurified water and fire pits. Your only camping option since it's not allowed inside the park.

Hotelito San Juan (☎ 777-0522; San Juancito; r with shared bathroom L$80) A last-resort option, this tiny, ultrabasic hotel has dark, musty rooms. It's located in the village of San Juancito, a block from the main road.

Eco-Albergue El Rosario (adult/child L$300/200) The lodge–like visitors center has nine simple rooms for visitors. Three have private bathrooms, while the other six share a toilet and shower. The digs are pretty basic, especially for the price. It's also located at the El Rosario entrance to the park

Cabañas & Eco-Albergue Jutiapa (adult/child L$300/200) This large eco-*albergue* (hostel or bunkhouse), similar to the one at El Rosario, has six simple rooms, each with one queen-size bed and one twin. Some have a private bathroom, while others share.

Cabaña Mirador El Rosario (☎ 9987-5835; s/d L$300/500) Simple charm, amazing views and easy access to the national park make this one of Honduras' most appealing getaways. There are just two units, side by side, one with a queen-size bed and the other with two twins, sharing a detached toilet and hot-water shower. With room for only four guests and a loyal clientele from Tegucigalpa, the Mirador is often full – definitely call ahead. English, Spanish and German spoken. The on-site restaurant offers breakfast and dinner (L$50 to L$70). It's at the El Rosario entrance to the park.

Comedores at the visitors centers in El Rosario (🕒 7am-8pm daily) and Jutiapa (🕒 7am-6pm Thu-Sun) serve basic meals to park visitors (mains L$50 to L$100). They may even make you a packed lunch to take with you hiking; ask the day before, if possible.

Pulpería El Rosario (🕒 7am-6pm Mon-Sat) has snacks and some basic groceries that you could use for lunch on the trail.

Shopping

Located across from the Pepsi kiosk near the steep road up to El Rosario, the **Bus Fantasma** (Phantom Bus; 🕒 open weekends, hrs vary) is an abandoned school bus that has been ingeniously converted into an *artesanía* shop.

Getting There & Away

The western entrance to the park, above Jutiapa, is the closest to Tegucigalpa, 22km away. To get there from Tegus, catch a bus (L$18, 1¼ hours, every 45 minutes, first bus between 6am and 7am) toward El Hatillo from the Dippsa gas station on Av Máximo Jérez at Av la Plazuela, across from a Banco Atlántida (or in front of Hotel Granada No 2; Map p71). Tell the driver you are going to La Tigra; most likely you'll be dropped at Los Planes, a soccer field about 2km short of the visitors center, but occasionally drivers take you all the way to the entrance. On the return trip, a few buses leave from the visitors center, but most leave from Los Planes; the first is at 6am, the last around 3pm. If you miss the last one, it's 4km to the next town (Los Limones) where buses run much later.

The eastern park entrance is at El Rosario, a small community perched on a steep hillside. It overlooks San Juancito, once a booming mining town, now a quiet mountain village. From Tegucigalpa, buses go only as far as San Juancito (L$18, 1½ hours), leaving from the Mercado San Pablo (3pm Monday to Friday; 8am, 12:40pm and 3pm Saturday; 8am and 12:40pm Sunday); from the Valle de Ángeles bus stop, opposite Hospital San Felipe (5pm Monday to Friday); and from Supermercado Más x Menos (4:30pm Saturday). Buses on their way back to Tegus from San Juancito leave from the kiosk on the main road (6am and 6:50am Monday to Friday; 6am, 6:40am, 12:30pm and 2:30pm Saturday; 6:20am Sunday).

From San Juancito, it is a very steep, winding 3km dirt road up to El Rosario – typically a 60- to 90-minute walk. It's much harder and sweatier than anything you'll encounter in the park itself. The guy at the Pepsi kiosk opposite Bus Fantasma takes travelers up the hill in his pickup for around L$200; Monika and Jeorg at Cabaña Mirador El Rosario (p83) will do the same for their guests.

OJOJONA

pop 9500

This dusty colonial town, located just 33km south of Tegucigalpa, is popular among *capitalinos* on weekend shopping trips, though surely more for its proximity to the city than for any other reason. The town's three 18th- and 19th-century churches are moderately interesting, as is watching *artesanía* being made in local workshops.

Ojojona has basic services, including **Ojojona Internet** (Main Plaza; internet per hr L$20; international calls per min L$2; ⌚ 8am-8pm Mon-Fri, 8:30am-12:30pm Sat) on the main plaza, **Hondutel** (☎ 767-0113; ⌚ 8am-5pm Mon-Fri, to noon Sat) a block north of the main plaza and a **police station** (☎ 777-0174; ⌚ 24hr) at the entrance to town.

Sights & Activities

Ojojona and the surrounding area is best known for producing simple clay pots, but in fact has a wide variety of clay handicrafts sold in shops…everywhere. A good place to start your browsing is in **Artesanía Manos Lencas** (☎ 767-0178; Main Plaza; ⌚ 9am-5pm), which sells high-end crafts from all over the country.

Ojojona has three beautiful late-colonial churches. The oldest is **Parroquía San Juan**, dating to 1783. Straight up the hill from there is tiny **Iglesia El Calvario**, which contains a remarkable painting of *La Sangre de Cristo* (The Blood of Christ), dated 1700. **Iglesia El Carmen** is in the middle of town, opening onto a shady plaza. All open on Sunday, but are frequently closed during the week.

A short steep road leads from town to **El Mirador** (the overlook), which offers fine views over Ojojona and the surrounding landscape. There's a small grassy area, good for picnicking. To get there, turn left one block past Arte Halagos, and just keep going up. It's 2km to the top.

Sleeping & Eating

If you can't swing the hotel but are interested in staying in town, there are several homestay options; hosts typically charge L$140 to L$200 per person for a private room with a hot-water bathroom. Stop by the *alcaldía* (city hall) to hook up with one of these places.

Hotel Ojojona (☎ 9914-0375; s/d L$400/500; Ⓟ) A nice surprise in this dusty town, this hotel has six new rooms with hot-water bathrooms, cable TV and fans. It is spotlessly clean with friendly service and has great views from the 2nd story. It's only downside is that it's at the top of a steep hill, a slow walk up a rutted dirt road (there's no way that Kia will make it up). The walk down is a breeze, however, and will take you to the main plaza in about 10 minutes. As you're coming into town, look for the signs after the police station.

Restaurante Joxone (mains L$40-100; ⌚ breakfast, lunch & dinner) Serves good basic meals in a large, somewhat dim, dining area.

You can also get a meal at the **food stands** (mains L$20) in the market.

Getting There & Away

Ojojona is 33km from the capital. Buses come and go from a stop in front of Iglesia El Calvario. Service to Tegucigalpa (L$11, 1½ hours) is every hour from 4:30am to 5:15pm, and more frequently on mornings and weekends. The Tegus stop is in Comayaguëla; if you prefer, you can get off in front of the airport and take a taxi or *colectivo* downtown or to Colonia Palmira instead.

LAS CUEVAS PINTADAS

Opposite the Ojojona turnoff is a dirt road leading to San Buenaventura and, beyond that, the village of El Sauce. From there an easy hour's walk leads you to the **Cuevas Pintadas** (Painted Caves), a handful of caves in a large rock outcropping. The caves vary in size, from narrow tunnels to large domes, and are filled with dozens of painted images, especially animals. It was believed (or perhaps hoped) that the paintings dated back several millennia, but recent analyses suggest they're closer to 600 years old. Local kids have left some cave paintings spray-painted, but the damage is relatively unobtrusive. For a guide, call or look for **Oscar Pineda** (☎ 767-0161) at the municipal offices in Ojojona; knowledgeable on the area and proficient in English, Oscar offers guided trips to Cuevas Pintadas and elsewhere for around L$100 per person.

EL PARAÍSO DEPARTMENT

This is the country's breadbasket, a series of fertile valleys ascending east from the capital all the way to the Nicaraguan border. The department's capital at Yuscarán is certainly a highlight, as are visits to the numerous cigar factories in the region. Those with a bit of time to spare should consider an adventure into the seldom-visited Reserva Biológica Yuscarán.

YUSCARÁN

pop 14,000

There's little to do other than bop around the twisted cobblestone streets of this white-washed village, perched on a mountainside, but after a few days in Tegus, that may be enough. There are some adventure hikes in the neighboring hills.

Information

Banco de Occidente (Parque Central; 🕑 8:30am-4:15pm Mon-Fri, to 11:30am Sat) US dollars exchanged. No ATM.
CCCC Internet (per hr L$20; 🕑 9am-7pm Mon-Sat) Located two blocks from Parque Central, near the police station.
Hondutel (🕑 7am-8pm Mon-Sat) Located just off Parque Central, next to the post office.
Police (☎ 793-7125; 🕑 24hr) Located one block from Parque Central near Casa Fortín.
Post office (🕑 8am-4pm Mon-Fri, to noon Sat) Located just off Parque Central.

Sights & Activities

The closest thing in Yuscarán to a regular 'sight' is **Casa de Fortín** (admission free), a 19th-century mansion that once belonged to one of Yuscarán's wealthiest families but now functions more or less as the town museum. The Fortín family had its finger in many pies, earning a fortune and gathering influence in mining, cattle, agriculture, trading and politics. One son, Daniel, served as Secretary of State in the 1880s. The family lived here until around 1910, when the house was all but abandoned and remained that way until 1979 when it was declared a national monument. Today it contains a random and mostly unorganized collection of era pieces; exploring the building itself is far more interesting than the majority of displays. The opening hours are variable but **Oscar Lezama** (☎ 793-7160, 357-6209), the de-facto caretaker, tries to open the museum from 8am until noon and 2pm to 4pm daily, and give free tours. If it's closed, you can call him, or ask for him at his house, opposite the church.

Yuscarán is home to **Distilería El Buen Gusto**, the manufacturer of Honduras' best-known brand of its best-known alcoholic drink: *aguardiente*. **Plant tours** (admission free; 🕑 7am-noon & 1-4pm Mon-Fri, 7am-noon Sat) are short but interesting. You can see the various stages of processing, from fermentation to bottling. There's no formal system for tours, and sometimes no one is available to do it. But ask at the door, and they will at least tell you when to come back.

JOURNEY INTO THE COUNTRY NEAR YUSCARÁN

Towering directly behind Yuscarán is the **Reserva Biológica Yuscarán**, with a triad of (nearly) 2000m-high mountains: Cerro El Volcán, Cerro el Fogón and Cerro Monserrat. An extremely steep dirt road leads 7km from a small bridge on the way into Yuscarán town to the top of Cerro Monserrat, where Hondutel has a communications antenna. A 4x4 truck can make it, or it's a sweaty three-hour hike. There may be some trails near the top, or you might be able to swashbuckle your way 4km north to the small town of Ocotal.

Near the town of Oropolí, 25km from Yuscarán, is a set of **petroglyphs**, whose origin is still unclear. **Cascada de Barro** and **Cascada La Fortuna** are two picturesque waterfalls beyond Oropolí, about 90 minutes' hiking from the town of La Cienaga.

For these and other excursions, consider hiring a guide in Yuscarán. Oscar Lezama (p85) at Casa de Fortín or the folks at Fundación Yuscarán (next to the *alcaldía*) should be able to help.

Festivals & Events

If you've ever wanted to bob for mangoes (and who hasn't?), look no further than Yuscarán's annual **Festival de Mangos**. Typically held the first weekend in June, it features folkloric dance performances, live music, art exhibits, any number of mango-related games: one year it even featured a polo match on donkeys.

Sleeping & Eating

Casa Colibri (☎ 793-7176; casacolibriyuscar@hotmail.com; Parque Central; s/d L$300/400) A renovated colonial home right on Parque Central, Casa Colibri offers two large rooms with hot-water bathrooms, cable TV and lots of hospitality. The rooms have high ceilings and are lovingly decorated with Guatemalan and Honduran *artesanía*. A large common area between the two guest rooms has couches with lots of good books, and a leafy patio makes a good place to write those postcards you've been meaning to get to. Staff speak English and German.

Hotel Colonial (☎ 3272-1697; Parque Central; s/d L$300/400) Next to the Casa Colobri on Parque Central, this place doesn't feel colonial at all – though the facade certainly harkens back to those days. Rather, it's surprisingly modern on the inside with four pleasant rooms, contemporary furnishings and warm service.

Comedor Chica (mains L$30-60; 🕑 breakfast, lunch & dinner) A tiny restaurant set up in what looks like a converted living room, this eatery serves some of the best *típica* in town. And lots of it. It's located half a block down from Parque Central.

Getting There & Away

Buses come and go right from the main park. Buses to Tegucigalpa (L$27, two hours) leave at 5am, 6am, 8am, 9am, 10:45am, 2:45pm, 3:15pm and 4pm. To get to Danlí, there is occasionally a direct bus in the morning, otherwise take any Tegus-bound bus (or one of the frequent microbuses) to the highway intersection, also known as El Palme (L$14, 30 minutes). Transfer there to any east-bound bus, which pass every 45 minutes or so.

DANLÍ

pop 175,100

Danlí is the largest town between Tegucigalpa and the border at Las Manos, but is only worth the visit if you're really interested in corn or cigars – or both. It was founded by Spanish settlers in 1667 as San Buena Ventura. The name was later changed to Danlí, which reportedly comes from the Nahuatl-Xallili word for 'water running over sand', probably a reference to several shallow rivers in the area. Following the Cuban revolution in 1959, Cuban cigarmakers made their way to Danlí and turned the area's low-key tobacco cultivation – then producing mostly low-grade tobacco for cigarettes – into a center for the production of world-class cigars.

Danlí's other claim to fame is the Festival Nacional de Maíz (National Corn Festival). This week-long event is held at the end of August and draws thousands of visitors for the parade, music and all things corn.

Information

Banco Atlántida (🕑 8:30am-3:30pm Mon-Fri, to 11:30am Sat) Exchanges US dollars and has one 24-hour ATM. Located half a block from Chat People.

Chat People (🕑 8am-10pm; a block from Hotel Apolo; internet per hr L$20) One of numerous internet cafes near the central park; most also have international phone calling.

Post Office (8am-4pm Mon-Fri, to 11am Sat) Located half a block from Parque Central.

Tourist Office (763-3631; Calle del Comercio; 8am-4pm Mon-Fri) The sign reads 'Festival Nacional de Maíz' – the office's main annual undertaking – but it provides good general information as well.

Sights & Activities

The **Museo Municipal** (Parque Central; admission L$10; 8am-noon & 1-3:45pm Mon-Fri), housed in the former city hall building that dates to 1857, is Danlí's municipal museum and makes for a mildly interesting visit, if it's actually open. The 1st floor has displays on the tobacco, cotton and mining trades. Or at least the tools used in those trades, like curved two-headed tobacco knives and large wooden *morteros* used to shell rice and other grains. Upstairs there are bios on notable *danlidenses* (citizens of Danlí) and important events, like the building of Los Arcos aqueduct in 1770 (Honduras' second oldest).

The tourist office has a map and information on a number of short excursions that can be done around town. You'll most likely need a car (your own or a taxi) as bus transportation is only along main roads. Ask about visiting **Acuaducto Los Arcos** and **Laguna de San Julian**, a manmade lake 25km from town that was built by mining companies for electricity generation.

Festivals & Events

The **Festival Nacional de Maíz** (National Corn Festival) is a popular celebration of all things corn, held every year during the last week of August.

Domingo Gastronómico is a relatively new event in Danlí, held on the last Sunday of every month. Townspeople crowd around tables set up by the city and staffed by local women who serve up traditional home-grown specialties such as *mondongo* (tripe soup), *sopa de pata de vaca* (cow's hoof soup), *sopa de olla* (stew) and *arroz de maíz* (corn meal with pork ribs or wild hen).

The **Founding of Danlí** is celebrated every April 12, with a small carnival, including music and street food. The highlight is the crowning of the *madrinas* (the town protectresses), but instead of just one 'Miss Danlí' there are three: child, young adult and senior citizen.

Sleeping

Hotel Esperanza (763-2106; s/d with shared bathroom $178/280, s/d with fan L$280/448, s/d with air-con L$392/662; P) The rooms are clean and basic, and that's about all you could need (or expect) in this agricultural backwater. It's located one block west of the gas stations on the main drag.

Eating

Rancho Mexicano (763-3307; mains L$40-100; lunch & dinner) Sombreros on the wall and ranchero on the radio are givens, but this Mexican restaurant goes a step further, with a collection of antique farming equipment in one corner – stirrups, wooden ploughs etc. On

A CIGAR MECCA

Danlí stands at the edge of the fertile Jamastrán valley, which is blessed with near-perfect conditions for tobacco cultivation, comparable to the Pinar del Río region of Cuba. Indeed, many master cigarmakers who fled the Communist revolution in Cuba settled here, and have since made Danlí the cigar capital of Honduras.

Danlí sees relatively few travelers, but most of those who come are cigar aficionados on a sort of pilgrimage. **Tabacaleras Unidas** (763-6072) is a small factory whose owner, Libardo Rico, has given tours to Peace Corps volunteers, among other groups, and is especially amenable to visitors. **Puros Aliados Cigar** (763-1486) shows curious visitors around its cigar-rolling plant, located 1km east of town. Tours are free and mainly entail visiting the plant floor, where 150-odd rollers, mostly women, roll the company's signature Puro Indio, Cuba Aliado and Roly Cigars. It's owned by noted cigarmaker Rolando Reyes, Sr. On a whole other scale is **Plasencia Tobacco** (763-2828), reputedly one of the largest cigar factories in the world, with some 2000 workers turning out tens of millions of cigars a year. It is owned by renowned Cuban tobacco baron Don Nestor Plasencia and his family, who also operate the smaller **Paraíso Cigars** (763-4918); both plants are on the highway toward El Paraíso and are open to visitors.

EL PARAÍSO & CROSSING INTO NICARAGUA

El Paraíso, the last town before hitting the Nicaraguan border at Las Manos, offers basic services to travelers on their way in or out of the country.

Hotel Isis (☎ 793-4251; Parque Central; s/d L$160/240; P) is a simple, clean hotel with private hot-water bathrooms; rooms near the front have better beds and better lighting. There's also a secure parking lot.

There are a handful of **comedores** (dishes L$20-80; breakfast, lunch & dinner) on Parque Central, all serving decent *típica*. One block from the parque you'll find **Banco de Occidente** (8am-4pm Mon-Fri, to noon Sat), which exchanges US dollars but has no ATM.

Buses to the Nicaraguan border at Las Manos (L$10, 30 minutes) leave near Hotel Isis every 40 minutes from 6:30am to 4pm; buses from the border to town operate from 7:50am to 5pm.

the menu are typical Mexican and Mexicanish dishes. It's half a block from park central.

Rincón Danlidense (mains L$40-100; lunch & dinner) It is a measure of just how limited Danlí's restaurant selection is that the next best restaurant is also next door. Smaller than Rancho Mexicano, with plastic tables instead of wood, Rincón Danlidense has loyal clients who come, above all, for the beef soup, a house specialty that's served on weekends only. Weekdays, a potpourri of other dishes are offered: enchiladas, tacos, Honduras *típico,* even hamburgers. It's also half a block from park central.

If you're passing though on the last Sunday of the month, skip the restaurants and head to the Domingo Gastronómico (p87) for some good home cooking at even better prices.

Getting There & Away

Danlí's main bus stop is on the outskirts of town; a taxi there costs around L$15. **Rapiditos del Oriente** (☎ 736-7411) operates minibuses (L$70, 1½ hours, every 30 to 40 minutes 4:30am to 4:30pm) between Danlí and its terminal is near the Mercado Jacaleapa in Tegucigalpa. A larger *ordinario* bus makes the same trip for about half the price, taking a half hour longer and departing every hour. There is also service to El Paraíso (L$15, 30 minutes, 6am to 5pm, every 20 minutes) where you can catch another bus the rest of the way to the Nicaraguan border.

THE FAR SOUTH

This hot, muggy coastal plain offers very little for visitors, though Isla del Tigre makes for a pleasant enough stopover for travelers moving from El Salvador to Nicaragua. Further inland, past the city of Choluteca, the land rises into the foothills and the mountains, forming the Sierra de la Botija range on the Honduras–Nicaragua border.

CHOLUTECA

pop 157,600

Choluteca, capital of the department of the same name, lies near Río Choluteca, the same river that runs through Tegucigalpa. It's the largest town in southern Honduras, and the fourth largest in the country. Which is not to say there's a whole lot to do here; the former mining town is now principally a commercial center for the agricultural region and a stopping-off point between the borders. Choluteca's annual festival day is December 8.

Orientation

The streets in Choluteca follow a standard grid, with *calles* (streets) running east–west, and *avenidas* (avenues) north–south. The city is divided into four zones: NO (*noroeste,* northwest), NE (*noreste,* northeast), SO (*suroeste,* southwest) or SE (*sureste,* southeast). Parque Central is in the middle.

The bus terminal is in the southeast zone, on Blvd Carranza and 3a Av SE. The Mi Esperanza bus terminal is just over a block north. The old market (Mercado Viejo San Antonio) is just three blocks south of Parque Central but nine long blocks west and two blocks north of the bus terminal. The old market is the center of activity, and several hotels, restaurants and banks are nearby.

Information

Banco Atlántida (6a Av NO; 8:30am-3:30pm Mon-Fri, to 11:30am Sat) One 24-hour ATM. Located a block south of Parque Central.

Farmacia Luar (☎ 882-0969; Calle Williams near 6a Av NO; 🕑 8am-noon & 1-5pm Mon-Fri, to noon Sat)
Global Cyber (6a Av NO near Calle Williams; internet per hr L$20; 🕑 7:30am-6pm Mon-Sat) Web-based international calls also made. Located on the 2nd floor of Pasaje Sarita, a small shopping center.
Hondutel (2a Calle NO near 3a Av NO; 🕑 7am-9pm) Call center with branches throughout the country.
Police (☎ 782-0951; Parque Central; 🕑 24hr)
Post Office (2a Calle NO at 3a Av NO; 🕑 8am-4pm Mon-Fri, to noon Sat)

Sights & Activities

There isn't much to see in Choluteca, but if you're wandering around town, check out the huge whitewashed *casona* (colonial-style mansion) on the southwest corner of Parque Central. Once the family home of José Cecilio del Valle (below), it now houses the town's public library.

Sleeping

Hotel Pacifico (☎ 782-3249; just off Blvd Enrique Weddle; s/d L$300/350; P ❄) Located half a block south from the Wendy's on the main road to Nicaragua, this place has moderately clean rooms with air-con, and secure parking.

Hotel Rivera (☎ 782-0828; Blvd Enrique Weddle; s/d L$400/500; P ❄) A step up in quality, the Riviera offers motel-style rooms with hot-water bathrooms and air-con. The hotel is attractive and well maintained, and the service is attentive. It's located on Blvd Enrique Weddle, a busy street with a smattering of fast-food restaurants. Coming into town from Tegucigalpa, take a left at the Banco de Occidente. The hotel is about a 25-minute walk from Parque Central.

Eating

In addition to the places listed here, you'll find a slew of small *comedores* along the streets bordering the old market.

Cafetería Frosty (Calle Williams near 6a Av NO; mains L$30-50; 🕑 breakfast & lunch) Food is served fresh and hot at this cafeteria-style diner – just be sure to get there early so you don't get left with the scraps. If that happens, there's an extensive hamburger menu.

Restaurante Yi Kim (☎ 782-5578; Av La Rosa; mains L$60-160; 🕑 lunch & dinner) Huge portions of Szechuan- and Cantonese-inspired food are served at this paper-lantern–laden restaurant. Food comes out at light speed – how do they make it so fast? Located one block west of Parque Central.

Mercado Viejo San Antonio (old market; Calle Williams btwn 6a Av NO & Av La Rosa) You'll find everything you need – and don't need – at this centrally located market. Great for last-minute items or just as a point of reference.

Getting There & Around

Virtually all the listed hotels, restaurants and services are within a few blocks of the central park, and are easily reached by foot. The

EL SABIO – REVEALING THE LIFE & TIMES OF JOSÉ CECILIO DEL VALLE

José Cecilio del Valle's role in Central American independence is often overshadowed by that of his contemporary, and sometime rival, General Francisco Morazán (who is known fetchingly as the 'George Washington of Central America'). Born in Choluteca in 1777, del Valle was a judge and law professor, nicknamed El Sabio (The Wise) for his carefully crafted opinions. In 1821, he drafted the Central American Declaration of Independence. Later, when Central America was annexed by Mexico, del Valle served as one of the region's representatives in the Mexican Congress. There, del Valle led efforts to limit the authoritarianism of Augustine del Iturbide (who had declared himself emperor, among other abuses), for which del Valle was eventually arrested and jailed. It was a brief detention: Iturbide was exiled shortly thereafter and del Valle rejoined Congress. In 1823 he made a famously impassioned argument before his fellow legislators that Central America should be granted independence: 'Free will is the basis of all agreements… The union of two nations demands the freely-given consent of both. For Mexico and [Central America] to unify, it is necessary that both Mexico and [Central America] want to be united.' Mexico ordered the withdrawal of troops, and del Valle returned to Central America in 1824.

Back home, del Valle helped draft the constitution of the new Central American federation, which included the abolition of slavery. Del Valle was narrowly defeated in his bid to be the federation's first president, and again in 1830. He finally won in 1834, but died before he could take office.

GETTING TO & FROM THE BORDER: NICARAGUA & EL SALVADOR

Choluteca is within striking distance of three border crossings: El Amatillo for entering El Salvador, and Guasaule and La Fraternidad/El Espino for entering Nicaragua.

El Amatillo (El Salvador) From the Choluteca terminal, buses (L$30, 2¼ hours, 4:30am to 4:30pm) leave every 25 minutes. Entering Honduras, you can take the same bus to Choluteca, or another for Tegucigalpa (L$50, three hours, every 30 minutes 4:30am to 3:30pm).

Guasaule (Nicaragua) Feels distinctly dodgy and you should stay alert for pickpockets or be wary of anyone being overly 'helpful.' From the Choluteca terminal, the *directos* (midrange bus) service (L$25, 45 minutes, 5am to 9pm) leaves every 25 minutes and returns until 5pm. Avoid the *ordinario* service as it can take twice as long. Microbuses (L$95, 1¾ hours, every 45 minutes 7:20am to 5pm) zip from here to the Salvadoran border at El Amatillo.

La Fraternidad/El Espino (Nicaragua) From San Marcos de Colón *colectivo* taxis and microbuses operate between 6am and 7pm and charge around L$20 for the 10-minute ride. Both wait until they fill up before leaving; they line up in front of Mi Esperanza bus terminal. A private taxi costs around L$70. There's identical service from the border until about 6pm.

exceptions – the Hotel Riviera and the bus terminals – are best reached by taxi, which are plentiful in the center of town.

Choluteca's bus terminal is on Blvd Carranza, at the corner of 3a Av NE. **Transportes Mi Esperanza** (☎ 782-0841) has its own station half a block down the street opposite the main terminal, while **Rey Express** (☎ 782-2712) and 1st-class **Saenz** (☎ 782-0712) have terminals around the block.

There are services to San Marcos de Colón (L$26, 1½ hours, 11 departures between 6:15am and 6:15pm), La Esperanza (L$28, 1¼ hours, six departures 7:30am to 7:15pm) and Rey Express (L$28, one hour, 9:45am, 2:25pm and 6:25pm). The last bus from San Marcos to Choluteca departs at 4pm

Tegucigalpa is served by Mi Esperanza (L$58; 3½ hours, hourly 4am to 5:30pm), Rey Express (L$70, three hours, 8:15am, 12:15am and 4:15am) and Saenz (L$150, 2½ hours, 6am, 10am, 2pm and 6pm).

EL CORPUS

pop 24,200

Just 17km from Choluteca, El Corpus' cool climate and quaint cobblestone streets seem a world apart from the hot, bustling department capital. Perched on a hillside, the small stone plaza has beds of flowers and benches overlooking the sloping valley below. The fortunes of El Corpus have long depended on those of its on-again, off-again mining industry (mostly gold). It was once one of the richest mining towns in the country but is now much reduced.

There are at least two good hikes around town. The toughest – and most rewarding – is to the top of Cerro Guanacaure, with an amazing 360-degree view from the summit. On a clear day, you can see into Nicaragua, the Gulf of Fonseca and all the way to eastern El Salvador. It's a steep 4km trail to the top, starting from the community of Aqua Fría, about 8km from El Corpus proper.

The other hike is up Cerro Calaire, with views of the Valle de Choluteca and sometimes the Golfo de Fonseca. It's a moderately tough 90-minute hike to the summit, starting from El Corpus. The **tourist office** (☎ 787-3523, Municipal Bldg; 🕑 8am-4pm Mon-Fri, to 11am Sat) can help arrange a guide and maybe even a homestay. March and April are burning season, pretty much spoiling the view.

You can also hire someone to show you some of the many abandoned mines that dot the area in and around El Corpus (there's even one right in town). Needless to say, this can be an extremely dangerous activity – the tourist office can help arrange a guide with the proper experience and know-how.

Buses to Concepción de María (L$14, one hour), the next town up, leave Choluteca's bus terminal hourly from 4:30am to 3:30pm, with a stop in El Corpus along the way. There are Corpus-only buses (L$14, one hour) at 7am, 11:45am and 3pm.

CEDEÑO

pop 1500

Considering it's the nearest beach to Choluteca, it's too bad Cedeño is not more appealing. Picture dark-brown sand leading to even darker brown water, makeshift food stands lining the beach in every direction, garbage strewn about and the water packed

10 deep with jean-clad swimmers. Add several sketchy dance halls blasting reggueton (hip-hop with Jamaican and Latin American influences), and you've got Cedeño. Weekends are particularly awful (unless, of course, this is your sort of scene) but walk down the beach1km or so, and it's not so bad. Just watch your belongings.

Cedeño is located 33km south of the Amatillo-Choluteca highway. Look for the turnoff at a Texaco gas station. Buses ferry passengers to and from Choluteca (L$30, 1½ hours, 4am to 4:45pm, every 30 minutes).

SAN MARCOS DE COLÓN

pop 23,900

San Marcos sees a steady stream of travelers passing through to catch a bus to or from Nicaragua. Very few stay, and the riches of this little colonial town – and the mountains around it, teeming with birds and wildlife – remain largely unknown.

Like most Honduran towns, Parque Central is the center of town. The one in San Marcos de Colón is particularly pleasant with plenty of shady trees, benches and a high-steepled church.

Being a small place, there aren't many traveler services: you'll find **Banco Atlántida** (8:30am-3:30pm Mon-Fri, to 11:30am Sat) one block east of Parque Central. It doesn't have an ATM so you should plan accordingly (the nearest one is in Choluteca). For medicine, try **Farmacia Familiar** (888-3410; 8am-noon & 1-5pm Mon-Fri, 8am-noon Sat), which is kitty-corner to the bank. **Hondutel** (7am-9pm Mon-Fri, to 2pm Sat & Sun) is 1½ blocks west of the park; the **police station** (788-3063; 24hr) is next door.

Sleeping & Eating

Hotel Shalom (788-3268; r L$250; P) Located in a peach-colored building at the top of a steep street overlooking Parque Central, the Hotel Shalom offers very clean rooms with hot-water bathrooms and cable TV. Many suffer from Stinky Bathroom Syndrome but a plastic bag over the drain should help. The best thing about this place is the view; well above the town, many rooms afford views of its colonial surroundings with a mountain backdrop.

Hotel Colonial (788-3822; r L$250; P) Two long corridors lead to several large rooms with high ceilings. The rooms are quiet, dark and spotless, though the beds are a bit squishy. All include private hot-water bathrooms and cable TV. There also is secure indoor parking. It's located two blocks from Parque Central.

La Esquisita (mains L$20-40; breakfast, lunch & dinner Wed-Mon) A pleasant cafe serving *típica* all day. The menu is about two sentences long, the meals are excellent and are served at picnic-style tables. Service is fast and friendly.

Pollo Campestre (mains L$30-80; lunch & dinner) As the name suggests, the 'Country Chicken' specializes in chicken – grilled, fried, rotisserie-style, whole, chopped up.

Getting There & Away

East of the park, **Transportes Mi Esperanza** (788-3705) has daily service to Choluteca (L$26, one hour) that continues to Tegucigalpa, **Rey Express/Blanquita Express** (788-3972) offers a more direct service on the same route (Choluteca L$28, 45 minutes) at 7:15am, 11:15am and 3:15pm. Otherwise, no-name buses shuttle back and forth to Choluteca (L$26, 1½ hours, every 30 minutes) all day; pick them up near Mi Esperanza.

Buses to Duyusupo leave twice a day at 7am and 1pm (L$30, two hours). The bus stop is in front of a yellow house a block east of Funerales San Martín. Return trips are at 8:30am and 2:30pm.

For info on getting to/from the Nicaraguan border at La Fraternidad/El Espino, see opposite.

REFUGIO DE VIDA SILVESTRE OJOCHAL

South of San Marco de Colón, the **Refugio de Vida Silvestre Ojochal** (Ojochal Wildlife Reserve) is a private wildlife reserve within the pristine Sierra de la Botija mountains along the Honduras–Nicaragua border. Precious few travelers make it here; those who do are rewarded with gorgeous pine and tropical forest brimming with wildlife, especially white-faced monkeys. There are no organized services for the refuge, and trail maintenance is uneven. The best way to visit is to contact **Dr Ángel Enrique Sándoval López** (788-3505, 9977-9442) and family, who own La Esquisita restaurant (above). Travelers may be able to stay the night in the family's home, or camp on the grounds. From Duyusupo, it's a two- to three-hour downhill hike into the protected area at Río Negro – it's a punishing return. You can also climb **Cerro de Águila**, one of several forest-clad mountains in the area. A shorter hike (30 minutes) is to **Chorro de la Mina**, a 20m waterfall with a natural swimming hole at the bottom. Ask Dr Sándoval about hiring guides; there's usually someone in Duyusupo or in the neighboring community of Zarzal that can accompany you.

For transportation information, see p91.

AMAPALA & ISLA DEL TIGRE

Amapala is a quiet fishing village on Isla del Tigre, a 783m-high inactive volcanic island. Founded in 1833, Amapala was once Honduras' main Pacific port town, before the port was moved to San Lorenzo on the mainland. Visitors come here for holidays during Semana Santa (the week before Easter), and in smaller numbers on weekends, but generally the place is very quiet. There's a picture of Amapala on the back of the L$2 note.

The few services that are available on the island are in Amapala. For basic information about the island or homestay options, go to the **tourist office** (☎ 895-8555; end of main pier; 🕒 8am-noon & 2-5pm Mon-Fri, 8am-noon Sat). The **immigration office** (☎ 795-8643; 🕒 8am-noon & 1-5pm Mon-Fri) is also on the pier. **Hondutel** (🕒 8am-5pm Mon-Sat) and the **post office** (🕒 9am-4pm Mon-Fri) sit side-by-side a block south of the main pier. And while there are no banking services on the island, the folks at Restaurante El Faro de Victoria (opposite) will exchange US dollars for a premium.

Sights & Activities

Del Tigre's main draw is its beaches, though none are exactly scintillating. **Playa El Burro** is the nearest beach to Amapala, reachable by foot in about 20 minutes. (It's also closest to Coyolito, and the boat can drop you here directly.) A large clean, tawny-sand beach, it faces inland and has almost no waves. At low tide, the shallows are muddy and unpleasant. This is where backpackers end up when they visit the island. A couple of restaurants sell simple food.

Located about 3km south of Amapala (about a 45-minute walk), **Playa Grande** is the most popular beach. It doesn't get muddy at low tide, and has a small cave at one end. Unfortunately clapboard eateries have been built right on the sand virtually from end to end, leaving very little actual open beach.

Most travelers prefer **Playa Negra**, which is less built-up. Small, with sparkling black sand, the beach is backed by high bluffs. A few stands sell simple meals, or you can eat at the restaurant at Hotel Playa Negra, which overlooks the beach. The main problem with the beach is that it's the furthest from Amapala (6km).

You can also climb **Cerro Vejía** (783m), the distinctive bulge in the middle of the island. The view from the summit includes the entire gulf and three countries. Take the dirt road that starts opposite the naval base, about 3km from Amapala; it winds its way to the top of the Cerro. The road is fairly well shaded, but the region's oppressive heat makes this a tough hike. Leave as early as possible and bring plenty of water; allow three hours up and nearly the same amount for the return.

Aquatours Marabella (☎ 795-8050; Playa El Burro) offers various boat trips, including around Isla El Tigre (L$800 to L900), to Isla Exposición (L$350 one way) and to Isla Las Almejas (L$350 one way).

Sleeping & Eating

Amapala has one hotel and one restaurant in town, plus two hotel/restaurant establishments at Playa El Burro. There are also homestay possibilities in private homes around the island for around L$400 per couple.

Veleros (☎ 795-8040, 9989-2285; Playa El Burro; d with fan/air-con L$400/600; ❄) A nice surprise, Veleros has spotless rooms with private bathrooms, tile floors and good beds, all overlooking the ocean. The service is friendly and there's a small outdoor patio and restaurant with tables, chairs and hammocks for guests to share. There are only three rooms, but staff can set you up with other homestays or small-time lodges in the area.

Hotel Aquatours Marbella (☎ 795-8050; Playa El Burro; r L$900; ❄ 🏊) Next to Veleros, this is another pleasant (though overpriced) find, offering 11 large clean rooms and a shady beachfront courtyard with hammocks slung between the trees. There's a tiny pool with a huge waterslide; the water is rather murky but nice to have during low tide when the beach is unswimmable.

Mirador de Amapala Hotel (☎ 795-8407, 795-8592; www.miradordeamapala.com; Amapala; s/d L$800/1000; ❄ 💻 🏊) The grounds are nice enough – built into the side of a hill, with lots of vegetation and a pool – and some rooms have fantastic views of the Golfo de Fonseca. The cramped quarters and gruff service can mar the experience though. Still, this is the best of Amapala's hotels, and the one to choose if you want something a little nicer than average.

EXPLORE MORE OF THE GOLFO DE FONSECA

The shores of Honduras, El Salvador and Nicaragua all touch the **Golfo de Fonseca**; Honduras has the middle, and the largest share, with 124km of coastline and jurisdiction over nearly all of the 30-plus islands in the gulf. In September 1992 the International Court of Justice eased previous tensions by ruling that sovereignty in the gulf must be shared by the three nations, barring a 3-mile maritime belt around the coast. Of the islands in the gulf, sovereignty was disputed by Honduras and El Salvador in three cases. The court found in favor of Honduras regarding the island of El Tigre, but El Salvador prevailed on Meanguera and Meanguerita.

The European discovery of the Golfo de Fonseca was made in 1522 by Andrés Niño, who named the gulf in honor of his benefactor, Bishop Juan Rodríguez de Fonseca. In 1578, the buccaneer Sir Francis Drake occupied the gulf, using El Tigre as a base as he made raids as far afield as Peru and Baja California. There is still speculation that Drake may have left a hidden treasure, but it has never been found.

In Amapala or Coyolito, you can hire a boatman to take you to **Isla Meanguera**, the largest of the islands in the gulf (and the closest to Honduras); it has pleasant black-sand beaches and a small town where you can stop for lunch. As you drift by, be sure to check out the islet directly in front of it, Meanguerita or **Isla de los Pájaros** (Bird Island), named for the thousands of birds that live there (it's a protected zone, in fact). Towards the northwest, the mountainous **Conchagüita** has good hiking. Just south, the island of **Martín Pérez** is uninhabited but great if you're looking for solitary beaches.

The islands are all part of El Salvador, so technically you should pass through Salvadoran immigration before visiting them. That said, there's very little chance you'll be 'caught' while on a day trip from Amapala. If you're considering staying a night or two, however, play it safe and go to the immigration office in La Unión first.

Hotel Playa Negra (☎ 795-8026, in Tegucigalpa 238-4323; Playa Negra; r L$1500; P) Well past its prime, the Hotel Playa Negra makes little effort to fix – or even hide – its deficiencies. The bathrooms have cement floors, the headboards are mismatched, the bedspreads and in-room chairs are raggedy. If that weren't enough, the tennis court has weeds growing on it (and it's not a grass court), none of the rooms have views despite sitting above the prettiest beach on the island, and the cloudy pool is surrounded by a chain-link fence. Not exactly what you expect when you're paying high-end rates. Perhaps the only reason to come here is to enjoy a meal at the restaurant (mains L$80 to L$200, open breakfast, lunch and dinner) with a view over the Golfo de Fonseca.

Restaurante El Faro de Victoria (☎ 795-8543; main pier; mains L$60-200; lunch & dinner) An open-air restaurant with tables overlooking the pier and gulf, El Faro would be hard to resist even if it weren't the only real option in the town. The seafood is excellent: try the *pescado sudado* ('sweating fish'; whole fish poached in foil). Hamburgers and sandwiches also available.

Hotel y Restaurante Dignita (☎ 795-8707; Playa Grande; mains L$60-200; breakfast & lunch) This is the most popular restaurant on Playa Grande. The seafood dishes are excellent. Clients sit at long wooden tables just a few feet from the ocean – perfect for throwing back a couple of beers over a plate of *ceviche* (raw fish marinated in lime juice).

Getting There & Away

Fiberglass *lanchas* (motorboats) ferry passengers to and from Coyolito and Amapala all day, every day. The ride takes about 15 minutes and costs L$15 per person on a *colectivo* boat; you may have to wait a while for one to fill up. If you're in a hurry, a private trip is around L$150.

From Coyolito, buses depart for San Lorenzo (L$19, one hour, every 40 minutes 5:30am to 4pm). In San Lorenzo, buses to Coyolito leave from the Mercado Municipal, the last departure at 5:30pm. To get to Choluteca or Tegucigalpa, transfer at San Lorenzo or at the gas station at the Coyolito turnoff.

A moto-taxi from the main pier to Playa El Burro costs L$20, and it's L$40 to Playa Negra. If you drive to Coyolito, it's best to pay to park your car (L$60 per day).

Central Honduras

Practically nobody goes here – we're talking a trickle of a few hundred foreign tourists a year at best – and what more reason do you need to visit this uncharted territory in an already uncharted country? Sure, the infrastructure is rustic and the developed attractions few, but sometimes a journey beyond the tourist trail is just what the doctor ordered.

Most people who visit the area come for a multi-day forest hike to the top of Olancho's highest mountain in Parque Nacional Sierra de Agalta. Along the route, you'll pass through numerous microclimates, ascending through jungle up to the cloud and dwarf forests near the summit. It's a tough tromp, but well worth the effort. There's also excellent hiking in El Boquerón Natural Monument, and cave exploration at the Cuevas de Susmay and de Talgua. If that doesn't tire you out, then prepare yourself for one of Honduras' truly great adventures – a 10-day float down the rivers Patuca or Plátano into La Moskitia.

And while this modern-day Wild West is a bit rough around the edges – anticipate a few unfriendly stares, and don't be surprised that nearly everybody is carrying a gun – it does offer a bit for the culture hound. One of Honduras' biggest archaeological discoveries took place near the city of Catacamas, where the 'Glowing Skulls of Talgua' were discovered in a cave in 1994. Unfortunately, you don't get to see the skulls (they really do glow, thanks to a coating of phosphorescent calcite) but it does go to show you that discoveries rating a perfect 10 on the 'Indiana-Jones-O-Meter' are still possible in this rugged little corner of the world.

HIGHLIGHTS

- Spirit your way through dripping rainforest to a bizarre dwarf forest on the dizzying summit of **La Picucha** (p103)
- Get dirty on a day hike through the **Monumento Natural El Boquerón** (p99), passing through river valleys, cloud forests and small-time coffee plantations along the way
- Imagine the possibilities as you duck through the **Cuevas de Talgua** (p101), where amateur spelunkers discovered dozens of 'glowing skulls' left there 3000 years ago
- Shiver your way through the dark as you follow a bone-chilling river to the limestone formations at the **Cuevas de Susmay** (p105)
- Test yourself in the seldom-visited **Reserva Biológico El Chile** (opposite), where waterfalls and untrammeled trails await

DANGERS & ANNOYANCES

Olancho's north-south highways have been the scene of numerous roadside assaults; the one via La Unión has the unsettling nickname *camino de la muerte* (road of death). The problem has abated somewhat – and President Zelaya, an Olanchano, once proposed paving these roads – but avoid driving here if possible and certainly don't do so at night. If you get to a road block, don't get out of your car, just turn around and return from where you came.

CENTRAL HIGHLANDS & BEYOND

Most people skip this area altogether, heading on instead to the more renowned attractions out in Olancho, but a day or two exploring the waterfalls of Reserva Biológico El Chile or visiting the local troop of howler monkeys in the Misoco Biological Reserve may be worth the effort. Stay in the dusty towns of Yoro and Cedros along the way.

RESERVA BIOLÓGICA EL CHILE

A beautiful and rugged stretch of highland forest, this protected area includes several peaks, including Pico de Navaja (2150m) and numerous rivers and important watersheds.

Access to the reserve is through **San Marcos**, a town of around 1000 people and about 1½ hours by rough dirt road from Guaimaca. There's a small **visitors center** (no phone; opening hrs vary) in San Marcos where you may be able to hire a guide. Two trails leave from San Marcos, taking you to either a set of waterfalls near the village of Piñuela or to a smaller waterfall known as Majastre II. Either trail will take you about an hour or two to hike.

You may be able to camp at, or near, the visitors center in San Marcos, or in a small cabin in Piñuela. Ask around town, or at the visitors center if it's open.

The park has a second entrance on its far side via the town of Teupasenti, near Danlí. There, a short but steep hike from the community of El Aguantal leads to an impressive waterfall of the same name. Hiking across the reserve is possible but very difficult – hire a local guide.

Admission to the reserve is free, but it is a good idea to stop in at the local **Honduran Corporation for Forest Development** (COHDEFOR; 8am-noon & 1-4pm Mon-Fri) before heading in. The office is 300m off the highway (behind a plywood factory, ironically) about 2km west of Guaimaca.

Any bus between Juticalpa and Tegucigalpa can drop you at the turnoff to Guaimaca. From there, buses leave for San Marcos (L$20, 1½ hours) at 1:30pm only; the return bus departs from San Marcos at 7am. Should you choose to hitch, mornings are best.

RESERVA BIOLÓGICA MISOCO

This even smaller reserve has one maintained trail and is known for its howler monkeys. The turnoff is 750m east from Guaimaca and the reserve itself is at the hamlet of Arenales up an extremely rough road. A **visitors center** (no phone; opening hrs vary) there has simple accommodation where you may be able to hire a guide.

CEDROS

pop 19,700

There's very little to do in this dusty mining berg, situated on the edge of the Montañas de Comayagua mountain range, aside from soaking in that good-ol' small-town atmosphere. If you do decide to poke around the surrounding hills, be extremely careful of unfenced, unmarked mine shafts.

The **police** (24hr) and **Hondutel Call Center** (7:30am-9pm Mon-Sat) are located on Parque Central. Across from the police station is the **Casa de Cultura** (admission free; 9am-noon & 2-4:30pm Mon-Fri), which occasionally has photo exhibits of the area.

El Cerrito is the name of a small hill in the center of town. At the top, there's a large shady kiosk and a rather obtrusive cell-phone tower. The view, of the town church on one side and the pine-covered valley on the other, is quite nice.

Sleeping & Eating

Doña Elinda (☎ 917-3138; r with shared bathroom per person L$60) Located in a simple home behind the *iglesia* (church), this guesthouse is the only place to stay in town. It's a lucky thing that it's comfortable. Doña Elinda also prepares meals (around L$50) for her guests.

Restaurante Típicos (mains L$40-100; breakfast, lunch & dinner Mon-Sat) Located kitty-corner from

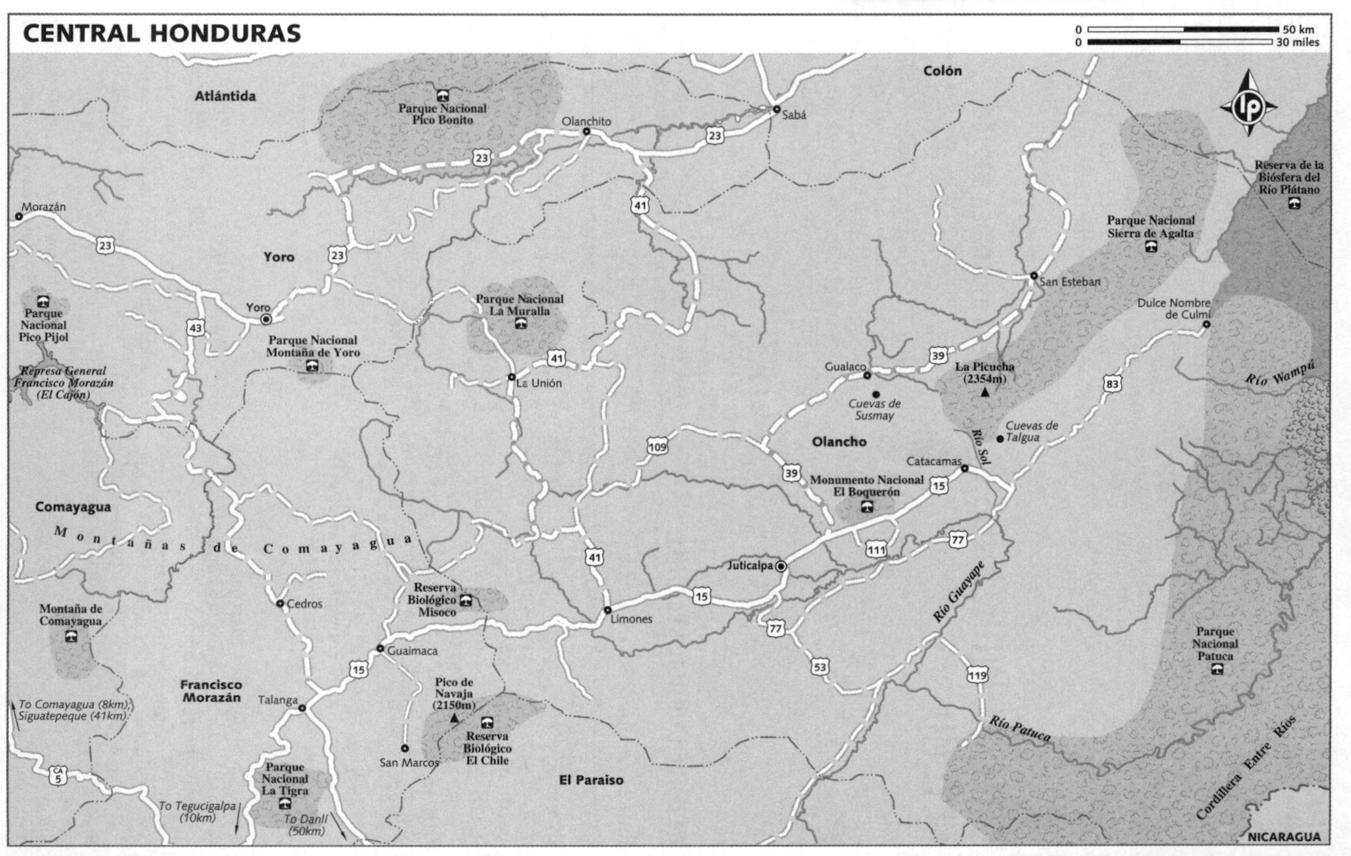
CENTRAL HONDURAS
0 50 km
0 30 miles
Atlántida
Parque Nacional Pico Bonito
Olanchito
Sabá
Colón
Reserva de la Biósfera del Río Plátano
Parque Nacional Sierra de Agalta
Morazán
Yoro
Yoro
San Esteban
Dulce Nombre de Culmí
Parque Nacional Pico Pijol
Parque Nacional La Muralla
Parque Nacional Montaña de Yoro
Represa General Francisco Morazán (El Cajón)
La Unión
Gualaco
La Picucha (2354m)
Río Wampú
Cuevas de Susmay
Cuevas de Talgua
Río Sol
Olancho
Catacamas
Monumento Nacional El Boquerón
Comayagua
Montañas de Comayagua
Juticalpa
Río Guayape
Reserva Biológico Misoco
Cedros
Limones
Montaña de Comayagua
Guaimaca
Parque Nacional Patuca
Francisco Morazán
Talanga
Pico de Navaja (2150m)
Reserva Biológico El Chile
San Marcos
To Comayagua (8km); Siguatepeque (41km)
Río Patuca
Cordillera Entre Ríos
Parque Nacional La Tigra
El Paraiso
To Tegucigalpa (10km)
To Danlí (50km)
NICARAGUA
23
41
43
39
83
109
15
111
77
53
119
CA 5

LOS TOLUPANES

The Tolupán people of Yoro may be one of the oldest living cultures in the Americas. Many linguists believe their language is descended from the Hokun Sioux tribe of North America, which dates back more than 5000 years. However, other researchers say the Tolupán are part of the Chibcha-speaking migration from South America around 3000 years ago that also gave rise to the Pech, Tawahka and Miskitu groups today found in La Moskitia.

What is certain is that the Tolupán territory once extended over most of present-day Honduras. But with the appearance of Spanish colonizers – and the brutality and suffering they brought with them – the Tolupán receded further and further into the mountains and forests of central Honduras.

Today there are only about 19,000 Tolupán left and of those only around 700 speak their ancestral language. They are deeply reclusive; most live in small villages in the departments of Yoro and Francisco Morazán, surviving through subsistence farming, mostly on communal property, growing corn, beans, manioc and coffee.

the *alcaldía* (city hall), in the building where the first national constitutional assembly was held, this is your spot for simple eats.

Getting There & Away

There are daily buses to Tegucigalpa that leave from Cedros' Parque Central (L$35, 2½ hours, 3am, 4am, 5am and 2pm). From Tegucigalpa to Cedros, buses leave daily at 6am, 7am, 10am, 3pm and 4:40pm (L$35, 2½ hours).

YORO

pop 82,200

A dusty, back-country town on the way to nowhere, Yoro is a good place to check out some off-the-beaten-track hikes and spelunking. It is also the site of one of the more bizarre phenomena in Honduras: the rain of fish (p98).

On the southeast corner of the park, **Banco Atlántida** (8:30am-3:30pm Mon-Fri, to 11:30am Sat) has an ATM and does cash advances on Visa cards. **Hondutel** (671-2116; 7:30am-9pm Mon-Sat) is opposite the bank.

Activities

Based out of the Tortuga Veloz eatery, **Eco-Aventuras No Solo Grotte** (Not Just Caves Eco-Adventures; 671-0012; nosologrotte@hotmail.com; Parque Central; 9am-9pm) offers hiking, rappelling and caving trips in the region. Call a day or two in advance to book a tour. English and Italian spoken.

If No Solo Grotte is booked, the **Asociación Ecológica para la Protección del Parque Nacional Pico Pijol** (AECOPIJOL; 691-0412; aecopijol@yahoo.es; Parque Central), the management arm of Pico Pijol National Park, can provide general information about the park (see p99) and help track down a guide.

Parque Nacional Montaña de Yoro lies south of the town of Yoro. It's a small but rugged park with dense forest and numerous caves, as well as a small number of trails. Unfortunately it is also widely known for its illicit marijuana production and the gun-toting men who patrol the area.

The **Asociación Ecológica Amigos de la Montaña de Yoro** (AMY; 671-2199; 8am-4pm Mon-Fri) has an office on the 2nd floor of the kiosk in the central park, but it (and others) tend to discourage casual travelers from visiting the area.

Sleeping & Eating

Hotel Palace (671-2229; Calle Principal; s/d L$250/350; P) Located on the main road in town, the Hotel Palace offers plain and cramped rooms above one of the biggest *pulperías* (minimarts) in town.

Hotel Marquez (671-2804; fax 671-2815; Calle Principal; r/tw L$400/500; P) Further down the main street, this place looks nicer on the outside than it really is. Rooms are clean, but the beds are saggy, the paint looks slapped on and many of the curtains are holding on by just a thread.

For eats, head to Parque Central, where several *comedores* (basic, cheap eateries) serve *típica* meals three times a day.

Getting There & Away

Ordinario (literally 'stopping') buses leave for San Pedro Sula (L$100, 3½ hours, every 90 minutes, 4:45am to 3pm) from out the front of Supermercado Cabañas on the main drag.

Buses to Tegucigalpa leave once daily at 7am (L$150, six hours), or take any bus to the highway turnoff at Santa Rita (*ordinario* L$60, 2½ hours) and catch a Tegucigalpa-bound bus there.

There is somewhat erratic service, usually once or twice per day, to La Unión and to Olanchito. Departures are usually in the morning and depend on the weather and road conditions.

OLANCHO

Famous for its cowboy mentality and Wild West ways – wide-brimmed Presidente Manuel Zelaya hails from here – Olancho offers adventures aplenty in the Monumento Natural El Boquerón and Parque Nacional Sierra de Agalta. The department's towns are essential nuisances for visiting the outlying areas.

JUTICALPA

pop 113,000

The only major town in northeastern Honduras is Juticalpa, the capital of the department of Olancho. While there's nothing to see here, it's a decent staging point for excursions further east. There are two bus terminals (across the street from one another) at the entrance to town. From there it's a congested kilometer to the city park, which is surprisingly pleasant, flanked by a huge, modern church and filled with trees and benches.

Information

HSBC (Parque Central; 8:30am-3:30pm Mon-Fri, to 11:30am Sat) Has an ATM.

Farmacia Santa Teresita (Parque Central)

Hondutel (5a Av near 1a Calle; 7:30am-9pm Mon-Sat) For phone calls.

Police (785-2110; 3a Av SO at 4a Calle; 24hr)

Post Office (Parque Central; 8am-4pm Mon-Fri, to 11am Sat)

Sleeping & Eating

Hotel Reyes (785-2232; 7a Av SO near Calle Perulapán; r with shared bathroom per person L$70, r per person L$90-140) A sad-looking hotel with a dark cement courtyard and worn, but relatively clean, rooms.

Hotel Riviera (785-1154; Calle Perulapán at 8a Av SO; s with/without bathroom L$270/200, d with/without bathroom L$370/300) Next to the Posada del Centro, this cheapie offers moderately clean rooms at affordable rates.

Hotel Posada del Centro (785-3415; www.olanchoweb.com; Calle Perulapán at 8a Av SO; s/d/tr incl breakfast $550/760/960; P) The Hotel Posada del Centro is one of the best hotels around with a great rooftop common area perfect for sorting gear before you head into the woods. Rooms have all the little details you'd expect in a nice midrange place: recessed lighting, matching bedspreads, good beds, silent air conditioners, big TVs, in-room phones, even extra towels.

Restaurante El Rancho (785-1202; 4a Av SE near 2a Calle; mains L$40-100; lunch & dinner Mon-Sat) Located directly behind the *iglesia,* the picnic tables are always hopping at this open-air restaurant. Grilled meats are the specialty.

Entertainment

Cine Maya (2a Calle near 3a Av NO; tickets L$20) Despite the odd *problemas técnicos* (technical problems), this old-timer still creaks out Hollywood releases every night.

Getting There & Away

The main bus terminal is about 1km from town on the entrance road from the highway. Buses leave from there for Limones, La Unión, Manguile, Gualaco, San Estéban,

LOCAL LORE: RAIN OF FISH

On a given day in June or July, dark storm clouds will gather over the small town of Yoro and unleash a tremendous summer rainstorm. In the downpour, in the low-lying neighborhood of El Pántano, will appear thousands of silvery fish flopping on the ground. It happens virtually every year and is known as the *aguacero de pescado* or *lluvia de peces* (rain of fish).

Yoreños believe the phenomenon is nothing less than an act of God. They trace its origin to a 19th-century Spanish missionary named Manuel Jesús de Subirana, who prayed fervently for three days and three nights for a miracle to feed the local indigenous people. Biologists say it can be explained scientifically, but have yet to provide any conclusive evidence. Either way you look at it, it's an occasion for a party: since 1997, the annual Festival de la Lluvia de Peces has been held around the middle of June and includes parades, music and, thank God, lots of fried fish.

DAY TRIP TO PICO PIJOL

Rarely visited by tourists, Parque Nacional Pico Pijol is a lush cloud forest with two imposing peaks – Pico Pijol (2282m) and Cerro El Sargento (1852m). In 1987 it was set aside as a 122-sq-km reserve in order to protect its natural resources, namely four rivers, which are a major water source for San Pedro Sula.

The park offers no tourist services or hiking trails, however. The only way to visit it is with a guide and his machete; it's an adventure, to say the least. Above 1800m, visitors are treated to the view of an untouched cloud forest heavy with vegetation and teeming with wildlife and tropical birds, including a few families of quetzal.

In Yoro, **Eco-Aventuras No Solo Grotte** (p97) offers day trips in the park.

Tocoa, Trujillo and La Ceiba. **Transportes Aurora/Discovery** (☎ 785-2237) has its own terminal across the street, with ordinary and 1st-class service to Catacamas and Tegucigalpa. Plenty of taxis run between town and both stations (L$20).

Daily services from the two stations include:

Catacamas (L$24, 40 minutes, every 30 minutes 7:30am to 6pm)
Gualaco (L$53, two hours, hourly 3:30am to 3pm) Take any Gualaco-, San Estéban-, or Trujillo-bound bus.
La Ceiba (L$150, nine hours, 4am & 6am)
Tegucigalpa (*ordinario* L$78, three hours, hourly 5am to 6pm; *directo* L$86, 2½ hours, 6:15am, 8:30am, 9:15am, 10:15am, 1:15pm, 2:15pm & 5pm)

MONUMENTO NATURAL EL BOQUERÓN

This 4000-hectare protected zone is anchored by two river canyons and the 1433m Cerro de Agua Buena. It contains primary and secondary tropical forests as well as cloud forests, and also boasts the scenic Río Olancho running through the middle. A number of small farming settlements are found within the protected area.

The area around present-day El Boquerón town was once known as San Jorge de Olancho and functioned as the department capital in the 16th and 17th centuries. It was a rich and vibrant town, fueled by gold mined from the surrounding hills – locals still uncover tools and other artifacts while plowing their fields. However, legend has it that the townspeople grew miserly and, in an act of divine justice, a volcanic eruption sent a wave of burning lava down the hillside, burying the town and killing its residents. That San Jorge de Olancho was mysteriously obliterated is well known, but the volcano story is unlikely – for starters, there are no volcanoes in the area. A more likely scenario, supported by recent geologic surveys, is that a mudslide from Cerro de Agua Buena's steep flanks was responsible for the tragedy.

Information

This is a great place for day hikes without the need for guides. Following the loop 'backwards' – that is, heading toward El Bambú first – the trail is clear as far as La Avispa. The section along the Río Olancho is harder to follow; it's faded in places and criss-crossed by hunting trails.

Jose 'Joche' Mendoza and his son Tonito Mendoza are both experienced and recommended local guides. They live in the community of El Boquerón, on the highway at the foot of the protected area. Neither has a phone, but any passerby can help you locate them. They typically charge L$100 per day per person.

If you do go sans guide, make it a habit to talk with every local you see, to double check that you're headed in the right direction. It's much slower going, but you'll have some good conversations and will be much less likely to veer too far, or for too long, off your path.

Hiking

Trails in the protected area form a large loop. Starting at **El Boquerón** community, the trail follows the Río Olancho through old-growth forest and passes several swimming holes. A half-hour detour leads to **Cueva de Tepisquintle**, prickled with stalagmites and stalactites – the path isn't well marked, but any passing local will be able to point you in the right direction. There are numerous butterfly and bird species visible here; while butterflies are most active in the hottest hours, birds emerge mostly at dawn and dusk.

The trail eventually leaves the riverbank and climbs up the main canyon to the small community of **La Avispa**. There are a few simple *comedores* if you get hungry – it takes most casual hikers around three hours to get here from the highway.

Locals in La Avispa can point you to the trail leading to **Cerro de Agua Buena** and the park's nuclear zone. The ascent is through a thick cloud forest, teeming with birds, including quetzals, toucans and mot-mots. The summit of Cerro de Agua Buena offers spectacular views of the protected zone.

Along the way you'll pass a temporary settlement, also called **Agua Buena**. Empty most of the year, the settlement swells between January and March for the *cosecha de café* (coffee harvest). If you're there then, many workers will be happy to chat, even to explain how coffee is cultivated and harvested. You can also buy simple meals of beans-and-rice from local families who have come for the season. From Agua Buena, a pleasant side hike is to the COHDEFOR (Honduran Corporation for Forest Development) radio antennae. *Campesinos* (farm workers) can point you in the right direction; a trail leads away from the coffee areas and deeper into the natural forest.

Otherwise, the trail continues over Cerro Agua Buena and winds down to the tiny hamlet of **El Bambú**, at last count just three families strong. From there it's a 45-minute walk down a rough dirt road back to El Boquerón.

Sleeping

You can camp for free at a number of points within the protected area. The zone near the community of Agua Buena, or near the summit of Cerro de Aqua Buena, are the most common spots.

Getting There & Away

Monumento Natural El Boquerón is halfway between Juticalpa and Catacamas. Any Juticalpa–Catacamas bus can drop you there (from either side L$15, 20 minutes).

CATACAMAS

pop 107,200

Deep in Olancho, where the pavement suddenly ends and 'the Wild' begins, is Catacamas – a small attractive city with a somewhat rough-and-tumble vibe. It is best known for the Cuevas de Talgua, where dozens of skulls left there more than 3000 years ago were discovered by amateur explorers in 1994. The skulls are off-limits but the cave is still a popular sight. More recently, Catacamas has been used as a jumping-off point for a machete-hacking ascent of La Picucha, the tallest mountain in the department and the centerpiece of the impressive Sierra de Agalta national park.

Orientation

There are no street signs in Catacamas; in fact you don't have to go far from the center for the streets to turn from pavement to dirt. The road from the highway into town is Calle Independencia, which quickly bumps into Parque Central. Just before reaching Parque Central, Calle Independencia intersects with Blvd La Mora, an impressive paved and divided roadway that extends, well, five or so blocks before turning to dirt. Three blocks down Blvd La Mora is a stoplight; to your right is the *mercado municipal* (city market), to your left is the road that leads to the steps up to La Cruzicita. Continuing straight at the stoplight brings you to the Cuevas de Talgua – a sign at the Independencia–La Mora intersection points the way.

To orient yourself, remember that Blvd La Mora runs east to west and Avenida Independencia north to south.

Information

BGA (🕒 8:30am-3:30pm Mon-Fri, to 11:30am Sat) Half a block from Hotel Papabeto, the BGA has an ATM and can extend cash advances on Visa cards.

Clínica Campos (☎ 799-5303; 🕒 24hr) Located just past the municipal market, opposite Plaza Monise.

COHDEFOR office (Honduran Corporation for Forest Development; 🕒 8am-4pm Mon-Fri) The director (see p103) is helpful and knowledgeable about the area, but he can be hard to track down.

Post office (Av Independencia; 🕒 8am-4pm Mon-Fri, to 11am Sat)

Sights & Activities

In town, the main sight is **La Cruzicita**, also known as Cerro de la Cruz. Follow the road straight past the COHDEFOR – you can't miss the long flight of green steps climbing the hillside to the cross and altar. It's a nice enough walk, with a great view of the city and surrounding countryside.

Ten kilometers outside of Catacamas is its main attraction, the **Cuevas de Talgua** (admission L$100, 🕒 9am-5pm, no entry after 4pm, closed Mon), a huge limestone cave system made famous by

A LIGHT IN THE DARK: THE SKULLS OF TALGUA

Six-hundred meters into the dark and then-undeveloped **Cuevas de Talgua** (Talgua caves), a group of two Hondurans and two Americans saw what appeared to be a chamber at the top of a wall. Standing on one another's shoulders they clambered up the wall and into history – literally.

What those amateur spelunkers found on that April 1994 day was an archaeological treasure trove: a cache of human skeletons, painted red and gathered into small bundles. And when they first trained their flashlights on the remains, the skulls seemed to glow eerily. The effect was caused by a layer of translucent calcite that had been deposited over the centuries by water dripping from the chamber's limestone roof – the same way stalactites are formed. The remarkable sight gave the spot its common name: los Craneos Brillantes de Talgua (the Glowing Skulls of Talgua).

To date, 23 deposits containing more than 200 skeletons have been discovered in these and nearby caves. By analyzing charcoal fragments found with the deposits – probably fallen from wood torches used while preparing the sites – archaeologists believe the remains date back an incredible 3000 years, to around 980 to 850 BC. Researchers have uncovered evidence of a densely populated village not far from the cave and theorize that the skeletons are the remains of that settlement's elite and were placed there as part of an elaborate secondary burial rite. Ironically, the calcite cap that makes the skeletons so distinctive also makes them extremely difficult to extract and study; most remain where they were found.

the discovery, in 1994, of hundreds of prehistoric skeletons arranged in chambers deep inside. Over the course of three millennia, water dripping from the roof encased the skeletons in a milky calcite that glows when lit up (above). There's an onsite **visitors center** (no phone; 9am-5pm, closed Mon) where you can arrange for a tour of the caves and get info on nearby hikes.

The area of the skeletons is closed to the public, unfortunately, but you can tour the cave up to that point. The 45-minute guided tour of the cave includes a more detailed account of the discovery and of the cave system itself, which is thought to be over 100 million years in the making. A small museum near the entrance has good displays (in Spanish only) of the area's geology, archaeology and present-day life. There is another cave a short distance away that your guide can take you to for a few extra lempiras.

Three tiny communities – Talgua Arriba, La Florida and Los Ángeles – are strung along a couple hours' hike from the visitors center. If you take the 6am bus from Catacamas, you can do some hiking and bird-watching before the cave opens; you'll avoid paying the rather inflated park fee, too. Calixto Ordóñez (p103) lives in Talgua Arriba and is an excellent guide. See p102 for information on reaching the caves.

La Cascada de los Jutes (Snail Shell Falls) is an 80m beauty within the Sierra de Agalta National Park. There are various places to swim along the way and the especially adventurous of the group can clamber up the waterfall's sheer rock face. Calixto Ordóñez (p103) guides this trip for L$150 per group.

You can also climb **Pico La Picucha** from Catacamas, thanks to a new route forged by Peace Corps volunteers and local guides. See p104 for details.

Sleeping & Eating

Hotel Colina (799-4488; s/d L$200/250; P) Located half a block south of Parque Central, this hotel opens onto a long, sparse courtyard. The rooms are dated but very clean, and have hot water, cable TV and fans – a good deal.

Hotel Juan Carlos (799-4212; s/d with fan L$250/350, r with air-con L$500; P) Located 1km down the road heading to the caves, and popular with conferences and visiting tour groups, the San Juan is large, modern, clean and forgettable. High-ceilinged rooms with ceramic floors and firm beds open onto two long, open-air corridors with a row of greenery in the middle.

Hotel Meyling (799-4746; Av Independencia; s/d/tr L$300/400/500; P) Located two blocks south of Parque Central, the Meyling is a modern hotel offering plain but spotless rooms with high ceilings, cable TV and in-room phone. A restaurant on-site offers three meals a day at very reasonable prices.

Hotel Papabeto (799-5060; hhgarciadiaz@yahoo.com; s/d L$600/700; P) The best hotel in town, with 10 large rooms, spotless bathrooms and lovely soft beds. There's a pool, complete with a swim-up bar, and breakfast is sometimes included in the fare. The restaurant here is worth checking out.

Taki-Mex (mains L$10-50; lunch & dinner) Two blocks west of Blvd La Mora on the road that leads to La Cruzicita, this corner restaurant serves good cheap Mexican and Honduran food in a spotless dining area.

Comedor Be-Tel (mains L$30-70; Parque Central; breakfast, lunch & dinner) This simple family-run *comedor* serves exactly what you'd expect it to – hello eggs and beans! – at plastic tables looking onto the central park.

Su Hogar Supermercado (8am-9pm) Stock up on supplies for a La Picucha climb at this large supermarket. To get here from the central park, go up a block on Av Independencia, turn right at the post office and walk another 2½ blocks.

Drinking

Olancho has a not-undeserved reputation as the 'Wild West' of Honduras, so the drinking scene here is necessarily a bit rowdy. Nights in Catacamas usually begin with tailgating at the Texaco (yes, as in the gas station), which puts up speakers and serves a mean Philly cheese steak. The party eventually moves to **Vaqueros** (Parque Central; 10pm-2am Thu-Sat), which has a small dance floor that gets packed Friday and Saturday night – it can get a little rough late at night.

Getting There & Away

Transportes Aurora and **Discovery** (☎ 899-4393, 222-4256) have a terminal on the road leading into town from the highway; it's a 15-minute walk from the center or a L$20 cab ride. Direct buses to Tegucigalpa (L$108, 3½ hours, every 30 minutes 5:45am to 4:45pm) pass Juticalpa on the way. Of the two lines, Discovery tends to be more comfortable.

Second-class buses shuttle between Catacamas and Juticalpa (L$20, 40 minutes, every 30 minutes 7:30am to 6pm). It's also pretty easy to catch a *jalón* (hitch) out on the highway.

There is no direct service to Gualaco. Instead take any Juticalpa/Tegucigalpa bus to the Gualaco turnoff (L$20, 45 minutes) which is notable for the large 'American' gas station at the corner. From here, wait for buses coming from Juticalpa, which pass hourly from 6am to 3:30pm.

For the Cuevas de Talgua (L$15, 30 minutes), a converted school bus leaves Catacamas at 6am, 11am and 3pm from a bus stop near Comercial Palmira, two blocks east and a block north of the stoplight on Blvd La Mora. The same bus leaves the caves at 7am, noon and 4pm. A taxi there should cost around L$150. You can usually hitch a ride all or part of the way there too.

PARQUE NACIONAL SIERRA DE AGALTA

The Sierra de Agalta range forms a steep, mountainous spine down the middle of Olancho, and extends (under a different name) nearly to the Caribbean Sea. Its forested flanks give rise to the Río Guayape to one side and the Río Grande on the other, both of which help nourish the massive Moskitia rainforest. The park protects an amazing range of climates and ecosystems – hiking here is tough, but certainly never dull.

Orientation

There are two main entrances to the Sierra de Agalta National Park – Gualaco and Catacamas – located on opposite sides of the protected area, separated by the jagged mountain spine that runs down its center.

Gualaco is the traditional and more frequently used entrance, especially for climbing La Picucha. The trail is better marked and maintained (though far from perfect) and the ascent is steep but manageable. Several one-day and overnight trips are also possible.

Catacamas is a more recent entry-point; climbing La Picucha from this side is steeper and more overgrown and much of the hike requires hacking through ground cover with a machete. Like Gualaco, the area has several shorter hikes as well.

Information

It is highly recommended that you have a guide for hikes of any length in Sierra de Agalta National Park. The trails are poorly maintained in places, grown over with brush and trees, and many paths that are visible are in fact hunting trails that do not lead where you'll be hoping they do. And if following the trail is hard, relocating it once you've gone off is even harder. You'll also need to bring along a fair amount of cash with you, as there is no bank in Gualaco.

JOURNEY INTO LA MOSKITIA & BEYOND

One of the truly great adventures in Honduras is rafting from Olancho down the Plátano or Patuca rivers, a one- to two-week journey through the heart of La Moskitia. Both trips offer unparalleled wildlife viewing and pristine rainforest experience, floating for days on end without seeing a single human trace. The rivers are sights unto themselves – the Patuca is the second-longest in Honduras (after the Río Coco) and the Plátano includes some legitimate Class III white water. Omega Tours and La Moskitia Ecoaventuras (in La Ceiba) offer both tours.

From Dulce Nombre de Culmí, it's a one- to two-day hike to the headwaters of the **Río Plátano**. From there, you paddle downriver for five to six days through the totally uninhabited biosphere reserve, with a good chance of spotting monkeys, river otter, tapir, deer and more. Side hikes to caves and waterfalls are possible. The river varies from wide and slow to narrow and roiling, and nights are spent camped on the beach. You eventually arrive at Las Marías, stopping at the petroglyphs along the way. The next day, you'll motorboat to Rais Ta and fly or overland out. Alternatively, you may be able arrange to stay on at Las Marías for extra hiking.

Most trips on the **Río Patuca** start outside of Juticalpa, where the Guayape and Guayambre rivers converge to form the Patuca. You paddle for six to seven days through Parque Nacional Patuca and Tawahka Biosphere Reserve, spending nights camped on the beach. There's great bird- and animal-spotting. Arrive at Krausirpe, the largest Tawahka community (all of 300 people!). Switch to a motorized canoe for the trip to Ahuas and catch a flight home. You can extend this by getting off at Wampusirpi, or flying to Belén for additional trips from there.

In Gualaco, **Ramón 'Moncho' Velíz** (☎ 789-2377, 9741-0026) does most of the guiding; he's a friendly, reliable guy who speaks a little English and knows the park well. **Francisco Urbina** (☎ 901-3400) is another good choice and, as head of the local COHDEFOR office, extremely knowledgeable on the area. However, his second job – evangelical minister – means he's very busy and can be hard to track down. Both charge around L$500 per day, plus food. The folks at Comedor Sharon (p105) can help locating either guide.

It's also worthwhile locating the local Peace Corps volunteer – just ask anyone where you can find *el voluntario de Cuerpo de Paz*. They have long served as the de facto tourism contact in town – in fact some bus drivers take it upon themselves to drop arriving backpackers at the current volunteer's front door.

For hikes from the Catacamas side, contact **Calixto Ordóñez** (☎ 9783-8259; calixtoo77@yahoo.com), an extremely reliable and enthusiastic man who has worked with Peace Corps volunteers on developing the Catacamas–Picucha route. Calixto lives in Talgua Arriba, a tiny hamlet about 1km past the Talgua caves – enter as you would to visit the park and follow the well-trodden path at the back of the visitors area. His house is across a small river, which you'll actually cross twice before arriving; ask as you go. He typically charges L$400 per day for La Picucha. He also offers a number of other hikes that take in activities including bird-watching (L$350), nearby waterfalls (L$400), a cave tour (L$350) and a tour of his own coffee farm (L$350).

Dangers & Annoyances

The biggest danger in the park is getting lost, which is why guides are recommended for hikes of any length. River and spring water is fairly abundant, at least on the Gualaco side, but you should fill up whenever possible, always using a filter or purification pills. Bring a change of dry clothes including a warm layer for night-time.

Do not attempt this hike if it has rained in the last two days as the trail gets extremely muddy and the rivers may be too high to ford safely.

Sights & Activities

Climbing La Picucha is, of course, the main draw, but there are several shorter hikes along the edges of the park, starting from either Catacamas (p100) or Gualaco (p105) that let you explore the area without taking on such a difficult climb. See those sections for details.

La Picucha is a mother of a mountain and, at 2354m, the highest point in Olancho. It is most commonly climbed from the Gualaco side, a difficult three- to four-day hike.

ASK A LOCAL: THINGS TO KNOW BEFORE CLIMBING LA PICUCHA

The journey here is intense and the route is completely beautiful. People should bring along a backpack, camping tent, [water filter or purification tablets] and a sleeping bag. The other stuff you can buy here. The trip takes three or four days for a young, fit person, a bit more if you are stopping frequently. People will run across several types of forest along the way, and will have the chance to see monkeys and quetzals, among other animals. While you can climb it year-round, the summer is best, but it can get hot. As far as safety, it's best to go with three to four people tops per guide. And there haven't been any assaults or robberies in the area.

Ramón 'Moncho' Velí is a guide extraordinaire

CLIMBING LA PICUCHA FROM GUALACO

The trail starts about 16km north of town, near the village of El Pacayal. From a small road sign reading 'Sendero a La Picucha', it's 1½ hours of level and moderately inclined hiking to the official park entrance. From here, it's another hour and a half – and at least two river crossings – to the first campsite. The site runs alongside the Río Sol (good for a swim) and has a tin-roofed shelter and fire ring.

For those summit-bound, you may want to make it a bit further so the following day isn't so long; however, the second campsite is a good five to six hours further on. Fortunately, there are several decent places between the two camps to pitch a tent and refill your water bottle. This part of the trail climbs steadily and is hard to follow in places; the second campsite is also somewhat hidden, below and to the right of the trail. The next day, leave your gear at the second campsite and head for the summit, another two to three hours of tough climbing through a dripping cloud forest. It's beautiful but so steep in places you'll be using branches and tree roots to pull yourself up. At the very top is a bizarre *bosque enano* (dwarf forest) and stunning views of the forested, cloud-wisped valleys below. It's possible to camp on the summit but that would mean dragging your pack and supplies up here as well – no easy task.

CLIMBING LA PICUCHA FROM CATACAMAS

Since 2003, Peace Corps volunteers in Catacamas have worked with local guides to forge a path, though it remains a very tough adventure route.

The hike from the Catacamas side is easier to describe – stay close to your guide and just keep going up. The first day starts at the Cuevas de Talgua, passing the cluster of homes known as Talgua Arriba about 15 minutes past the visitors center (guide Calixto Ordóñez lives here) and La Florida in another 1½ hours. From there it's five hours of steady climbing on a well-marked path to the first camp. Dubbed *el Hotel de Lujo,* it is anything but a 'Hotel of Luxury', with rough-hewn wood walls, dirt floor and no latrine. The setting, however, could hardly be more beautiful: a thick tropical forest teeming with howler monkeys, toucans and quetzals.

Day two is when things get tough: a full day of slow, steady climbing with all your gear while your guide hacks a path through the underbrush. Starting early, you can get to the summit by 2pm, with time to set up camp amid the dwarf forest and explore the summit area. The following day you should be able to make it all the way back to the Cuevas de Talgua visitors center and the bus back to Catacamas.

Sleeping

Climbing La Picucha takes a minimum of two days and most people take three or four – in any case, you'll be spending at least one or more nights on the trail. Ideally you should have your own camping gear; if not, guide Francisco Urbina (p103) rents some basic equipment but, as he's hard to get a hold of, you can't depend on it. The Peace Corps volunteers in either Gualaco or Catacamas town may be able to help, but again it's no sure thing.

On the Catacamas side, you can stay overnight at guide Calixto Ordóñez's house (see p103), where there's a simple room with cement floor, tin roof and space for six (L$120), or you can pitch a tent nearby (L$40 per person). In either case, it's latrine toilet only; bring a flashlight and candles. Calixto's wife will make simple meals for a few extra lempiras too.

You also can camp at the Talgua Caves visitors center (p101) for as many days as you like, for the price of admission. It's not as homey as at Calixto's, but you do have access to the center's flush toilets.

Getting There & Away

You can access the park from Gualaco or Catacamas. For more details on getting to Gualaco see p106, or for Catacamas, see p102.

GUALACO

pop 23,300

This tiny, dirt-road town lies at the foot of the Sierra de Agalta National Park and has been the site of bitter and sometimes violent conflict between environmentalists and loggers/developers. For travelers, it is most notable as a point of departure for a multi-day hike up La Picucha.

Orientation & Information

At the town entrance is a triangular intersection known simply as *el triángulo;* Parque Central is just beyond there. There is an internet cafe, **Cibermass** (Parque Central; internet per hr L$20; 8am-9pm), that also offers telephone service to the US (L$5 per minute). Unfortunately there is no bank in town – take out money in Juticalpa or San Francisco de la Paz.

Sights & Activities

Gualaco is best known to travelers as the main jumping-off point for climbing **Pico La Picucha**, the highest mountain in Olancho department. See opposite for details on climbing the peak from Gualaco, or taking an even more challenging route from Catacamas. **La Chorrera** is a pretty little waterfall a short distance from the first campsite on the Gualaco–La Picucha trail. A nice one-night trip would be to hike here in the morning, pitch your tent at the campsite and spend the afternoon relaxing by the falls.

Would-be spelunkers can get some thrills at the **Cuevas de Susmay**, a series of caves, each known according to its prevailing feature: Water, Sand and Dry (not to be confused with Earth, Wind and Fire). The Water cave has a large cavern a short distance inside, but to get there you have to wade and swim through the bone-chillingly cold river that gives the cave its name. Around your ankles swim tiny black fish while overhead sleep thousands of bats – not for the faint of heart. Dry cave is a short but steep clamber above Water cave and has two entrances. Sand cave is also nearby, its floor covered in ankle-deep sand.

Just finding the entrances can be a little tricky – you'll walk about 90 minutes toward the village of Jicalapa, then cut through two pastures to a short forest path that leads to the cave entrances. It's recommended that you go with a guide, especially if you are interested in entering the caves. The local Peace Corps volunteer may well be free to take you, or can set you up with a guide. You can also ask at Comedor Sharon (below); in fact, one of the pastures you have to cut through belongs to the same family.

North of Gualaco on the road to San Esteban, the **Chorros de Babilonia** were once a beautiful series of eight waterfalls tumbling 50m down; a dam built upriver has left the falls a wisp of their former selves and not really worth the effort. The dam was deeply controversial when it was approved in 2001 – among other things, opponents argued it would ruin the falls while developers insisted it would not. One of the dam's most outspoken opponents, 28-year-old Carlos Roberto Flores, was gunned down in 2001 in his home in broad daylight.

Sleeping & Eating

The establishments listed here are all located on the highway.

Hotel Mi Palacio (r/tw L$150/200; P) Opened in 2005, the 12 rooms in this place still seem brand new; they've got gleaming tile floors, nice hot-water bathrooms, firm beds, fans and big TVs. Look for the peach building just past *el triángulo*.

Hotel Los Encuentros (913-7918; s/d L$150/250, r with air-con L$350; P) Just a few hundred meters from Mi Palacio, this hotel has five rooms over a hardware store and several out back around a gravel parking lot. The latter are less appealing, but have air-con. All are smallish but very clean, with new beds and a bright pink paint job. To stay the night – and to buy barbed wire – stop in the hardware store.

Restaurante El Muelle (mains L$30-100; breakfast, lunch & dinner) A favorite among locals, mostly because of the variety – customers can choose from smoked pork chops, sausage, steak, fried chicken and even fish – this eatery is located in a bright yellow house with pillars, facing *el triángulo*.

Comedor Sharon (mains L$40-70; breakfast, lunch & dinner) A large, dimly lit eatery serving *típico* at wood tables covered with red tablecloths.

Photos of area hikes are mounted on the wall and owners Santiago and Delicias have helped many travelers find guides and make arrangements for climbing La Picucha.

Getting There & Away

Buses come and go from *el triángulo* on the highway. Buses to Juticalpa (L$50, two hours) leave at 6:45am, 7am, 8am, 9am, 10am, noon, 1pm, 2pm and 4pm. There is no direct service to Catacamas; instead take any Juticalpa bus to the highway intersection (L$50, two hours, look for the 'American' gas station) and wait for a Catacamas bus there (L$20, 45 minutes, last bus at around 5pm).

From Juticalpa, take any Gualaco-, San Esteban- or Trujillo-bound bus from the 2nd-class bus station. Between the three, there's a bus leaving roughly every hour from 5:30am to 3pm.

Two ordinary buses leave daily for Tegucigalpa at 5:40am and 7am (L$100, five hours) and at least one bus a day passes by en route from Trujillo. The quickest route to the capital is to go to Juticalpa first and catch a direct bus from there.

LA UNIÓN

pop 8600

La Unión is a small, typical Honduran mountain town, nestled into a valley surrounded by pine-covered mountains. It's the gateway to Parque Nacional La Muralla and makes a convenient stopover on the scenic route between Tegucigalpa and Trujillo.

A note of caution: La Unión isn't particularly dangerous, but the long, lonely highway on either side of it has a reputation for highway robberies. Police say the problem has abated, but do not stop for strangers, or drive in the area alone or at night.

Activities

Although the main attraction here is La Muralla National Park, there are a couple other worthwhile jaunts you can take. **El Chorrón** is a pleasant and refreshing waterfall, only about 6m high but with a fine swimming hole at the bottom. To get there take the road to La Muralla until it crosses a small river, the Río Camote. The falls are 150m along the river from there. You also can hike to the nearby village of **Los Encuentros** (4km) where many houses are decorated with interesting hand-painted designs. If you're there during the sugar-cane harvest in March, you may be able to see old wooden *trapiches* (ox-driven sugar mills) in use.

Sleeping & Eating

Hotel Karol (s/d with shared bathroom L$60/90) Basic rooms surround a shady courtyard – brace for avocados crashing onto the corrugated tin roof. Cleanish, shared bathrooms have padded seats, perhaps the only ones in the country. There's no sign, but the building is painted purple. It's two blocks south of the *iglesia,* across from BanhCafé.

Hotel La Muralla (r L$60) is another suitable option.

There are a handful of *comedores* and street food stands around Parque Central that serve fried chicken and other standard fare, plus hot drinks in the early morning.

Getting There & Away

Bus traffic is decidedly light in La Unión, especially in the afternoon. Arrival/departure times might vary with the weather, the day or the mood of the driver. Wherever you're headed, you'll likely have one to three transfers, so get an early start to avoid getting stuck in the middle of nowhere.

From Tegucigalpa, take a Juticalpa-bound bus and transfer at Limones (L$40, two hours). From Juticalpa, only two buses go to La Unión (L$70, 3½ hours, noon and 1pm) or take any bus to Limones and transfer.

To Tegucigalpa, one direct bus leaves La Unión around 5am, or take a Limones bus and transfer. Alternatively, two Tegus-bound buses from Sonaguera pass La Unión at 9am-ish and 11am-ish (L$120, five hours).

For the north coast, take the 6:45am bus that's bound for Olanchito (L$70, 3½ hours); transfer at Mamé to reach La Ceiba (L$40, two hours); to reach Trujillo continue to Olanchito, where you can catch a direct bus, or connect through Savá and Tocoa.

PARQUE NACIONAL LA MURALLA

Deep in the heart of Olancho, **Parque Nacional La Muralla** used to be one of the gems of the national park system – a spectacular virgin cloud forest and a well-organized COHDEFOR office that did a good job maintaining trails, cabins, camping sites, even a youth guide service. For a number of reasons – not the least of which was ongoing and sometimes violent conflict between environmentalists and illegal loggers – the visitors center was closed and maintenance halted.

The park remains a gorgeous piece of the planet. Owing to the ship-shape condition of the park before the problems started, it is still, in fact, in pretty good shape.

Information

The COHDEFOR office in La Unión and the visitors center at the park entrance were closed indefinitely at the time of research. It's worth stopping by both, in case they have since reopened. You may be able to hire a guide in La Unión for about L$200 per trip. Be sure to bring along a sweater or jacket, good hiking boots and rain gear; it's quite cool in the park. You can likely camp out by the visitors center or stay in a hotel in La Unión, and you'll need to bring your own food, water and supplies.

Sights & Activities

Four well-maintained trails start at or near the visitors center – at least one short loop is relatively easy to follow, though the longer trails have started to fade, criss-crossed by fallen trees and branches, or swallowed up by fast-growing bamboo. Toucanettes and quetzals can be seen from certain spots on the trails. February is the best time for seeing birds; you'll see the most wildlife if you come early in the morning.

Getting There & Away

The park entrance and visitors center is a long 14km from La Unión along a good dirt road. It's uphill the entire way, so allow at least four hours to walk it. If you stay a night in La Unión, you usually can hitch a ride on pickups carrying coffee workers beginning at 5:30am; the stop is several blocks north of the park so ask to be sure you're in the right place. A taxi will cost upwards of L$500. A ride back can be trickier, especially if you're making this a day trip: ask the driver in the morning when the last truck returns, but in general you should be on the road with your thumb out by 1pm or plan on hoofing it.

OLANCHITO

pop 96,300

This tidy agricultural town has very little in the way of tourist attractions but can be a good stopover on your way to or from the interior. It has a surprisingly pretty Parque Central, with well-tended plants, and paths and benches beneath large leafy trees. A charming little church completes the scene. **Banco Atlántida** (1a Av; 8:30am-3:30pm Mon-Fri, to 11:30am Sat) has an ATM and is located on the main road into town, across from the Esso gas station.

Hotel Colonial (446-6972; 1a Av NE; r with shared bathroom L$120; s/d with air-con L$250/300; P) is your best bet in town for accommodations. You can also try across the street at the **Hotel Olimpic** (446-2487; 1a Av NE; s/d L$200/250, r with air-con L$300; P). Food is available at **Comidas Rapidas El Centro** (Parque Central; mains L$30-70; breakfast, lunch & dinner) across the street from the *iglesia*.

Christina (446-2861) has a terminal three blocks south and one block west of the stoplight on the main drag. First class buses to Tegucigalpa (L$250, nine hours) leave at 4:10am and 7am Monday to Saturday and at 7am and 9am on Sunday.

All other buses leave from the main terminal, half a block from the Dippsa gasoline station on the main drag.

Bus services include:

La Celba (*directo* L$217, two hours; *ordinario* L$200, three hours, every 30 to 60 minutes 5:30am-3pm)
La Unión Take any Tocoa or Trujillo bus and transfer at *desvío* (turnoff) Sococo.
San Pedro Sula (L$155, 5½ hours; 10 departures between 3am & 12:45pm, plus 2pm Saturday & Sunday)
Tocoa (L$40; 1½ hours, 10 departures 7am to 5:30pm)
Trujillo Take any Tocoa bus and transfer.
Yoro (L$70, three hours, 5am, 10am & 3:45pm)

Western Honduras

Honduras' rich past is remarkably evident here. You see it in the faces of the Lenca farmers as they head out at dawn to work the earth, in the expressionist gaze of the Maya carvings at the Copán archaeological site, and in the natural cycle that smites out death and decay each year with new growth in the wildlife reserves protecting the region's forests and mountains.

For the intrepid explorer, there are mountain romps in the pine and cloud forests of Montaña de Celaque National Park, and early-dawn bird-watching excursions in Parque Nacional Cerro Azul Meámbar and around the nearby Lago de Yojoa. And while most travelers end up spending the majority of their Western Honduran time ascending bird-towers, visiting butterfly farms and tromping through the tunnels and mysterious pyramids of Copán, it's definitely worth your while to extend your trip in the region for a few days, maybe even a few weeks, leaving time to visit the small whitewashed villages along the Ruta Lenca, witness the unique pageantry of the Semana Santa processions at Comayagua or venture further afield to towns and wild areas still untouched by the tourist trail.

Trips to the region generally begin and end in the crowded city environs of San Pedro Sula. It's not the prettiest – or safest – city in the world. But there are a few nearby sights and city-bound cultural attractions worth checking out before you put your nose to the wind and head out into the unspoiled wilds of this unique region.

HIGHLIGHTS

- Spirit yourself through tunnels and up ancient stairways in Honduras' only major Maya site, **Copán archaeological site** (p126)
- Hold your breath and watch your step as you tread lightly through the excellent bird-watching territories around the mist-shrouded **Lago de Yojoa** (p151).
- Find yourself on the **Ruta Lenca** (p133), where you can climb Honduras' highest peak in **Parque Nacional Montaña de Celaque** (p141) or simply get away from it all in the traditional whitewashed pueblos of **La Campa** (p143) and **San Manuel de Colohete** (p145)
- Leave **San Pedro Sula** (opposite) – it's the smartest move you'll make all day!
- Ascend to spiritual heights at **Comayagua's Semana Santa** (p160) celebration, where intricate *alfombras* (colorful sawdust carpets with religious iconography) mark the righteous path.

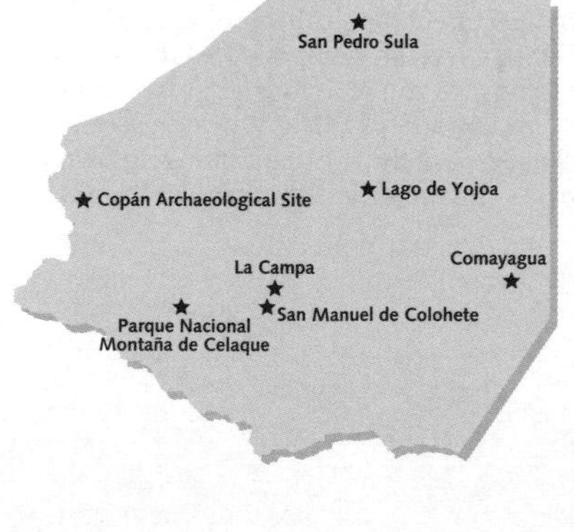

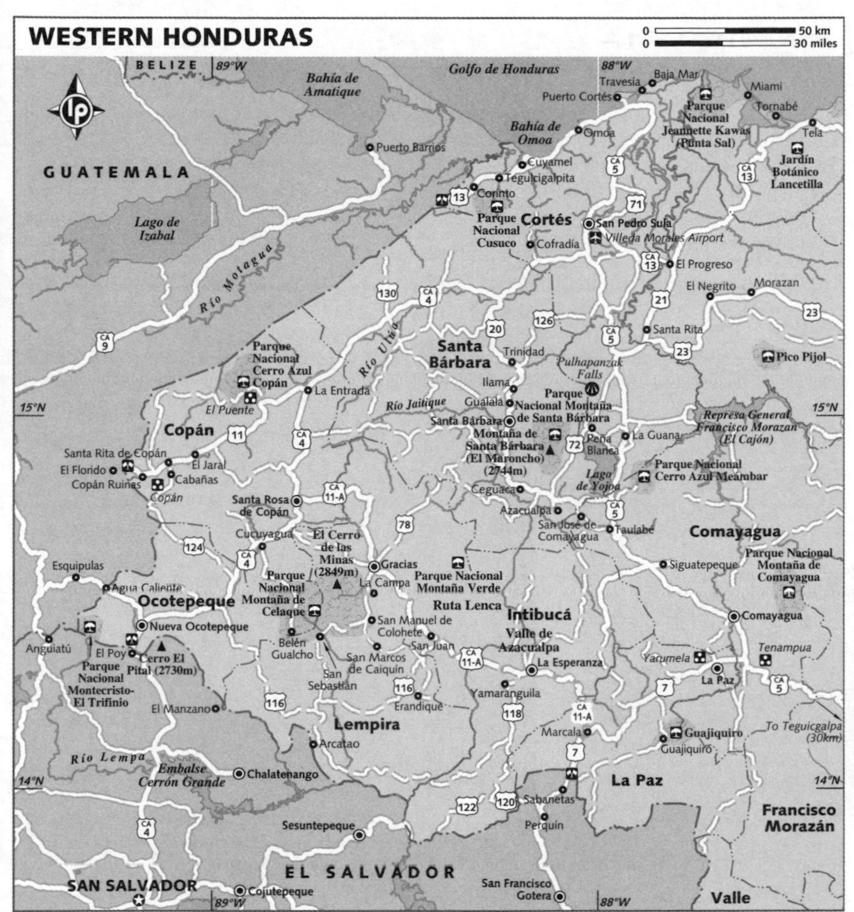

SAN PEDRO SULA

pop 710,000

There's nothing really pretty about San Pedro Sula. There's a lot of pollution, it's dangerous (especially at night), and there are few museums or other urban attractions to make it worth your while. Go figure that most people leave Honduras' second city as soon as possible.

But with most international flights coming through here (it really is the easiest entry point into the country), you're bound to spend at least a day here. So might as well enjoy the modern conveniences that this manufacturing city has to offer – malls, good restaurants, some decent museums and neighboring open-space, and plenty of air-conditioning – before you head out for your next adventure.

San Pedro can get extremely hot and humid, especially April to September. The rain starts around May, which helps cool things off.

HISTORY

San Pedro Sula – originally named San Pedro de Puerto Caballos – was founded by Pedro de Alvarado in June 1536. Located near the Río Chamelecón, the town was an important commercial center, where goods from the interior – cocoa, indigo, leather, sarsaparilla – were collected before being sent to Spain.

Unfortunately, San Pedro's wealth attracted pirates who repeatedly sailed up the Río Chamelecón to attack and loot the town;

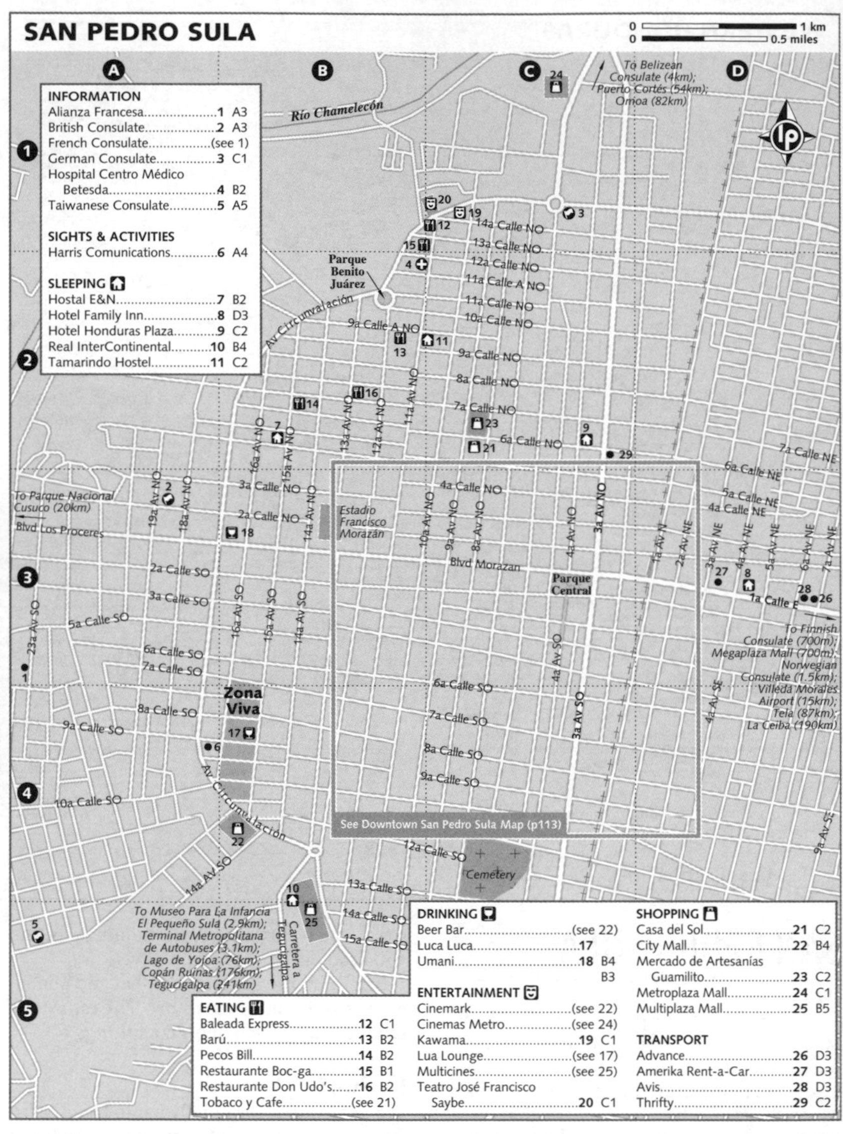

it was finally sacked and burned in the 17th century. The town's survivors moved south to Azula, an indigenous village, to restart. The new site – renamed San Pedro Sula – is where the city stands today.

During the 20th century, San Pedro Sula experienced a rapid boom. The population, 5000 in 1900 and 21,000 in 1950, increased to 150,000 by 1975. At the time of research, the estimated population was 710,100. This growth is due to the more than 200 factories that are headquartered in San Pedro Sula; they have attracted Hondurans with little to no job prospects in the rest of the country. The city's population continues to grow at a rate of 5% to 7% each year.

The growth of the city has also brought crime, air pollution and AIDS. San Pedro Sula bears the unfortunate distinction of being the AIDS capital of Central America; whereas Honduras has only 20% of Central America's population, it has 32% of its AIDS cases. A third of these are in San Pedro Sula. Suffice to say that practicing safe sex is extremely important, and nowhere more than here.

ORIENTATION

San Pedro Sula is belted by Av Circunvalación – a large boulevard that has shopping centers, gas stations, banks and fast-food restaurants. Inside the beltway, streets are divided between *avenidas* (avenues; abbreviated to Av), which run north–south, and *calles* (streets), which run east–west. The numbering begins where 1a Av and 1a Calle meet in the center of the city. From that point, the numbered *avenidas* and *calles* extend in four directions: northeast (*noreste;* NE), northwest (*noroeste;* NO), southeast (*sureste;* SE) and southwest (*suroeste;* SO). As a result, every address is given in relation to a numbered *calle* or *avenida,* and is further specified by the quadrant that it lies in.

Parque Central, two blocks west of the 1a Av–1a Calle axis point, is truly the city center. It's a pleasant bustling place, with a number of good places to eat, cool off with an ice cream, or people-watch over a cup of coffee.

INFORMATION

Cultural Centers

Centro Cultural Sampedrano (Map p113; ☎ 553-3911; 3a Calle NO near 3a AV NO; 🕑 9am-noon & 1-6pm Mon-Sat) Sponsors theater productions and art exhibits, and offers long-term art and music courses.

Alianza Francesa (Alliance Française; Map p110; ☎ 553-1178; www.afhonduras.com; 23a Av SO btwn 5a & 9a Calles SO) Offers cultural events and French-language courses.

Emergency

Tourist police (Map p113; ☎ 550-3472; 12a Av NO at 1a Calle O; 🕑 24hr)

Internet Access

Many hotels now have wi-fi, and the town's malls all have internet cafes. You can make international calls from most internet cafes.

Internet y más (Map p113; 5a Calle SO btwn 7a & 8a Avs SO; per hr L$20)

Diosita.net (Map p113; Parque Central; per hr L$25) Behind Dunkin' Donuts.

Laundry

Lavandería Jil (Map p113; 4a Calle NO btwn 7a & 8a Avs NO; 🕑 7am-6pm Mon-Sat) Wash and dry for L$75 a load.

Medical Services

Hospital Centro Médico Betesda (Map p110; ☎ 516-0900; 11a Ave NO btwn 11a & 12a Calles NO; 🕑 24hr)

Super Farmacia Siman (Map p113; ☎ 553-0321; 6a Calle SO btwn 5a & 6a Avs SO; 🕑 8-11am & 2:30-6pm Mon-Fri)

Money

All of the city's malls have banks (open 10am to 6pm Monday to Saturday) with ATMs.

BAC/Credomatic 5a Av (Map p113; 5 Av NO btwn 1a & 2a Calles NO; 🕑 8am-7pm Mon-Fri, to 2pm Sat); Airport (🕑 9am-5pm Mon-Fri, to noon Sat) Exchanges traveler's checks and has 24 hour ATMs.

Post

Post office (Map p113; ☎ 552-3185; 9a Calle SO at 3a Av SO; 🕑 7:30am-6pm Mon-Fri, 8am-noon Sat)

Tours

Fundacion Ecologigoca HR Pastor (☎ 557-6598; fundeco@netsys.hn; 12a Av NO at 1a Calle; 🕑 8am-noon & 1-5pm Mon-Fri, 8am-noon Sat) May have some useful information for trips to nearby Parque Nacional Cusuco.

Travel Agencies

Arrecife Tours (Map p113; ☎ 207-4081; www.arrecifetours.com; 7a Av SO btwn 1a Calle O & 2a Calle SO; 🕑 8am-5pm Mon-Fri, to noon Sat)

Mundirama (Map p113; ☎ 550-0490; www.mundiramatravel.com; 2a Calle SO btwn 2a & 3a Avs SO; 🕑 8am-5pm Mon-Fri, to noon Sat)

DANGERS & ANNOYANCES

San Pedro Sula has a serious crime and gang problem, but it's perfectly possible to enjoy the city's offerings if you just use some basic common sense. Use taxis after dark (especially in the downtown area) and avoid buying drugs or getting way too blotto at the nightclub. The municipal buses are also best avoided. If you are subjected to a stick-up, however, the safest thing to do is cooperate and not resist.

COURSES

Harris Communications (Map p110; ☎ 552-2705; Av Circunvalación & 9a Calle SO) Offers expensive (L$11,400 per month) Spanish tutoring. There's a one-month minimum.

DAY TRIPPING TO PARQUE NACIONAL CUSUCO

Just 45km from San Pedro Sula, but remarkably difficult to access, **Parque Nacional Cusuco** (admission L$200; 8am-4:30pm) is a cloud forest nestled in the impressive Merendón mountain range. The park has abundant wildlife, including parrots, toucans and a large population of quetzals, best spotted from April to June. Its highest peak is Cerro Jilinco (2242m). The park's visitors center is the starting point for five different **hiking** trails. Two trails – Quetzal and Las Minas – pass waterfalls and swimming holes. Guides can be hired at the visitors center for around L$100 per trip.

Access to the park is very difficult. From San Pedro Sula, take an early bus west to Cofradía (L$15, 45 minutes, every 10 minutes from 5:50am) in time to catch a pickup at Parque Central for the rough ride to the village of Buenos Aires (1½ hours, morning only). From there you'll have to rent a car, hitch a ride or walk to the visitors center – it's 20 minutes by car, an hour on foot.

You can camp at the visitors center, though there are no services there. Otherwise, **Fundación Ecologista HR Pastor** (557-6598; fundeco@netsys.hn; 12a Av NO at 1a Calle; 8am-noon & 1-5pm Mon-Fri, 8am-noon Sat) manages a very simple **cabaña** (r per person L$300) in Buenos Aires.

Merendón Adventures (984-0719; www.hikinghonduras.com) offers one- and two-day guided excursions in the park.

WESTERN HONDURAS

SIGHTS & ACTIVITIES

San Pedro's **cathedral** (Map p113; Parque Central) is worth peeking into. Opening times vary.

Don't let its '70s look fool you: the **Museo de Antropología e Historia de San Pedro Sula** (Map p113; 557-1496; 3a Av NO at 4a Calle NO; admission L$38; 9am-4pm Mon-Sat, to 3pm Sun, closed Tue) is an excellent museum that walks visitors through the changes in the Valle de Sula from the pre-Columbian era to the modern day.

The **Museo de la Naturaleza** (Map p113; 557-6598; 1a Calle O near 12a Av NO; admission L$20; 8am-4pm Mon-Fri, to noon Sat) has over 80 exhibits that cover the gamut of natural history, from paleontology and human biology to ecology and the universe. The level of detail is on a par with a college textbook, which can get a bit old given the signs are in Spanish. If the door's closed, enquire around the corner at the Fundación Ecologista HR Pastor (p111).

More a children's learning center than a museum, the **Museo Para La Infancia El Pequeño Sula** (off Map p110; 556-5114; sulaykili@yahoo.es; Carr a Tegucigalpa; adult/child L$40/20; 3-5pm Mon-Fri) offers monthly workshops in the sciences and arts. It's 3km from Av Circunvalación.

FESTIVALS & EVENTS

The **Feria Juniana**, a celebration in honor of the city's patron saint, is one of the biggest parties in Honduras. It takes place the entire last week of June, when San Pedranos hit the streets to dance, eat and watch cultural performances. The height of the *feria* is on June 29, when a huge parade makes its way down Av Circunvalación.

SLEEPING

The city's nicest hotels are near the malls but removed from downtown. Several budget options are just south of Parque Central, but the area can get dodgy at night.

Budget

Hotel Marina No 1 (Map p113; 557-2953; 6a Calle SO near 6a Av SO; r with shared bathroom & fan/air-con L$150/250; P) Numero 1 has horrific shared bathrooms and dark, hot rooms. But it is cheap.

Hotel San Jose (Map p113; 557-1208; 6a Av SO btwn 5a & 6a Calles SO; s/d/tr L$150/196/252) Don't be turned off by the prison-like exterior of this beat-and-cheap hotel. The rooms are actually decent. The sheets are clean, though the pillows are dirty, and you get a private shower that's actually fairly well bleached.

Tamarindo Hostel (Map p110; 557-0123; www.tamarindohostel.com; 9a Calle A NO btwn 10a & 11a Avs NO; dm L$200, r with air-con L$760; P) The best spot in town to meet fellow travelers, this unique hostel also has some of the best bunk rooms in all of Honduras. The cold-water private rooms probably aren't worth the price. There's also a huge fully equipped kitchen for guests. Linens, towels, soap, a locker and internet access are included in the daily rate. The hostel's owners are super friendly, we only wish the same could be said for their staff. A shared water jug would be nice, too.

our pick Hotel Real (Map p113; ☎ 550-7929; www.hotelrealhn.com; 6a Av SO btwn 6a & 7a Calles SO; s with fan L$323, s/d with air-con L$475/532; ❄ 💻) Without a doubt, this is the best downtown hotel for budget travelers. A welcoming place with hand-carved furnishings, Lencan pottery and lots of hanging plants, the rooms are a real surprise. A good one. Few things are better at the end of the day than a comfortable bed, cable TV, a sparkling bathroom and charming decor. The only downers are the cold-water showers and the sketchy location. It's fine by day, but cab it at night.

Hotel Marina No 3 (Map p113; ☎ 557-8722; 3a Calle SO btwn 5a & 6a Avs SO; r L$350-500; P ❄) Far better than Numero Uno, 'The Tres' has private bathrooms and air-con. The beds are spongy and the pillows feel a bit like day-old porridge, but the bathrooms are clean and you get hot water. This said, these are no great shakes, and you'll do much better at the Hotel Real.

Midrange

Hostal E&N (Map p110; ☎ 552-5731; www.hostaleyn.com; 15a Av NO at 5a Calle NO; s/d incl breakfast L$855/950; P ❄ 💻) This converted home is a bit Brady Bunch, but nonetheless a comfortable option in a quiet upscale neighborhood. Rooms all have hardwood floors, thin pillows, oddly odiferous hot-water bathrooms, cable TV and free in-room internet access.

Hotel Family Inn (Map p110; ☎ 552-1508; www.hotelfamilyinn.com; 1a Calle Este btwn 4a & 5a Calle NE; s/d incl breakfast L$950/1102) With a low-class, Willy

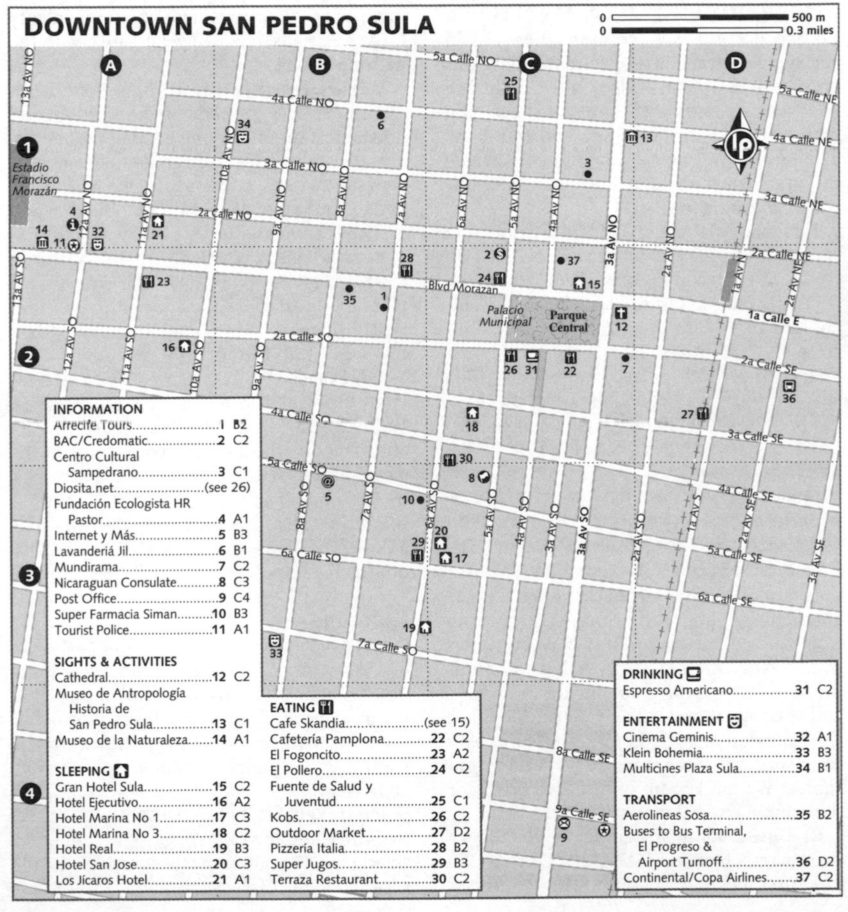

Loman–breakdown feel, the Family Inn has large, clean rooms and is well located for drivers passing through. Those on foot should look elsewhere.

Top End

Hotel Ejecutivo (Map p113; ☎ 552-4289; www.hotel-ejecutivo.com; 2a Calle SO at 10a Av SO; s/d/tr incl breakfast L$1212/1425/1653; P) This classic businessperson's hotel is spacious, tastefully decorated, sparkling clean and equipped with the amenities you'd expect: cable TV, air-conditioning, in-room telephone, internet access and a small rooftop gym (with a fantastic view of the mountains, no less). If you like cityscapes, ask for a room on the 5th floor.

Hotel Honduras Plaza (Map p110; ☎ 553-2424; www.hotelhondurasplaza.net; 4a Av NO at 6a Calle NO; s/d/tr incl breakfast L$1254/1463/1596; P) Greco-Roman decor – well, columns, heavy gold curtains and overstuffed furniture – make this hotel unique in San Pedro Sula. You'll find good-sized rooms with scratchy sheets, big bathrooms, air-conditioning and minibars. The company was building a hotel across the street when we passed through. Might be worth checking out.

Los Jícaros Hotel (Map p113; ☎ 550-0715; www.usula.com; 11a Av NO at 2a Calle NO; s/d incl breakfast L$1322/1432; P) Opened in early 2006, Los Jícaros is just six blocks west of Parque Central – far enough to be in a decent part of town but close enough for it to be an easy stroll there. Everything in the dark rooms is brand-spanking new – the tiles, the beds, the TVs, the furniture, the 'Frankenstein' shower fixtures. It's attractive but also kind of sterile, like a showroom.

Gran Hotel Sula (Map p113; ☎ 545-2600; www.hotelsula.hn; Parque Central, 1a Calle O btwn 3a & 4a Avs NO; s/d incl breakfast L$2314/2534, ste incl breakfast L$2534-2755; P) The rooms aren't worth the price of admission, but they are comfortable enough, and you are right on Parque Central. South-facing rooms have balconies overlooking the park, city hall and cathedral – ask for a top floor for the best view and least street noise. The view on the other side, overlooking the hotel's pool and leafy courtyard, isn't too shabby either – there you should ask for a room on the 2nd floor, for the double-size balconies.

Real InterContinental (Map p110; ☎ 553-0000; www.intercontinental.com; r from L$2850; P) The top hotel in town, but not as glamorous as the InterContinental in Tegucigalpa, this place still exudes a cool elegance, from the understated lobby to the thick, crisply folded towels in the bathrooms. The pool is only average – the one surprise in this otherwise 1st-class hotel. It's just off Av Circunvalación, next to Metroplaza Mall.

EATING

Budget

Outdoor Market (Map p113; 1Av S) Come here to pick up everything from belts to *baleadas* (flour tortilla smeared with beans and melted butter).

Baleada Express (Map p110; 14a Calle NO at Av Circunvalación; mains L$12-30; 7am-noon & 4-10:30pm Mon-Sat, 4-10:30pm Sun) The *sencilla* (simple) *baleada* has just beans and cream, but the huge array of options here, including plenty for vegetarians, lets you get creative with the national snack.

Cafetería Pamplona (Map p113; Parque Central, 2a Calle SO; mains L$50-150; breakfast, lunch & dinner) A good honest restaurant serving good honest meals. There's nothing spectacular about the menu – club sandwiches, chicken and rice, garlic fillet of fish, and a few daily specials – but the food is always good and service always friendly.

Pizzería Italia (Map p113; ☎ 550-7094; Blvd Morazan & 7a Av; dishes L$60-120; 10am-10pm, Tue-Sun) This place has great pizza and a funky hole-in-the-wall atmosphere. It got its start in 1976, when SPS was a fifth the size.

Café Skandia (Map p113; ☎ 552-9999; Parque Central, 1a Calle O btwn 3a & 4a Avs NO; mains L$60-200; 24hr) In Gran Hotel Sula, Skandia is surprisingly pleasant for a hotel restaurant; you can sit in the air-conditioned dining area or at shaded tables by the pool. The menu includes Honduran standbys – eggs, fried fish, roast chicken – plus a bunch of items you rarely see, like waffles, onion rings, apple pie and milkshakes.

Midrange

Pecos Bill (Map p110; ☎ 557-5744; 15 Av NO btwn 6a & 7a Calles NO; mains L$95-180; lunch & dinner Tue-Sun, lunch Mon) They do all kinds of grillin' in this large open-air restaurant with a Texas showdown theme. Movies or sports are shown on the giant TV every night – dinner and a movie all in one.

Terraza Restaurant (Map p113; ☎ 550-3108; 6a Av SO btwn 4a & 5a Calles SO; mains L$100-200; breakfast, lunch & dinner) Don't be put off by the location – inside a budget hotel of the same name, this restau-

QUICK EATS & DRINKS IN SAN PEDRO

Check out these quick and cheap eats.

- **Super Jugos** (Map p113; 6a Av SO at 6a Calle SO; $L10-20; 8am-9m Mon-Sat, to 6pm Sun) The motto here is 'the best *licuados* in Honduras' and who are we to disagree? (*Licuados* is a fresh fruit drink, blended with milk or water.)
- **Espresso Americano** (Map p113; Parque Central; coffee L$20-40; 6:30am-8pm) The cappuccino and mocha here are great.
- **El Pollero** (Map p113; cnr Blvd Morazan & 5a Av NO; mains L$50-100; breakfast, lunch & dinner) This chain's fried chicken is greasy enough to clog even the healthiest of arteries. Of course, that's how we like it!
- **Kobs** (Map p113; Parque Central; ice cream L$10-40; breakfast, lunch & dinner) A nice spot for an afternoon ice-cream cone.
- **Tobaco y Café** (Map p110; cnr 6a Calle NO & 9a Av NO; mains L$60-100; breakfast, lunch & dinner) Try the paella stand in front of this quaint outdoor cafe.

rant is one of the best downtown. Honduran classics like coconut shrimp and chicken tacos are served alongside international faves like BLTs and veggie pasta. Save some lemps with the *plato del día* (daily special).

El Fogoncito (Map p113; 553-3000, 1a Calle O at 11a Av NO; mains L$100-200; lunch & dinner) The best-known Mexican restaurant in town, this cantina-style place offers classic Mexican and Tex-Mex dishes.

Fuente de Salud y Juventud (Map p113; 553-7010; 5 Av NO btwn 4a & 5a Calle NO; mains L$100-300; lunch Mon-Fri) Mainly a natural goods store (vitamins, supplements etc), the Fount of Health & Youth also prepares a modest vegetarian buffet. The food is pretty underwhelming, but for vegetarians surviving on rice, beans and *licuados* (smoothies), it's a welcome change. Spa treatments are offered here, too.

Top End

Restaurante Boc-ga (Map p110; 991-0077; 11 Av NO at 13 Calle NO; mains L$120-300; lunch & dinner) This is a classy Korean restaurant whose name means 'house of blessing'. Go for Western tables with chairs and table legs, or normal ones, which in here means low to the floor with cushions to sit on. Either way, you've got a grill in the middle for do-it-yourself dishes like Boc-ga teriyaki or *tukpegi bulgogi* (spicy beef), a house favorite.

Barú (Map p110; 553-0499; 9a Calle NO btwn 11 & 12 Avs NO; mains L$150-300; lunch & dinner Mon-Sat) It's a bit expensive but this Columbian restaurant – with food that tastes distinctly Honduran – has friendly service, indoor and outdoor seating and yummy salads and meat from the grill.

Restaurante Don Udo's (Map p110; 557-7992; www.donudos.com; 13 Av NO btwn 7 & 7a Calle NO; mains L$150-400; lunch & dinner) You don't have to be a bigwig to eat here, though plenty do. Don Udo's is one of San Pedro's top restaurants, with excellent food and service and a cool colonial elegance. Live music and a cozy outdoor patio add to the experience.

WESTERN HONDURAS

DRINKING & ENTERTAINMENT

San Pedro has a raucous nightlife, with bars open most of the week and clubs open Thursday to Sunday. The Zona Viva (at 15a and 16a Avs SO, between 7a and 11a Calles SO) has a good selection of bars and restaurants. For more partying options see p116.

Bars & Nightclubs

Umani (Map p110; 557-3281; 1a Calle NO at Av Circunvalación; 6pm-3am) The age minimum (24 for men, 20 for women) and dress code (men must wear a collared shirt and dress shoes; women, well, dress to kill) are strictly enforced.

Beer Bar (Map p110; 580-1343; 3rd fl, City Mall; 2pm-midnight Tue-Sat, 2-7pm Sun) Yes, it's in a mall, but they have a huge selection of international beer.

Kawama (Map p110; Av Circunvalación, btwn 10a & 11a Avs NO; cover L$40-100; 9pm-3am Tue-Thu, to 5am Fri-Sun) This discotheque plays mostly Latin music.

ASK A LOCAL: BEST PLACES TO PIJINEAR (PARTY) LIKE A ROCK STAR

- **Klein Bohemia** (Map p113; ☎ 552-3172; www.kleinbohemia.com; 7a Calle SO at 8a Av SO; ⏲ 4:30pm-midnight Wed, Thu & Sat, to 1am Fri) If what you are looking for is a great time – and to learn a bit about national culture – then this is the spot. There's no cover charge, and live music most nights.
- **Luca Luca** (Map p110; 15 Av SO btwn 8 & 9 Calles SO, Zona Viva) The ambiance is very nice at this lounge. And normally you don't have to pay a cover, but it can get a bit crowded.
- **Lua Lounge** (Map p110; 15 Av SO btwn 8 & 9 Calles SO, Zona Viva) This is a great dance spot with '80s music, techno and house.

Ángela Bendeck, rocker & owner of Tamarindo Hostel

Cinemas

Downtown, **Cinema Geminis** (Map p113; ☎ 550-9060; 1a Calle O at 12a Av NO) and **Multicines Plaza Sula** (Map p113; ☎ 557-3860; 10a Av NO btwn 3a & 4a Calles NO) are small theaters with just a couple of screens. Theaters that are in the malls – **Cinemark** (Map p110; City Mall), **Multicines** (Map p110; Multiplaza Mall), **Cinemas Metro** (Map p110; Metroplaza Mall) – are larger and more modern. Tickets are L$40–60, with discounts on Tuesday and Thursday.

Theater

Teatro José Francisco Saybe (Map p110; ☎ 225-5117; Av Circunvalación, near 11a Av NO) This modern theater near the Universidad de San Pedro Sula hosts San Pedro's finest live performances year-round.

SHOPPING

Casa del Sol (Map p110; ☎ 557-1371; 6a Calle NO btwn 8a & 9a Avs NO; ⏲ 8am-6pm Mon-Sat, to noon Sun) This place sells the highest-quality *artesanía* (handicrafts) in town.

Mercado de Artesanías Guamilito (Map p110; 8a & 9a Avs NO btwn 6a & 7a Calles NO; ⏲ 7am-5pm Mon-Sat, to noon Sun) Stall upon stall of handicrafts from all over Honduras, Guatemala and El Salvador fill this sprawling market.

Malls include **City Mall** (Map p110; Av Circunvalación near Carr a Tegucigalpa), Metroplaza Mall (Map p110) just down the street from City Mall, Multiplaza Mall (Map p110) and Mega Plaza Mall (off Map p110).

GETTING THERE & AWAY

Air

Aeropuerto Internacional Ramón Villeda Morales (15km east of San Pedro Sula) is the country's busiest airport. Departure tax is L$646 for international flights and L$32 for domestic. Planes come and go from all the major cities in Central America plus several from the US, Mexico and Europe, and of course domestically to Tegucigalpa and La Ceiba.

Aerolineas Sosa (Map p113; ☎ 550-6545; www.aerolineasosa.com; Blvd Morazán btwn 7a & 8a Avs SO; ⏲ 8am-noon & 1-5pm Mon-Fri, 8am-noon Sat)

American Airlines (☎ at airport 668-3244; www.aa.com; ⏲ 8am-noon & 1-5pm Mon Fri, 8am-noon Sat)

Continental/Copa Airlines (Map p113; ☎ 550-7132; www.continental.com; 4a Av NO btwn 1 & 2 Calles NO; ⏲ 8am-noon & 1-5pm Mon-Fri, 8am-noon Sat)

Spirit Airlines (☎ in the US 1-800-772-7117; www.spiritair.com) Has amazingly cheap flights to Fort Lauderdale, Florida.

TACA/Isleña (☎ at airport 668-3183; www.taca.com; ⏲ 8am-noon & 1:15-5pm Mon-Fri, 8am-noon Sat)

Bus

San Pedro Sula is a land transportation hub, connecting the North Coast to Western and Southern Honduras. However, if you're not planning to stop, you can sometimes save time by transferring buses at El Progreso instead of going into San Pedro proper.

The **Terminal Metropolitana de Autobuses** (Metropolitan Bus Terminal; off Map p110), 5km south of town, is your one-stop shop for buses. Taxis go here for around L$60 from the city center. The free tourist magazine *Honduras Tips* has a very helpful section on bus routes around the country.

For long-distance buses from San Pedro Sula see the table, opposite.

INTERNATIONAL BUSES

Fuente del Norte (☎ 9843-0507; Metropolitan Bus Terminal) leaves at 6am for San Salvador (L$500), Guatemala City (L$500) and a few other spots in Guatemala.

Tica Bus (☎ 516-2022; www.ticabus.com; Metropolitan Bus Terminal) has deluxe service leaving at 5am for Managua (L$608), San José Costa Rica (L$988) and Panama City (L$1653).

GETTING AROUND

To/From the Airport

San Pedro's Villeda Morales airport, the largest and most modern in the country, is about 15km southeast of town. There is no direct bus to the airport, but you can get on any El Progreso bus and ask the driver to let you off at the airport turnoff (L$8). From there, it's a long shadeless walk (25 minutes); if you have heavy bags or it's late, consider springing for a taxi. A taxi ride to/from the airport costs L$200. Coming from the airport, you can get a taxi just to the turnoff (L$60) and catch a bus into town.

Bus

It's best to avoid taking local public buses in San Pedro Sula or any large town or city in Honduras. They are all too often the target of gang attacks and drivers often have to pay 'tax' to go through certain neighborhoods. **Buses** (Map p113; cnr 2Av SE & 2a Calle SE) to the airport turn-off (L$8), bus station (L$6) and Progresso (L$18.50 to L$20) are reputed to be safer, and often have transit police aboard.

Car & Motorcycle

Driving in San Pedro is a relatively painless experience. Always check if the street you're turning into is only one way. Signage is sparse and the police *will* pull you over for going the wrong way. Av Circunvalación is orderly and fast and often better than cutting through town.

Some car-rental agencies:

Advance (Map p110; ☎ 552-2295; at airport 668-0284; www.advancerentacar.com; 1a Calle Este btwn 6a & 7a Av NE; 🕑 8am-6pm Mon-Sat, 9am-5pm Sun)
Amerika Rent-a-Car (Map p110; ☎ 552-6082; 1a Calle E btwn 3 & 4 Avs SO)
Avis (Map p110; ☎ 553-0888, at airport 668-3164; www.avis.com.hn; 1a Calle Este btwn 6a & 7a Avs NE; 🕑 6am-10pm Mon-Fri, 8am-6pm Sat & Sun)
Thrifty (Map p110; ☎ 552-5498; www.thrifty.com; 3a Av NO btwn 5a & 6a Calles NE)

LONG-DISTANCE BUSES FROM SAN PEDRO SULA

Destination	Bus line	Phone	Fare	Frequency	Duration
Agua Caliente	Sultana	516-2048	L$164	6am, 8am, 10:30am & 1:30pm	5hr
Comayagua	Rivera	516-2156	L$72	hourly 6am-5pm	3¼hr
Copán Ruinas	Casasola	516-2031	L$110	6 departures 7am-2:40pm	2¾-3hr
Copán Ruinas**	Hedman Alas	557-2273	L$323	3-4 departures 7am-2:50pm	2½-3hr
La Ceiba	Catisa & Tupsa	no tel	L$94	hourly 6am-6pm	3hr
La Ceiba*	Diana Express	516-2014	L$95	10am, noon & 4:15pm	3hr
La Ceiba**	Hedman Alas	557-2273	L$320-380	4 departures 6am-6pm	2¾-3hr
Gracias	Torito	516-2046	L$110	every ½hr 4:30am-8am	4-6hr
Lago de Yojoa	Rivera	516-2156	L$43	hourly 6am-5pm	3¼hr
Pto Cortés	Impala/Citul	553-3111	L$42	every 15min 4:30am-9pm	1-1¾hr
Santa Rosa de Copán	Torito	516-2046	L$65	every ½hr 4:30am-8am	2½hr
Tegucigalpa**	Saenz	516-2222	L$400	every 2hr 6am-6pm	5hr
Tegucigalpa	Sultana	516-2048	L$99	every 60-90min 5:30am-6pm	4½hr
Tegucigalpa	El Rey de Oro & El Rey Express	516-2179	L$120-141	hourly 6:30am-6:15pm	4-6hr
Tegucigalpa**	Hedman Alas	557-2273	L$350	7 departures 5:45am-5:45pm	3½hr
Tela	Catisa & Tupsa	no tel	L$80	hourly 6am-6pm	1½hr
Trujillo	Cotuc & Contraibal	520-7497	L$165	11 departures 6am-3:30pm	6hr

*direct service
**luxury service

FIGHTING FOR SOME LAND TO STAND ON

In September 2005 some 1500 Maya-Chortí indigenous people marched onto the Copán archaeological site, blocking the entrance and demanding the Honduran government complete the land reforms it promised almost a decade ago. The occupation, which lasted five days, was one in a series of such actions, the most recent of which happened in March 2009.

The immediate conflict stems from an agreement reached in 1997 that the government would buy the Chortí around 14,000 hectares of privately owned land, worth around US$6 million. Only 2700 hectares had been distributed by 2005.

The root of the matter is considerably older, of course. The Maya-Chortí – descended from the builders of Copán ruins – have lived in the Valle de Copán for generations as subsistence farmers. In the 1950s wealthy landowners bought up thousands of hectares of traditional Chortí farmland, forcing the Chortí into plantation labor. They and other poor farmers eventually organized themselves into large peasant unions, whose actions, sometimes militant, prompted the adoption of Honduras' agrarian reform laws in the 1960s and '70s.

But even as laws gave poor farmers more rights, intimidation and repression increased. In 1997 Chortí leader Cándido Amador was brutally murdered – he was stabbed, shot, scalped and dumped by the side of the road – in a crime many say was orchestrated by local landowners. It remains unsolved. Amador was the 25th indigenous leader to be killed in a period of just five years, and one of dozens over the preceding decades. His murder galvanized Chortís and gained international attention; thousands marched on Tegucigalpa a month later, which led to the land distribution agreement that Chortí activists today say remains unenforced.

Taxi

It's easy to flag down a taxi, especially downtown and near the malls. Cabs don't have meters, however, so agree on a price before you get in. Average fares in town are L$20 per person; an airport run costs around L$200, and the bus terminal starts at L$60 from downtown.

VALLE DE COPÁN

This broad valley is the cultural crossroads of Western Honduras. Aside from the pyramids and mystical staircases at the Copán archaeological site, there are butterfly gardens, bird reserves, century-old coffee *fincas* (farms or plantations) and hot springs to be explored. And best of all, each attraction lies within an easy day-trip distance from the cooled-out colonial city of Copán Ruinas.

LA ENTRADA

pop 14,700

This is the *entrada* (entrance) to the fertile Copán Valley. Guess we know where the town got its name. But other than its unique geographic distinction, there's nothing really distinguished about this crossroads town. There is a Maya ruin just outside town that makes it worthwhile spending at least a few hours in the area before you head on to the 'bigger' sights along the Ruta Lenca and in the Valle de Copán.

Information & Orientation

La Entrada is a one-road town lined with hotels, restaurants and other services. The main intersection is at the south end of town – coming from San Pedro Sula, bear right for Copán Ruinas and the Guatemalan border, or bear left for Santa Rosa de Copán and the Ruta Lenca.

Farmacia La Milagrosa (☎ 661-2097; 🕑 8am-6pm Mon-Sat) is next door to the Hotel Tegucigalpa. Two-and-a-half blocks north of there is **Banco Atlántida** (🕑 9am-4pm Mon-Fri, 8:30-11:30am Sat), which has an ATM. There's an **internet cafe** (per hr L$20) on the 2nd floor of a mini-mall located 100m west of the Hotel El San Carlos.

Sleeping & Eating

Hotel Alexandra (☎ 661-2263; s/d with fan L$200/250, with air-con L$300/400; P ❄) If all you want is to hole up somewhere cheap, take a hot shower and watch some TV, this is your place. A short walk from the main intersection means you've got easy access to/from all the buses, so you can catch an early morning bus out.

Hotel y Restaurant El San Carlos (☎ 661-2228; www.hotelelsancarlos.com; s with fan L$350, s/d with air-con L$500/700; P ❄ 🏊) Something must have gone wrong for you to be stuck in La Entrada, so why not treat yourself with spotlessly clean rooms and an inviting pool area? The hotel is 50m from the main intersection on your way to Copán Ruinas.

Pollolandia (mains L$60-100; breakfast, lunch & dinner) At the main intersection, across from Hotel Alexandra, Pollolandia is the Honduran answer to KFC, except with a better name.

Getting There & Around

The intersection at the south end of town is a good place to catch a bus. Buses to Copán Ruinas, however, stop at a small kiosk under an almond tree about 75m past the Hotel San Carlos, on the turnoff toward the ruins. To get around town, three-wheeled moto-taxis (red and white scooters with a small cab attached) zip around town, charging L$6 to L$10 per person, depending on the length of the ride. Buses go to the following destinations:

Copán Ruinas (L$40, two hours, every 40 minutes 6am to 4pm)

Nueva Ocotepeque (L$80, 2½ to three hours, every 45 minutes 6am to 4pm)

San Pedro Sula (*ordinario* L$53, one to 1½ hours, every 30 minutes 5:30am to 6pm; *directo* (direct) L$82, one hour, 8:10am, 10:10am and 3:10pm)

Santa Rosa de Copán (*ordinario* L$20, 1¼ hours, every 30 minutes 6am to 7pm; *directo* L$32, 45 minutes, every one to 1½ hours 7am to 3pm)

EL PUENTE

Ten kilometers southwest of La Entrada, **Sitio Archeológico El Puente** (admission L$95; 8am-4pm) sees only a trickle of visitors. With one large-ish pyramid and no stelae, El Puente (the Bridge) doesn't begin to compare in size or artfulness to Copán, but having a Maya site all to yourself is a memorable and increasingly rare experience. Unfortunately, there are no buses to the site. If you have a car – or better yet, a bike – it's well worth a trip out there. By taxi, well, you're better off spending that money on a guide at Copán.

El Puente consists of more than 200 structures, though only nine have been excavated. Entering the site, you'll see a well-restored step pyramid in the middle of a long grassy plaza. Along the edges are lower, tree-shaded structures, including what may have been living quarters for the political or religious elite. The west flanking structure has rooms and passages hidden inside – look for the metal access ladder. Behind that is a short nature path, where voracious mosquitoes are poised for attack.

A small but intriguing museum at the entrance displays artifacts uncovered in El Puente's two major excavations (1985–89 and 1990–93). Among them are *líticas* (obsidian blades and tools), which this region is known for, and human remains from several burial sites. Signage is in Spanish only.

There is no direct bus to El Puente. The turnoff to the archaeological site is 4.5km south of La Entrada, on the road toward Copán Ruinas, and another 6km from there. You could easily catch a bus to the turnoff but would have to walk the rest of the way, and back, and there's a large hill in the middle. There's little traffic on this road, so hitching isn't a sure thing. Taxis don't have a fixed price; a ballpark figure is L$400 to L$600 round-trip, including waiting for you while you check out the site.

COPÁN RUINAS

pop 38,600

It feels as if all roads lead to this charming hill-perched colonial town just 1km northwest of Honduras' most famous Maya site. Here you'll reconnect with old friends from the road, make new ones and, of course, get the chance to head out from the cobblestone confines of town to the butterfly gardens, nature centers and nearby ruins that have transformed this small pueblo into mainland Honduras' Number One traveler attraction.

Orientation

Parque Central is the heart of town – almost everything is within a few blocks of it. The ruins (p126) are 1.5km outside of town, on the road to La Entrada – a pleasant 15-minute stroll along a footpath alongside the highway. Las Sepulturas archaeological site is 2km further along.

There are no street names in Copán Ruinas, but with the town being so compact, it's easy enough to find your way around.

Information

BOOKSTORES

Biblioteca Pública de Copán (Antiguo Mercado de Artesanías, Parque Central; 9am-noon & 1:30-6pm) Offers book exchange of mostly English-language books.

La Casa de Todo (☎ 651-4185; www.casadetodo.com; 7am-9pm) Small book exchange tucked into this gift shop, one block east of Parque Central.

EMERGENCY

Police (☎ 651-4060; 24hr) It's 300m west of the park.

INTERNET ACCESS

Many hotels now have wi-fi and internet machines for their guests.

@ngel Internet (per hr L$20)

LAUNDRY

Maya Connection (per load L$100; 7am-9pm) Does same-day laundry and has an internet cafe (L$20 per hour).

MEDICAL SERVICES

Farmacia Santos (☎ 651-4383; 8am-6pm Mon-Sat) Also open two Sundays per month.

Proyecto Clinico Materno Infantil (24hr) In El Jaral, the only area hospital specializes in pediatrics and obstetrics, but no one is turned away. Located 20km northeast of Copán Ruinas on Hwy CA-11.

MONEY

BAC (Parque Central; 9am-5pm Mon-Fri, to noon Sat) Exchanges US dollars, quetzals and traveler's checks; one 24-hour ATM.

Banco Atlántida (Parque Central; 9am-4pm Mon-Fri, 8:30-11:30am Sat) Offers same services as BAC but has longer lines.

POST

Post office (8am-noon & 2-5pm Mon-Fri, 8am-noon Sat) Half a block west of Parque Central.

TELEPHONE

Hondutel (7am-noon, 12:30-6pm & 6:30-9pm) Offers international calling and is located next to the post office, half a block west of Parque Central.

TOURIST INFORMATION

Cámara de Comercio y Turismo (☎ 651-3829; 8am-5pm Mon-Fri, 9am-4pm Sat, 9am-noon Sun) Offers brochures and basic information.

ViaVia Café (☎ 651-4652; www.viaviacafe.com) Excellent bulletin board with information on area sites and beyond; 1½ blocks west of Parque Central.

Sights & Activities

Although in need of some updating, the 1970s-era **Museo Regional de Arqueología Maya** (☎ 651-4437; Parque Central; admission L$57; 9am-5pm) gives a good overview of the Maya and their presence in the Valle de Copán. The exhibit contains some excellent pieces: painted pottery, carved jade, Maya glyphs and the original Stela B, portraying King 18 Rabbit. Don't miss the Tumba de la Bruja, the round tomb of a *shamana* who was buried with several spectacular offerings, including two human heads (neither of which were hers).

The **Casa K'inich** (☎ 651-4105; www.asociacioncopan.org; Antiguo Mercado de Artesanías, Parque Central; admission free; 8am-noon & 1-5pm) was closed when we passed through. If it reopens, it's a fine children's museum that explores everything Maya.

Recreational Center Camino Maya (☎ 651-4648; adult/child L$50/30; 8am-5pm Mon-Thu, to 6pm Fri & Sat) This well-maintained recreational area with lush grounds and a pool is just off the road to the Hedman Alas bus terminal. At night, Las Piscinas – the center's bar and discotheque – keeps the place hopping.

For a fine view over the fertile Copán valley, head to the **Mirador El Cuartel**, an abandoned jail five blocks north of Parque Central. It's also fun to do as the Hondurans do, and take a picnic lunch down to the **Río Copán** (Copán River), just south of town.

Courses

Ixbalanque Spanish Language School (☎ 651-4432; www.ixbalanque.com) Probably the best school in town, Ixbalanque offers one-on-one Spanish classes 20 hours per week (L$3990), including a homestay (private room with bathroom, three meals per day and laundry). Volunteer opportunities in elementary schools, medical centers and municipal offices also can be arranged in conjunction with language study.

Guacamaya Spanish Academy (☎ 651-4360; www.guacamaya.com) Virtually the same setup as Ixbalanque.

Seed of Light (☎ 9888-5057; www.seedoflightcopan.com) If hauling your pack around Honduras has left you aching for a good stretch, drop in on a class (L$150, 1½ hours) at this Krípalu yoga studio. Yoga sessions at the Copán archaeological site, Hacienda San Lucas (p122) 2km southeast of town, and Macaw Mountain (p125) are also offered; prices vary depending on the package.

Tours

Copán Ruinas offers much more than an archaeological site, thanks primarily to the large number of creative, quality excursions offered by local tour operators. You can hike, bird-watch, horseback ride or motorcycle ride, or visit Maya villages, natural hot

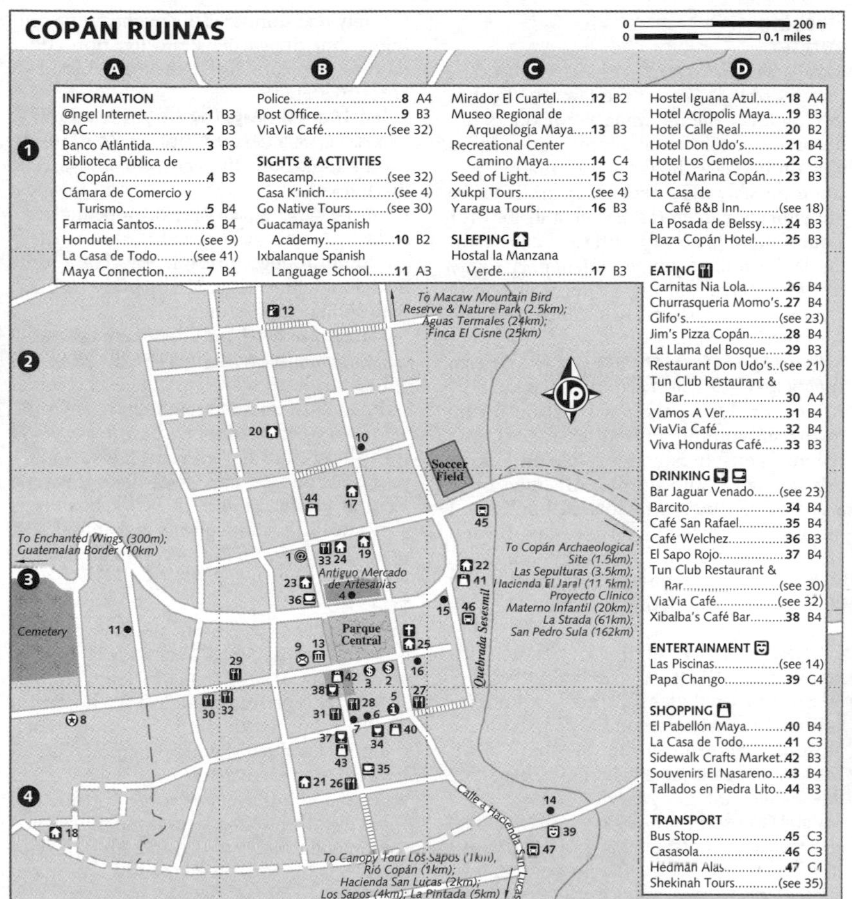

springs and a working coffee plantation. In addition to the tours listed here, see p125 for additional tours and outings.

Inside the ViaVia Café, **Basecamp** (☎ 651-4695; www.basecamphonduras.com; 8am-6pm) is easily one of the best operations in Honduras. It offers a variety of excursions, from a two-hour walking tour of the 'real' Copán village to an all-day hike through the hills and rural communities around Copán.

The longtime and locally owned **Go Native Tours** (☎ 651-4410; www.copanhonduras.org; gnative4@yahoo.com) offers hiking, caving and horseback-riding trips around Copán, as well as to Lago de Yojoa and Gracias. Some of the local trips involve and benefit local villagers. The office is in Tun Club Restaurant & Bar (p123).

Xukpi Tours (☎ 651-4435) is operated by the ebullient and extremely knowledgeable Jorge Barraza, whose specialized ruins and bird-watching tours are justly famous. He'll do trips to Lago de Yojoa and elsewhere, even into Guatemala.

Just east of Parque Central, the reliable **Yaragua Tours** (☎ 651-4147; www.yaragua.com; 7am-10pm) offers various excursions, including tubing and horseback trips along the Copán River, bird-watching, waterfall hikes and coffee plantation tours. Ask for Samuel Miranda.

Festivals & Events

The annual Feria de Copán Ruinas – a huge fair complete with rides and games – is celebrated from March 15 to 20.

Sleeping

BUDGET

Hostal la Manzana Verde (☎ 9097-9178; www.lamanzanaverde.com; dm L$95) One of the few true hostels in Honduras, the Manzana Verde offers hip decor, spotlessly clean rooms and a killer bulletin board with all the information you could possibly need about Copán. Beds are individually named (eg Barbie and Ken for a queen) and match up with food cubbies in the fantastically equipped kitchen. A shady hammock area and lounge serve as comfy common areas. Lockers are included but bring your own towel and soap.

Hostel Iguana Azul (☎ 651-4620; www.todomundo.com/iguanaazul; dm L$100, r with shared bathroom L$250) A bit retired from the major action in the town center (and the better for it), the Iguana Azul offers comfortable and clean private rooms and dorms. All open onto a common room with lots of books and magazines and there is a pleasant garden area as well. No kitchen facilities are available, which is a bummer but not the end of the world considering there are so many options in town.

Hotel Los Gemelos (☎ 651-4077; r with shared bathroom per person L$100; P) A great budget buy run by a very friendly family, this longtime favorite has 14 private rooms with good beds, mosquito nets and a fan; all share clean cold-water bathrooms. There is a beautiful flower-filled interior garden.

Hotel Calle Real (☎ 651-4230; hotelcallereal@yahoo.com; s/d with fan $265/380, with air-con L$560/660; P) It's a steep three-block hike to get here, but this colonial-styled hotel may be worth it. The rooms are a bit damp, and you'll have to double up the Frito Lay–thin pillows, but they're relative clean and you get excellent city views from the rooftop hammock area.

La Posada de Belssy (☎ 651-4680; r L$300; P) The biggest draw of the Belssy – beyond the spotless rooms – is the rooftop lounge. Tables, comfy chairs, hammocks and even a small pool (about the size of a Volkswagen bug) make it one of the best hangout spots in town. The 1st floor also has an open-air common room and a modern kitchen that you may be able to use if you ask first.

MIDRANGE

La Casa de Café B&B Inn (☎ 651-4620; www.casadecafecopan.com; s/d incl breakfast L$881/1102; P) The rooms at this friendly B&B are fairly simple – the only real stunner is the pitched pine ceilings – but the gardens and location add a pastoral old-world feel to the place. Massages are also offered.

Hotel Acropolis Maya (☎ 651-4634; hotelacropolis@hotmail.com; s/d/tr L$900/950/1100; P) Twenty rooms look onto the central courtyard of this fine colonial-style hotel. Each all-business room has two queen-size orthopedic beds, scratchy towels, dark-wood furniture, silent air-conditioning and cable TV. The rooms next door at the Brisas de Copán are cheaper, with similar appointments.

Plaza Copán Hotel (☎ 651-4508; www.plazacopanhotel.com; Parque Central; s/d L$1083/1197; P) While this hotel offers surface-level colonial styling, it just doesn't seem to have any soul. The somewhat dated rooms have heavy wood furnishings and flower-print bedspreads – rooms 210 and 213 have great views of Parque Central. A small but very well-kept pool is a nice feature, although it's a shame that it opens directly onto the reception area.

TOP END

Hotel Don Udo's (☎ 651-4533; www.donudos.com; s/d incl breakfast with fan L$760/874, with air-con L$1197/1235, ste incl breakfast L$1653-2204; P) This colonial-style hotel is perfect if you like the hominess of a B&B but not the intimacy of one. Each room is decorated slightly differently but all have a Guatemalan theme, with whitewashed walls and colorful hand-woven bedspreads. Don't miss the rooftop Jacuzzi and the sauna – they're great places to unwind after a day of exploring the ruins. Breakfast is served at the recommended hotel restaurant.

Hotel Marina Copán (☎ 651-4070; www.hotelmarinacopan.com; s/d L$1763/1983, ste L$3967-5510; P) This classy colonial-style hotel has 51 rooms amid flower gardens, gurgling fountains, koi ponds and plush seating areas. Rooms are clean and modern, with details like marble sinks, thick linens and old-world furnishings. Ask for one with a balcony, as many of these have spectacular views over the town. An excellent restaurant, live music on weekends, a well-tended pool and a small gym make it especially nice.

our pick **Hacienda San Lucas** (☎ 651-4495; www.haciendasanlucas.com; s/d/tr incl breakfast L$2394/2755/3420; P) This beautifully restored hacienda has eight guest rooms, all built like the original *casa grande,* including high sloped ceilings and ceramic-tile floors. Delight is in the details: redolent cedar headboards, colorful Guatemalan bedspreads, stone showers, fresh flowers and (best of all) candles lit nightly in your room and all over the property, a custom held over from the hacienda's pre-electricity days. The hacienda also offers spa treatments, yoga courses, hiking and horseback-riding excursions, and a pricey but terrific restaurant. Hacienda San Lucas is about 2.5km southeast of town; a taxi costs around L$60.

Eating

BUDGET

Viva Honduras Café (☎ 651-4097; mains L$20-90; 🕒 6:30am-9:30pm; 📶) Head all the way upstairs for the best views in town in this friendly cafe, which serves good smoothies, *baleadas* and other local fare. There's free wi-fi for the laptop set.

La Llama del Bosque (☎ 651-4431; mains L$30-90; 🕒 breakfast, lunch & dinner) From the outside, this place looks forgettable. But eat one meal here and you're likely to remember it for a long time. The menu is extensive and varied with dishes that are delicious, beautifully presented, abundant and cheap.

ViaVia Café (☎ 651-4652; mains L$35-90; 🕒 breakfast, lunch & dinner) A hip boho atmosphere with outdoor and indoor seating; the daily specials are the way to go at this place. Each day the chef takes a crack at various world-food dishes and often pulls them off with flair.

Tun Club Restaurant & Bar (mains L$50-150; 🕒 breakfast, lunch & dinner) You wouldn't expect it from the outside, but the dining area in this longtime restaurant and bar is quite large and, with a leafy interior courtyard, stone floors and wood tables, downright outdoorsy. (Well, almost.) The food is tasty and the portions large, and the menu includes a number of vegetarian options.

Vamos A Ver (☎ 651-4627; mains L$70-200; 🕒 breakfast, lunch & dinner) This cozy little patio restaurant dishes up good food: tasty soups, fruit or vegetable salads, homemade breads, a variety of international cheeses, and lots of teas. Plus, every evening, pretend that you're back at camp and make your own s'mores over an open fire.

Churrasqueria Momo's (☎ 651-3692; mains L$80-200; 🕒 breakfast, lunch & dinner) A meat-lover's haven, Momo's, one block south of Parque Central, serves beef in four basic styles: *pincho* (kebab), *churrasco* (Argentinean-style beef), *puyaso* (a choice cut of steak), and *parrillada* (a sampler, including sausage, beans and tortillas). There are a few chicken, pork, and shrimp dishes, but you might as well go somewhere else for those. Meals are served in an open-air dining area overlooking the Valle de Copán.

MIDRANGE & TOP END

Restaurant Don Udo's (☎ 651-4533; mains L$80-200; 🕒 breakfast, lunch & dinner) Overlooking Hotel Don Udo's grassy courtyard, Don Udo's is known as the place to head for seafood. Try the salmon-stuffed ravioli or the *camarones pil pil* (white-wine flambé shrimp) to give your taste buds a treat.

Carnitas Nia Lola (mains L$100-315; 🕒 breakfast, lunch & dinner) An American bar-and-grill planted firmly on the Honduran mainland, this restaurant feels a bit more upscale than other spots in town and draws an older – we mean 'more mature' – crowd.

Jim's Pizza Copán (mains L$130-200; 🕒 lunch & dinner) This thatch-roof restaurant serves some of the best pizza around. Choose from a variety of ingredients – pepperoni, ham, sausage, bell peppers, onion, mushrooms, olives – and it's baked before your eyes in the open-air kitchen. A steady stream of clients keeps the place going late.

Glifo's (☎ 651-4070; mains L$120-250; 🕒 breakfast, lunch & dinner) A bit stuffy but still considered one of the classiest places to eat in town, this restaurant in Hotel Marina Copán offers a wide selection of fine international dishes. The Honduran specialties with a traditional Maya twist, however, are the way to go. Service is excellent.

One of Copán's best hotels, **Hacienda San Lucas** (opposite) also offers one of its most memorable dining experiences. It's open just for dinner and reservations are required. Call a day in advance and make a request and the chefs will do their best to accommodate; wood-fired roast chicken, beef, *tamales* (boiled or steamed cornmeal filled with chicken or pork, usually wrapped in a banana leaf), green salad and fresh tortillas frequently figure in the four-course meal (prix fixe L$570); The view is amazing, including a sliver of the main ruins – come early for a glass of wine and sunset over Templo 21.

Drinking & Entertainment

Café San Rafael (☎ 651-4402; 🕒 7:30am-8pm) This tiny eatery 1½ blocks south of Parque Central sells coffee from the family *finca*.

Barcito (until midnight) A little hole in the wall with upholstered milk crates for seats, good music and friendly staff.

Café Welchez (☎ 651-4070; Parque Central; 6am-10pm) Although it looks like money, the Café Welchez is a relatively affordable place.

El Sapo Rojo (noon-midnight or later) This 2nd-story bar and grill is a good place to meet the local ruffians, who aren't so rough after you get to talking.

ViaVia Café (☎ 651-4695; www.viaviacafe.com; 8am-midnight) One of the hottest nightspots in town, the ViaVia is a hipster lounge bar-restaurant with low lighting, urban tunes and lots of seating. It shows movies Sunday, Monday and Tuesday night at 7pm (L$20), and has music and dancing the rest of the week. Next door, the Tun Club (p123) serves two-for-one drink specials from 7pm to 8pm, sometimes later (closes midnight).

Xibalba's Café Bar (☎ 651-4182; 2-10pm Mon-Sat) If this is the afterlife, things are looking up. Borrowing its name from the Maya underworld, Xibalba is a loud, lively pub with a young vibe and great music, and even live performances sometimes.

Bar Jaguar Venado (☎ 651-4070; 11am-10pm) In Hotel Marina Copán, this fancy-pants bar is geared towards an older crowd.

Las Piscinas (Recreational Center Camino Maya; cover L$50; 8am-midnight Mon-Thu, to 3am Fri & Sat) A hacienda-style recreational area by day, Las Piscinas becomes a hopping karaoke bar and discotheque by night. If it's not happening, check out Papa Chango across the way.

Shopping

For a town that sees so much steady tourism, it's a surprise that the shopping isn't much better. There's a fair number of tacky gift shops – even the *artesanía* (handicraft) market got hit with the kitsch stick – but at least there's a handful of hopefuls.

Tallados en Piedra Lito (☎ 651-4138; 7am-9pm) Perhaps the most enticing souvenirs in Copán are the high-quality Maya replicas made by Don Lito Lara and his son.

El Pabellón Maya (☎ 651-4066; 9am-7pm) This warehouse-type store has a variety of *artesanía* from Honduras, Guatemala and Costa Rica.

Souvenirs El Nasareno (☎ 651-4201; 8:30am-8pm) Although this small shop may look like one of the pack, the tropical hardwood *artesanía* and the leatherwork are among the best around.

La Casa de Todo (☎ 651-4185; www.casadetodo.com; 7am-9pm) As the name suggests, the House of Everything has just about…well, everything.

Every afternoon, a small **sidewalk crafts market** sets up just off Parque Central. You'll see Guatemalan women sitting side by side with hippie-ish traveler-jewelers, each loaded down with shell necklaces, bead bracelets and feather earrings.

Getting There & Away

Buses to La Entrada (L$40, two hours, every 40 minutes 5am to 5pm) leave from a small dirt lot at the entrance to town, just across the bridge. From there, you can transfer to Santa Rosa de Copán, Gracias or elsewhere on the Ruta Lenca. There's more frequent service from the same stop to Santa Rita (L$7, 15 minutes), if you're just headed to El Jaral or Cabañas. For other destinations in the country, you'll need to transfer in San Pedro Sula first.

Shekinah Tours (☎ 651-3955, 9687-8593) has direct shuttles to Antigua, Guatemala (L$228), Tikal, Guatemala (L$760), San Pedro Sula (L$152), La Ceiba (L$304) and Tegucigalpa (L$760). Buses leave at 6am and noon. And they pick you up right at your hotel.

Hedman Alas (☎ 651-4037; www.hedmanalas.com; Calle a Hacienda San Lucas; 4:30am-6pm) has a new terminal a few hundred meters southeast of town, just across the bridge on the road to Hacienda San Lucas. All domestic buses go first to San Pedro Sula (three hours) with departures at 5:30am, 10:30am and 2:30pm. From there, connect to your final destination. See the bus timetable on p117 for more information.

Casasola Express (☎ 651-4078) has a direct service to San Pedro Sula (L$110, 2¾ to three hours, 5:30am, 6am, 7am and 2pm) from a dirt lot a block east of Parque Central.

Getting Around

CAR

Driving in Copán Ruinas can be an exercise in frustration. The streets are too narrow for the number of cars on them, and the system of one-way streets has no rhyme or reason – you'll go a dozen blocks out of your way just to get to your hotel garage. Luckily, you don't really need a car for any of Copán's attractions – leave it parked at the hotel and you'll be a lot happier.

TAXI

Moto-taxis run from 6am to 11pm every day. Drivers charge L$8 (L$20 at night) per person in town, L$10 to the archaeological site and more for longer distances. As with all cabbies, be sure to confirm the fare before you get in.

AROUND COPÁN RUINAS

Finca El Cisne (☎ 651-4695; www.fincaelcisne.com; 8am-6pm) is the well-run tourism arm of a century-old family farm, located 25km north of Copán Ruinas; trips combine beautiful scenery with an inside-look at a working *finca* and include horseback riding through coffee and cardamom fields, swimming in the Río Blanco, soaking at Agua Caliente hot springs and a stop at the coffee-processing plants (February to October). Lodging is in a homey solar-powered cabin. Per person costs (minimum two people) are: day trips L$1000; overnight L$1300; and two-night stays L$2100; they include transportation to/from Copán Ruinas and meals. The *finca* shares an office with Basecamp tours, opposite ViaVia Café in Copán Ruinas.

Canopy Tour Los Sapos (☎ 9856-3758; www.hcanopytours.com; 8am-6pm) is on the road to the Hacienda San Lucas. This small-scale operation has several ziplines running you down the hill from La Pintada. It's a fun ride, but you're better off saving your lemps for a canopy tour elsewhere – like where they actually have a rainforest canopy.

From Hacienda San Lucas in Copán Ruinas, a pleasant 10-minute (2km) walk brings you to **Los Sapos**, a Maya site purportedly dedicated to women and fertility. Some archaeologists believe it was a place for royal women to conduct fertility ceremonies, or even to give birth. Others say it was simply a place for stone carvers to practice their trade. In any case, the actual pieces – roughly hewn rocks, one in the shape of a *sapo* (toad), hence the site's name – are significantly eroded but the hike there, with great views over the valley, is half the fun.

From Los Sapos you can continue another 10 minutes (1km) to **La Pintada**, a picturesque Maya-Chortí village known for the production of corn-husk dolls. (You may be swarmed by kids trying to sell them to you.) The town has beautiful views, including of the acropolis at the Copán archaeological site (p126). The name of the town comes from a little-known painted stela nearby. The folks at Hacienda San Lucas can provide a guide to point it out (free, but a tip is expected).

There are two excellent artisan cooperatives in town. The first is located right on the 'main square' and sells corn-husk creations. Down the hill, **Jardín de Mujeres Tejiendo Maya Chortí** (☎ 9815-0102; 8am-6pm) is a woman's art cooperative focusing on traditional textiles. Stop by for a loom demonstration. And – Green Travel Alert! – by buying goods, or eating in the excellent little **restaurant** nearby, you are doing your small part to support local business people and avoid the massive urbanization that plagues many countries in this part of the world.

The trails to these sites are maintained by Hacienda San Lucas, and non-guests may be charged L$30 for their use.

A short distance west of town, **Enchanted Wings** (☎ 651-4133; www.copannaturecenter.com; adult/child L$115/50; 8am-4:30pm) has a terrific *mariposario* (butterfly enclosure), bursting with tropical plants and dozens of moths and butterflies flitting about. Come before 11am and you may see new butterflies breaking out of their cocoons (the adults are more active then, too). An attached *orquidiario* has 150 different species of orchids, all native to Honduras.

Set on 4 hectares of tropical forest, **Macaw Mountain Bird Reserve & Nature Park** (☎ 651-4245; www.macawmountain.com; entrance L$200; 9am-5pm) has large enclosures with birds ranging from brilliant Buffon's macaws to manic keel-billed toucans. The ticket price (a bit steep, but good for three days) includes a one-hour guided tour (English and French spoken). There's also a 20-minute nature loop through an adjacent coffee plantation, a small swimming hole and a cafe. It's 2.5km north of Copan Ruinas, mostly uphill; a taxi is L$20 per person.

A set of hot springs, **aguas termales** (admission L$20; 10am-10pm), are 24km north of Copán Ruinas, an hour's drive through fertile mountains and coffee plantations. There are a couple of artificial pools or you can sit in the river, where the boiling hot-spring water mixes with the cool river water. Plans are in place to redevelop the area, but nothing was happening when we visited. Bring warm clothes if you come in the evening.

Just a few minutes east of Copán is the cheerful little farming community of **Cabañas**. Peace Corps volunteers have helped community members organize a day-long **rural tour** (per person L$400); highlights include hiking or horseback-riding through coffee fields and tiny farming communities, visiting traditional houses 'painted' with colored mud, a 25m waterfall, and lunch at a *campesino*

THE DEBATE GOES ON

History is never a permanent thing. And the history of Copán – the true stories that drove everyday life – is constantly morphing as archaeologists slowly unravel the mystery of the Maya. Or were they actually Maya?

'Actually, history and tradition assume Copán to be ethnically Maya, but current anthropological debates contest this,' says Kristin Landau, an archaeologist who has worked since 2005 on the Copán Urban Planning Project. 'Maya presence at Copán may have been an archaeologically visible elite veneer on a non-Maya (possibly Lenca) general populace.'

(farm worker) home. Visitors can also stay overnight with a family in Cabañas. It is vital that you call in advance, so the trip can be organized.

Doña Magaly Alvarado (☎ 656-7004), who operates the Comedor Calle Real, is the contact person. **Comedor Calle Real** (Parque Central; mains L$40-80; breakfast, lunch & dinner) serves good *comida típica* (Honduran fare).

To get to Cabañas from Copán Ruinas, take any Santa Rita, La Entrada or San Pedro Sula bus to Santa Rita (L$7, 15 minutes); get off at the gas station and walk to Parque Central, where buses leave for Cabañas (L$5, 10 minutes) every half-hour until 4:30pm.

The large, rather cheesy **Hacienda El Jaral** (☎ 9986-5665; admission L$100; 9am-5pm Mon-Fri, to 6pm Sat & Sun) resort-hotel-waterpark-museum-foodcourt-minimall-movie theater (did we miss anything?) is what Disneyland might have been if it had US$10,000 in seed money rather than US$10 million. It's located 11.5km east of town.

COPÁN ARCHAEOLOGICAL SITE

While Copán lacks the massive pyramids to the north in sites like Tikal and Chichén Itzá, it does have some of the world's best preserved stelae, intricately carved stone sculptures depicting former leaders. As Honduras' only major archaeological site, it may be just a bit over-hyped, and is certainly overpriced, but this Unesco World Heritage Site does have a top-notch museum, and a day-trip through here is well worth the price of admission.

History

PRECLASSIC PERIOD

Ceramic evidence shows that people have been living in the Valle de Copán since at least 1400 BC and probably before that. Ceramics dated to that period show clear influence from El Salvador, Guatemala and even Mexico.

The Preclassic was a period of rapid and fundamental change in the Maya region, but Copán seems to have lagged behind in that important era. Archaeologists aren't sure why: occupying a small self-contained valley with rich agricultural lands, the city had the fundamental elements needed for physical and cultural expansion. Instead Copán experienced a decline in population between 400 BC and AD 100.

CONSOLIDATING POWER

Around AD 426 a mysterious king named K'inich Yax K'uk' Mo' (Great Sun First Quetzal Macaw) came to Copán, ruling until AD 435. Archaeological evidence indicates that he was the progenitor to Classic period Copán; later kings revered him as the semidivine founder of the city. His dynasty ruled throughout Copán's florescence during the Classic period (AD 250–800).

Of the early kings who ruled from about 435 to 628 we know little. Little more than the names of some of the rulers have been deciphered: K'inich Popol Hol (Mat Head), the second king; Ku Ix, the fourth king; B'alam Nehn (Waterlily Jaguar), the seventh; Moon Jaguar, the 10th; and Butz' Chan, the 11th. We now know that Moon Jaguar constructed 'the famous Rosalila, an elaborately stuccoed and painted monument venerating the founding dynast. It is perhaps the best example of how all such structures in the royal precinct of Copán may have appeared in antiquity; facades of the structure are visible and accessible to tourists in the archaeological tunnels, and a full-size replica is the centerpiece of the Copán Sculpture Museum,' says Kristin Landau, an archaeologist working at the site. 'An associated offering of nine eccentric flints is displayed in the town's museum.'

Among the greatest of Copán's kings was Smoke Imix (Smoke Jaguar), the 12th king, who ruled from AD 628 to 695, longer than any other Copán king. Smoke Imix was wise and powerful, and 'he brought Copan to its political height and set the stage for artistic and cultural renovation exemplified during Ruler 13's reign,' according to Landau. He might have even taken over the nearby princedom of Quiriguá, as one of the famous altars there bears his name and image. By the time he died in 695, Copán's population had grown significantly. At its peak, Copán may have supported as many as 20,000 people.

Smoke Imix was succeeded by the 13th king Waxaklajuun Ub'aah K'awiil (popularly – but incorrectly – known as 18 Rabbit; 695–738), who willingly took the reins of power and pursued further military conquest. '[Ruler 13] developed an in-the-round sculptural style exemplified by his stelae in the Great Plaza, constructed the final phase of the Ball Court, and commissioned Temple 22, his potential throne room,' says Landau. In a war with his neighbor K'ak' Tiliw Chan Yoaat of Quiriguá – in present-day Guatemala – King 13 was captured and beheaded, to be succeeded by Smoke Monkey, who was known in those days as K'ak' Joplaj Chan K'awiil, and ruled from 738 to 749. Smoke Monkey's short reign left little mark on Copán. In 749 Smoke Monkey was succeeded by his son K'ak' Yipyaj Chan K'awiil (Smoke Shell, 749–763), one of Copán's greatest builders. He doubled the length of Ruler 13's great Hieroglyphic Stairway, which immortalizes the achievements of the dynasty from its establishment until 755, when he finished and dedicated the stairway in its final form. It is the longest such inscription and historical chronicle ever discovered in Mesoamerica.

Yax Pasaj Chan Yoaat (First Dawned Sky Lightening God, 763–820), Smoke Shell's successor and the 16th king of Copán, continued the beautification of Copán through the construction of Temple 11, a literal diagram of the Maya cosmos, and Altar Q, the famous representation of all of Copán's kings, a family tree of sorts. However, by the middle of his reign it seems that the dynasty's power was declining and its residents had fallen on hard times.

THE DECLINE

Until recently the collapse of the civilization at Copán has been a complete mystery. Now, archaeologists are starting to understand what happened, though it is still a hotly debated topic. The traditional scenario claims that, near the end of Copán's heyday, the population grew at an unprecedented rate, straining agricultural resources. In the end, Copán was no longer agriculturally self-sufficient and had to import food from other areas. The urban core expanded in the fertile lowlands in the center of the valley, forcing both agriculture and residential areas to spread onto the steep slopes surrounding the valley. Wide areas were deforested, resulting in massive erosion that further decimated agricultural production and flooding during rainy seasons. Skeletal remains of people who died during the final years of Copán's heyday show marked evidence of malnutrition and infectious diseases, as well as a decreased lifespan. However, new data collected by archaeobotanists suggest quite the opposite. Pollen samples taken from the Copán Valley indicate that there was a good balance between forested and cultivated lands. Rather than a protracted decline, rapid *re*forestation at the end of the Late Classic indicates a dramatic drop in population. And it seems unlikely that local or even regional ecology had anything to do with the collapse. While we may never truly know what caused this collapse – seen throughout the Maya area – archaeologists have found only a few settlements on nearby hillsides dating from the Postclassic. Whether these settlers were ethnically Maya, Lenca or of some other indigenous group is another hotly debated topic. Nonetheless, by the time European explorers traversed the area, the royal city of Copán had been claimed by jungle.

EUROPEAN DISCOVERY

The first known European to see the ruins was Diego García de Palacios, a representative of Spanish King Felipe II, who lived in Guatemala and traveled through the region. On March 8, 1576, he wrote to the king about the ruins. Only about five families were living there and they knew nothing of the history of the ruins. The discovery was not pursued, and almost three centuries went by until another Spaniard, Colonel Juan Galindo, visited the ruins and made the first map of them.

Galindo's report stimulated Americans John L Stephens and Frederick Catherwood to come to Copán on their Central American journey in 1839. When Stephens published the book *Incidents of Travel in Central America, Chiapas, and Yucatán* in 1841, illustrated by Catherwood, the ruins first became known to the world.

THE RISE & FALL OF THE MAYA

Creation (13.0.0.0.0, 4 Ajaw, 8 Kumk'u)

According to the *Popol Vuh*, the K'iche' Maya book of creation, it took the gods four attempts to create a being powerful enough to maintain the world. On the first attempt the gods made deer, birds and other animals, but when the gods called upon the animals to pronounce the names of their creators, they only squawked and grunted and roared. Not being able to speak properly to honor the gods, they were deemed unworthy and condemned to be eaten.

The second attempt was a human made out of mud. The mud person spoke 'without knowledge and understanding' and soon he fell apart and dissolved back into the mud, to be replaced by men of flesh. The fleshed beings, however, turned to wickedness and were wiped out in a great flood. The gods' third attempt was a person carved from wood. These were better than the mud people, but still not perfect. They could speak, walk around, and even began to populate the world with their children. But they 'walked without purpose,' and did not remember their Framer or their Shaper, and so they were destroyed, ground up on their own grinding stones. The survivors became chattering monkeys found in trees throughout Mesoamerica.

The gods finally got it right when they discovered maize, from which they made the flesh of mankind. The *Popul Vuh,* one of the great religious texts of all time, describes the event: 'Thus their frame and shape were given expression by our first Mother and our first Father. Their flesh was merely yellow ears of maize and white ears of maize…'

Preclassic Period (2000 BC–AD 250)

For their part, archaeologists (mud people?) say the Copán Valley had its first proto-Maya settlers by about 1100 BC, and a century later settlements on the Guatemalan Pacific coast were developing a hierarchical society. Without question, the most significant event of this period occurred about 1000 BC, not in the traditional Maya lands, but in nearby Tabasco and Veracruz, Mexico. The mysterious Olmec people developed a hieroglyphic writing system, perhaps based on knowledge borrowed from the Zapotecs of Oaxaca. They also developed what is known as the Vague Year calendar of 365 days and the *tzolk'in* (ritual calendar) of 260 days. Although aspects of Olmec culture lived on among their neighbors, paving the way for the later accomplishments of Maya art, architecture and science, the Olmecs themselves disappeared; historians assume they were overpowered by waves of invaders.

From 800 BC to 300 BC, known as the Middle Preclassic period, rich villages already existed in Honduras' Copán Valley and trade routes flourished, with coastal peoples exchanging ever important salt for highlanders' tool-grade obsidian. There was a brisk trade in ceramic pots and villages were founded at Tikal, in northern Guatemala.

Improved agricultural techniques led to surpluses, an accumulation of wealth, class divisions and monumental construction projects, particularly temples. The first temples were modest affairs, consisting of raised-earth platforms topped by a thatch-roofed shelter similar to a normal *na* (hut). In the lowlands, where limestone was abundant, the Maya began to build platform temples from stone. As each succeeding local potentate had to have a bigger temple, more and larger platforms were put over other platforms, forming huge step pyramids with a hut-style shelter on top. More and more pyramids were built around large plazas, with working-class homes around the outskirts. The stage was set for the flourishing of Classic Maya civilization.

Classic Period (AD 250–800)

Armies from Teotihuacán (beneath modern-day Mexico City) invaded and conquered the Maya highlands, imposing their rule and culture for a time, but were eventually absorbed into Maya daily life by the late 6th century. The so-called Esperanza culture, a blend of Mexican and Maya elements, was born of this conquest and acculturation. It was during this period that the Maya produced the western hemisphere's most brilliant ancient civilization. Stretching from Copán, through Guatemala and Belize to Mexico's Yucatán Peninsula, they constructed great ceremonial and cultural centers including Quiriguá, Tikal, Uaxactún, Río Azul and Yaxhá in Guatemala, Caracol in Belize, Yaxchilán and Palenque in Chiapas and Calakmul, Uxmal and Chichén Itzá in the Yucatán. Maya astronomers could predict lunar eclipses, and their calculation of the orbit of Venus was off by less than one day for every 1000 years.

At its peak, most Maya lands of the Late Classic period were ruled as a network of independent, but interdependent, city-states. Each city-state had its noble house, headed by a king who was the social, political and religious focus of the city's life. The king propitiated the gods by shedding his blood in ceremonies where he pierced his tongue, ears or penis with a sharp instrument. Not blood shy, he also led his soldiers into battle against rival cities, capturing prisoners for use in human sacrifices.

Postclassic Period (AD 800–1500)

Beginning in AD 800, Maya civilizations entered a rapid and mysterious decline. The ruling dynasties apparently lost power, the construction of new structures and stelae halted, and the population dropped, likely by a combination of death, migration and lowered birth rate. The once mighty Maya cities of Tikal, Yaxchilán, Copán, Quiriguá, Piedras Negras and Caracol all reverted to little more than villages with residues of ceremonial grandeur. Over the centuries the people living in those villages – still Maya, of course – lost all collective memory of their fabled past. By the time European explorers arrived in the 16th century, the ruins had been swallowed by their jungle surroundings and were as much a mystery to the local people as to the explorers themselves.

Why and whether Classic Maya civilization crashed suddenly or gradually is still a matter for debate. Most researchers agree that a combination of factors are to blame, mostly related to a population boom that taxed the food supply and exhausted fertile farmland. However, new data may suggest otherwise. Devastating droughts, each of several years' duration, around AD 810, 860 and 910 would have exacerbated the problem. Maya royalty derived its legitimacy, to a large degree, from a divine connection with the gods. When kings and priests proved unable to induce the gods to improve the increasingly desperate situation, disenchantment and even rebellion may have swept the region. In any case, when Toltec invaders arrived in the Yucatan from Central Mexico, the Maya could do nothing but retreat into their villages.

An End is Near (Present–December 23, 2012)

When discussing the 'Maya Collapse' it is often assumed that the Maya disappeared altogether. In Honduras, the modern Maya- Chortí are thought to descend from the builders of Copán, and remain mostly subsistence farmers. They, like indigenous people everywhere, contend with an array of modern challenges, including cultural preservation and land rights (p118).

But there is solace in knowing the end, or at least rebirth, is near. The Great Cycle of the present age will last for 13 *bak'tun* cycles, which in maize people's time ends on December 23, 2012, the winter solstice. Death and life must dance together for the succession of days to continue, so while 2012 may well be the end of us, it will not be for the cosmos. In fact, there are stelae that refer to a period of time 41,341,050,000,000,000,000,000,000,000 years long. By comparison, the chattering monkeys say the Big Bang occurred a mere 15,000,000,000 years ago. And even that incomprehensibly long cycle will be repeated, over and over, infinitely.

with contributions from Dr Allen J Christenson & Kristin Landau

DIGGING UP HISTORY

The history of ancient Copán continues to unfold today, as archaeologists continue to probe the site. 'Some of the most important new discoveries have been made outside of the site core, and more nuanced understandings of Copán as an urban center supporting activities of the royals, elites and general population are developing every field season,' says Landau. 'Although efforts have been made to protect these areas and open them to tourism, the majority of the ancient city remains on private lands, inaccessible to tourists and archaeologists alike.'

The remains of 3450 structures have been found in the 24 sq km surrounding the Principal Group, most of them within about 500m of the Principal Group. In a wider zone, 4509 structures have been detected in 1420 sites within 135 sq km of the ruins. These discoveries indicate that, at the peak of Maya civilization here, around the end of the 8th century, the valley of Copán possibly had over 20,000 inhabitants – a population not reached again until the 1980s.

In addition to examining the area outside the Principal Group, archaeologists are continuing to explore and make new discoveries within the Principal Group itself. Five separate phases of building on this site have been identified; the final phase, dating from AD 650 to 820, is partially what we see today. But buried underneath the visible architecture are residues of other yet earlier buildings, which archaeologists are exploring by means of underground tunnels.

Orientation

There are three buildings at the entrance to the archaeological site: the visitors center, the Sculpture Museum and the Rosalila Cafeteria–gift shop. Behind the visitors center are signs for the ruins themselves and the Yax Ché nature trail.

Information

Admission to the **Copán archaeological site** (☎ 651-4108; admission L$285; 🕑 8am-5pm, museum closes 4pm) includes entry to Las Sepulturas (p133). The tunnels (opposite) cost an additional and exorbitant L$285, while the extra L$133 fee for the Sculpture Museum (p133) is totally worth it. Near the ticket booth are a small gift-shop, restrooms and a booth where you can arrange a guide (L$475 for a group up to 10 people). Across the parking lot, near the Sculpture Museum, is a much larger *artesanía* shop, and the Rosalila Cafeteria – which sells simple meals plus chips, Gatorade and other snacks; both places are surprisingly good. You can also take horseback rides from near the visitors centre for around L$380 per person.

Dangers & Annoyances

The biggest safety concern at Copán is falling down the steep stone steps, which, besides being endlessly embarrassing, can be quite painful, even bone-breaking. Copán doesn't have the high structures other ruins do, but wear good shoes and watch your step at all times.

Sights

THE PRINCIPAL GROUP

The **Principal Group** is the royal urban core of Copán, and includes the **Great Plaza** in the north, and the massive architectural complex known as the **Acropolis** to the south. Located about 400m beyond the visitors center, the Principal Group was Copán's commercial and political hub, both introducing outside visitors to its grandeur and supporting royal headquarters, stages for ritual performance, and kingly residences.

THE GREAT PLAZA

The north sector of the group is located on the left-hand side as one enters the site walking along the western *sak'be* (white road). The stelae in the center of the Plaza all date from Ruler 13's reign (AD 695–738). Their curious and precise placement has long been investigated by archaeologists and archaeoastronomers alike. All seem to have been painted; a few traces of red paint survive on Stela C. Many stelae had quadripartite or cross-shaped chambers beneath them in which offerings were placed at the time of stela dedication.

Many of the stelae in the Great Plaza portray Waxaklajuun Ub'aah K'awiil as himself or in the guise of Copán's patron gods, including Stelae A, B, C, D, F, H and 4. Perhaps the most beautiful stele in the Great Plaza is **Stela A** (AD 731); the original has been moved inside the Sculpture Museum; the one outdoors is a reproduction. Nearby, and almost equal in beauty, are Stela 4 (February 3, 731); **Stela B** (August 22, 731), depicting the 13th ruler within the great Mo' Witz' (Macaw Mountain); and the double-sided **Stela C**

(December 5, 711), with a turtle-shaped altar in front. **Stelae E and I** were both erected by earlier rulers and flank the east and west sides of the Plaza. At the northern end of the Great Plaza, at the base of Structure 2, **Stela D** (July 26, 736) portrays Ruler 13 wearing the mask and beard of an unknown god. On its back are two columns of rare full-figure hieroglyphs; at its base is an altar with dual representations of a fleshed and skeletal jaguar. In front of the altar is the burial place of Dr John Owen, an archaeologist with the expedition from Harvard's Peabody Museum who died during the work in 1893.

On the east side of the plaza is **Stela F** (October 13, 721), which shows the ruler in almost three-dimensional relief, involved in the story of Copán's patron gods. Designed by Yax Pasaj, the **Altar G complex** (G1 – February 19, 766; G2 – September 15, 795; G3 – August 19, 800), is an ancestral veneration monument showing double-headed feathered snakes and the last ruler's desire to communicate through trance with Ruler 13. **Stela H** (December 5, 730) depicts Ruler 13 as the Maize God in the dance of creation.

THE ACROPOLIS

The Acropolis is a collection of imposing structures at the south end of the site. In Copán's heyday this would have been the heart of the city and government. The lofty flight of steps to the south of the Hieroglyphic Stairway is called the **Temple of the Inscriptions** (Temple 11). On top of the stairway, the walls are carved with groups of hieroglyphs in mirror images of each other. On the south side of the Temple of the Inscriptions are the East and West Courts. In the **West Court**, be sure to see **Altar Q** (March 2, 776), among the most famous sculptures here; the original is in the Sculpture Museum. Around its sides, carved in superb relief, are depictions and the names of the 16 great kings of Copán, ending with the altar's creator, Yax Pasaj. Below the altar was a sacrificial vault in which archaeologists discovered the bones of 15 jaguars (one for each previous king) and several macaws that were sacrificed to the glory of Yax Pasaj and his ancestors.

TUNNELS

In 1999 archaeologists opened up two tunnels that allow visitors to get a glimpse of the Early Classic pre-existing structures below the visible structures. The first, **Rosalila tunnel**, is very short and takes only a few visitors at a time. Behind thick glass, the famous Rosalila temple is only barely exposed. The other tunnel, **Los Jaguares**, was originally 700m in length, but a large section has been closed, reducing it to about 80m, running along the foundations of Temple 22. This tunnel exits on the outside of the main site, so you must walk around the main site to get back in again. While interesting, it's hard to justify the L$285 extra you pay to get in.

Rosalila, dedicated in AD 571 by Copán's 10th ruler, Moon Jaguar, was apparently so sacred that when Structure 16 was built over it the temple was not destroyed but left completely intact.

The original Rosalila temple is still in the core of Structure 16. Under it is a still earlier temple, Margarita, built 150 years before, as well as other earlier platforms and tombs.

BALL COURT & HIEROGLYPHIC STAIRWAY

Linking the open expanse of the Great Plaza with the massive architectural complex to its south is the **Ball Court** (final phase January 10, 738), the second-largest in Mesoamerica. The one you see is the third one on this axis; the other two were buried by this construction (a second ball court can be found along the nature trail). Note the macaw heads carved at the top of the sloping walls. The central three markers in the court were the work of the 13th ruler, and are now on display in the town museum. The previous versions of the macaw heads are in the Sculpture Museum.

South of the Ball Court is Copán's most famous monument, the **Hieroglyphic Stairway**, the work of Rulers 13 and 15. Today it's protected from the elements by a tarp, which is replaced every 10 years or so. This lessens the impact of its beauty, but you can still get an idea of how it looked. The flight of 64 steps bears the dynastic history – in several thousand glyphs – of the royal house of Copán; the steps are bordered by balustrades inscribed with more reliefs and glyphs. Unfortunately, when archaeologists first uncovered the stairway in the late 19th century, its upper section had collapsed. The bottom 15 stairs are in their original position, but the rest of the stones were jumbled and cemented in random order. Today a group of the best Maya epigraphers in the world are working to digitally scan, reorder and decipher this magnificent stairway.

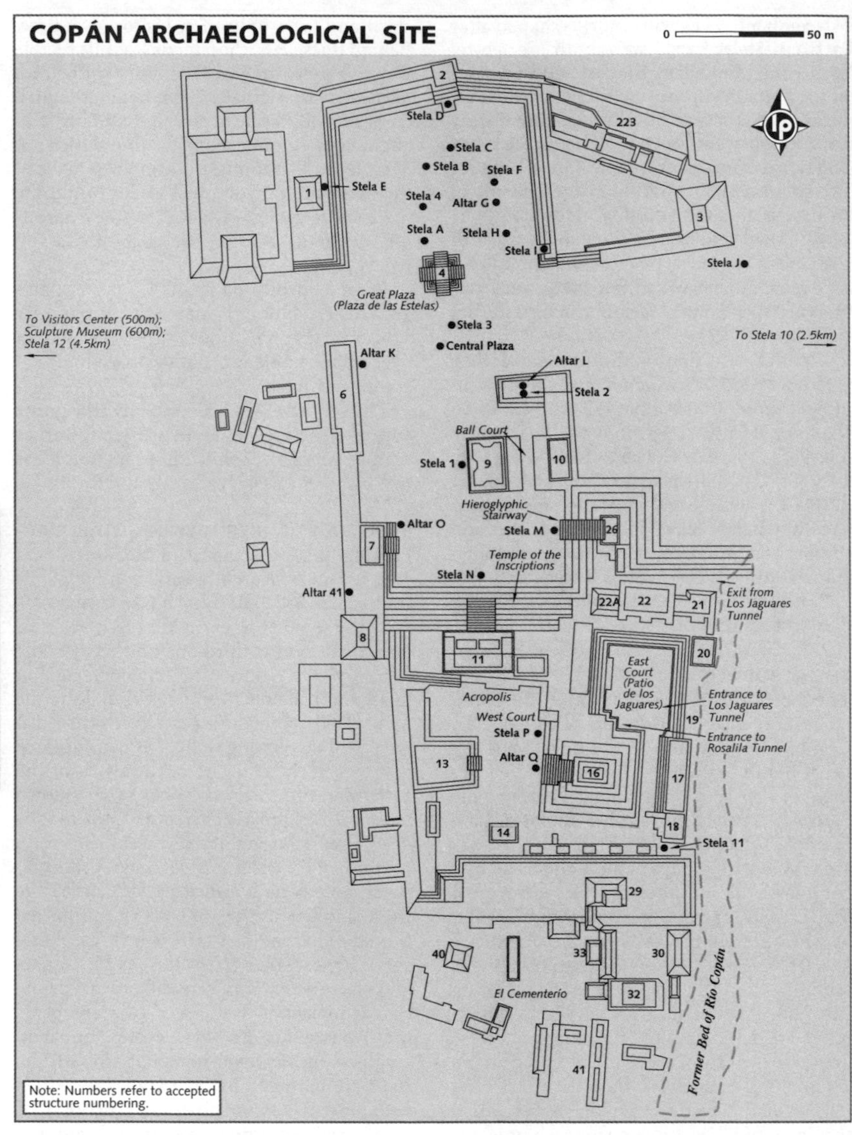

At the base of the Hieroglyphic Stairway is **Stela M** (April 12, 756), bearing a figure (probably Smoke Shell, Ruler 15) in a feathered cloak; glyphs tell of the solar eclipse in that year. The altar in front shows a plumed serpent with a human head emerging from its jaws.

Beside the stairway, a tunnel leads to the tomb of the 12th king, Smoke Imix, buried in a large crypt called Chorcha. The tomb, discovered in June 1989, held a treasure trove of painted pottery and beautiful carved jade objects. A series of 12 incense burners capped with portraits of Smoke Imix and his 11 predecessors were also found. You can see them in the town museum, though the tomb and this tunnel have not yet been opened for tourists.

LAS SEPULTURAS, EL BOSQUE & OUTLYING AREAS

Excavations in the 1980s at **Las Sepulturas** and more recently at other outlying areas have shed light on the daily life of ancient Copanecos since the Early Preclassic period (2000–1000 BC). Las Sepulturas, named for the great amount of burials found there and once connected to the Great Plaza by a *sak'be,* might have been a residential area where powerful noble scribes lived. The huge, luxurious residential compound seems to have supported as many as 50 buildings arranged around seven courtyards. The principal structure, called the **House of the Bakabs** (Bakabs were officials), had outer walls carved with the full-size figures of scribal patrons holding writing implements; inside was a hieroglyphic bench. To get to the site, you have to go back to the main road, turn right and follow the sidewalk, then right again at the sign (2km).

Hopefully accessible to tourists in the near future, the **El Bosque Zone** in the western forest of the archaeological park was excavated between 2005 and 2007. Although more than 400m from the Principal Group, a stunning subterranean tomb was unearthed there, the likes of which had never been found outside of the royal precinct. The tomb's occupant is not from Copán and lab analysis is ongoing. Impressive digital reconstructions, an interactive map of Copán, and a short documentary about the tomb and other important outlying areas of ancient Copán can be found at www.papacweb.org.

SCULPTURE MUSEUM

Whereas Tikal is renowned for its tall temple pyramids and Palenque for its elegant design and limestone relief panels, Copán is known as the Paris of the Maya world for its sculpture. Some of the best pieces are displayed at the site's excellent museum, built in 1996 and a highlight of any visit to Copán. Entering the museum is an impressive experience in itself: you go in through the maw of a serpent and wind through the entrails of the beast before suddenly emerging into a fantastic world of sculpture and light. The centerpiece of the museum is a huge full-scale replica of the Rosalila temple, the ornate brightly painted structure found at the core of Structure 16, the central building of the Acropolis. Two floors of wide corridors connected by long ramps open to the middle for better views of Rosalila. On the walls are examples of Copán's incredible stonework, with well-organized displays explaining the iconography, imagery and hieroglyphs found there.

STELAE 10 & 12

Dating to AD 652 and erected by Smoke Imix, Stelae 10 and 12 are found on two hills approximately 7km apart: a line connecting them would cross the southern edge of the Acropolis. These monoliths measure around 3m, each with inscriptions on all four sides. On two days a year – April 12 and September 7 – the sun sets directly behind Stela 10 as you look at it from Stela 12. No one knows the meaning; some believe they are a calendar for planting and harvesting, others think that they have an astronomical significance. In any case, both make pleasant hikes, with sweeping views of the valley. It's best to go with a guide – most agencies in town offer day trips that include a visit to one or both sites.

Tours

Independent travelers are often loath to hire guides, but those at Copán Ruinas tend to be better than most. Fees are steep at L$665 per group for the ruins and tunnels, or L$475 per group for the ruins only. Tours last about two hours; don't be shy about asking other travelers if they want to go in together for a guide. Guides speaking Spanish, English, German, French and Italian are available.

You can also pick up a copy of the booklet *History Carved in Stone: A Guide to the Archaeological Park of the Ruins of Copán,* by William L Fash and Ricardo Agurcia Fasquelle, which is usually available for a couple of dollars at the visitors center.

Getting There & Away

The archaeological site is about 1km outside of Copán Ruinas on the road to La Entrada – a pleasant 15-minute stroll along a footpath to one side of the highway. Las Sepulturas is 2km further along. A taxi to the ruins costs L$10 per person, L$15 to Las Sepulturas.

LA RUTA LENCA

Well removed from the mainstream Honduran Tourist Trail, the Ruta Lenca (Lenca Route) of-

LOCAL LORE: LA SUCIA

One of the most widely told tales in Honduras is of La Sucia (the Dirty Woman). The story varies widely, but the basics stay the same: a man encounters a woman, usually by a river or lake. Usually her face is obscured, whether because it's night-time or because she's just washed her hair. The woman seduces the man, or attempts to, and soon begins to cackle loudly. The man looks at her to discover she is in fact a toothless old hag. She has gargantuan breasts, which she thrusts at him, crooning *'Toma tu teta, toma tu teta!'* (a vulgar way of saying, 'Drink your milk, drink your milk!'). Horrified, the man runs off.

The story often involves a soon-to-be-married groom or a wayward son. A version of La Sucia is told by the Lenca, who call the woman the *ciguanaba;* by English-speaking blacks, who call her Bubbly Susan; and by Garífunas, who call her Agayuma and often set the story to music. The story must be intended to dissuade men from cheating on their wives, lest they end up with La Sucia, but is told with such relish and humor that it's hard to detect much moralizing in it.

fers the opportunity to visit traditional Lenca villages, explore lost countryside and ascend the country's highest peak. The route officially starts in Santa Rosa de Copán – though most people begin in Gracias – and includes San Juan, La Esperanza and others, continuing to Marcala, nearly to the Salvadoran border. You may get some unfriendly snarls – outsiders are looked at with extreme circumspect, especially in the larger cities – but don't let a few sour grapes ruin your day.

The landscape changes dramatically with the seasons, becoming lush and green in the rainy season (April to November) and hot and brown in the dry season. The best time to come is the end of the rainy season, when the trees are still green but the roads and trails have started to dry out.

SANTA ROSA DE COPÁN

pop 48,000

Santa Rosa de Copán is a small, cool colonial mountain town, with cobblestone streets, clay-tiled roofs and a lovely church with *azulejo* (glazed tile) floors. There's not a ton to do here, but with a bustling city center and vibrant festivals throughout the year it provides a wonderful window into everyday Honduran life.

History

Since the early 1700s Santa Rosa has been key to the region's prosperity because of its tobacco production. In 1765 the Spanish crown chose the town as the site of La Real Factoría del Tabaco, a government office responsible for setting tobacco prices, marketing the product and distributing the seeds and equipment necessary for its production. This official presence helped to market the region's cash crop even more, which in turn increased the wealth of this city. It became such an economic force, in fact, that by 1812 Santa Rosa de Copán was declared the capital of what is now the Lempira department. Today, although the department capital has moved to Gracias, Santa Rosa remains a strong presence in the tobacco industry; cigars produced here are considered among the best in the world.

Orientation

Santa Rosa is up on a hill, about 1km from the bus terminal on the highway. Ascend the road leading up the hill just west of the bus terminal to the Centro Histórico (historical center). This takes you on 4a Av NO to the city center. Parque Central is three blocks west of 4a Av NO and bordered by 1a Calle NO, Calle Real Centenario, 1a Av NO and 1a Av NE. As with most towns in Honduras, *avenidas* run north–south, and *calles* run east–west. They extend out in four directions: northeast (*noreste;* NE), northwest (*noroeste;* NO), southeast (*sureste;* SE) and southwest (*suroeste;* SO). Almost everything you'll need is within walking distance of Parque Central.

Information

Banco Atlántida (1Av NE btwn 2 & 3 Calles NE; 8am-4pm Mon-Fri, 8:30-11:30am Sat) Exchanges traveler's checks and US dollars. Has a 24-hour ATM.

Casa de Cultura (☎ 662-0800; Av Alvaro Contreras at 1a Calle SO; 8am-noon & 2-5pm Mon-Fri) Occasionally presents art exhibits and theater productions.

Farmacia Central (☎ 662-0465; Parque Central; 8am-noon & 2-6pm Mon-Sat)

Hondutel (Parque Central; 7am-9pm) For international calls.

Hospital del Occidente (☎ 662-0112; Barrio El Calvario; 🕑 24hr)
Lavandería Wash & Dry (1a Calle NE near 4a Av NE; per load L$80; 🕑 7am-9pm)
Pizza Pizza (☎ 662-1104; Calle Real Centenario near 6a Av NE; 🕑 11:30am-9pm, Thu-Tue) Decent book exchange of mostly English-language books.
Police (☎ 662-0214; Parque Central; 🕑 24hr)
Post office (Parque Central; 🕑 8am-noon & 2-5pm Mon-Fri, 8am-noon Sat)
Tourist office (☎ 662-2234; turismosrc@yahoo.com; Parque Central; 🕑 8am-noon & 1:30-5pm Mon-Sat) In the kiosk in Parque Central; has good information on area sights and services. Also has internet access (L$15 per hour). English is spoken.
Zona Digital (1a Calle NE at 3a Av NE, Plaza Saavedra; internet per hr L$20; 🕑 8am-10pm) Internet access; also offers international calls.

Sights & Activities

Fine hand-rolled cigars are produced in **La Flor de Copán** (☎ 662-0185; Carr a Nueva Ocotepeque; 🕑 8:30am-4:30pm Mon-Fri) factory, just 2km from town. You can learn about the entire process – from the trimming of the tobacco to the packaging of *puros* (cigars) – by taking a tour (L$40, 10am and 2pm); call to reserve a spot. If you want a smoke without a tour, stop by the factory outlet store in town (Calle Centenario near 3a Av Norte), open from 8am to noon and 2pm to 5pm Monday to Friday, 8am to noon Saturday.

Learn how coffee is roasted, classified, and prepared for export at **Beneficio Maya** (☎ 662-1665; www.cafecopan.com; Colonia San Martín; 🕑 7am-noon & 2-5pm Mon-Fri, 7am-noon Sat), a coffee processing plant. Visitors are welcome year-round but **tours** (no cost; 🕑 same time as opening hours) are only offered during the coffee season (November to February).

At the western end of town, **Parque El Cerrito** (8a Av NO to 12a Av NO btwn Calle Real Centenario & 1a Calle NO) has a nice lookout point –105 steps to the best view around.

Courses

Although it's mainly dedicated to teaching English to Hondurans, the **International Language Institute** (☎ 662-1378; www.spanish-ili-copan.com; Barrio Santa Teresa) just up the street from the Casa del Obrero, also offers Spanish courses. Classes are one-on-one and cost L$228 per hour, with a one-time L$190 registration fee. Homestays, including three meals per day, can be arranged for an additional L$237 per day.

Tours

Lenca Land Trails (☎ 662-1128; max@Lenca-Honduras.com; Calle Real Centenario near 3a Av NO) offers personalized day trips and multi-day excursions to the colonial villages on the Ruta Lenca and the Parque Nacional Montaña de Celaque.

Festivals & Events

Santa Rosa de Copán is known for its religious processions during **Semana Santa**. Beginning on Thursday, re-enactments of the six processions surrounding Jesus' death and resurrection take place. The most spectacular is the Holy Cross Procession, where Jesus – under the weight of a cross and the eyes of guards – is led on a 2km walk over *alfombras* (intricate, colored carpets made of sawdust, flowers and seeds) that are created overnight by townspeople. The Holy Cross Procession takes place on Friday morning in the historic town center. Be sure to find a place to stand before 9am so you can check out the artwork before it's trampled.

La Feria de los Llanos is an artisanal fair that showcases crafts made in and around Santa Rosa. It is held three times a year: Semana Santa, August 25 to 30 and the second week in December.

A lively event, the **Noche de Fumadores** (held the third Friday of August) is an evening dedicated to fine cigars. A variety of locally produced stogies are offered by La Flor de Copán and sampled by festival-goers.

Sleeping

BUDGET

The tourist office can also arrange **homestays** (r with breakfast L$200), which may be the best option for budget travelers.

Hotel El Rosario (☎ 662-0211; 3a Av NE near 2a Calle NE; s/d with shared bathroom L$150/300; **P**) Two doors down from Blanca Nieves, this is probably your best budget bet. The rooms are musty and the showers only have cold water, but the sheets feel clean and, well, the price is right.

Hotel Blanca Nieves (☎ 662-4480; 3a Av NE near 2a Calle NE; s/d with shared bathroom L$180/360) Rooms at the Snow White are not the fairest of them all, but if next door is packed, you might want to check them out. Enter through the motorcycle shop.

MIDRANGE

our pick **Posada de Carlos y Blanca** (☎ 662-1028; posadacarlosyb@yahoo.com; Calle Real Centenario near 4a

Av SO; s/d incl breakfast L$440/661; (P) (computer)) A warm family setting with comfy rooms makes this converted home your best midrange bet in town. There's a welcoming living room with lots of table games and books too.

Hotel VIP Copán (☎ 662-0265; hotelvipcopan@hotmail.com; 1a Calle NE at 3a Av NE; s/d with fan L$445/695, with air-con L$645/845; (P) (air-con) (pool)) The rooms at this largish hotel are cramped and dark, but they are at least clean and up-to-date. The air-conditioned rooms are much nicer, but they have ridiculous bathtub showers. There's a pleasant pool on the premises.

Hotel Elvir (☎ 662-0103; www.hotelelvir.com; Calle Real Centenario near 3a Av NO; s/d with fan L$775/1001, with air-con L$982/1246; (P) (air-con) (computer)) Not much to look at from the outside – don't worry, it gets at least a little better once you're inside – this is Santa Rosa's only 'fancy' hotel. Accommodations are clean but lifeless, with particle-board furniture, dated decor and poor lighting – all in all a disappointment given the price and grand surroundings.

Eating

Every afternoon, street vendors sell steaming corn *tamales* and sweet breads (L$10 to L$20) from their baskets and Tupperware on Parque Central. **Manzanitas Supermarket** (Calle Real Centenario near 2a Av NO; ⏲ 8:30am-7pm Mon-Sat, to noon Sun) is a full-on supermarket in the center of town, while the **Mercado Central** (1a Calle NE at 2a Av NE; ⏲ 6am-4pm Mon-Sat, to noon Sun), behind the church, sells everything from carrots to clothing.

BUDGET

Ten Napel Café (☎ 662-3238; Calle Real Centenario near 4a Av NO; mains L$20-40; ⏲ 9am-noon & 1:30-7pm) Next to the Hotel Elvir, this cozy coffee shop is perfect if you need a caffeine or sugar fix (or both).

Tio Kike (☎ 662-3249; 1a Av SE near 1a Calle SE; mains L$20-60; ⏲ breakfast, lunch & dinner) An unexpectedly appealing hole-in-the-wall that serves up good *típica*. The roasted chicken and fruit smoothies are particularly good.

Hemady's Típico (☎ 662-1124; Calle Real Centenario near 2a Av NO; mains L$30-90; ⏲ breakfast, lunch & dinner Mon-Sat, lunch & dinner Sun) Housed in a renovated colonial building with original *azulejo* floors, this place serves reliable Honduran fare, sandwiches and hamburgers. It's a 'family friendly' establishment, which means no booze.

our pick **Pizza Pizza** (☎ 662-1104; Calle Real Centenario near 6a Av NE; mains L$65-100; ⏲ lunch & dinner, Thu-Tue) This popular pizzeria that serves brick-oven pizza made with hand-tossed dough, homemade sauce and any number of toppings is one of our faves in Honduras. It's owned by Warren Post, a friendly American who is a great source of information if you can catch him.

MIDRANGE

Restaurante Flamingos (☎ 662-0654; 1a Av SE near 1a Calle SE; mains L$80-130; ⏲ lunch & dinner) Considered one of the best restaurants in town, Flamingos has a pleasant atmosphere and good food. Seafood is the specialty here. There's live music on Sundays.

El Rodeo (☎ 662-0697; 1a Av SE btwn 1a & 2a Calles SE; mains L$100-170; ⏲ lunch & dinner) This cavernous steakhouse doubles as a boho bar Thursday through Saturday nights. Meals are well prepared and portions are hefty; they always come with a complimentary *anafras* (bean fondue) for the table too. The menu has a few options if meat isn't your thing, but if it is, definitely go for it – you'll leave satisfied.

Drinking & Entertainment

El Rodeo (☎ 662-0697; 1a Av SE btwn 1a & 2a Calles SE; no cover; ⏲ 10:30am-midnight) Fairly hip, believe it or not.

Zotz (Calle Centenario btwn 1 & 2 Calles SO) A locally recommended nightspot.

Xtassi's Discotec (1a Av SE near 2a Calle SE; cover L$100; ⏲ 9pm-4am Wed-Sat) Just down the street from El Rodeo, this disco attracts a young – as in teenaged – crowd on weekends. Not much of a scene unless you're into braces and cliques.

Cinema Don Quijote (☎ 662-2625; Plaza Saavedra; 1a Calle NE at 3a Av NE; tickets L$35) Late-release Hollywood films are shown on one screen at 7pm every night.

Getting There & Away

Buses from Santa Rosa de Copán come and go from the Terminal de Transporte on the main highway, about 1km from the center of town. **La Sultana de Occidente** (☎ 662-0940) has a ticket office behind JM for express buses to San Pedro Sula, La Entrada, Agua Caliente (at the Guatemalan border) and San Salvador, with connections to Copán Ruinas and Tegucigalpa. Toritos & Copaneca has a stop two blocks down the highway, with buses to San Pedro Sula and Tegucigalpa (*directo* and *ordinario*) plus Gracias and Belén Gualcho. Destinations include the following.

Agua Caliente Guatemalan border (L$75, 2½ hours, 5am, 9:30am, 10:30am, noon, 1pm, 2:30pm, 3:30pm, 5pm and 6pm)
Copán Ruinas (L$75, three hours; 11:30am, 12:30pm and 2pm) Or take any bus heading to San Pedro Sula and transfer at La Entrada.
Gracias (L$40, 1½ hours, 47km; every 45 minutes 7:10am to 6pm)
La Entrada (*directo* L$30, 45 minutes; *ordinario* L$20, 1¼ hours) Take any San Pedro Sula bus.
Nueva Ocotepeque (L$120, two hours) Take any Agua Caliente bus.
San Pedro Sula (*ordinario* L$55, 3½ hours, every 30 minutes 4:30am-5pm; *directo* L$80, 2½ hours) La Sultana bus company (6am, 7:30am, 9am, 10am, 11am and 1pm); Toritos & Copaneca (8am, 9:30am & 2pm)
Tegucigalpa (L$300, 6½ hours) Take any San Pedro Sula morning bus and transfer.

Getting Around

CAR & MOTORCYCLE

All of the streets in downtown Santa Rosa are one lane and one way; before you turn down any street, check to see if you'll be going with the flow of traffic – checking to see if parked cars are facing away from you is a good trick.

TAXI

From 7am to 7pm, taxis circle the city or are at taxi stands at Parque Central and the bus terminal. To book a cab call the **Asociación de Taxis Copán** (☎ 9983-9892). Rides within town cost L$10 and it's around L$6 to the bus station; for destinations further afield, be sure to agree on a price before you get in.

BELÉN GUALCHO

pop 6100

If you are headed down toward Nueva Ocotepeque, consider taking a little side trip from the highway at Cucuyagua to Belén Gualcho, a picturesque colonial village bordering Parque Nacional Montaña de Celaque. The town is especially known for the busy Lenca market held there every Sunday morning.

To reach someone in Belén Gualcho, call **Hondutel** (☎ 651-9600, 601-5030, 601-5029; half a block from Parque Central; 🕑 7:30am-noon & 1-5pm). There's an internet cafe, **Internet Cecob** (per hr L$20; 🕑 11am-1:30pm & 4-10pm Mon-Fri, 11am-10pm Sat & Sun), next to the Hotel Olvin. **Farmacia El Carmen** (Parque Central; 🕑 8am-5pm Mon-Sat, to noon Sun) has basic medicines and supplies.

Activities

There's an entrance to Parque Nacional Montaña de Celaque (p141) on the outskirts of Belén Gualcho. There's no checkpoint and no services but the one trail starting here follows the southern edge of the mountain to San Sebastián and San Manuel De Colohete. It's a steep four-hour hike but a beautiful one. Just be sure to stay on the trail – even locals can get lost in the area.

A picturesque hike to a set of waterfalls, the **Cataratas de Santa María de Gualcho**, is also a good way to explore the area. From Belén Gualcho, walk to the hamlet of Lentago, which is on a turnoff from the dirt road that leads to the highway; you should get there in about 10 minutes. Once there, ask someone to point you in the direction of the *sendero* (trail) to the falls. About a 30-minute trek will take you right there.

Sleeping & Eating

Hotels fill up on Saturdays with market vendors; if you plan to stay over that night, check in early to guarantee a spot.

Hotelito El Carmen (s/d with shared bathroom L$40/80, s/d L$80/160; Ⓟ) Belén Gualcho's best hotel is a very simple but surprisingly pleasant place, two blocks downhill from the church and Parque Central. Rooms are small and boxy but clean and comfortable – a few have square windows with swinging wood shutters with a view of town and the valley beyond. If this is full, check for a room at the Pulperia Ovin. It's not as nice, but it'll keep you dry for the night.

There are three basic eateries in town within a couple of blocks of each other on the main drag – Pulpería y Comedor Onan, Comedor y Golosinas Raquel and Pollera Lety. All serve cheap *típica* for breakfast, lunch and dinner.

Getting There & Away

To get here, two daily buses arrive from Santa Rosa de Copán. To return, buses to Santa Rosa de Copán (L$50, two to three hours, hourly 3am to 8am) leave from the church. On Sunday the schedule is 4am, 5am, 7am, 9:30am, noon and 1pm. You may also be able to hitch a ride on a pickup.

NUEVA OCOTEPEQUE

pop 19,100

In the southwest corner of Honduras, Nueva Ocotepeque is the crossroads town from buses to Agua Caliente (Guatemala) and El Poy (El Salvador). Most travelers stop only long enough to transfer buses. Hotels, restaurants and services are either on or near the main street, Calle Intermedio.

Information

Banco Atlántida (Calle Intermedio; 9am-4pm Mon-Fri, 8:30-11:30am Sat) Next to Hotel Internacional; has no ATM. Your closest ATM is probably in Santa Rosa de Copan.

Immigration (653-2162; Calle Intermedio; 7:30am-3:30pm) Across from the Congolón bus terminal.

Police (Carr a Santa Rosa de Copán) Located 500m from the town entrance.

Sights

Not far from town, the magnificent **Parque Nacional Montecristo–El Trifinio** straddles Honduras, Guatemala, and El Salvador, whose borders join at the peak of the park's showcase mountain, Cerro Montecristo, also known as El Trifinio. The three countries manage the park jointly, but only El Salvador has made it reasonably accessible to the public, from the town of Metapán.

Sleeping & Eating

Hotel Turista (653-3639; Av General Francisco Morazán; s/d L$150/200) The best of several cheapies clustered around the Toritos & Copaneca and Transporte San José bus stops. The rooms are cheap and clean, and they have hot-water showers.

Hotel Internacional (653-2357; Calle Intermedio; s/d incl breakfast with fan L$406/580, with air-con L$493/643; P) Probably the best hotel in town, this hulking building has newish rooms, and a rather unique architectural style (for Ocotepeque at least). The rooms are clean and rather sterile.

Servi Pollo (mains L$60-100; 9am-7pm) This bright, glossy joint specializes in fried and roast chicken, but also has hot dogs and hamburgers. Go south from the local bus stop, left at the Banco Occidente, then take the second right.

Getting There & Away

Nueva Ocotepeque has two long-distance bus companies, charging almost identical prices. **Congolón** (653-3064) is half a block south of Parque Central, on the road to El Poy (El Salvador). **Toritos & Copaneca** (653-3405) is two blocks north of the park, near the entrance town. Buses run to various destinations, including the following.

San Pedro Sula (L$130, 4½ hours); Toritos & Copaneca (3am, 4am, 6:30am, 7:15am, 8am, 8:40am, 10am, 10:40am, 12:30pm, 1:45pm, 2:30pm, 4:30pm and 5:30pm) Congolón (midnight; 3am, 5:30am, 6am, 9:30am, 11:30am, 12:30pm, 1pm and 3:30pm)

Santa Rosa de Copán (L$120, 1½ hours) Take any San Pedro Sula bus.

La Entrada (L$100, 2½ hours) Take any San Pedro Sula bus.

CROSSING INTO EL SALVADOR OR GUATEMALA

Transportes San José operates buses from Nueva Ocotepeque to both borders from its dirt-lot terminal two blocks north of the park, near the Toritos & Copaneca office.

Buses to the Salvadoran border at El Poy (L$12, 15 minutes, 7km) leave every 20 minutes from 6:30am to 7pm. Buses to the Guatemalan border at Agua Caliente (L$25, 30 minutes, 22km) leave every half hour from 6am to 6pm. Once past Honduran immigration, catch a truck or moto-taxi to the Guatemalan post (L$10, 2km). The border areas can get tense, especially crossing into Guatemala, with pushy money changers and paper-runners; watch your pockets and belongings.

GRACIAS

pop 43,600

Gracias is a peaceful mountain town with cobblestone streets, colonial churches and a sense that time here moves at a slower pace. It is the most visited stop on the Ruta Lenca. Gracias itself has a new museum with some fine pieces, and is the gateway to smaller towns like La Campa and San Manuel De Colohete.

But Gracias is perhaps best known for its proximity to Parque Nacional Montaña de Celaque, a rugged swath of dense forest that's home to the country's highest peak.

History

Gracias was founded in 1526 by Spanish captain Juan de Chávez; its original name was Gracias a Dios (Thanks to God). The Sede de la Audiencia de los Confines, the

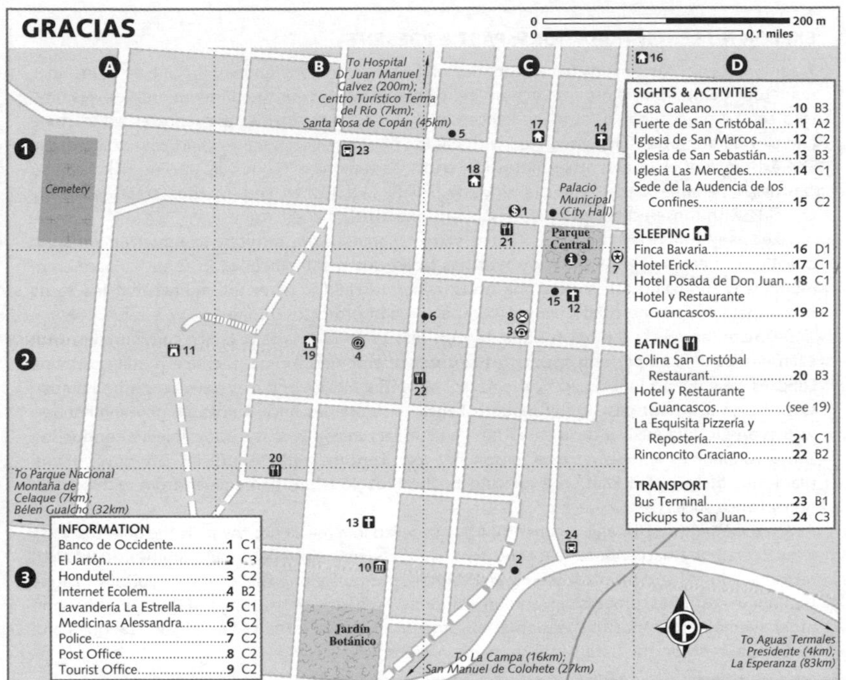

governing council for all Central America, was established here on April 16, 1544; the buildings that the council occupied are still here. The town was important and grew for several years, and for a short time served as the capital of the Spanish empire in Central America. It was eventually eclipsed in importance by Antigua (Guatemala) and Comayagua, and slowly returned to its small-town roots.

Information

There are no ATMs – or street names! – in Gracias, and the banks don't offer advances on credit cards. Bring extra cash, as the nearest 'real' bank is in Santa Rosa de Copán.

Banco de Occidente (Parque Central; 8:30am-4:30pm Mon-Fri, to 11:30am Sat) Exchanges traveler's checks and US dollars.

El Jarrón crafts shop (656-0627; guiamarcolencas@yahoo.com) On the road to La Esperanza.

Hondutel (7am-6:30pm & 7-9pm) Next to the post office; offers international calling.

Hospital Dr Juan Manuel Galvez (656-1100; Carr a Santa Rosa de Copán; 24hr) Near the entrance to town, across from a Texaco station.

Internet Ecolem (per hr L$20; 8am-9:30pm) Also offers web-based calls to the USA and Canada (per min Monday to Friday L$16, Saturday & Sunday L$10).

Lavandería La Estrella (per load L$50; 8am-5pm Mon-Sat) This laundry is two blocks west of Iglesia Las Mercedes.

Medicinas Alessandra (656-1275; 7:30am-12:30pm & 1:30-8pm) This pharmacy is two blocks west of Hondutel.

Police (656-1326, 656-1327; Parque Central; 24hr)

Post office (8am-noon & 2-5pm Mon-Fri, 8-11am Sat) One block southeast of Parque Central.

Tourist office (Parque Central kiosk; 8am-noon & 1:30-4:30pm Mon-Fri) Information binders are more helpful than the well-meaning staffers. Staff only speak Spanish.

Sights & Activities

Gracias has several colonial churches: **San Marcos**, **Las Mercedes** and **San Sebastián** (at last check, closed and falling apart in a dirt park surrounded by enormous trees). Next door to the Iglesia de San Marcos, the **Sede de la Audiencia de los Confines** is now the *casa parroquial,* the residence for the parish priest.

Built in response to the tumultuous times of the 18th century, the striking **Fuerte de San**

WESTERN HONDURAS

EXPLORING LENCA TRADITIONS: PAST & PRESENT

Traditional Lenca *cosmovisión* (an explanation of the origin and operation of the universe), includes numerous deities and spirits. Interaction and communication with the different entities was (and is) a central preoccupation of many Lenca communities. Some deities are represented in stone and clay figures, others are associated with natural phenomenon, such as wind, rain or lightning. The existence of elves and other fantastical creatures is a given, though as they're tricksters you can never be sure of their intentions. Many beliefs, like 'Father' and 'Mother' creators loosely coincide with those espoused by Catholic missionaries.

Like many American indigenous belief systems, animals are thought to represent different qualities or personalities. A tradition that has faded but is still practiced in some isolated communities is sprinkling ash around the house where a child is born; the animal that leaves its prints there will be the child's *nahual* (companion and protector for life).

Shamans, healers and other spiritual leaders play important roles in Lenca communities, with each empowered to perform specific rituals and ceremonies. Animal sacrifice is still practiced; Lencans were deeply influenced by the Aztecs of central Mexico and may have performed human sacrifices in a distant past. Many modern Lenca communities have municipal governments, as well as an Alcaldía Auxiliar de la Vara Alta – an auxiliary mayor who is responsible for conducting Lenca ceremonies and serves as a liaison between Lencans and the 'official' city government. (Vara Alta, literally 'Tall Staff,' is a rotating political-religious position chosen from within traditional Lenca society.)

A fascinating pre-Hispanic custom that has survived in a few Lenca towns is the *guancasco,* an annual ceremony that confirms peace and friendship between neighboring communities. *Guancascos* take many forms and have adopted many Catholic symbols along the way, but typically include traditional costumes, processions and an elaborate exchange of greetings, statues of saints and other symbolic rites (not to mention a fair amount of revelry). The towns of Yamaranguila and La Campa, both on the Ruta Lenca, host *guancascos.*

Cristóbal (San Cristóbal Fort; admission free; 8am-4pm) has fantastic views of Gracias and the San Marcos church below. Beyond that, there's not much else to see up there, save the tomb of Honduran Juan Lindo, the former president of El Salvador (1841–42) *and* Honduras (1847–52). That, and a few teenage couples looking for a quiet corner to make out. It's five blocks west of Parque Central.

Lenca pottery is arguably the best and most widely recognized *artesanía* in Honduras. Yet the country has long lacked a 1st-class museum to exhibit and preserve this unique folk art. Now there are two: one in Gracias – the **Casa Galeano** (625-5407; admission L$30; 9am-6pm) and the other in La Campa (p143).

The **Jardín Botánico** (admission free; 8am-5pm Mon-Sat, to noon Sun) is at the southern end of town, five blocks south of the old Mercado Municipal, and takes up half a city block. Local flora can be admired all year long from a sidewalk that meanders through the park.

The hot springs at **Aguas Termales Presidente** (admission L$100; 6am-8pm) are one of Gracias' main attractions. Four kilometers southeast of town, the hot springs have several pools at various temperatures. You can walk there in one to 1½ hours: take the road to La Esperanza until you reach the right-hand turnoff for the Aguas Termales, then follow the road or take the first right onto a footpath, which is a shortcut but requires fording a (usually) small river. You should be able to hitch a ride back – everybody does. Cabs don't usually come here; hiring a private truck costs around L$200, with an hour at the springs (ask at Hotel Guancascos).

Centro Turístico Terma del Río (admission L$100; 7am-9pm) is located 7km from town on the road to Santa Rosa de Copán. This hot spring is more relaxed than its 'presidential' counterpart.

Tours

You can arrange tours at the El Jarrón crafts shop, located on the road to La Esperanza, where **Marco Aurelio** (656-0627; guiamarcolencas@yahoo.com) arranges city tours (L$350), hikes in Celaque (L$300 to L$750), trips to La Campa and San Manuel De Colohete (L$500 to L$700), three-hour horseback-riding trips

(L$200 per person) and bike rental (per hour/day L$30/75). Hotel Guancascos (below) also offers tours.

Sleeping

Hotel Erick (☎ 656-1066; s/d with cold water L$100/150, d with hot water & fan L$200; P) A longtime favorite of budget travelers, rooms here are basic but clean, with little niceties like complimentary drinking water and a small table to make up for the saggy beds and flat white light. Guests can leave their luggage here while camping in the national park – a big plus.

Finca Bavaria (r L$200) A bit retired from the city center, the Finca Bavaria offers a lot of space and poorly maintained gardens. The rooms are slightly ripe, but you get thick mattresses and old-but-clean sheets. This is a good alternative for those craving a little quiet.

Hotel Guancascos (☎ 656-1219; www.guancascos.com; s/d/tr L$370/420/600; P) Fifteen comfortable, thoughtfully decorated rooms, all with hot-water bathrooms and some with terrific views (especially rooms 12, 13 and 14), make Guancascos hard to beat. The terrace restaurant has excellent food and views – though the service was abysmal when we visited – and is a good place to meet travelers heading to Parque Nacional Montaña de Celaque. You can leave bags here while you're hiking; there are sleeping bags (but no tents) for rent. Ask too about Cabaña Villa Verde, a fully equipped house at the entrance to Celaque.

Hotel Posada de Don Juan (☎ 656-1020; www.posadadedonjuanhotel.com; s/d with fan L$771/991, s/d with air-con L$1212/1432; ❄ 💻 🏊) The rooms here are way overpriced – and you are better off at Guancascos – but they are modern and clean, and you get a pool. Things like the internet, and even water for your shower, seem to be eternally on the fritz. Rates include breakfast.

Eating

Rinconcito Graciano (mains L$20-60; 🕑 breakfast, lunch & dinner, closed Mon) This artsy place with Lencan art on the walls, handmade menus and rustic clay dishes, has a menu rife with traditional Lencan food – *ticucos* (cornmeal patties, stuffed with beans), *anafres* (bean fondue with tortilla chips), *mulitas* (corn tortilla filled with beans, eggs, avocado and cheese) and *chilate* (a sweet drink). Opening hours can be very irregular.

Colina San Cristóbal Restaurant (☎ 656-1543; mains L$20-100; 🕑 7am-9pm) Known mostly for its outstanding pizza, La Colina also offers grilled meats, hamburgers, sandwiches and *comida típica*. The two dining rooms are understated and classy, with huge windows, muted colors and silk flowers.

La Esquisita Pizzería y Repostería (mains L$30-70; 🕑 breakfast, lunch & dinner) Almost always jam packed with locals, this pizzeria is half a block west of Parque Central. The daily special – whatever it is – is the way to go; it's served fast and comes loaded with a couple of sides and a drink.

Getting There & Away

Gracias is 45km from Santa Rosa de Copán and 37km from San Juan, on good paved roads. From the bus terminal, numerous buses go to Santa Rosa de Copán (L$38, 1¼ hours, hourly 5am to 5pm) and two *directos* to San Pedro Sula (L$100, four hours, 8:30am and 9am); otherwise transfer at Santa Rosa de Copán. For Copán Ruinas, take the San Pedro bus and transfer at La Entrada. The whole trip takes three to four hours and costs about L$100.

The best way to get to San Juan is by *jalón* (hitchhiking); just wave down a pickup truck on the road toward San Juan. Be sure to offer the driver some money when you arrive – L$35 is fair.

Buses for La Campa, San Manuel De Colohete and that region leave the terminal daily around noon. See each town section for prices and information on return buses.

PARQUE NACIONAL MONTAÑA DE CELAQUE

One of Honduras' most impressive national parks, the Montaña de Celaque is a lush, steep cloud forest, just over 6km from Gracias. It boasts El Cerro de las Minas (2849m), the highest peak in Honduras – a good, tiring hike.

Celaque, which means 'box of water' in the local Lencan dialect, is an appropriate name: Celaque's 11 rivers supply water to all of the surrounding communities, northern Honduras and parts of El Salvador. It also has a majestic waterfall that is visible from the entire valley.

The park is rich in plant and animal life: 232 plant, 48 mammal, 269 bird and 18 reptile species make Celaque their home. Jaguars, pumas, ocelots and a number of rare endemic species have been spotted by lucky hikers.

More common, but still elusive, are spider monkeys and quetzals. You have to be very quiet, and up very early, to see much wildlife, but if you don't see many animals the rugged pine and cloud forests are still rewarding.

Information

The entrance fee (L$50) is payable at the visitors center, as is the additional cost of staying overnight – L$50 per person regardless of whether you stay in the dorm or in a tent.

For information on hiking in Celaque, look for Marco Aurelio at El Jarrón crafts shop (p140), or enquire at Hotel Guancascos (p141), both in Gracias. Also see right.

Dangers & Annoyances

Although it may be tempting to follow that spider monkey into the mist, don't wander off the trail. The forest is so dense that it can be hard, even impossible, to find your way back. A Dutch hiker disappeared here in 1998 and was never found; a Honduran hiker got lost and died in 2003.

Temperatures in the park are much chillier than in Gracias, so bring warm clothes. Also be prepared for dampness and rain; it's a cloud forest, after all, and the park gets around 2000mm to 4000mm of annual precipitation.

Hiking

The trails are well marked throughout the park and, unlike hiking in other parts of the country, it's safe to take on a hike here without a guide. The main hike in Celaque is to **El Cerro de las Minas** (2849m) – a 1449m ascent from the visitors center. It is a steep, challenging hike that takes most hikers two to three days to complete. Many people misjudge the time they need for the climb. Some do the whole thing in a single day, but it's a very long haul. Even spreading it over two days, you should start hiking early. The trail is somewhat unclear in places – look for the colored ribbons.

The original nameless trail (it should be called Switchback Heaven) heads up the northern side of Río Mecatal, directly to **Campamento Don Tomás**; it passes over several streams, through a dense pine forest, with switchback upon switchback until it reaches the campsite. After about two hours, you'll come to a fork in the trail – continue left (south), as the trail to the right goes to Santa Lucia Waterfall (below). It takes about 4½ to five hours to get to the campsite.

A second trail – **Rooster Trail** – heads up the southern side of Río Mecatal, passing a waterfall vista and taking hikers through Monkey Valley, an area known to be inhabited by spider monkeys (keep your eyes peeled – they're fast little buggers). It also leads to Campamento Don Tomás in about 3½ hours.

Most hikers set up camp at Don Tomás but if you can handle a couple of more hours of steep climbing – literally, pulling yourself up the mountain by tree roots and rocks – it's worth the sweat to get to **Campamento El Naranjo** to set up for the night. From there, it's another 1½ to two hours on a beautiful rolling trail through the cloud forest to the summit. Because of clouds and tree cover, you might not see anything from the top, but there's a sign there telling you that you've made it to the top all the same.

A third steep trail leads to **Santa Lucia Waterfall**, a majestic cascade emerging from the cloud forest. It's a four- to five-hour hike from the visitors center; follow 'Switchback Heaven' until you reach a fork in the trail, about two hours up; go right (north) to reach the falls. There's no campsite along this trail, so start early to be sure you'll be back before dark. With a lunch break, it could take you nine to 11 hours to complete.

A couple of short trails start at the visitors center – one to a little waterfall due north, the other east down Río Arcagual. It'll be very tempting to jump into the latter after a long grueling hike; however, the river provides drinking water downstream, so swimming is strictly prohibited.

Tours

In Gracias, Marco Aurelio (p140) and Hotel Guancascos (p141) offer guided trips to the park, which must be arranged at least one day in advance. Costs vary, and you can save big by teaming up with a group of four or more, where you'll get a group discount. Average prices (per person without a group discount): La Cascada L$1300 per person, El Gallo L$1300 per person, two-day ascent of El Cerro de las Minas L$2600 per person.

Sleeping & Eating

The **visitors center dorm** has bunks that can sleep up to 15 people. Half of the bunks have mattresses, while the rest are just wood frames; either way, bring your own bedding. There's also a decent communal kitchen.

The good folks at Gracias' **El Jarrón** (☎ 656-0627) rent out tents (L$70 to L$80 per night) and they can also track down binoculars and walkie-talkies for you.

From the visitors center, a four-hour uphill walk along a well-marked trail leads to **Campamento Don Tomás** (2060m). The camp has a sketchy two-bunk shack reminiscent of the abandoned house in *The Blair Witch Project;* you're better off just camping. There's also a small latrine on site but no running water. Remember to collect some from the streams that you pass on your way up (be sure to purify it with tablets or a filter).

A second campsite, **El Naranjo** (2560m), is only 500m away, but the trail up is very steep (one to two hours). It's a pretty camp though – just inside the cloud forest – and worth staying at if you can handle carrying your gear up.

For meals, **Comedor Doña Alejandra** (mains L$30; breakfast, lunch & dinner) and **Los Melgares** (mains L$30; breakfast, lunch & dinner) are both located near the visitors center. Los Melgares also offers basic rooms for L$50 per person.

Getting There & Away

From Gracias, it's a 6.5km steady climb to the park entrance; it takes around one to two hours to get there – look for the well-marked shortcut for those *a pie* (on foot). From there, it's another half-hour uphill to the park visitors center.

If you opt to get a lift to the park entrance, the cheapest option is a bumpy ride in a moto-taxi (L$70 per person). Otherwise, you can either cab it (L$250 to L$300) or arrange a ride through **Marco Aurelio** (☎ 656-0627; guia marcolencas@yahoo.com, El Jarrón crafts shop, Gracias) or the **Hotel Guancascos** (☎ 656-1219; www.guancascos.com) in Gracias.

Another option is to enter the park at Belén Gualcho, but there are no park services available at that entrance; besides, the forest is much more pristine on the Gracias side.

LA CAMPA

pop 5300

The first town you reach headed south from Gracias is La Campa, a scenic little community at the bottom of a steep-walled river valley. La Campa's natural beauty and proximity to Gracias (16km) make it a good place for travelers to stop, and the townspeople are renowned for their handcrafted pottery. Two new hotels, a good museum and two *artesanía* cooperatives make this the most accessible of the remote villages along La Ruta Lenca. Hiking and other excursions are possible as well, though travel here still requires a fair amount of improvisation.

Information & Orientation

The road from Gracias descends through several switchbacks before reaching the bottom. There, a large grassy field is effectively the Parque Central, with a pretty colonial church on the near side and municipal buildings across the way. Passing the center, the road crosses a bridge and climbs abruptly, up and out of town.

The *alcaldía* (city hall), also on the park, is a logical place to ask for help, though results will vary. For internet access, head to the **Centro Comunitario de Conocimiento y Comunicación** (CCCC; per hr L$20; 9am-9pm Mon-Fri) behind the large municipal building.

Sight & Activities

The Lenca region, and La Campa in particular, is known for its *alfarería* (handmade pottery). The **Centro de Interpretación de Alfarería Lenca** (admission L$30; 9am-noon & 1:30-4pm) is a museum dedicated to this art form, complete with several excellent displays of pottery and historical information. It's housed in a beautiful colonial-style building overlooking the center of town.

Local workshops have long been open to drop-in visitors. **Doña Desideria Pérez' workshop** (8-11am & 1-4pm), 700m past the church, specializes in giant *cántaros* (urns), made entirely by hand without the use of a wheel. The pieces take a week to make and sell for around L$1200 each. Most are used as decoration in gardens and outdoor patios, though traditionally they served as storage for corn, beans or water. Doña Desideria is a charming woman who's been making pottery for over four decades and is happy to chat with visitors; occasionally she's taken on volunteer assistants/apprentices for a month or two.

The nearby community of **Cruz Alta** has two artisan collectives, one making pots, mobiles and other clay items, the other *tejado de pino* (pine-needle basketry). The artwork is modest and is made and sold in private homes amid chickens, children and other trappings of everyday life; ask for Suyapa Pérez or Máximo Velásquez. Cruz Alta is 4km from La Campa, up an extremely steep dirt road past the basketball court. There is no regular transport.

A couple of guided area **hikes** (L$70-140) are available: one to Cuevas del Gigante, a trek through the countryside to a set of caves; and another to El Cañon de la Mujer Cabra, a relatively easy hike through a lush canyon. Both trips can be done on **horseback** (L$130-200) and can include lunch (around L$40). Hikes last approximately three hours; contact Alan Reyes at Hostal JB for more information. Another fun adventure would be to backpack from town to town along the Ruta Lenca.

Sleeping & Eating

our pick **Hostal JB** (☎ 9925-6042; hostal_jb@yahoo.com; r L$200) One of the best hotels on the Ruta Lenca, this is more like a huge house with five rooms for rent. All have new queen-size beds with thick comforters and hot-water bathrooms; guests share a fully equipped kitchen and a spacious living room with sofas, folk art and high wood-beamed ceilings. It's at the hairpin turn just before the church.

Hotel Vista Hermosa (☎ 625-4770; r L$200) Just up the street from the JB, this is your second choice in town. The hotel does have some pretty views, as the name indicates, and is clean and polished, but it doesn't quite fit into the whole 'colonial La Campa' thing.

Getting There & Away

The once-daily bus from Gracias to San Manuel de Colohete (L$20, one hour) passes through La Campa on the main road in town at around 1pm. Going in the other direction, to Gracias, the bus passes around 6:30am (L$15, 45 minutes). It's also possible to hitch a ride in either direction.

SAN MARCOS DE CAIQUÍN

pop 5200

Five kilometers past La Campa, the road splits: go left 5.5km to Caiquín and right 6km to San Manuel de Colohete. As the town has few tourist accommodations, it's best to visit as a day trip. You'll love the brilliant whitewashed church and interesting adobe architecture. Plus, kids still say hi to you as you walk by.

Check your email at the municipal **Sala de Computo** (🕑 9am-noon & 2-9pm; internet per hr L$20), a surprisingly modern computer center in the building next to the *alcaldía*.

Sights & Activities

There's not a lot to do in Caiquín, beyond soaking in the small-town atmosphere. The interior of the **Iglesia de San Marcos de Caiquín** was recently restored and is quite beautiful, but it's all but impossible to get in (even for insistent guidebook writers) on any day other than Sunday.

It is possible to **hike** from here across the mountains to Erandique, which takes you through small towns, pine forest and areas once controlled by Lempira, the famous 16th-century Lenca chieftain. The road appears on some maps, though it's very rough in places, passing through Cualaca and Arcamón, then over the mountain to the community of Santa Cruz and down into Erandique. Budget at least two days; the *alcaldía* may be able to locate a guide.

There's a shorter hike along the dirt road that connects Caiquín to Cruz Alto, the small, artistically inclined *aldea* (hamlet) of La Campa.

Sleeping & Eating

In a pinch, you can stay the night in **La Casa de Doña Josefina Santos** (☎ 915-4347; r L$60), 1½ blocks from the school, but the conditions are pretty rough: the kids are kicked out of their room whenever a backpacker shows up, and everyone shares a rather gross cold-water bathroom. Doña Josefina, a gruff but friendly lady, also runs a *comedor* (a basic and cheap eatery) and *pulpería* (corner store or mini-mart).

You may also be able to camp somewhere in or around town – there's certainly no shortage of open space. Ask at the *alcaldía* for advice and permission.

There are three *comedores* in town, including Doña Josefina's place, and finding them isn't a problem. Comedor Daniela and a no-name eatery in a quaint adobe building opposite the church both serve cheap *típica* meals.

Getting There & Away

There's just one bus daily in and out of Caiquín. It leaves from in front of the church at 6:30am bound for Gracias, returning at 12:30pm (L$35, 1½ hours). Walking to Gracias will take you about half a day, but is a nice alternative. An ordinary car can easily make it in the dry season, but you'll need a 4x4 vehicle in the winter to cross over the mud, especially after a heavy rain.

SAN MANUEL DE COLOHETE

pop 14,000

There's a split in the road 5km past La Campa: head to the right 6km to get to our favorite village along the Ruta Lenca, San Manuel De Colohete. Sitting literally in the shadow of the Parque Nacional Montaña de Celaque, it's the largest town in this neck of the woods, but there are still more horses here than cars, and the townspeople welcome visitors with open arms.

It's impossible to get lost in San Manuel, though it's easy enough to get disoriented on the narrow curving streets. There's no post office or internet cafe in town. The small pharmacy and health clinic have no signs or regular hours.

Sights & Activities

San Manuel is justly known for its **colonial church** (Sun) a beautiful colonial structure with 400-year-old fresco paintings inside; its altar and wood columns were recently restored by a Spanish NGO. The **cemetery**, located 100m from the town center on the road to San Sebastián, is also worth checking out.

On the 1st and 15th of every month, the town hosts a large **market** (6am-noon), similar to the one held in Belén Gualcho. People come from all over the region to buy and sell domestic and farm goods; you won't find much *artesanía*, but it's a good place to stock up on rubber boots, machetes, tin buckets and the like. You never know when you'll need an extra colander.

For a nice day hike, follow the road past Parque Central out of town up to San Antonio, a small community on the edge of the national park, with a nice little plaza and school.

A longer **hike** goes from San Manuel to Belén Gualcho. Take the road toward San Antonio that veers off across a swinging bridge and onto a trail over the ridge. Alternatively, take one of two trails off the road to San Sebastián, one 2.5km west from San Manuel at a small river, the other 2km further on at the community of San José. No matter how you go, take time to ask around San Manuel about the latest conditions. On the trail, ask locals you pass if you're headed in the right direction; there are plenty of side trails that can take you off the track. Plan on staying the night in Belén Gualcho – it's a good six to seven hours each way.

It's also possible to climb **Pico Celaque** from here, but you'll need an experienced guide.

Sleeping & Eating

It's slim pickings on the hotel and eatery front in this town.

Hotel Emanuel (Calle Principal; s/d with shared bathroom L$50/100, r L$70-150) Nine clean simple rooms – three with private bathroom, one of which has hot water – occupy this two-story building on Calle Principal. Room 6 is the best: spacious, with a private bathroom and a view of the valley below.

For meals, ask at the front desk of the hotel; they'll help set something up. You also can get snacks at Pulpería Eben-Ezer across the street.

Getting There & Away

The bus from Gracias to San Manuel (L$35, 1½ hours) leaves Gracias between noon and 1pm, dropping passengers at the center of town before continuing to San Sebastián. The return bus passes through San Manuel between 6am and 6:30am. Travel times can be considerably longer in the rainy season.

SAN SEBASTIÁN

pop 10,000

Another 13km of rough roads – impassable in a regular car – brings you to San Sebastián, a small, somewhat tense town. From here, a decrepit dirt road continues to Belén Gualcho, a scenic and moderately tough **hike** that takes four to six hours. Other than doing that hike (or finishing it) there's not much reason to come here.

The road to Belén Gualcho begins about 750m outside of San Sebastián, right where the road from San Manuel makes a sharp left and starts up a hill into town. Look for a barbed-wire fence with wood posts. The hike is very doable on your own, but you can also hire the services of **Victor Manuel Pasqual**, a friendly local farmer and sometime guide who lives in the first house on the right past the Belén Gualcho turnoff.

You may need to stay a night in San Sebastián, either to get an early start or if you arrive late from the other direction. The best option are four **rooms for rent** (r with shared/private bathroom per person L$50/60) owned by Don Adrian, who is typically at a *pulpería* near

Parque Central. The rooms are cramped and a bit grubby but adequate.

You can get snacks and simple meals at Don Adrian's or head down to Parque Central where Doña Alicia runs a small *comedor* (no sign). There's also a fruit-and-veggie shop on the park.

Buses to San Sebastián (L$40, 3½ hours) leave Gracias between noon and 1pm. Return buses leave from San Sebastián's Parque Central, near the Hotel Mejilla Melgar, at 5:30am.

SAN JUAN

pop 3100

Once little more than a crossroads between La Esperanza and Gracias, San Juan is slowly making its way onto the Ruta Lenca, thanks to the good hiking to be had out of town. Head to Parque Central for internet, police matters, health issues and tourist info (at the police station). The visitors center on the main road was closed when we passed through, but ask for Gladys Nolasco to see if it's re-opened.

Activities

Local guides can take you on a number of interesting hikes in the region. The most worthwhile include the **Cascada de los Duendes**, a trek through a cloud forest with a small set of waterfalls that ends with a *finca de café* (coffee plantation) tour (the best time for this hike is between December and March, when coffee is in full production); and **El Cañon Encantado**, a hike in the lush San Juan Valley complete with legends of the ghosts who inhabit it (Spanish-speaking guides only). Both hikes are moderately difficult but have decent trails. Prices are kind of steep (L$400/500/600/700 for one/two/three/four people) but the trips last from 8am to 4pm and include lunch. The same excursions can also be taken on horseback for a bit more. A hike to **Piedra Parada**, the enormous rock where the famous Lencan chieftain Lempira was killed, can also be arranged for L$1300 (up to six people); it includes transport to the hamlet of La Laguna and a hike to **Congolón**, one of the highest peaks in the country.

Ask about guides at your hotel. All tours must be reserved a day in advance.

San Juan also has two cultural tours: a **coffee roasting and tasting** demonstration in a local home (translation: watch a tourist official's mother, Doña Soledad, roast coffee beans on her wood-burning stove and then try it yourself) and a **clay artisan demonstration** (head 5km south of town to watch and learn how to make a terracotta brick or tile – ask for Don Amadeo). Not the most scintillating activities but a great way to interact with locals and learn a little about daily life in a Lencan village. Both tours cost L$30 per person; no advance notice needed. Ask around town (or at your hotel) for more tour information.

If you're in the mood for a swim, head to **La Piscina de Don Nicho** (adult/child L$20/10; sunrise-sunset), a set of spring-fed pools 5km south of town near the road to Esperanza. It's nothing fancy, but it's refreshing.

Bicycle rentals (half/full day L$30/60) may be an option if the visitors center is open.

Sleeping & Eating

Cabaña en el Campo (r per person L$70) This simple wood-construction guesthouse, with outdoor toilet and shower, is near the Opalaca Biological Reserve, about a half-hour's walk from San Juan. The guesthouse is often closed, so ask in town before you head out. Reservations are required and can be made at the visitors center, if it's open.

Posada de Doña Soledad (Calle Principal; r per person L$100) Meeting Doña Soledad, a straight-talking octogenarian, is surely the best reason to come to this otherwise simple guesthouse. The two rooms – one large, one small – are reasonably comfortable, with hot-water bathrooms and separate entrances. Home-cooked meals are an extra L$50.

Comedor Yamilet (Calle Principal; mains L$30-40; breakfast, lunch & dinner) This cool, spacious eatery is a good bet.

Getting There & Away

The mainly dirt road leading to La Esperanza is passable year-round with a normal car. There are several unmarked splits in the road: be sure to ask if you are headed in the right direction.

Buses to La Esperanza pass through the center of town at 6am, 7:30am, 8:20am and 9:30am daily (L$35, 1½ hours). For the same fare, there is also a *busito* (minivan) that heads to La Esperanza at 1:30pm every day.

There is an iffy bus service to Gracias that sometimes passes through town between 6am and 8am (L$30, one hour); if you prefer not to hold your breath (and pass out) waiting, it's easy to get a *jalón* from drivers headed there.

Stand on the main road and just wave a pickup truck down. Also, be sure to offer the driver some money for the ride – L$30 is fair.

ERANDIQUE

pop 14,500

An attractive colonial town 24km south of San Juan, Erandique has some good hiking but is most famous for its opals, which are extracted from three mines in the area. A number of valuable varieties can be found here, including black seam, black matrix and white opals. You are sure to be approached by locals selling them, some rather aggressively.

There is an internet cafe near Parque Central (per hour L$20), which has international calling.

Erandique is a 'dry' community – no alcohol is permitted.

Sights & Activities

One of Erandique's three **opal mines** is a half-hour walk from town, in the direction of Gualguire. As with any mine, you should never venture beyond the entrance without an exceptional guide or companion. Another good half-day hike is to **Las Cuatro Chorreras** (the Four Waterfalls), 3km to 4km away.

For something more challenging, **Peñol de Cerquín** and **Piedra Parada** – the fortress of 16th-century Lenca chieftain Lempira and the place where he was assassinated – can be reached from here, though the trip is at least two days round-trip on foot.

Sleeping & Eating

Erandique has three hotels. All have basic rooms with cable TV and private bathrooms with hot water: **Hotel Steven** (Barrio Gualmaca; s/d L$100/160; P), **Hotel Sinai** (Barrio Gualmaca; s/d L$100/160; P), and **Hotel Torre Fuerte** (Barrio Centro; s/d L$100/160; P), one block south of the church.

Comedor Rossie (Barrio Gualmaca) and **Comedor Los 3 Reyes** (Parque Central) are both open for all three meals and serve good cheap Honduran *típica*, plus sandwiches and snacks.

Getting There & Away

The bus to Gracias (L$50, two hours) leaves from Barrio Gualmaca at 5am; to return, the same bus leaves Gracias at noon, from the bridge opposite the electricity company (EENE). The bus to La Esperanza (L$60, 2½ hours) leaves Erandique's Parque Central at 5am, while the return bus leaves La Esperanza at noon. The bus is marked 'San Francisco' and leaves from behind the soccer stadium.

LA ESPERANZA

pop 9000

La Esperanza is Intibucá's capital and largest city, though you'd never guess from the dusty streets and small-town atmosphere. This is one of Honduras' poorest departments, and it shows. The town is best known for its Sunday market, when Lencans from the surrounding area buy, sell and trade goods of all sorts.

Orientation & Information

Most of La Esperanza's restaurants, hotels and services face or are within a few blocks of its Parque Central, either on the road that runs between the park and the police station, or one street over (Av Los Próceres), which eventually turns into the main highway, connecting La Esperanza to Siguatepeque and Gracias.

Banco Atlántida In front of the market. Has an ATM.

Explored (Plaza María; internet per hr L$20; 9am-11pm) Across from Hotel Mejia Batres; offers cheap international phone calls too.

Farmacia Santa Isabel (☎ 783-0427; 8am-noon & 2-6pm Mon-Sat, to noon Sun) Behind the church.

Hondutel (Parque Central; 7am-noon, 12:30-6pm & 6:30-9pm) Phone center.

Police (☎ 783-1007; Parque Central; 24hr)

Post office (Parque Central; 7:30am-4pm Mon-Fri, to noon Sat)

Sights & Activities

A number of very interesting sights are found outside La Esperanza, including the Lenca town of Yamaranguila and the Valle de Azacualpa, which make for excellent day trips.

Closer to town, **Cicai** (Centro Indigenista de Capacitación Artesanal Intibucano; ☎ 783-0565; Calle a Azacualpa; 7am-3pm Mon-Fri, Feb-Nov) is a semi-boarding school, 1.5km north from the center, where around 80 indigenous students learn folk art and vocational skills. The school welcomes visitors – some of the teachers are foreign volunteers – and you can sit in on a class or talk with the students or teachers. Mornings are best; check in at the administrative office first. Sadly, the school is often without enough supplies or materials.

Ask about things to do in La Esperanza, and you'll invariably hear about the **bosque enano** (dwarf forest), a few kilometers from town. It sounds intriguing, but the 'forest' is actually a low bulge of hard earth dotted with tiny gnarled shrubs (and not a small amount of litter). It's right alongside the road, in view of a large earth-excavation project. Tree enthusiasts may derive some enjoyment from the sight, but a more typical response is 'Huh?'

Sleeping

La Esperanza also has an on-again, off-again system of homestays. Try **Casa de Luz** (☎ 783-1142), **Casa de Eneyda** (☎ 783-0124) or **Casa de Leyda Villanueva** (☎ 783-1169); all offer a room with a queen-size bed and private hot-water bathroom (single/double L$100/180).

Hotel Mejia Batres (☎ 783-7086; r with/without bathroom per person L$250/125; P) Although suffering from seriously stinky and cramped bathrooms, this is a clean hotel offering basic, somewhat worn rooms. Its location is prime – one block west of Parque Central.

Hotel Mina (☎ 783-1071; s L$350-550, d L$700; P) Two blocks east and one block south of the bus terminal, this is the nicest hotel in town. It's a bit pricy, but a good option if you are looking for some creature comforts like hot water and comfy beds.

Eating

Café Jardín Colonial (☎ 783-0988; Av Próceres; mains L$20-60; breakfast, lunch & dinner) This great little cafe, three blocks from Parque Central, will assuage the pain of anyone missing their favorite coffee spot back home. The menu also includes fresh sandwiches and a long list of crepes, from chicken and ham to jam, banana or *melacatón* (passion fruit), served with a scoop of ice cream.

El Recreo (mains L$40-120; breakfast, lunch & dinner) A favorite among young volunteers, El Recreo has a friendly owner who serves a fixed menu for breakfast, mostly *baleadas* for lunch, and dishes like coconut chicken or a barbecue sampler for dinner. There's music and dancing Friday and Saturday. It's a block south and a block west of Parque Central.

our pick **El Fogón** (mains L$70-120; 9am-10pm Mon-Thu, noon-midnight Fri & Sat) Everything from pork ribs to mixed tacos is served up in this friendly bar and restaurant located one block from Parque Central. The patio out the back is excellent, and the breakfasts are some of the best in town. There's even karaoke, on occasion.

Opalaca's Restaurant (☎ 783-0503; mains L$100-200; breakfast, lunch & dinner) Ask for the best restaurant in town and most people will point to this one. It certainly looks the part, housed in a colonial-era building with high wood-beamed ceilings, and offering cloth napkins and real water glasses. All of which makes the menu that much more surprising, with grilled beef, grilled pork chops, Honduran barbecue, plus hamburgers and sandwiches.

Getting There & Away

Most buses leave from the *mercado quemado* (burned market) a huge dusty lot south of the park. Some depart from *el estadio* (the stadium, located near the bridge on the highway to Siguatepeque) and others from individual terminals down the main drag. You can always catch buses to Siguatepeque, San Pedro and Tegucigalpa at the Texaco station at the edge of town – be sure to take a *directo*, which takes half as long and costs only pennies more. Taxis around town cost L$15 per person or slightly more at night.

Gracias (L$70, four hours, morning departure, time varies) Pickup service might be available.
Marcala (L$40, 1½ to two hours, three departures daily, roughly 8am, noon & 3pm) Stops in front of Hotel La Esperanza.
San Juan (L$35, 1½ hours, 11:30am, 1pm, 2:45pm and 4:45pm)
San Pedro Sula (L$100, 3½ hours, every two hours, 4:15am to 12:15pm Monday to Saturday, Sunday 12:15pm and 1:30pm only)
Siguatepeque (*directo* L$50, one hour) Take any San Pedro Sula or Tegucigalpa bus.
Tegucigalpa (L$100, 3½ hours, every one to 1½ hours, 4:40am to 2pm)

AROUND LA ESPERANZA

Yamaranguila

pop 1200

Yamaranguila is a quaint, predominantly indigenous, mountain town 9km from La Esperanza. It is notable for preserving a system of traditional Lenca governance that coexists with the 'modern' elected municipal government. Yamaranguila is one of a dwindling number of indigenous communities that celebrate **guancascos**, usually held around the first week of December. Yamaranguila also celebrates not one, but two patron saints' days: San Francisco in early October and Santa Luca in mid-December.

The other attraction of Yamaranguila is a tall wispy **waterfall** that's an easy walk from town. From the park, all roads lead downhill to the school; there, hop the small creek that runs between the road and the soccer field, duck through the barbed-wire fence and continue downstream through the pine forest less than 1km to the falls. The viewing area is at the top of the falls – at the lip of a huge sinkhole. Ask around town for someone to show you how to get to the bottom. It's a long, roundabout route and a steep climb back out.

Buses run from La Esperanza to Yamaranguila daily (L$7, 20 minutes, every one to 1½ hours, 6am to 5pm). They return at the same frequency from 6am to 2pm.

Valle de Azacualpa

If you have a car – or better yet, a mountain bike – a great way to spend a day is exploring the Valle de Azacualpa, a fertile rolling valley covering more than 300 hectares and only a short distance from La Esperanza. The valley is mostly populated with Lenca families who get by on farming and *tejido y hilado* (weaving and stitch work), the latter aimed at their neighbors as much as visitors. That's because Lenca women here wear traditional clothing, including brilliant pink, blue and scarlet blouses and equally bright headscarves. Driving or riding through the valley, it is common to see women working the fields, their distinctive clothing set against the dark browns and greens of the landscape.

Following Calle Azacualpa out of town, you'll pass Cicai (p147); 6.5km later you'll reach a fork in the road. Turning right, the road winds 2.5km through fringe forest and beside fields and flower nurseries, to **Laguna Chiligatoro**, a pretty little pond with a stout white church just beyond. On Sundays after service, the grounds are a sea of color, filled with churchgoers in traditional clothing. Another 4km brings you to the hamlet of **Cacao**, where a local cooperative produces handkerchiefs, tablecloths and other woven items. There's no formal store or workshop, but a *pulpería* on the left is run by one of the cooperative's member families, who may show you their modest loom and supply of products. From Cacao, the road continues into the mountains, growing steeper and rougher until only 4x4 vehicles can reliably pass to the community of Río Grande. **Cascada Río Grande** is an impressive 60m waterfall a short distance from town. The view is even better if you hire a local to show you the way to the bottom.

The road makes a long rough loop, but for most it's easier to turn around at Cacao and head to **Cerro de los Hoyos**. The 'Hill of Holes' is a tree-covered hill pocked with holes, more like wells, 1m wide and up to 20m deep – keep your eyes on the ground when you walk! No one seems to know who made them or why, or even when, but scratching away some of the topsoil reveals a clue: obsidian. The hill seems to be a huge bubble of volcanic glass, and the holes may have been used to gather large, unbroken pieces. The hill is near the hamlet of Los Olivos, about 10km (and three turnoffs) down the left-hand fork back at the first intersection – ask as you go, it's part of the fun.

MARCALA

pop 30,900

Plopped at the southern end of the Ruta Lenca, Marcala is a quiet mountain town with a strong indigenous history and character. The town is known for producing world-class coffee beans. In fact, coffee from Marcala was the first in Central America to receive the prestigious 'Denomination of Origin' stamp, protecting the authenticity of beans from this region. An organic coffee and produce cooperative – the first of its kind in Honduras – offers tours of its member plantations and processing plants. The area also has a few mildly interesting hikes.

Orientation & Information

There are no street names in Marcala, but you can orient yourself according to the tourist kiosk in Parque Central: it's on the southeast corner.

Banco Atlántida (entrance to town) ATM and banking needs.
Clínica Moreno (☎ 764-5478; ⏲ 9am-9pm Mon-Sat, to 2pm Sun) Medical clinic near the police station.
Farmacia Danli (⏲ 7am-9pm) On Parque Central.
Global Online (☎ 764-5562; internet per hr L$20; ⏲ 7am-9pm) Internet access; half a block west of Parque Central.
Hondutel (☎ 764-5398; ⏲ 7am-9pm) On the main road into town; for international calling.
Lavandería Bourcas (⏲ 8am-6pm Mon-Fri, 8am-noon Sat) Charges around L$70 to L$100 per load; 1½ blocks north of Parque Central.
Police (☎ 764-5715) In front of the Catholic church.
Post office (⏲ 8am-noon & 2-4pm Mon-Fri, 8am-noon Sat) On the main road into town.
Tourist office (Parque Central; ⏲ 8am-noon & 1-4pm, closed Wed) Kiosk with helpful staff offering information, brochures and maps on area sights. English is spoken.

Sights & Activities

The tourist office has pamphlets describing eight hikes in the area as well as detailed descriptions of getting there and back.

Among the options is **La Estanzuela**, a short hike to a pretty waterfall and swimming area, and a large cavern (La Cueva del Gigante) with a few prehistoric paintings on its walls 1km further. By bus, it's a 2.2km walk to the town of La Estanzuela and another 2km to the falls. With a car, you should have enough time to combine this with the nearby **Cascada de Santa Rita** or **La Isla** hikes.

RAOS (☎ 764-5181, 9911-5315; cooperativaraos@yahoo.com; 8am-noon & 1-4pm Mon-Fri, 8am-noon Sat), half a block north of Parque Central, is Honduras' first organic farming cooperative. **Finca tours** (per person L$100-300) includes visiting two to three plantations, learning about organic farming and talking to the farmers. From November to March, you can visit the *beneficio húmedo* (wet processing plant, where coffee beans are de-pulped) and the *beneficio seco* (dry processing plant, where the beans are dried before toasting). The tour can also include a lunch break at **El Chiflador** waterfall. Stop by the RAOS office or tourist information kiosk to arrange a visit.

Festivals & Events

Held at the beginning of April, the **Feria de Café** has coffee-tasting competitions, displays on the picking and processing of coffee and, of course, coffee for sale. The *fiesta patronal* (patron saint festival) is held during the last two weeks of September.

Sleeping & Eating

Hotel San Miguel (☎ 754-5793; r L$160; P) Near the police station, this hotel's small, clean rooms (with one queen or two twin beds) open onto a dirt courtyard that doubles as a parking lot.

Hotel Jerusalén Medina (☎ 764-5909; s/d L$220/270; P) This two-story motel has several simple, clean rooms with private hot-water bathroom, a fan and cable TV. It's two long blocks east of Parque Central.

Restaurante Riviera Linda (☎ 764-5630; mains L$30-100; breakfast, lunch & dinner) One block north of Parque Central, this airy restaurant comes with an extensive menu – you'll find everything from sandwiches to chop suey here. The food is just OK and the service frustratingly slow.

Casa Gloria (☎ 764-5869; mains L$60-120; lunch & dinner) Sure it's *comida a la vista* (buffet), but Casa Gloria is still the most pleasant of Marcala's eating options, occupying a high-ceilinged colonial-style building right on Parque Central.

Centro Comercial Junior (8am-6:30pm Mon-Sat, to 5pm Sun) is a good-sized supermarket on the main drag into town, one block north of Parque Central. Near Hondutel and the supermarket, **Mercado de Marcala** (7am-4pm Mon-Sat, 7am-noon Sun) sells a good variety of fruits, vegetables and grains.

Shopping

Artesanía de la Ruta Lenca (☎ 393-9061; 8am-noon & 1-6pm) One block east of Parque Central, this folk-art store has a little of everything from the Lenca region (and some from beyond).

Getting There & Away

Buses leave from various points, but all pass the Texaco gas station at the east end of the main road in and out of town, making it a good de facto bus stop. Buses to El Salvador

GETTING TO PERQUÍN, EL SALVADOR

From Marcala there's a twice-daily bus service to Perquín, El Salvador (L$50, three hours, 5am and noon) continuing to San Miguel, El Salvador (L$70, five hours). Unfortunately, due to a long-standing border dispute, there is no Salvadoran immigration post at this border. This may not be a problem if you are only interested in going to Perquín and coming back the same way – technically you will be in El Salvador illegally, but it is unlikely you'll be checked. However, if you plan to travel further into El Salvador or leave from a different border, you may be fined for having entered illegally once your status is discovered – even going directly to the immigration office in San Miguel or San Salvador won't help. The only sure alternative is to exit or enter through another location, like El Amatillo. That said, definitely ask in Marcala about the latest – local businesses and NGOs on both sides of the border frequently lobby the Salvadoran government to rectify the situation.

VISITING THE PULHAPANZAK FALLS

Centro Turístico Pulhapanzak (☎ 9995-1010; admission L$30; 🕑 6am-6pm) is a magnificent 43m waterfall on the Río Amapa surrounded by a lush and well-kept park. This is a popular swimming spot, and there also are guides who will take visitors to a small cave behind the falls. It takes just a few minutes to get there – and anyone can do it – but it feels like something out of Indiana Jones: jumping off boulders, swimming across roiling pools, inching around rocks amid a maelstrom of crashing water and swirling air, and finally squeezing up the narrow passage into the cave. There's no set price, but it's worth a good tip: L$40 to L$60 per person is fair.

If you like it enough to stay, there is a simple **hospedaje** (guesthouse; r L$400). If you bring gear, **camping** (per person L$30) is permitted in a grassy area surrounded by *monticulos* (unexcavated pre-Columbian mounds). For meals, a simple **eatery** (mains L$40 to L$80) serves *típica* and snacks until nightfall.

From Peña Blanca or Los Naranjos catch any San Pedro Sula bus (or pickup headed in that direction) and ask to be let off at the San Buenaventura turnoff (10km). From there, it's a little more than a kilometer down a dirt road to the village and the falls just beyond.

leave from behind the *alcaldía*. The road between here and La Esperanza is dirt most of the way, but is passable by car.

Tegucigalpa Transportes Lila (L$85, 3½ to four hours, 4:30am, 5:30am, 8:45am, 10:30am, 1:30pm and 2pm); Transportes Vanesa (L$60, 3½ to four hours, 5:50am)
San Pedro Sula Transportes Lila (L$120, five hours, 5:15am); Transportes Vanesa (L$120, five hours, 4:45am)
Comayagua (L$65, three hours, 6:30am, 8am, 11am, 1pm and 3pm)
La Esperanza (L$40, 1½ to two hours, 6:30am and 8:30am, plus 7:30am Saturday and Sunday)
La Paz (L$35 to L$37, two hours, eight departures daily 7:15am to 3:45pm)

THE WESTERN CORRIDOR

With star natural attractions like Parque Nacional Cerro Azul Meámbar and the Lago de Yojoa – and a few worthwhile colonial cities including Santa Bárbara, Siguatepeque and Comayagua – this less-traveled region has loads of potential. The corridor stretches some 240km along the Valle de Comayagua between Tegucigalpa and San Pedro Sula. Also on this route are turnoffs for two archaeological sites, two cave systems and the thermal waters at Azacualpa.

This region has long been an important commercial corridor. Settled at least 3000 years ago, it was an important trading route for early indigenous groups. Today, the valley is transected by the country's only 'real highway,' Hwy CA-5, which seems to be under constant construction but rarely gets any better.

LAGO DE YOJOA

You'll love the mist-shrouded Lago de Yojoa, Honduras' largest natural lake (89 sq km) and surely its most beautiful. This is slowly emerging as Honduras' next tourism hot spot…but it's not there yet. It has long been a favorite among bird-watchers, who have recorded over 375 species around the lake. This is also a good base for exploring two national parks: Cerro Azul Meámbar, with well-marked, moderately challenging trails, and Santa Bárbara, with the country's second-highest peak. Several easy day trips are also possible, including boat rides on the lake, a Lenca eco-archaeological site and the impressive Pulhapanzak Falls.

Orientation

Lago de Yojoa is 157km north of Tegucigalpa and 84km south of San Pedro Sula. Peña Blanca (pop 3700), a small town near the lake's north shore, is the best place to base yourself, with two adequate hotels in town and several better options a short distance away. From the CA-5 Hwy, the turnoff to Peña Blanca is 200m north of the town of La Guama – look sharp, as it's very easy to miss.

Information

Most of the lake region's basic services are in Peña Blanca, 15km northwest from the highway turnoff at La Guama.

Asociación de Municipios del Lago de Yojoa y su Área de Influencia (Amuprolago; ☎ 9988-2300; CA-5 Hwy; 🕑 8am-4pm Mon-Fri) Detailed information about the lake and the surrounding area; guide services can be arranged with advance notice. An excellent glossy map of the area is also for sale (L$20). It's 300m south of Honduyate Marina.

Banco Occidental (Peña Blanca; 8am-3:30pm Mon-Fri, to noon Sat) No ATM or currency exchange. At the eastern end of Calle Principal.

Clínica Santa Cecelia (650-0010; 24hr) Medical clinic near the turnoff to Los Naranjos.

Medicinas Marantina (650-0106; Peña Blanca; 8am-5pm) At the western end of Calle Principal.

Peña Blanc@net Café (Peña Blanca; internet per hr L$20; 8am-9pm) At the western end of Calle Principal; internet and web-based phone calls.

Police (Peña Blanca; 650-0026; 24hr) Opposite Hotel La Maranata.

Sights & Activities

Lago de Yojoa is a good jumping-off point for Cerro Azul Meámbar and Santa Bárbara national parks.

PARQUE ECO-ARQUEOLÓGICO DE LOS NARANJOS

On the northwest side of the lake, the **Parque Eco-Arqueológico de los Naranjos** (9654-0040; admission L$114; 8am-4pm) is a Lencan archaeological site dating to approximately 700 BC. The ruins themselves are not terribly interesting; they're made of clay so have only been semi-excavated (to protect them from environmental damage). The main reason to visit, however, is the wildlife. The park has 6km of trails that wind through the forest over hanging bridges and on a lakeside boardwalk, providing fantastic opportunities for spotting birds. A small museum at the visitors center gives a general overview of Lencan civilization, which is mildly interesting. The park is 5km south of Peña Blanca.

BOATING ON LAGO DE YOJOA

If you have a hankering to get on the lake, **Robert Dale** (9949-9719) at D&D Bed & Breakfast can arrange for you to rent a **rowboat** (per day L$50) from a local fisherman. For another L$50, a kid will come along to row, and if you arrange it for the early morning, he'll be able to guide you to the best places to see birds.

Hotel Agua Azul (opposite) rents out **kayaks** (per hr s/d L$100/160) as well as **pedal boats** (4-person maximum, per hr L$250). If you want a little more wind in your hair, Honduyate Marina (opposite) can arrange for a guided **motor boat tour** (9-person maximum; per 30min L$480) of the lake.

Ask about including fishing in your boat trip. The lake is famous for its bass.

BALNEARIO Y CENTRO TURÍSTICO PARADISE

Almost 5km south of Peña Blanca, the **Balneario y Centro Turístico Paradise** (357-0469; daylight hr) is a beautiful coffee and flower plantation with a river running through it. It doubles as a recreational area with picnic spots and plenty of swimming holes to jump into the cool, refreshing river. Although it's free most of the year (a small admission is charged during Semana Santa), it's far enough off the beaten track to keep visitors to a minimum. It also has a few rooms for overnight guests.

AGUAS TERMALES DE AZACUALPA

Most hot springs are a trickle of hot water burbling quietly out of a rock, but not at **Aguas Termales de Azacualpa** (admission L$10; 7am-5pm; P). Here, superheated water spits and boils out from the ground – one spot whistles like a teapot. A natural stone arch over the site conveniently contains the thick sulfurous steam, and there's a makeshift sauna if you really want to sweat. The water streams into the nearby Río Jaitique, forming shifting semi-hot pools. Upstream are large swimming holes flanked by high stone cliffs that are perfect for cooling off – there's even a wee sandy beach. Parking costs around L$50.

From the hot springs it's possible to **hike** to caves on the Río Ulua. Ask the attendant about guides.

A Honduran NGO has a large dorm and camping area next to the hot springs; if it's not being used, the caretaker, **Juan Ramón Henríquez** (608-9781), aka Moncho, will let you camp (L$100 per tent). On the other side of Azacualpa, 1km from town, the **Centro Turística Acosta** (608-7204; admission L$10) has cabins in the works, plus three very nice swimming pools (use of pools L$20) and a soccer field with sheep grazing on it.

Azacualpa is 25km southwest of Pito Solo, at the southeastern edge of Lago de Yojoa; the springs are a 1.5km walk from town. To get to Azacualpa, catch a *rapidito* (microbus) at Pito Solo. They generally leave at 8:30am, 11am and 1pm (L$25, 45 minutes). Others go as far as Zacapa, where you may be able to hitch the rest of the way.

Buses from San Pedro Sula pass through Pito Solo around 2:30pm and 5:30pm, and there's direct service from Santa Bárbara. To return, buses leave Azacualpa for San Pedro Sula at 6:30am and noon, and for Santa Bárbara at

6:30am and 8am. You may also be able to hitch to the Santa Bárbara–Pito Solo road, where the last bus to Santa Bárbara passes the turnoff at 5:30pm, and the last to Pito Solo at 3pm.

Sleeping & Eating

AROUND THE LAKE

The hotels around the lake all have their own restaurants. Most visitors end up having most meals at their hotels or in Pena Blanca.

Honduyate Marina (☎ 608-3276; www.honduyatemarina.com; CA-5 Hwy; campsite L$100, s/d L$1500/1690; P ❄ 💻 🏊) You'll almost think you're in Nantucket for all the nautical gear around. It does feel a bit too mainstream for the lake's otherwise rustic feel, and the grounds are seriously lacking, but camping is allowed. The rooms have the best lake views around and are large and clean, with amenities like air-con and TVs with DVDs.

Posada El Cortijo del Lago (☎ 9906-5333; s L$200 d L$400-600) All in all, not a bad deal for the price. The grounds are the highlight here: right on the lake, carpeted with pine needles, with canoes and sailboats available for rent. The rooms are basic, but the tile floors and clean bathrooms are a welcome sight, though the walls could use a bit of artwork. El Cortijo is 2km from La Guama turnoff.

D&D Bed & Breakfast and Micro Brewery (☎ 9994-9719, 3396-1279; www.dd-brewery.com; s/d L$180/250, cabins incl breakfast L$500-700; P 🏊) American Robert Dale says he started D&D because he wanted a place to get a real hamburger and a real beer, and listen to good music. He's done all that and added rooms for travelers of various budgets: simple, slightly dirty cement rooms and newer cabins that sleep up to four. Add a small clean pool and lush grounds and it's no wonder D&D has such a loyal clientele. The beer is home brewed, by the way, and the restaurant menu goes way beyond burgers: try the tilapia (a type of fish) for dinner and the blueberry pancakes for breakfast. D&D is off the road to El Mochito.

Hotel y Restaurante Colonial (☎ 380-5266; s/d L$300/400; P ❄ 🏊) One kilometer from Parque Eco-Arqueológico Los Naranjos, this hotel is good for birders who want to be at the park at dawn. Five smallish but comfortable rooms have gleaming hot-water bathrooms and cable TV. A teeny, immaculate pool faces the driveway, but is refreshing nonetheless.

Hotel Agua Azul (☎ 9991-7244; aboesch87@hotmail.com; r with fan/air-con L$480/690; P ❄ 🏊) Past its glory days but still just fine, Agua Azul offers simple wood cabins with painted cement floors, soft beds and clean bathrooms. There are great views from the extremely buggy grounds and tip-top restaurant, but the rooms lack views of any kind. Considering it's right on the lake, it seems like an architectural blunder. It's 3km from the highway on the north side of the lake.

Hotel Finca Las Glorias (☎ 566-0461; www.hotellasglorias.com; s/d L$870/928, 2-/3-bedroom cabin L$2088/2842; P 💻 🏊) A sprawling resort set down on the lake's shore, this is a great spot for larger groups. The resort's immaculately tended grounds lead you to the rustic but comfy enough cabins, most of which have screened-in porches, kitchens and living rooms. Solo travelers or couples have better options elsewhere.

La Posada de Don Julio (☎ 8938-0760; laabuelitafide@hotmail.com; road to Los Naranjos; apt L$1140; P ❄) Overlooking a coffee *finca* on the road to Los Naranjos, this new hotel has full apartments with kitchens and living areas. Each apartment has beautiful hardwood floors, porches with hammocks and two well-appointed bedrooms, making this a great spot for families or large groups. We only wish it were lakeside. Call ahead for reservations.

PEÑA BLANCA

Hotel La Maranata (☎ 650-0160; r with/without bathroom L$220/100) The cheapest rooms in town are about what you'd expect – small, spongy beds and cold-water bathrooms – but adequate and convenient if you're on a tight budget.

Hotel La Finca (☎ 566-0461; www.hotellasglorias.com; s/d L$260/360; P) A sister hotel to Finca Las Glorias, this is the better of the two sleeping options in Peña Blanca proper. Occupying a converted townhouse, with a large yard and fountain as remnants of a more glamorous youth, the hotel has six comfortable but plain rooms and a common area with sofas.

La Copaneca (mains L$20-60; 🕑 breakfast, lunch & dinner) A few tables set up in the front room of this family home, at the western end of Calle Principal, make up a good *pupusa* (cornmeal stuffed with cheese or refried beans) and *típica* eatery. Food is abundant and cheap.

The well-stocked minimart **Mini-Super Eben Ezer** (🕑 7am-6:30pm) is located where the road to El Mochito meets the Calle Principal.

Getting There & Away

From San Pedro Sula, the 'El Mochito' bus passes through Peña Blanca – get off there for

GONE SPELUNKIN'

South of Lago de Yojoa are two cave systems, one very well developed, the other down and dirty.

The **Cuevas de Taulabé** (CA-5 Hwy, Km 140; admission incl guide L$35; 8am-5pm), located alongside the highway, 25km north of Siguatepeque, were discovered in 1969 when the highway was being built, and have been explored to a depth of 12km, with no end in sight. The first several hundred meters have lights and a cement pathway; guides lead you on a 30-minute tour, describing the formation of the cave and pointing out stalagmites and stalactites with recognizable shapes (Jesus, Buddha etc). Tipping the guide is customary; for a bit extra, they'll take you to deeper, less-visited areas.

Not far away, **Cuevas de San José de Comayagua** (tours 1-3 people L$200) are two completely undeveloped caves. The first has a narrow crawl-through entrance, with spectacular stalactites and stalagmites. The second has a dramatic high-ceilinged entrance, huge formations and a crystalline river through the middle, which you have to wade through in places (1m to 1.25m deep). You can explore 300m into each cave; the first has no bats, the second does. Guides are required; tours last four hours, including two hours' hiking and an hour in each cave. The trip can also include lunch and a stop at a swimming hole on the Río Jaitique (extra L$100 per person). Flashlights, a hard hat, gloves and rope are provided; wear shoes that can get wet. The caves are 3km from the town of San José de Comayagua, which can be reached by bus from Taulabé (45 to 60 minutes, several departures daily) or by hitching. This same road connects with the thermal waters in Azacualpa (p152). **Daniel Espinoza García** (☎ 9922-0232; dedaniesp@yahoo.com) is one of several guides.

hotels in town, or catch a second bus toward La Guama and hotels along the lake (L$10, 10 minutes, every 20 minutes). For D&D and Balneario y Centro Turístico Paradise, stay on the Mochito bus past Los Naranjos to the signed access road. The last bus back to San Pedro Sula leaves at 4:30pm.

From the CA-5 Hwy, ask the bus driver to let you off at the *desvío* (turnoff) to Peña Blanca – it's just north of La Guama and very easy to miss. From there, buses to Peña Blanca run until 5pm. To get to D&D or Balneario y Centro Turístico Paradise, take a cab from Peña Blanca (L$10 to the access road, L$20 to their front gates).

To access Parque Nacional Santa Bárbara, take a bus from Peña Blanca to San Luis Planes (L$20, one to 1½ hours, 10:30am only) or to Los Andes.

PARQUE NACIONAL CERRO AZUL MEÁMBAR

Just east of Lago de Yojoa, Parque Nacional Cerro Azul Meámbar (Panacam) is easily one of the country's best equipped – and most unappreciated – national parks. A lush cloud forest measuring 312 sq km and reaching 2074m at its highest point, the park is a key source of the region's water, providing 70% of Lago de Yojoa's water, 20% of Francisco Morazán hydroelectric reserve, and drinking water for over 40 communities. All that water means waterfalls, green surroundings and lots of wildlife, including over 334 species of birds. Add some 15km of well-maintained hiking trails, an excellent visitors center (including guest rooms and a *comedor*), affordable fees and relatively easy access, and you have a true gem.

Information

A L$20 park fee is payable at the **visitors center** (☎ 608-5510, in Tegucigalpa 773-2027; www.infohn.com/parquesnacionales/azul_meambar.html). Staffers are very knowledgeable and can help arrange guide services (L$160 to L$250). There's also a rudimentary but useful trail map available.

A second entrance is planned for the small community of Cerro Azul, 7km east of the main highway. The turnoff is 5km south of Lago de Yojoa, marked by a sign for the national park; one bus passes daily (L$10, 15 minutes, noon) and hitching is easy. A 10km trail, due to be completed any day now, will connect the two entrances. There are basic accommodations in Cerro Azul; ask at the coffee *pulpería* in the center of town.

Hiking

The park has three main trails totaling 15km. They form intersecting loops, making it possible to hike on several without returning to the visitors center. The intersections are mostly well marked and the trail map is handy in clearing up any confusion.

Sendero El Sinai (8km, about four hours) is the hardest of the three trails, climbing from 750m at the visitors center to the system's highest point (1060m). The trail can be hiked in either direction; making a counterclockwise loop, it starts out with a moderate incline, up to an observation tower. Then it turns much steeper, shadowing a river (you'll cross at least four bridges) to Cascada El Sinai, a pretty 10m waterfall at about the 90-minute mark. As tempting as it will be, swimming is not allowed as the water is used for drinking. From the waterfall, the trail climbs more evenly, cresting at 1060m in about an hour. Heading down you'll come to a *mirador* (look-out point; 975m) with terrific views of Lago de Yojoa, the Represa Yure (Río Yure Dam), and the surrounding countryside. A steep winding descent follows; just before the visitors center you'll intersect with Sendero El Venado – turn left for that trail, or right to return to the center.

Sendero El Venado is only 1.2km long but it's moderately difficult. Following it clockwise, the trail intersects with the end of the Sinai trail, climbing through predominantly secondary forest before intersecting with the Sinai trail again, this time the first part. Continuing straight on, you'll descend steeply to the river, where the trail dead-ends into the third trail, **Sendero Los Vensejos**. Turning left, you'll cross a hanging bridge to Cascada Los Vensejos, a small falls pouring from a stone chasm into a welcoming pool. This one you can swim in – there's even a makeshift changing area. The other direction is the first part of Sendero Los Vensejos, which loops around less than 1km before emerging at the visitors center playing field.

Sleeping & Eating

The accommodations here are among the best in the country's national-park system. Visitors can choose between simple and spotless **cabins** (per person L$100) with bunk beds, hot-water bathroom, and linens (and even soap); or **camping** (per person L$20) on a grassy field overlooking a beautiful valley. The visitors center also rents camping gear (L$30 per night for a tent and sleeping bag) and sells basic toiletries.

The park can provide meals in the cafeteria as long as two prerequisites are met: at least seven people are interested and advance notice is given. That probably means you're on your own for food. Plan to bring your own eats and either enjoy them raw or rent the cafeteria kitchen (L$160 per day) to cook them.

Getting There & Away

The park entrance is at the end of a dirt road that starts at La Guama, just off CA-5 Hwy. Pickups typically head part of the way up every five to 11 minutes (6am to 7pm), shuttling locals to their villages. For a sure bet, call **Junior Molina** (☎ 9924-8448), who regularly takes visitors to the park in his van. The one-way trip costs L$160 per vanload (up to 15 people).

An alternative entrance is being established from the town of Cerro Azul (opposite), along the southwestern edge of the park.

PARQUE NACIONAL MONTAÑA DE SANTA BÁRBARA

Overlooking Lago de Yojoa, the Parque Nacional Montaña de Santa Bárbara is home to the majestic Montaña de Santa Bárbara – or El Maroncho, as many locals call it. At 2744m, it is the second-highest peak in Honduras – and looks absolutely mammoth from afar. A protected area since 1987, the park is a 321-sq-km combination of tropical, pine and cloud forest. It is also composed entirely of limestone, which means there are lots of caves and tunnels, and no visible water at higher elevations, as it is absorbed by the porous rock.

The park is accessible through the villages of **El Playón** (south side), **San Luis Planes** (north side), and **San José de los Andes** (east side). There is no direct access through the town of Santa Bárbara, but you can still catch a bus from there to one of the entry points.

Information

Santa Bárbara National Park does not have any tourist infrastructure – trails are unmarked, there are no campgrounds and no park services. But it is free.

For general information about the park, and for help with the logistics, contact Sandra Barahona in the Santa Bárbara **tourist office** (☎ 643-2338; turismosb@yahoo.com).

Hiking

There are several unmarked trails ranging in difficulty from intermediate to challenging. It takes most hikers two to three days to hit the summit, depending on where they enter the park. Along the way, visitors will have the opportunity to see almost four dozen orchid varieties, 407 bird species, 15 endemic plants, and animals like spider monkeys, anteaters and, if you're incredibly lucky, jaguars.

As there is only minimal development, a guide is essential. Fortunately, each of the three villages that border the park have highly recommended guides: **Mario Orellana** (☎ 9904-4457) in El Playón; **Adán Teruel** (☎ 674-3304) in San Luis Planes; and **Marcos Chavez** in Los Andes (ask around town to contact him). Most charge between L$200 and L$300 a day for their services; if you enjoy the trip, a tip is also appreciated.

Sleeping & Eating

Visitors have to bring their own gear and food to camp in the park. If you need equipment, Mario Orellana (above) in El Playón rents tents and sleeping bags for a nominal fee. For food, its best to stock up in the villages before you head out; it's also customary to buy food for the guide.

Getting There & Away

To enter the park through El Playón, take a bus from Santa Bárbara (L$20, 45 to 60 minutes) at 6:30am, 11:30am or 2pm Monday to Saturday; it returns at 6:30am, 7:30am and 2pm. To San Luis Planes, a bus leaves from Peña Blanca at 10:30am daily (L$160, one to 1½ hours); to return, take the daily 6am bus back to Peña Blanca. There is also a bus from Santa Bárbara at 11:30am (L$20, 1½ to two hours); there is a return at 6:30am daily. Finally, to head into the park through Los Andes, take a bus from Peña Blanca.

TRINIDAD

pop 19,100

The largest of the villages north of Santa Bárbara, Trinidad is a small colonial town with big-time charm – cobblestone streets, whitewashed homes and a beautiful old church. Be sure to check out the spectacular view from the hilltop cemetery. There aren't many services in town.

Two blocks behind the main church, the pleasant **Hotel y Pulpería López** (☎ 9933-7814; Calle Principal; r with fan/air-con L160/200; ❄) – the only one of its kind in town – has good beds, cable TV and spotless bathrooms.

Outside of town, **Estancia El Pedregal** (☎ 552-6365, 552-6359; www.estanciaelpedregal.com; r L$800-1000; P ❄) is a comfortable lodge 7.5km up a dirt road from Hwy 20, with horseback-riding and views of Pico Santa Bárbara.

For meals, stop in the modest *comedores* on Parque Central.

Buses traveling between Santa Bárbara and San Pedro Sula stop alongside the highway at the entrance to town. Once here, walk or use moto-taxis (in town L$6 per person, to El Pedregal L$220).

SANTA BÁRBARA

pop 36,800

About 53km west of Lago de Yojoa, Santa Bárbara, capital of the department of the same name, is a medium-sized colonial town known for its *junco* (straw-weaving) handicrafts. Despite its name, this is not the jumping-off point for Parque Nacional Santa Bárbara. The town has a pleasant old-fashioned air – many evenings, teenagers in school uniforms circle Parque Central (currently under renovation) in a courting ritual reminiscent of the 1950s.

Santa Bárbara was founded in 1761 by Spanish families from the towns of Gracias and Tencoa. Its residents are nicknamed *pateplumas* (winged feet), a reference to their speedy withdrawal into the mountains during the civil unrest that followed the dissolution of the Central American Federation in the late 1830s. Though the name was probably first used pejoratively, locals have embraced it as evidence of their peace-loving nature.

Orientation & Information

As a point of reference, the cathedral is on the east side of Parque Central, Betty's is on the west. There are no street names in town.

Andromeda.com (☎ 643-2678; internet per hr L$20; 🕒 8am-9pm Mon-Sat, 8am-12:30pm Sun) Half a block south of the cathedral for internet and web-based phone calls.

Banco Atlántida (🕒 8:30am-3:30pm Mon-Fri, to 11:30am Sat) Half a block north of the cathedral; traveler's checks are exchanged and there's a 24-hour ATM on site.

Hondutel (🕒 7am-noon, 12:30-5pm & 5:30-9pm) Next to the post office.

Hospital Integrado Santa Bárbara (☎ 643-2721; 🕒 24hr) At the entrance to town.

Police (☎ 643-2647, 643-2120) Downhill from Parque Central.

WESTERN HONDURAS

EXPLORING THE VILLAGES AROUND SANTA BÁRBARA

Several small towns between Santa Bárbara and the CA-4 Hwy are worth a short stop, whether for their *artesanía*, colonial churches or simple small-town appeal. Between Gualala and Ilama, several roadside *junco* (basket-weaving) stands have a good selection of hats, bags and hammocks.

- **San José de los Colinas** (22km from Santa Bárbara) is a picturesque village set in the hills and has one of the oldest churches in the country.
- **Gualala** (400m from CA-4 Hwy) features whitewashed homes with red-tile roofs, and lots of bougainvillea and *junco* products sold in front of local homes.
- **Ilama** (300m from CA-4 Hwy) is built into the hillside, and is bigger and less picturesque than other villages but has a few nice shops.

Post office (8am-4pm Mon-Fri, 8-11:30am Sat) One block south of the cathedral.
Tourist office (643-2338; turismosb@yahoo.com; 8am-noon & 2-5pm Mon-Sat, 8am-noon Sun) Two blocks east of Parque Central; has good information on area sites, including Parque Nacional Santa Bárbara.

Sights & Activities

Santa Bárbara's colonial Parque Central is the heart of the town, with a strikingly white church and a number of popular eateries around its edges.

It's definitely not a reason to stop in Santa Bárbara, but if you're in town and can't stand the heat, take a dip at **Balneario La Torre** (643-2440; adult/child L$50/25; 7am-6pm Sat & Sun), three blocks east of Parque Central.

To get sweeping views of the valley, head to **Castillo Bográn** (2.8km southeast of town), a steep hike to the shell of what was once a colonial-style building. The property itself is enclosed in barbed wire and the structure isn't particularly interesting but the view is nice. Be sure to bring a hat and bottled water – there's little shade and no *pulperías* along the way.

Sleeping & Eating

Hotel Boarding House Moderno (643-2203; Calle El Progresso; s/d with fan L$250/350, with air-con L$500/600; P) This old-fashioned hotel has a spacious tiled lobby and large, rather dirty rooms. All in all, you might be better off at the Colonial.

Gran Hotel Colonial (643-2665; s/d/tr incl breakfast L$550/640/790; P) Most travelers who stay in Santa Bárbara end up here – while no Ritz, it's an affordable, reliable choice close to the center, and there's hot water. It's 1½ blocks east of Parque Central.

Cafetería y Repostería Betty's (643-3006; Parque Central; mains L$20-50; breakfast, lunch & dinner) An air-conditioned hole-in-the-wall, Betty's has quick service, huge portions and cheap food.

Mesón Casa Blanca (mains L$50-90; breakfast, lunch & dinner) Housed within a cluttered converted living room – there are a couple of mounted deer heads, oil paintings and plants galore – this colonial-style restaurant is known as one of the best in town. Food is *típica*, served buffet-style for lunch and à la carte for breakfast and dinner. If it looks closed, just ring the bell; someone is almost always home. It's three blocks southeast of Parque Central.

Behind the cathedral, the **Mercado Municipal** (6am-5pm Mon-Sat, to noon Sun) is a rambling city market with a huge variety of fruit and vegetable stands.

Drinking

Billares Berpsa (10am-10pm Mon-Fri, 8am-10pm Sat & Sun) Definitely a guy's-guy scene – pool halls generally are in Honduras – but if you're looking to shoot a game or two, this is a relatively friendly place for travelers to go. It's behind the cathedral.

Getting There & Away

Los Junqueños (643-2113) buses to Tegucigalpa leave from 1½ blocks north of the plaza, past Banco Atlántida. All other buses leave from or near the main terminal, a block west of Parque Central. Buses go to various destinations, including:

Azacualpa/Aguas Termales (L$25, 1½ hours, 10am and 4pm) Or take a Tegus-bound bus and transfer – be sure to take the bus to Azacualpa, Zacapa, not Azacualpa, Valle.

Colinas (L$10, every 15 minutes, last bus at 7pm) Take any Ilama bus and transfer.

Copán Ruinas or Santa Rosa de Copán Take an *ordinario* toward San Pedro Sula and transfer at La Ceibita.

Ilama (L$10, 30 minutes, every 15 minutes 6:30am to 9:30pm, until 5pm Saturday and Sunday)

San Pedro Sula (*directo* L$50, 1½ hours, every 30 minutes 8am-5am; *ordinario* L$35, two hours, every 30 minutes 4am to 5pm)

Santa Bárbara National Park El Playón (L$20, 45 to 60 minutes, 6:30am, 11:30am and 2pm Monday to Saturday); San Luís Planes (L$22, 1½ to two hours, 11:30am)

Tegucigalpa (L$100, four hours) Los Junqueños has two to three morning departures and one at 2:30pm.

SIGUATEPEQUE

pop 81,600

There's no real reason to stop here, frankly, except if it's getting late and you want to get off the road. And even then, you're much better off continuing on to the pleasant colonial city of Comayagua.

Siguatepeque was founded by Spanish colonists in 1689 as a center for religious and monastic training. Some of the vows were evidently optional though, as the town's population grew quickly from the extensive intermixing of colonists and Lencans. The name Siguatepeque reportedly means 'town of beautiful women' in Nahuatl, which may have had something to do with it.

WESTERN HONDURAS

Orientation

Siguatepeque has two large plazas with the town's hotels, restaurants and services nearby. The pleasant Parque Central has trees and shady benches with a huge spider-like structure in the center. Plaza San Pablo, three blocks west, is ratty and unappealing and has been for years. Calle 21 de Junio and Calle 21 de Agosto connect the two.

Information

You'll find banks with ATMs, laundry, post and Hondutel on Parque Central and Plaza San Pablo.

Police (☎ 773-0042; Calle 21 de Agosto; 🕑 24hr)

Zona Virtual (1 block west of Parque Central; internet per hr L$20; 🕑 8am-8:30pm Mon-Sat) Internet access plus web-based phone calls.

Sleeping & Eating

Hotel Zari (☎ 773-0015; hotelzari@yahoo.com; Calle 21 de Junio; s/d L$200/320; P) The best value in town – though we aren't crazy about the jaguar skin in the lobby – this hotel near Parque Central offers good-sized but stark rooms that are sparkling clean. Each room has hot water, cable TV and a strong fan. Secure parking is also available.

Hotel Gómez (☎ 773-0868; Calle 21 de Junio; s/d with fan L$200/350, with air-con L$400/522; ❄) Although it's showing some wear and tear, the Gomez is a clean place with decent beds and private bathrooms. There is secure courtyard parking, a cafeteria (mains L$20 to L$60) open for breakfast and dinner Monday to Saturday, and free drinking water. Not bad for a cheapie.

Hotel Plaza San Pablo (☎ 773-0700; www.hotelplazasanpablo.com; Plaza San Pablo; s/d with fan L$345/470, with air-con L$455/580; P ❄ 💻) If you can get past the King Arthur castle motif, rooms here are really very comfortable and spacious with hot-water bathrooms and cable TV. It's popular with business travelers, so you'll need a reservation most weekdays.

Chicken's Friends (☎ 773-1122; Parque Central; dishes L$40-80; 🕑 lunch & dinner) This is one chicken who could really use some new friends: the ones he's got let him get chopped up, fried and served to backpackers for 60 lemps a plate. (Pretty tasty, though.)

Pizzería Venezia Centro (☎ 773-2999; Calle 21 de Junio; mains L$60-160; 🕑 lunch & dinner) One of Siguatepeque's longest-running restaurants, the Venezia serves fresh, thick-crust pizzas with just about any combination of meats and veggies. A medium pie easily serves two, though you may find yourself wanting more.

Entertainment

Cinemas Park (Parque Central; tickets L$30) Once-a-night shows start at 7:15pm.

Getting There & Away

Siguatepeque's buses leave from west of Plaza San Pablo. Most leave from a large walled lot at the corner of El Boulevard and Calle 21 de Junio, or just outside of it. You can also catch Tegucigalpa- and San Pedro Sula–bound buses at the highway.

Tegucigalpa (L$55, 2½ hours, hourly 5:15am to 5pm)

San Pedro Sula (L$57, 2¾ hours, every 45 minutes 4:40am to 4:10pm)

Comayagua (L$25, 40 minutes, every 15 minutes 6am to 5:15pm) Use 'Directos Rapiditos'.

La Esperanza (L$40, 1½ hours, 5:30am and 7am) From in front of the Hospedaje Central, a half-block from the terminal. After that, take a taxi (L$20) to La Esperanza turnoff, where buses leave at 8:30am, 9:30am, 11am and noon.

Lago de Yojoa (L$25, 40 minutes) Take San Pedro Sula buses.

COMAYAGUA

pop 114,500

Comayagua, 84km northwest of Tegucigalpa, is the historic first capital of Honduras and was a religious and political center for over three centuries, until power shifted to Tegucigalpa in 1880. The town's colonial past is evident in its several fine old *iglesias,* an impressive cathedral, colonial plazas and two interesting museums. A very Catholic city, it's also considered the best place in Honduras for visitors to witness Easter celebrations.

This is also a good staging point for trips along the Ruta Lenca and for hiking expeditions in the nearby Parque Nacional Montaña de Comayagua.

History

The city was founded as the capital of the colonial province of Honduras in 1537 by Spanish captain Alonso de Cáceres, fulfilling the orders of the Spanish governor of Honduras to establish a new settlement in the geographic center of the territory. The town was initially called Villa de Santa María de Comayagua; in 1543 the name was changed to Villa de la Nueva Valladolid de Comayagua.

Comayagua was declared a city in 1557, and in 1561 the seat of the diocese of Honduras was moved from Trujillo to Comayagua because of its more favorable conditions, central position and proximity to the silver- and gold-mining regions.

Orientation

As in most Honduran towns, life and essential services focus around Parque Central, which has been tastefully refurbished with gardens, benches and even piped-in music. Comayagua is a very walkable city, though the area between Parque Central and where most of the hotels are can feel very lonely after dark. Solo travelers, especially women, should consider taking a cab home if it's late.

The numbering begins where 1a Av and 1a Calle meet in the center of the city. From that point, the numbered avenidas and calles extend out in four directions: northeast (*noreste*; NE), northwest (*noroeste*; NO), southeast (*sureste*; SE) and southwest (*suroeste*; SO).

Information

Banco Atlántida (⌚ 8:30am-3:30pm Mon-Fri, 8:30-11:30am Sat) El Bulevar (4a Calle NO); 1a Av NO (btwn 2a & 3a Calles NO) Both branches have an ATM and change traveler's checks.

Centro Médico Comayagua Colonial (☎ 772-1126, 772-4026; 3a Calle NE; ⌚ emergency 24hr, pharmacy 8am-5pm Mon-Fri, to noon Sat)

Ecosimco (Ecosistema Montaña de Comayagua; ☎ 772-4681; ecosimco@hondutel.hn; Camara de Comercio; ⌚ 9am-noon & 1-5pm Mon-Fri) Manages the Montaña de Comayagua National Park; 500m north of town.

Farmacia Santa Fe (☎ 772-2459; 1a Av NE at 2a Calle NO; ⌚ 8am-12:30pm & 1:30-5:30pm)

Hondutel (1a Av NE btwn 4a & 5a Calles NO; ⌚ 7am-noon, 12:30-6pm & 6:30-9pm)

L@ Red Internet (Parque Central; per hr L$25; ⌚ 8am-8pm Mon-Sat, 3-8pm Sun)

Lavandería Ebenezer (Parque La Merced; per 1kg L$20; ⌚ 7am-6:30pm Mon-Sat, noon-6:30pm Sun) Laundry services.

Police (☎ 772-3040; ⌚ 24hr) At the eastern end of 5a Calle NO.

Post office (1a Av NE btwn 4a & 5a Calles NO; ⌚ 8am-4pm Mon-Fri, to 11am Sat)

Red Cross (☎ 195, 772-1997; ⌚ 24hr) For emergencies.

Sights

The **Catedral de la Inmaculada Concepción** (Parque Central; ⌚ 7am-8pm) is a colonial gem. Built between 1685 and 1715, it contains fine art in the Renaissance, baroque and neoclassic styles, both inside and out. The impressive three-paneled altar is similar to that of Tegucigalpa's cathedral; both are believed to have been made by the same unknown artist. The clock in the *iglesia* tower is the oldest in the Americas and one of the oldest in the world. The Moors built it around 1100 for the palace of the Alhambra in Granada. It was donated to the town by King Phillip II of Spain.

Other fine *iglesias* include the 1584 **Iglesia y Ex-convento de San Francisco** (1a Av NE btwn 6a & 7a Calles NO; ⌚ 7am-8pm), which has a remodeled plaza; the 1585 **San Sebastián** (3a Av NE near 6a Calle SO; ⌚ 7am-8pm), at the south end of town; and the 1730 **Nuestra Señora de la Caridad** (7a Calle NO at 3a Av NO; ⌚ 7am-8pm). Comayagua's first *iglesia* was **Nuestra Señora de la Merced** (1a Av NE at 1 Calle NO, Parque La Merced; ⌚ 7am-8pm), built from 1550 to 1558; it has a great little plaza in front. Another colonial *iglesia,* San Juan de Dios (1590), was destroyed by an earthquake in 1750, but samples of its artwork, along with artwork from all the other *iglesias,* are

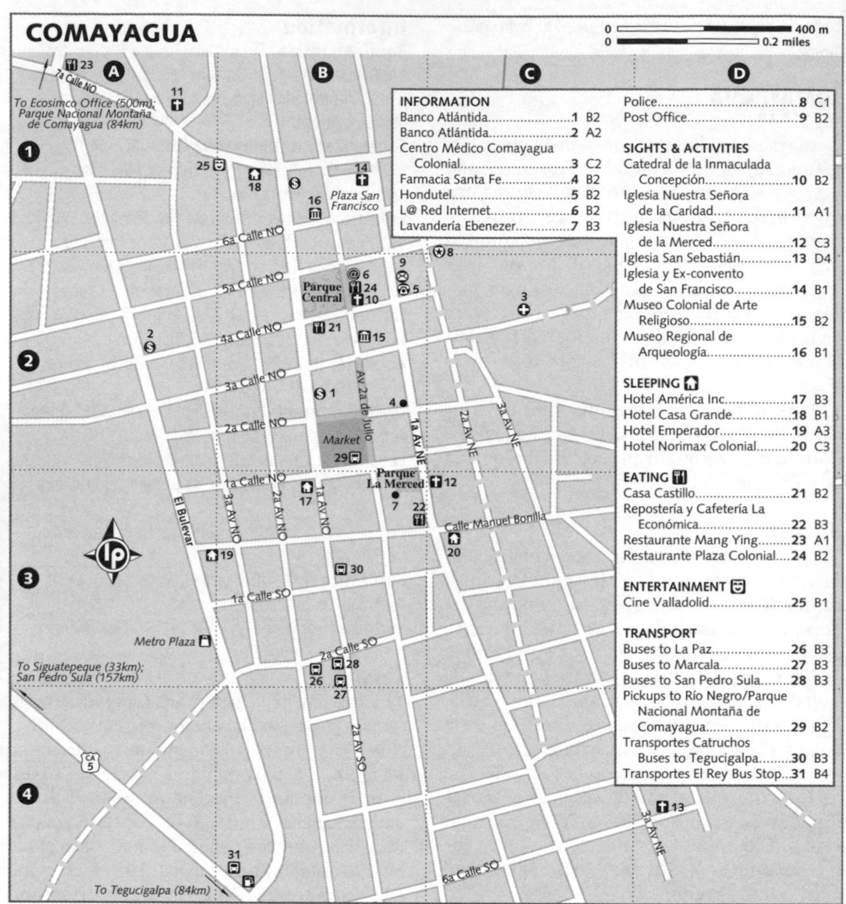

on display in the Museo Colonial de Arte Religioso. If you read Spanish, look for a small book entitled *Las Iglesias Coloniales de la Ciudad de Comayagua*, which contains an interesting history of Comayagua and its churches. It's available at both museums in town.

Housed in the former presidential palace, the **Museo Regional de Arqueología** (☎ 772-0386; 6a Calle NO near Av 2 de Julio; admission L$76; ⌚ 8:30am-4pm) has six excellent exhibits displaying artifacts from ancient Lenca communities, including pottery, *metates* (stone on which grain is ground), stone carvings and petroglyphs. It's way overpriced for foreigners, and signage is in English and Spanish.

Opened in 1962, the **Museo Colonial de Arte Religioso** (☎ 772-0169; Av 2a de Julio near 3a Calle NO; admission L$25; ⌚ 8am-noon & 2-4:30pm Tue-Sun) was once the site of the first university (1632) in Central America, which operated for almost 200 years. Priests have occupied the building even longer, since 1558. Totally renovated in 2005, the museum contains artwork and religious paraphernalia culled from all five churches of Comayagua, spanning the 16th to 18th centuries. The price of the ticket includes a guide.

Festivals & Events

One of the most Catholic cities in Honduras, Comayagua holds religious processions and special masses the entire week of **Semana Santa**.

The height of the celebration is on Good Friday morning, when the Vía Crucis – the procession representing Jesus carrying the cross down the streets of Jerusalem – makes its way around the historical center. The procession walks upon *alfombras*, which townspeople create throughout the night; watching these being made can be as interesting as the procession itself. The procession takes place from 8am to 2pm but be sure to arrive early so that you get a good look at the *alfombras* – and take a couple of photos – before they're trampled by thousands of feet.

Sleeping

If you're planning to visit during Semana Santa, be sure to call a couple months in advance to reserve a room.

Hotel Norimax Colonial (☎ 772-1703; Calle Manuel Bonilla near 1 Av NE; s/d with fan L$250/300, with air-con L$300/400; P ❄) Just half a block from charming Parque La Merced, the Norimax Colonial has clean, airy rooms, with high ceilings and lots of sunlight; be sure to ask for one facing away from the busy street. A sister hotel, called simply Norimax, is nearby, but the tiny rooms and surly service make it a far inferior choice – be sure you're at the right one.

Hotel América Inc (☎ 772-0360; www.hotelamericainc.com; 1a Av NO near 1a Calle NO; s with fan L$292, s/d with air-con L$361/699; P ☒ ❄ 💻 🏊) The best deal in town, the rambling Hotel América offers spacious, spotless rooms with cable TV, hot-water bathrooms and orthopedic beds. Add about L$150 for a new room, which has wood furnishings, brand-new floor tiles, and refurbished bathroom. There is also a well-kept pool on-site, a restaurant and secure parking.

Hotel Emperador (☎ 772-0332; Calle Manuel Bonilla near El Bulevar; s/d L$325/348; ❄) Despite the lofty name, the 'Emperor' is a basic, no-frills place far from the center of town. It is well kept – but can get a bit stinky. Consider spending a bit extra to have an interior facing room; they're super dark but the noise from the interminably busy boulevard in front is muffled by a couple of thick walls.

Hotel Casa Grande (☎ 772-0772; www.hotelcolonialcasagrande.com; 7a Calle NO near 1a Av NO; s/d incl breakfast L$952/1142; P ❄) This is the cutest spot in town. Set in a restored 19th-century *casona* (colonial-style mansion), the Casa Grande is a class act. Rooms are simple but elegant with handcrafted furnishings, warm earth tones and *azulejo* tiles. All open onto a lush central courtyard that leads to an outdoor dining area.

Eating

Restaurante Plaza Colonial (Parque Central; snacks L$25-50, mains L$100-125; 🕑 breakfast, lunch & dinner) This cute little cafe-bistro has metal tables and chairs right on Parque Central. The menu includes *golosinas* (traditional snacks), a hefty club sandwich, as well as beef, chicken and seafood dishes. Even if you're not hungry, it's a nice spot for coffee, postcards or evening beers.

Repostería y Cafetería La Económica (☎ 772-2331; 1a Av NE at Parque la Merced; mains L$40-100; 🕑 breakfast & lunch Mon-Sat) This small pastry shop serves typical Honduran dishes at tables behind a display case full of cakes. The windows let in plenty of light, but a nicer option is when tables are set up out the front, with a view of the church and Parque La Merced.

Casa Castillo (☎ 772-3528; Parque Central; mains L$60-160; 🕑 lunch & dinner, Tue-Sun) The Casa Castillo has two dining areas: a courtyard at the back and a high-ceilinged foyer that looks onto the park. The pasta is bland but the seafood and other dishes – like sweet-and-sour chicken with tartar sauce – are reasonably tasty. Head to the ice-cream shop next door for dessert.

SOUTHERN COMMAND: LA PALMEROLA

Fifteen kilometers from Comayagua is the Soto Cano air base, better known as La Palmerola and a longtime nerve center of US military presence in Central America. Up to 2000 US soldiers were stationed here during the 1980s, when the US was waging the Contra War in Nicaragua. Since then it's been converted to a Honduran base – on paper, anyway – and the force reduced to around 550 American soldiers. Periodic reports have called the mission at Soto Cano 'not critical,' but after the pullout of US forces from Panama in 1999, La Palmerola now represents the 'front-line' of US forces in the Americas. Far from scaling back, in 2005 the US Air Force underscored its intention to remain at La Palmerola by replacing hundreds of old soldier barracks with modern new apartments.

Restaurante Mang Ying (7a Calle NO at El Bulevar; dishes L$100-160; ⌚ 10am-10pm) If you're hungry – really hungry – order the Chop Suey Mang Ying. A mound of noodles, veggies, chicken, beef and shrimp, it's gotta weigh at least a couple of kilos.

Entertainment

Cine Valladolid (2a Av NO at 7a Calle NO; tickets L$20) Although it has seen better days, this old movie house still cranks out a feature every night at 7pm.

Getting There & Around

Taxis around town cost L$20 per person, more at night (L$30) or for longer trips.

Comayagua's town center is about 1km east of the highway. Bus companies servicing La Paz, Marcala and San Pedro Sula are located on the corner of 2a Calle SO and 2a Av SO. **Transportes Catrachos** (1a Av NO btwn Calle Manuel Bonilla & 1a Calle SO) services Tegucigalpa, as does **Transportes El Rey**, which stops at the Texaco gas station at the highway turnoff. El Rey drops you off in a better part of Tegucigalpa.

Some bus services:

La Paz (L$14, 30 minutes, every 15 minutes 5:40am to 6pm)
Marcala (L$50, three hours, 6:15am, 8am, 10am, noon and 2pm)
Río Negro (L$35, four hours) Pickups leave from the south side of the market at 11am, noon and 1pm. It's a long bumpy road, with no benches in the truck to sit on.
San Pedro Sula Transportes Rivera (3¼ hours; *ordinario* L$72, *directo* L$100, hourly 5am to 4pm)
Tegucigalpa Transportes Catrachos & Transportes El Rey (L$38, 2½ hours, hourly 5:15am to 5pm)

PARQUE NACIONAL MONTAÑA DE COMAYAGUA

Spanning more than 30,000 hectares of primary and secondary forest, Parque Nacional Montaña de Comayagua (Panacoma) has a few decent hiking trails and provides the bulk of fresh water used by some neighboring 60 communities, including Comayagua.

The national park is managed by **Ecosimco** (☎ 772-4681; ecosimco@hondutel.hn; ⌚ 9am-noon & 1-5pm Mon-Fri), which operates out of a small office next to the Camara de Comercio about 500m north of Comayagua; look for the big green gates. Admission to the park is L$35, payable at the Ecosimco office. That said, no one in the park collects your ticket, so it's a strictly karmic exercise.

Hiking

There are two official trails in the park. Both start from near the village of Río Negro, a small cluster of homes along the road 42km north of Comayagua – you'll pass the trailhead, marked Paseo de los Leones, about 1km before the village. The first trail is to **Cascada de los Ensueños**, a 75m waterfall about an hour's hike away through mostly secondary forest. The trip takes longer if you stop to read the more than 20 placards along the way, explaining the flora, fauna and ecology of the area. The second trail veers off the first just before reaching Los Ensueños, and leads to another waterfall, **El Gavilán**. Swimming is not permitted in either falls, however, as they both provide drinking water for several communities downstream.

A guide is recommended and can be hired in Río Negro. Dania Morales Alvarado (ask for him in Río Negro) is very knowledgeable about the park's ecology and leads most hikes. The walk to Los Ensueños/El Gavilán for one to three people costs around L$200 per person. The Morales Alvarado house is on the left in Río Negro, just before the road goes steeply downhill. In addition to hiking, there is a pool with a waterfall (and a cave behind it – ask any kid to show you how to access it) about 300m from the Morales Alvarado home.

Sleeping & Eating

Simple **accommodations** (☎ 9990-0802; r L$60-120) are available at the house of Don Avilio Velásquez, which also serves as the de facto visitors center. They're basic eco-casitas with four bunks apiece, cold-water bathrooms, sturdy wooden furniture and no electricity. There are also places to camp and simple meal service. It's a short walk from Dania Morales Alvarado's place.

Getting There & Away

Pickup trucks bound for Río Negro leave from the south side of the market in Comayagua at 11am, noon, and 1pm (L$35). From Río Negro, they leave at 5am and 6am only. It's four long, bumpy hours, standing the whole way, since there are no seats in the truck.

YARUMELA

Located on the Río Humuya between Comayagua and La Paz, Yarumela is a mostly unexcavated **archaeological site** with mounds that simply look like hills covered in brush.

Lencans occupied the city from 1000 BC until AD 250, when it was abruptly abandoned. Because of the number of administrative and religious buildings, it also is believed to have been a seat of government.

The site has two major mounds worth checking out. The central structure is 20m high; archaeologists believe it was the residence of a chieftain. From the top, the view of the Valle de Comayagua is fantastic. The smaller mound sits right beside the river; it has been reconstructed on one side, revealing a step pyramid with several platforms and a stairway going up the middle. The remaining half of the mound looks like a grassy knoll.

Yarumela is accessible by cab or private vehicle only. From Comayagua, take CA-5 Hwy toward Tegucigalpa. Take the turnoff to La Paz and go over the Río Humuya. Just before you come to a roundabout, take a right on the dirt road. Stay on it until you come to the large mound on the right-hand side of the road. This is the site. There are no set prices for a cab ride from Comayagua. A taxi from La Paz costs around L$250 round-trip.

TENAMPUA

The Tenampua archaeological site sits on a large hill and was constructed between AD 900 and 1000 – a time of war in the valley. Its structure reflects the era: it is both well protected and easy to defend. The sweeping views it had of the entire valley allowed the inhabitants to see approaching enemies; the ascent is very steep on three sides, and on the fourth side a high, 2m-thick wall was constructed. Features that can be seen today include a handful of unexcavated mounds, walls and a ball court, an example of the influence that the Maya had over the region.

Tenampua is about 20km south of Comayagua. Take a Tegucigalpa-bound bus and ask to be let off at the *sendero* for Tenampua; it's on the east side of the highway, just north of the Restaurant Aquarios. It's a steep climb and takes one to 1½ hours.

LA PAZ

pop 38,400

La Paz is a gateway to La Esperanza and the Ruta Lenca, though Comayagua, just 20 minutes away, serves the same function and is much more pleasant.

The town has basic services for travelers. There is a **Banco Atlántida** (Parque Central; 8:30am-3:30pm Mon-Fri, to 11:30am Sat), which exchanges traveler's checks and American dollars. The **post office** (8am-4pm Mon-Fri, 8-11:30am Sat) is three blocks from Parque Central.

Sleeping & Eating

Valle de Piedras B&B (774-3713; Blvd Los Pinos; s/d with fan L$220/300, with air-con L$400/450; P) A short distance from the main square, this is a great little B&B with just seven rooms. Upstairs air-conditioned rooms are clean and bright, with ceramic floors and large TVs. The second 'B' in 'B&B' must stand for something other than breakfast, but fresh coffee plus a fridge, microwave and sunny little terrace are available to guests upstairs.

Comedor y Golosinas La Chalupa (mains L$20-60; breakfast, lunch & dinner Mon-Sat) An old school eatery, this *comedor* has high ceilings, shutters pulled to keep the heat out, and a menu replete with Honduran *típica*. It's two blocks from Parque Central.

Getting There & Away

Buses come and go from the busy intersection at the entrance to town. Buses to Marcala (L$30, two hours, every 30 minutes 5am to 4pm) and Comayagua (L$14, 40 minutes, every 15 minutes 5am to 6pm) park right on the shoulder. Buses to Tegucigalpa (L$30, 1½ hours, every 30 to 60 minutes 4:30am to 4pm) leave from a small terminal next to the Shell gas station. Buses to San Pedro Sula (L$90, three hours) originate in Marcala and pass the La Paz terminal at around 5:30am and 6:30am; be sure to arrive at the bus stop 30 minutes early.

A taxi in town costs L$13 per person, or L$16 at night.

The North Coast

This is truly a wild coast, with nearly a dozen protected areas between Omoa and Trujillo. There are howler monkeys and glimmering beaches at Parque Nacional Jeannette Kawas to the west, excellent rafting and jungle lodges just inland from La Ceiba in the middle, bird-choked lagoons to the far east, and the chance to get away from it all just about everywhere in between.

The region is home to the Garífuna people – descendents of Arawak Indians and West Africans who escaped from slave ships in the 16th century – and spending time in funked-out Garífuna communities such as Miami or Santa Fe is surely a highlight for any traveler interested in exploring Honduras' unique culture. There are also colonial forts; a diverse ethnic mix of coastal Caribs, Garífuna, ladinos and expats resolved to spend the rest of their days in paradise; and a series of festivals that'll leave your head spinning. These festivities culminate during Semana Santa (Holy Week), when the entire coast fills up with vacationing Hondurans. It may be tough to get a room, but it won't be hard to find a good party.

With all that coastline, you'd think there'd be some better beaches. But Honduras' North Coast is not really about the sand and the water – though you'll certainly find some totally adequate plots of sand on the nearby Cayos Cochinos, and in tourist towns such as Trujillo and Tela. It's more about the people and the adventures you'll encounter along the way.

HIGHLIGHTS

- Get wet on the **Río Cangrejal** (p189), one of the best stretches of white-water in Central America, before heading off for some canoeing at **Refugio de Vida Silvestre Cuero y Salado** (p187)
- Howl at the dawning sun in chorus with the local troupe of howler monkeys at **Parque Nacional Jeannette Kawas** (Punta Sal; p174) by day, and party it up in **Tela** (p169) by night
- Break the surface in **Cayos Cochinos** (p191), the best diving and snorkeling spot along the coast – it has beaches, too!
- Leave the tourist trail behind in the remote villages surrounding **Trujillo** (p192), leaving time for a jungle tromp in **Parque Nacional Capiro-Calentura** (p198)
- Shake it – hopefully not like a 'celluloid picture' – at the **Garífuna Festival** (p166) at Baja Mar

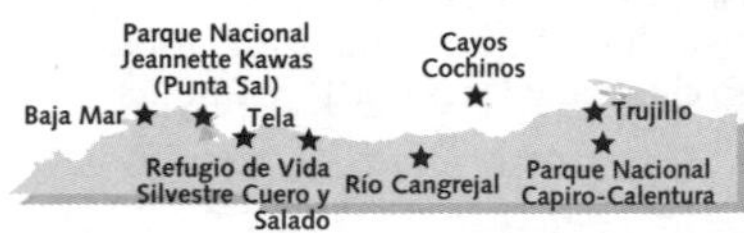

DANGERS & ANNOYANCES

We've heard of occasional reports of travelers being accosted and robbed on beaches along the North Coast, typically by groups of young men. Most of the incidents have happened on lonely stretches of beach outside La Ceiba and, to a lesser degree, Tela and Trujillo. Some people have reported having belongings swiped from the beach while they were in the water. The simple solution, of course, is not to walk along these beaches without company and certainly never at night, and to not leave valuables unguarded. It's best to cab-it at night in La Ceiba.

The North Coast also has a very high rate of HIV infection: plan accordingly.

PUERTO CORTÉS & AROUND

OK, Puerto Cortés is pretty damned ugly – it's one of the busiest deepwater ports in the Americas, so go figure – but the nearby beach towns of Omoa, Travesía and Baja Mar are worth the visit. To the west, Omoa is the most developed of these resort areas, with a smattering of restaurants and hotels, and a dark honey-colored beach. East of Puerto Cortés, Travesía and Baja Mar are small Garífuna villages with fairly decent lodging options, and the best beaches on this section of the coast. The latter hosts the annual Garífuna festival. Unfortunately, this area lacks the national parks you'll find outside of Tela, La Ceiba and Trujillo – beach-bums only need apply.

PUERTO CORTÉS

pop 118,100

There just isn't much reason to stop in this large port city, and most people only pass through on their way to the neighboring beach areas. You can also catch a twice-weekly ferry from here to Belize. If you end up spending the day, visit the Parque Central, then head over to Playa Cienaguita in front of the **Hotel Playa** (☎ 665-0453; www.hotelplaya.hn). The beach is clean and open to all.

Puerto Cortés' annual fair is held on August 15.

History

More interesting than the town itself is its history. Puerto Cortés was founded in 1524 by Spanish colonizers drawn to its potential as a deepwater port. The port was originally called Puerto Caballos (Port of Horses); as the story goes, when explorer Gil González Dávila arrived, a powerful storm blew in and he had to throw several horses overboard in order to survive. How throwing the poor horses in the ocean improved the situation remains unclear, but the name stuck until 1869, when it was changed to Puerto Cortés.

Information

Banco Atlántida (2a Av near 4a Calle Este; 9am-4:30pm Mon-Fri, to noon Sat) Exchanges traveler's checks; ATM accepts Visa cards only.
Centro Medico Bahía (☎ 665-4325; 2a Av at 7a Calle Este; 6:30am-5pm Mon-Fri, to noon Sat) Emergencies handled 24/7.
Farmacia FarmaUNO (☎ 665-1579; 4a Av btwn 2a & 3a Calles Este; 7am-6pm Mon-Fri, to noon Sat)
Hondutel (1a Calle btwn 1a & 3a Av; 7:30am-8:30pm) To make phone calls.
MultiNet (Parque Central; per hr L$20) Internet access.
Police (☎ 665-0420; 24hr)
Post office (1a Calle btwn 1a & 3a Av; 8am-4pm)

Dangers & Annoyances

As a port town goes, Puerto Cortés has its fair share of roughnecks and shady characters. It's perfectly fine during the day, but exudes a certain toughness at night, especially anywhere drinking is going on.

Sleeping

Hotel El Centro (☎ 665-1160; 3a Av btwn 2a & 3a Calles Este; s with fan/air-con L$324/442, d with fan/air-con L$453/576; P) Near the bus terminals, this well-kept hotel has gleaming tile-floored rooms. Each room has a cable TV and hot-water bathroom. The rooms are small but not oppressively so – the framed posters on the walls help a lot.

Hotel Buenos Aires (☎ 665-4580; 5a Av btwn 12a & 13a Calles Este; s with fan L$324, d with fan/air-con L$453/576; P) Nicer than El Centro, but owned by the same family, the BA has clean tile floors, hot water, cable TV and an easy-peezy feel. It's in a quiet neighborhood nine blocks from Parque Central – a short walk by day, but one that you should cab at night.

Hotel Villa del Sol (☎ 665-4938; villadelsol.hn@hotmail.com; Blvd El Porvenir; r L$1387) Across the street from the municipal beach, this newish hotel block has clean, business-style rooms with thick mattresses, a little pool

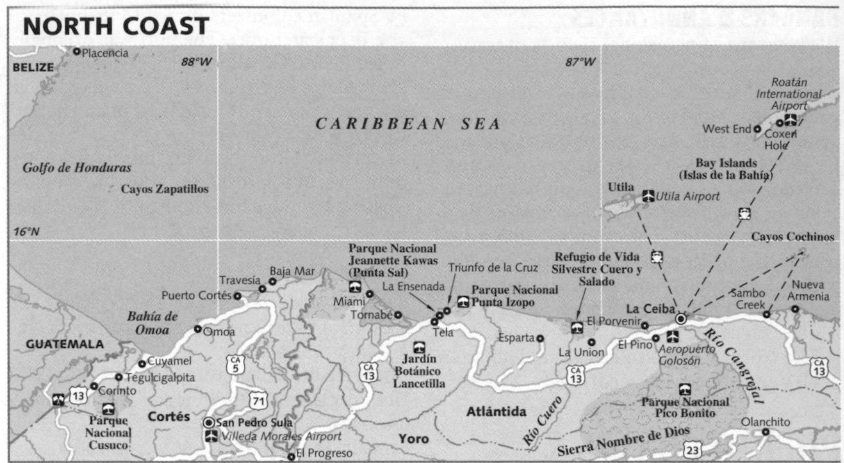

out back and wi-fi for it's business clients. It's expensive, but the nicest hotel in town.

Eating

Repostería y Comida Buffet Plata (3a Av at 2a Calle Este; mains L$30-80; breakfast, lunch & dinner Mon-Sat) Near the bus terminals, this bustling cafeteria serves tasty *típico* (Honduran fare) and tempting baked goods.

Parrillada Joché (3a Av at 11a Calle Este; mains L$40-80; lunch & dinner) This popular barbecue place serves grilled meat and chicken. Seating is on the front lawn of a private home. Arrive early for a seat on weekends – it's hopping with customers at peak hours.

Getting There & Away

BOAT

Boats to Belize leave Barra La Laguna, near Puerto Cortés, twice a week – on Monday they go to Dangriga (L$950, two hours). Departure is at 9am, though it is often delayed for up to two hours. You must come with your passport the day before to sign up (yes, it's a pain). The office is about 3km west of Puerto Cortés – take any Omoa-bound bus and get off at La Laguna. The office is in the fish market, under a bridge about 200m from the highway.

BUS

Both **Impala** and **Caribe** (☎ 665-0606) service Puerto Cortés from side-by-side terminals on 4a Av between 3a and 4a Calles. Between them, buses leave for San Pedro Sula every five to 10 minutes from 4am to 9pm (L$42).

For transportation information to Travesía and Baja Mar, see opposite.

Citral Costeños (☎ 655-0888; 3a Calle Este) provides a daily service to Omoa (L$20, 30 minutes to the turnoff) every 20 minutes from 5am to 5:40pm.

TRAVESÍA & BAJA MAR

pop 2400

Travesía and Baja Mar, just east of Puerto Cortés, are traditional Garífuna villages with houses built along the shore and fishing boats pulled up onto the sand. The beach at Travesía is cleaner than the one at Baja Mar. Beyond Travesía and Baja Mar, and a good distance inland, is a non-Garífuna town called Brisas del Chamelcón, although very few visitors make it that far.

Festivals & Events

Baja Mar is best known as the home of the **Garífuna Festival**, held here every year between July 9 and 24. Members of the three dozen or so Garífuna communities in Honduras come together, making it one of the best opportunities to experience Garífuna culture. The height of the party is typically July 16, when an all-night dance competition keeps everyone moving until the sun rises.

Sleeping & Eating

Hotel Frontera del Caribe (☎ 665-5001, 9981-1033; r L$350; P) The best buy in the Travesía-

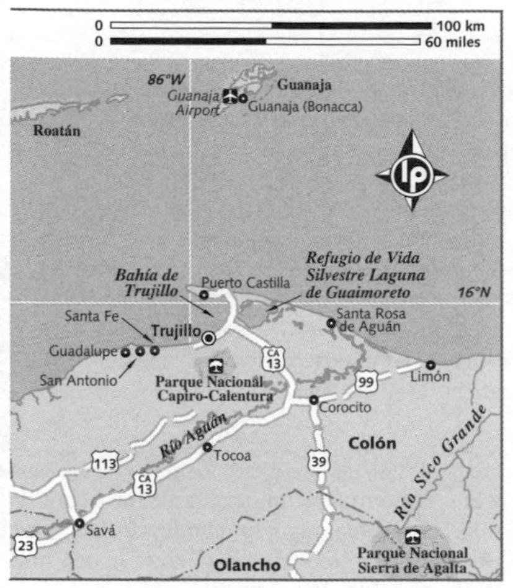

Baja Mar area, this little gem is right on the beach, at the western entrance to Travesía. The rooms are small and hot, but perfectly clean, and the tiled baths are a welcome sight. Some of the sheets are pilled up, but clean, and there's a big water jug to fill your water bottle. It serves meals onsite (L$20 to L$40).

Blue Bayou (☎ 3382-1865; hammock L$50, campsites L$300, s/d L$450/550; P) Just 6.5km east of Puerto Cortés, this beachfront spot was just getting started when we passed by. It has squishy mattresses, but the rooms are clean and the service friendly, and there was talk of building a restaurant onsite.

Hotel Victoria (☎ 9739-7348, 9587 6769; eastern end of Baja Mar; r with/without bathroom L$400/300; P) This pepto-pink beachfront hotel just feels a bit dirty: the bathrooms are dirty, the concrete floors are dirty and the grounds are litter-strewn. But the 'Return of the Jedi' sheets are clean, and it's close to the beach.

Getting There & Away

The road to Travesía is so-so, worse to Baja Mar, and awful to Brisas. In the summer an ordinary car can make it to all three, driving carefully; otherwise only 4x4s can manage the mud. Accordingly, departure times and durations may vary considerably.

Buses from Puerto Cortés to Travesía (L$6, 15 minutes), Baja Mar (L$8, 30 minutes) and Brisas del Chamelecón (L$10, 45 minutes) usually depart from a stop at the corner of 5a Calle Este and 4a Av at 7am, 9:30am, 10:30am, 12:15pm, 2pm, 4pm and 5:30pm. The bus returns from Brisas, in front of the Pulpería Lester, at 8am, 11am, noon, 2pm and 4pm.

A taxi will take you between Puerto Cortés and Travesía for around L$100.

OMOA

pop 37,300

Omoa is a sleepy seaside town, 18km west of Puerto Cortés. A weekend getaway for San Pedro Sulans, Omoa also attracts a steady stream of backpackers with its pervasive shorts-and-flip-flops atmosphere and brown-sugar beach. For some, however, Omoa is simply a convenient stopover before or after crossing the Guatemalan border. Omoa's annual festival is held on May 30.

Information

Buses to/from Omoa stop on the main highway, 1km from the beach. There is a cluster of

LOCAL LORE: THE FOUNTAIN OF YOUTH

A growing body of historical research calls into question the accuracy of the famous tale of Don Juan Ponce de León's 'discovery' of Florida in his quest for the fountain of youth. In fact, that search may have been conducted by another sailor altogether, Juan Díaz de Solís, who reckoned the mythical fountain must have been somewhere along Honduras' North Coast.

While de León was certainly the first European to land at Florida (where he was fatally wounded by a Native American's arrow) records of his journey mention nothing of a search for a fountain of youth – he was there to look for gold and 'wealthy land.' The mistake seems to have stemmed from misreadings of coordinates in the original documents, and a comment by 16th-century Spanish historian Gonzalo Fernández de Oviedo, who snickered that de León's ill-advised adventuring must have been done in search of a fountain of youth to cure his *enflaquecimiento del sexo* (flaccid member). They don't seem to mention that theory at the 'Fountain of Youth' theme park in St Augustine, Florida. For his part, Solís searched the Golfo de Honduras as far as Belize, with no luck.

THE PIRATE LIFE FOR ME!

In his book *Villains of All Nations* (2004), University of Pittsburgh professor Marcus Rediker debunks the popular conception of pirates as ruthless killers and plunderers – or at least as *only* killers and plunderers. He points out that life for sailors on lawful merchant ships was no picnic. A standard merchant ship might have 15 or 20 miserably overworked crew members, while a pirate ship of similar size might have 80 or 90. Sailors who were injured onboard commercial ships were jettisoned at the nearest port, if not before. The semi-comical picture of a pirate with peg-leg and eye-patch may more accurately portray destitute crippled sailors, scores of whom could be found begging on the streets of Atlantic port cities. On pirate ships, injured crew members were still entitled to a portion of the booty – an early form of welfare. Moreover, captains were elected democratically. Those who abused their crew could be removed, punished or even killed. And captains never received more than twice what the ordinary sailors got – propose *that* to the average oil-company CEO.

shops and services at the highway intersection and on the road to the beach.

Banco de Occidente (8:30am-4pm Mon-Fri, to 11:30am Sat) Just west of the Omoa turnoff; exchanges traveler's checks but has no ATM.

Bubbles (road to the beach) Does laundry for L$70 per load.

Dr Jorge Mejia (☎ 658-9070; from 5pm) For medical emergencies; recommended by locals and expats. It's 40m west of the Farmacia San Antonio.

Farmacia San Antonio (☎ 658-9198; 8am-6pm Mon-Sat, to 1pm Sun) At the highway turnoff.

Internet & Video Club (☎ 933-0271; per hr L$20; 8am-10pm) Internet access; located 150m from the highway.

Sights & Activities

Omoa's claim to historical fame is the **Fortaleza de San Fernando de Omoa** (☎ 658-9167; admission L$76, guided tour max 10 people L$100; 8am-4pm Mon-Fri, 9am-5pm Sat & Sun). Located on the main street to the beach, this fort was built under King Fernando VII of Spain between 1759 and 1775 by enslaved Indians and, later, by enslaved Africans. It was constructed to protect the coast and the region's treasures – gold, silver and indigo – that were shipped out from there. The plan only worked for four years; in 1779 the fortress was captured by the British after a two-day battle. It's still in good shape today, and features 31 rooms, a small museum, about three dozen cannons and hundreds of cannonballs. It's way overpriced for your average indie traveler.

Omoa has a pretty **waterfall** and **swimming hole** about 2km to 3km south of the highway turn-off. To get there, follow the road past the bank, bearing right until you reach a small garbage dump. Bearing left, stay on the road until it crosses the river, where you turn left and walk along the river to the falls. There were some much-publicized assaults on this hike several years ago, though reportedly none of late. Definitely check at your hotel, and leave valuables at home.

Ask a local boatman if they can take you to **Cayos Zapatillos**, a collection of eight spectacular Belizean islands 45km offshore.

Sleeping

Roli's Place (☎ 658-9082; roli@yaxpactours.com; campsite/dm/s/d L$60/80/150/180, s/d with private bathroom L$220/250, d with air-con L$330; P) The aggressive, surly service is certainly a turnoff. The digs are basic and the rules are strict, but backpackers will appreciate the free bikes and kayaks, and communal kitchen.

Bahía de Omoa (☎ 658-9076; heinz.windmann@gmail.com; r L$500; P) This hotel across from the Flamingo has four 2nd-floor rooms with high ceilings, hot-water bathrooms and cable TV. Beds are hit or miss but the rooms are clean. Little details like *artesanía* (handicrafts) and posters on the walls add a bit of personality. Bicycles are free for guests.

Flamingo's (☎ 658-9199; flamingosomoa@yahoo.com.ar; s/d incl breakfast L$870/1740; P) Located on the beach, and the top dog in town, Flamingo's has large modern rooms with spotless floors and bathrooms, high ceilings and brightly painted pine walls. The restaurant has views over the beach and pier. Service is friendly and professional.

More hotels along the main drag:

Chompa Julie (☎ 658-9174; s/d with fan L$150/300; d with air-con L$500) At the budget end; comes with the bare basics.

Hotel Bar y Piscina Michelle (☎ 3364-7973; hotelmichelle@yahoo.ca; s with fan L$300; d with air-con L$600;) The beds are concave, but the pool is awesome.

ispy-clean rooms also have air-con, two ouble beds, cable TV and hot-water bathoom. There's 24-hour security too.

IDRANGE

otel Colonial (448-3222; cnr 8a Av NE & 9a Calle NE; s/d/tr L$590/650/850;) This new hotel is a great deal if you don't mind not being beachfront. It's pert and clean, but lacks a bit of character. Would it kill them to put some art on the walls? The interior rooms are dark, but quieter than those looking onto the street.

Hotel Presidente (448-2821; www.hotelpresidentecaribe.com; Parque Central; s/d L$735/1157;) A rambling hotel right near Parque Central, the Presidente is reminiscent of Holiday Inn – pleasant but impersonal. Rooms have furniture sets, matching bedspreads, big bathrooms and electrical hot water. Features such as a pool, game room and gym (even if it is an oversized closet) are nice surprises.

Hotel y Restaurante Maya Vista (448-1497; www.mayavista.com; off 8a Calle NE btwn 9a & 10a Avs NE; r with fan L$570, s/d with air-con L$760/855, ste L$1140-1330;) Wake up to one of the best views in Tela at this jungle gym of a hotel. Built on a hill and climbing several stories into a windswept sky, the hotel seems to have acres of patio space to take in the ocean vistas. Rooms have warm, tasteful décor and some have a private patio. The only drawback: it's a hell of a hike to the beach.

Hotel Gran Central (448-1099; www.hotelgrancentral.com; Calle José Trinidad Reyes at 5a Av NE; s/d L$760/950;) While there's nothing central about the Grand, and it's overpriced given there's no beach here, this rancho-style hotel does have its charms, offering seven artsy rooms on the 2nd floor of a renovated colonial building. Each is decorated differently, with details such as handcrafted light fixtures, checkerboard floors and hand-painted designs on he walls.

OP END

ésar Mariscos Hotel y Restaurante (448-2083; ww.hotelcesarmariscos.com; Calle Peatonal at 3a Av NE; s/d cl breakfast L$1052/1327;) Charming ooms with a modern beachy feel open on two sunny decks and a mezzanine-level finity pool with Jacuzzi. Most rooms have lconies looking out to sea. And the view om the pool – well, it's classic Caribbean. s right on the boardwalk, and also has a achfront restaurant.

Hotel y Restaurante Sherwood (448-1065; w.hotelsherwood.com; Calle Peatonal at 3a Av NE; L$1100/1500;) A bit darker and drear than neighboring César, this is your seco choice in the top-end range along t boardwalk. The 3rd-floor rooms are de nitely the way to go at this place – hardwo floors, wood paneling and great views. pool and a breezy beachside restaurant nice features.

Hotel Villas Telamar (448-2196; www.hoteltela.com; r with garden view L$2413, r with ocean view L$3 2-/3-/4-bedroom villa L$5396/7600/8816;) Tela's heavy hitter, this mega resort off brand-spanking-new hotel rooms, w maintained Caribbean-style bungalows a villas, and the best stretch of beach arou Although it's not an all-inclusive, it is set like one; there's daily programming (da classes, water aerobics, beach-volleyball co petitions), two restaurants (including a bu of course) and on weekends guests wear w bands to keep the riff-raff out. The resort a boasts three tennis courts and an 18-hole course, all complimentary for guests. It's 2 west of town.

Eating

Seafood soups are a particular delicacy of town; fish, shrimp, lobster and *caracol* (con are found in many restaurants. Another s cialty is *pan de coco* (coconut bread); yo see Garífuna women and children sellin around town. Try it – it's delicious.

BUDGET

Auto Pollo Al Carbón #1 (11a Calle at 2a Av; brea lunch & dinner) Just a wishbone's throw from beach, this simple open-air chicken sh serves up good roast chicken.

Tuty's (9a Calle NE at 5a Av NE; mains L$40-60; 10pm) This gleaming air-cooled pastry *licuado* (smoothie) shop and the hot, cran chicken place next door are one and same – a culinary Dr Jekyll and Mr H The chicken place serves up good gr meals. Cut the grease with a *licuado* f next door.

Luces del Norte (448-1044; 11a Calle NE at NE; mains L$98-240; breakfast, lunch & dinner) longtime favorite has a casual atmosp inexpensive meals and a postcard-star boot. The menu has all the standard breal and *platos fuertes* (main dishes) plus sandwiches – fish, chicken, BLT, even p

Hotel Tatiana (658-9186; s/d with fan L$200/400, with air-con L$500/700;) Our favorite; also at the budget end.

Eating

Omoa has a gaggle of beachside restaurants – just walk around and pick the one that most fits your fancy.

Escapate (beachside; mains L$80-300; breakfast, lunch & dinner) Next to Flamingo's, this is our favorite beachside eatery in town. Try a whole fish (with head and all). There's live music on the weekends.

Punto Italia (658-9125; mains L$120-300; lunch & dinner Wed-Sun) Punto Italia serves tasty, slow-cooked Italian specialties and well-prepared pizza and pasta. A grocery is attached, with gourmet items such as anchovies, olives and wine, plus everyday stuff like rum, sunscreen and condoms. It's halfway between the fort and the highway.

Other longtime favorites include **Champa Johnson** (mains L$80-200; lunch & dinner) and the somewhat funkier **Jardín Romántico** (mains L$60-160; breakfast & dinner)

Getting There & Away

Buses to Omoa depart from Puerto Cortés every 20 minutes from 5am to 5:40pm (L$20, 30 minutes) from the **Citral Costeños terminal** (655-0888; 3a Calle Este). It stops on the highway, a 15-minute walk from the fort and beach. From Omoa to Puerto Cortés, buses depart every 20 minutes from 5:20am to 6pm.

If you're headed to Guatemala, jump on a bus headed to Corinto; the green and yellow buses pass Omoa every hour from 6:50am to 3:50pm (L$40, 1¼ hours). Just flag one down on the highway. In Corinto, be sure to get your exit stamp (L$60) and then jump into the back of a *colectivo* (shared) pickup for the 10km ride to the border.

Bike taxis – and more recently moto-taxis (red and white scooters with a small cab attached) – ferry people back and forth from the highway to the town and beach. A ride in either direction is L$10 – way better than lugging your pack down that long, hot road.

TELA & AROUND

The best beaches on the mainland can be found in the small resort town of Tela and the small communities surrounding it. There are also excellent national parks and reserves nearby – travelers shouldn't miss a day trip to Jeannette Kawas or Punta Izopo nature reserves, or a bike over to the Lancetilla botanical gardens.

TELA

pop 88,100

A quiet coastal town with beat-down wooden houses and a welcoming resort atmosphere, Tela has a fine beach and a pleasant beachfront boardwalk. It's the best vacation spot on the coast, and can get overcrowded on weekends – reserve well in advance for Semana Santa. Most people visiting the area choose to stay here, taking day trips to the outlying national parks.

History

Tela was founded in 1524 by Cristóbal de Olid, one of several Spanish conquistadores who vied for dominance in the new-found colony. In fact, not long after founding Tela, Olid was betrayed by his own men to his main rival, Gil González Dávila, who had Olid beheaded.

The precise day of Tela's founding was May 3 (the day of the Holy Cross) so the town was named Triunfo de la Cruz, which was eventually shortened to Tela. (Later, a Garífuna community established east of the city adopted the full original name, which it still has today.) Through the early 1900s, Tela survived largely on small-time banana farming. In 1913 the United Fruit Company acquired the Tela Railroad Company and in exchange for building the railroad was awarded rights to most of the farmland around Tela. For the next half century, workers – eventually organized in unions – battled with United for better wages and working conditions. It is a fight workers are still waging, though international oversight has improved workers' rights considerably.

Orientation

The town is divided into two sections: Tela Vieja, the 'old town,' on the east bank of the Río Tela where the river meets the sea; and Tela Nueva, on the west side of the river, where the Hotel Villas Telamar hugs the best stretch of beach around.

INFORMATION

Banco Atlántida (4a Av NE at 9a Calle NE; 8:30am-3:30pm Mon-Fri, to 11:30am Sat) Has an ATM and can exchange travelers' checks and give cash advances on Visa cards.

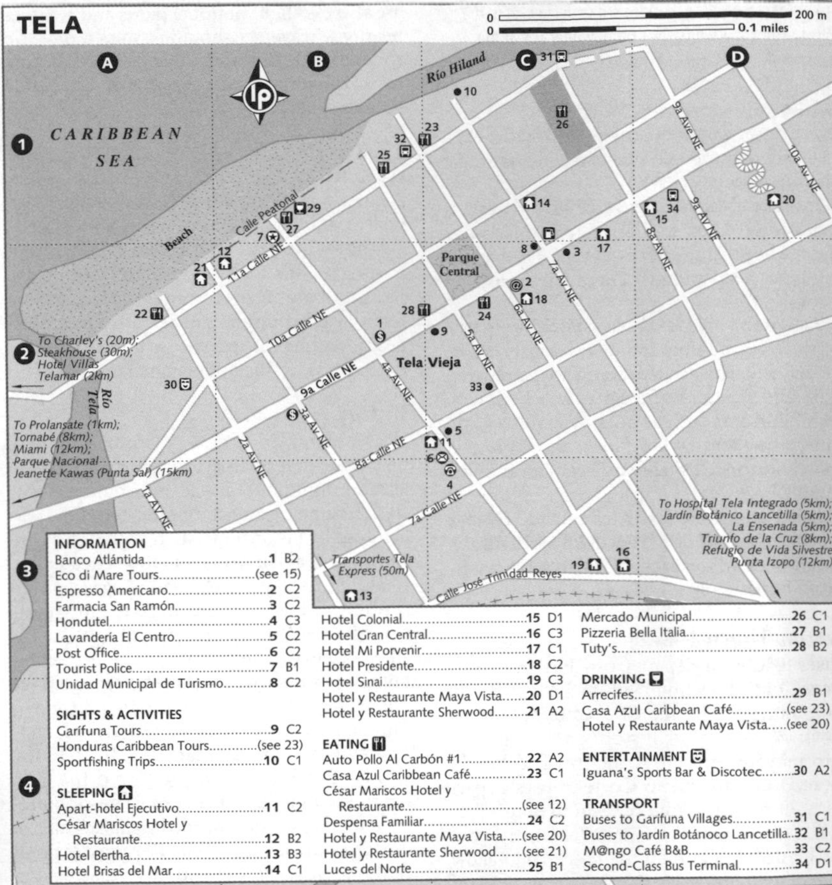

Espresso Americano (cnr 9a Calle NE & 6a Av NE) Has coffee and internet (per hr L$15).

Farmacia San Ramón (☎ 448-1007; 9a Calle NE; 🕑 7:30am-6pm Mon-Fri, to 2pm Sat) Opposite the Texaco gas station.

Hondutel (4a Av NE btwn 7a & 8a Calles NE; 🕑 7:30am-9pm)

Hospital Tela Integrado (☎ 442-3176; 🕑 24hr)

Lavandería El Centro (4a Av NE btwn 7a & 8a Calles NE; laundry per load L$70; 🕑 7am-5pm Mon-Fri) For laundry services.

Post office (4a Av btwn 7a & 8a Calles NE; 🕑 8am-noon & 1-4pm Mon-Fri, 8am-noon Sat)

Prolansate (☎ 448-2042; www.prolansate.org; Edificio Kawas, Calle del Comercio; 🕑 8:30am-noon & 1:30-5:30pm Mon-Fri, 8:30am-noon Sat) Has brochures and other material about the protected areas. It also oversees Parque Nacional Jeannette Kawas, Punta Izopo Wildlife Reserve and Jardín Botánico Lancetilla.

Tourist police (☎ 448-3535; 11a Calle NE at 4a Av NE; 🕑 24hr)

Unidad Municipal de Turismo (tourist office; ☎ 448-1463; cnr 7a Av NE & 9a Calle NE; 🕑 8am-noon & 1-4:30pm Mon-Fri, 8am-noon Sat) May be able to help with some tourist info.

Dangers & Annoyances

Several years ago, there was a spate of as saults on travelers, especially on the beache in and around Tela. While the problem ha diminished significantly with the inaugura tion of a tourist police force, it is still no advisable to walk on the beaches aroun town after dark.

Sights & Activities

Tela's main attraction is its **beaches**, which stretch around the bay for several kilometers. The beach in town is OK, though sometimes littered; the one at Hotel Villas Telamar (see p172) is better, and open to the public.

Several **Garífuna villages**, including Tornabé (p176) and Triunfo de la Cruz (p177), are also within easy reach of Tela, as are the **Jeannette Kawas** (p174) and **Punta Izopo** (p175) reserves, and **Lancetilla Botanic Gardens** (p174).

Sportfishing trips (enquire at Restaurante La Costa, 7a Av NE on the beach; per person L$580), for a minimum of six people, are also on offer.

Tours

Eco di Mare Tours (☎ 439-0110; www.ecodimare tours.com; cnr 8a Av NE & 9a Calle NE) Slightly cheaper than Garífuna Tours, but new and untested. Inquire at the Hotel Colonial (p172).

Garífuna Tours (☎ 448-2904; www.garifunatours.com; 9a Calle at 5a Ave; 🕑 7:30am-6:30pm) Offers all-day boat excursions to Parque Nacional Jeannette Kawas (per person L$646), bird-watching excursions to Los Micos Lagoon (per person L$835) and kayaking in Punta Izopo wildlife reserve (per person L$620).

Honduras Caribbean Tours (☎ 448-2623; www honduras-carribean.com; 11a Calle NE at 6a Av NE) Has tours similar to Garífuna Tours, but also sportfishing (per boat L$5491), trips to Lancetilla (L$550), Pico Bonito (L$1045) & Cayos Cochinos (L$1121) and rafting on the Río Cangrejal (L$1121). Enquire at Casa Azul Caribbean Café (p173).

Festivals & Events

Tela is somnolent most of the year, but it's quite another story during **Semana Santa** (Holy Week, the week preceding Easter), when the town fills with Honduran vacationers. During that time, hotel rates can double and advance bookings are essential. In July ar North American and European tra scend upon the town and things get too, though room rates remain un Tela's annual festival is held on June

Sleeping

BUDGET

Hotel Sinai (☎ 448-1373; 5a Av NE at Calle José Reyes; s/d with shared bathroom L$150/200, d with con L$250/300; ❄) Located near the train tr the Sinai is a decent budget option. It's a hotel with exposed brick walls, 19 rooms concave beds and clean bathrooms. Servic especially friendly, too. The only down sid that it's not close to the beach.

Hotel Mi Porvenir (9a Calle NE btwn 7a & 8a Avs N s L$150-250/, d L$400) This three-story hotel offer several small rooms with fans. It's noisy and a bit dirty, but cheap. There are no toilets seats, if that's the sort of thing you are into.

Hotel Bertha (☎ 448-3020; 2a Av NE near 7a Calle NE; r with fan/air-con L$230/340; ❄ P) Housed in a relatively new building near the Tela Express bus terminal, this hotel is kept clean – spotless really – and has lots of plastic hanging plants and framed posters, but you are a ways from the beach. The rooms are small but not suffocating and all have private bathrooms.

Hotel Brisas del Mar (☎ 448-2486; 7a Av NE at 10a Calle NE; s/d L$300/500) Closer to the ocean most budget digs, the Brisas is a totall ceptable, if somewhat drab, hotel. The r are breezy and clean, with bathrooms a Lilliputian.

Apart-hotel Ejecutivo (☎ 448-1607; www.ejec .com; 8a Calle NE at 4a Av NE; d/tr L$600/650; Consider staying here if you plan to while – having even a small kitchen c you save on going out for every me

ASK A LOCAL: THREE BEST DAYTRIPS FROM TELA

- Parque Nacional Jeannette Kawas (p174) – This park offers three components you won' in other parks: tropical forest, good beaches and coral reefs for snorkeling.
- Refugio de Vida Silvestre Punta Izopo (p175) – This is nice because it mixes adventure [kayaking] with natural beauty. It also offers beaches and a chance to experience local in the Garífuna villages along the way.
- Ecofinca San Silvestre (on the road to San Pedro Sula; entrance L$95) – This is a new tion, about 20 minutes from town by car. There are three nature trails that'll take fron six hours. It's one of the best spots around for bird-watching, and there's a cold-wate and two small waterfalls.

Flabio Irias, owner of Honduras Caribt

butter and banana – and a long list of soups, such as vegetable clam and one called Queen's Seafood Soup.

In New Tela, two side-by-side restaurants offer good, hefty meals in a lively atmosphere. **Charley's** (mains L$100-250; lunch & dinner) and **Steakhouse** (mains L$100-250; lunch & dinner) have excellent, moderately priced steaks, plus chicken and pork dishes and sandwiches.

Despensa Familiar (Parque Central; 7am-7pm Mon-Sat, to 6pm Sun) is a large supermarket on Parque Central. The **Mercado Municipal** (8a Av NE btwn 10a & 11a Calles NE; 7am-5pm Mon-Sat, to 2pm Sun) is a small but packed public market selling fresh fruits, veggies, breads, dried foods and seafood.

MIDRANGE

Casa Azul Caribbean Café (☎ 415-3072; 11a Calle NE at 6a Av NE; mains L$75-95; lunch & dinner Thu-Tue) This longtime favorite now has a mostly Caribbean-Garífuna menu, with some southern Florida flare such as deep-fried fish, and holdovers from the old restaurant, including pizza and spaghetti.

Hotel y Restaurante Sherwood (☎ 448-1065; Calle Peatonal at 3a Av NE; mains L$50-160; breakfast, lunch & dinner) Offering reliable meals and overlooking the beach, the Sherwood has a classic hotel-restaurant menu – there's something for everyone, including *típico,* sandwiches, pasta, grilled meats and seafood. There's also live music on the weekend.

César Mariscos Hotel y Restaurante (☎ 448-2083; Calle Peatonal at 3a Av NE; mains L$80-250; breakfast, lunch & dinner) This bustling open-air restaurant, right on the boardwalk, is known for serving up great fresh seafood – it's regarded by some as one of the town's best restaurants.

Pizzería Bella Italia (☎ 448-1055; 4a Av NE at Calle Peatonal; mains L$80-300; lunch & dinner Tue-Sun) The friendly Italian owners spent almost a decade in Santa Rosa de Copán before moving to Tela to be near the beach. Pizza here is terrific – from *personal* to 16-piece *gigantes* (extra large) – but the specialty is the *panzerotti,* a variation of calzone stuffed with salami, ham, mushrooms and more.

Hotel y Restaurante Maya Vista (☎ 448-1497; mains L$105-245; breakfast, lunch & dinner) Off 8a Calle NE between 9a and 10a Avs NE, this restaurant has friendly service, excellent home-cooked dishes and a spectacular view from its breezy, outdoor dining area. A full meal will set you back a bit but the seafood dishes are well worth it. The view is at least worth a coffee and cake in the afternoon.

Drinking & Entertainment

A number of restaurants around town stay open late on weekends for bar service. Casa Azul Caribbean Café (left) and the Hotel y Restaurante Maya Vista (left) both have mellow bar scenes. On the boardwalk, Arrecifes serves cheap beers and sometimes has a guy with his keyboard belting out tunes.

Iguana's Sports Bar & Discotec (10a Calle NE near 2a Av NE) is the only true *discoteca* in town.

Getting There & Away

Direct buses to La Ceiba (L$56, 1½ hours) don't enter Tela proper; instead, take a taxi to the Dippsa gasoline station on the highway, where buses from San Pedro Sula on the way to La Ceiba pass every 30 to 45 minutes. Alternatively, ordinary buses to La Ceiba (L$40, two hours) or Progresso (L$30, two hours) leave from the second-class bus terminal on 9a Calle NE every 25 minutes from 4am to 6pm.

Transportes Tela Express (2a Av NE) operates direct buses to San Pedro Sula (L$70, 1½ to two hours) from its terminal a block past the train tracks. There are eight departures from 6am to 5pm Monday to Saturday and from 7am to 5:30pm on Sunday.

Buses to various Garífuna villages leave from a dirt lot at the corner of 8a Av NE and 11a Calle NE. Buses go to Triunfo de la Cruz (L$15, 30 minutes) and continue to La Ensenada (L$16, 45 minutes) hourly from 9am to 5pm (until 4pm only on Sunday). Buses to San Juan (L$16, 25 minutes) and Tornabé (L$17, 30 minutes) leave from the same lot on roughly the same schedule.

Buses to Jardín Botánico Lancetilla leave from the corner of 6a Av NE and 11a Calle NE.

Getting Around

You can rent a bicycle from **M@ngo Café B&B** (☎ 448-0388; 8a Calle NE at 5a Av NE) for L$100 per day. Tela abounds with taxis; a ride in town costs from L$10 to L$15.

PARKS & RESERVES

Most travelers choose to visit Lancetilla, Punta Sal and Punta Izopo as day trips from Tela, but intrepid explorers may be able to camp for the

INSIDE THE HONDURAN SEX TRADE

While prostitution is legal in Honduras, sex tourism is not as obvious here as it is in the resort towns of the Dominican Republic or in Costa Rica, where dozens of websites advertise what amounts to sex-tour packages. It may be because the preferred victims in Honduras are less visible: children.

In May 2006, FBI and immigration agents arrested a 58-year-old Florida man who they accused of arranging trips to Honduras for men interested in having sex with underage girls. The man was the commander of a local US Navy children's program, teaching youngsters the navy's values of honor, courage and commitment. In 2004, a Brooklyn, US pediatrician was sentenced to 21 years in prison for having lured children in Honduras and Mexico into sexual encounters.

Casa Alianza (www.casa-alianza.org.uk), the Latin American affiliate of Covenant House, a children's advocacy group, issued a report that said 8000 to 10,000 children were involved in sex work in Honduras alone. Honduran teenagers are among the most frequently trafficked children in Central America, most going to brothels and resorts in Guatemala, Mexico and El Salvador, where the patrons are mainly American, European and Australian men.

Groups like Casa Alianza have worked to raise awareness of the problem in Central America, which they say has grown in the wake of crack downs in Thailand and other Asian countries long known for their prostitution and pedophilia rings. In a bitter irony, Casa Alianza fired the 15-year director of its Tegucigalpa office in 2004 after reports surfaced that he had paid a 19-year-old staying in one of the group's youth shelters to have sex. The director, a British citizen, was a well-known children's advocate, and had even been awarded an Order of the British Empire Medal in 2000 for his work with homeless children.

In 2000, advocates across the political spectrum joined in pressing the US to pass a law against human trafficking. The law has been particularly effective in Asia and Eastern Europe, breaking up numerous trafficking rings and returning victims to their homes and countries. While Latin America has been generally slower to respond, the Honduran government has taken some positive steps forward, and a recent US State Department Human Rights Report says that approximately 7000 police, prosecutors and judges, and 10,000 students have been trained on human trafficking. The law here is tough, but due to corruption, can be hard to enforce. Fines for prostitution, human trafficking and pornography range from L$100,000 to L$500,000, with prison terms up to 20 years.

night in the reserves or in one of the villages along the way (see p176).

Jardín Botánico Lancetilla

One of the largest tropical botanical gardens in the world, **Lancetilla Botanical Garden & Research Center** (www.lancetilla.org; admission L$95; 7:30am-5pm, no entry after 4pm) spans some 1680 hectares and has 1200 species of plants from four continents. The garden has hundreds of bird species – migratory species are present from November to February – and generates 60% of Tela's fresh water. Well-marked trails wind through the main garden and arboretum areas. The trees are divided and labeled according to their major characteristic: ornamental, medicinal, fruit-bearing, timber and poisonous. At the far end of the garden is a long tunnel formed by an arch of bamboo, leading to a swimming hole.

There are cabins (L$400) and rooms (L$260 to L$300) available for rent. Call the **visitor information office** (448-1740; 7am-4pm Mon-Fri, 8am-noon Sat) ahead of time to make reservations.

Small buses from Tela to the gardens (L$16, 20 minutes) leave from the corner of 6a Av NE and 11a Calle NE, opposite Casa Azul Caribbean Café, at 6:30am (Monday to Friday only) and 8am, 10:50am, 1:30pm and 3:30pm daily. The return is at 6:20am (Monday to Friday only) and 9am, 11:30am, 2pm and 4pm daily. The bus stops at the ticket kiosk for anyone who needs to pay (many of the passengers are workers) and continues to the main garden and hiking area.

A great way to get to the gardens is by bike, which can be rented in Tela (p173).

Parque Nacional Jeannette Kawas (Punta Sal)

Standing on the beach at Tela, you can look to the west and see a long arc of land curving out to a point. This point, Punta Sal, is part of the **Parque Nacional Jeannette Kawas** (entrance fee L$100), one of the most scenic places on the North Coast. The park has several white-sand beaches, the prettiest and most popular being **Playa Cocalito**. From Cocalito, a number of trails, both marked national-park trails and unmarked ones, lead to less-visited beaches, including **Puerto Caribe** and **La Ensenada**; you may spot howler monkeys on the way. Offshore are coral reefs that make for fine snorkeling. The park was formerly known as Parque Nacional Marino Punta Sal; it was renamed after Jeannette Kawas, a former director of Fundación Prolansate, who was murdered in 1995 during a bitter struggle to protect the park from development (see below).

On the park's east side is the **Laguna de los Micos** (Lagoon of the Monkeys), containing extensive mangrove forests. It's a habitat for hundreds of species of birds (especially from November to February, when migratory species flock here) and for the monkeys that the lagoon is named for.

There are a few ways to visit the park. Most tours from Tela (p171) leave at 8am and return at 3pm. You can also negotiate a trip with Tela's local *lancheros* (boat operators), who charge L$2000 to L$2600 for groups up to 12. They tie up under the bridge between old and new Tela.

It's also possible to make the trip from the town of Miami. From there you can do a day trip by boat or even walk to Punta Sal and camp there which, among other things, means you will have the beach to yourself after 2pm.

Refugio De Vida Silvestre Punta Izopo

Standing on the beach at Tela and looking to the east, you can see another point: Punta Izopo, namesake of the **Punta Izopo Wildlife Reserve**. Rivers flowing through the wildlife refuge splinter out into a tangled network of canals and thick mangrove forests. Many animals make their home here, including

THE LIFE OF AN ENVIRONMENTAL MARTYR: JEANNETTE KAWAS

Born in Tela in 1947, Blanca Jeannette Kawas Fernández did not become involved with environmentalism until late in life. In 1992, having returned to Tela after many years of living in the US, Kawas was approached by a Peace Corps volunteer to participate in an ecological organization. She accepted and eventually became president of the group, known as Fundación Prolansate (the Foundation for the Protection of Lancetilla, Punta Sal & Texiguat).

By all accounts, Kawas was a tireless advocate for the environment and a stickler for the law. She would personally patrol the park at night, looking for poachers. Among the people caught by Fundación Prolansate and fined for environmental violations were cattle ranchers, former military officers, even a former congressman-turned-resort owner (who was fined US$1000 for illegally catching dolphins).

In 1995 Kawas and Fundación Prolansate were embroiled in a bitter three-way struggle over development in the then Punta Sal Marino National Park. The Unión Nacional de Campesinos (UNC), the country's largest *campesino* organization, had been granted rights to clear a huge portion of the park to turn it into agricultural land for thousands of poor farmers. At the same time, the palm-oil company Hondupalma had secured a concession to clear part of the park to grow oil-palm trees.

Kawas, who sympathized with the farmers if not with Hondupalma, opposed both concessions, arguing they were shortsighted and would destroy the park. Among other efforts, she organized a 200-person march against the projects, in which she was photographed with a sign that read *No prostituyan el decreto del parque* (Don't prostitute the park decree). Two days later, on February 6, 1995, gunmen shot Jeannette Kawas through an open window in her home. A bullet struck her in the head as she sat doing paperwork at her kitchen table.

Kawas' murder was one in a string of assassinations of environmental and indigenous-rights activists, including Carlos Luna in 1997, Carlos Escaleras in 1998 and Carlos Flores in 2001. Of the four murders, only one has resulted in an arrest. Kawas has been compared to Chico Mendes, the Brazilian environmentalist whose killing brought international attention to efforts made to save the Amazon rainforest. Kawas' legacy certainly lives on – the UNC and Hondupalma projects did not go forward, and Punta Sal was renamed in her honor. More importantly, Fundación Prolansate continues its work protecting natural areas on the North Coast.

monkeys, crocodiles, turtles and many species of birds, including toucans and parrots. It's best to get here with a tour from Tela (p171), as you get the use of a kayak – a big plus for wildlife watching (no engine noise means more birds).

VILLAGES

The villages of Tornabé and Miami are east of Tela, while La Ensenada and Triunfo de la Cruz are off to the west.

Tornabé

The largest and most developed of the Garífuna villages in the area is Tornabé, around 8km west of Tela. The name comes from 'Turn Bay,' a name given to this inlet by English pirates in the 16th century. When we passed through, there was no place to stay in town, but there was work in progress on a large golf resort, so this is sure to change.

A taxi from Tela to Tornabé costs L$40, but costs less from Tornabé to Tela. Buses leave Tela for Tornabé every hour; see p173 for details. If you're driving or cycling, you can get to San Juan on the beach road heading west from Tela and continue on to Tornabé. Be careful when you cross the sandbar at the Laguna de los Micos between San Juan and Tornabé; vehicles regularly get stuck.

Miami

Miami is often described as a 'pure' Garífuna village, a cluster of thatched huts at the end of a long, sandy road, free of outside influence. There's only one catch: it's not a Garífuna town! It's a designated Garífuna area, and many of the lots are owned by Garífuna people, but almost all of Miami's full-time residents are ladinos (people of mixed Indian and European parentage) who have moved here from Tela, some recently, some generations ago. Most of Miami's Garífunas spend most of their time in Tornabé, where there are jobs, shops, schools and bars (not to mention electricity and running water).

This is not to say Miami isn't a worthwhile place to visit. The beach is scenic and the village appealingly rustic, assuming you don't mind latrine toilets, dirt floors and no electricity. It's also a great jumping-off point for trips, by boat or by foot, to Parque Nacional Jeannette Kawas (Punta Sal; p174) and the Laguna de los Micos (p175).

ACTIVITIES

Miami local **Alejandro Alas** (☎ 9950-6853) is one of a half-dozen boat operators in Miami who take travelers on day trips to Punta Sal for L$1500 per boat (up to seven people, 30 minutes) and Laguna de los Micos for L$500 per boat (up to six people). It is also possible to walk from Miami to Punta Sal and camp there, if you've got camping gear. There is a L$100 park fee for all visitors. Trips by boat should start as early as possible because you have to return no later than 2pm; after that, the wind and waves pick up, and the boat passage can be dangerous.

On foot, cross the mouth of the lagoon and continue 7km along the beach – allow two hours – before passing a marked national park trail. Rather than take that, however, look for an unmarked trail a short distance further that leads over the sea cliffs to Playa Cocalito, about another 30 minutes of hiking. You can camp on Playa Cocalito – after 2pm the tour groups leave and you'll have it all to yourself. To get back, try hitching a ride with one of the tour groups, which ought to cost from L$100 to L$200.

We have heard secondhand reports of assaults on this hike – it's a lonely stretch between Miami and Playa Cocalito. Others have done it with no problems, but still it's best not to go alone. And be sure to bring camping gear: if you don't manage a boat ride back, you'll have to stay the night and try to get a lift the following day.

If you're going by boat to Laguna de los Micos, it's advisable to leave early for the best bird and wildlife viewing. The trip lasts about an hour (or more if you can negotiate it) and includes a short hike on a small island and a stop at an observation town.

SLEEPING & EATING

Alejandro Alas (☎ 9950-6853) has three extremely simple cabins – dirt floors, thatched roofs, mud-plastered walls.

It's also possible to camp; just be sure to find out who owns the plot you're looking at and ask their permission. You may want to arrange to have use of the latrine and shower as well, for which you should offer a small fee.

You should be able to buy water and snacks in Miami for everyday use, but if you're planning to hike to Parque Nacional

Jeannette Kawas (Punta Sal), stock up in Tela or Tornabé.

GETTING THERE & AWAY

Miami is 8km northwest of Tornabé down a narrow sand road, passable by car in the summer, but by 4x4 only in the winter. Pickups leave Tornabé for Miami (L$20, 45 minutes) at 6am and 1pm, and leave Miami for the return trip at 7:15am and 2pm, daily except Sunday. You may be able to hitch a ride, if one happens by, or even walk, though the road is hot and exposed most of the way – bring a hat and plenty of water.

La Ensenada

The closest village to Tela is La Ensenada, 5km east along the arc of the beach, just before you reach Punta Triunfo, which is crowned by the Cerro El Triunfo de la Cruz. La Ensenada is a charming little village with seafood restaurants (although most are only open on the weekend, when it can get pretty crowded). The beach here isn't bad.

Local resident Gerardo Colón can take travelers in a horse-drawn *carreta* (a type of carriage, with a sun shade) to various points along the beach, most commonly to Punta Izopo. Trips cost L$300 per person and last about four hours.

Hotel Laguna Mar (☎ 9811-5558; d L$600; P ❄), toward the western edge of town and just 100m from the beach, is the cleanest, nicest spot to stay with meticulously maintained gardens and neat little rooms.

From Tela, buses headed to La Ensenada (L$15, 30 minutes) leave from a dirt lot at the corner of 8a Av NE and 11a Calle NE hourly from 9am to 5pm (until 4pm only on Sunday). The last bus back to Tela leaves La Ensenada at 3:30pm.

If you're driving, the turnoff to La Ensenada (and Triunfo de la Cruz) is 5km east of Tela on the coastal highway. From there, take the road 500m until you come to a fork in the road: La Ensenada is 500m down the left prong.

TRIUNFO DE LA CRUZ

Triunfo de la Cruz is larger and more developed than La Ensenada. At the same time, food, lodging and services are better and more abundant here, and the pretty, off-white beach is good for swimming, with waves neither too strong nor too wimpy.

Cabañas y Restaurante Colón (☎ 9989-5622; s/d L$300/450; P ❄), in the center of town, has several cabañas, but is a little rough around the edges. There's cold-water bathrooms and saggy beds, but you are just feet from a well-maintained beach. The hotel restaurant (mains L$60 to L$200) specializes in seafood.

This small **Hotel Caribbean Coral Inn** (☎ 9994-9806; www.caribbeancoralinn.com; s/d incl breakfast L$1080/1300; P 💻), at the eastern end of town, offers a great alternative to staying in overcrowded Tela. Each of the rustic but comfortable rooms has its own porch with hammock. All have queen beds and hot-water bathrooms. A breakfast buffet is served beachside at the hotel eatery, La Banana Restaurant (mains L$60 to L$200), which is also open for lunch and dinner.

Buses (L$16, 30 minutes) leave roughly every hour from a dirt lot at the corner of 8a Av NE and 11a Calle NE in Tela.

The turnoff to Triunfo de la Cruz is 5km east of Tela on the coastal highway. Take this road 500m to a fork in the road (look for the dilapidated 'Bienvenidos' sign). Triunfo de la Cruz is 700m down the right-hand road. A taxi here from Tela costs L$80, but it's just L$25 the other way.

LA CEIBA & AROUND

While the city of La Ceiba itself is quite ugly, it could hardly be better situated: the city stands at the foot of Parque Nacional Pico Bonito and the towering Sierra Nombre de Dios, and most travelers only use the town as a staging ground for forays into the wild. To the west is the Cuero y Salado Wildlife Reserve, home to monkeys, tropical birds and even manatees. East of town is the Río Cangrejal, where adventurers will find some of Central America's best whitewater. Further east are the Garífuna villages of Nueva Armenia and Sambo Creek, and the jumping-off point to the remarkable Cayos Cochinos. La Ceiba is where you come to catch the ferry to Roatán and Utila, and is a good place to organize (and begin) trips into La Moskitia.

LA CEIBA

pop 178,300

It's not the most attractive city in the world – the town is a spider web of electrical wires,

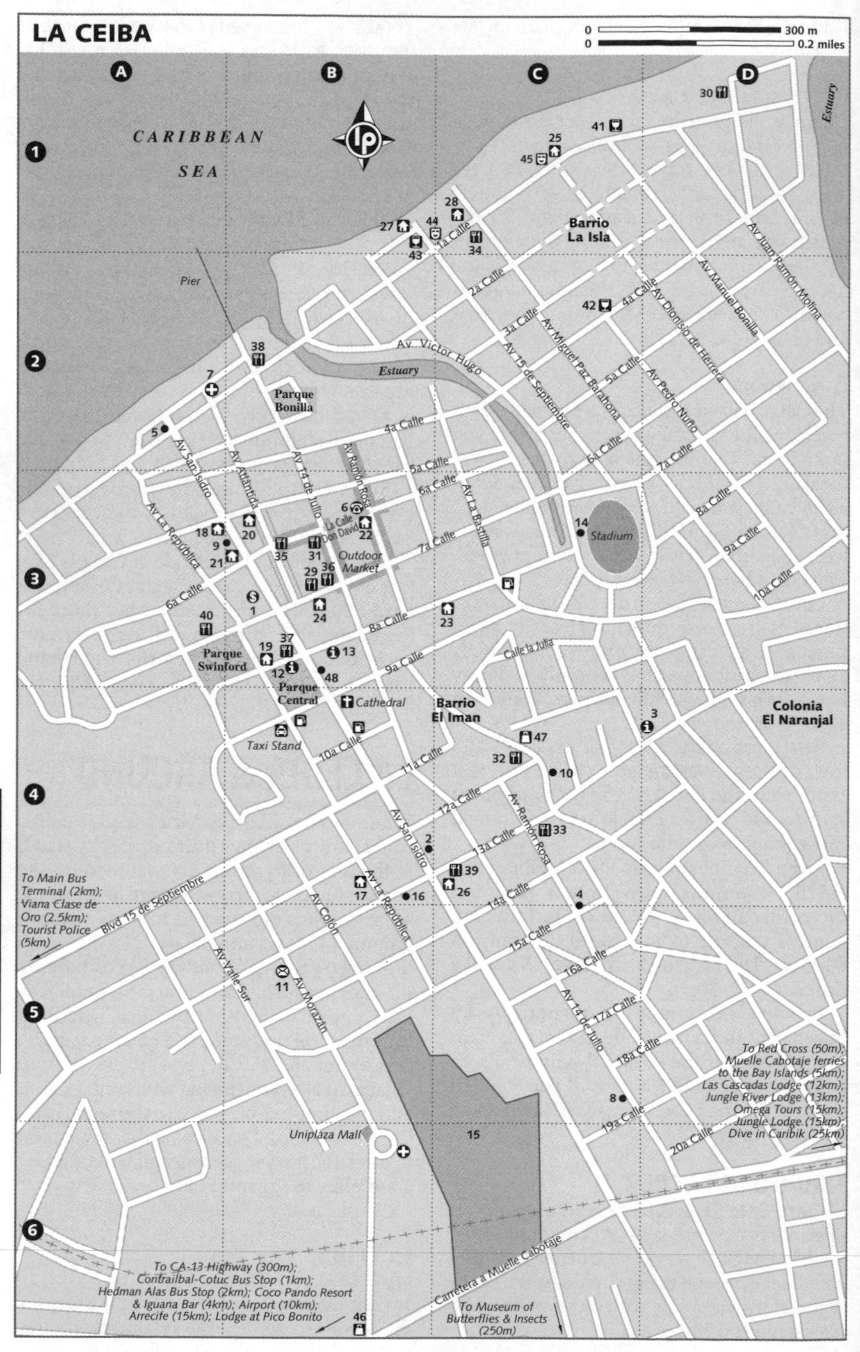
LA CEIBA
0 300 m
0 0.2 miles
CARIBBEAN SEA
Pier
Estuary
Parque Bonilla
Parque Swinford
Parque Central
Cathedral
Taxi Stand
Outdoor Market
La Calle Don David
Stadium
Barrio La Isla
Barrio El Iman
Colonia El Naranjal
Uniplaza Mall
Av Victor Hugo
Av San Isidro
Av Atlántida
Av 14 de Julio
Av Ramón Rosa
Av La República
Av La Bastilla
Av 15 de Septiembre
Av Miguel Paz Barahona
Av Dionisio de Herrera
Av Manuel Bonilla
Av Juan Ramón Molina
Av Pedro Nuño
Av Colón
Av Valle Sur
Av Morazán
Calle la Julia
Blvd 15 de Septiembre
Carretera a Muelle Cabotaje
To Main Bus Terminal (2km); Viana Clase de Oro (2.5km); Tourist Police (5km)
To Red Cross (50m); Muelle Cabotaje ferries to the Bay Islands (5km); Las Cascadas Lodge (12km); Jungle River Lodge (13km); Omega Tours (15km); Jungle Lodge (15km); Dive in Caribik (25km)
To CA-13 Highway (300m); Contraibal-Cotuc Bus Stop (1km); Hedman Alas Bus Stop (2km); Coco Pando Resort & Iguana Bar (4km); Airport (10km); Arrecife (15km); Lodge at Pico Bonito
To Museum of Butterflies & Insects (250m)

THE NORTH COAST

INFORMATION
BAC....(see 47)
Banco Atlántida....**1** B3
Central America Spanish School....**2** B4
Fundación Cayos Cochinos....**3** D4
Fundación Cuero y Salado....**4** C5
Garífuna Tours....**5** A2
Hondutel....**6** B3
Hospital Eurohonduras....**7** A2
Immigration Office....**8** C5
Internet Café....(see 19)
Lafitte Travel....**9** B3
Lavandería Express....**10** C4
Multi-net....(see 47)
Post Office....**11** B5
Tourist Information Kiosk....**12** B3
Tourist Office....**13** B3
Wash & Dry....**14** C3

SIGHTS & ACTIVITIES
D'Antoni Golf Club....**15** C6
Jungle Rivers Tours....(see 17)
La Ruta Moskitia....**16** B4

SLEEPING
Banana Republic Guesthouse....**17** B4
Gran Hotel Ceiba....**18** A3
Gran Hotel Paris....**19** B3
Hotel Caribe....**20** B3
Hotel Iberia....**21** B3
Hotel Italia....**22** B3
Hotel Monserratte....**23** C3
Hotel Principe....**24** B3
Partenon Beach Resort....**25** C1
Posada Catracha....**26** C4
Quinta Real....**27** B1
Rotterdam Beach Hotel....**28** C1

EATING
Cafetería Cobel....**29** B3
Chabelita....**30** D1
Comidas Royale....(see 19)
Despensa Familiar....**31** B3
Expatriates Bar & Grill....**32** C4
Laura's Bakery....**33** C4
Mango Tango....**34** C1
Mercado Municipal....**35** B3
Mixers....**36** B3
Pizza Hut....**37** B3
Pupusería Univeritaria....**38** B2
Ristorante Bella Italia....**39** C4
Supermercado Paiz....**40** A3

DRINKING
Espresso Americano....(see 37)
Hibou....**41** C1
La Casona....**42** C2
Restaurante La Palapa....**43** B1

ENTERTAINMENT
Cine Milenium....(see 47)
Del Mar Casino....**44** B1
Le Pacha....**45** C1

SHOPPING
Mall Megaplaza....**46** B6
Souvenir El Buen Amigo £3....**47** C4
Tourist Office Gift Shop....(see 13)

TRANSPORT
Aerolineas Sosa....**48** B3
Taca Regional....(see 47)
Union Rent A Car....(see 21)

honking horns, blaring music and curiously pungent smells – but hopefully you'll be out and about all day, exploring the hiking and rafting opportunities, the canopy tours and the butterfly farms up in the hills surrounding the city. Nature lovers should definitely consider staying in one of the many eco-lodges around town.

History

Pech indigenous people occupied much of the North Coast before – and well after – the arrival of Spanish explorers. The first non-Indians to settle in present-day La Ceiba arrived in 1810 and were not Spanish, but Garífunas from Trujillo. They were followed by waves of immigrants from Olancho, who were fleeing the violence that broke out there in 1828 and lasted a half-century. The Spanish finally showed up in 1846, followed by French settlers in 1857. The city – officially chartered in 1872 – was long known as La Ceiba for a large ceiba tree that stood near the coast, used as a mooring and a community gathering place. (The tree was cut down in 1917 to make room for a new customs house.) Cuban and Arab wayfarers also settled here before the end of the century.

La Ceiba's modern history began in 1899, with the arrival of the Vacarro brothers, who founded a banana exporting business that would become the Standard Fruit Company, today known as the Dole Food Company. La Ceiba was its longtime headquarters, and much of the city's early infrastructure, including the port, railroad tracks, electrical system, hospitals, parks, housing and the first bank, was built by Standard to support its massive operations.

Orientation

Most travelers find all they need in La Ceiba's center. The shady central park has a cathedral on one corner and a Pizza Hut on another. Av San Isidro is the main north-south corridor; it runs alongside Parque Central, north to the ocean and south to the highway. Along the ocean is 1a Calle, which extends east across a small inlet to Barrio La Isla, a mostly Garífuna neighborhood that's also home to the Zona Viva, La Ceiba's nightlife district. Two blocks south of the park, 11a Calle turns into Av 15 de Septiembre and runs west 2km to the main bus terminal; you can also catch passing buses on the highway. The airport is 10km west of town, the ferry pier 8km to the east.

Information

EMERGENCY

Red Cross (☎ 195, 443-0707; Carr Muelle Cabotaje near Av 14 de Julio; 24hr)
Tourist police (☎ 441-0860; Residencial El Toronjal; 24hr) Three blocks south of Carr a Tela.

IMMIGRATION

Immigration office (☎ 442-0638; Av 14 de Julio btwn 19 Calle & 18 Calle; 7:30am-3:30pm Mon-Fri)

INTERNET ACCESS

Internet Cafe (next to Gran Hotel Paris; per hr L$20)
Multi-net (Carretera a Muelle Cabotaje at Av Morazán; per hr L$20; 9am-8:30pm Mon-Sat, 10:30am-8:30pm Sun) At the Mall Megaplaza.

LAUNDRY

Lavandería Express (Barrio El Iman; per 10lb L$60; 7am-noon & 1-5pm Mon-Sat) Near the end of 12a Calle.

Wash & Dry (Av Victor Hugo in front of the stadium; per 10lb L$60; 8am-6pm Mon-Sat)

MEDICAL SERVICES

Hospital Eurohonduras (440-0927; Av Atlántida; 24hr) Between 1a Calle and the beach.

MONEY

BAC Mall Megaplaza (Carretera a Muelle Cabotaje at Av Morazán; 10am-6pm Mon-Fri, to 5pm Sat); Airport (9am-5pm Mon-Fri, to noon Sat) Both have 24-hour ATMs and exchange traveler's checks.

Banco Atlántida Av San Isidro (btwn 6a & 7a Calles; 9am-4pm Mon-Fri, 8:30-11:30am Sat); Mall Megaplaza (Carretera a Muelle Cabotaje at Av Morazán; 10am-6pm Mon-Fri, to 5pm Sat) Both have 24-hour ATMs.

POST

Post office (Av Morazán at 13a Calle; 8am-4pm Mon-Fri, to noon Sat)

TELEPHONE

Hondutel (Av Ramón Rosa near 6a Calle; 7am-9pm) International calls are cheaper at most internet cafés.

TOURIST INFORMATION

Fundación Cayos Cochinos (Honduras Coral Reef Fund; 442-2670, 443-4075; www.cayoscochinos.org; 13a Calle, Barrio El Iman; 8am-5pm Mon-Fri) Manages the Cayos Cochinos Marine Reserve.

Fundación Cuero y Salado (/fax 443-0329; fucsa@televicab.net; 2nd fl, Av Ramón Rosa at 15a Calle; 8-11:30am & 1-5:30pm Mon-Fri) Manages the Cuero y Salado Wildlife Reserve.

Fundación Parque Nacional Pico Bonito (Funapib; 442-3044; www.picobonito.org; Hwy to Tela, before the airport; 7:30am-5pm Mon-Fri, 8-11am Sat) Manages Parque Nacional Pico Bonito.

Tourist information kiosk (440-1562; Parque Central; 8am-6pm Mon-Sat) Dispenses basic information and brochures.

Tourist office (440-3044; www.conozcalaceiba.com; 8a Calle near Av San Isidro; 8am-4:30pm Mon-Fri) Offers a bunch of brochures and maps on area sites. It also has an office at the airport. Some English is spoken.

TRAVEL AGENCIES

Lafitte Travel (Av San Isidro btwn 5a & 6a Calle; 7:30am-4:30pm Mon-Fri, 7:30am-11am Sat) To book travel; next to the Hotel Iberia.

Dangers & Annoyances

La Ceiba is the country's third-largest city and you should take the same common-sense precautions you would in any urban area. The Zona Viva is safe overall, but has its fair share of drugs, prostitutes and pickpockets. It's safest to take a cab after dark, and not wander into the neighborhoods outside the city center (where there are fewer people and police). The beach is also unsafe at night.

Sights

Created by the Standard Fruit Company, the beautifully manicured **Parque Swinford** (Av La República btwn 7a & 8a Calles) is arguably the prettiest city park in all of Honduras. Palm trees tower over hundreds of plants and flower beds, small bridges lead to gleaming bronze sculptures, and antique train cars remind visitors of the city's role in the banana industry.

The one-room **Museum of Butterflies & Insects** (442-2874; www.hondurasbutterfly.com; Etapa 2, Casa G-12, Calle Escuela Internacional, Colonia El Sauce; adult/child L$60/30; 8am-5pm Mon-Sat) houses an amazing collection of butterflies, moths and other insects – 13,000 creepy-crawlers in all, stuck with pins and preserved in glass cases on the walls.

A **city tour** (440-7562; per person L$30; 6-10pm Mon-Wed, Fri & Sat) on a caboose pulled by a tractor (a cabractor? a traboose?) takes visitors to La Ceiba's highlights. Tickets are sold at the information kiosk in Parque Central; the tour leaves from just in front.

THE NORTH COAST

PARTYING IT UP AT LA FERIA DE SAN ISIDRO

La Ceiba is known to be a party town, but no ordinary Saturday night in the Zona Viva compares to the one during the city's patron saint festival, **La Feria de San Isidro**. Also known as the Gran Carnival Nacional (Great National Carnival), it is the largest celebration in Honduras and, some say, all of Central America. Nearly a quarter of a million visitors descend on La Ceiba for a weekend of live music, cultural performances and all-night food and drink stands. It culminates with a huge parade of horses, floats and dancers in costume down Av San Isidro. The official festival and parade takes place the third Saturday in May. The festival is known to be friendly and safe, but be on the alert for pickpocketing and the occasional drunken brawl.

Activities

CANOEING & KAYAKING

Experienced kayakers can take on the Río Cangrejal; Omega Tours has rentals and organized trips. The most popular flat-water boat trips are in the Refugio de Vida Silvestre Cuero y Salado (p187), which can be arranged either independently or through most tour operators in town. Omega Tours also offers paddling trips in the less-visited Cacao Lagoon (L$1178), 24km east of La Ceiba, which may well turn up more birds and howler monkeys than in Cuero y Salado.

CANOPY TOURS

Jungle River Tours opened the North Coast's first canopy tour, an eight-cable circuit that begins at Jungle River's lodge on the Río Cangrejal and ends with a 660ft (200m) slide across the river (L$760 per person, two to three hours, reservation required). Like all Jungle River's tours, a free night at the river lodge is included. There's another canopy tour near Sambo Creek (p190).

GOLF

If you're itching to play a round of golf, the **D'Antoni Golf Club** (☎ 440-2736; Carr Muelle Cabotaje near Av San Isidro; ⏰ 6am-sunset) is your only option.

HIKING

The primary hikes in the area are to two waterfalls in the buffer zone of Parque Nacional Pico Bonito. (The park's core is closed to hiking.) See p188 for details.

Another option for hikers is through **Guaruma Servicios** (☎ 406-6782; www.guaruma.org), a new community-based tour operator in the small town of Las Mangas, on the Río Cangrejal, that offers inexpensive guided hikes. See p190 for details.

HORSEBACK RIDING

Omega Tours offers excellent, one- to three-day horseback riding trips (L$1862 per day), a step up from the plodding non-adventures you may have been suckered into elsewhere. Trips start on the beach west of La Ceiba, and cross through the lowland lagoons and waterways to the town of El Pino. Multi-day trips include an overnight stay at a private home – or The Lodge at Pico Bonito (p184), if you want to treat yourself – and either return the next day via an alternative route or continue another day into the Pico Bonito buffer zone.

MOUNTAIN BIKING

Jungle River Tours offers a handful of guided mountain-bike trips, ranging from mellow to challenging. The most difficult is a five-hour trip west of La Ceiba, through the Pico Bonito buffer zone to a picturesque waterfall. The ride is mostly on single-track paths, and includes a stop in a small community for lunch (L$1200 per person). Other trips follow the dirt road upriver from the jungle lodge, and include excellent views of the Río Cangrejal valley and/or a stop at the Coloradito petroglyphs.

Jungle River also rents out mountain bikes (per day L$285) that you can take down the same road, where you can stop in villages or at vista points along the way.

WHITE-WATER RAFTING

The Río Cangrejal forms the eastern border of Parque National Pico Bonito and is considered by many to offer the best white-water rafting in Central America. The river tumbles down a narrow river gorge, with plenty of swimming holes, ledges to clamber up and leap off, and short hikes into the park's buffer zone. Omega Tours (p182) and Jungle River Tours (p182) both offer trips; the standard outing includes two to three hours on the water and covers Class II to Class III water. Omega Tours, which costs a bit more but generally receives higher marks for service, also offers a three- to four-hour trip from further upriver, where Class IV to Class V rapids form in high water. Trips cost around L$760, and both outfits include lunch and a free night's stay at their jungle lodges. Be sure to ask what stops you'll make – some travelers have written to say the trips felt too short. During high water you should ask to stop and scout the Revolcadero Rapid – it's dangerous. If it looks like it's too much, skip it.

Courses

Central America Spanish School (☎ 440-1707; www.ca-spanish.com; Av San Isidro btwn 12a & 13a Calles) offers intensive Spanish classes for students of all levels. Classes (L$3000 per week) include 20 hours per week of one-on-one instruction, weekly excursions and cultural events like Latin dance or Honduran cooking classes. Homestays (L$1330 per week, including meals) and other housing options can be arranged.

Tours

Most operators offer similar prices for their tours: rafting (L$760), canopy (L$760), hiking (L$760), mountain biking (L$285), Pico Bonito (L$646), Cayos Cochinos (L$836) and Cuero Salado ($1026), and generally have a two- to four-person minimum.

Dive in Caribik (☎ 373-8620; www.dive-in-caribik.com) Based at Hotel Palma Real, an all-inclusive resort 25km east of La Ceiba, this German-run dive shop offers recommended diving and snorkel trips to Cayos Cochinos. See also p191.

Garífuna Tours (☎ 440-3252; www.garifunatours.com; Av San Isidro at 1a Calle) Runs several excursions on the North Coast. Most trips are based on a four-person minimum, though this is rarely a problem, since large tour groups are the norm (and kind of a bummer).

Jungle River Tours (☎ 440-1268, 408-0059; www.jungleriverlodge.com; Banana Republic Guesthouse, Av República btwn 12 & 13 calles, La Ceiba) offers white-water rafting trips, canopy tours, mountain biking and hiking. A free night at its jungle lodge is included with every trip.

La Moskitia Ecoaventuras (☎ 441-2480, 9929-7532; www.honduras.com/moskitia, moskitiaecoaventuras@yahoo.com; Colonia El Toronjal, La Ceiba) Run by Jorge Salverri, an expert birder and one of the most knowledgeable guides to La Moskitia. Call ahead.

La Ruta Moskitia (☎ 3391-8833; www.larutamoskitia.com; Edificio Cenit Color, Local 6, Calle 13 btwn Av San Isidro y La República, La Ceiba) One of the most popular operators for trips to La Moskitia.

Omega Tours (☎ 440-0334; www.omegatours.info; Omega Jungle Lodge, Calle a Yaruca Km 9) Located along the Río Cangrejal on the way to the town of Yaruca.

Festivals & Events

Though none are the size of the Feria de San Isidro (see p180), La Ceiba does have a number of other celebrations. **Semana Santa** certainly rivals the *feria* in sheer numbers; all of Honduras is on vacation and hankering to cool off at the beach, making La Ceiba one of the country's major Holy Week destinations. The **Carnaval del Aniversario de La Ceiba** is held in the third week of August and celebrates the founding of the city with live music and street performances in the Zona Viva. The **Festival del Amor y Amistad** (Festival of Love & Friendship) is held in February around Valentine's Day. The city's peaceful **Festival Navideño** (Christmas Festival) is held in the first week of December.

Sleeping

La Ceiba has some terrific nature lodges outside of town (p184), with easy access to the area's many outdoor attractions.

BUDGET

La Ceiba's cheapest bunks are the ones you get for free – in a riverside jungle lodge, no less – when you book a trip with Omega Tours or Jungle River Tours (left).

Banana Republic Guesthouse (☎ 440-1268, 408-0059; www.jungleriverlodge.com; Av La República btwn Calle 12 & Calle 13; dm L$114, r with/without bathroom L$285/247; P ✖ 🖳) A fairly cool affair in an old wooden house, this is La Ceiba's only hostel. Upstairs you have simple fan-cooled private rooms and a little internet area. Downstairs are the dorm rooms, which sleep 11 total (bring your earplugs). It's all relatively clean, and you get a hangout area, lockers and a good spot to meet fellow travelers.

Rotterdam Beach Hotel (☎ 440-0321; Av Miguel Paz Barahona at 1a Calle, Barrio La Isla; s/d L$200/250) Clean, medium-sized rooms open onto a small garden at this quiet Barrio La Isla hotel. It's better value than a like-priced room in town, and you're near La Ceiba's nightlife and the beach, making this one of the best budget buys.

Hotel Caribe (☎ 443-1857; 5a Calle btwn Avs San Isidro & Atlántida; r with fan/air-con L$225/450; ✖ P) The bare-bones basic rooms at this second-story hotel have unpainted concrete floors, industrial fans and cold-water showers – but they are cheap. The 'deluxe' rooms have tiled floors and air-con, but are expensive for what you're getting.

Posada Catracha (☎ 442-2812; cnr Av San Isidro & 13 Calle; s with/without bathroom L$350/250, d with/without bathroom $350/500; P ✖ 🅿) This second-story option is owned by the folks at Bella Italia. The rooms are simple with clean sheets and absolutely no adornments to speak of – never heard of a framed picture? You're a bit out of the busy city center, which means less traffic noise at night.

Partenon Beach Resort (☎ 443-0516; 7a Calle btwn Avs Atlántida & 14 de Julio; s/d L$400/500; ✖) This is an adequate choice for those who are on a budget but will pay a bit extra if it means they don't have to wear flip-flops in the shower. Plain rooms with ceramic floors, and clean sheets and bathrooms come in either hospital white or bright blue. The best rooms (105, 106, 145 and 146) have large windows facing a wide outdoor passageway. (You'll definitely get traffic noise in the morning, though.)

Hotel Principe (☎ 443-0404; 1a Calle at Av Dionisio de Herrera; s/d L$400/600; ✖ 🅿) The beds are concave and soft, the sheets threadbare, and the grounds are rather windblown and dirty, but at least you are beachfront and get air-con in every room. You are also in the Zona Viva, making it easy to get out and about at night.

Hotel Italia (☎ 443-0150; hotel@carrion.hn; Av Ramón Rosa near 6a Calle; r L$528; P) Comfortable, clean and well-kept sums up the Italia pretty well. Add air-con, hot water, cable TV, and in-room phones and it's a steal. Weigh in the sparkling garden-side pool and welcoming bar-lounge and it's downright dreamy. The only drawback is that it's smack dab in the middle of the outdoor market, which is fine during the day but kind of sketchy at night. Definitely cab it after sunset.

Hotel Iberia (☎ 443-0100; Fernando_Ferndz@hotmail.com; Av San Isidro btwn 5a & 6a Calle; s/d L$580/596; P) A smidge better than the Gran Hotel Ceiba and a dollop worse than the Italia, this is a solid buy in the center of town. The beds are rock hard, but the sheets are good and the rooms look onto a central courtyard, making for a bit more quiet come lullaby time.

Gran Hotel Ceiba (☎ 443-2747; www.hotelceiba.net; Av San Isidro at 5a Calle; r L$588; P) It's not as nice as the Italia, but it's in a slightly better neighborhood. Rooms have large, bright bathrooms and clean ceramic floors, though the beds can be a bit spongy. Almost all have private balconies; there are better views and less street noise on the upper floors.

MIDRANGE

Hotel Monserratte (☎ 440-4133; www.corporacionmonserratte.com; 9a Calle; s/d L$740/880; P) This is the most modern hotel in the downtown area. It's clean but rather run-of-the-mill with firm beds, well-appointed rooms, and a small gym and pool. The service can get a bit uppity.

Gran Hotel Paris (☎ 443-2391; hotelparis@psinet.hn; Parque Central; s/d L$819/972; P) Fancy things like card keys – that don't work – and a pleasant courtyard pool set this hotel apart. Plus, you're right on the Parque Central. Many rooms have aging air-con units and spongy beds, but there are a few renovated units worth asking about. The rooms facing the park can get downright loud.

Coco Pando Resort & Iguana Bar (☎ 9969-9663; www.cocopando.com; Colonia Ponce; s/d L$950/1140; P) Four kilometers west of town, the Coco Pando can be inconvenient if you don't have a car; then again, many guests come not so much to explore the area as to just sit back and relax for a while. And for that it's well suited: large, comfortable rooms, with fridge, purified water, free internet and use of kayaks and hammocks.

TOP END

Quinta Real (☎ 440-3311; www.quintarealhotel.com; Av 15 de Septiembre at 1a Calle; Barrio La Isla; s/d incl breakfast L$1691/2299; P) A quantum leap from the other hotels in town with grand staircases, marble tiles just about everywhere and a removed resort-like feel, this is the best (and only) top-end hotel in town. It has all the modern comforts you'd expect for the price, including a spa, business center, pool, restaurant, shops and pool-side bar, plus 81 comfortable rooms, with hot water, air-con, high-speed internet and big, plush beds.

Eating

Outside of town, The Lodge at Pico Bonito and Omega Tours Jungle Lodge (see boxed text, p184) both serve terrific food and are open to nonguests, provided you call in advance.

BUDGET

Laura's Bakery (☎ 443-1494; 13a Calle; 7am-6:30pm Mon-Fri, to 5pm Sat) This bakery is known for its breads – most notably the wheat and French loaves – sold piping hot in the mornings.

Espresso Americano (Parque Central; coffee drinks L$15-50; 8am-6pm Mon-Sat) Serving some of the best coffee in the country, this Honduran chain is well worth a stop.

Pupusería Universitaria (☎ 440-1070; 1a Calle near Av 14 de Julio; pupusas $15, mains L$75-85; lunch & dinner) One of our favorite budget spots, this friendly hole-in-the-wall is immensely popular with tourists and locals alike. It serves – you guessed it – *pupusas* (stuffed patties) of every shape, size and flavor.

Cafetería Cobel (☎ 442-2192; 7a Calle near Av Atlántida; mains L$30-60; breakfast & lunch Mon-Sat) Always jam-packed with regulars, the Cobel is an institution in La Ceiba. And for good reason – *típico* is served hot and fast, and it's a steal.

Mixers (☎ 443-4166; Centro Comercial Panayotti, 7a Calle near Av 14 de Julio; mains L$30-60; breakfast, lunch & dinner Mon-Fri, breakfast & lunch Sat) Cafeteria-style eating is what you'll get at this locale. Every day a new variety of *típico* is served – there's always beans, rice and a vegetable dish though – so you won't get bored if you eat here more than once. It's on the 2nd floor of a peach-colored shopping center.

LA CEIBA'S ECOLODGES

La Ceiba has four ecolodges: three along the Río Cangrejal and another near the town of El Pino, 19km west of La Ceiba. They run the gamut in price and amenities, but all offer respite from the city and easy access to the area's impressive natural riches.

The Lodge at Pico Bonito (☎ 440-0388, in US 888-428-0221; www.picobonito.com; Carr a Tela, El Pino; per 2 people L$4560, extra person L$955; P ⊠ ✲ ▣ ⛱) This hotel boasts a whopping 300 hectares of private forest with terrific hiking on guest-only trails. There's also a butterfly and reptile enclosure, observation tower, library and pleasant swimming pool. Cabins are spaced well apart for privacy, and have polished wood floors, tile bathrooms and a private patio with hammock. While the Lodge is no longer the area's most luxurious digs – that would be Las Cascadas on the Río Cangrejal – it still offers first-class service and installations in a gorgeous setting. Meal plans (with breakfast, lunch and dinner) cost L$760 per day.

Las Cascadas Lodge (☎ 9805-2200, www.lascascadaslodge.com; Calle a Yaruca, Km 6; per person incl meals & wine L$2185; P ⊠ ▣ ⛱) With just three rooms, expertly prepared meals and a no-kids policy, Las Cascadas offers supreme comfort and relaxation in a beautiful setting. The lodge is built beside a gurgling creek with three scenic waterfalls – the namesake *cascadas* – and is surrounded by thick forest. Large rooms have canopy beds, hardwood floors and stone showers, while the high-ceilinged common area has sofas and chairs, and a beautiful wooden table for family-style eating. Outside are nooks and crannies with wood chairs, perfect for relaxing. Rafting, hiking and other excursions can also be arranged.

Omega Tours Jungle Lodge (☎ 440-0334; www.omegatours.com; Calle a Yaruca, Km 9; s/d with shared bathroom L$200/300, cabins L$500-1500) Nestled in a 40.5-hectare lot a few hundred meters from the road and river, this friendly, well-managed lodge has something for every budget. Backpackers rates are low – or free, if you book a trip – in large no-frills rooms with shared bathrooms. For a bit more, two new split-level cabins sleep five and have hot water, firm beds and nice views from upstairs. Or ask for the cozy Creek Cabin, built right over a creek, which will babble you to sleep every night. There's a small pool and a great outdoor shower, and guests can hike up behind the lodge for views of Cascada El Bejuco, across the river.

Jungle River Lodge (☎ 440-1268; Calle a Yaruca, Km 7; dm L$190; r L$665-950) The Río Cangrejal tumbles by just meters from this simple but attractive lodge, operated by Jungle River Tours. Wood-constructed rooms feel somewhat cramped but are free if you book a tour (call ahead, as they may actually require a tour for your stay). Two private rooms offer a bit more space. The restaurant-bar serves family-style meals at open-air tables (breakfast and lunch L$80, dinner L$100). But the best reason to come is for the youthful, mellow atmosphere and easy access to the river, which is wonderfully swimmable when the water isn't too high. To get here, take a Yaruca bus from the main bus terminal and look for the sign on your right.

Comidas Royale (☎ 443-2391; Parque Central, Av La República at 8a Calle; mains L$45-75; ⏲ breakfast, lunch & dinner) Right on Parque Central, this is one of the best buffets in town. Not only is it open all day, every day, but the trays always seem to be brimming with fresh food. Dishes vary by the hour – *típico* of all sorts is served up alongside Honduran-style chow mein, fried rice, sweet-and-sour chicken, and ribs.

MIDRANGE

Ristorante Bella Italia (Av San Isidro at 13a Calle; mains L$100-220; ⏲ lunch & dinner) This European-style cafe has a good ambiance, and serves a wide range of homemade pastas, freshly made Italian desserts and espresso drinks. You can choose between eating indoors in an intimate dining area or outdoors at sidewalk tables with big umbrellas.

Chabelita (☎ 440-0027; 1a Calle; mains L$110-230; ⏲ 10am-10pm Tue-Sun, to 3pm Mon) This Garífuna-style restaurant, at the far end of the Zona Viva, is well worth the walk. Seafood is the specialty – try the hefty fish fillet or Chabelita's famous *sopa marinera* (seafood soup). The dining area is unremarkable, but a little patio out the back is perfect for a late-afternoon or evening meal and a cold beer.

Mango Tango (1a Calle at Av Miguel Paz Barahona; mains L$120-180; ⏲ dinner Wed-Sun) Across the street from Amsterdam 2001 and the Rotterdam

Beach Hotel, this breezy restaurant-café-bar is a good place to start any Zona Viva outing: for many, it's the main destination. Its claim to fame is the well-stocked salad bar, one of the few in Honduras. The rest of the menu is typical north coast and Ceibeño fare – lots of seafood – served fresh at *palapa*-shaded tables. The bar stays open late, with sport showing on the large TVs.

our pick **Expatriates Bar & Grill** (☎ 440-1131; 12a Calle; mains L$129-239; 4pm-midnight Mon-Thu, 4pm-2am Fri & Sat, 11am-11pm Sun) Aptly named, this is a longtime favorite of foreigners living in La Ceiba. The specialty is barbecue chicken wings, but just about everything is grilled and good – ribs, shrimp, chicken breasts, veggies. There's also a full bar, occasional live music, book exchange, community board, large-screen TV with major sporting events, and high-speed internet.

Pizza Hut (☎ 443-7492; Parque Central; mains L$85-200; lunch & dinner) Don't forget to eulogize Dom DeLuise, who played 'Pizza The Hutt' in Mel Brooke's *Spaceballs*.

TOP END

Arrecife (☎ 441-4353; Carr a Trujillo; mains L$200-300; lunch & dinner Tue-Sun) Local food buffs and hotel concierges have started calling Arrecife the best restaurant in town. An upscale but understated place 15km east of town, it offers terrific seafood dishes and a good wine list. The only drawback is the location – if you don't have a car, you may end up paying more in taxi fare than you do for dinner.

SELF-CATERING

Self-caterers should try the **outdoor market** (6am-5pm Mon-Sat, 7am-noon Sun), a noisy place winding its way through the downtown area, or head inside the **Mercado Municipal** (cnr Av Atlántida & 6a Calle).

Supermercado Paiz (across from Parque Swinford; 7am-6:45pm Mon-Sat, to noon Sun) and **Despensa Familiar** (cnr Av 14 de Julio & 6a Calle; 9am-9pm) are large supermarkets.

Drinking & Entertainment

Head to the Zona Viva in Barrio La Isla to get jiggy with it. Nightlife moves at a good clip on weekends, but is dead during the week. It's relatively safe, but robberies and pickpocketing occur now and then – keep your radar on and take a cab home at the end of the night.

Del Mar Casino (cnr 1a Calle & Av 15 de Septiembre; 24hr) Loose slots – and you check your gun at the door.

La Casona (4a Calle btwn Av Pedro Nuño & Dionisio de Herrera, Barrio La Isla; cover from L$100; 9pm-late Wed-Sat) Two blocks off the main drag, this huge wood-paneled building may look more like a ski lodge than a nightclub, but it's a favorite destination for La Ceiba's late-20s and early-30s set.

Le Pacha (1a Calle btwn Av Dionisio de Herrera & Av Miguel Paz Barahoria; cover from L$100; 9:30pm-late Thu-Sat) It was just under construction when we passed through, but this massive beachfront disco, under a tent-like canvas, promises to be one of the best in town.

Hibou (1a Calle at Av Manuel Bonilla; cover from L$100; 9:30pm-late Thu-Sat) This is the preferred club for La Ceiba's moneyed, mostly 20-something crowd. Dress sharp.

Restaurante La Palapa (☎ 443-3844; 1a Calle at Av 15 de Septiembre, Zona Viva; no cover; 9pm-late Wed-Sat) In front of the Quinta Real hotel, this breezy bar-restaurant has a large dancing area on one side, wooden tables encircling a bar on the other, and the namesake *palapa* roof high above.

Cine Milenium (Mall Megaplaza, 22a Calle at Av Morazán) Two screens feature Hollywood films daily; tickets cost L$30 before 7pm, and L$45 after 7pm.

Shopping

Souvenir El Buen Amigo #3 (☎ 442-0716; Barrio El Iman; 8am-6:30pm Mon-Sat) Although somewhat out of the way (near the eastern end of Calle 12), you'll find a great selection of Honduran *artesanía* (handicrafts) here.

Tourist Office Gift Shop (☎ 440-3044; 8a Calle near Av San Isidro; 8am-6pm Mon-Fri, to noon Sat) A corner of this city office houses a gift shop with a small selection of quality crafts from around the country.

Mall Megaplaza (22a Calle at Av Morazán; 10am-9pm) Near the entrance to town, the Megaplaza is a two-story giant.

Getting There & Away

AIR

La Ceiba's **Aeropuerto Golosón** (☎ 443-3925) has frequent flights to San Pedro Sula, Tegucigalpa, the Bay Islands and La Moskitia. There's a L$29 airport tax for domestic flights, and L$646 for international. Services at the airport include a bank, internet café and several car-rental agencies.

There are a few airline companies in La Ceiba:

Aerolineas Sosa (☎ 443-1309, at airport 440-0692; www.aerolineasosa.com; Av San Isidro btwn 8a & 9a Calles; 🕑 7am-5pm Mon-Fri) Flies to San Pedro (L$1370), Guanaja (L$1390), Tegucigalpa (L$1670), Roatán (L$1000), Utila (L$1065) & numerous destinations in La Moskitia.

Taca Regional (☎ 441-3191, at airport 443-2683; www.tacaregional.com; Mall Megaplaza, 1st fl, 22a Calle at Av Morazán; 🕑 9am-6pm Mon-Fri, 9am-1pm Sat) Has flights to Roatán & Utila for the same price as Aerolineas Sosa.

BOAT

Two comfortable, air-conditioned ferries – leaving from La Ceiba's Muelle Cabotaje, about 5km east of downtown – ply the water between La Ceiba, Roatán and Utila. **Yate Galaxy** (☎ Roatán 445-1795, La Ceiba 414-5739) provides a fast, comfortable ride between Roatán and La Ceiba (children 12 & under/economy/first class L$284/524/624, 1¼ hours). There are daily departures from La Ceiba to Roatán at 9:30am and 4:30pm, and from Roatán to La Ceiba at 7am and 2pm. **The Utila Princess** ferries passengers between La Ceiba and Utila's main pier every day (L$420, one hour). The ferry makes two trips each way, leaving Utila at 6:20am and 2pm, and returning from La Ceiba at 9:30am and 4pm. The ferry often suspends service for bad weather (and even occasionally if there aren't enough passengers) – plan accordingly. If you sit at the back, you're gonna get wet.

BUS

Most buses – but not all – leave from the **main bus terminal** (Mercado San José, Blvd 15 de Septiembre), about 2km west of the center. **Cristina** (☎ 441-6471), **Diana Express** (☎ 441-6460) and **Catisa-Tupsa** (☎ 441-2539) have offices there, serving Tela and San Pedro Sula.

Contraibal-Cotuc (☎ 441-2199) stops at an office on the main highway, with service to/from Trujillo and San Pedro Sula. **Kamaldy** (☎ 441-2028) goes to Tela, Progreso and Tegucigalpa. **Hedman Alas** (☎ 441-5347; www.hedmanalas.com) is located next to the Supermercado Ceibeño #4 on the main highway near the eastern end of town and has luxury service to Tela and San Pedro, with connections to Tegucigalpa and Copán Ruinas.

Another luxury line, **Viana Clase de Oro** (☎ 441-2330), uses the Esso gas station 500m west of the main bus terminal and serves San Pedro Sula and Tegucigalpa. Buses go to various destinations, including:

Corozal (L$10, 30 minutes) Take any Sambo Creek bus.

Copán Ruinas Transfer from San Pedro Sula.

El Naranjo/Río Cangrejal (L$12, 15 minutes; last return bus 2pm) Take any Las Mangas or Yaruca bus.

El Porvenir (L$12, 45 minutes) Same bus as to La Unión.

Las Mangas/Río Cangrejal (L$13, 20 minutes; 9am, 11am, noon, 2:30pm & 4pm; last return bus 2pm) Take the Yaruca bus.

La Unión/Cuero y Salado (L$16, 1½ hours; 6:30am to 6:00pm Monday to Saturday every 45 minutes; 8am to 5pm Sun hourly; last return bus 4pm)

Nueva Armenia (L$26, 1½ hours; 9:30am, 10:30am, 12:30pm, 2:30pm, 3:30pm & 4:30pm; last return bus 11am)

Olanchito (L$217, *ordinario* 3¼ hours, *directo* two hours; 6:45am to 4pm hourly)

Sambo Creek (L$12, 45 minutes; 6:10am to 6:10pm Monday to Saturday, 8am to 5pm Sunday every 35 minutes; last return bus 4pm)

San Pedro Sula Diana Express & Catisa-Tupsa (L$95, 3½ hours); Hedman-Alas (luxury service L$320-380, three hours; 5:15am, 10am, 2pm & 5:45pm); Contraibal-Cotuc (L$90; 6am & 3pm)

Tegucigalpa Kamaldy (L$217, seven hours; 6:15am, 7:30am, 9:30am, 11am, 12:30pm & 5:30pm); Cristina (L$217, 6½ hours; 5:15am, 10am & 2pm); Contraibal-Cotuc (L$182; 6:30am & 3pm)

Tela Diana Express & Catisa-Tupsa (L$80, 1½ hours; 5:30am-6:30pm hourly); Kamaldy (L$57, 1½ hours; 5:30am to 6:30pm hourly)

Tocoa (L$75, 2½ hours; 4:30am to 5:30pm every 30 minutes) For faster service, catch any Trujillo-bound bus at the Cotuc-Contraibal stop on the main hwy (L$80, 1½ hours; 8:30am to 7pm every 45 minutes)

Trujillo Cotuc-Contraibal (L$100, three hours; 8am to 7pm every 30 to 45minutes)

Getting Around

TO/FROM THE AIRPORT

Taxis from the airport cost L$100, but you should be able to get a ride for half that just by walking about 100m outside the airport gate. Chances are a taxi will be waiting there; otherwise walk to the highway – another 100m – and flag one down there.

BUS

Buses depart from in front of the Banana Republic Guesthouse (p182) to Muelle de Cabotaje for ferries to the Bay Islands (L$6, one hour).

IF YOU HAVE A FEW MORE DAYS

There are a number of tawny-sand beaches near La Ceiba that are easy to explore by bus (and even easier with a rental). Most are 1km or 2km off the highway, usually down dirt roads. They're empty during the week but often see action – *fútbol* games, food vendors, bodysurfing and general ocean- and sun-worshipping – on weekends. As always, be aware of your surroundings and your belongings; don't take valuables as they have a way of walking while you're practicing your synchronized swimming moves just a few meters away.

Although this coast is sprinkled with decent beaches, try these to get started: the windswept **Playa de Peru** (9.5km east), the town beach at **Villa Nuria** (17km east), the ocean and river beaches at **El Porvenir** (15km west) and the often-packed **Cuyamel** (18.5km west) with its spectacular barbecued-fish stands.

CAR

Daily rental rates range from around L$760 to L$1140.

Econo Rent A Car (☎ 442-1688, 442-8686; airport; 8am-6pm Mon-Fri)
Thrifty (☎ 442-1532; www.thrifty.com; airport; 8am-6pm Mon-Fri)
Union Rent A Car (☎ 440-0439; 8am-noon & 1:30-5:30pm Mon-Fri, 8am-noon Sat) Located next to Hotel Iberia.

TAXI

Taxis in La Ceiba are easy to find; in fact, they normally find you. The cost of a ride depends on the distance and time of day. In town, a cab costs L$20 per person from 5am to 8pm, and from L$30 to L$50 between 9pm and 5am. Rides to the airport are about L$80 per person, and L$50 to L$80 per person to Muelle Cabotaje (the main pier). For other destinations, prepare to negotiate, and be sure to agree upon a price before you get in.

REFUGIO DE VIDA SILVESTRE CUERO Y SALADO

On the coast about 30km west of La Ceiba, the Cuero y Salado Wildlife Refuge takes its name from two of three rivers, Cuero and Salado (the third is San Juan), which meet at the coast in a large estuary, creating waterways, mangrove forests and coastal lagoons along the way. A reserve since 1987, it protects varied and abundant wildlife; manatees are the most famous and most elusive, but there are also howler and white-faced monkeys (among others), sloths, otters, iguanas, caimans and 196 bird species.

Orientation

Cuero y Salado is 9.5km northwest of La Unión. Visitors must take a train from there to the visitors center (see p188) in Salado Barra, which is in the heart of the reserve.

Information

A brand-new visitors center in Salado Barra overlooks the estuary at the end of the railroad track; all guests must pay the park fee here (adult/student L$190/95), and can book a tour, eat at the cafeteria or reserve a bed for the night. Also inside is a small but very good exhibition on the refuge, and its flora and fauna. Signage is in English and Spanish.

For information on the refuge before you arrive, contact La Ceiba-based Fundación Cuero y Salado (see p180), which manages the reserve.

Sights & Activities

To see the most wildlife, visit the reserve early in the morning or late in the afternoon. During the heat of the day, animals hide from the sun. Be sure to bring plenty of water, sunscreen and insect repellent. For tours, make a reservation a day in advance so that guides can be ready for your arrival.

Just 500m from the visitors center, **Coco Beach** is a rustic but relatively clean gray-sand beach.

Without a doubt, the best way to see the wildlife in this reserve is on the water. Guided **canoe tours** (1-2 people L$320, canoe hire only L$120), lasting 3½ hours, take visitors silently down the rivers and through mangroves, which are perfect for spotting birds, monkeys, crocodiles, and sometimes even a manatee. Guided two-hour **motorboat tours** (1-2 people L$425) are also offered. You can save money by going with a larger group. Although the boats take visitors to lagoons and channels further afield, the noise of the outboard motor can startle animals into flying or scurrying away before you can admire them.

Canoe and boat tours can be arranged at the visitors center; for early morning tours, make a reservation a day in advance.

You can learn how *casabe,* a yucca-based Garífuna flat bread, is made on a tour of the **Casa de Casabe** (admission L$20; 8am-6pm), a community production center. It's in a yellow house, 3km from La Unión on the railroad track.

With advance notice, a 2½ hour **Garífuna cultural tour** (up to 8 people L$855) can be arranged, complete with a guided tour of the community, a stop at the Casa de Casabe, and dance and musical performances. Ask at the visitors center for details.

Sleeping & Eating

A wooden-plank building on stilts houses a very well-maintained **dorm** (per person L$150), about 200m from the visitors center. Each room is spacious, has large windows with screens, and two to three bunk beds apiece with linen included. The shared bathroom is clean and has running water 24/7. No worries about the house full of soldiers next door; they're posted on the reserve to protect against poachers. **Camping** (campsite per person L$80) is also permitted. Tents can be rented for L$150 (no sleeping bags, unfortunately).

Breakfast, lunch and dinner (mains L$30 to L$60) are prepared and served in the airy cafeteria at the visitors center; you'll get standard Honduran fare – mostly chicken, eggs, fried bananas, rice and beans. It's run by the friendly Doña Fátima.

Getting There & Away

To get to the reserve, you can either take a bus from La Ceiba's main terminal to La Unión (L$16, 1½ hours, 6am to 4pm, every 45 minutes) or spring for a taxi (L$320 to L$450). From La Unión, jump on the *trencito* (roundtrip per person for two or more L$114, 45 minutes, 7am to 2pm, departs every 1½ hours) for the 9.5km ride on the old banana railroad to the visitors center in Salado Barra. If you arrive between *trencitos* (little trains), consider taking a *burra,* a railcar basket pushed gondola-style by a couple of men with poles (roundtrip per person L$400, one hour). Be sure to tell the *trencito* or *burra* drivers when you'd like to return; the last bus from La Unión to La Ceiba is at 4pm. You also can walk along the railway tracks to the visitors center; it takes about 1½ hours at a brisk pace.

PARQUE NACIONAL PICO BONITO

One of Honduras' best-known national parks, **Pico Bonito National Park** has the country's third-highest peak (Pico Bonito; 2436m) and an unexplored core area of 500 sq km. It was already the largest national park in Honduras when additional forest territory was included in July 1992. Its magnificent and varied terrain includes thick forests, rivers, waterfalls and abundant wildlife, including jaguars, armadillos, wild pigs, *tepezcuintles* (pacas), monkeys, doves and toucans.

Now for the bad news: the vast majority of the park is off-limits to intrusion of any kind, including hiking. Fortunately, trails to two waterfalls on the park's perimeter make for great day hikes, and still offer a glimpse into this rugged and pristine area.

There are two entrances to the park, at **El Pino** and at **Río Cangrejal**. Almost every tour agency in La Ceiba offers Pico Bonito tours, mostly to the El Pino side though others can be arranged. Entrance to Pico Bonito National Park is L$114 – if you take a tour, be sure to ask if admission is included or separate from the tour price.

For additional information about the park, contact the Fundación Parque Nacional Pico Bonito (see p180). And in case you were wondering, climbing Pico Bonito itself requires technical climbing experience and takes several days and special permissions. Few groups have attempted it, even fewer have made it.

El Pino

The original entrance to Pico Bonito is at the town of El Pino, 19km west of La Ceiba on the highway toward Tela.

HIKING

El Pino Tourism Committee (☎ 386-9878) offers several guided trips. The prices are surprisingly high for day hikes – as much as L$500 per person. The tourism committee does not have an office, but you can call, or get information and arrange tours a day in advance, at **Vivero Natural View** (☎ 368-8343) in El Pino (look for the purple tourist information sign).

The Lodge at Pico Bonito (☎ 440-0388, in US 888-428-0221; www.picobonito.com; Carr a Tela, El Pino) also has a number of trails in its private protected forest at the foot of the mountain. Access is free for guests, but day trips for nonguests can be arranged.

THE OCEAN'S FILTER: UNDERSTANDING MANGROVE ECOLOGY

Mangrove forests – often referred to as swamps – are vital to the protection of coastal lands. Providing a buffer zone between the ocean and the land, their extensive root systems slow waves, which ultimately prevents erosion. They are also home to a rich and varied wildlife; in Honduras, this includes birds such as snowy egrets, neotropic cormorants and yellow-crowned night herons as well as larger creatures like American crocodiles, Caribbean manatees, leatherback turtles and howler monkeys.

The trees and bushes that make up mangroves grow along coasts and have developed the unique ability to withstand daily inundation and high levels of salinity. They survive – and thrive – by having an exposed root system that allows them to get oxygen directly from the air during low tide. They do so either by having roots that elevate them above the low tide level or by having roots that stick out of the muddy silt that they grow in.

Today, the biggest threat to mangrove forests is agricultural development. More and more farmers are settling in coastal regions, clearing lands and draining wetlands to create plots suitable for planting or ranching. The result has been the destruction of key wildlife habitats and the increased vulnerability of the mainland, and its swelling population, to the wrath of tropical storms and hurricanes.

There are several mangrove forests on Honduras' coastlines; those that are protected include Parque Nacional Jeannette Kawas, Refugio de Vida Silvestre Cuero y Salado and Refugio de Vida Silvestre Laguna de Guaimoreto.

The park's first trail is still a favorite, with a moderately difficult three hour hike to **Cascada Zacate** (per person incl guide, transport & park entrance fee L$210). You'll hear the falls before you see them; in fact, they are also known as Cascada Ruidoso, or 'noisy falls.' When the water is high, it thunders through a narrow chasm, throwing up a thick cloud of vapor. The pool at the base is enticing, but a community downstream uses the water for drinking so swimming isn't allowed. Fortunately, there's a smaller waterfall, with an equally appealing swimming hole, at the trailhead.

Other options (not in the park) include **Sendero La Montura** (per person L$380), a tough eight-hour hike that forms a loop through varied forest, stopping at a small waterfall and passing overlooks with views of Parque Nacional Cayos Cochinos and Refugio de Vide Silvestre Cuero y Salado; a three-hour **cacao and butterfly tour** (per person L$310); and a three-hour hike along the **Río Coloradito** (per person L$190). The folks at Vivero Natural View have booklets detailing all the available outings.

SLEEPING & EATING

Posada El Buen Pastor (Carr a Tela; r L$310-450) El Buen Pastor has four surprisingly comfortable rooms, all with private bathroom, fan, hot water and homey décor. There's a common TV room, a garden at the back and a patio in the front. Noise from passing buses and trucks is the main drawback here, but traffic is fairly light at night. Morning toast and coffee are included.

Centro Ecoturístico Natural View (☎ 368-8343, r L$220) Two kilometers north of the highway, this place has a couple of simple rooms that sleep two, and camping is possible on the large grassy plot. It's also a good place to eat and relax après-hiking, with *palapa*-covered tables and shady hammocks.

The Lodge at Pico Bonito (☎ 440-0388, in US 888-428-0221; www.picobonito.com; Carr a Tela, El Pino; per 2 people L$4560, extra person L$955; P ☒ ✣ ☐ ☒) This is certainly the nicest option in El Pino and not far from the Cascada Zacate trailhead. See also p184.

GETTING THERE & AWAY

Any bus headed toward Tela or San Pedro Sula can drop you at El Pino. To get to Vivero Natural View look for the purple tourist information sign on your right.

Río Cangrejal

Access to part of Parque Nacional Pico Bonito is also available along the Río Cangrejal, a narrow, lively river that forms much of the park's eastern border. The most common way to experience the river is to raft it, a popular excursion offered by a number of outfits (see p181) that usually includes stopping for a short hike or two into the park. You can stay at any of three jungle lodges along the river (p184) – two of the lodges are operated by the rafting operators, which offer a free night with any trip.

For a more cultural experience, there is a nascent ecotourism project involving the communities of Las Mangas and El Naranjo, with guided hikes, community tours and a stay at a guesthouse (see right).

Guaruma Servicios (☎ 427-2678; www.guaruma.org; Centro Cultural, Las Mangas; 🕑 7am-7pm) is a guide service run jointly by students and community members. The community guesthouse is also located there. Check out its website to learn about volunteer opportunities.

In the town of El Naranjo, the **Centro de Información Turística** (Tourist Information Center; 🕑 7am-7pm) has simple displays and photos about the hikes and other activities available in the area.

SIGHTS & ACTIVITIES

On the Río Cangrejal side, the one main trail leads to **Cascada El Bejuco**, a 60m falls that's a good one- or two-hour climb from the river, depending on the condition of the trail. You'll pass several smaller falls along the way that are nice for swimming.

Guaruma Servicios offers several guided **hikes**. The longer hike (per person L$180, four hours) takes you to the village of La Muralla, stopping at a swimming hole to take a dip, while the shorter hike (per person L$140, two hours) starts just beyond the river bridge south of town and winds through thick forest before reaching a pleasant swimming hole. Tours start at the Centro Cultural, where, if you're interested, you can have a quick introduction to the various community programs, from computer training to photography lessons.

El Naranjo is a timber town, and groups of men hike far into the forest to cut tropical hardwoods. They hew the logs with handsaws and carry them on their shoulders back to town. The leftover scraps used to be discarded, but a few enterprising residents have learned to turn them into *artesanía*, which they sell along the roadside. El Naranjo also has a very modest orchid garden containing about 15 species of orchids.

Guaruma rents **bicycles** (per day L$100) – a great way to explore the area and other communities along the main road.

SLEEPING & EATING

Consisting of three cabins and a *comedor* (a small eatery), **Cabañas Aventuras del Bosque** (r L$285) is jointly owned and operated by a group of three families. The cabins have two rooms apiece, each with a hot-water bathroom. They are rustic, built of hand-hewn wood slats that add to the charm but leave gaps here and there – a mosquito net would come in handy. A large terrace has hammocks, and the *comedor* (open for breakfast and lunch) serves simple fish, chicken and pork dishes (mains L$70 to L$80).

GETTING THERE & AROUND

Take a Yaruca-bound bus from the main bus terminal, departing at 9am, 11am, noon, 1pm, 2:30pm and 4pm. The bus can drop you anywhere along the road, including El Naranjo (L$12, 30 minutes) and Las Mangas (L$13, 40 minutes). A taxi from La Ceiba will cost between L$240 and L$300.

Just about everything here is built on or near the main dirt road, which itself hugs the river, climbing steadily from the highway turnoff. (Whether on foot or bike, it's always easier headed south.) Buses pass every couple of hours, and you can always hitch a ride with a passing pickup truck.

SAMBO CREEK

pop 2600

This Garífuna fishing village 21km east of La Ceiba is most notable as a jumping-off point to Cayos Cochinos. There's a decent beach too.

While you are in town, you might as well swing by the **Sambo Creek Canopy Tour** (☎ 3355-5481, 3349-1075; 🕑 8am-4pm), which has a massive 18-zipline canopy cruise that includes a dip in their hot springs and mud baths (L$855). If you want to skip the canopy, the baths are L$475. It's 500m east of the Hotel Canadien turnoff on the main highway. Cash only.

Sleeping & Eating

The second and third hotels listed here are reached via a dirt road, 200m past the main Sambo Creek entrance, while the others are in Sambo Creek proper.

Hotel Avila (☎ 9775-0840; s/d L$250/300) There's a decent restaurant (mains L$80 to L$180) and a handful of passable rooms at this little hotel on the eastern corner of town.

Hotel-Restaurante Helen's (☎ 408-1137; s/d/ste L$665/722/912, cabins L$800-1000; P ❄ 💻 🏊) The best deal in town, this hotel boasts a tropical bar and restaurant, and excellent common areas. The rooms are fairly basic with hot-water bathrooms, air-con and small refrigerators. There are also seven cabins, most of which come with living rooms and kitchens.

Hotel Canadien (☎ 408-9912; www.hotelcanadien.com; r L$1197; P) This beachfront family place has nice, clean rooms with separate sitting areas, a funky pool area with a frog in the middle, and a good onsite restaurant with the best views in town. To get here, walk along the beach from town or take the road from the highway.

Restaurante Sambo Creek (mains L$60-200; breakfast, lunch & dinner) A Massachusetts transplant, the owner of this longtime watering hole is a good source of information and can also organize trips to Cayos Cochinos. The whole fish and fresh jumbo shrimp are tasty. It's in the center of town, and has cheap and decent rooms available for rent at times.

Champa Kabasa (☎ 440-3360; mains L$109-200; 10am-8pm) This popular restaurant at the entrance to town has branches in La Ceiba and San Pedro Sula. Garífuna and seafood dishes are the specialty: the seafood sampler makes a good appetizer, while the *sopa marinera* is a classic. Grab a table right on the beach, or head to the 2nd-floor patio for views of the ocean.

Getting There & Away

Local buses connect Sambo Creek with La Ceiba (L$12, 45 minutes, 5:30am to 7pm, every 35 minutes).

CAYOS COCHINOS

Comprised of two small islands and 13 little cays, the Cayos Cochinos are a classic Caribbean beauty with white-sand beaches, impossibly turquoise water and palm trees galore. It was designated a Marine National Monument in 2003 after 10 years of hard lobbying by the Fundación Cayos Cochinos (see p180). As a result, commercial fishing is not allowed in Cayos Cochinos and instead the 489-sq-km reserve is filled with pristine reefs and a flourishing marine life that make for excellent diving and snorkeling. The islands are also known for their unique pink boa constrictors, which aren't dangerous.

As a protected reserve, there is a fee to visit any part of the Cayos Cochinos; it's L$95 per person if you come with a tour operator, L$190 if you come with an independent boatman – payable at the Fundación Cayos Cochinos research station at Cayo Menor.

Sights & Activities

Cayos Cochinos have spectacular **diving** and **snorkeling**. There are over 60 named dives in the area – and hundreds more without names. You'll be able to see black coral reefs, sea mounds and even a two-engine Cessna. Whether you want to drift through the deep or stay in the shallows, the dives here are certainly out of this world. See below for information about dive packages.

Fundación Cayos Cochinos (see p180) coordinates various **volunteer programs** at its research facility on Cayo Menor, the smaller of the two main islands in Cayos Cochinos. The center is used by scientists to monitor the flora, fauna and reef in the reserve; volunteers can participate in projects like reef surveying (Open Water dive certification required), sea-turtle watching and studying the islands' pink boa constrictors.

Sleeping & Eating

Plantation Beach Resort (☎ 3371-7556, 440-0265; www.plantationbeachresort.com; r per night/week L$2644/18,183, nondivers L$2204/13,317) Opened as a fishing camp in the 1960s, Plantation Beach is still the only resort and dive shop based in Cayos Cochinos. Dive packages include lodging, meals, three boat dives per day, unlimited shore diving, and use of kayaks and snorkels. It's no Hilton, of course. While there is a set of newly built rooms with a beachy, modern feel, most are older, a little worn, and look like they haven't been significantly updated in 40 years. The setting, however, is one of a kind.

Dive in Caribik (☎ 361-6584, 3373-8620; www.dive-in-caribik.com) In 2006 this well-regarded dive shop, based at the Hotel Palma Real 25km east of La Ceiba, began offering overnight accommodations and diving at a private home on one of the smaller cays. The home is a classic wood-frame beach house – comfortable but not luxurious, with boxy rooms and a large common area. Dive packages are a good deal: five nights with full board, 10 dives and transfer to/from La Ceiba are around L$9000 per person (double occupancy). Customized packages are available too.

The tiny Garífuna village of **Chachauate**, named after the cay it lies on, has lodging with several families who will happily rent you a room, or in some cases, their entire house. Homes are rustic – sand floor, no running water, no electricity, a communal town latrine – so don't expect much beyond a thin foam mattress and a thatch roof over your head. Rates run between L$60 and L$200 per night. There is also a handful of simple eateries on the cay; a standard meal (L$40 to L$80) includes fried fish, rice, beans and a side of *plátanos* (plantains).

You may be able to stay at the Fundación Cayos Cochinos (see p180) research station on Cayo Menor, if they aren't already booked with scientists and volunteers. It offers three simple dorms with foam-mattress bunk beds and indoor bathrooms that open onto the beach. It's way overpriced – L$500 per person – and the staff seems to much prefer hosting volunteer groups over independent travelers. For meals, there's a hilltop eatery offering *típico*.

Getting There & Away

Day trips and dive packages from La Ceiba (p182) typically include transportation to/from the islands, and cost around L$836. If you're interested in getting to Cayos Cochinos on your own, **Soledad Bernardez** (☎ 3344-5625) in Sambo Creek can arrange trips. Boats leave Sambo Creek most days at 7am, returning at 3pm and cost L$570 per person (minimum six people) and L$1500 for a private launch. If all else fails, you can simply go to Sambo Creek or Nueva Armenia and arrange a ride with the local fishermen, who make the trip daily.

You might be able to get a boat here from the Muelle Cabotaje in La Ceiba; ask around.

TRUJILLO & AROUND

It's a long way from the major tourist draws of the North Coast, but Trujillo and its surrounding wild areas are well worth the visit. Up in the verdant mountains above the city you have the uncharted Parque Nacional Capiro-Calentura, and to the east there's great bird-watching in the Refugio de Vida Silvestre Laguna de Guaimoreto. The beach around Trujillo itself is one of the North Coast's best.

TRUJILLO

pop 60,000

Capital of the department of Colón, Trujillo sits on the wide arc of the Bahía de Trujillo. It's famous for its coconut palm–lined beaches and gentle seas. At the end of that long arc is Puerto Castilla, another of Honduras' major deepwater ports. There's nothing much to see out there, but the seaward side of the peninsula has fine, rustic beaches.

History

It was near Trujillo that Christopher Columbus first set foot on the American mainland, on August 14, 1502, on his fourth and final voyage. The first Catholic Mass on American mainland soil was held on the spot where he and his crew landed. Trujillo was founded two decades later, in 1525, and served as Honduras' provincial capital until 1537.

Trujillo's deepwater port was used by ships carrying gold and silver to Spain, and was attacked numerous times by pirates, including A-list scallywags such as Nicolas Van Horn and Henry Morgan. The Spanish built fortresses – including Fortaleza Santa Bárbara – to repel the pirates but to no avail. After being sacked by Dutch pirates in 1643, the city was abandoned for over a century.

Orientation

Trujillo is much smaller and quieter than many people expect, and the center is easy to navigate on foot. However, the bus station is 1km from town, and a few popular hotels are even further. Taxis are plentiful and hitching is very common.

Information

Banco Atlántida (Parque Central; 🕒 9am-4pm Mon-Fri, 8:30-11:30am Sat) Exchanges traveler's checks and has a 24hr ATM.

Cyber Net Café (per hr L$20; 🕒 8am-10pm) For internet access.

Farmacia Almim (☎ 434-4526; 2a Calle; 🕒 8am-8pm Mon-Sat) Pharmacy.

Fundación Calentura y Guaimoreto (Fucagua; ☎ 434-4294; 7am-noon & 1:30-5pm Mon-Fri) On the road toward Parque Nacional Capiro-Calentura; manages the national park and the Laguna de Guaimoreto Wildlife Reserve.

Hondutel (3a Calle; 🕒 7am-9pm Mon-Fri, 8am-noon Sat & Sun)

Hospital Salvador Paredes (☎ 434-4093; Calle Principal; 🕒 24hr)

Lavandería Colón (2a Calle; per 10lb L$60; 🕒 8am-5pm Mon-Fri) Offers laundry services.

WILLIAM WALKER – THE GRAY-EYED MAN OF DESTINY

It's tempting (if clichéd) to accuse Tennessee-born William Walker of having a Napoleonic complex: he was 5'2", and had suffered childhood taunts of 'missy' while caring for his ailing mother. His social life thus lacking, by age 22 he spoke several languages and had degrees in medicine and law. Walker became editor of the left-wing *San Francisco Herald,* where he spoke out against slavery, but after the death of both his fiancée and his beloved mother, Walker decided to pursue other interests.

Filibustering, a word derived from an old Dutch term for pirate, became the Spanish verb for invading another country as a private citizen, then unofficially receiving aid from your home government. Walker's first filibustering gig in 1852 targeted La Paz, Mexico, where he pulled off a stunning, if short-lived, victory against the larger, better-equipped (but totally unprepared) Mexican army. The venture played well in the press and two years later, in 1854, Walker was invited by liberals in Nicaragua to help defeat conservatives for control of the country. Dubbed 'the Immortals', Walker's army easily took Granada and before long he had installed himself as dictator, abolished Spanish as the native language and reinstated slavery. The rest of Central America seemed to pooh-pooh the development – some liberals even hailed it – until Walker declared his intention to conquer the whole region and launched an attack on Costa Rica. Neighboring countries joined together and fell on Walker who, after a year of bloody fighting, accepted a US-brokered truce and retreated to New Orleans.

Walker returned to the USA a hero, and immediately began planning his return. In 1860 he and 200 soldiers set sail for Roatán, but discovering the island was still controlled by Britain, landed in Trujillo instead and captured the fort. Walker intended to unite with liberal commander Trinidad Cabañas, but after sailing up the Río Negro, Walker found Cabañas' camp abandoned. By then British and Honduran forces were closing in; after five days of fighting, Walker surrendered to the British, assuming he'd be returned to the US. But Britain handed him over to Honduran authorities in Trujillo, who promptly had him executed.

Walker is buried in Trujillo, though the cemetery is usually locked. To learn more, check out Guillermo Yuscarán's *Gringos in Honduras* or the critically panned and somewhat hallucinogenic movie *Walker,* directed by Alex Cox (of *Sid and Nancy* and *Repo Man* fame).

With contributions by Paige Penland

Police station (☎ 434-4038; Parque Central; 🕑 24hr)
Post office (4a Calle; 🕑 8am-noon & 2-4pm Mon-Fri, 8-11am Sat)
Tourist information office (☎ 434-3140; Parque Central; 🕑 8am-4pm Mon-Fri)

Dangers & Annoyances

There have been daytime robberies reported on the beaches just outside Trujillo, especially on the way to Santa Fe. Though Trujillo's main beach is safe by day, it's best to skip the moonlight stroll.

Sights & Activities

Trujillo is best known for its attractive **beaches**, with pale sand fronting a glassy, waveless ocean. Some of the best are near the airstrip, over 1km east along the beach from town. Several beachside thatched-roof restaurant-bars provide shade, food and a cool drink for beachgoers, and keep the beaches clean.

Often called El Castillo (the Castle), **Fortaleza Santa Bárbara de Trujillo** (☎ 434-4535; Parque Central; admission L$50; 🕑 9am-5pm) is a 17th-century Spanish fortress with a small museum containing pre-Columbian artifacts, religious relics, slave chains, Garífuna masks, and antique weaponry – each item a glimpse into the area's history. The grounds have excellent views of the coast, several old cannons and a stone marker of the execution site of adventurer and would-be conqueror William Walker (see above).

The **Museo Riveras del Pedregal** (☎ 434-3245; adult/child L$50/25; 🕑 7am-5pm) has a huge collection of antiques and artifacts, ranging from the wacky to the sublime.

The most 'substantial' excursions around Trujillo are an all-day hike to the upper reaches of **Parque Nacional Capiro-Calentura** or a bird-watching trip through the tangled mangrove channels of **Refugio de Vida Silvestre Laguna de Guaimoreto**.

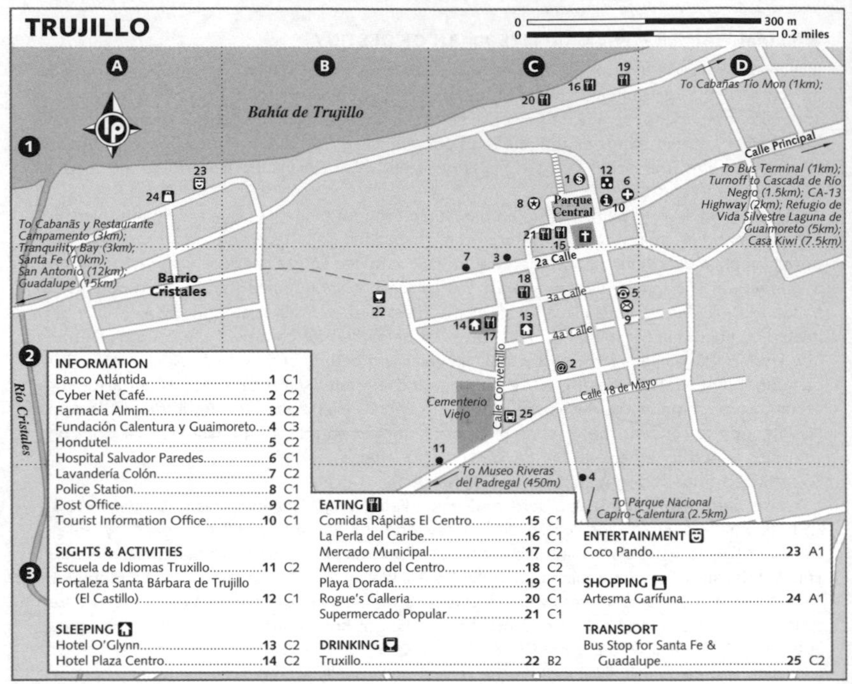

The bay has several good places to go **snorkeling**. Cayo Blanco and the Banco de Estrellas Marinas (Sea Star Bank) are the best spots, with a healthy coral reef teeming with fish, starfish (of course) and the occasional turtle. There's another spot 2km east along the beach to a sunken boat; its rusted hull sticks partway out of the water just a short distance from shore.

The short hike to **La Cascada de Río Negro** is another pleasant excursion. On the road into Trujillo, turn at the 'Mahogany & Cacao Reforestation & Research Facility' sign, circle behind the stadium and then turn right down a dead-end street. Veer right down a dirt road and through a gate; where the road bends right, look for a small path with a water tube partially buried in the middle. Follow the path (and the tube) about 1km to the falls.

There are undeveloped **hot springs** along the Río Silin, just 20km east of town.

Courses

The **Escuela de Idiomas Truxillo** (☎ 434-4135; 20hr per week L$2000, with homestay incl materials L$3500), 50m east of Hotel Trujillo, offers one-on-one Spanish classes, four hours per day.

Festivals & Events

Every other Sunday a Garífuna Mass, including traditional singing, is held at Iglesia San Juan Bautista at 6:30pm.

The annual fair in honor of Trujillo's patron saint, San Juan Bautista, takes place the last week of June.

Sleeping

While staying in town is a good way to get to know Trujillo, it's small enough that most travelers can visit it on a day trip from one of the outlying hotels. Each is just a short *jalón* (hitch), bus or cab ride away.

IN TOWN

Hotel Plaza Centro (☎ 434-3006; Calle Conventillo; r with fan/air-con L$250/350; P ❄) When we visited, this clean, well-tended hotel was home to many construction workers who are breaking ground on a major resort-home development nearby. It's well worth the extra 100 lemps to go for the air-con rooms, which are cleaner and brighter, and, well, they have air-con.

Hotel O'Glynn (☎ 434-4592; 4a Calle; s/d L$380/500; P ❄) For the price, you are better off at the Centro, but this is a good alternative in the center of town. The common areas are beautiful, modern and clean, but the rooms have seen better days, with threadbare sheets and sparse furnishings.

OUTSIDE OF TOWN

Casa Kiwi (☎ 434-3050; www.casakiwi.com; Calle a Puerto Castilla; dm L$70, s with/without bathroom L$130/110, d with/without bathroom L$260/130, cabins L$500-600; P ❄) Although it's over 7km east of Trujillo, the isolation here has its advantages: guests get to know each other over beers and billiards in the airy dining area, and the beach out front is almost entirely yours. Dorms are clean but cramped, private rooms are a bargain for couples (get one on the ocean side), and cabins are pricey for what you get but a worthwhile splurge if you prefer some anonymity. There are bikes, beach gear and snorkel gear for rent (guests only). A cab from town or the bus terminal is around L$100. Hitching is possible too.

Cabañas Tío Mon (☎ 9605-3790; r from L$500; P) These beachfront cabins were under construction when we passed by. It looks like they'll be fairly decent. It's 2km east of town on the beach.

our pick **Tranquility Bay** (☎ 9928-2095; www.tranquilitybayhonduras.com; r L$570, cabañas L$760-855; P) Three kilometers west of Trujillo, Tranquility

A BRIEF HISTORY OF THE BANANA

Bananas are big business. And it would be hard to underestimate the impact that this little yellow fruit has had on Honduras, and Central America as a whole, in the last century. In virtually every arena – political, economic, military, social, environmental, health – American fruit companies have left their mark.

In the early part of the century, banana companies gobbled up land as quickly as they could. Banana baron Samuel Zemmuray helped orchestrate a 1908 coup in order to win a concession for more land. In 1913 the United Fruit Company secured a deal under which it would complete and operate two new national railways in exchange for huge tracts of land along the route. The railroad never extended more than a few hundred kilometers, but thousands of small-time farmers were left landless.

Despite having acquired so much land, the banana companies used only a fraction of what they had. In 1954 Guatemalan president Jacobo Arbenz undertook a plan to buy back unused land from the United Fruit Company – at the value United itself had declared for tax purposes – in order to distribute it to landless peasants.

But land reform was slow to work, if it ever worked at all. In 1962 Honduran president Ramón Villeda Morales signed into law an ambitious agrarian reform – the country's first – designed to redistribute unused land to poor farmers. The law was undermined by the fruit companies, and Villeda Morales was ousted by the military a year later, but an even more aggressive law was put into effect 10 years later by the same military government. Standard Fruit, followed by United, could see the inevitability of reform, and began voluntarily returning some lands. The companies turned the situation to their favor, of course. Entering into exclusive contracts to buy bananas from the small-time farmers and collectives, the fruit companies reaped nearly the same profits but assumed none of the political or economic risk of owning the land.

In recent years, the environmental and health impact of the banana industry has gained more attention. Researchers estimate that plantations in Central America use 10 times more pesticides than those in industrialized countries. One pesticide, a soil fumigant called Nemagon, was banned in the US in the 1970s after it was shown to cause migraines, vision loss, infertility, cancer and birth defects.

In Honduras, as elsewhere, landless farmers have been forced to clear and cultivate undesirable plots, namely on Honduras' steep mountain slopes, thereby contributing to deforestation. Others have migrated to cities like San Pedro Sula and Tegucigalpa, living in shanty towns along riverbanks and unoccupied hillsides. When Hurricane Mitch hit in 1998, thousands of Hondurans died in mudslides on those very same denuded hillsides and overcrowded shantytowns.

Bay offers sunny, beachfront cabañas, all charmingly decorated with Guatemalan bedspreads and Maya prints. Some of the cabins have kitchenettes, but the two smaller rooms are the real buy here. There's a restaurant onsite serving wood-fired pizza.

Cabañas y Restaurante Campamento (jehimyclari@hotmail.com; d L$1200, cabins L$1200-1300; P) You are much better off at the Tranquility Bay, but this resort-like hotel, 3km west of town, does give you cable TV, a big pool and seafront porches.

Eating

Merendero del Centro (☎ 434-3034; mains L$20-60; breakfast & lunch) This popular place serves up *típico* hot and fast. The *baleadas* (flour tortilla filled with beans and cream) and *pasteles* are particularly tasty although the daily lunch specials (L$30) are hard to resist.

Comidas Rápidas El Centro (☎ 434-4567; Parque Central; mains L$40-100; breakfast, lunch & dinner) A standard cafeteria-style eatery, this place has outdoor tables that it shares with an ice-cream shop next door. Be sure to get there early to get the freshest food.

Just below the main plaza, there are over a dozen virtually identical **beachside restaurants** (mains L$80-180; breakfast, lunch & dinner). All offer *típico* with a focus on seafood, and have similar prices. Favorites include **Playa Dorada** (☎ 434-3121), **La Perla del Caribe** (☎ 434-4486) and **Rogue's Galeria** (☎ 434-4668).

For groceries, try **Supermercado Popular** (Parque Central; 7:30am-7:30pm Mon-Sat, 8am-noon Sun) or the **Mercado Municipal** (3a Calle; 6am-4pm Mon-Sat, 6-11:30am Sun), where you'll find a little of everything (including a few mangy dogs).

Drinking & Entertainment

Truxillo (2a Calle; cover L$50) Regguetón, merengue and Latin rock keep the locals moving from 8pm until the early morning hours. Thursday night is karaoke night.

Coco Pando (☎ 443-4748; Barrio Cristales; cover L$20; from 9pm Fri-Sun) This is a popular dance spot on the beach, in a mostly Garífuna neighborhood.

There are a few other dancing spots around here. Cab it home.

Shopping

Artesma Garífuna (☎ 434-3583; Barrio Cristales; 7am-11pm) This place offers a good selection of Garífuna handicrafts and souvenirs. Try some *guifiti* (Garífuna-brewed fire water).

Getting There & Away

There are no commercial air services to Trujillo.

BOAT

There used to be a ferry from Trujillo to Guanaja, but service was suspended at the time of research. It's theoretically possible to get a ride on one of the many cargo or fishing ships going to the Bay Islands or La Moskitia. Go to the pier and try your luck. Check out the vessel (and the weather) before you sign up.

BUS

Buses arrive and depart from the main terminal about 1km east of town. The two main bus lines – **Contraibal** (☎ 434-4932) and **Cotuc** (☎ 444-2181) – rotate service, so ask which is leaving next.

Buses for San Pedro Sula (L$164, six hours) – making a stop in La Ceiba (L$100, three hours) – leave the terminal every 45 minutes from 1:45am to 1:45pm. There's a 2:30pm bus to La Ceiba only, where you can transfer to the San Pedro Sula bus that originates there. Transfer in San Pedro Sula for buses to Tegucigalpa.

Although both are technically direct, you can usually get off at any of the intermediate points, including Corocito (L$25, 30 minutes), Tocoa (L$40, 45 minutes), Savá (L$60, 1¾ hours) and Tela (L$75, five hours).

Five daily buses for Puerto Castilla (L$15, 30 minutes), passing Casa Kiwi (L$8) along the way, leave the Trujillo terminal between 7:15am and 4pm (usually).

For Santa Fe (L$20, 45 minutes) and Guadalupe (L$21, 55 minutes) buses leave from in front of the Cementerio Viejo (old cemetery).

Getting Around

Cabs out of town generally cost L$100 to L$150. If you hitch – very common here – definitely offer the driver money, although most likely they won't accept it.

AROUND TRUJILLO

Garífuna Villages

West of Trujillo are three pleasant Garífuna villages, all with houses stretching along the beach.

EXPLORING THE CULTURAL INTRICACIES OF THE GARÍFUNA

Their culture, dance, language and customs are unique to the world, but who are the Garífuna? How did they get here, where are they going, and will I ever learn to shake my hips as well as them?

Originally from South America, this tribe was known for its fighting skills and use of poison darts, and migrated to the Caribbean in the 13th century. The Caribs mingled with the Arawak, an Amerindian group that had made the same northward journey 1000 years prior, to form the Calinago, or Island Caribs.

Columbus' arrival to the Caribbean in 1492 heralded disease, enslavement and near extermination for the Calinago – but never total subjugation. Over the next three centuries, the Calinago mixed with escaped African slaves to form a new race known as Black Caribs. British soldiers finally conquered the group in 1796 and, fearing an uprising, deported 5000 of them to the island of Baliceaux, then to Roatán. More than 2000 died in the process, while the survivors became the first Garífunas. April 12 – the date in 1797 when they were ignominiously abandoned on Roatán – is today celebrated as 'Arrival Day.'

The Garífuna settled the Bay Islands and then the coast, establishing communities from La Moskitia to Belize. When banana jobs dried up in the 1930s, many Garífuna men joined the US and British merchant marines. Today there are about 300,000 Garífuna people around the world. The largest number still live in Honduras – around 100,000 – but almost the same amount live in the US, especially Houston, Chicago, Los Angeles, Miami, New York City and New Orleans.

Garífuna life and culture has evolved with the times, but certain elements have survived from antiquity. Yucca was a staple of the Arawak Indians in the 2nd century AD, and of the Caribs after them, and present-day methods of cultivating and preparing the starchy root have changed little over the millennia. (The word Garífuna comes from a Carib phrase meaning 'people who eat yucca.') The most famous yucca product is *ereba,* better known by its Spanish name of *casabe,* a large wafer-like cake made from yucca flour. The yucca must first be grated and dried, and it is traditional for women to sing while doing so, their distinctive and melancholy songs harkening back centuries. The Garífuna are also well known for their dances – the *coreopatea, hunguhungu, wanaragua* – which often portray ancient fables.

In May 2001 Unesco named the Garífuna language and culture as one of its inaugural 'Masterpieces of the Oral and Intangible Heritage of Humanity.' Storytelling is a deeply important custom among the Garífuna and *urugas* (storytellers) are much revered, but it's only recently that Garífuna stories have been written down. Garífuna language is a mixture of Arawak, Carib and West African words, and there is still no official orthography: Garífunas from English-speaking Belize and Spanish-speaking Honduras and Guatemala disagree on how to properly spell numerous words, such as *gifity* versus *guifiti* (a traditional drink), or *hana* versus *jana* (a mortar for mashing plantains).

Garífuna communities face very modern challenges as well, from AIDS to the lasting impact of Hurricane Mitch. Unemployment is high in many communities, something that remittances from abroad both mitigate and perpetuate. There are few definitive works of Garífuna history and culture. Online **www.stanford.edu/group/arts/honduras** and **www.ngcbelize.org** have good, basic information.

SANTA FE

pop 8200

Ten kilometers west of Trujillo, Santa Fe is a friendly Garífuna village – people still stop to say hello – with a decent swath of beach. It doesn't receive much tourism except during its annual fair, Feria de Santa Fe (July 15 to 30), when the town bursts at the seams with party-goers.

A small white two-story building on the beach, **Hotel Las Tres Orquidias** (☎ 9163-5360; r L$250) offers just four rooms, each with two queen beds (with annoying plastic mattress covers) and a cold-water bathroom. If these are booked, try across the street at the **Mar Atlántico**.

There are a handful of small eateries along the road as you come into town. **Comedor Caballero** (mains L$40-240; 🕑 breakfast, lunch & dinner), on the main street two doors west of the church, is considered the best restaurant around.

Buses to Santa Fe (L$20, 45 minutes) leave from the old cemetery in Trujillo at 9:30am, 10:30am, noon, 1pm, 3pm and 5pm (Monday to Saturday). On Sunday, there's just one bus that leaves Santa Fe at 7.30am and returns from Trujillo at noon.

SAN ANTONIO & GUADALUPE

These two very small, very isolated villages (12km and 15km, respectively, from Trujillo) sit on opposite sides of a wide river. They are classically Garífuna, with little outside influence, evidenced in the people's dress, their language, their faces and the watchful but not unwelcome attitude toward newcomers.

At the eastern end of the main street in Guadalupe, **Hotel Franklin** (☎ 429-9046; r/tw L$110/170) offers dark, cramped rooms that are, frankly, pretty grim. If it's closed, head to the Pulpería Franklin – someone there will let you into the hotel.

Daily buses depart from the old cemetery in Trujillo (about five daily) for San Antonio and Guadalupe (L$21, 1¼ hours). On Sunday, there's just one bus that leaves Guadalupe at 7am and returns from Trujillo at noon.

Parque Nacional Capiro-Calentura

The mountain behind Trujillo, Cerro Calentura (1235m), is part of the Parque Nacional Capiro-Calentura. A dirt road leads all the way to the top, about 10km, with a number of side trails cutting into the forest along the way. A hike to the top takes about four hours, the return about three.

On the way up the hill, you'll pass through a couple of distinct vegetation zones. At around 600m to 700m the vegetation changes from tropical rainforest to subtropical low-mountain rainforest, and you'll find yourself in a zone of giant tree ferns, with lush forest, large trees, vines and flowering plants. About a third of the way up, a couple of trails diverge off from the road to the left, leading to a waterfall and a tiny reservoir; although they're not marked, you can see them distinctly from the road.

While it might be sunny, clear and warm in Trujillo, it might be cloudy and much cooler at the top of the hill. If the weather isn't cloudy, you can get a great view from the summit over the beautiful Valle de Aguán, along the coast as far as Limón, and across to the Bay Islands and Cayos Cochinos. There is a radar station at the summit.

Fundación Capiro-Calentura Guaimoreto (Fucagua; ☎ 434-4294; 7am-noon & 1:30-5pm Mon-Fri) oversees the park and ostensibly provides information, though service can be pretty hit-and-miss. You'll pass the office, clearly marked on your left, on the road to the park. Park entrance is free.

Refugio de Vida Silvestre Laguna de Guaimoreto

Five kilometers east of Trujillo, **Refugio de Vida Silvestre Laguna de Guaimoreto** is a large lagoon with a natural passageway into the bay. About 6km by 9km, the lagoon is a protected wildlife refuge; its complex system of canals and mangrove forests is home to abundant animal, bird and plant life, including thousands of migratory birds between November and February.

Ask at the tourist office in Trujillo or at Casa Kiwi, 7km east of Trujillo (see p195), about arranging an early-morning bird-watching trip. The going price is around L$1200 for up to 10 people. You also can rent a dugout canoe from a fisherman and paddle yourself through the long channel toward the lagoon. Go early – or better yet, the evening before – to arrange it with a fisherman. A few hundred lempira ought to do it.

More information on the lagoon is available at the Fundación Capiro-Calentura Guaimoreto (see above), on the road toward Parque Nacional Capiro-Calentura. There's no fee to enter the park.

Santa Rosa de Aguán

pop 3900

Paul Theroux's remarkable novel, *The Mosquito Coast,* which was later made into a movie starring River Phoenix (RIP), features this small, pleasant town. Just 40km outside Trujillo, the town has an engaging, frontier-like atmosphere, and you can hire boats to take you up the Río Aguán, where you might see 4.3m (14ft) alligators.

There's an annual Garífuna festival here from August 22 to 29. Two very basic hotels charge around L$70. Buses to Santa Rosa de Aguán leave Trujillo daily at 10:30am.

The Bay Islands

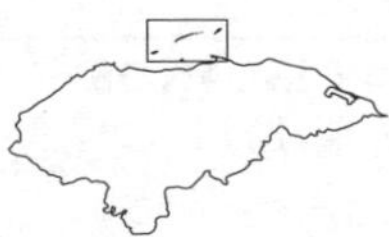

World's apart from mainland Honduras, the Bay Islands (Islas de la Bahía) – Utila, Roatán and Guanaja – move to a lyrical reggae beat, and offer some of the best diving and snorkeling in Central America.

Most people visiting Honduras will chunk out at least a week or two to explore the islands, taking advantage of the dirt-cheap diving courses, the laid-back island rhythm, and the endless sunsets and parties that set this little corner of our planet apart. Perched on the southern terminus of the Mesoamerican Reef – the second largest barrier reef in the world – this is a water-lovers dream, with amazing reef systems and enough marine life to keep divers and snorkelers busy for days on end.

But there's more to these islands than the azure-dream waters of the Caribbean. There are peaced-out Garífuna villages, salty sailor hangouts, wilderness hikes and a history that harkens to those wispy-tailed days when the Garífuna people first landed here, and bold, cold-hearted pirates plied the crystalline tropical waters.

Backpackers and indie travelers will love the sand streets and cheap accommodations of Utila, while mainstream Roatán – the most visited of the islands – appeals to an older crowd, families and folks looking for a bit more on the creature-comfort scale. And while oft-forgotten Guanaja is difficult to reach (and too expensive for most budget travelers), it is certainly not without its bonuses: fewer travelers, lost Caribbean cays, and tremendous diving on a pine-crowned island far from the standard travel circuit.

HIGHLIGHTS

- Take advantage of some of the cheapest dive courses in the world in the aquamarine wonderworlds surrounding **Utila** (p223)
- Rent a scooter for the day as you head out to explore the small Garífuna villages, lost beaches and hidden snorkeling spots of **Roatán** (p219)
- Feel the burn as you kayak from island to island in the **Utila Cays** (p229), stopping to snorkel, picnic and just absorb some good old Vitamin D on the postcard-perfect coral beaches
- Head out at dawn for a **whale shark expedition** (p223) off Utila's north shore, leaving time for some serious 'hammocking' in the syrupy afternoon sun
- Blaze your own trail to **Guanaja** (p230), the least visited and most enigmatic of the islands, for great snorkeling and wide-open views

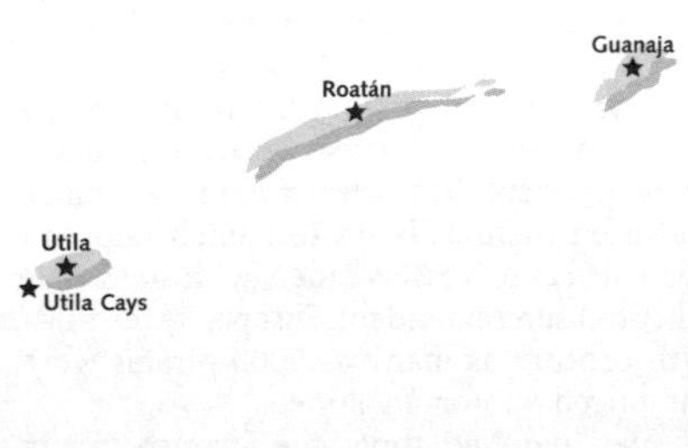

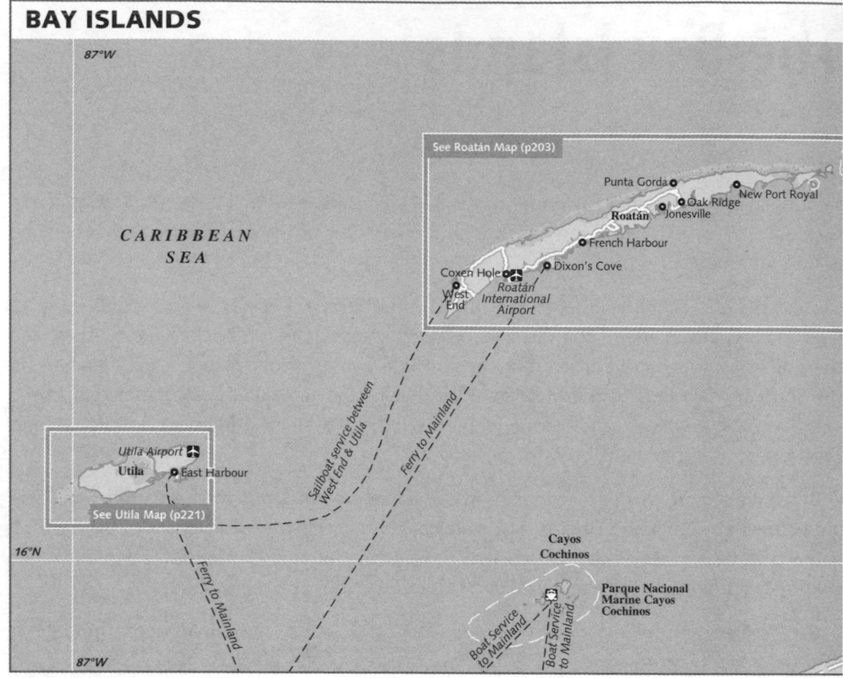

HISTORY

Little is known about life on the Bay Islands before the arrival of European explorers in the 16th century. All three islands were surely inhabited by AD 1000, and perhaps as early as AD 600, but who those early island inhabitants were and where they came from remains unclear.

Christopher Columbus, on his fourth and final voyage to the New World, landed on the island of Guanaja on July 30, 1502. Alerted to a large indigenous population there and on the other islands, Spanish slave-traders kidnapped some of the islanders and sent them to work on plantations in Cuba, and in the gold and silver mines of Mexico.

Meanwhile, English, French and Dutch pirates (including English buccaneer Henry Morgan) established hideaways on the islands, and used them as bases to launch raids on Spanish cargo vessels laden with gold and other treasures bound for Europe. By the mid-17th century as many as 5000 pirates were ensconced on Roatán alone.

After many attempts, the Spanish finally captured the town of Port Royal in March 1782, killing most of the pirates and selling the rest off as slaves. The islands were left largely unoccupied until 1797, when British marines dumped more than 2000 Black Caribs, the surviving participants of a massive uprising on the island of St Vincent, on Roatán. That group settled in Punta Gorda and became known as the Garífuna.

The Bay Islands were controlled by the British until 1859, when Great Britain finally ceded the territory to Honduras.

PEOPLE

The population of the Bay Islands is very diverse. Most *isleños* (islanders) have a mixed heritage that includes African, Carib and European. English, spoken with a broad Caribbean accent, is the dominant language, with Spanish following as a distant second. On Roatán, there is a Garífuna settlement at Punta Gorda, where Garífuna, English and Spanish are all spoken.

There are still some descendants of early British and Irish settlers, especially on Utila. You're likely to meet people who look like they just got off the boat from England, Scotland

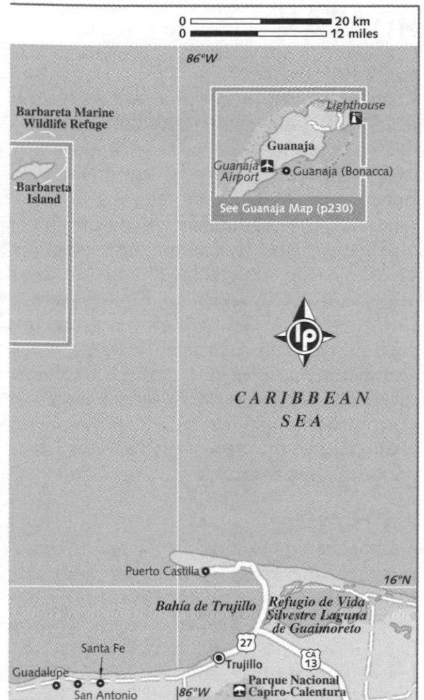

or Ireland, though their ancestors came to the islands over a century ago.

More recently, there has been a large influx of ladinos (people of mixed Indian and European parentage) from the mainland, especially to Roatán, where the tourism boom has created lots of new jobs in the construction, service and security industries. The ladino migration is changing the language on the island; you will hear much more Spanish spoken here now than even just a few years ago.

There is also a significant population of foreign whites, mostly from Europe and the US. Most work at dive shops and other tourist-oriented businesses; in these establishments, you'll hear a variety of languages, including German, Italian, French and Hebrew.

COSTS

The Bay Islands are much more expensive than the mainland – expect to pay about twice what you were paying in the rest of the country – and prices are generally quoted in US dollars. Guanaja is the most expensive of the three islands, and well out of backpacker range. Roatán is more reasonable, but food, accommodations and dives can add up fast. Keep costs down by renting a place with a kitchen so you don't have to eat out every meal. Diving prices on Utila are slightly cheaper than on Roatán, and it has cheaper hotels and restaurants. Many dive shops offer free or discounted accommodation packages in both Utila and Roatán.

Visiting the islands will eat into your budget for sure, but if you want to dive, it truly doesn't get any cheaper (or much better) in the Caribbean. If you can only afford to dive a few times, or not at all, you can snorkel and kayak cheaply, or swim and sunbathe for free.

DANGERS & ANNOYANCES

The islands are generally safer than the mainland. It's best to avoid walking on the beach between West End and West Bay on Roatán at night, as some assaults have been reported. Water taxis are a faster and safer option than walking. Also, when swimming or snorkeling, don't leave valuables unattended on the beach – they have a way of walking away. Better to not bring them at all.

Mosquitoes and sand flies are voracious on the islands, especially during the rainy season. You'll need plenty of repellent, and light long-sleeve shirts and pants. The Center for Disease Control recommends taking malaria pills for your visit to the islands. Mosquitoes also carry dengue fever; see p277, for more information on both malaria and dengue fever.

Sand flies don't carry diseases, but they're tiny – the size of a grain of sand – and can turn your back and legs into a forest of red welts in one afternoon on the beach.

DIVING

Diving is by far the most popular tourist activity on the Bay Islands, and it's known as one of the cheapest places in the world to get certified. Most dive shops offer a range of courses and recreational dives, from an introductory resort course (basic instruction plus a couple of dives) to a full PADI-certification course qualifying you to dive worldwide. Most dive shops are affiliated with PADI (www.padi.com). NAUI (www.naui.org) and SSI (www.divessi.com) courses are available on Utila. An Open Water diving certification course will last from three to four days and includes two confined-water and four open-water dives. Open Water courses cost anywhere from L$5000 to L$6000. Dives cost from around L$665 (one-tank) to L$1050 (two tanks). Advanced diving courses are also offered. Despite the low cost, safety and equipment standards are reasonable. Run by the course director at Coconut Tree Divers, www.bayislandsdiver.com has loads of information on diving the islands, and you can get laminated dive maps at www.mantamaps.com.

Utila (p223) has the lowest certification and fun-diving prices, followed closely by Roatán (p207). Guanaja (p231) is the most expensive. When comparing prices, check whether study materials, extra dives or a free stay are included; ask about reef taxes too. Rental equipment is usually included in all the rates; if you have your own, ask about discounts.

Don't make the mistake of selecting a diving course purely on the basis of price though – you'll find the differences are small anyway. Instead, find one that has a good record and where you feel comfortable (see boxed text, p204).

Qualified divers also have plenty of options, including fun dives, 10-dive packages, night dives, deep dives, wreck diving, shark diving (off Roatán), customized dive charters and dives to coral walls and caves. There is a great variety of marine life, the water temperature is balmy, and the visibility is hard to beat. The waters between Roatán and Utila are also among the best places in the world to view whale sharks, which are typically in the region between May and September. There are shark dives on Roatán, visit www.sharkdiveroatan.com for more info.

GETTING THERE & AROUND

You can reach all three Bay Islands by airplane. All flights come and go from La Ceiba (p185), as do the ferries for Roatán and Utila. At the time of writing there was no ferry service to Guanaja, but you may be able to pay for board on a local boat from Trujillo (or chip in with friends to charter a boat from Roatán), though it could be several days' wait. Captain Vern (right) sails his catamaran between Utila and Roatán – and back again – daily. When there are high seas, especially during Norte season (September through December), it can be tough to get ferries to and from the Bay Islands. Be sure to add a bit of flexibility in your schedule.

For information on getting around the islands, check out: Roatán (opposite), Utila (p228 and Guanaja (p232).

ROATÁN

pop 28,400

Roatán is much bigger than you'd imagine, nearly 50km long, with rugged mountains in the center, wind-scrubbed beach to the north, and protected coves to the south and west. But it wears its heft well, offering the widest variety of accommodations and activities of the three islands. The main draw here is, of course, the spectacular diving, but there are also isolated beaches, punta-rhythmed Garífuna villages, and terra firma attractions such as butterfly farms and canopy tours. And while mainstream tourism is bounding in steadily – with a new cruise-ship dock and several more in the works – Roatán remains resilient, and the laissez-faire pace of island life is unlikely to change anytime soon.

Where to Stay

Backpacker types looking for good restaurants, cheaper lodging and a hopping party scene generally stay in **West End** (p205), while those looking for a relaxed beach vacation head down the beach to **West Bay** (p213). Looking for a break from the crowds? Head east to the resorts around **French Harbor** (p218), the beach and dive resorts of **Oak Ridge** (p219) and **Paya Bay** (p220), or the traditional Garífuna village of **Punta Gorda** (p219). While **Coxen Hole** (p216) is the largest town on the island, it's not really worth staying there.

Getting There & Away

AIR

Roatán's **Aeropuerto Juan Ramón Galvez** (RTB) is located a short distance east of Coxen Hole.

Taca Regional (☎ 552-9910; www.tacaregional.com) and **Aerolineas Sosa** (☎ 445-1658, 445-1154; www.aerolineassosa.com) have offices in Roatán's airport; both offer daily flights between Roatán and La Ceiba (around L$1000 each way), with domestic and international connections. At the time of research, **Continental** (☎ 445-0224, 550-7132; www.continental.com) operated nonstop flights from Houston to Roatán, Wednesday through Sunday. **Delta** (☎ 1-800-791-9000; www.delta.com) had flights from Atlanta on Saturday only. You might save some dough by flying to San Pedro Sula (p116) then taking a bus and a ferry (about five hours) to Roatán. Airport departure taxes are L$642 (international) and L$29 (domestic).

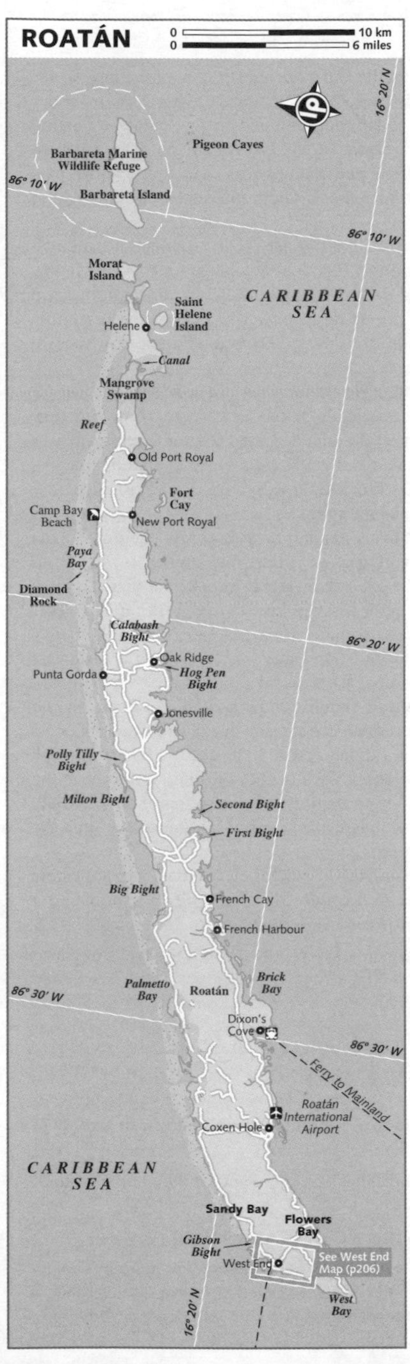

BOAT

Yate Galaxy (☎ Roatán 445-1795, La Ceiba 414-5739) provides a fast, comfortable ride between Roatán and La Ceiba (children 12 & under/economy/first class L$284/524/624, 1¼ hours). There are daily departures from La Ceiba to Roatán at 9:30am and 4:30pm, and from Roatán to La Ceiba at 7am and 2pm.

Captain Vern (☎ 3346-2600, 9910-8040; vfine@hotmail.com) offers catamaran sailboat trips between Roatán's West End (the pier in front of Coconut Divers), and the Alton's Dive Center and Driftwood Café piers in Utila (daily, L$1038 one-way, four to five hours), leaving Roatán at 1pm and Utila at 6:30am. Call ahead.

Getting Around

BICYCLE

Captain Van's Rentals (above) rents mountain bikes for L$170 per day.

BOAT

Water taxis are most commonly used between West End and West Bay (L$50, 10 minutes) and for getting around Oak Ridge; just stick your hand up and they should stop. You can hire the same boat drivers to take you on a private tour of the island, or to reach places inaccessible by car. There are no fixed or standard prices for such excursions, however, so be prepared to negotiate.

BUS

Roatán has two bus routes, both originating in Coxen Hole.

Bus 2 is the one most visitors use. It travels west from Coxen Hole past Sandy Bay (L$13) and on to West End. Minibuses depart from both ends and take about 25 minutes in each direction (L$20, every 15 minutes from 6am to 6pm).

Bus 1 travels east from Coxen Hole past the airport to French Harbour, past Polly Tilly Bight, through Punta Gorda and on to Oak Ridge (L$20 to L$40, every 30 minutes from 6am to 5:30pm); the cost depends on the destination. Travel time varies by driver, taking up to a painful one hour to get to Oak Ridge.

CAR & MOTORCYCLE

Car rentals cost L$850 to L$1130 per day. Car rental agencies on Roatán include:

Avis (☎ 445-0122; www.avis.com.hn; 🕒 7am-5pm)

Best Car Rental (☎ 445-2268; www.roatanbestcarrental.com; airport; 🕒 7am-5pm)

GUIDELINES FOR SAFE DIVING

Diving safety must be taken very seriously. Do not let the laid-back atmosphere of the Bay Islands translate into a blasé attitude toward safety guidelines. That goes for all aspects of the sport, from setting up your gear, to riding on the boat, to entering and exiting the water, to floating on the surface, to exploring the depths below. It's true that the Bay Islands have an excellent safety record, and diving itself demands relatively little physical prowess or technical know-how. But it is vitally important that you do not skip or hurry basic safety measures, nor dive with a shop or instructor that does.

The single biggest concern for a student diver should be quality of instruction and supervision. Turnover of divemasters and instructors can be very high – at any given time, even a highly recommended shop might be short on instructors. Understaffing can lead to larger groups and less attentive supervision. Ask how many people will be in your course; eight is the maximum allowed by PADI, less is better. If the number is high, consider going to a different dive shop or starting a day later.

You should like and trust your instructor. Ask other divers for recommendations, not just for shops but for specific instructors and divemasters. It's perfectly OK to ask instructors how long they have been teaching and how long they have been on the island. Ask to see the equipment – as a beginner there's not a lot you'll be able to determine, but you'll get a sense of your instructor's attitude toward you and your concerns. If you're uncomfortable with a particular instructor, ask to move to a different course or simply go to a different shop.

Quality of equipment is also important. While it takes training to truly assess equipment, you can and should check certain things, like that the O-ring on your tank isn't broken or frayed and whether your regulator hisses when you turn on the air. Arrive early to check your gear; if you're uncomfortable with something – even if the instructor assures you it's OK – ask for a replacement. Being comfortable and confident in the water is a crucial part of safe, enjoyable diving. Shops should also have their air analyzed three to four times per year, and have a certificate prominently displayed to prove it. If you don't see one, ask about it.

There are certain boat safety guidelines that shops should follow as well. All boats should have a captain who stays on board (make sure the captain is not also your divemaster). All boats should have supplies of oxygen, usually carried in a green first aid kit, and a VHF radio – cell phone service is not reliable. Don't be afraid to ask about each of these things, and to have the instructor actually show you the items on board – if enough divers did so, more shops would follow the rules; in the rare case of an emergency, they can make the difference between life and death.

Finally, no matter where you sign up, do not rely on your instructor or divemaster to anticipate every problem. Check your own equipment, assess your comfort level and be vocal about your concerns. Actively monitor your own safety using the following guidelines:

- Accept responsibility for your own safety on every dive. Always dive within the limits of your ability and training.
- Use and respect the buddy system. It saves lives.
- Do not surface if you hear the motor of a boat, unless you are pulling yourself slowly up by the dive-boat mooring line. Accidents have occurred when boats have hit divers who were on the surface or just under it.
- Do not go into caves unless you're certified to do so. Go through tunnels and swim-throughs only with qualified guides.
- Don't drink or use drugs and dive – it's stupid and can kill or injure you or the people around you.
- Avoid flying the same day after a dive (24 hours after a dive is a good target).
- If you haven't dived for a while, consider taking a refresher course before you jump into deep water. It takes about an hour and only costs around US$15. It's much better to discover that you remember all your diving skills in 3m of water than to realize that you don't in 20m.

Budget (☎ 445-2290; www.budget.com; airport; 🕑 7am-5pm)

Captain Van's Rentals (Map p206; ☎ 445-5040; www.captainvans.com; West End) Rents out motorcycles for L$850 to L$1040 per day plus insurance, as well as scooters for L$740 per day.

Thrifty (☎ 445-1729; www.thrifty.com; airport; 🕑 7am-5pm)

TAXI

Plenty of taxis operate around the island. Many are *colectivos* during the day, which means they stop along the way to pick up additional passengers and don't charge much more than buses. Cabbies will assume you want a taxi *privado,* or direct service, so be sure to let the taxi driver know what type of service you want before you get in. Unfortunately, there are no *colectivos* between West End and the ferry terminal in Dixon Cove; if you are short on lempira and long on time, catch a *colectivo* between West End and Coxen Hole (L$35), then take a private cab between Coxen Hole and Brick Bay (L$100). *Colectivos* to the airport cost from L$50 to L$65. A private cab from West End to the ferry terminal costs around L$280; it's L$190 to L$285 to the airport. As with everywhere in Honduras, always clarify the price of the ride before you get in. Fares are higher after 6pm.

WEST END

Curled around two small turquoise bays West End is where virtually all independent travelers end up. It feels less 'roots' than say Utila, but still offers a pretty cool scene with beach front reggae bars, dive shops and a wide selection of restaurants. Unfortunately, the beach isn't as nice as in neighboring West Bay.

Orientation

The road through West End runs almost exactly north-to-south, making for spectacular sunsets from anywhere in town. The road from Coxen Hole intersects West End's main road at the east side of Half Moon Bay, the first of West End's two small bays. Buses and taxis to Coxen Hole wait at that intersection. To the north (your right as you enter town) you'll find a handful of hotels, restaurants and dive shops. South of the main intersection, the road curls around Half Moon Bay, passes the First Baptist church and continues to where most of West End's restaurants, bars and dive shops are concentrated. The road continues south until the buildings eventually end at an expansive beach that leads to West Bay.

Information

There's a handful of internet cafés along the strip, charging around L$40 per hour. More and more hotels are offering free wi-fi for those with laptops. Most internet cafés in West End also place national and international calls. Rates are relatively uniform (and uniformly high): domestic fixed line per minute L$5, domestic cell phone per minute L$10, international calls per minute L$15 to L$20. It's much cheaper to call from Coxen Hole (p216).

There's an ATM in front of the **Coconut Tree Market** (Half Moon Bay). Head over to Coxen Hole if you need a bank.

Bamboo Hut Laundry (up to 5lbs L$75; 🕑 8am-4pm Mon-Sat) Laundry services.

Barefoot Charlie's (☎ 403-8721; 🕑 9am-9pm) Offers 2-for-the-price-of-1 books or buy one, get the second one at half-price. Opposite Foster's Bar.

Mariposa Lodge (☎ 445-4450; 🕑 24hr) A 1-for-1 book exchange of English-language books is offered at the reception kiosk of this lodge (see p210).

Tourist Police (☎ 199) The office is just off the strip. For more serious matters, head over to the police station at Coxen Hole.

Sights

Half Moon Bay has a small, clean beach and good snorkeling if you get past the sea grass. It is a popular spot for kayaking and sunbathing too. While you're there, check out **Sandy Bay & West End Marine Park** (☎ 445-4206, 445-4208; www.roatanmarinepark.org; Half Moon Bay; 🕑 8am-noon & 2-6pm Mon-Sat), a marine preservation office with a small exhibit on the marine park and island ecology. Check out the website or drop by to learn about volunteering opportunities.

Nearby **West Bay beach** (p213) is one of the most beautiful beaches in the country and is great for snorkeling, too. Frequent water taxis (p215) make it a quick and easy trip over. You can also walk there – just keep heading south along the beach – although it's not recommended to do so at night (see p201).

Lady Slipper, Queen and Sunset Langwings, Helicopter, Common Owl and Orange Dog are just a few of the 30-plus species of moths and butterflies at the **Roatán Butterfly Garden** (☎ 445-4481; www.roatanbutterfly.com; adult/child

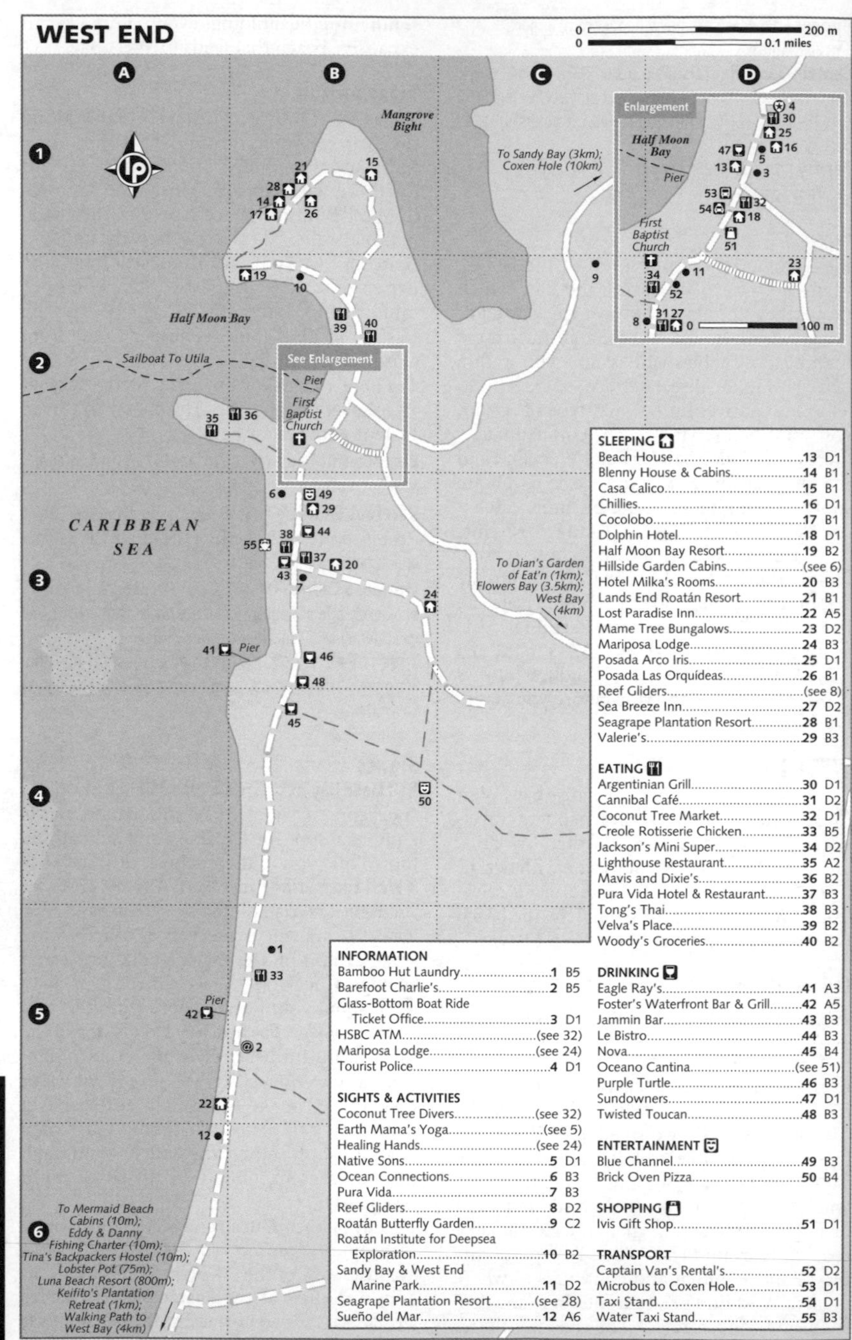
WEST END
0 200 m
0 0.1 miles
A
B
C
D
1
2
3
4
5
6
Mangrove Bight
Half Moon Bay
Sailboat To Utila
Pier
First Baptist Church
See Enlargement
Enlargement
Half Moon Bay
0 100 m
To Sandy Bay (3km); Coxen Hole (10km)
CARIBBEAN SEA
To Dian's Garden of Eat'n (1km); Flowers Bay (3.5km); West Bay (4km)
To Mermaid Beach Cabins (10m); Eddy & Danny Fishing Charter (10m); Tina's Backpackers Hostel (10m); Lobster Pot (75m); Luna Beach Resort (800m); Keifito's Plantation Retreat (1km); Walking Path to West Bay (4km)
INFORMATION
Bamboo Hut Laundry 1 B5
Barefoot Charlie's 2 B5
Glass-Bottom Boat Ride Ticket Office 3 D1
HSBC ATM (see 32)
Mariposa Lodge (see 24)
Tourist Police 4 D1
SIGHTS & ACTIVITIES
Coconut Tree Divers (see 32)
Earth Mama's Yoga (see 5)
Healing Hands (see 24)
Native Sons 5 D1
Ocean Connections 6 B3
Pura Vida 7 B3
Reef Gliders 8 D2
Roatán Butterfly Garden 9 C2
Roatán Institute for Deepsea Exploration 10 B2
Sandy Bay & West End Marine Park 11 D2
Seagrape Plantation Resort (see 28)
Sueño del Mar 12 A6
SLEEPING
Beach House 13 D1
Blenny House & Cabins 14 B1
Casa Calico 15 B1
Chillies 16 D1
Cocolobo 17 B1
Dolphin Hotel 18 D1
Half Moon Bay Resort 19 B2
Hillside Garden Cabins (see 6)
Hotel Milka's Rooms 20 B3
Lands End Roatán Resort 21 B1
Lost Paradise Inn 22 A5
Mame Tree Bungalows 23 D2
Mariposa Lodge 24 B3
Posada Arco Iris 25 D1
Posada Las Orquídeas 26 B1
Reef Gliders (see 8)
Sea Breeze Inn 27 D2
Seagrape Plantation Resort 28 B1
Valerie's 29 B3
EATING
Argentinian Grill 30 D1
Cannibal Café 31 D2
Coconut Tree Market 32 D1
Creole Rotisserie Chicken 33 B5
Jackson's Mini Super 34 D2
Lighthouse Restaurant 35 A2
Mavis and Dixie's 36 B2
Pura Vida Hotel & Restaurant 37 B3
Tong's Thai 38 B3
Velva's Place 39 B2
Woody's Groceries 40 B2
DRINKING
Eagle Ray's 41 A3
Foster's Waterfront Bar & Grill 42 A5
Jammin Bar 43 B3
Le Bistro 44 B3
Nova 45 B4
Oceano Cantina (see 51)
Purple Turtle 46 B3
Sundowners 47 D1
Twisted Toucan 48 B3
ENTERTAINMENT
Blue Channel 49 B3
Brick Oven Pizza 50 B4
SHOPPING
Ivis Gift Shop 51 D1
TRANSPORT
Captain Van's Rental's 52 D2
Microbus to Coxen Hole 53 D1
Taxi Stand 54 D1
Water Taxi Stand 55 B3

THE BAY ISLANDS

L$130/95; ⌚ 9am-5pm Sun-Fri), a 900-sq-meter enclosure a few hundred meters from the West End turn-off. The best time to visit is noon or early afternoon, when the sun is hottest and the butterflies are most active. The garden also has a large collection of orchids and other tropical plants, as well as bird enclosures with keel billed toucans, collared aracari and several species of parrots.

Activities

DIVING

Roatán is a diver's paradise, with near-perfect Caribbean conditions and innumerable dives, from wrecks and reefs, to swim-throughs and drift-dives. There is plenty of great diving within a few minutes' boat ride of West End, including spots like Hole in the Wall, Texas, Sponge Emporium, Black Rock and Lighthouse.

Dive Shops

Dive shops in West End have worked hard to standardize prices for courses and fun dives, and to end the destructive price wars of past years. Prices have gone up, yes, but only because they were ridiculously low before. Most dive shops offer three single-tank dives per day, starting at 9am and spending the surface interval back at the shop. At the time of research, Open Water courses cost around L$6050, including the PADI-required manual and marine park fee. Rescue and advanced courses cost L$5700, and divemaster courses start at L$9500, plus materials. Fun dives cost L$660 per tank, but you can save big by booking more than one dive. A resort course – this is for first timers not looking to do the full four-day certification course – costs L$1900. Night dives and two-tank trips to the south side cost a bit more.

Most shops have joined the Sandy Bay & West End Marine Park, and voluntarily charge all divers a one-time L$189 park fee. The money goes toward anti-poaching and reef-protection programs. Please only use shops that are part of this effort – there's a list of member shops at the marine park's website (www.roatanmarinepark.org). It costs a little more, but one dive will show you why it's so important. Most shops can arrange a shark dive. Check out www.sharkdiveroatan.com for more on the trips. Many dive shops now offer discounted lodging with an Open Water course.

Coconut Tree Divers (☎ 445-4081; www.coconuttreedivers.com) The only shop to regularly offer advanced two-tank dives in the morning. Experienced instructors lead most dives; after-dive beers draw a younger crowd. It has basic dorms for divers (per person L$100). Next to Coconut Tree Market.

Native Sons (☎ 445-4003; www.nativesonsroatan.com) A solid, professional outfit run by Alvin Jackson, a local instructor with almost three decades of experience. Fast, modern boats mean this shop is more willing than most to go to distant dive spots. It's at the entrance to Chillies hotel.

Ocean Connections (☎ 8948-2988; www.ocean-connections.com) With small classes and a friendly, noncompetitive atmosphere. It's operated by a friendly Canadian couple. Enquire about rates on its cabins with your course. Across from Blue Channel.

Pura Vida (☎ 445-4110; www.puravidaresort.com; Pura Vida Hotel & Restaurant) Another shop with a good, long-standing reputation.

Reef Gliders (☎ 403-8243; www.reefgliders.com) Capably managed by a young American-Canadian couple who used to work in Utila; known for friendly service and small groups. Dorms are offered for divers (see p209).

Seagrape Plantation Resort (☎ 445-4297; www.seagraperoatan.com) A hotel dive shop that gets good reviews. It's at the northern end of town.

Sueño del Mar (☎ 445-4343; www.suenodelmar.com) This place is a bit junky, and, when we visited, the service was borderline rude and they wouldn't show us their PADI credentials. It's near Lost Paradise Inn.

Dive Sites

Roatán has dozens of dive sites and most shops do a good job of making sure divers who buy multi-dive packages don't end up going to the same place again and again. If there's a site you are keen to try, don't be afraid to ask. At the same time, weather and water conditions dictate most site selection, and some aren't practical or able to be dived for days at a time. Some favorites – among many, many others – include:

- **Mary's Place** Fissures in the coral form a deep, sheer-faced maze at this one-of-a-kind site. Winding through, you'll likely see jacks, lobsters and crabs, and huge schools of silversides; near the mooring, keep an eye out for seahorses. Mary's Place is near French Harbour, and is usually combined with another south-side dive and lunch at Hole in the Wall restaurant.
- **Texas** Part of the same area known as West End Wall, Texas is so called for its wide open terrain and Texas-sized barrel

ASK A LOCAL: DISCOVERING ROATÁN'S TOP SNORKELING SPOTS

It's important to know your reef topography. From lagoons, it's tough to get past the grass to the coral, and the north side of the island gets deep quick, while the south side has shallower coral gardens [better for snorkeling]. Always be careful of boat traffic, and consider renting gear from the **Marine Park Office** (p205).

From **Land's End** you can walk out and the stuff is right there. **West Bay** (p213) is quite nice, but you have to swim over the reef crest, and can get cut up on fire coral, or you can just swim out from **Half Moon Bay** (p205). When there are strong storms, check out **Flowers Bay**. **Cocoview**, between Jonesville and Oakridge, has a wreck you can see, but it can be difficult to access. And at **Sandy Bay** (p215) near the Bay Island Beach Resort, you can swim to the famous 'spooky channel,' about 100m out, or to Lawson Rock.

Will Welbourn, Course Director at Coconut Tree Divers

sponges. A deep, strong current means you can sometimes fly over the reef at three to four knots without lifting a fin. It's not uncommon to see free-swimming morays, large groupers and the occasional hammerhead. You may even spot the elusive sargassum triggerfish.

- **Hole in the Wall** Another amazing dive. Dropping through a hole in the reef at 6m, you descend through a narrow sloping channel before it spits you out 30m down. Be sure to look up at the spectacular vertical vista above you.
- **El Águila Wreck** Scuttled in 1997 just opposite Anthony's Key Resort, the Águila was a good dive until Hurricane Mitch came along and broke the ship into three pieces – and now it's even better! As you descend, you may draw a crowd of huge groupers looking for a snack, and resident moray eels may join in the swimabout. (Cool to see, but a good reason not to feed animals while diving or snorkeling since they can get annoying – and sometimes even aggressive.)
- **Blue Channel** A 9m-deep channel running parallel to shore just off West End, Blue Channel has some easy swim-throughs and an incredible array of fish and reef life, including triggers, damselfish, grunts and barracuda.
- **Overheat** A shallow dive site that's good for novice divers. Its proximity to the Águila wreck makes it a good place to spot giant groupers.

SNORKELING

Many dive shops loan snorkel gear to their students for free; non-students can rent for about L$100 a day. **Captain Steve** (☎ 9704-5084; www.roatanseaadventures.com) offers booze cruises, snorkeling trips and occasional trips to Cayos Cochinos on his yacht. See above for more on snorkeling around the island.

BOAT TRIPS

The **Roatán Institute for Deepsea Exploration** (RIDE; ☎ 3359-2887; www.stanleysubmarines.com; Half Moon Bay) is the fancy name for an American kid with a homemade submarine, which he uses to take tourists into the deep-sea trenches just off Roatán's north shore. This is one of only two operations in the world that take Joe Public deeper than 91m. And the *Idabel*, as the sub is called, goes much deeper than that – more than 610m down, for as long as seven hours. There is no vegetation after 91m (and no light after 520m) and only the strangest of life forms: bioluminescent sponges, swimming sea cucumbers, six-gilled sharks, all amid huge limestone boulders and fossilized coral formations. The sub's creator, Karl Stanley, got into submarine building with no formal engineering training, or even advanced welding, for that matter. He admits he has no special insurance (nor the international certification he'd need to secure it); if anything happens, says Karl, he's not coming up either. The sub does have redundant safety systems and three days' worth of air and supplies, and has had no major incidents in hundreds of outings. Up to three passengers can take trips of varying lengths: 1½ hours to a maximum depth of 300m (L$7560), 2½ hours to 460m (L$11,340), or 3½ hours to 610m (L$15,120).

For **glass-bottom boat rides** (☎ 3271-3873; per person L$475) head to the small kiosk across from the Beach House at Half Moon Bay. There is no fixed schedule, and at least two people are needed to take the 45- to 60-minute trip. It also offers snorkeling tours.

FISHING

At the far end of town, **Eddy & Danny Fishing Charter** (☎ 9833-7820; west of Sueño del Mar; 🕑 8am-9pm) is a friendly family operation that takes groups trolling (for tuna, dorado, barracuda, and sometimes wahoo and marlin in season), deep-sea fishing (for grouper, and snapper) and flat fishing (catch-and-release bone fish). On a full-day trip (L$6650 to L$11,400 depending on the boat), you can combine different types of fishing, and even stop for snorkeling or lunch on a deserted beach. Half-day trips cost from L$3800 to L$6650. At the end of the day, you can have your catch cooked up, along with potatoes, garlic bread and veggies, for an extra L$100 per person. Ask at the Barefeet Bar for bookings.

HIKING

A loop starting in West End heading to Flowers Bay, then continuing south almost to the tip of the island, over the ridge to West Bay and back up the beach to West End, makes a good five- to six-hour hike. Tack on a couple of hours enjoying the beach at West Bay, and it's a whole day's excursion. For a shorter trek, simply do the West End to Flowers Bay leg – when you reach the ridge, look out over both sides of the island. In either case, bring plenty of water to stay hydrated and adequate repellent to ward off the numerous ticks and sand flies.

KAYAKING

There are plenty of places to push off in West End; Half Moon Bay is one of the easiest – and prettiest – places since it's so well protected. A few hotels provide kayaks for their guests to use. Cannibal Café (p211) and Mavis and Dixies (p212) rent kayaks for around L$95 per hour or L$340 per day.

MASSAGE & YOGA

If carrying tanks on and off the dive boat has put a kink in your neck, book a massage at **Healing Hands** (☎ 445-4450; per hr L$950), located at the Mariposa Lodge (p210).

Earth Mama's Yoga meets next to Native Sons dive shop (p207) for informal yoga courses Tuesday through Thursday at 5:30pm, and Sunday at 9am. Classes are L$100 to L$160 per person.

Courses

Saguey Ariza (☎ 9855-3180, saguey_ariza@yahoo.com) offers private Spanish classes…on an island where everybody speaks English.

Sleeping

With such a steady number of tourists arriving in West End every day, there is an excellent selection of hotels. Be aware that some taxi drivers will try to shepherd you to ones where they get a commission – if you have a place in mind, insist on stopping at it.

BUDGET

Reef Gliders (☎ 8913-5099; www.reefgliders.com; dm L$100) This dive shop's new owners previously ran a dive shop on Utila, so it's no surprise that one of their first moves was to open a dorm exclusively for its students. It has just four beds, an in-room bathroom and a small deck with excellent views. It's right over the classroom, so you can stumble out of bed and be calculating surface intervals within seconds. It's next to Purple Turtle (p212).

Tina's Backpackers Hostel (☎ 445-4144; dm L$133) There are six beds total at this basic backpacker spot. The sheets are clean, there's a shared kitchen and you are just steps from the beach. Unfortunately, there are no lockers to keep your stuff safe. Enquire at the Barefeet Bar just next door.

Valerie's (☎ 403-8757; www.roatanonline.com/valeries; dm L$150, r with shared bathroom L$300) The architectural integrity is definitely questionable at this dirt-cheap (and just plain dirty) backpacker place. The rooms are some of the cheapest in town, but beware: there have been reports of things getting stolen. Single female travelers might not feel comfortable here.

Hotel Milka's Rooms (☎ 445-4241; milkasroom@yahoo.com; dm L$200, r with/without bathroom L$600/L$500) Pretty beat down from the outside, this budget option has cramped dorms and smallish rooms. It's located on the road to Mariposa Lodge, just a few steps from the main drag. The rooms are pretty dirty, but you do get discounts for extended stays.

Chillies (☎ 445-4003; www.nativesonsroatan.com; r with shared bathroom L$400, cabins with shared bathroom & kitchen L$450, cabins with private bathroom & kitchen L$570) Affiliated with Native Sons dive shop (p207), Chillies offers simple clapboard rooms and cabins on a tidy lot. There are plenty of hammocks around for 'chillin' at Chillies' – sorry we couldn't resist – plus a shared kitchen.

The cabins are the real buy here. It's behind Native Sons.

Dolphin Hotel (445-4499; d L$475-550;) This is a basic but clean hotel in one of the most coveted locations in West End – on the main drag overlooking Half Moon Bay, near Coconut Tree Market. Room 201 has the best ocean views, but can get a bit noisy. It's fairly rundown on the outside, but the rooms are relatively clean, and all come with cable TV.

Hillside Garden Cabins (8948-2988; www.ocean-connections.com; cabins L$475-570) These clean hillside cabins are a great deal. It's hard to find, so enquire at Ocean Connections (p207).

MIDRANGE

our pick **Mariposa Lodge** (445-4450; www.mariposa-lodge.com; r with shared bathroom L$490, r with air-con L$750-1115;) This is the best deal in West End, but it's a bummer its not beachside. Accommodations are set up in three buildings: the main house has five modern apartments with fantastically equipped kitchens; a small annex houses two private rooms with air con; and the Little Mariposa House is a cottage with three private rooms that share a kitchen and bathroom. The Canadian owners are friendly hosts and have tons of information about the island, plus there are water jugs and wi-fi.

Sea Breeze Inn (445 4026; www.seabreezeroatan.com; r with fan/air-con L$660/790, studio with fan/air-con L$1510/1700;) A cute, three-story building behind Cannibal Café, the Sea Breeze has wood-slat construction, excellent patios and a few rooms with kitchenettes (although the kitchenette rooms end up stinking of propane). Also has free kayaks and wi-fi.

Keifito's Plantation Retreat (9575-8710; www.keifitosplantation.com; d L$720-1300;) A towering riot of pine stairs leads up from the beach to this hilltop retreat. If you want a beach getaway, than this is the place to be, but you're definitely a long walk from town, and there's no restaurant or kitchen onsite. Choose from old back-to-basics rooms or 'deluxe' renovated models.

Blenny House & Cabins (3303-2328; www.bayislandsconnection.com; cabins with fan/air-con L$850/945, apt up to 8 people L$1890-3600;) An excellent choice for large groups, the Blenny House (next to Cocolobo) has a big apartment with ocean views, a full kitchen and rosy hardwood floors that'll sleep up to eight. There are two rustic cabins next door with chill porches and mossie nets. It feels more like staying in someone's house than a hotel.

Half Moon Bay Resort (445-4442; www.roatanhalfmoonresort.com; s/d L$870/1100;) On the quiet end of Half Moon Bay, this small resort offers 14 wood bungalows dotting the water's edge in a studied, wasting-away-in-Margaritaville setting. The rooms are no frills – except for the air-con – but are clean. A huge plus is a deck right on the water, and the free kayak and snorkel gear rentals.

Posada Arco Iris (445-4264; www.posadaarcoiris.com; Half Moon Bay; r with fan/air-con L$900/1200;) Nicer than the Mariposa, but also a bit more expensive, this Argentinean-owned place offers consistent attention to detail. There are hardwoods throughout this lush and well-maintained lot, and all the rooms have private porches and are charmingly decorated with Guatemalan bedspreads and Honduran handicrafts.

Posada Las Orquídeas (445-4387; posadalasorquideas@globalnet.com; s with fan/air-con L$910/1190, d with fan/air-con L$1025/1310;) Quiet and removed from the hub of the main strip, the Orquídeas has a private dock and clean, easy-going rooms with hardwood floors – but the ocean-front location is the real sales point. It's next to Seagrape Plantation.

Seagrape Plantation Resort (445-4428; www.seagraperoatan.com; d L$1130;) At the far northern end of town, Seagrape is an old-timer that's holding on strong. Come here for the oceanfront bungalows, highlighted by private porches and beautiful views. The hotel rooms, unfortunately, lack character. The one surprise – perhaps even a bummer – is that there's no beach. Instead of sand at the front, it's ironshore – a sharp, black rock made of coral, mollusk shells and limestone. Not exactly a great tanning spot, but it is dramatic.

TOP END

Lands End Roatan Resort (9817-8994; www.landsendroatan.com; r incl breakfast L$945-1870;) Ten Spartan, Euro-styled rooms make up this modern hotel. Rooms are spacious, spotlessly clean, and most have a balcony with a hammock. Although the hotel is alongside the ocean, it doesn't have a beach; ironshore is where you'd expect the sand to be. Still, guests can enjoy the ocean – and the fantastic reef out front – via a swim ladder. Or, if you opt to stay out of the Caribbean, you can still wade in its waters in the saltwater infinity pool that lines the front of the property. Call in Thursday through Sunday for sunset cocktails from 4pm to 8pm.

Casa Calico (☎ 445-4231; www.casacalico.com; d incl breakfast L$1230; P) This place is nice – clean, condo-like rooms in an airy, wood building, granite in the baths and a few rooms with their own kitchens – but it's missing something to bring it all together…something like soul. A big breakfast is included in the rate, as is the use of kayaks. Service was begrudgingly given when we visited.

Mame Tree Bungalows (☎ 403-8245; www.mametreebungalows.com; d L$1285-1500, apt L$2740-2920; P) Perched on a verdant hill overlooking Half Moon Bay, the Mame Tree offers modern, well-appointed rooms with travertine tiling and some of the most modern bathrooms in town. The grounds do leave a bit to be desired, but the two apartments are perfect for families, with large kitchens and delicious ocean views. Free international calls and wi-fi round out the offers, and plans are in the works to build a yoga center.

Lost Paradise Inn (☎ 445-4210; www.lost-paradise.com; d L$1285; P) Or Paradise Lost? Actually, this is one of the few places in West End that actually feels like a real beach resort, with genuine sand beaches (a rarity here) and gazebos overlooking the water. The service is hit or miss, and the rooms are a bit dated.

Luna Beach Resort (☎ 403-8773; www.lunabeachresort.com; d L$1460-2600, q L$2890, apt L$3650-6690; P) The closest thing to a beach resort near West End – though it's down the beach from the town's main strip – Luna Beach offers comfortable beachside hotel rooms and enormous hillside homes; you can see the money here. Like a mega-chain hotel or a bad TV show, it lacks a bit of character and depth. In fact, *Temptation Island* has been filmed here seven times.

Cocolobo (☎ 9898-4510; www.cocolobo.com; s/d/tr L$1800/2280/2890, apt L$2116; P) This boutique hotel is our favorite in the high-end category. The 10 ocean-front rooms have a great, lyrical feel, with Honduran pine everywhere, excellent patios and wicker headboards. There's also a two-story cabin – unfortunately no ocean views here – with a kitchen and sitting area downstairs that's good for families. There's cable TV, iPod docks and wi-fi for the laptop set. The infinity pool offers some of the best sunset views in town. Rates include breakfast.

Other acceptable options include **Mermaid Beach Cabins** (☎ 445-4335; www.roatanmermaidbeachcabins.com; r L$850-890; P) and the **Beach House** (☎ 445-4260; www.roatanbeachhouse.com; r L$2835-3325; P). Both are fine hotels, but they're simply overpriced – the last, spectacularly so.

Between West End and West Bay, the hilltop **Villa Delfin** (www.villadelfin.com; per week L$13,230-81,270; P) offers tremendous ocean views, weekly rentals and special meals prepared by Chef Frank and his lady, Mikey.

Eating

With such a good variety of restaurants, eating out in West End can be a real delight. Just be aware that prices are much higher here than on the mainland.

BUDGET

Cannibal Café (☎ 445-4026; snacks L$50-85, mains L$140-225; 7am-10pm) A favorite spot for afternoon snacks, the open-air Cannibal specializes in Mexican food – and the owners guarantee that no meat of the Homo sapiens variety makes it onto the menu. It serves up a mean *baleada*, but you might be disappointed by the entrées.

Velva's Place (7am-10pm Mon-Sat) This low-key, outdoor restaurant is away from the hubbub of West End's main strip. An 'Island breakfast' of eggs, bacon, beans and toast costs L$100, burgers are about the same, and fish and shrimp dishes range from L$70 to L$110. It's two minutes north of the intersection.

Creole Rotisserie Chicken (mains L$100-140; 3pm-midnight Tue-Sun) Super tasty roast chicken is served in quarter-, half-, or whole-bird portions at this small, open-air eatery, along with large sides of rice, beans, potato salad or coleslaw for a buck and change each. The fish fingers don't disappoint, either. This is a longtime backpacker haunt, but you don't have to be on a budget to appreciate the good food.

There are three markets/grocery stores in West End. None are cheap or have the selection of HB Warren in Coxen Hole or Eldon's in French Harbor, but will do for supplies and making simple meals. **Coconut Tree Market** (Half Moon Bay; 7am-8pm) and **Jackson's Mini Super** (near First Baptist church; 7am-8pm) are the best stocked; **Woody's Groceries** (past Posada Arco Iris; 7am-6pm

Sun-Thu, to 5pm Fri) is less so. You can also get fresh fruit and veggies from a **produce truck** (7am-6pm) that is usually parked near the First Baptist church.

MIDRANGE

Pura Vida Hotel & Restaurant (445-4110; mains L$80-300; breakfast, lunch & dinner) There's no shortage of Italian food to be had in West End, but Pura Vida still takes the cannoli for quality and service. For lunch, the grilled veggie focaccia sandwich is humongous and terrific, while the black fettuccine with shrimp is a delectable departure from the typical spaghetti and meatballs dinner (though they have that too). It's on the turnoff to Mariposa Lodge.

Argentinean Grill (445-4264; Posada Arco Iris; L$95-280; 10am-10pm Thu-Tue) The hottest restaurant in town, this is the place to splurge if your lemps are burning a hole in your wallet. As the name suggests, steaks are the specialty – the filet mignon is spectacular – but if red meat isn't your thing, the seafood and chicken dishes are just as good. We aren't too stoked that all the waitstaff are foreigners, on an island with a high unemployment rate.

our pick **Mavis and Dixie's** (445-4013; mains L$132-340; breakfast, lunch & dinner) This beachfront restaurant delivers, with delicious seafood dishes – from coconut-stung wahoo to blackened mahi-mahi – and some of the friendliest service on the island. Its location, on the spit leading out from Half Moon Bay, offers a welcome respite from the traffic of Main Street.

Tong's Thai (mains L$150-300; lunch & dinner, closed for lunch Mon & Thu) You really can't beat the ambiance – right over the water with ceiling fans warping overhead, pine everywhere and views of the Caribbean night on all sides – and the Thai cuisine isn't bad either. But the service moved at a snail's pace when we visited, so be sure you have the next couple of hours free before you commit.

The Lobster Pot (916-7165; mains L$160-240; breakfast, lunch & dinner) Right on the beach, this mellow restaurant serves fine Caribbean cooking. It's not cheap (or fancy for that matter) but it's worth the splurge. The dessert choice is killer – key lime pie, yucca cake or coconut brownies (L$60).

Dian's Garden of Eat'n (368-1098; road btwn West End & West Bay; mains L$160-400; erratic opening hr) While it's often closed, Dian's Thai-Caribbean fusion cuisine is reputed to be some of the best on the island. The restaurant is a three-minute drive or taxi ride from the West End turnoff toward West Bay.

Lighthouse Restaurant (445-1209; mains L$250-400; breakfast, lunch & dinner) Everyone loves an inside tip, and Lighthouse Restaurant is that easy-to-miss 'secret spot' that hoteliers like to recommend to their guests. It's pricy, but has great views and a landed-elite British Caribbean feel. The coconut prawns and Thai-style seafood bowl are reliable, and the daily specials usually have some intriguing items. The setting is the real highlight: it's hidden from the main road and (amazingly enough) is one of only a couple of restaurants with seating right on the water. Service is a bit hit and miss. It's near Mavis and Dixie's.

Drinking

Eagle Ray's (445 4283; 11am-late) This bar-restaurant built on stilts over the water is a good spot for sunset drinks. It's on the pier across from Twisted Toucan.

Foster's Waterfront Bar & Grill (11am-midnight Sun-Thu, to 2am Fri & Sat) One of two bars-on-a-pier jutting out over the water, Foster's has occasional live music and the best dancing in town. It's a bit 'gangster,' as one local put it, but you can't beat the location.

Jammin Bar (4pm-midnight) This positive vibes bar kicks out roots reggae at painful decibel levels.

Le Bistro (11am-midnight) The food here is tremendously bad, but it has karaoke on Thursday and Sunday night – a must see.

Nova (10pm-late) This hoppening joint gets going late.

Oceano Cantina (7:30am-10pm) A realtor-turned-restaurateur from California opened this *palapa*-roofed cantina in early 2009. It was wildly popular when we passed through. There are good tacos and plenty of hammocks.

Purple Turtle (7am-10pm Sun, to midnight Mon-Thu, to 2am Fri & Sat) They play a lot of metal at this open-air bar.

Sundowners (to 10pm) This is a small, Jimmy Buffet kind of bar right on the beach at Half Moon Bay. The view makes it a popular place to start the night, before migrating downstream. Happy hour is from 5pm to 7pm. It's across from Native Sons.

Twisted Toucan (7am-10pm Sun, to midnight Mon-Thu, to 2am Fri & Sat) Somewhat eclipsed by upstart

Purple Turtle, this longtime West End bar still knows how to throw a party. It's across from Eagle Ray's.

Entertainment

Movies are a popular diversion in West End, especially on nights when you're wiped from multiple dives and you're not up for another all-nighter at the Purple Turtle. **Brick Oven Pizza** (mains L$160-300; dinner, closed Tue) shows recent-release movies almost every night, usually at 5pm and 7pm. Schedules are on those white flyers plastered all over town. The pizza here is decent, but overpriced. It's past Twisted Toucan.

Blue Channel (☎ 445-4133; mains L$180-280; breakfast, lunch & dinner) serves up a decent pizza pie, and has live music on weekends. It's across from Ocean Connections.

Shopping

Ivis Gift Shop (Half Moon Bay; 7am-6pm) The very friendly proprietor here has packed her small wood-shack shop with Honduran, Salvadoran and Guatemalan *artesanía* (handicrafts), plus T-shirts and other knick-knacks – some are good, some not so good, but it's worth a browse if you're in the market for souvenirs.

Getting There & Around

The best way to get to West End from the airport or ferry terminal is by taxi (*colectivo* L$50 to L$65, direct L$190 to L$285). You can also take *colectivos* (L$35) or buses (L$20) from here to Coxen Hole. To get to West Bay, take a water taxi (L$50). For the most part, you'll need a rental car or scooter to visit the rest of the island. See p203 for the low-down on costs.

WEST BAY

Most people call this the best resort destination in Honduras. And, they are probably right. The sands are pitch perfect, it's well-manicured, and there's excellent swimming and snorkeling along the entire length (head to the west end for the best snorkeling). There are less budget hotels here, and most people end up eating and partying over in West End, but if a beach vacation is what the doctor ordered, then this is your spot.

Activities

Dive courses cost more here than they do at West End (L$6175 for an Open Water course). Fun dives cost L$760 for one dive, and you can save some lemps by booking multi-dive packages. Whereas shops in West End are pretty firm in their prices, those in West Bay seem more willing to extend discounts, especially on fun-dive packages.

Bananarama Diving Center (☎ 445-5005; www.bananaramadive.com), West Bay's first dive shop, is also the largest and busiest. It offers a number of good lodging-diving packages, but you may have to contend with large groups.

Las Rocas (☎ 408-5760; www.lasrocasresort.com) is a small professional shop, befitting the more intimate setting of the hotel it's a part of. It's at the north end of the bay.

Gumbalimba Park (www.gumbalimbapark.com; 9am-4pm), a family recreation park, has something for everyone: beach, kayaking, canopy tour, snorkeling, SNUBA, nature path, botanical garden, monkey and bird enclosures, and, of course, restaurants and gift shops. Aimed squarely at cruise-shippers, it can still be a fun outing for independent travelers with kids. The park is only open to the general public on days when there are no cruise ships on the island. Even more strange, the park does not have set individual admission prices – they negotiate package deals with cruise ship companies – so be sure to call the day you plan to go to see what the fee is. It's a 10-minute walk north on the beach from West Bay.

You can rent **jet skis** from the tourist information kiosk in front of Bananarama (L$1140 for 40 minutes).

Festivals & Events

The **Bay Islands International Triathlon** (www.bayislandstriathlon.com) is an Olympic- and sprint-distance event that takes place every March. An International Triathlon Union (ITU)–rated race, it is considered a challenging course primarily because of the steep cycling section that includes 16%, 18% and 20% grades. The race starts and finishes on West Bay beach and makes several loops, and extends as far east as Anthony's Key Resort. A beach party is typically hosted at the close of the race.

Sleeping

West Bay has a reputation for being Roatán's 'resort capital,' but in fact there are as many non-traditional options as traditional ones. Prices aren't cheap, of course, but it is possible to get a nice little place on Honduras'

DON'T TOUCH THE CORAL

Coral comes in many shapes, sizes and colors, especially in the Bay Islands. Some coral, such as fan coral, resembles a plant. Other coral, such as brain coral, looks more like a rock. But coral is neither a plant nor a rock, it's an animal.

'Don't touch the coral' is a refrain you will often hear in the Bay Islands, where thousands of divers and snorkelers come every year to explore the magnificent reefs just a few yards offshore.

Coral is fascinating and beautiful, and many divers – beginner and experienced – are tempted to touch it. Even if you resist that temptation, it's easy to accidentally brush the coral with your fin or tank, either as you swim past or if you are still learning to maintain neutral buoyancy.

Avoiding such contact is extremely important. Give yourself a wide berth, and snorkelers should remember to avoid the reef crest, instead swimming on the edges of the reef. Coral has an invisible covering of slime that protects it, much like skin on other animals. Touching the coral can damage this protective covering, exposing it to infection and disease. Large segments of coral can be killed by a single brush of a diver's fin.

If you hit it hard enough, you can even break it; some places are littered with coral fragments, broken by divers or heavy surf. Under ideal conditions, most coral grows about 1cm (less than half an inch) per year; even the fastest growing sponges grow only an inch per year. The coral and sponge formations you see in the Bay Islands are the result of centuries of growth.

Another good reason not to touch the coral is that it will sting you. Fire coral is the most famous for this – you'll feel like you're on fire if you touch it. Even coral that doesn't sting can be surprisingly sharp or prickly, and cuts from it are notoriously slow to heal. (If you are stung by coral, vinegar will help stop the stinging and anti-bacterial cream will help it heal; no such luck for the coral, though.)

Historically, the reefs around the Bay Islands have been healthy and pristine, thanks to the low number of divers and inhabitants on the islands. But both of those numbers have increased dramatically in recent years, and the coral is beginning to show signs of damage. So much so that in 1998, the Honduran government invited the nonprofit Coral Cay Conservation to study the reef and propose solutions to sustaining it, and initiatives have now been adopted by island communities and businesses to secure the reef's health. So far, the effort is slowly working. It remains crucial – especially with even more divers expected (not to mention legions of snorkeler-toting cruise shippers) – for everyone to help preserve the coral reef.

best beach without paying the premium that brand-name places charge (or suffering the cookie-cutter treatment). Looking for an all-inclusive? Check out the numerous resorts run by Henry Morgans (www.hmresorts.com).

Bananarama Resort & Diving Center (☎ 445-5005; www.bananaramadive.com; cabins L$1770-1995, villas L$4450-4860; P) The atmosphere is best described as 'frenetic' – dive instructors, guests and students all colliding in a beehive of movement. But the simple cabins are a decent value. The only problem: you're not on the beach, and it can be far from relaxing.

Las Rocas (☎ 408-5760; www.lasrocasresort.com; r incl breakfast L$1770-2700; P) With just 13 units, Las Rocas is the sort of place where guests really get to know each other: over breakfast, on the dive boat, at the bar. Bungalows are simply but comfortably appointed, with polished wood floors, air-con and firm beds (too firm in some cases); superior rooms have peaked ceilings, king-size beds and (in some cases) awesome ocean views. True to its name, Las Rocas is built on a rocky outcrop and doesn't have a beach of its own. West Bay beach is a short walk away, and the hotel has a teeny-tiny salt-water pool and a waterfront wooden deck for sunbathing, but hardcore beach-hounds may be disappointed. It's at the north end of the bay.

Infinity Bay Spa & Beach Resort (☎ 445-5016; www.infinitybay.com; studio L$3550, apt L$5500-10,250; P) We love the green technology they've put into this brand-spanking-new resort and timeshare complex at the end of West Bay. There's a monster infinity pool that's kept clean without chlorine, and a green septic system (you can even drink the water out of the tap). We also love the high-ceilinged studios and apartments. Choose from a cozy suite (it still has granite countertops and a full kitchen) or a three-bedroom luxury apartment. A spa and health club are in the works.

Casa de Paradise (☎ 9961-5311; www.casadeparadise.com; units per week L$11,400-38,000;) About half a block from the beach, the Casa de Paradise has five fully furnished apartments, complete with kitchens and living rooms. Units range from a studio to a four-bedroom apartment. It's good for larger groups. There's a three-night minimum and you'll need to book ahead.

West Bay Village (☎ 403-8022; www.westbayvillage.com; weekly rentals L$11,875-38,000; P) This set of five luxury homes is right on West Bay beach. Each house has a different owner, which accounts for the vastly different styles. All, however, are modern and come fully equipped with all the amenities you'd expect: cable TV, DVD player, stereo, hot water and air-con. Check out the website to choose from one- to three-bedroom homes. It's a great deal, especially if you're traveling in a group.

Eating

Out of the Blue Mini Mart (8.30am-7pm) This small, expensive bodega at the north end of the beach is good for water, soda, and snacks, and has a limited selection of canned foods.

Las Rocas (☎ 408-5760; north end of bay; mains L$100-240; breakfast, lunch & dinner) This establishment has a fine restaurant, open to guests and non-guests alike, just a few steps from Bite on the Beach. Seafood is the specialty – surprise, surprise – and comes in various incarnations: fish fillet, grilled shrimp sandwiches, shrimp and gorgonzola, seafood linguini, even seafood pizza (which is terrific, by the way).

Bite on the Beach (mains L$180-280; lunch & dinner Tue-Sat) Perched on a rocky outcrop at the north end of the beach, this was West Bay's second establishment, and the first restaurant, when it opened in 1996. (How times have changed!) The friendly American owners, who took over in 2001, serve an eclectic menu, from hamburgers and blue-cheese-and-sundried-tomato chicken to Thai curry and conch soup. Its large garden salads are made with vegetables from Roatán's hydroponics garden, and the key lime pie is divine. The view isn't too shabby either – from the restaurant's raised two-level eating area, the bay and ocean spread out below you, both endlessly blue.

Drinking & Entertainment

Most folks head over to West End for nighttime ribaldry. At West Bay, Bite on the Beach (left) stays open relatively late for drinking, with a happy hour between 4pm and sunset. The bar at Las Rocas (left) can also be lively. It's easy to stagger between the two.

Getting There & Away

A regular taxi from West End to West Bay costs an outrageous L$200 (sometimes more) each way. Unless you're in a large group, a better option is a water taxi, which charges L$50 per person. In West Bay, you can flag down a driver at any of the piers or right from shore, if you don't mind sloshing through the shallows. The last boat in either direction is around 6pm. You can also walk along the beach between West End and West Bay. It takes about 45 minutes, but isn't recommended at night (see p201).

SANDY BAY

Heading from West Bay, about 4km before you reach West End is Sandy Bay, a quiet bend of seashore with several homes and a handful of hotels tucked away in the trees.

Sights & Activities

Across the road from Anthony's Key Resort, the **Carambola Botanical Gardens** (☎ 445-3117; carambolabg@yahoo.com; admission L$152; 7am-5pm Mon-Sat) has well-maintained trails through 40 acres of protected forest, extending up a hillside known as Carambola Mountain. It's about 1km to the 'summit,' where you can see all the way to Utila on a clear day and, at the right time, down into the dolphin show at Anthony's Key Resort. Along the trail you'll encounter dozens of species of native plants, including orchids, spice plants, medicinal plants and fruit trees. You'll also pass Iguana Wall, a cliff favored by iguanas and parrots, as well as remnants of pre-Colombian settlements. Reservations are required for guided tours.

Anthony's Key Resort (p216) has a resident population of some 20 bottlenose dolphins, and offers a number of programs for both guests and non-guests. It's worth checking out the **dolphin show** (admission free) held daily at 10am and 4pm. For more interaction, you can sign up for one of several 'dolphin discovery' programs; from the **Dolphin Beach Encounter** (L$1310) where you wade and interact with a single dolphin in waist-deep water to a **Dolphin Snorkel** (L$2185) or **Dolphin Dive** (L$2915), which include interacting with a group of dolphins in the open water. Dolphin programs like these definitely vary in their quality (especially for the dolphins), but Anthony's Key does a good job of treating its dolphins humanely and as something more than just show animals.

Anthony's also houses the **Roatán Museum** (admission L$40; 8am-5pm), a smallish historical center with displays spanning island history from prehistoric times to Maya occupation to Columbus' arrival and the beginning of the colonial period. There's surprisingly little on Garífuna history though, in which Roatán played an important role (see boxed text, p197). Overall, however, the artifacts and displays (in Spanish and English) are quite good. A visit takes about 30 to 45 minutes.

Sandy Bay has excellent **windsurfing** conditions, including warm water, a broad obstacle-free bay and strong steady wind. Advanced sailboarders may wish there was a bigger swell, but the flat shallow water is ideal for those just learning the sport. **Wind & Fun Windsurf School** (☎ 445-3292; www.windsurfroatan.blogspot.com; 10am-5pm Tue-Sun) offers private lessons for L$800 per session (1½ to two hours, including equipment); equipment rental only is L$400 per hour. It's west of Blue Bahía Resort.

Island's Gym (☎ 445-3123; 10am-8pm Tue-Sun) is a top-notch gym located next door to Rick's American Café.

Massage and personalized treatments of various kinds are available at **Spa at Baan Suerte** (☎ 445-3059; www.spabaansuerte.com; treatments L$2000-3000; 9am-9pm). Go for a tropical body smoothie (yummy!). Appointments required.

Sleeping & Eating

Anthony's Key Resort (☎ 445-3003; www.anthonyskey.com; all-inclusive dive package with fan/air-con per person L$3880/L$4560; P) Anthony's Key Resort is one of the best dive resorts on Roatán. But it also offers plenty of options for non-divers, including kayaking, snorkeling and the island's only dolphin encounter programs. However, there's no beach. Accommodations are in individual bungalows that, while not exactly luxurious, are quite comfy, all with a sundeck; the best ones have king-size beds, air-con and ocean views.

Mayoka Lodge (☎ 445-3043; www.mayokalodge.com; 6-12 person per week L$427,500; P) No, that isn't a typo: for a couple of grand each, you and the other jurors can deliberate in style at this stunning six-bedroom, 1980-sq-meter beachfront home, surely one of the most beautiful houses (and most luxurious accommodations) in the whole country. Overlooking Sandy Bay, the home features a wine cellar, cigar humidor, infinity pool, flat-screen TVs, multilingual book and DVD library, pool and poker tables, tennis courts, kayaks, sea scooters, wireless internet, maid, chef and chauffeur service...the list goes on and on. Rates include meals and most drinks, but not taxes.

Rick's American Café (☎ 445-3123; www.ricksamerican.com; mains L$220-500; dinner Tue-Sun) This is a pricey restaurant with a fine view, superb meats and big salads. The specialty is the baby back ribs, though the lamb is a favorite among regulars. During the NFL season, this is the place for Sunday brunch. It's located west of Anthony's Key Resort.

Getting There & Away

Anthony's Key marks the eastern end of Sandy Bay, while a small dirt road with a sign for the windsurfing school marks the western end. Taxis and buses pass right by and drop you at either end.

COXEN HOLE

There's really no reason to come to Coxen Hole, expect maybe as a quick stop before a day of exploring the rest of the island. Sure, it's the largest town on Roatán; there are banks, a cruise-ship dock with plenty of T-shirt shops nearby, a post office and grocery stores – and you're close to the ferry terminal and airport – but it's a fairly ugly little town. It's right on the sea, but alas there's no beach. Avoid walking around Coxen Hole at night, as discos and bars can get rowdy.

Orientation

The commercial section of Coxen Hole is only a few short blocks. The HB Warren supermarket, with the tiny city park beside it, is at the center of town; just about everything of interest is situated nearby or on the road leading into town. Buses and taxis arrive in front of the city park. The main road through Coxen Hole is one-way; if you are driving a rented car, be careful as there are no signs alerting you to this fact.

Information

Coxen Hole's banks are located on Front St. They have ATMs, and will exchange traveler's checks

Banco Atlántida (9am-4pm Mon-Fri, 8:30-11:30am Sat)

LOCAL LORE: DUPPIES IN THE BUSH

Ghosts, or *duppies* as they're known on the Bay Islands, are alive and well here. They are said to live in the forests and mangroves, stuck on earth because of unfinished business. With a history so rich with pirates – the Bay Islands, after all, were a refuge for those famous for looting Spanish galleons – it is no wonder that the *duppies* who walk these shores are said to be guarding hidden treasure. It's only when they tire of protecting their stash and are ready to move to a higher plane that they reveal where their treasure is, typically by visiting a descendant in a dream. Father Red Cape, a *duppy* well-known in West End, used to be spotted often, but locals say it's been a while since he's appeared. Some speculate that the development on Roatán has run him deeper into the bush. Others think that perhaps Father Red Cape just spilled the beans.

Burgo Store/Farmacia (☎ 445-1480; 🕑 8am-6pm Mon-Fri, to 5pm Sat) Near city hall.
Casi Todo Bookstore (☎ 445-1944; averyl@globalnet.hn; 🕑 9am-4pm Mon-Fri) New and used English-language books to buy or trade. Located at the west entrance to town.
Hondutel (☎ 445-1329; 🕑 7am-8:30pm) On the same passageway as Martínez Cyber Center.
Martínez Cyber Center (☎ 445-0396; 🕑 8am-10pm Mon-Sat) Internet & international calls for L$1 per min. It is located down a narrow passage across from the plaza.
Migración (☎ 445-1326; Parque Central; 🕑 9am-noon & 1:30-4pm Mon-Fri)
Paradise Tours (☎ 445-1747; 🕑 8:30am-3:30pm Mon-Fri, to noon Sat) Handles domestic and international plane tickets. Second-floor office west of HB Warren.
Police (☎ 445-3438; Parque Central; 🕑 24hr)
Post office (🕑 8am-noon & 2-4pm Mon-Fri) East of HB Warren.
Wood Medical Center (☎ 445-1080; 🕑 24hr) Largest private clinic with an emergency room, pharmacy, on-site laboratory, and English- and Spanish-speaking staff. It's near old ferry pier.

Sleeping & Eating

Hotel Cay View (☎ 445-1202; s/d L$580/730; ❄) Unless you really hate West End (or love Coxen Hole) it's hard to imagine a good reason why anyone would stay here. It's not that the rooms are awful – they're small and worn, but have hot-water bathrooms, air con and cable TV – but for the same price (a short bus or cab ride away) you can stay in a better place in a better location. The hotel restaurant (mains L$80 to L$160, open for lunch and dinner, Monday to Saturday) has a nice patio out the back overlooking the water, and serves typical Honduran fare, plus a few specials such as garlic or coconut-milk shrimp. It's near the ferry pier.

Comedor Jaylin (Front St; mains L$70-90; 🕑 6am-7pm) Locally recommended, this little hole in the wall is cheap and clean, with good local fare. Go for a *baleada* for just L$10. It's adjacent to the Wood Medical Center.

HB Warren (☎ 445-1208; 🕑 7am-7pm Mon-Sat) The largest supermarket on this end of the island, this is a good place to stock up on groceries. It also has a popular cafeteria (mains L$20 to L$60) with counter seating, low prices and possibly the best fried chicken on the island.

Shopping

Yaba Ding Ding (🕑 9am-5pm Mon-Sat) Located on the ground floor of a two-story commercial center next to HB Warren, this friendly shop has a surprisingly complete selection of Honduran *artesanía*, including Lenca pottery, Garífuna paintings, glasswork from Tegucigalpa, junco baskets from Santa Barbara, even some *talavera* dishes and clay masks from El Salvador for good measure. Also on display – but not for sale – are several pieces of *yaba ding ding*, an island term for pre-Colombian artifacts.

Getting There & Away

Taxis and minibuses arrive in front of the Plaza. Hop on a bus (L$20) back to West End from the mercado municipal (just a few blocks inland from Front St) or take a *colectivo* (L$35).

FRENCH HARBOUR

It's fun passing through French Harbour on a day trip, but there's really no reason to stay here. The second-largest town on Roatán, it's an important port and is home to a large fishing, shrimp and lobster fleet,

Information

Banco Atlántida (☎ 455-7484; 🕑 9am-4pm Mon-Fri, 8:30-11:30am Sat) Has an ATM and exchanges traveler's checks. It's on main hwy, 100m before turnoff to French Harbour center.

Martínez Cyber Center (☎ 455-5228; per hr L$40; 8am-10pm Mon-Sat) National and international phone calls offered too.
Police (☎ 455-5099; 24hr) Located at the entrance to town, 250m past Eldon's supermarket.

Sights & Activities

The area's main attraction is the impressive **Arch's Iguana Farm** (☎ 445-7743; admission L$160; 8am-3:30pm) in French Cay, just outside of town. Less a farm than the house of a serious iguana-phile, everywhere you look you see iguanas – on the driveway, in the trees, under bushes, everywhere. In all, around 3000 iguanas live here, some as long as 1.5m. Midday is feeding time, and the best time to visit. There's also an enclosed pool with a school of huge fish, several small sea turtles and dozens of conches. It's a worthwhile stop.

Sleeping & Eating

Roatán's Yacht Club (☎ 455-5233; r with fan L$1400, with air-con L$1800-2000; P) This is a comfortable hotel with a pool and restaurant that's simply overpriced. Accommodations are modern and clean with nice views of the harbor, but on this island, a couple of thousand lemps ought to give you some bang; this place is more like a sparkler. Worth it, perhaps, if you've arrived by yacht – there is a private marina where you can park your boat.

Gío's Restaurant (☎ 455-5214; Calle Principal; mains L$120-400; lunch & dinner Mon-Sat) Long considered one of the best restaurants on the island, Gío's specializes in seafood – especially crab and lobster, for which they issue bibs – but serves up a pretty mean *churrasco* (Argentinean-style beef) and filet mignon. All dishes come with salad and garlic bread, and are served in the air-cooled dining room or on a patio overlooking the harbor.

Casa Romeo's Hotel and Restaurant (☎ 455-5518; www.casaromeos.com; mains L$150-400; lunch & dinner Mon-Sat) A fine Italian restaurant right on the harbor's edge, Casa Romeo's offers excellent, though pricey, meals. Seafood is the focus – the conch chowder and Caribbean king crab are superb. A wine list featuring Italian, French, Chilean and Californian wines rounds out the menu nicely. The hotel rooms are best avoided.

Eldon's (☎ 455-7484; 7am-7pm Mon-Fri, to 8pm Sat, 8am-1pm Sun) The island's largest supermarket is on the access road to French Harbour, just off the main cross-island highway. Dollars, traveler's checks and credit cards (no commission) are all accepted.

Getting There & Away

Bus 1 (L$20, 20 minutes) runs once or twice an hour between Coxen Hole and French Harbour from 6am to 5:30pm daily. *Colectivo* taxis to Coxen Hole cost L$30 to L$35, while a private one costs around L$150.

AROUND FRENCH HARBOUR

Brick Bay

This sheltered bay on Roatán's south side has a large, secure marina frequented by long-range sailors and yachters. Those folks seem to leave their boats only rarely, and the community's one hotel, **Hotel Brick Bay** (☎ 445-1127; Brick Bay Rd; r with air-con L$1000; P), is a dark, lonely place, made even creepier for almost always having no clients. All in all, it's hard to imagine the average traveler having much interest or reason to come here.

Palmetto Bay

There aren't many places left on Roatán where you have a whole beach to yourself, and even fewer that don't assault the shoreline with their gaudy buildings, giant pools and matching lounge chairs. **Palmetto Bay Plantation** (☎ 9991-0811; www.palmettobayplantation.com; r L$1990-5130, all-inclusive package per person extra L$1045) is one of those select few, an understated luxury resort hidden several kilometers down a dirt road, sharing a beautiful stretch of beach with hundreds of palm trees and not much else. The resort has 31 bungalows (with two to three bedrooms, one to two bathrooms), all with gorgeous hardwood floors, high-peaked ceilings, and spacious kitchens with gas ranges and full-size stainless steel refrigerators. An infinity pool, free kayaks, wireless internet, and airport pickup and drop-off are all included in the rates (which vary by season, number of guests, and category of lodging). The resort's bar and restaurant (mains L$140 to L$400, open for lunch and dinner) is popular with guests and non-guests alike, with live music Friday and Saturday night. Reservations are recommended.

Subway Watersports (☎ 3387-0579, 445-5707; www.subwaywatersports.com) operates out of the resort, but is open to the public. Open Water dive courses cost L$7220, while fun dives are L$665. The resort can also arrange **sunset horseback rides** (per person L$665), which last from 1½ to 2½ hours (advance reservations required), or if you're feeling brave, try the 1½-hour **canopy tour** (per person L$665), located near the main road.

Santé Wellness Center

A great way to pamper yourself is at the **Santé Wellness Center** (☎ 408-5156, 9991-0474; www.santewellnesscenter.com; Parrot Tree Plantation; 9am-4pm, or by appointment), a day spa located on a tiny, private island about 5km east of French Harbour. Treatments cost anywhere from L$600 to L$1900. If you find it hard to leave, you don't have to – there is a high-end bed and breakfast (room L$2375) here as well. Base prices include breakfast, but all-inclusive packages including meals, spa treatments and diving are also available.

EASTERN ROATÁN

Eastern Roatán has almost none of the rapid, large-scale development that has consumed the other side of the island. Here, paved roads turn to dirt and construction sites and crowds of suntanned foreigners give way to grassy bluffs and solitary fishermen plying rough coastal waters. It is a much poorer area, too, visible in the shanty houses of towns like Oak Ridge and Punta Gorda. A drive out to eastern Roatán is, in many ways, a drive into its past, when island residents lived isolated island lives, before the arrival of planes, resorts and foreigners. This is also a great spot to escape that famed Gringo Trail. Stay the night in Punta Gorda to see what authentic experiences turn up.

Oak Ridge

This tiny town hugs a protected harbor surrounded by colorful wooden stilt houses. And while it's not especially worth the trip, most folks at least stop for an hour or two. More homes and shops are on a small cay a two-minute motorboat ride from shore. It's officially called José Santos Guardiola, but almost no one calls it by its Spanish name.

SIGHTS & ACTIVITIES

Water taxis at the Oak Ridge dock take visitors on a pleasant tour through mangrove canals to **Jonesville**, a small town on a nearby bight. A 45- to 60-minute boat tour costs L$500 for up to eight people. You can stop and eat at the famous **Hole in the Wall** restaurant, which has a way-over-priced, all-you-can-eat shrimp feast on Friday and Sunday (Sunday only during low season) for L$475; if you do stop, be sure to give your boat driver an extra large tip for waiting.

Dive sites here receive a fraction of the traffic of those around West End, making them that much more pristine.

SLEEPING & EATING

Reef House Resort (☎ 445-2297; www.reefhouseresort.com; 7-night all-inclusive dive package s/d per person L$19,855/17,000) One of the oldest dive resorts on Roatán, this comfortable hotel, restaurant and diving center features large rooms with two queen-size beds, private bathroom, air-con and cable TV. Most guests come on seven-night packages, which include a room, meals, three dives a day, unlimited shore diving, a night dive and transport to or from the airport. Snorkel and room-and-board only packages are also available.

GETTING THERE & AROUND

Oak Ridge is 25km east of Coxen Hole. Buses leave from Coxen Hole for Oak Ridge every half-hour from 6am to 5:30pm (L$40, one hour). *Colectivo* taxis are rare; rates for a private cab must be negotiated – L$400 is a good target.

Water taxis take passengers around the harbor and across to the cay for about $40; they dock in front of the bus stop.

Punta Gorda

History and culture buffs will love this lost little town – the first Garífuna village ever – where a band of more than 2200 Black Caribs settled after they were dumped in 1797 by British colonizers fearful of a slave uprising. Unfortunately, the town's historic significance has not preserved it from the degradation and decay so many Garífuna communities have suffered; it is run down, with few job prospects, an inadequate social service network, and a lot of litter (consider it beachside art) on the beach.

SIGHTS & ACTIVITIES

The **Punta Gorda Festival** is the main reason for travelers to visit. The festival, which typically runs from April 8 to 12, includes a re-enactment of the arrival of the first Caribs on Roatán, the crowning of a Garífuna queen, and lots of Garífuna music and dancing.

WANARAGUA – THE MASKED WARRIOR DANCE

The story goes like this: Barauda, the wife of Satuye, an important Black Carib chieftain on the island of St Vincent, was berating her husband for his army's inability to rid the island of British invaders once and for all. Working up a head of steam, she declared that the women may as well do the fighting while the men, who evidently lacked the *cajones* to get the job done, could dress in their wives' clothing and hide. (Ouch!) But this gave Satuye an idea. The next time the British invaded, they found the Carib men gone. When they let down their guard, the men, disguised as women, fell upon the unsuspecting Redcoats, defeating them soundly.

The *wanaragua* dance recounts the tale of the cross-dressing army, and is one of the most beloved and memorable of Garífuna dances. The dance is performed by men only, and is notable for its extremely elaborate costumes – a long woman's dress decorated with ribbons, a headdress made of feathers and mirrors, and a mask made of painted metallic mesh set on an oval frame. The dancers wear shell rattles on their legs, and are accompanied by a drummer.

The dance is performed rather half-heartedly for visiting cruise-shippers at Yübu – The Garífuna Experience (below), hardly doing it justice. To see the real thing, visit the Garífuna village of Punta Gorda or a Garífuna town on the mainland.

It's also fun just passing through Punta Gordon for the day, checking out the honey-sand beach and maybe even joining the pick-up soccer game.

Outside of Punta Gorda is a new attraction that is either an economic boon for the town, or a gross reduction and repackaging of Garífuna culture for material gain. Maybe both. **Yübu – The Garífuna Experience** (☎ 455-6713; admission L$100; ⏰ 10am-3pm Tue-Fri) is an utterly artificial cultural center that was built as a tourist trap for cruise-shippers, and which seems to be working its magic perfectly well. The experience begins with a 30- to 35-minute historical talk about the Garífuna's beginnings and their brutal passage to Roatán. After that, a dance demonstration ought to be uplifting, but the dancers are obviously not having much fun. You can also shop in the gift shop, learn to make *casabe* (a traditional yucca flatbread) or eat Garífuna specialties at the small comedor, but the food, like the overall experience, is pretty bland.

SLEEPING

North Side Garden Hotel (☎ 435-1848; d L$300) One of the keys to sustainable tourism is to leave the 'tourist trail' behind. And there's no place better than in Punta Gorda. By staying in this cheap – and relatively clean – spot just across from the beach, you are bringing much needed cash into the community, all the while broadening your horizons in a village far removed from the hustle and flow of West End.

GETTING THERE & AWAY

Buses do not go beyond Oak Ridge. Most travelers interested in exploring the far east rent a car or hire a taxi for the day.

Paya Bay & Camp Bay

Eight kilometers beyond Oak Ridge, Paya Bay and Camp Bay see very few visitors, local or foreign, despite their dramatic cliff lines and rustic golden sand beaches. Both are reachable by car or taxi, even by bike or foot if you're up for it. The lack of visitors makes the one hotel there – the **Paya Bay Beach Resort** (☎ 3361-1732, in US 866-323-5414; www.payabay.com; r with 3 meals L$2850; P ❄) – all the more attractive. The clifftop rooms offer tremendous views, cozy amenities and a level of privacy befitting even the sexiest of honeymoon couples. Guests have access to a private, clothes-optional beach on the west side of the hotel, but anyone can eat at the restaurant and make use of Paya Beach proper. The big drawback here is there are no restaurants or shops for miles (or is that an asset?). Diving packages are also offered.

EXPLORING THE EAST-END ISLANDS

Paya Bay Beach Resort (above) offers day-long tours to Roatán's eastern islands, with their beautiful deserted beaches and clear, snorkel-friendly waters. Excursions typically include Pigeon Cayes and Barbareta Island and cost approximately L$4000 for one to four people.

Camp Bay is further east, and has calmer water and an even more isolated feel. It's reachable by car, though for an adventure you can borrow a kayak from the beach resort (guests free, non-guests L$100) and paddle there.

UTILA

pop 2800

Smaller and less developed than its big brother to the east, Utila moves at a slower pace and appeals to a younger, backpacker crowd. The streets are still paved with sand, and you can still get your Open Water certificate for less than almost anywhere else in the world. Top that off with a cooler-than-Coolio traveler scene (honestly, sometimes it's too cool for us), great diving, crystalline waters and snorkeling at your doorstep, remote cays just a kayak away, and a laid-back Caribbean chill, and you might just have found your perfect sliver of paradise. The beaches, unfortunately, leave a bit to be desired.

EAST HARBOUR (UTILA TOWN)

Utila's only town is officially called East Harbour, though most people use 'Utila' to refer to both the town and the island. Virtually everything a traveler needs – hotels, restaurants, dive shops, bars crowded with tanned and tempting fellow journeyers, banks, medical service and the ferry pier – are located here. It's also where most of the island's residents live, though their homes are found more on the outskirts rather than in the tourist-oriented center.

Orientation

The public jetty, where the ferries arrive and depart, is at the intersection of the town's two main roads. Facing away from the pier, you can turn right (east) or left (west) on the main road, or go straight onto Cola de Mico Rd (north). If you turn left on the main road, you'll run into a third road, Mamey Lane, which runs north from the fire station. It's nearly impossible to get lost.

Information

BOOKSTORES

Bundu Café (east main st; ⌚ 8am-9pm) Decent selection of books for sale or exchange, including a range of pre-loved Lonely Planet titles.

EMERGENCY

Police (☎ 425-3145; Mamey Lane; ⌚ 24hr) Facing the soccer field.

IMMIGRATION

Migración (☎ 425-3365; main st; ⌚ 9am-noon & 2-5pm Mon-Fri) Extend visas here. Located on 1st floor of the Palacio Municipal building next to the public jetty.

INTERNET ACCESS

Utila has numerous internet centers, and some dive shops also offer internet access to

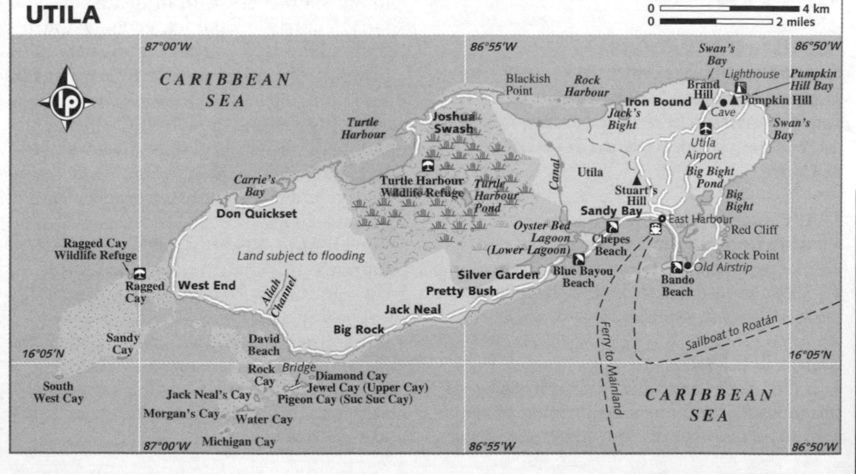

their students. Many hotels now have wi-fi. Internet access costs around L$40 per hour. Most internet cafe's offer international calling (L$3 per minute).

LAUNDRY

There are a number of private homes that will wash clothes. A load should cost around L$70. Look for handwritten signs along the main street, especially in the vicinity of the Central American Spanish School.

MEDICAL SERVICES

Hyperbaric Chamber (☎ 425-3378; west main st) By the Utila Lodge.

Medi-Servicios de la Fe (☎ 9819-4509; west main st; 🕒 24hrs) Just east of Bandu Café.

Utila Community Clinic (☎ 425-3137; west main st; 🕒 10am-3:30pm Mon-Fri) Run by Dr John McVay, an eccentric but well-regarded American doctor. There's also a pharmacy on site.

MONEY

Most dive shops and many hotels accept lempira, US dollars, traveler's checks and credit cards (usually with a service fee).

Banco Atlántida (east main st; ☎ 9am-4pm Mon-Fri, 8:30-11:30am Sat) Has an ATM.

HSBC (main st, facing pier; 🕒 8am-3:30pm Mon-Fri, 8:30-11:30am Sat) Changes traveler's checks and gives cash advances on Visa cards.

Unibanc ATM (east main st) Takes European cards. It's next to Café Mariposa.

POST

Post Office (🕒 9am-4pm Mon-Fri, 9am-noon Sat) Located just off the ferry dock.

TOURIST INFORMATION

Captain Morgan's Dive Centre (☎ 425-3349; www.divingutila.com; main st) Across from the pier, Captain Morgan's offers straightforward info and advice, and you can even leave your backpack there while you look for a hotel.

TRAVEL AGENCIES

Morgan's Travel (☎ 425-3161; utilamorganstravel@yahoo.com; at pier opposite ferry office; 🕒 8am-noon & 2-5:30pm Mon-Sat) Arranges plane tickets off the island and taxis to and from the airport.

Sights & Activities

Utila doesn't have much in the way of beaches, so someone finally took matters into their own hands and made one. **Bando Beach** (☎ 425-3190; east main st; admission L$60; 🕒 9am-5pm), at the old airport, doesn't have the deep, soft shoreline of a natural beach, but it's pleasant enough, with beach chairs wrapping around a small point nicely shaded by low tangled trees. The main drawback is the *regguetón* (hip-hop with a blend of Jamaican and Latin American influences) that blasts all day long.

Located just beyond the western edge of town, **Chepes Beach** is a white-sand beach with a few shade trees and lots of shallow, clear water. It's a pleasant place, made even better by a handful of simple beachside restaurants and a new thatch-roofed bar-discotheque.

A scientific center that is open to the public, the **Iguana Research & Breeding Station** (☎ 425-3946; www.utila-iguana.de; east of Mamey Lane; admission L$40; 🕒 2-5pm Mon, Wed & Fri) is dedicated to studying, protecting and breeding the island's endangered iguana, known locally as 'swamper' or 'wishiwilly'. Overhunting of eggs and development on the island has led to the iguanas' near demise. Visitors get a tour of the research station, learn about the species and see lots of wishiwillies. If you're interested in volunteering, check the website for information.

Based out of the Bay Island College of Diving, the **Whale Shark & Oceanic Research Center** (WSORC; ☎ 425-3760; www.wsorc.com; west main st; 🕒 9am-noon & 2-5pm Sun-Fri) is one of the only programs in Honduras that is 100% dedicated to advanced whale shark research. Divers and snorkelers can participate in various whale shark programs, ranging from one-time shark-spotting trips (L$1026 per person without snorkel gear), to in-depth three- to six-day courses on theory, ecology and research methods, plus training in spear guns and whale identification. There are plans to offer internship and summer camp programs as well. Just visiting the WSORC office is fascinating, with its numerous displays about whale shark biology, identification, safe diving practices and more. It hosts free talks Sunday night at 7:30pm.

Deep Blue Resort (p226) also offers programs in whale shark identification to its guests. See its website or call for more information.

Utila has a full service public gym, **Ocean Fitness** (☎ 425-3935; west main st, Sandy Bay; per day/month L$60/700; 🕒 6am-noon & 2-8pm Mon-Fri, 6am-2pm Sat), with free weights, machines, and treadmills.

BOUNTY & BEAUTY UNDER THE SEA: WHALE SHARKS

You put your snorkel gear on, slip into the water and when the bubbles clear and your eyes adjust, before you is a truly massive creature: dark-gray, white spots, long bony ridges down its body, and the fixed pectoral fins and slow sweeping tail that scream *shark!* A whale shark to be exact, and no matter what you've heard – they are, in fact, totally harmless – you'd have to be cold-blooded to not get a certain stomach-in-the-throat feeling. Because once you're in the water, you're in the shark's realm, and between that very big animal and the very big sea all around, you suddenly feel very small.

Whale sharks *(Rhincodon typhus)* have been spotted around all the Bay Islands, including Cayos Cochinos, but they are far more prevalent in Utila than anywhere else. Underwater currents around Utila stir up seabed nutrients that support plankton, the whale shark's favorite food. The sharks are present year-round, but, as migratory animals, tend to be most numerous from March to May and August to October.

The biggest fish in the sea, whale sharks can grow up to 16m (50ft) and weigh 15 tons. Fishermen in Utila tell of a resident whale shark that's 18m (60ft) long and known as Old Tom. The name may be quite apt, as whale sharks can live to be 150 years old. Whale sharks are filter feeders, swimming at or near the surface straining plankton out of the water with structures called 'gill rakes.' When not feeding, they dive: scientists now believe whale sharks spend two-thirds of their life at depth, possibly as far down as 1000m.

But there is a lot scientists do not know about whale sharks. The first order of business is simply determining whale shark populations and migration routes. To that end, researchers on Utila and elsewhere have been tagging sharks and using their spots – captured with underwater cameras – to create a database of individual animals. On Utila, the Whale Shark & Oceanic Research Center (WSORC; opposite) leads much of the current research and has a number of ways divers and snorkelers can be involved.

WSORC has also developed guidelines for shark encounters, including not touching or grabbing a shark, no flash photography, no more than eight snorkelers in the water at a time, and only one boat within 100m of a shark at a time. It's vital that travelers know and follow the rules, and insist their guides and boat captains do the same.

DIVING

As in Roatán, dive shops on Utila have largely standardized their prices. Shops charge between L$4920 and L$5255 for Open Water and advanced courses, including materials and equipment rental, and around L$665 (one tank) and L$1045 (two tank) for fun dives. Most shops offer two to four nights of free lodging with every course (usually in a dorm), and maybe a few free fun dives. It's a good idea to check out the lodging before you commit to a dive shop.

There is also a mandatory reef tax (per day L$57), with a dollar going to support the hyperbaric chamber, a dollar to the municipal government for garbage collection and the planned desalination plant, and a dollar for Utila Dive Safety & Environmental Council (UDSEC) projects, such as repairing buoys and paying for tourist police. Everyone pays this, divemasters and instructors included.

Most dive shops start Open Water and other courses almost every day, and offer advanced courses up to divemaster. Specialty courses, including Nitrox and technical diving, are also available. Recommended dive shops:

Alton's Dive Center (☎ 425-3704; www.diveinutila.com; east main st) Longtime local shop – 'Alton' is Alton Cooper, Utila's mayor until 2010 – with good equipment and a laid-back atmosphere. Courses include four night's accommodation – in little, basic, cold-water rooms right at the shop – and two fun dives. The service can be a bit hit and miss. It also offers NAUI courses.

Bay Islands College of Diving (☎ 425-3291; www.dive-utila.com; west main st) Well-established shop that appeals especially to nervous first-time divers. Its policy is to have only four divers per course or fun dive, but the shop's popularity can stretch the staff thin at times. It offers discounts at nearby hotels.

Captain Morgan's Dive Centre (☎ 425-3349; www.divingutila.com; main st) Small operation with an office at the intersection, but its dive shop and lodging are on Jewel Cay (Upper Cay), a 20-minute boat ride from Utila. Three to four nights of lodging are included with your Open Water

EXPLORING THE REST OF THE ISLAND

Hiking

If island life is making you a little claustrophobic, you can stretch your legs on a walk or hike to Pumpkin Hill Bay, about 3km across the island. Pumpkin Hill itself has some caves; one was supposedly a hideout for the pirate Henry Morgan. As with any cave, do not venture in beyond the opening without a guide.

The Iguana Research Station (see p222) occasionally offers guided hikes around the island as well.

Kayaking

Kayaking to Rock Harbour, a beautiful white-sand beach that is only accessible by boat or foot, is also a good way to spend the day. Start by paddling into Oyster Bed Lagoon, then continue into the mangrove canal, which will lead you straight to Rock Harbour. A round-trip from town, with a couple of hours at the beach, takes about four hours. Most dive shops rent kayaks for around L$100 per day.

course in the clean and comfy lodge – a good bet if you want to get away from the Utila scene.

Cross Creek (☎ 425-3397; www.crosscreekutila.com; east main st) Owned by the Utila Diver Center, Cross Creek is a bit more expensive, but has friendly multilingual staff and professional instruction. Breakfast and accommodation are included with an Open Water course, and the rooms are some of our favorites on the island. All guests can use the big, shared kitchen and lounge.

Deep Blue Diving (☎ 425-3211; www.deepblueutila.com; west main st) This dive school offers free hostel stays for students (L$100 non-guests) in its clean, 3rd-floor digs across the street. There's a shared kitchen and wi-fi. It's across from Piccola.

Ecomarine Dive Shop (☎ 425-3350; www.ecomarineutila.com; west main st) Low-key and unpretentious, with small classes and solid instruction. Located in a residential area a 10-minute walk west of the center, which can be a bummer or a blessing. The backpacker lodge across the street is free for students and L$40-100 for non-divers, and has a small shared kitchen and even smaller rooms.

Underwater Vision (☎ 425-3103; www.diving-utila.com; east main st) Friendly, local shop founded by Jernigan Cooper, father of Mayor Cooper, and run by members of the family. Courses included four nights accommodation and two fun dives. Centrally located, but still low key.

Utila Dive Center (UDC; ☎ 425-3327; www.utiladivecentre.com; east main st) Utila's first and biggest dive shop, UDC issued more Open Water certifications in 2004 than any other shop in the world. Groups can get big (up to 12 people) but there's at least one staff member (whether instructor, assistant or divemaster) for every two students. Courses are more expensive, but include four nights at the Mango Inn (p226) and two fun dives.

Utila Water Sports (☎ 425-3264; www.utilawatersports.com; east main st) One of the few locally-owned shops, this operation also manages the Agressor (p226) and the high-end Laguna Beach Resort (p226). It has excellent gear and a well-trained and well-supported staff. It offers both PADI and SSI certification. Open Water courses include three free nights in its clean and cozy dorms (some private rooms are available), plus four free fun dives.

SNORKELING

There's good snorkeling at Bando Beach, the Utila Cays (p229), inside the harbor, and at both ends of the main road: at Airport Reef, just past the old landing strip and at Blue Bayou on the far western end of the road. Airport Reef is somewhat better, but Blue Bayou has a nice pier and a small patch of sand. In either case, beware of the rocky shallows – they're loaded with sea urchins, whose needles deliver a painful sting. Look for the white buoys, which mark diving spots, and be sure to watch for boat traffic. You can also make your way across the island to Turtle Harbour, part of a like-named marine reserve and protected turtle nesting area, for fine snorkeling.

Many dive shops will loan or rent snorkel gear to their students, some to non-students as well. **Utila Snorkel Centre** (info@utilasnorkelcentre.com; west main st) is a brand-new shop (next to Munchies) offering snorkeling day trips (L$450 per person) to Jack Neal Cove and Water Cay. It may also be able to arrange a day trip to Cayos Cochinos for L$1615 per person.

Courses & Volunteering

Utila isn't the most logical place in the world to take Spanish classes – most of the locals speak English – but all of the professors at the **Central American Spanish School** (☎ 425-3788; www.ca-spanish.com; east main st; per week L$2280; 8am-noon & 1-9pm) are native speakers from La Ceiba, and there are more and more mainland transplants working and living here. Homestays aren't available yet, but with a little effort you should have no trouble finding people to practice your skills on. Classes are offered for all levels, usually one-on-one, four hours per day, five days per week. All books and materials are included, along with five hours of internet access per week, and the school can help arrange long-term lodging. It's opposite Rubi's Inn.

Drop the kids off for a few hours at **L'Atelier** (☎ 3254-6808; patriciasuarez@hotmail.com; west main st) with Argentinean artist-in-residence Patricia Suarez, who offers art classes for L$200 per hour. She teaches big kids, too.

The **Utila Centre for Marine Ecology** (www.utilaecology.org) accepts volunteers for marine research projects.

Sleeping

Utila has a bunch of cheap places to stay, but there is a good selection of midrange and top-end options too. It doesn't take long to walk around and find something that suits your needs. Most dive shops offer free lodging while you're taking a class, though the quality of the lodging varies considerably. Be sure to book ahead during the high seasons (July and August, and mid-December to Easter).

BUDGET

Tony's Place (☎ 425-3376; Cola de Mico Rd; s/d with shared bathroom L$100/150) Two buildings with breezy porches house eight acceptable rooms in this cold-water affair. The walls need a coat of fresh paint, or at least a scrubbing, but the sheets are clean and the price is right. There's a *pila* (hand-washing station) in the yard and plenty of clothesline to dry your clothes on. Located kitty corner from Mango Inn.

Hotel Bavaria (☎ 425-3809; petrawhitefield3@hotmail.com; Cola de Mico Rd; s/d/tr L$247/304/361, plus L$57 for hot water) A simple place with six rooms on the 2nd floor of a big house, accommodations here are small, spotless, and boast polished hardwood floors and tile bathrooms. All rooms share a wrap-around porch, which is great for relaxing after a day of diving. It's one of the best deals around, though it can get a bit noisy next door. German is spoken. Look for the Bavarian flag near Mango Inn.

Hotel Rose (☎ 425-3027; west main st; s with fan/air-con L$300/500, d with fan/air-con L$400/600;) There's sweet beauty-parloresque furniture in the oh-so-'60s-lobby of this fairly clean budget spot opposite Deep Blue Diving. It's quite dark, but you get electrically-charged hot water and the cable TV. It doesn't even charge extra for the stale smell.

Hotel Roses Inn (☎ 425-3283; Mamey Lane; r L$380) Situated out in the countryside, this bare-bones option has a shared kitchen and a pleasant backdoor porch. There's no night watchman, so security might be an issue. Enquire at the Supermarket Rose (on the main street).

Bayview Hotel (☎ 425-3114; bayviewinternet@yahoo.com; west main st; r with fan L$475-665, with air-con L$665-855;) While it's a bit west of the action, this smallish hotel has better rooms than those at Rubi's – though they are a bit smaller – a sundeck looking out onto the water, and decently manicured grounds.

MIDRANGE

Margaritaville Beach Hotel (☎ 425-3366; margaritavillehotel@yahoo.com; west main st, Sandy Bay; r with fan/air-con L$380/760, cabañas with air-con L$1330;) About 100m from Chepes Beach, Margaritaville is a two-story Caribbean-style house with two wrap-around porches. Rooms are simple and cramped (two beds, a fan and a cleanish bathroom) while across the street, the cabañas are a slight step up – updated furnishings, private porches and bay views.

Rubi's Inn (☎ 425-3240; rubisinn@yahoo.com; east main st; r with fan/air-con L$475/760, r with air-con & ocean view L$910;) While bugs often get into the rooms at night, and the beds are a bit concave, this remains a solid buy. Topping the amenities list are clean, comfortable rooms, a nice sundeck and mini-fridges in all the rooms. Best of all, the owners are friendly and you are oceanfront. It's next to Reef Cinema.

Colibri Hill Resort (☎ 425-3329; www.colibri-resort.com; west main st; d L$950, 1-bedroom apt L$1330-1900;) Located on a hilltop overlooking the bay – but still just a minute's walk to the main drag – the Colibri has stunning grounds, a nice pool area (though there's green water in the pool), and even a *colibri* (hummingbird) or two. Rooms have polished wood floors, white-washed walls and nice tile bathrooms. They're modern in a stark sort of way. All this greenery means there are a lot of mossies around.

Caribbean Dreams (☎ 425-3692; east main st; apt per night/week/month L$950/4750/8550;) Ideal for long-stay visitors, these fully furnished apartments are brand-spanking new. You're not beachfront, but they have hardwood floors, cable TVs and decently appointed kitchens, plus, you'll save a bundle over the long haul.

Mango Inn (☎ 425-3334; www.mango-inn.com; Cola de Mico Rd; r L$1045, cabin L$1615-2090;) Straight up the hill from the pier, the Mango Inn sits on lush grounds with two sundecks and a great three-tiered pool with hot tub. Rooms and cabins are clean and comfortable, with polished hardwood floors, hot-water bathrooms and air-con, but the service was some of the worst on the island when we visited.

our pick **The Lighthouse Hotel** (☎ 425-3164; www.aboututila.com; east main st; d with/without ocean view L$1235/950;) Based on the plans of the New Canal Lighthouse in New Orleans, this hotel sits over the water and has the best rooms in town. The only thing it lacks is a good beach or sunning deck. But it does have tastefully appointed clean rooms, deliciously new sheets and kitchenettes. The friendly owners seem to know just about everything when it comes to the island's culture and history. There's a minimum two-night stay.

TOP END

Jade Seahorse (☎ 425-3270; www.jadeseahorse.com; Cola de Mico Rd; s/d L$1330/1425;) A bizarre boutique hotel, the Jade Seahorse features five oddly shaped but comfortable bungalows, each eclectically decorated with bottle art, mosaic tiles and iridescent glass stones. It took the owner, Neil Keller, 15 years to produce this dreamlike world, and staying here will certainly invoke your inner artist. The lush grounds are an extension of the rooms – pod-like steps, ocean tunnels, glass bubbles with funkadelic masks. It's a trippy place, but the service, unfortunately, was less than friendly when we were there.

OUTSIDE EAST HARBOUR

On the west end of the island are Utila's higher-end resorts. At the time of writing, there were just two modest establishments, and Utilans have so far rebuffed large-scale development there, partly to preserve the island's low profile and partly because Utila's water and power supplies would be severely strained. But as Roatán gets bought up, the pressure to build more and bigger resorts will keep growing

Laguna Beach Resort (☎ 425-3263; www.utiladiveventures.com; dive-package d per person per night L$3325-4750, per week L$20,900-26,500;) Utila's best resort has 13 bungalows set on a narrow peninsula across from Blue Bayou Beach, with the ocean on one side and the lagoon on the other. Cabins are clean and quaint, with hot water, air-con and a covered porch overlooking the lagoon. Guests can use the kayaks and bicycles, and the resort provides a free water taxi service into town. Dive equipment and staff are top notch, but the meals can get a little monotonous. Dive packages include full board, three dives per day, two night dives and unlimited shore diving.

Deep Blue Resort (☎ 425-3211; www.deepblueutila.com; all-inclusive 7-day dive package per person L$22,800) This low-key, 12-room dive resort is one of just a handful of establishments – more surely to come – on the mostly uninhabited west end of the island. Rooms are comfortable if not luxurious, with dark wood floors, hot-water bathrooms, air-con and a private patio. The common area, including a bar, dining area, and pool table, is distinctly lodge-like. Meals here are just OK, but then few resorts offer gourmet dining. The hotel owners and staff help out with rides to and from town, but some guests may be frustrated at not having easier access to Utila town. Others prefer it that way. Deep Blue Resort is also a Whale Shark Research Center and offers special programs and packages for those interested in the world's biggest fish.

Ask at Laguna or at Utila Water Sports (p224) about the 'radical' live-aboard diving packages on the **Utila Agressor** (☎ in US 800-348-2628; www.agressor.com), which had a rainy maiden voyage in February 2006.

Eating

There's a surprisingly good selection of eateries considering the size of Utila. If you plan on cooking your own food, however, remember that fruit and vegetables are more expensive here than on the mainland; consider bringing a small stockpile over on the ferry.

BUDGET

Thompson's Café Bakery (Cola de Mico Rd; breakfast L$40-70; 6am-6pm) Don't leave Utila without stopping here at least once to try the famous Johnny cakes – a doughy biscuit that is like manna from heaven when fresh

DIVING NEAR UTILA

Utila's south shore has warm, crystal-clear water filled with tropical fish, coral, sponges and other marine life. On the north side, a plunging wall makes for great drift- and deep-diving. Utila is famous for the magnificent whale sharks that gather here from March to May and August to October.

Black Hills A beautiful sea mound rising from 40m to 10m with a truly stunning array of sea life, from giant tube and barrel sponges to huge schools of jack, snapper and spadefish, plus hawksbill turtles and even whale sharks in the right season. Drop to 25m and just wind your way up.

Blackish Point Drift along the sheer wall at 20m, checking out pillar coral, and huge rope and tube sponges. Caves and crevices shelter spotted drum, porcupine fish and blue Creole wrasses, peculiar because they swim nose down.

CJ's Dropoff Another wall dive featuring numerous outcrops and caves, pillars and overhangs. Schools of damsel fish and sergeant majors forage among massive barrel sponges.

The Maze A series of deep canyons with steep walls, home to huge Goliath groupers and dainty peppermint shrimp. Divers can also explore several large caverns, including Willy's Hole.

from the oven and smeared with butter. For something heartier, have it with egg and ham: a Ferrari to the Egg McMuffin's Pinto. Thompson's opens early (and starts baking even earlier) so you can snag breakfast before an early dive. Good egg-and-bean breakfasts, fresh bread and cinnamon roles are also served.

Munchies (☎ 425-3168; west main st; mains L$65-110; 🕑 breakfast, lunch & dinner Mon-Sat) Located on the 1st floor of an island home built in 1864, this restaurant has a great Caribbean vibe, with pleasant outdoor seating on the front porch and at the back. The menu is a bit limited, but includes good vegetarian options and big breakfasts, which keeps it busy with travelers.

RJ's BBQ (east main st; mains L$80-135; 🕑 5:30pm-11pm Wed, Fri & Sun) Huge, cheap, well-prepared dishes attract a crowd here – it's lucky for the other restaurants in town that RJ's is only open three days a week. Choose from barbecued chicken, wahoo, kingfish, pork or beef, all of which are served with mashed potato and salad. The selections are written on a chalk board near the cash register, and erased one by one as the night wears on and the food runs out. Needless to say, come early. It's across from Alton's Dive Shop.

Bundu Café (east main st; breakfast L$60-110, mains L$80-195; 🕑 breakfast, lunch & dinner) Its panini sandwiches are enough to keep you fueled all day, and the breakfast is legendary. Unfortunately, hygiene is a bit circumspect. The large book exchange has a few good finds, if you search hard enough.

Dave's Restaurant (west main st; mains L$105-110; 🕑 lunch & dinner) In front of the Cocoloco, this is a massively popular spot serving grilled chicken or pork with your choice of sauces, from cilantro to basil and garlic.

Ultralight Café (☎ 425-3514; west main st; mains L$90-150; 🕑 breakfast, lunch & dinner Sun-Thu) An Israeli restaurant run by a Utila native named after a doomed flying machine – you know there's a story here. Joya, the owner, leased her burger joint to an Israeli couple, who switched from hamburgers to hummus, but were mainly interested in flying their ultralight. They were better chefs than pilots though: the ultralight crashed (no one was hurt) while the restaurant took off – the aircraft's propeller still hangs in the little wood eatery. Joya returned, the Israelis left, and Joya planned to go back to burgers. But the Israelis' kitchen assistant had memorized all the recipes and convinced Joya to stick with *shakshuka* (a popular Israeli egg dish), falafel, *sabich* (a pita sandwich) and what is still the best fresh pita bread in Central America.

Bush's Supermarket (east main st; 🕑 6:30am-6pm Mon-Sat, to 11am Sun) is the island's largest and best-stocked grocery store, while **Supermarket Rose** (main st; 🕑 8am-noon & 2-8pm Mon-Sat) is run by the folks at Hotel Roses Inn.

La Tienda del Pueblo (main st, across from Munchies; 🕑 6am-noon & 2-6pm Mon-Sat) has a wide selection of food, plus hippies selling their wares out the front – groovy.

There is a handful of simple **beachside restaurants** (mains L$50-110; 🕑 breakfast, lunch & dinner) on Chepes Beach that serve snacks, *típica*, and good seafood dishes. They're great places to escape the heat of the sun over a couple of beers and a plate of *ceviche* (seafood marinated in lemon or lime juice, garlic and seasonings).

MIDRANGE

La Dolce Vita Pizzeria (mains L$75-260; breakfast, lunch & dinner) In the courtyard of Mango Inn, this place serves great brick-oven pizza and decent seafood pastas, as well as breakfasts. It's a good place to come for drinks, too, before Tranquila and Coco Loco get fired up.

Jade Seahorse Restaurant (425-3270; Cola de Mico Rd; mains L$80-220; 7am-3pm & 5-7pm) This restaurant is just as eclectic as the hotel it's a part of. The rambling, artsy dining area has groovy tile work, unexpected colors and hardly a symmetrical shape in sight. The menu is nearly as creative, consisting mostly of vegetarian, seafood and pasta plates. The attached Treetonic Bar stays open till midnight.

La Piccola (425-3746; west main st; dishes L$95-250; lunch & dinner Wed-Mon) This classy restaurant serves excellent homemade Italian food – and a few traveler favorites. Most of the pasta is made fresh by hand and served at tables with candles and tablecloths in a second-floor patio setting.

Café Mariposa (east main st; sandwiches L$95-115, mains L$155-175; 11am-10pm) Housed in a canary-yellow building jutting out above the sea, the Mariposa has friendly service, yummy snacks and tremendous views. Don't miss the pan-seared prawns accompanied with a freshly-mixed Piña Colada (after all, we're in the tropics). You can save some duckets by going with the snacks and sandwiches.

Drinking

Bar in the Bush (Cola de Mico Rd) It's popular, but this place can get rowdy. Lone travelers should take care at night, since the pathway to the bar is unlit. It's past the Mango Inn.

Coco Loco (west main st) Just meters away from Tranquila and virtually identical in appearance, it would be easy to stagger out for a pee and return to find yourself in the other bar without realizing it – which is maybe just what happens, because at some point Tranquila starts to empty and the party moves to Coco Loco.

Driftwood Café (west main st) A way's west of the ferry dock, this 'yachtie' hangout has decent pub grub. Try the 'Monkeyball,' made with home-crafted Kahlua and a few other secret ingredients.

La Pirata (main st & Cola de Mico) This third-floor drinkery is a good sunset spot. And if its sign is any indication, this may be a boys-only club.

Thatch-roofed bar-discotheque (admission free; 2pm-3am) Facing Chepes Beach, this is a great place to strut your stuff on a starry night. Cheap beers and good mixed drinks make it even better.

Tranquila (west main st) Perched on a wood jetty over the water, this is the place to start your night before migrating all of 15 steps to Coco Loco.

Entertainment

Reef Cinema (425-3254; east main st; tickets L$45; video store 11:30am-6pm Mon-Sat, cinema 7:30pm) Next to Rubi's Inn, this cinema plays a creative selection of recently released movies every night. It also rents videos and sells books.

Shopping

Gunter's Driftwood Gallery (425-3113; west of Cola de Mico Rd) The gallery and gift shop of Gunter Kordovsky – multimedia artist, accomplished diver, and Utila institution – is worth a stop. Most of Gunter's art is made from materials he's found on the beach or in the ocean – driftwood, shells, shark jaws – which are reworked and then shellacked to hell. Open every afternoon except Sunday; look for it near the Mango Inn.

Bay Island Originals (east main st; 9am-noon & 1-6pm Mon-Fri, 9am-noon Sat & Sun) Across from Reef Cinema, this small shop has a good selection of *artesanía,* clothing and souvenirs.

Getting There & Away

AIR

At the time of writing, flights between Utila and La Ceiba were only offered by **Aerolineas Sosa** (452-3161; www.aerolineassosa.com). Tickets cost L$1064 one way from Utila (6am Tuesday, Thursday and Saturday) or La Ceiba (3:30pm Monday, Wednesday and Friday). Double-check the schedule if you are thinking of flying, and bear in mind that even marginally bad weather can cause the flight to be cancelled. Utila has an airstrip, but no terminal; buy tickets at **Morgan's Travel** (425-3161; utilamorganstravel@yahoo.com; 8am-noon & 2-5:30pm Mon-Sat), at the pier opposite the ferry office, which can also arrange an early morning taxi to the airstrip. It's a small plane and fills up fast, so book a spot as early as possible and always reconfirm the day before.

BOAT

The Utila Princess ferries passengers between La Ceiba and Utila's main pier every day (L$420, one hour). The ferry makes two trips each way, leaving Utila at 6:20am and 2pm, and returning from La Ceiba at 9:30am and 4pm. The ferry often suspends service for bad weather (and even occasionally if there aren't enough passengers) – plan accordingly. If you sit at the back, you're gonna get wet.

Captain Vern (☎ 3346-2600, 9910-8040; vfine@hotmail.com) offers catamaran sailboat trips between the Alton's Dive Center and Driftwood Café piers in Utila and Roatán's West End (daily, L$1038 one way, four to five hours), leaving Roatán at 1pm and Utila at 6:30am. Call ahead.

Getting Around

A few golf-cart taxis ply the streets of Utila, charging a standard L$20 for any distance. You can usually find one at El Paisano Restaurant (next to Bundu Cafe on east main street), Bush's Supermarket, or near the pier (ask at Morgan's Travel).

Some golf cart, scooter and bicycle rental places include:

Captain Hank's (☎ 3355-8705) Rents electric scooters by the hour/day (L$95/570). It's next to Banco Atlántida.

Rita's Club Car Rental (☎ 425-3692; east main st; 9am-noon & 2-6pm Mon-Sat) Rents golf carts for around L$950 a day. At Rita's Boutique.

Utila Bike Rental (☎ 425-3940; east main st; 9am-noon & 2-6pm Mon-Sat) Rents bicycles by the hour/day (L$25/100).

UTILA CAYS

Several cays on Utila's southwest shore make nice day trips, and even overnighters for travelers looking to take a break from the groovie-groupie Utila scene. **Jewel and Pigeon Cays**, connected by a small bridge, are home to a charming village of just 600 residents (and five churches!). **Captain Morgan's Dive Centre** (p223) operates from here, and rents kayaks (L$100) and snorkel gear (L$100) to non-guests – students are free. There's excellent snorkeling on Jewel Cay just east of the main dock.

Water Cay, just beyond Pigeon and Jewel Cays, is a beautiful 3-acre island covered with palm trees and surrounded by warm turquoise waters. It's uninhabited, but there's a caretaker who keeps it clean and charges L$50 per visitor for the upkeep of the island. Ask first for overnight camping. The best snorkeling is about 100m out from the western shore, but watch for boat traffic. You can get to the cay by renting a kayak from Captain Morgan's Dive Center (L$100). The island is the third cay west of Jewel Cay, and is about a 30-minute paddle away. You can also hire a local fisherman to take you there (L$100 per person). Be sure to bring water and snacks.

Festivals & Events

What started out in 1997 as a 50-person party on Water Cay is today a 1500-person event known as **Sun Jam** (www.sunjamutila.com), an all-day/all-night party with a troupe of bad-ass DJs spinning tunes for a dancing, drinking, and general mayhem-creating crowd of locals and travelers. It's held every August, and information is released just a few weeks before the party; check the website early and often to secure a spot.

SWAN ISLANDS

Located approximately 156km from mainland Honduras, the Swan Islands are a chain of three rocky islets measuring a mere 8 sq km. Stumbled upon by Christopher Columbus in 1502, they were later occupied by the filibuster William Walker (see p193). After Walker's execution in 1860, Honduras claimed the chain of islands as its own. The US, however, also laid claim to them in 1863 under the Guano Islands Act, a legislation 'enabling' the US to take possession of any island caked in guano – a fancy word for bird shit, which was highly valued as fertilizer at the time – as long as the island wasn't inhabited or owned by another country. In 1971, over 100 years later, the US relinquished its claim to them.

The Swan Islands are most famous for having housed Radio Swan (later called Radio Americas), which began broadcasting during the period leading up to and after the US invasion of Cuba at the Bay of Pigs. Believed to be owned by a private steamship company, it was eventually discovered that the radio station was owned by the US government and allegedly operated by the CIA to transmit coded messages to Cubans who were going to support American forces during the invasion. Radio Swan was closed in the late 1960s and its main transmitter relocated for use in the Vietnam War.

Today, the Swan Islands are uninhabited except for a small Honduran military base.

Sleeping & Eating

Hotel Kayla (r with dive course free, non-divers L$190) Located on Jewel Cay (Upper Cay) and operated by Captain Morgan's (p223), Hotel Kayla is a large, airy, wooden building with a long foyer framed with arches that's kind of southern belle-ish. Rooms are large and clean.

Hotel Kayla II (☎ 408-5133; r L$250) There's another Hotel Kayla located across from Myrna's Café. It offers immaculately clean rooms and friendly service.

Harbor House (☎ 9937-5457; www.islandlifetours.com; mains L$70-110; 🕑 7am-8pm) The brand new Harbor House does it all: there's a gym, internet café (L$1 per minute), a second-story diner-style restaurant, and a third-story bar. It also rents out a studio apartment for a three-day package (per person L$4750). The American owners, Henry and Victoria, are especially proud of their cookbook that features local dishes, with proceeds benefiting the town's park.

Myrna's Café (mains L$7-30; 🕑 4:30am-7pm) Down Jewel Cay on the north side of the main road, this hole in the wall serves *baleadas*, enchiladas and *tajaditas* at budget-busting prices.

Fish Burgers (🕑 9am-9pm) On the east side of the bridge to Pigeon Cay, this waterfront eatery offers up – surprise, surprise – fish burgers. There are a few more options on the menu, but why would you even try.

Getting There & Around

Ask at Captain Morgan's in town about arranging transport to the cays. The fare is L$100 per person roundtrip (30 minutes each way, minimum four people), and they normally leave around 7am.

If you stay on Jewel Cay (Upper Cay), you can easily kayak or hire a boat to Water Cay or to some of the cays further out. Each of the Utila Cays can be covered by foot in just a few minutes.

GUANAJA

pop 5800

While a trip to pine-shrouded Guanaja is probably way too expensive for your average budget traveler – there's no ferry service here – folks with a bit more cash will enjoy the charms of this seldom-explored

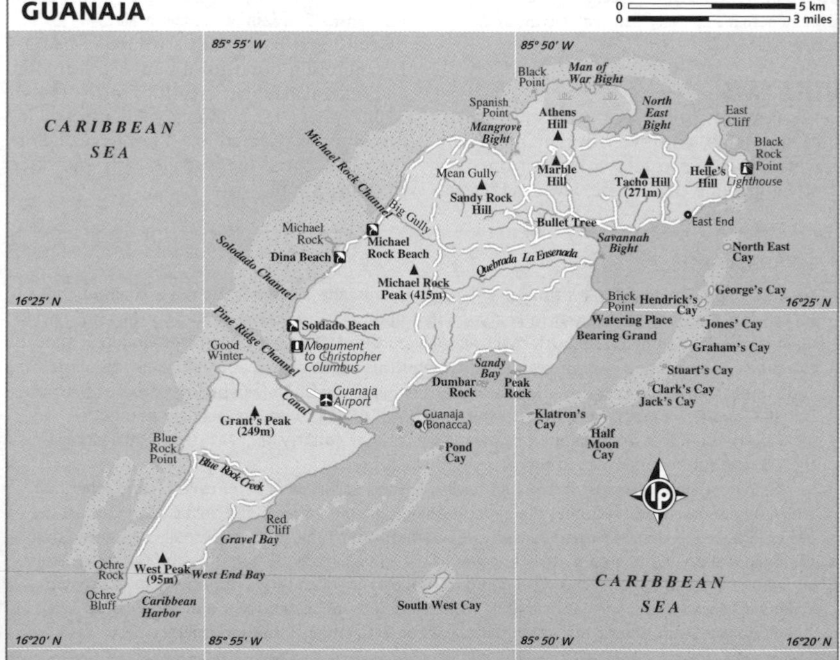

DIVING AROUND GUANAJA

Declared a marine reserve, the waters around Guanaja are home to 38 terrific dives sites, most teeming with marine life and a flourishing reef. The northside sites are known for their coral forests and dramatic drop-offs, the southside sites for being shallower and sprinkled with channels. Some of the top sites include

The Pinnacle Located in Pine Ridge Channel near Soldado Beach, this pinnacle rises 41m from the ocean floor, down to a point about 16m below the ocean's surface. Known for its incredible varieties of black coral, divers will also be treated to views of gorgonians, sea whips, arrow crabs, flamingo tongues, and seahorses. The best way to enjoy it is to descend to 24m or 27m, and slowly spiral up and around it.

Volcano Caves (Black Rocks) An excellent drift dive, this site is made up of hundreds of volcanic caverns and tunnels that extend along a 2.5km wall. There isn't much sponge or coral growth here, but there are lots of fish. Silversides, glassy sweepers, grouper and barracuda can be seen in and around the tunnels, and some divers have been lucky enough to come across sleeping sharks. Be sure to bring a dive light.

Jado Trader One of the most famous dive sites in the Caribbean, this 73m freighter lies 33m under the surface on a sandy shelf. Next to the wreck, there is a wall that rises to a depth of about 13m and a bit further off, a 21m volcanic chimney. Scuttled in 1987, the ship has an abundant growth of coral, sponges and algae. Fish are often fed here, so don't be alarmed if you're approached by a 2m-long green moray eel frisking you for food. Grouper and yellowtail are common fish to spot, and the occasional hammerhead shark is seen here as well.

Jim's Silver Lode An excellent drift dive, this site begins at a 21m-deep tunnel that is often crowded with silverside sardines. It leads to a large sandy bowl covered in fans and lush coral where grouper, yellow goatfish, stingrays and moray eels are commonly seen. Be sure to check out the holes and crevices along the wall; they're prime places to spot black durgon, fairy basslets, butterflyfish, and bigeyes. It's a top-notch site for underwater photographers.

Caribbean paradise. Like its brethren to the west, Guanaja also has excellent diving and plenty of open space – about 90% of the island has been declared a national forest reserve and marine park.

A vibrant coral reef encircles the 18km-long island and its 15 or so cays. It's this reef – and the ships it has sunken – that makes Guanaja attractive for snorkeling and diving. Guanaja Town (Bonacca), the largest settlement, is a dirty maze of stilt houses and pathways – hardly worth the visit – and most travelers end up staying at all-inclusive dive resorts on the mainland. There are a few tiny settlements on the main island, including one on Savannah Bight and another on Mangrove Bight; the latter was badly hit by Hurricane Mitch in 1998.

The island was surely inhabited when Christopher Columbus landed here in 1502, naming it the *Isla de Pinos* (Island of Pines). Its original name is not known.

GUANAJA TOWN (BONACCA)

Sitting on a small cay just off the mainland's eastern coast, Guanaja town – the locals call it Bonacca – is the biggest town around. Tour brochures often call this the 'Venice of Honduras' – there are no roads on the cay and therefore no cars, and narrow canals allow the residents to pull their boats right up to their stilt houses. Sound beautiful, right? In reality, it's a bit cramped and dirty.

Most lodging options here are upscale resorts; basic hotels start at L$600. And with no ferry service, even getting here can be expensive.

Information

Guanaja's few public services are located in Bonacca. There's a **Banco Atlántida** (🕑 9am-4pm Mon-Fri, to noon Sat), which exchanges traveler's checks and gives cash advances on Visa card; however, the bank uses a manual machine, so your card should have raised numbers (the smooth 'electronic use only' cards won't work). There's also a **post office** and telephone calls can be made at **Hondutel** (🕑 7am-9pm Mon-Fri, to 4pm Sat).

Sights & Activities

Snorkeling, diving and visits to the cays and beaches are the main activities on Guanaja.

IF YOU HAVE A FEW MORE DAYS

After you've spent a few days unwinding, consider booking a boat to take you beach-hopping along the north side of the island (it's mostly uninhabited). Start at **Dina Beach**, just west of Michael Rock, an empty, tawny-sand beach with patches of seagrapes and a backdrop of pines. From there, hike or take the boat to **Soldado Beach**, the site where Columbus is reputed to have landed in 1502. There's a ramshackle monument commemorating the event, but far more striking is the pretty inlet with clear turquoise blue waters – be sure to bring your snorkel gear. Finally, set off for **West End Bay**. Located on the southwestern end of the island, it's a long, white-sand beach with a lush pine and deciduous tree forest alongside it – absolutely perfect for beachcombing.

Most hotels on the mainland have dive shops, and offer courses, fun dives and multi-dive packages. Dive gear can be rented (usually for an additional fee) if you don't have your own. It's possible to snorkel right off Bonacca, although it's much better off Black Point on the main island, and around South West and Jones' Cays. Surprisingly, snorkeling gear is not readily available on the island; you should bring your own. The main island has a number of hiking trails and a waterfall too.

Sleeping

There are a few places to stay in Bonacca (Guanaja town), but if you can afford them, the options on the main island are worlds more appealing.

Hotel Miller (☎ 453-4327; Bonacca; r incl breakfast with fan/air-con L$950/1140;) This simple hotel has cable TV, private hot-water bathrooms, air-con and an onsite restaurant. In addition to this hotel, the Miller family owns half of South West Cay, an excellent spot to spend the day snorkeling, swimming and beachcombing. Ask at the front desk for details about trips.

Bo Bush's Island House (☎ 9963-8551; www.bosislandhouse.com; all-inclusive per person per week diver/non-diver L$13,300/11,400) This small, laid-back resort offers basic but clean rooms in a hillside building with great views of the Caribbean. It's owned by islander Bo Bush who knows the island – and its reefs – like the back of his hand. It's on the north side of island.

West Peak Inn (☎ in US 831-786-0406; www.westpeakinn.com; all-inclusive per person $1805) Situated on three miles of pristine, secluded beach, the all-inclusive West Peak Inn specializes in sea kayaking packages around Guanaja. There's good hiking nearby, and diving, snorkeling and fishing trips can also be arranged. Individual cabins are comfortable and appealing in a simple, beachy sort of way. The service is excellent. It's on the southwest side of island.

Villa at Dunbar Rock (☎ in US 952-953-4124; www.usdivetravel.com; Dunbar Rock; all-inclusive per person per week L$26,380-30,800) This picture-perfect hotel accommodates up to 14 people at a time and is located on a strikingly beautiful rocky outcrop directly across from Sandy Bay. It has basic rooms but phenomenal views – the Caribbean sea in every direction and the lush main island directly in front.

Nautilus Dive Resort (☎ 453-4506, in US 952-953-4124; www.usdivetravel.com; all-inclusive per person per week L$26,380-30,800) Villa's sister hotel, located just 500m away on Sandy Bay, the Nautilus has humbler digs, on a not-so-humble 27-acre plantation. Be sure to hike the trail up the mountain out the back.

Eating

Many of the hotels on the mainland provide meals to guests, either à la carte or as part of a package. On Sunday, the West Peak Inn holds a popular barbecue. Graham's Place offers good meals, and is a 15-minute boat ride (L$600) from Bonacca.

Getting There & Away

AIR

Aerolineas SOSA (☎ 453-2459; www.aerolineasosa.com) offers a 25-minute flight between Guanaja and La Ceiba (L$2546 roundtrip). There's a dock near the airport where a motorboat meets incoming visitors for the five-minute ride to Bonacca. For departing flights, a water taxi meets passengers at the pier near the joint airline office in Bonacca to take them to the airport. If you're staying at one of the resorts, transportation to and from the airport is typically provided.

BOAT

There is no longer a ferry service between Trujillo and Guanaja. Some travelers report you can hop on Guanaja-bound cargo or fishing ships from Trujillo for around L$600 (though you'll likely wait several days for a ship to leave). You may also be able to charter a boat here from Roatán (around L$11,400 for up to eight passengers).

GETTING AROUND

Wherever you stay in Guanaja, travel is by boat. Almost everyone has one so rides are easy to arrange; ask at the front desk of your hotel for information on a trusted driver.

La Moskitia

Life in La Moskitia begins at dawn, the new-day's sun kicking off a whirling dervish of activity under the verdant rainforest canopy to the west and out on the great pine savannah to the east. Jaguars are finishing up the night hunt as the rest of the forest dwellers – the tapirs and toucans, monkeys and macaws – begin their day of foraging. Along the numerous twisted rivers and broad, salt-water lagoons that make this landscape so unique, the rugged frontiersmen also begin their day, heading out to fish or tend their crops as many have done for centuries. Among the five distinct ethnic groups that call this land home, there are few hard-won commonalities: a proximity to the land – to the wild – that brings each community together.

Taking on a trip to the 'Mosquito Coast' is no small task – it costs a lot of money, you may wait for several days for a boat or a plane, and normal-day creature comforts that we now take for granted seem a lifetime away. But with new trails, new hotels and new routes opening up, it's much easier to visit today than it has ever been.

Generally speaking, a trip will take at least five days and could last for several months. The most visited route takes you by land and water to the Laguna de Ibans, and into the vast Reserva de la Biósfera del Río Plátano. Less visited even still are the chalkboard-flat grassland savannahs of eastern Moskitia. It's tough travel, and in that lies the biggest draw: a chance to get back to the beginning.

HIGHLIGHTS

- Visit La Moskitia the hard way, gliding past Tawahka villages as you journey down the **Río Patuca** (p252) on a 10-day cruise
- Head into the wilds of this massive swath of rainforest from **Las Marías** (p243), visiting the petroglyphs at **Walpaulban Sirpi** (p246) or tromping out on a three-day journey to **Pico Dama** (p246)
- Cut your teeth with a few Miskitu phrases as you visit with folks in the tranquil villages of **Cocobila** (p241), **Rais Ta** (p241) and **Belén** (p241)
- Discover the modern legacy of the Garífuna in traditional villages such as **Plaplaya** (p240)
- Leave the tourist trail, and this guidebook, behind as you forge new trails into the wilds of this last great frontier

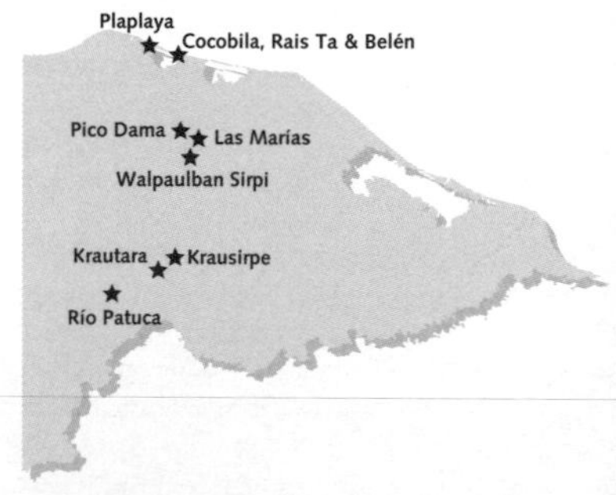

HISTORY

La Moskitia was inhabited as long as 3000 years ago by Chibcha-speaking Amerindians, who migrated here from present-day South America. Today's Pech and Tawahka indigenous groups are descended from those early migrants, and speak variations of Chibcha dialects. The pre-Hispanic population reached its peak between AD 800 and 1200, around the time groups to the west, especially the Maya, were in near collapse.

Christopher Columbus was the first European to reach La Moskitia, on his fourth and last voyage in 1502. Sailing east from the Bay Islands, he landed briefly near the mouth of a large river – which one is unknown, though it was likely the Patuca or the Sico – before rounding the cape (which he dubbed Cabo Gracias a Dios, or 'Thank God Cape,' reportedly after weathering a fierce storm). But the unforgiving terrain and environment of La Moskitia prevented any serious exploration for over a century. A cursory exploration in 1564 was not followed up until 1607 and 1609, and the first church – the point of early expeditions – was not founded until 1610. However, that church, and another founded a year later, were both sacked and burned and their occupants killed by Tawahka Indians. It took another 80 years for Spanish missionaries (supported by Spanish troops) to gain a foothold in the jungle.

In the 1700s, Spanish influence waned as that of English pirates (and some Dutch and French) rose. The slow-moving Spanish galleons laden with precious metals and raw materials made easy targets for pirates, who found refuge in La Moskitia's lagoons and river inlets. The English made little attempt to convert the indigenous people to Christianity – one supposes the pirates were not themselves big church-goers – but rather formed alliances with them against the Spanish. In fact, it was arming one group with muskets that gave rise to the term *mosqueteros* and eventually 'Miskitu' and 'Moskitia,' according to many historians.

Britain maintained control over eastern Honduras until 1786 when, through a treaty with Spain, it essentially traded La Moskitia for present-day Belize. But having gained nominal control of the territory, Spain did little to exert any real influence there. The status of the colony was in constant flux: the Central American Federation came and went, and a meddlesome British government briefly recognized La Moskitia as a sovereign nation, before Honduras finally became an independent republic in 1838. Through it all, life in La Moskitia stayed relatively unchanged. Moravian missionaries began arriving in the late 1920s, setting up schools, clinics and churches. The Honduran government didn't take up true civic responsibility in La Moskitia until the 1950s, around the same time indigenous rights organizations began forming to focus on land rights and other issues.

In the 1980s, La Moskitia was used as a base for the Contra War, the US-supported effort to unseat the new Sandinista government in Nicaragua. Puerto Lempira had major military installations, as did many of the small border towns. Countless indigenous people, especially Miskitus, whose traditional lands spanned the Honduran-Nicaraguan border, were killed and displaced during the conflict.

PEOPLE

With five distinct ethnic groups – Miskitu, Pech, Garífuna, Tawahka and ladino – La Moskitia is arguably the most culturally diverse region in the country. The single largest ethnic group in the region is the Miskitu, whose present members arose from a mixing of a landed indigenous group and escaped African slaves, and later English pirates. Historically, they occupied areas along the coast and around La Moskitia's three large lagoons, as well as along the Río Coco. They form the majority in all of the towns frequented by travelers, including Brus Laguna, Belén, Rais Ta, Ahuas, Wampusirpi, and a large part of Las Marías.

Another group, the Pech, once occupied large parts of what is now the Reserva de la Biósfera del Río Plátano, and as far south as the Sierra de Agalta mountains in Olancho and west to the Valle de Aguán. However, a longtime rivalry with the Miskitus along the coast, and encroachment by ladino farmers in Olancho, squeezed the Pech into the middle reaches of the Río Plátano, where they remain today. Even Las Marías, once a vital Pech village, now has a large number of Miskitu residents thanks to migration and intermarriage. In 1990, about 40 Pech people moved from Olancho to Las Marías, in part to re-establish Pech presence in the area.

Even more isolated than the Pech are the Tawahka, who live mostly along the Río Patuca and number about 1000 people. They, too, once controlled large portions of present-day Moskitia, but are today concentrated in just five communities, the largest being Krausirpe, in the Tawahka Asangni Biosphere Reserve. The Tawahka were the last of the indigenous groups in La Moskitia to be contacted by Europeans, and fiercely resisted their intrusion. The first two missionary expeditions to the region, in 1610 and 1611, both ended when Tawahka Indians attacked and killed the interlopers and the soldiers accompanying them.

La Moskitia has a small number of Garífuna people, living along the coast in the towns of Plaplaya, Batalla and Iriona. Descended from Carib indigenous people and African slaves on the island of St Vincent, and then deported by Britain to Roatán in the late 1700s, the Garífuna did not reach La Moskitia until the turn of the 20th century. Nevertheless, Plaplaya is considered one of the 'purest' Garífuna villages in Honduras, isolated from many modern-day intrusions.

Ladinos, considered 'mainstream' Hondurans, have moved to La Moskitia in ever-increasing numbers, mostly drawn

LA MOSKITIA PLANNING GUIDE

Here's a quick planning guide to get you started on your travels. Remember, there are very few stores in the region, so you'll need to come prepared. Most guesthouses do not have telephones, so it's all but impossible to make a reservation from outside La Moskitia for hotels or transit. Within La Moskitia, ask your hotel owner to call by radio to the next town to let them know you're coming. All that said, it's very rare that every single room is filled. But if so, arrangements can usually be made with local families – ask one of the guesthouse owners for help. Generally speaking, you eat your meals at your guesthouse in a family setting. Dinner is whatever was caught or killed that day.

What To Bring

It's best to travel light here. A small rucksack with a long-sleeve shirt and pair of light pants, a swimsuit, a couple of T-shirts and shorts, a rain jacket, sun hat, flashlight (torch), bug spray, water purification drops (you can pick up Microdyn-brand tablets in pharmacies in La Ceiba), sunscreen, malaria pills, general toiletries, foot powder, and plenty of socks and underwear should do. Most people also recommend bringing knee-high rubber boots. If you are bringing a camera, it's a good idea to take a few ziplock bags to keep your gear dry, and a big plastic bag to cover your pack. There is more good planning info at www.larutamoskitia.com.

Costs

You'll need a lot of money – small bills are preferable – as there are no banks in the region (except for Puerto Lempira). We suggest bringing a money belt and dispersing the cash between the members of your group. You can figure on anywhere between L$60 and L$400 a night for accommodation (less if you are willing to camp or arrange stays with local families), meals from L$40 to L$100, *colectivo* boat trips (following a set route) from L$300 to L$500 per leg, and flights between L$1171 and L$2450.

Three Great Itineraries

- Five days – This is the most common trip in the area (see p239 for more details on the overland route here). Begin your trip in the Laguna de Ibans area (p239). Get up early the next day to hike to Las Marías (p243). Spend a day or two in Las Marías, taking a tour, then following the route back to civilization.
- Twelve days (the hard way) – Hike one to two days from Dulce Nombre de Culmí (p103) to the headwaters of the Río Plátano, spending five days on the river as you travel down to Las Marías, then reconnecting with the five-day itinerary above.
- More time – With more time, you can take a raft or *colectivo* trip down the Río Patuca (p249), then hook up with the five-day itinerary above, leaving more time for tours in Las Marías.

by the availability of land for farming and ranching. A great deal of controversy surrounds ladino occupation of Moskitia lands, especially in areas traditionally used by the region's indigenous groups. Environmentalists worry, too, that ladino clear cutting, to make room for cattle, is contributing to the erosion of the region's rivers and leading to flooding downstream. See p39 for more in-depth coverage of Moskitia's ethnic groups.

DANGERS & ANNOYANCES

As in any large swath of rainforest or wilderness, travel in La Moskitia has a unique set of difficulties, dangers and annoyances.

First and foremost, never venture into the rainforest without a guide. Trails are faint and overgrown, and even experienced hikers can become hopelessly lost within a matter of minutes.

Traveling at night (by boat, truck or foot) can be dangerous, so avoid trying to do too much in any one day. Boats can break down, paths can be washed out, rivers can become impassable: you should always leave yourself several hours of daylight as a cushion in case problems arise. Remember that guides and boatmen – eager to please – may go along with an overly ambitious plan, assuming you understand the risks.

Likewise, avoid crossing Laguna de Ibans and especially Brus Laguna and Laguna de Caratasca late in the day – afternoon winds create large waves that can swamp or sink a boat. Though such incidents are rare, it's even rarer for boats to have lifejackets or radios in case of an emergency. Better to plan ahead so your crossings are in the morning, even if it means having to wake up extra early or 'losing' an afternoon along the way.

This is a malaria zone, so you should take the appropriate precautions (see p276). And with all that water, foot fungus (*masamora*) can become a real problem. Consider bringing foot powder, and try to dry off your feet at the end of every day.

The region is being used as a stopover for drugs from South America to the US, which has created a fair share of drug-related violence. Though attacks on tourists are rare, it's best to avoid the towns of Ironia and Palacios

LOCAL LORE: SEARCH FOR THE WHITE CITY

In 1519, Hernán Cortés first heard reports of La Cuidad Blanca (The White City), a glorious city named after elaborately carved white stones that were said to exist there. Stories of its immeasurable wealth in gold spurred Cortés to find the city, but, as it was supposedly hidden deep in the jungles of La Moskitia, he never did.

Many Pech legends refer to The White City as the birthplace of gods and a city filled with golden idols. The basis of countless expeditions, these stories have been fueled by 'sightings' as early as 1544, when Cristóbal de Pedraza, the then bishop of Honduras, wrote to the king of Spain to tell him about an impressive metropolis that he had seen from a mountaintop in La Moskitia; his guides assured him, he related, that nobles there ate from plates of gold.

In modern times, pilots and hunters have reported seeing or stumbling upon this elusive city; expeditions to find it have increased considerably since the 1940s because of this. Many treasure-hunters, in fact, claim to have already discovered it, but no proof or directional coordinates have ever been revealed.

in western Moskitia – they are dirty, dangerous and offer very little for travelers anyway. Puerto Lempira and Brus Laguna can get a bit dodgy at night.

And remember, all plans in La Moskitia are provisional. Planes, boats, trucks and buses can all be delayed for hours or days. On the same note, you may well find you want more time than you planned for. Build flexibility into your itinerary to account for unexpected changes of either sort. Changing tickets or plans is usually fairly easy, as all the towns are connected by radio.

TOURS

A pre-arranged tour is definitely worth considering, especially if your time (or Spanish speaking ability) is limited. Tours have the advantage of having all the transport and lodging planned ahead of time, something that can take a lot of time and energy for indie travelers. Most outfits offering tours to La Moskitia have good guides and track records – it's rare to get suckered into a total fiasco. The cost is higher than traveling independently, though not by as much as you might think. Going independently can be a terrific experience if you have the time, language skills and, to a certain degree, the money, to take things as they come. Otherwise, a tour can take the guesswork out of going to La Moskitia, letting you sit back and enjoy it.

Recommended tour operators include:

Jungle River Tours (☎ 440-1268, 408-0059; www.jungleriverlodge.com; Banana Republic Guesthouse, Av República btwn 12 & 13 calles, La Ceiba) Multi-day hiking and rafting trips.

La Moskitia Ecoaventuras (☎ 441-2480, 9929-7532; www.honduras.com/moskitia, moskitiaecoaventuras@yahoo.com; Colonia El Toronjal, La Ceiba) Run by Jorge Salverri, an expert birder and one of the most knowledgeable guides to La Moskitia. Tours range from five to 12 days and are cheap, though sometimes rough around the edges. Call ahead.

La Ruta Moskitia (☎ 3391-8833; www.larutamoskitia.com; Edificio Cenit Color, Local 6, Calle 13 btwn Av San Isidro & La República, La Ceiba) One of the most popular operators, sort of 'tour-lite': you don't travel with a dedicated guide, but transportation is prearranged and you are told who to ask for in each town. Every penny goes to the guides, guesthouse owners and boatmen you use, but traveling with this company also means other independent hotel operators, boatmen and restaurants receive fewer visitors.

MC Tours (☎ 551-8639; www.mctours-honduras.com; Col Tara Local No 3 Adobe 30, San Pedro Sula) An upscale outfit.

Mesoamérica Travel (☎ 557-8447; www.mesoamerica-travel.com; 8a Calle 709 at 32a Av NO, Col Juan Lindo, San Pedro Sula) Recommended from among the more upscale outfits.

Omega Tours (☎ 440-0334; www.omegatours.info; Omega Jungle Lodge, Calle a Yaruca Km 9) German owned and operated, offering highly recommended multi-day rafting trips down the Plátano and Patuca rivers. It's located along the Río Cangrejal on the way to the town of Yaruca.

Turtle Tours (☎ 429-2284; www.turtle-tours.com) German-run tour operator with an established reputation for small groups and professional service.

GETTING THERE & AWAY

Air

All flights to La Moskitia depart from La Ceiba. At the time of research, Aerolineas Sosa had daily flights to Puerto Lempira (L$2450, one way), and service to Brus

Laguna (L$2242, one way) on Monday, Wednesday and Friday. There was no scheduled service to Palacios, though SAMI (aka Air Honduras) occasionally connects to and from La Ceiba through there. Service in the region is irregular, and it's not uncommon to wait several days for a flight.

Aerolineas Sosa (www.aerolineasosa.com) La Ceiba (☎ 443-1849; Av San Isidro btwn 8a & 9a Calles; 🕑 7am-5pm Mon-Fri); Puerto Lempira (☎ 433-6558); Brus Laguna (☎ 433-8042)

SAMI Puerto Lempira (☎ 433-6016); Brus Laguna (433-8031)

Overland

You can get to the towns around the Laguna de Ibans – Cocobila, Rais Ta, Belén – in a day from either La Ceiba or Tocoa. These towns are the jump-off points for trips up the Río Plátano to Las Marías or to eastern destinations such as Ahuas and the Río Patuca. From La Ceiba take a 6am bus to Tocoa (L$75, 2½ hours). From there, grab a 4x4 – ask for a *paila a Batalla* – in the market (L$400), which will take you to Batalla. They'll take you right to the water taxis (L$200, two hours), which will take you to the villages around the Laguna de Ibans. See p246 for info on getting to and from Las Marías.

RETURNING

To return from the villages around Laguna de Ibans in a day, you'll need to take the first *colectivo* to Batalla at 3am, retracing your steps from there.

GETTING AROUND

Different seasons present different challenges in terms of getting around the Moskitia. The rainy reason is probably the most difficult, especially November through January, as the rivers get swollen with debris, and the trails and roads get muddy. Plus, getting caught in the rain while hiking or on a five-hour boat ride is no fun. During the driest months (February to April) some rivers may get too shallow in places to navigate.

Air

Within La Moskitia, **SAMI** (☎ in Brus Laguna 433-8031, in Puerto Lempira 433-6016) has semi-regular flights to and among all the main towns: Puerto Lempira, Brus Laguna, Palacios, Belén/Rais Ta, Ahuas, Wampusirpi, and Barra Patuca. Using tiny propeller planes, these flights are not for the faint hearted, but can be a convenient way to cut your travel time. That said, the flights do not follow a regular schedule – planes arrive and depart any time between 7am and 4pm, with no advance notice, and you may end up waiting a day (or more) for your flight. Fares vary widely, but average from L$1100 to L$1330 each way.

Boat

Most transportation in and around the Moskitia is by boat. Way upriver, the most common boat is a *pipantes,* a flat-bottomed boat made from a single tree trunk that's propelled by a pole or paddle. However, for longer trips or those on the lagoons, a *cayuco,* a wood-planked boat with an outboard motor, is more commonly used.

There are two types of service: *expreso* is like a private taxi and can be fairly expensive depending on the route (L$1000 to L$4000); and *colectivo,* which is like a bus following a set route picking up passengers as it goes. Prices are somewhat more manageable on *colectivo* services, ranging from L$300 to L$800.

Truck

A single dirt road along the Laguna de Ibans runs from the town of Ibans west through Belén, Rais Ta and Cocobila, and east to the town of Río Plátano (at the mouth of the river). Pickup trucks ply the route several times a day; the entire trip takes about an hour and costs around L$60.

AROUND LAGUNA DE IBANS

Most trips to La Moskitia begin in the sleepy villages around the Laguna de Ibans, the smallest of the three lagoons in the Moskitia. Along the low narrow strip of land that separates the lagoon from the ocean is a string of classic coastal villages with simple wood homes built on stilts, separated by patches of sandy grass or small plots of yucca and beans, and connected by small footpaths. It's fun just to spend a day or two bopping from village to village – it's about a 30-minute walk between most villages – being sure to take an afternoon

GAPS ON THE MAP: WESTERN MOSKITIA

No, La Moskitia does not start in the Laguna de Ibans, but given the ease of getting there in a day, it might as well. Once the staging points for expeditions into the region, Western Moskitia towns such as Palacios and Ironia are no longer necessary stops, and most folks skip them altogether.

The second largest city in La Moskitia, Palacios is a downright dangerous and dirty place. There's no reason to come here, and we'd recommend you skip it altogether. The tourist trail now skips Iriona, a pastoral Garífuna village perched on the edge of the sea. You can still take a bus from Tocoa to Ironia (L$100, four to five hours), than a speedboat (L$500, two hours) on to Belén. But it is much easier, and safer, to get to the area around Laguna de Ibans via Batalla (p236).

off for a little beach action. Arriving by boat from Batalla, you can choose to be dropped off in Plaplaya – the only Garífuna village in the area and home to an excellent sea turtle project – or head on to the jumping-off points for trips up the Río Plátano in the towns of Cocobila, Rais Ta or Belén. Rais Ta has the nicest (and most expensive) lodging, while Cocobila and Belén offer cheaper digs, and have a few stores and restaurants to stock up.

PLAPLAYA

pop 700

It's easier to get to Las Marías and the Reserva de la Biósfera del Río Plátano from the Laguna de Ibans towns to the east – Cocobila, Rais Ta and Belén – but travelers with a few extra days shouldn't miss Plaplaya, Honduras' easternmost Garífuna community. This quiet community is spread out between the lagoon and a scenic ocean beach. Basic wooden homes with thatched roofs and dirt floors are sprinkled along the narrow peninsula, connected by dirt paths that angle through small yucca plots. It is common to see women outside planting, harvesting, grating or compressing yucca, or in their homes standing before a hot wood-burning stove turning the flour into huge, slightly toasted, white *casabe* wafers.

Many consider Plaplaya to be the most traditional of Honduras' Garífuna villages. People here still live by fishing and yucca and banana cultivation, and have not suffered the outside encroachment or massive emigration, especially of young men, common in other communities. (Not that there is no emigration at all – many Plaplayans live and work in La Ceiba, the Bay Islands, San Pedro Sula and the United States.) A visit to the turtle protection project is well worth it, as is just walking around town and speaking with the local people.

You can make phone calls and buy food at **Pulpería Yohanna** (☎ 433-8221; 🕒 7am-noon & 1-7pm). Rates are L$10 for domestic calls, and start at L$18 for international calls. It is a five-minute walk west of Hospedaje Doña Sede.

Sights & Activities

Visitors to Plaplaya should try to track down Doña Patrocinia Blanco, an extremely friendly and capable woman who lives in Barrio Berijales, west of the center. Doña Patrocinia happens *not* to be Garífuna, but moved to Plaplaya from Tegucigalpa more than 30 years ago after marrying a Garífuna man. Her house serves as the de facto visitors center, and she can help you to see (and participate in) *casabe* being made, Garífuna dancing and the turtle project.

Plaplaya maintains a very successful **sea turtle preservation program** (🕒 Feb-Sep), which brings many foreign tourists to the small town and is the source of no small amount of pride for local residents. The project was started in 1995 with the help of a Peace Corps volunteer, and protects up to 50 turtle nests every year. Four different species nest here: *caray, verde* (green), *caurama* (*Caretta caretta* or loggerhead) and *baula* (leatherbacks, the largest sea turtles in the world). Between February and September, travelers can accompany volunteers on nightly patrols, in search of new nests and turtles laying their eggs. The turtles are measured and the eggs removed to a large nursery, where they have 24-hour protection against other animals and poachers. In 65 days – usually between June and August – the eggs begin to hatch and visitors can help release them into the ocean. The project also goes to schools in various communities to educate children about turtle preservation. *Día de la Tortuga* (Day of the Turtle) is celebrated every year on May 22, in commemoration of the day, in 1995, when the project's first turtles were born.

There's not much to see or do outside of the nesting season, unfortunately. A sea-turtle mural at the local school is worth a peek, though.

Sleeping & Eating

Hospedaje Doña Sede (main rd; r with shared bathroom L$120) This *hospedaje* (guesthouse) offers three basic rooms with cement floors and a corrugated tin roof. Beds have mosquito nets and there is a generator on-site (which means rooms get electricity until 10pm) – both a huge plus. As with every hotel around, the bathroom is located in an outhouse; the shower, in this case, is a hose with a pail. *Típica* (Honduran fare) meals are provided upon request (L$60).

Doña Vazilia (on lagoon; r with shared bathroom per person L$80) Just down the way from Doña Sede's place, this is a very simple, two-room structure with worn beds. The outhouse is pretty basic – prepare to hold your breath. Meals are provided upon request (L$50 to L$60).

Getting There & Away

From almost any pier on the lagoon, you can wait for a passing *colectivo* boat to go east to Belén (L$160, 45 minutes) or to any of the points along the way, including Ibans, Cocobila, and Rais Ta. The boat to Batalla (L$60, 45 minutes) passes around 4am. You can also walk east from here to Cocobila (two hours) and it's neighboring towns.

COCOBILA, RAIS TA & BELÉN

Connected by little pathways and large swaths of green grass and foliage, these three towns are just 30-minutes apart by foot. Belén has the soccerfield/airstrip, making it the most important of the three. But there's also a soccer field in Cocobila – take that Belén! – plus a few hotels and stores. Rais Ta is little more than the ecolodge run by the Bodden family. Continue east from Belén (about 30 minutes walking), and you'll run into Nuevo Jerusalén, a traditional Miskitu village with no guesthouses but nonetheless worth a visit. The white-sand beach is easily accessible from any of these villages; just head north and you'll find it.

Information

Clínica Privada Judith (24hr; Cocobila) This clinic is run by Judith Sandoval, a nurse trained in Tegucigalpa with over three decades of experience (her diplomas and licences are prominently displayed to prove it). Look for the green-and-white striped building on the main road.

Pulperías (general stores; 7am-6pm Mon-Sat; Belén & Cocobila) Next to the airstrip in Belén, there are several stores selling basic groceries and snacks. In Cocobila, there are two *pulperías* between Hospedaje Ethelinda and Hospedaje El Nopal.

Teléfono comunitario de Belén (community phone; 8am-7pm Mon-Sat; Belén) In a large building next to the airstrip, unmistakable for the antennae and satellite dishes on its roof. Rates are L$10 for domestic calls, and start at L$18 for international calls.

Teléfono comunitario de Cocobila (7:30am-8pm Mon-Sat, noon-8pm Sun; Cocobila) Similar prices to those in Belén, and located several hundred meters apart on the main road. One is in a private home next door to Hospedaje El Nopal, and the other is at nearby Hospedaje & Comedor Ethelinda.

Sights & Activities

A few different excursions can be arranged in Rais Ta. These are by no means a *National Geographic* jungle expedition; they're mellow and easy, a chance to see some rainforest, talk with the guide, and get your shoes dirty. The Rais Ta Eco Lodge (p242) is the best place to make arrangements, whether or not you're a guest there. Visiting early morning is best, not only for animal spotting, but because by afternoon the lagoon gets windy and rough, making your return journey tougher (and a whole lot wetter).

A popular half-day trip is to **Paru Creek** (trip per person L$200). Taking a *cayuco* across the lagoon, a guide leads you on a mild winding hike through the rainforest, checking out the multitudinous varieties of trees, flowers and insects. Two troops of howler monkeys live in this area, but spotting them is never guaranteed. You end up at Paru Creek, where the *cayuco* will be waiting. Shedding everything but your swimsuit – you may want to keep your shoes on too – you then float down the creek in inner tubes, the water clear and cold, the canopy swaying overhead, before returning to Rais Ta. Similar options are the **Brans Jungle Hike** and a trip to the community of **Banaka**, where you'll see ancient petroglyphs.

A very nice walk – which Mario Miller of Pawanka Beach Cabins (see p242) is likely to take you on as a matter of course – is from the cabins through Nuevo Jerusalén to the beach. Mario has numerous stories to tell about the town, various people and events, presenting an interesting snapshot of the area. You can return via the beach, collecting shells and driftwood. Ships are often moored offshore; many are lobster ships, which Mario can also describe, having been a lobster diver himself. You can do the same trip on horseback – there's nothing quite like galloping on the beach with the wind in your hair. Ask Mario for details.

Mario can also arrange any of these hikes and has other outings in the works, including manatee-spotting and nighttime crocodile-spotting. None had been finalized at the time of research, but are worth asking about.

Most guests at the Pawanka Cabins are treated to – or roped into, depending on your taste for these things – a bonfire on the beach with traditional music, singing and dancing by local community members. Of course, the foreigners are always pulled up to dance, usually several times over the course of the hour-long gathering. You can try feigning a sprained ankle, but it's easier to just go with the flow. The rough folksy songs, accompanied by a guitar and washboard, are the highlight of the evening. Kids often perform a dance that appears to be a Miskitu version of 'London Bridge is Falling Down,' which can be fun.

A knowledgeable Miskitu guide, Alberto Chow Tinglas, takes visitors overland to Las Marías. The trip takes one or two days, depending on how fit you are. During the rainy season, you're likely to be in *lodo* (mud) up to your knees. The rest of the year it's highly passable. Alberto can arrange for accommodation along the way. Inquire for him at the Hospedaje & Comedor Ethelinda in Cocobila. Alberto charges L$1000 for the journey (normally one to two days), and it costs L$400 (up to six people) to cross the Laguna de Ibans in *expreso*. He can also arrange horseback trips up there for L$100 per day. Note that Alberto only speaks Spanish and Miskitu.

Sleeping & Eating

COCOBILA

Hospedaje & Comedor Ethelinda (r L$70) Walking from Rais Ta you'll pass this bare-bones-basic guesthouse first. It's rather dirty with paper-thin foam mattresses – ask the owners if you can double them up – and toilets that are just plain nasty. But it's cheap and traditional, and there's a friendly *comedor* next door, where you can ask for Alberto Chow Tinglas, who guides folks overland up to Las Marías.

Hospedaje El Nopal (r L$100) A couple of hundred meters further on is this small hotel with a huge nopal cactus in front – totally out of place in this tropical town, but thriving nonetheless. Rooms are clean and well kept, with cement floors, candles, lace curtains and surprisingly thick mattresses. The latrine and shower – rainwater or well water, depending on the season – are out the back. If no one is around when you arrive, ask for René or Ana at the wooden building across the street and just east of the hotel.

RAIS TA

Rais Ta Eco Lodge (☎ 449-0198; s/d with shared bathroom L$200/360) This hotel opened in 2006 with help from La Ruta Moskitia, and is undeniably the nicest in the area. The Bodden family owns the whole village, including the eight-bedroom lodge. Rooms are rustic, but well built and comfortable, with sturdy beds, mosquito nets, and small porches with hammocks. The shower and bath area is spic-and-span. Doña Elma also cooks large tasty meals (L$60).

BELÉN

Pawanka Beach Cabins (per person L$180) Too bad there are only two cabins here, because these are some of the nicest ones around. They're identical in design to the Yamari Cabañas outside Brus Laguna, with screen walls, mosquito nets, thick firm mattresses and crisp linens. The ocean waves lull you to sleep at night, while Pico Baltimore, off in the distance, greets you in the morning. And Pawanka has real flush toilets and even a standup shower with shower head if you could use some creature comforts. Meals are L$65.

Doña Exy (r with shared bathroom per person L$100) A huge bougainvillea bush greets visitors as they enter the humble grounds of this *hospedaje*. The rooms themselves are basic – wood-plank walls with a tin roof and squishy beds – but clean. Meals are served upon request (L$50). The on-site generator, which runs from 6pm to 9pm nightly, is a plus. It's on the road from Rais Ta to the airstrip.

Doña Mendilia (r with shared bathroom per person L$60) A beautiful and well-tended garden is the highlight of this huge old place, the 2nd floor of which houses the guestrooms. Each room has a foam bed with clean linens and is divided from the others by paper-thin walls. Located right on the airstrip – don't worry, planes seldom land here – this guesthouse has a rickety balcony, a great vantage point for watching afternoon soccer games.

Comedor y Hospedaje Diana (r with shared bathroom per person L$120) Looking onto the airstrip, the Diana serves up excellent meals (L$60) in its dirt-floor *comedor*. The rooms are basic, but a decent value, though the separate bathrooms leave a bit to be desired.

Getting There & Away

There is a landing strip/soccer field in Belén. Half-way down one side of it is a small wood building that houses the **SAMI office** (6:30am-5pm Mon-Sat). Be sure to check in at 6.30am since flight departures change on a whim. Prepare to wait anywhere from half an hour to a day or two.

An early morning *colectivo* takes passengers from Belén (3am), Rais Ta (3am) and Cocobila (3:30am) to Batalla (L$200), in time to catch a 4x4 back to Tocoa. For the town of Río Plátano, a *colectivo* pickup truck passes about twice a day (L$50, 45 minutes); another passes in the other direction at the same frequency, making stops in Cocobila, Ibans and Plaplaya. For Brus Laguna, you can take a *colectivo* boat (L$200, two to three hours) or hire an *expreso* (L$2000, two hours). You may have better luck finding a *colectivo* by taking the truck to Río Plátano first.

There is an occasional *colectivo* service to Las Marías (L$500 to L$800, about twice a week, five to seven hours). Ask around Belén, Cocobila and Nuevo Jerusalén to see if there's a boat heading up. *Expreso* service to Las Marías is L$4000 (roundtrip) for the boat. Better yet, talk to the young men around town for a dugout canoe trip up to Las Marías (around L$1500 roundtrip, two days), or Alberto Tinglas on Cocobila (p245), who guides hikers up to Las Marías (one to two days, L$1400 roundtrip).

RESERVA DE LA BIÓSFERA DEL RÍO PLÁTANO

The Río Plátano Biosphere Reserve protects a wide array of species – monkeys, peccaries and birds aplenty…oh my! – and is by most assertions the most magnificent nature reserve in all of Honduras. But the rainforest reserve is not just for the birds – there are plenty of indigenous communities that call this place home, and on a trip up the Río Plátano, you'll see less rainforest and more small-scale farming than you probably expected. It takes a concerted hike into the jungle to really get a picture of the reserve's wild inhabitants, and that sort of trip is likely to cost you a pretty penny. The best time of year to visit this World Heritage Site, founded in 1980 by Honduras and the UN, is between November and July; the best time for bird-watching is February and March, when many migratory birds are in the area.

LAS MARÍAS

Ideally situated in the heart of the biosphere reserve, Las Marías is the jumping-off spot for most jungle expeditions in the region. It is a town of mixed ethnicity, with around 100 Miskitu and Pech families living in relative harmony. The Pech population had declined significantly, but the arrival of several families from upriver in Olancho has reinvigorated the normally reticent group. Men and women from both communities participate in the guide program – if your guide is Pech, they'll likely let you know.

Orientation

Arriving at Las Marías by river, you first come to the *hospedajes* run by Doña Diana and Doña Rutilia. A path leads from behind Doña Diana's up a small rise to a third guesthouse – Doña Justa – that is definitely worth checking out. One of the town's two *pulperías* is a short distance from the entrance to Doña Justa's. Continuing on the path you'll reach the center of town – so to speak – a grassy and little-used airstrip/soccer field with the clinic on one side and another guesthouse, Hospedaje Don Ovidio, on the other. The path meanders on, over a bridge, and past two churches and a fourth guesthouse (Don Luís), before reconnecting with the river near the put-in for *pipante* trips upriver. The path forms a loop – touted as the 'Village Trail' – that makes for a pleasant walk if you have some free time. Bring a flashlight if there's any chance you'll be out past dusk – when it gets dark it gets *dark*.

Information

There isn't much in the way of services in Las Marías. There's no running water or

UNRAVEL THE TRADITIONS OF THE MISKITU

The Miskitu indigenous group – the namesake of La Moskitia, aka the Mosquito Coast – occupies coastal and inland areas in the state of Gracias a Dios and parts of Olancho. Although they are arguably the most 'modernized' of the ethnic groups in La Moskitia, most essentially still subsist as they have for centuries, through small-time agriculture and fishing.

How the Miskitu came to be is not fully understood. And to this date, there hasn't even been agreement as to how to spell the tribe's name and language, though most scholars now go with a 'u' instead of an 'o' at the end.

Fairly dark skinned, the Miskitu are almost certainly descended from an as-yet-unknown indigenous group and escaped or shipwrecked African slaves. The name definitely did not come from 'mosquito' as Paul Theroux led us all to believe, although its true origin is disputed. There was an early king named Miskut, and some argue Miskitu is derived from a phrase meaning 'people who follow Miskut'. A more widely accepted theory is that it comes from the English word 'musket,' which the Miskitu were given (and quickly mastered) by British meddlers seeking to erode Spanish control of mainland Honduras. In fact, Miskitus probably have a fair amount of British blood, too. Some 30% of Miskitu words come from English, including *landing, kitchen, work,* and the days of the week. We include a few Miskitu phrases in our language chapter. Some say Miskitu culture is so mixed – indigenous, African, English – that it lacks a core identity. Yet it may be their multi-ethnicity that has made the Miskitu so well prepared to adapt to the many challenges and changes they face.

Traditional Miskitu territory straddles the Nicaragua-Honduras border, marked by the Río Coco. Through the colonial and early independence periods – and even in modern times – the Miskitu passed back and forth freely, whether for family, fishing or farming. The border became intensely militarized, however, following the Sandinista revolution in Nicaragua, when US-funded Contras launched incursions from camps just across the border. The CIA recruited untold numbers of Nicaraguan Miskitus as guides, translators, foot soldiers, even platoon leaders, while the Sandinista government killed and imprisoned Miskitus they suspected of colluding with the Contras. The US seized upon the deaths as evidence that the Sandinistas would kill their own people to stay in power. Whether Miskitu deaths amounted to a massacre, as the US claimed, or were ordinary casualties of war exaggerated by American propaganda, as the Sandinistas said, may never be officially determined.

Miskitu people on both sides of the border have returned to a more ordinary existence, still surviving largely on fishing, small-time farming, and, increasingly, tourism. In both countries, but especially Honduras, Miskitu men have been drawn to quick money as lobster divers, but hundreds have been crippled or killed by decompression sickness, stemming from a lack of proper training and the failure of boat owners and the government to enforce basic safety regulations.

electricity, and there is only one phone in town (at Hospedaje Doña Rutilia, p246). For medical emergencies, head to the **Clínica de Salud** (🕑 7:30am-3pm Mon-Fri, emergencies 24hr), in the center of town, which is staffed by two nurses with a meager medical supply.

Dangers & Annoyances

When walking around town, stay on the trail and do not venture on your own into the forest – this is still the jungle, after all. At night, do not leave anything outside, even laundry. While just about everyone you meet in Las Marías is gracious and friendly, modern shoes, clothes and electronics – so far beyond the means of most residents – make tempting targets.

Tours

It's a bit of a racket – and wildly expensive – but you are basically required to take a tour to visit the areas around Las Marías. Ask around for the **Centro de Visitantes** (☎ 9943-9706, 433-8165), an unmarked building on the road to town from the river, which may or may not be manned. For detailed itineraries of the tours, see p246).

This being national patrimony, you *could* head off on your own, but it's really quite dangerous to venture into the jungle without a guide, so you're basically forced to work within the system. Here's how it works: Sometime after you arrive, most likely in the early evening, you will be visited by the current *sacaguía* (head guide). Elected every six months, the *sacaguía* is responsible for greeting newly arrived visitors, helping you determine what tours you'd like to take, and assigning the necessary guides. The *sacaguía's* fee is L$100 per group per tour, which you typically pay on the spot. They'll probably also ask for a small donation for trail maintenance and the like; it's not required, but a couple of dollars is definitely appreciated.

Prices for a given tour depend on the number of guides required – the Cerro de Zapote tour requires just one guide for one day, while Pico Dama takes three guides for three days. On any tour, the lead guide is paid L$250 per day, while secondary guides receive L$150 per day. If your group has more than seven people, you'll need additional guides. You are not required to pay for the guides' food or supplies, but a 10% tip is customary for good service. The cabins en route to Pico Dama and Cerro Baltimore cost L$130 per person per night, a mossie-net and sheet run to L$130, and canoes cost L$150 per day. This can start to add up – all told, a Pico Dama trip costs more than L$2000 – so be sure you bring enough cash, always in small bills. Neither the prices nor the number of required guides is negotiable.

Ask the owner of your guesthouse in Las Marías about stowing gear you won't need on your hike. It should be perfectly fine, but do put a lock on your rucksack, and bring along especially important items, including your passport, plane tickets and cash

Finally, 7am is the standard departure time, which, after introductions, gathering up gear, walking to the boat or the trailhead, and explaining one thing or another, can easily turn into 9am – way too late for bird- or animal-spotting. If you're up for it, tell the *sacaguía* you want to start at 5:30am or 6am; with any luck you'll be on your way no later than 7am and have a better chance of seeing creatures.

A fun alternative to the Las Marías tours is to take the one- to two-day hike to Las Marías from the Laguna de Ibans – you see plenty of rainforest along the way, and also get a chance to see small-time farming operations, learn about the medicinal uses of rainforest plants, and ford a river or two. Alberto Tinglas is a knowledgeable local guide. He can arrange for overnight stays along the way, and knows quite a bit about local flora and fauna (though he only speaks Spanish and Miskitu). Ask for him at the Hospedaje & Comedor Ethelinda in Cocobila (p242). This trip is best done during the dry season, as the trails become nearly impassable (lots of mud) during the rainy season. And do not attempt this trip on your own, it's far too easy to get lost in the maze of trails. To get back to Laguna de Ibans or to destinations upriver, check with locals to see if they can take you in a dugout canoe (around L$500 per day, for up to four passengers).

The only informal tour in town is the Crocodile Tour (L$790 for two people) – a two-hour twilight walk around a crocodile-infested lagoon. Sounds a little edgy, but no one has been hurt so far. Plus the photo opps are excellent. Stop by Hospedaje Doña Justa to set it up. And you can always ask a kid with a horse if they can take you for a horseback ride (around L$100).

Ask the *sacaguía* about Danzas Culturales (Cultural Dances), your chance to witness the traditional dances of the Miskitu and Pech. At L$100 per dancer, the dance normally ends up costing L$1000.

Sleeping & Eating

Hospedaje Doña Justa (center of town; r with shared bathroom per person L$100) Super friendly, the Doña Justa is a thatch-roofed building with several airy rooms overlooking a huge flower garden. Each room is well-kept and has decent beds with mosquito nets. There's a big patio with lots of hammocks, perfect for whiling away an afternoon with a book. Meals are prepared upon request (L$50).

Hospedaje Doña Diana (on the river; r with shared bathroom per person L$100) Two plank-wood buildings overlooking the Río Plátano house four private rooms. Each has a couple of foam beds with mosquito nets and is kept reasonably clean. Meals can be prepared upon request (L$60) and are served on the porch outside your room; it's convenient and pretty, but, unfortunately, can attract roaches.

Hospedaje Don Ovidio (center of town; r with shared bathroom per person L$100) This thatch-roofed building is located right on the airstrip. There are several private rooms, all with squishy, thin mattresses and no window screens (lather on the bug repellent and ask for a mossie net). The bathroom facilities are a serious highlight: there's a toilet seat and the outdoor shower

INTO THE WILD: TOURS FROM LAS MARÍAS

There are half a dozen different tours available from Las Marías, of varying lengths and difficulty. Some involve rigorous hiking, others only moderate; some have lots of boat time, others none at all. If you're up for it, Pico Dama and Cerro Baltimore are truly terrific hikes, and afford the best chance of seeing birds, animals and primary forest (which is why you came, right?). Cerro Mico and Cerro de Zapote are good if you want something less strenuous. The one-day Walpaulban Sirpi petroglyph (rock-carving) tour is popular, especially with groups, but involves an awful lot of boat time, especially considering you just spent five hours on a *cayuco* to get here and will spend another five to return.

Pico Dama

Duration Three days
Guides Three
Difficulty Difficult

The toughest tour starts with a two-hour *pipante* ride upriver, then a mild three- to four-hour hike through primary and secondary forest to a cabin with simple beds and an area for camping (linens and mosquito nets can be rented in Las Marías for L$130 per night). Day 2 involves a steep three- to four-hour hike through thick vegetation to the base of Pico Dama's distinctive rock pinnacle. The views are spectacular, and the bird and animal life abundant throughout. You return to camp that afternoon, and hike out the following day. For an even longer trip, add the second half of the Cerro Mico tour, with a stop at the lower petroglyphs.

Cerro Baltimore

Duration Two days
Guides Two
Difficulty Moderate to difficult

This hike begins from Las Marías with a rolling five- to seven-hour hike through primary and secondary forest, teeming with wildlife. You overnight at a rustic camp-house then wake up early to climb the summit – a two-hour hike with incredible views of Laguna de Ibans and the Caribbean Sea beyond. Return to Las Marías on the same day via a different route.

Cerro Mico

Duration Two days
Guides Three

is attached to the main building. Meals are prepared upon request (L$60).

Hospedaje Don Luís (toward the river; r with shared bathroom per person $100) The *hospedaje* of last resort in town, the two rooms here are on the wrong side of clean and the beds are so saggy, you might as well sleep on the floor. The cement bathroom with ceramic toilet bowl would be a plus if you didn't have to push pigs out of the way to get to it.

Hospedaje Doña Rutilia (on the river; r with shared bathroom per person L$150) Twenty-one beds distributed in several private rooms make up this rambling guesthouse. Some beds have outright mattresses (as opposed to foam cushions) and rooms are relatively clean. The only generator and telephone in town are here too – both a plus if you need, or just like to have, these modern conveniences. Meals (L$60) are also offered.

Hospedaje Wehnatara (r with shared bathroom per person L$150) Located a 35-minute canoe trip upriver (inquire with the *sacaguía*) this is an alternative place to stay if you want to explore the petroglyphs, Cerro Mico or Pico Dama. It offers two rooms in a wood building that overlooks the river. Accommodations are basic but adequate. All meals are prepared upon request (L$60).

Pulpería Yehimy (center of town; 5am-6pm Mon-Sat) Basic foodstuffs and medicines are sold at this tiny bodega.

Getting There & Away

An *expreso* from Rais Ta to Las Marías has a fixed price of L$4000 (roundtrip, five to six hours each way) – ouch – though you can

Difficulty Moderate
This tour begins as the petroglyph tours do, making your way by *pipante* and foot to Walpaulban Sirpi. Camp along the river or stay at a nearby *hospedaje*, and the next day climb Cerro Mico – which is not called 'Monkey Hill' for nothing – returning on a different path to the river where the *pipante* is waiting to take you downstream to Las Marías. You could add a day to this trip by continuing upriver to Walpaulban Tara, the second set of petroglyphs.

Cerro de Zapote
Duration One day
Guides One
Difficulty Moderate
This up-and-back hike is essentially the first part of the Cerro Baltimore trip. Starting from Las Marías, you hike through fairly flat terrain, with only one steep hill before turning back. This hike has good bird-watching opportunities without having to stay the night outside of Las Marías – be sure to start early!

Walpaulban Sirpi
Duration One day
Guides Three
Difficulty Easy
Las Marías' most popular tour begins with a two-hour *pipante* ride upriver before disembarking at the beginning of the Kuyuzqui trail. A moderate 1½- to two-hour hike includes stopping at a new observation tower. Birds and animals are relatively rare, owing to the foot traffic and because you get here relatively late. After seeing the petroglyphs – an evocative, but small archeological remnant – and lunching by the river, you return to Las Marías.

Walpaulban Tara
Duration Two days
Guides Three
Difficulty Easy
Start out as the Walpaulban Sirpi tour does, but rather than return, camp or stay the night at the nearby *hospedaje*. The next day is similar, continuing upriver in the *pipante*, with short hikes along the way. Return to Las Marías in the afternoon.

often join up with other travelers, or even a tour group, to share the cost. The boatman waits in Las Marías, so after the second night it'll cost you an extra US$8 per night. There is occasional *colectivo* service (about three days a week) between here and the Laguna de Ibans area (L$500 to L$800, five to six hours). Ask in Cocobila, Belén or Nuevo Jerusalén.

Our favorite way to get to Las Marías is to talk with Alberto Tinglas (ask for him at the Hospedaje & Comedor Ethelinda in Cocobila, p242) who guides trekkers overland from the Laguna de Ibans to Las Marías (one to two days). The trip costs L$400 for the Laguna de Ibans crossing, and L$1000 for the guide (for the entire trip).

The best way down is to take a dugout canoe (a seven- to 10-hour trip) downriver to the Laguna de Ibans for around L$1500 per boat (up to four passengers). Ask at your hotel for information. You might be able to hire a canoe to take you to and from the Laguna (around L$1500), but it's two days up, and you'll need to camp along the way.

BRUS LAGUNA & AROUND

You won't see many foreign faces in the areas surrounding Brus Laguna (pronounced 'Bruce', as in Springsteen) – there just isn't that much to see or do in the pine savannah surrounding the town. But you can head out for adventures around the lagoon or upriver to the Río Patuca or Río Plátano. And, well, it's kind of nice in this day and age to not see another traveler for a few days. The pirate Bloody Brewer used the lagoon as his hideaway, hence the name. Today, Brus Laguna (the town) is tucked into a sheltered corner of Brus Laguna (the lagoon) and is one of two towns in La Moskitia receiving regular flights from La Ceiba (the other is Puerto Lempira).

BRUS LAGUNA TOWN

pop 13,900

Brus Laguna is a dusty, one-road town. There's little to do here, and most people go straight from the airport to the boat dock to hop on a motorboat for Rais Ta or head straight to Las Marías. The boat trips are highlights in and of themselves. However, if you're not crunched for time, consider spending a night at Yamari Cabañas (opposite), a set of cabins outside of town.

There is world-class flat fishing in and around the lagoon, including snook, grouper and record-size tarpon.

Orientation & Information

Brus Laguna has one main drag (main st), a wide, dirt road that extends uninterrupted from the pier to the airport, several kilometers away. Just about everything you need is on or near the main road, within a few blocks of the pier. If you're ever unsure, just ask the first person to pass – locals are very friendly, though there's an increasing problem with public drunkenness in town.

CESAMO (☎ 443-8082; ⏲ 7:30am-noon & 2-5pm Mon-Fri) is the only medical center in town; services are very basic, but there is always a doctor and nurse on staff. It's located in a blue-and-white building next to the **police station** (☎ 443-8015; ⏲ 24hr). On the other side of the main drag is **Hondutel** (⏲ 7:30am-3:30pm Mon-Fri), where you can make national and international calls. The town's electricity does not start till 5pm.

Sleeping & Eating

Stay in town if you're here just to catch a flight; otherwise, the best accommodations are a short boat ride away (see Yamari Cabañas, opposite). When we visited, there was a fancy Centro Turistico Restaurant being built (opposite the Hotel Laguna Paradise), which looked like it'd be the nicest restaurant in town.

Hotel Tukrun Tangni (r with shared bathroom L$150) Just down from the pier, this budget-buster has cardboard walls and thinner-than-thin-mint mattresses. But, it's darn cheap, and you get mossie nets. It's just west of the pier.

Hotel Laguna Paradise (☎ 433-8039; s/d L$200/300) Located over Pulpería Vanesa, this place is fairly janky, but the sheets appear to be clean and the service is friendly, making it the best 'middle-of-the-road' buy. Beds are a little saggy, but it'll do for a night or two. All rooms have fans, cable TV and private bathrooms.

Hotel Casa Blanca (s/d L$350/450; ❄) Though the air-con wasn't working when we passed through, this is the best hotel in town, with mossie nets on the crisp, new beds, clean showers and cable TV. It's 1½ blocks west of main st but a bit tough to find, so ask around for directions.

Comedor Doña Nohemy (main st; meals L$60; ⏲ breakfast, lunch & dinner) The only restaurant in town, Doña Nohemy will feed you every day of the week as long as you're not picky about what you get. Just be sure it's freshly made – items sit around until they're eaten. Scrambled eggs and sandwiches are safe bets.

Pulpería Vanesa (main st; ⏲ 6am-7pm) The biggest *pulpería* in town, this place also has the best variety of goods. Apart from lots of foodstuffs, you will also find repellent, mosquito nets, rain gear and batteries (but no sunblock, unfortunately).

Entertainment

Brus Laguna has a **movie theater** (admission L$10; ⏲ 7pm daily & 1pm, 3pm & 7pm Sun) – sort of. It's a digital projector connected to a DVD player, with a dozen or so plastic chairs set up in a private house on the main drag. (It's run by the same family that operates the bus to the airport, in fact.) Most movies are dubbed in Spanish and action-oriented: *King Kong*, yes, *Capote*, no.

Getting There & Away

AIR

At the time of research, **Aerolineas Sosa** (☎ 9818-8272; www.aerolineasosa.com; office by the pier) had flights from La Ceiba to Brus Laguna (L$2260 one way, one hour) at 10am on Monday, Wednesday, and Friday, returning from Brus Laguna the same days at 11am. They're small planes, so it's recommended you make reservations well in advance (and double-check fares and schedules while you're at it).

SAMI (☎ 433-6016; ⏰ 6:30am-5pm Mon-Sat) has even smaller planes – taking six to nine passengers – and serves towns within La Moskitia, including Puerto Lempira, Ahuas, Belén, Wampusirpi and Palacios. Tickets cost between L$1171 and L$1333, one-way. The ticket office accepts cash only and is at a bodega several blocks up the main drag from the pier. Flights leave anytime between 7am and 2pm (Monday to Saturday only); plan on waiting around all day, and cross your fingers the wait's not two or three days. The flight may make a few stops along the way, depending on where you and the other passengers are headed.

Brus Laguna's airport – a narrow, dirt strip with a kiosk on one side for passengers to wait under – is several kilometers from town. A small school bus ferries passengers to and from all Sosa flights (per person L$50 – ouch again!), while the SAMI guy usually takes passengers there in his pick-up (and charges the same).

BOAT

Motor boats carry passengers from the town pier to various points in and outside the lagoon. *Colectivos* from Brus Laguna to Belén leave the main pier between 5am and 6am daily (per person L$200, three hours). An *expreso* for the same trip costs around L$1600 for up to six people. It's a great trip, passing through mangrove channels, small fishing villages and wild spots along the lagoon's edge.

You can also arrange a boat straight from Brus Laguna to Las Marías. The *expreso* trip takes five to six hours and costs around L$6000 roundtrip. The boat holds up to eight people, but costs the same if there are only two. It's important you hire a reliable boat driver, as the trip across the lagoon and up the Río Plátano can be tricky. Juan Membreno and 'El Chele' are recommended, or ask the Woods (see Yamari Cabañas, right) for more suggestions. There is an occasional *colectivo* service from here to Las Marías (L$500 to L$800) and a daily service to Ahuas (L$325). Ask around at the dock.

Whether you're headed to Rais Ta/Belén or Las Marías, you may be able to get a ride (for a fee) with a tour group; there's likely to be one on the plane from La Ceiba. If you go the same day, don't dally, as wind and waves on the lagoon grow dangerously strong in the afternoon.

OUTSIDE BRUS LAGUNA TOWN

An hour's boat ride from Brus Laguna, **Yamari Cabañas** (☎ 433-8265, 9589-9533; per person L$180) are two rustic but very comfortable wood cabins built on stilts on a broad, grassy savannah. The grassy expanse is bisected by a long meandering creek, and studded here and there with clusters of small tique palms. It is an unusual landscape – you almost expect a giraffe to appear – certainly not what most people would expect when they plan a trip to La Moskitia. And there's nothing else out here, save a few ranchers and the occasional cow. The cabins are operated by Macoy and Dorcas Wood, a serious but friendly couple who will go out of their way to make your stay pleasant.

A visit to Yamari Cabins typically includes a long walk through the savannah. If the water is high, you can float back down the creek to the cabins on inner-tubes. When the water is low, there's still a great little swimming hole a few meters from the cabins. At night, Macoy can take you in the boat to go crocodile-spotting.

The cabins themselves are thatch-roofed, with four individual beds apiece and mosquito nets hanging down. The mattresses are surprisingly thick – the sort you'd find in a good hotel – and the linens fresh and clean. But what makes the cabins lovely is their screen walls, which let in all the sounds and sights around you. Sunsets and sunrises are sublime, accompanied by the songs of countless birds. Meals (L$80) are served in a separate building. It also offers free kayaks for guests.

The cabins are about an hour by motorized *cayuco* from Brus Laguna, and transportation is included in the price. Macoy or Dorcas will meet you at the airport or pier and accompany you, along with a guide and a cook, for your stay at Yamari. Do not simply make your own way there – not only do few boatmen in town know the way, the cabins are opened only when the Woods (who live in Brus Laguna proper) are expecting guests.

RÍO PATUCA

Most people never make it this far…sounds perfect! The Patuca is Honduras' second-

CANNON ISLAND

Cannon Island, a small outcropping on the southwest corner of Brus Laguna (the lagoon), has seen its fair share of history. British marines occupied the islet in the 1700s and fortified it with cannons, which gave the island its name. (The cannons are still there.)

Later, it was a temporary camp for around 250 Scottish settlers who arrived in 1822 and 1823, lured by tales of fertile lands, pliant natives, even government jobs in a newly-formed nation called Territory of Poyais. It was all an elaborate self-indulgence of Scottish adventurer Gregor MacGregor (what a name!), who evidently believed he had been given sovereign rights to some 34,500 sq km at the mouth of the Río Negro by the Miskitu king. The settlers soon realized the folly of their situation and ensconced themselves on Cannon Island, refusing to venture into what was then unconquered indigenous territory. They were eventually evacuated by British ships from present-day Belize, but not before disease and despair had taken root – at least one settler committed suicide and 180 died of various causes stemming from the ordeal. MacGregor managed to escape blame – survivors even defended him in the British press – and he concocted several similar schemes before retiring to Venezuela, where he died in 1845. Author David Sinclair delves into the madness in *The Land that Never Was: Sir Gregor MacGregor and the Most Audacious Fraud in History* (2004).

More recently, Cannon Island became known among anglers for its snook and tarpon flats. Record tarpon have been landed here, including several 200-pounders. A fishing camp opened on the island in 1995, but has since changed hands, and disputes over leasing rights have stalled its re-opening. Some tours include a stop here to check out the cannons and a small museum created by the original fishing-camp operators. Tour guides and boat drivers can also arrange a brief stop on the island. You may need to negotiate a fee.

longest river, stretching some 500km from its headwaters in Olancho to the Caribbean Sea. It passes through the pristine Patuca National Park, the Tawahka Asangni Biosphere Reserve, and along the edge of the Reserva de la Biósfera del Río Plátano. Most travelers reach this remote area by plane, via Ahuas or Wampusirpi, though week-long rafting expeditions starting in Olancho are possible (p103).

AHUAS

pop 9300

Ahuas is the largest town along the Río Patuca, which is not to say it's huge: about 9000 people live here and in the surrounding areas, mostly Miskitu. It is a quiet place a few kilometers from the river itself, with wood homes, a few churches and an airstrip. It also has a hospital that is run by volunteer doctors from abroad and considered one of the best in the region. Ahuas used to be the main jumping-off point for trips into the Tawahka region, but the travelers who make it here – very few indeed – now tend to fly all the way to Wampusirpi and start upriver from there. The *colectivo* trip from here to Puerto Lempira or destinations upriver is a highlight in and of itself. But don't expect lots of jungle hiking opportunities: this is pine savannah, and while there's excellent bird-watching, those expecting a Bungalow Bill experience will be sorely disappointed.

Walk into town to check out the lodging options. Budget travelers can save some lemps by asking to stay at a *hospedaje* (guesthouse), which will run to around L$150.

Hotel Mi Estrella (r L$250) is the only 'real' hotel in town, and has extremely thin mattresses and very basic rooms. Ask to see the rooms upstairs, which offer more ventilation and better light. Meals (L$60) are served upon request.

Getting There & Away

SAMI (☎ in Puerto Lempira 433-6016) is the only airline with services to Ahuas. Virtually all flights come from Brus Laguna (L$1171) or Puerto Lempira (L$1171). There is no fixed schedule, and as with all SAMI flights you may have to wait a day or two before getting on a plane.

Boats from Barra Patuca stop in Ahuas to load and unload cargo, and either continue upriver to Wampusirpi, or turn around and go back. You may be able to talk your way onto one of those boats, though they have no fixed schedule. Prices should be around L$250 to L$350 in either direction. **Transporte Fluvial Jaaciel** (☎ 3252-8421, 3287-7935) runs *colectivo* boats between here and Brus Laguna (L$325, two to three hours). Note that the river is a solid hour's walk from Ahuas town. **Gamisu Transporte Fluvial** (☎ 9801-9775), on the pier in Puerto Lempira, runs *colectivo* boats between here and Puerto Lempira (L$350, one to two hours), including transfers to and from the town center.

WAMPUSIRPI

pop 6000

An appealingly rustic little town, Wampusirpi is of Tawahka origin, but most of its residents are now Miskitu. They live simple though somewhat precarious lives, surviving on small plots of rice, beans, bananas and yucca, supplemented by fish from the Patuca River and whatever small game they can hunt down in the surrounding hills. Wampusirpi proper is a collection of wooden homes on stilts – the river and a nearby lagoon are prone to flooding – while some 23 smaller communities (some just a cluster of homes) are scattered nearby.

Wampusirpi is by no means a tourist town, though townspeople are accustomed to a trickle of foreign missionaries, service workers and travelers. A number of people pass through on their way to Tawahka, further upriver. It's easy to spend a day or more quietly exploring the town, meeting local folks and soaking up the small-town atmosphere.

There are no formal services in Wampusirpi, save a small *centro médico* (health center) on the road between the town and the airport. The lagoon is used by children for swimming and by women for laundry. A thick pipe drawing a good flow of cold spring water is used for bathing and for drinking. You may be able to find bottled water at one of the *pulperías* in town – locals drink straight from the pipe – but it's essential travelers in this area carry plenty of water purification tablets or a small bottle of chlorine. See p279 for more info.

February and March is the best and driest time of year to come. During the rainy season, especially June and July, the paths get extremely muddy and the mosquitoes are especially voracious. No matter what time of year, a pair of good boots is a must; if you only packed flip-flops, a pair of rubber boots costs about L$150 in the small market here, or in any Moskitia town.

Sleeping & Eating

At least three families rent rooms in their homes to travelers and volunteers. None of the houses have signs, but anyone in town will be able to point you in the right direction. All are very basic, with cots and latrine toilets. One guesthouse, known as **La Cabaña** (r L$100), is in the middle of town and has largish rooms. The others are near the *puente roto* (broken bridge) at the far end of the main road, near the lagoon. The one on the right as you approach charges L$80 per person, and the hosts can help you arrange river transport. Some travelers have reported staying at the **Catholic Mission** (dm L$40), which has dorm-like lodging.

There are no *comedores,* per se, but you should be able to arrange a meal at your guesthouse or another home in town, just by asking around. The Catholic Mission may have a kitchen guests can use, provided you pay for the gas.

Getting There & Away

As usual, **SAMI** (☎ in Puerto Lempira 433-6016) has the only air service to Wampusirpi. Flights typically come from Puerto Lempira (L$1171), usually stopping at Ahuas on the way in or out, though you may be able to swing a flight from La Ceiba (L$2755).

Wampusirpi's grass airstrip is a 15-minute walk outside of town. Trucks meet arriving planes, charging L$10 for a ride into town. SAMI has a small office on the road into town where you can buy and confirm tickets.

Boats, mostly carrying cargo, come and go occasionally and you may be able to convince a passing captain (and pay him enough) to give you a ride upriver to Krausirpe in the Tawahka region, or downriver to Ahuas and Barra de Patuca, on the ocean. A more reliable, and more expensive, alternative would be to negotiate with a local boatman or young men with a dugout canoe for a trip of a certain time and distance, depending on your designs and his availability.

TAWAHKA REGION

Further up the Río Patuca, and deep in the rainforest, are the towns of Krausirpe and Krautara. Both are considered Tawahka communities, though Krausirpe, like Wampusirpi, has a growing Miskitu population. Krautara is smaller and more isolated, and remains 100% Tawahka.

Community leaders in Krausirpe have tried to establish eco-tourism programs like the ones in Las Marías and elsewhere in La Moskitia, though with little lasting success. Whether this is due to a lack of infrastructure or experience, the remoteness of the area, or reticence on the part of ordinary Tawahka – or some combination of these factors – is not entirely clear. But as tourism in La Moskitia grows, it stands to reason that the Tawahka region will slowly open to foreign visitors as well.

Sights & Activities

By far the best way to see the Tawahka region – and the Moskitia rainforest as a whole – is on a seven- to 10-day rafting expedition down the Río Patuca (see p103). That trip, and a similar one down the Río Plátano, are among the most adventurous to be had in Honduras, and an unforgettable way to experience La Moskitia in its full glory. The Patuca trip starts near the town of Catacamas in Olancho and takes you right through the Tawahka Asangni Biosphere Reserve, with stops along the way, including Krausirpe. Omega Tours and La Moskitia Ecoaventuras, both based in La Ceiba, offer recommended trips down the Patuca and Plátano rivers; see p238 for more info.

In Krausirpe, it's possible to arrange **hikes** through the rainforest, which has abundant birds and wildlife (though spotting them, as always, can be tough). Local guides can also take you to nearby **caves** and **petroglyphs**. Lorenzo Macling, a local resident and leader, is a good source of information and assistance.

Sleeping

There is a rural medical center in Krausirpe where travelers can ask to stay the night. There is no fee, but the doctors and staff certainly appreciate small donations. Krautara has no formal accommodations or guesthouses, but you can ask around for a room or a place to camp.

Getting There & Away

Without a doubt, the best way to visit the Tawahka region is on a rafting trip down the Río Patuca (above). If you're already in La Moskitia (the raft trips start in Olancho) you can visit the region by catching a boat upriver from Barra Patuca, Ahuas or Wampusirpi. There are no fixed prices or schedules – you may have to wait several days in any of those towns before a boat (with room for passengers) passes by. You also can catch a flight on SAMI to Ahuas or Wampusirpi from Puerto Lempira or Brus Laguna, and take a boat from there.

LAGUNA DE CARATASCA

Out on the Laguna de Caratasca – by far the largest of La Moskitia's lagoons – the natural cycle of life continues much as it has for thousands of years. This shallow lagoon, averaging just 3m in depth, is home to a remarkable array of fauna, with sizable populations of manatee, seabirds and small coastal mammals. And while few travelers make it out here – this area is mostly pine savannah, and lacks the big-time rainforest drawcards further west – it might be a good start or end point for an expedition into the region, given that this is where you'll find La Moskitia's largest town, Puerto Lempira – a good place to launch a river trip off to the Río Patuca or over to the Río Coco on the Nicaraguan border.

PUERTO LEMPIRA

pop 35,700

While Puerto Lempira has grown big (note that the population above includes the outlying communities) it's not so big that the townsfolk have become too busy to wait out the numerous rainstorms that trundle through the region on a daily basis. And it's still not big enough to merit paved roads – though the fishermen and merchants that call this town home would certainly appreciate it if the Honduran government would build some. But it is big enough to have some of the infrastructure – including churches, parks, restaurants, a bank and internet access – that smaller towns in the region lack.

Most travelers come (or leave) by plane, spending only the time necessary to make onward travel arrangements. Some are on their way to or from Nicaragua's back door, via the town of Leimus on the Río Coco, others just want to get a taste of this odd frontier town with its lagoon-front piers and restaurants, dusty roads leading to nowhere and memorable street scenes around every corner.

If you stay, there are at least two interesting side trips to Mistruk (p254) and Kaukira (p254), both manageable in a day, but more pleasant as overnight excursions.

Information

Banco Atlántida (8am-4:30pm Mon-Fri, 8:30-11:30am Sat) No ATM, but the teller can exchange traveler's checks and issue credit card advances on Visa cards. Often has long queues.
Cyberphone (☎ 419-0024; near Hotel Flores; Internet per hr L$40; 8:40am-10:30pm)
Hondutel Centro Comunitario (☎ 433-6270; to USA per min L$3; 6:30am-10pm). Calls to other parts of the world start at L$10. It's situated a half-block west of Parque Central.
Hospital Puerto Lempira (☎ 433-6078, emergency 433-6978; 24hr) Located 1.5km southwest of town. From the airport, go roughly 10 blocks west until you cross a small concrete bridge. Turn left (south) and continue another 750m. If in doubt, ask any passerby.
Immigration office (☎ 433-6055; 8am-noon & 2-5pm Mon-Fri) Located on the 2nd floor of a commercial building, a half-block from Calle Principal on the same street as Hotel El Gran Samaritano.
Pharmacy (24hr) Located inside the hospital.

Dangers & Annoyances

As a port town and La Moskitia's largest town, Puerto Lempira is somewhat edgier than other places in the region, but not overly so. Most problems have something to do with alcohol, or sometimes drugs. Avoiding drugs and drunks altogether is the best way to stay safe.

Sleeping & Eating

Hotel Flores (☎ 433-6380; s/d/tr L$400/600/750;) A half-block from the Parque Central east of Calle Principal, the Hotel Flores has cleanish rooms – though the pillows are downright nasty – and welcome air-con. For all that, you're better off at the Yu Baiwan.

our pick **Hotel Yu Baiwan** (☎ 433-6348; s/d/tr L$450/500/600;) The best deal in town, the Yu Baiwan has plenty of space, firm beds, clean linens, cable TV and friendly service. The original nine rooms are all on the ground floor, while a rather grand, curving stairway leads to nine new rooms that were being built on the 2nd floor when we visited. To get here, look for a narrow cement passageway off Calle Principal, a half-block from the pier.

Hotel Pinares (☎ 433-6679; www.hotelpinares.com; s/d/tr L$800/900/1100;) This is the most expensive hotel in town. But sometimes you actually get what you pay for: firm beds, a swimming pool looking out to sea (albeit through a chain-link fence), and a newness and brightness seldom seen in La Moskitia. Unfortunately, you only get cold-water showers. It's 500m east of Calle Principal.

Kabu Payaska (mains L$90-180; breakfast, lunch & dinner) This is an excellent sea-view restaurant, located around 300m east of Calle Principal. It specializes in grilled meats, but you can also get a few seafood options.

Restaurante Lakou Payaska (mains L$130-220; breakfast, lunch & dinner) Miskitu for 'lake breezes,' the Lakou Payaska gets plenty of them – and strong – on its 2nd-floor open-air dining area a few steps from the lagoon. Operated by (and opposite) Hotel Yu Baiwan, this is easily the most reliable meal in town, if not the most creative. Chicken, beef, lobster and conch are served with the standard accompaniments, and sometimes a serving of loud country music. The main restaurant is out the back of the bar-snack joint that faces the street and is decidedly less appealing.

Getting There & Around

The most reliable plane service to/from Puerto Lempira is on **Aerolineas Sosa** (☎ 433-6558; www.aerolineasosa.com; 8:30am-5:30pm Mon-Fri, to noon Sat & Sun), which has a large office facing the airstrip. **SAMI** (☎ 433-6016; 6am-5pm) has an office in the turquoise building at the end of the airstrip.

Sosa has frequent flights – usually every day, check in at 7am – to Tegucigalpa (L$4156), La Ceiba (L$2470) and San Pedro Sula (L$3861). SAMI serves destinations inside La Moskitia, including Ahuas (L$1171), Wampusirpi (L$1171), Brus Laguna (L$1171), Belén (L$1240) and Palacios (L$1333). Departure times vary, but you should be able to catch a flight from Puerto Lempira to any of those towns within a day or two. Note that prices and schedules change frequently and unexpectedly – always call ahead.

A taxi into town from the airport is L$50, or you could walk it in about 20 minutes.

Gamisu Transporte Fluvial (☎ 9801-9775), near the pier, operates a regular *colectivo* service between here and Ahuas (L$350, one to two hours), but boats do not necessarily run everyday.

You can usually rent a bike from one of the repair shops along the main drag – look for handwritten '*Se repara bicicleta*' signs, especially near the pier. You'll have to negotiate a price, probably between L$100 and L$150 per day.

GETTING TO NICARAGUA

Getting to Nicaragua is easier than it used to be, thanks mainly to changes on the Nicaraguan side. From Puerto Lempira, trucks leave once a day for the town of Leimus along the Río Coco (L$200, 7:30am, four to five hours). You can pick up the truck outside its owners' house – three blocks west and two blocks south of the pier – or on Parque Central, near Banco Atlántida. Look for a large truck with a canvas covering. In Leimus, you pass Honduran immigration on one side of the river, and Nicaraguan immigration on the other. A new road means you can board a bus right there for Puerto Cabezas (five hours).

Before the new highway was built, you had to take a boat or 4x4 downriver to Waspán to clear Nicaraguan immigration and catch a bus to Puerto Cabezas. That remains an alternative, if there are no buses from Leimus or the immigration office there is closed.

It costs L$140 to enter Nicaragua, L$60 to enter Honduras; neither is supposed to charge an exit fee, but occasionally officials ask for a nominal one. Trucks return from Leimus to Puerto Lempira twice daily, around 7am and 4pm.

A small number of travelers take the overland route between Puerto Lempira and Puerto Cabezas, in Nicaragua. See boxed text, above, for details on getting to and from the border.

MISTRUK

A great one- or two-day trip from Puerto Lempira is to Mistruk, a tiny Miskitu community 18km south of town along the banks of the Laguna de Tansing. The 400 or so people of the village make their living from agriculture and fishing. The beach is grainy and attractive, shaded by tall, long-armed almond trees, with a long pier to avoid walking in the shallows. The water is clear and fresh (not salted), a nice change from most of the Moskitia's rivers.

A handful of wooden **bungalows** (r L$300-500), spaced well apart along a pleasant, freshwater beach, are popular with visiting tours and service groups. The bungalows have two good beds apiece, private bathroom with flush toilets, wood floors and high thatched roofs. Sunlight coming through the walls by day means mosquitoes by night – bring a mosquito net or plenty of bug spray. Solar panels charge batteries. There's not much to do here but relax on the beach and strike up a conversation with local kids and boatmen.

A bike is by far the best and most pleasant way to get here. The well-maintained dirt road winds through expansive grassland with a thin sprinkling of spindly pine trees; there are no major climbs, just a few mild rollers to keep it interesting. Follow the road past the airport out of Puerto Lempira – anyone can point you in the right direction. At 13km, the road splits, left to Leimus and the Nicaraguan border, right to Mistruk. In another 3km, you'll reach a simple wood gate, which you can easily open or go around, and the town is a short distance further.

The bungalows are big enough to store a bike or two inside, which is probably the smart thing to do. Bikes can be rented in Puerto Lempira (p253). Taxis regularly take locals and visitors to Mistruk, charging L$800 for the roundtrip, including time at the beach.

KAUKIRA

Red and blue macaws can sometimes be seen flying around this medium-sized town, tucked away on the northeast side of Laguna de Caratasca. There's a nice beach a 15-minute walk from town, but the town is better known for its bird-watching, wildlife and *pesca deportiva* (sport fishing). **Ralston Haylock** (☎ community telephone 433-6081) can arrange excursions of just about any kind and length, and maintains a simple lodge for overnight trips. He's a fount of information and lore, and speaks excellent English.

From Puerto Lempira, *colectivo* boats leave the main pier at around 10am to 11am (L$100, 1½ hours). Getting back the same day can be tricky, however, as the boats 'live' in Kaukira; they leave every morning between 5am and 6am, but if there aren't enough passengers, they may not make an afternoon run. Ask the boat driver in Puerto Lempira – or Ralston by phone (above) – about an afternoon service the day you're thinking of going. You may need to hire an *expreso* boat, which costs around L$1800 each way.

Directory

CONTENTS

ACCOMMODATIONS

Honduras has all types of hotels, from luxury resorts to colonial guesthouses to super-cheapies. There is a smattering of bed-and-breakfasts and hostels, though both are still pretty rare. No matter where you stay, it's almost always a good idea to see a few rooms since the hotel receptionist may have a different opinion about which is the most desirable room in the place. Hotels of all levels sometimes suffer from what could be called Stinky Bathroom Syndrome, which is caused by bad plumbing; covering the shower drain usually helps significantly.

At the low-budget end, hotels tend to have cold-water bathrooms and ceiling fans. Rooms with shared bathrooms are less and less common, though the state of some bathrooms being what they are, you may wish you didn't have to sleep next to it. Cable TV is increasingly standard, even in cheap rooms.

In this book we list high-season prices, with the exception of Easter Week when prices can double. The budget range goes up to L$600 (US$31.75) per night. Travelers who generally think of themselves as midrangers may be perfectly happy in one of the nicer budget listings. In those, you are likely to have hot water – though the hot water often comes from an electric shower head that heats the water (kind of) as the water runs through it – and can often choose between fans and air-con. Rooms are still modest, but beds are usually newer, the paint fresher and the bathrooms cleaner.

Midrange hotels – L$600 (US$31.75) to L$1200 (US$63.50) – will certainly have hot water and air-con, and may include parking, breakfast or a pool. They tend to be in more secure neighborhoods, which often translates to 'away from downtown.' You may need to take cabs to and from the sights in the center.

Top-end hotels are typically high-rise chain hotels, plus a handful of deluxe, private resorts on Roatán and outside La Ceiba. These start at L$1200 (US$63.50) per night. Most hotels in this range have all the amenities you'd expect at a Real InterContinental in any country, including marble bathrooms, air-con, quality beds, bellhop and taxi service, room service, in-room telephones, safety deposit boxes and parking.

You're better off booking your hotel online through an aggregator like www.hotels.com if you want to stay in a top-end hotel. For budget and midrange, you can just show up.

PRACTICALITIES

- **DVD & Video** DVD and VHS systems (NTSC) are commonplace.
- **Electricity** The standard current is 110 volt AC (like the US and Canada); three-prong outlets, however, are uncommon.
- **Laundry Service** Most cities and large towns have full-service laundromats that charge L$60 (US$3) to L$80 (US$4) per 10lbs. Many hotels also provide laundry service, but often charge per item of clothing, which adds up pretty fast.
- **Newspapers & Magazines** *Honduras Tips* (www.hondurastips.honduras.com) is an essential English/Spanish language tourist magazine with up-to-date information. *Honduras This Week* (www.hondurasthisweek.com) is Honduras' only English-language weekly newspaper. *El Heraldo, La Tribuna, La Prensa, El Tiempo* and *El Nuevo Día* are the country's daily newspapers. Occasionally, day-old *New York Times* and the *Miami Herald* are sold at top-end hotels and English-language bookshops.
- **Radio & TV** Honduran TV consists largely of programming imported from Mexico and the US – some English-language programs are dubbed, some subtitled straight from American providers. FM radio plays a mix of ballads, Mexican ranchero music and American rock.
- **Water** As a rule, don't drink the tap water. Instead, bring along a water bottle and refill it in your hotel (many now have large water coolers). Greenies could even bring a steripen or water filter and filter their own tap water.
- **Weights & Measures** The metric system is used for everything except gasoline, which is measured in gallons, and laundry, which is weighed in pounds.

Around Christmas and Easter weeks hotel rooms fill up quickly in the Bay Islands, along the Coast and in Comayagua (for Easter only). If you are coming during these times, you'll want to book at least a month in advance. During the low-season and off-peak times – September to December on the Bay Islands – you can often negotiate a better price.

Wireless internet access is increasingly available in both midrange and top-end hotels.

B&Bs

True bed-and-breakfast hotels are few and far between in Honduras; you'll see plenty of places with 'bed & breakfast' in their name, though just 'bed' would be more accurate. Ask if morning eats are included before you plunk down your cash. Actual B&Bs can be found in places with large expat populations, including Roatán, Copán Ruinas and Tegucigalpa.

Camping

Camping is not pursued by many Hondurans and, as a result, campsites such as those in the USA or Europe are scarce. Camping is allowed, however, in several national parks, including Parque Nacional Montaña de Celaque, Parque Nacional Cerro Azul Meámbar, Parque Nacional Santa Bárbara and Parque Nacional Sierra de Agalta. Running water and latrines are sometimes available, and occasionally even a kitchen.

Camping on the fly – on beaches, in the countryside, in the forest – is typically hassle-free. Just be sure to ask permission at the *alcaldía* (city hall) or at the nearest home – you never know if you're camping on someone's property.

There have been reports of attacks on tourists walking or camping on the beaches of the North Coast at night. We address these issues in the Dangers & Annoyances sections in the regional chapters.

Plan on bringing your own gear; visitor centers rarely have tents or sleeping bags (with the notable exception of the one at Cerro Azul Meámbar). Travelers, however, can occasionally rent gear from guides or establishments that cater to foreign travelers – they can at least help track some down.

Finally, as you would at home, leave any campsite as you found it (or better). Carry out your trash, throw dirt or sand on any leftover ashes, and tidy up the site for the next camper.

Homestays

Staying in a home with a local family – sharing their space and meals – gives travelers a rare insight into everyday Honduran life; depending on the length of stay, and the family, of course, it often becomes a highlight of any trip here.

Homestays typically cost L$100 (US$5) to L$200 (US$10.50) per person and include a private room, private bathroom and at least one meal. The quality of rooms varies from home to home, but in general, they are modern and clean. In fact, most homestay rooms (and families) must be 'approved' by the local tourism board, city hall or Spanish-language school before they are added to a roster of recommended places.

Places with established homestays include Copán Ruinas, which can be arranged through the Spanish-language schools (p120), Santa Rosa de Copán (p135) and Ojojona (p84). Outside these locales, you can just ask around at the local *alcaldía* or any restaurant.

Hostels

There are a handful of hostels in Honduras, which are great for saving a few lemps and meeting other travelers. All have dorms, shared bathroom and at least one common area to relax. There are also hostels with extras including kitchens, lockers and internet access. You'll find hostels in Copán Ruinas, San Pedro Sula, Tegucigalpa, La Ceiba, Trujillo and Roatán. Utila doesn't have any true hostels, but has plenty of cheap dorm-style lodging, used especially by backpackers taking Open Water diving courses.

Hotels

Most travelers will stay most nights in a hotel. Note that a 'motel' is not the same thing, and is usually used for prostitution and people having affairs (hence the high walls, lack of windows and individual garages).

ACTIVITIES

Honduras has a host of outdoor activities for travelers – from flying high through the forest to dropping to the ocean floor, from birdwatching in national parks to rafting down a raging Class V river. Whatever interests you, you may be surprised at how much Honduras has to offer. See our Honduras Outdoors chapter (p58) for more coverage.

Canopy Tours

Canopy tours involve donning a special harness and sliding along fixed cables high in the treetops. Honduras' first such tour is along the Río Cangrejal near La Ceiba (p181). It has since been copied by other outfits, one east of La Ceiba (see p181), two on Roatán (p219 and p213), one near Copán Ruinas (p125), and another by Sambo Creek (p190).

Caving

There are plenty of caving opportunities here. The best spots are in Central Honduras in the Cuevas de Susmay (p105) and the Cuevas de Talgua (p101). You'll definitely want to bring along a guide for these adventures.

Diving & Snorkeling

Honduras' Bay Islands – Roatán, Utila and Guanaja, plus Cayos Cochinos off the North Coast – are famous for their diving, with clear warm water and a magnificent coral reef. You can learn to dive here for less money than just about anywhere in the world, without sacrificing an iota of quality. Dozens of dive shops, especially on Roatán and Utila, offer all levels of courses, from beginner to instructor. Snorkeling gear can be rented or bought, or you can bring your own, for snorkeling right off the shore or on inexpensive tours. The majority of shops here are PADI certified (www.padi.com), though there's one NAUI (www.naui.com) shop on Utila.

Fishing

Anglers can go trolling, deep-sea fishing or flat fishing on the Bay Islands, especially Roatán where local outfits have experienced guides. La Moskitia is also an excellent place for fishing, especially Brus Laguna.

Hiking & Trekking

Honduras has excellent hiking, especially in the national parks. Most of the best hikes involve climbing one of Honduras' many peaks, so hikers should be well prepared for moderate to challenging outings. Some parks have well-maintained trails and permanent visitors centers, others have little or no infrastructure at all. In the latter case, it is highly recommended that you hire a guide, as it's very easy to get lost (and much harder to be found).

Some favorite hiking areas include Parque Nacional Montaña de Celaque (p141), Parque Nacional La Tigra (p82), Parque Nacional Cerro Azul Meámbar (p154), Parque Nacional Sierra de Agalta (p102), and Parque Nacional Montañ de Santa Bárbara (p155) as well as around Copán Ruinas (p120) and the Reserva de la Biósfera del Río Plátano (p244).

Horseback Riding

Horseback riding is a popular activity at Copán Ruinas (p121), though travelers should steer clear of the rides offered by local kids on the street, which are notoriously bad. It's much better to go with one of the listed tour operators instead. Horseback riding is also available in La Ceiba (p181).

Mountain Biking

At least two tour operators in La Ceiba (p181) offer half- and all-day mountain biking trips. It is rare to see independent travelers exploring Honduras by bike, though not for shortage of good dirt roads or places to go. A few highways in Olancho are known for roadside robberies, however, and are best avoided.

River Running & Kayaking

White-water rafting is popular on the Río Cangrejal near La Ceiba; several companies in La Ceiba offer rafting tours on this river. For even more adventure, try one of the week-plus expeditions down the Río Plátano or Río Patuca, starting in Olancho and ending in La Moskitia (p103).

Small-boat tours are a good way to visit a number of national parks and wildlife refuges along the north coast, including Parque Nacional Jeannette Kawas (Punta Sal, p174), Refugio de Vida Silvestre Punta Izopo (p175), Refugio de Vida Silvestre Cuero y Salado (p187) and Refugio De Vida Silvestre Laguna De Guaimoreto (p193). A number of the trips in La Moskitia are also conducted by small boat.

Bird-Watching

Birding is becoming a popular activity in Honduras, where you can spot hundreds of species, including quetzals, toucans, scarlet macaws (Honduras' national bird) as well as brilliant green and green-and-yellow parrots. Many of the national park and wildlife reserves are excellent birding locations, including Parque Nacional Cusuco (p112), Parque Nacional Montaña de Celaque (p141) and Parque Nacional La Tigra (p81).

Lago de Yojoa (p151) is another excellent place for birding – 375 species have been counted there so far.

Migratory birds are present along the North Coast during the northern winter months from November to February. They are easiest to spot in the lagoons and coastal reserves, like Parque Nacional Punta Izopo and Jardín Botánico de Lancetilla, both near Tela. The Lodge at Pico Bonito (p184), outside of La Ceiba, has 300 hectares of private forest, with viewing platforms and guided tours.

BUSINESS HOURS

Businesses are open during the following hours. (Exceptions to these hours are noted in specific listings.)

Banks 8:30am to 4:30pm Monday to Friday, 8:30 to 11:30am Saturday
Bars & pubs Generally open around noon and close around midnight
Nightclubs 9pm or 10pm to 3am or 4am
Restaurants 7am to 9pm
Shops 9am to 6pm Monday to Saturday, 9am to 1pm or 5pm Sunday

CHILDREN

Like most of Latin America, Honduras is very open and welcoming of children. There's no taboo about bringing children to restaurants or performances, and pregnant women are ushered to the front of the line in banks, government offices and many private businesses.

Practicalities

Travelers will be hard-pressed to find child-specific amenities like car seats, high chairs and bassinettes, except perhaps in top-end hotels and resorts. Hondurans simply do not have the quantity and variety of kid-specific paraphernalia that Americans, at least, are accustomed to. Disposable diapers, wipes, formula and other basics, however, are available in most large supermarkets.

Sights & Activities

The North Coast, Western Honduras and the Bay Islands are the best areas for those traveling with children. Assuming the little ones are up for some outdoor excursions, Tela and La Ceiba have a number of good options, including canopy tours, mangrove tours, short hikes, a butterfly and insect museum in La Ceiba and (as a last resort) the beach in Tela. The north also has a number of forts, including in Omoa and Trujillo, which kids might enjoy too. In the west, the area around Copán Ruinas has a number of activities suitable for children, including a butterfly enclosure, bird park and of course the ruins. The Bay Islands have a number of kid-friendly resorts, notably Anthony's Key Resort, which has dolphin encounter programs (p215).

CLIMATE

The temperature in Honduras does not change dramatically by the season, perhaps by 5°C throughout the year (see p13 for more details on when to visit). Instead, the temperature is entirely dependant on the elevation. For instance, the mountainous interior ranges from 16°C to 20°C, and is a little warmer in the dry season. Tegucigalpa, at 975m, has a temperate climate, with temperatures between 24°C and 29°C during the day in the dry season (it's a bit cooler in the rainy season). The coastal lowlands on the Pacific and Caribbean sides are warmer and more humid year-round. Temperatures there range from 28°C to 32°C in the dry season; it's about 3°C cooler (and more comfortable) in the rainy season.

In general, the rainy season in Honduras runs from May to November in the interior and from September to January along the North Coast and Bay Islands (with a chance of severe storms any time of the year). Heavy rains can cause flooding in the lowlands and mudslides in the mountains, and both can cause serious damage and impede travel. Hurricane season is from August to November; direct hits are uncommon, but are devastating when they do hit. Travelers should take evacuation orders very seriously.

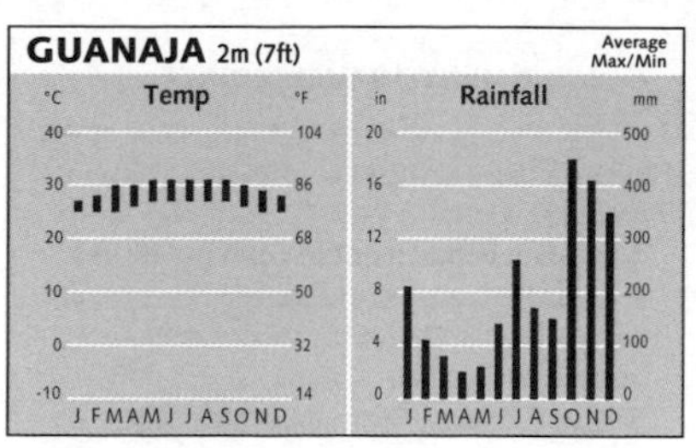

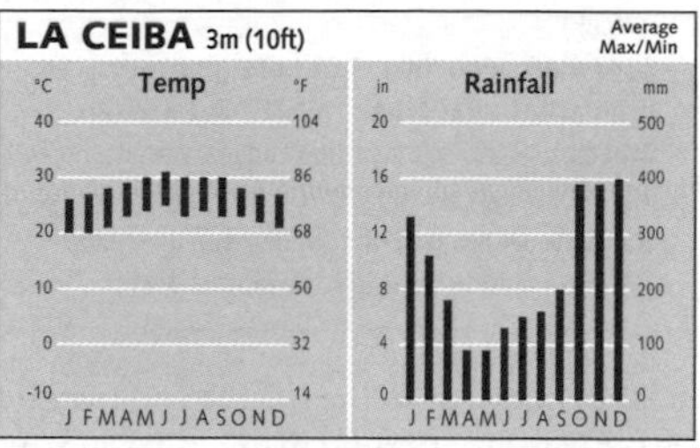

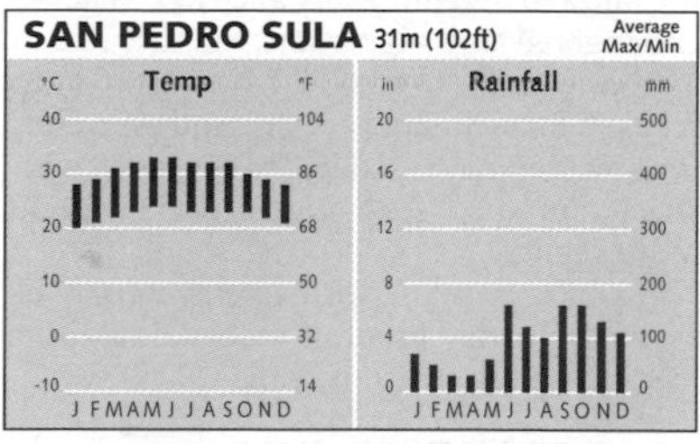

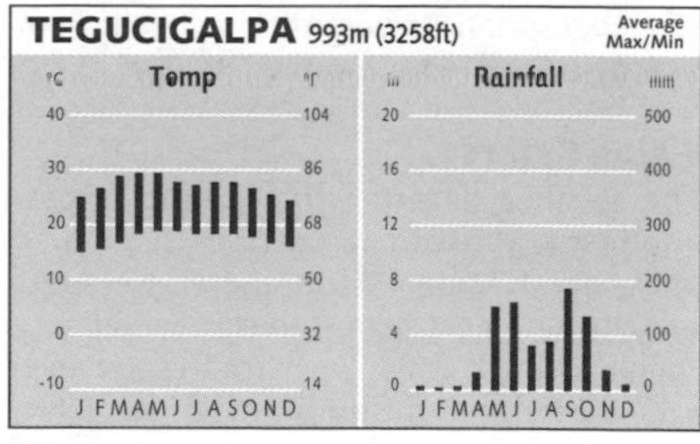

COURSES

Scuba diving courses bring thousands of travelers to Honduras every year because of the world-class dive sites and the bargain basement prices. Besides Open Water and Advanced Open Water certifications, dive shops offer upper-level courses and specialties, including nitrox, divemaster and instructor. While the vast majority of dive shops are on the Bay Islands, there is also a fully-equipped shop servicing Cayos Cochinos. The North Coast has no dive shops (though plans are in the works to open one in Tela).

Spanish language courses are becoming increasingly popular. Travelers have the option of studying in Copán Ruinas (p120), San Pedro Sula (p111), La Ceiba (p181), Valle de Ángeles (p81) and the Bay Islands (p224).

There are art courses available on Utila (p225).

CUSTOMS REGULATIONS

Customs officers are pretty lax; while police and customs officers are entitled to search you at any time, especially in border areas, they rarely do. Even searches at the airport tend to be perfunctory. The exception is if something about your appearance or de-

GOVERNMENT TRAVEL ADVICE

The following government websites offer travel advisories and information on current hot spots.

Australian Department of Foreign Affairs & Trade (☎ emergency helpline 1300 555 135 in Australia, 61 2 6261 3305 from Honduras; www.smarttraveller.gov.au)

British Foreign & Commonwealth Office (☎ 020-7008 1500, 0845 850 2829; www.fco.gov.uk)

Canadian Department of Foreign Affairs & International Trade (☎ 800-267-8376 in Canada, 613-996-8885 outside Canada; www.dfait-maeci.gc.ca)

US State Department (☎ 888-407-4747, 202-501-4444 outside US; http://travel.state.gov)

meanor suggests to the officer you may be carrying drugs. Beyond drugs, travelers are not allowed to remove any ancient artifact or endangered animal or plant, whether live or a product made from one. It's smart to keep receipts for any item you buy, and especially for any that may be confused for being a restricted product, such as an especially good Maya replica.

If you're traveling with a pet, you may be asked to provide proof of vaccination and a medical certificate from home.

DANGERS & ANNOYANCES

We cover specific issues in the regional chapters. Also see p15 for more safety tips.

Hiking Hazards

The greatest hazard while hiking is getting lost – at least two travelers have died in Parque Nacional Montaña de Celaque, evidently after getting off the trail and being unable to find it again. Even in a well-traveled park like Celaque, the trails can be overgrown in places, and secondary paths used by animals and hunters can easily lead hikers astray. Guides are readily available at most hiking areas, and it is strongly recommended you use them.

Although mostly found on the North Coast and in La Moskitia, you should be alert for poisonous snakes throughout Honduras; coral snakes, rattlesnakes and barba amarilla (fer-de-lance, otherwise known as the lancehead) are among the most common types seen. Wear long pants and boots, and be careful where you step.

See also p61 for more safe-trekking tips.

Thefts & Muggings

Honduras has a very high crime and violence rate, though the vast majority of travelers experience no problems. Pickpocketing and petty theft are most common, and assault is possible. Take the usual precautions, like not wearing flashy jewelry, walking around with your camera out or pulling out a wad of cash. Tegucigalpa and San Pedro Sula are the worst places for street crime; the downtown areas of both are fine during the day, but less so after dark. Consider taking a cab when it gets late. If you are mugged, do not resist.

In general, small towns are much safer than the big cities. Watch yourself on the North Coast, especially on the beach: avoid leaving items unattended and do not walk on the beach at night. It seems to be a favorite tactic of thieves to wait in the trees along a deserted stretch of beach, especially after dark, and wait for someone to happen by.

It's also best to skip municipal buses, as these are common targets for gang attacks.

EMBASSIES & CONSULATES

Check out www.embassiesabroad.com for listings of embassies and consulates in Honduras, and Honduran embassies abroad.

Honduran Embassies & Consulates

TEGUCIGALPA

Belgium (☎ 232-3954; fax 231-1974; jomen45@yahoo.com; Edif Banco Atlántida, 3rd fl, Blvd Centro America; ⏲ 8:30am-2pm Mon-Fri)

Belize (Map p74; ☎ 238-4614; fax 236-5873; consuladobelice@yahoo.com; Honduras Maya, Av República de Chile; ⏲ 9am-noon & 2-5pm Mon-Fri)

Canada (☎ 232-4551; fax 239-7767; www.canadainternational.gc.ca; Edif Financiero Banexpo, Local 3, Blvd San Juan Bosco; ⏲ 8am-4:30pm Mon-Thu, to 1:30pm Fri)

Costa Rica (☎ 232-1768; embacori@amnettgu.com; Residencial El Triángulo, 1a Calle 3451; ⏲ 8:30am-3:30pm Mon-Fri)

Denmark (☎ 236-6407; omaduro@inversioneslapaz.com; Edif La Paz, Av de los Próceres 206, 2nd fl; ⏲ 8am-4pm Mon-Fri)

El Salvador (☎ 239-0901; embasalva@cablecolor.hn; 2a Av & 5a Calle No 620, Colonia Rubén Darío; ⏲ 8am-3:30pm Mon-Fri)

Finland (Map pp66-7; ☎ 236-7322; fax 236-6740; luiskafie@hotmail.com; Edif Comercial, Av de los Próceres; 8am-5:45pm Mon-Fri)
France (Map p74; ☎ 236-6800; fax 236-8051; www.ambafrance-hn.org; 3a Calle at Av Juan Lindo, Colonia Palmira; 8am-12:30pm Mon-Fri)
Germany (☎ 232-3161; fax 232-9018; www.tegucigalpa.diplo.de; in front of the Ministerio Público de Salud; 9am-noon Mon-Fri)
Guatemala (☎ 232-1580; embhonduras@minex.gob.gt; Calle Arturo López Rodezno 2421, Colonia Las Minitas; 9am-1pm Mon-Fri)
Italy (Map pp66-7; ☎ 236-6801; fax 236-5659; www.ambtegucigalpa.esteri.it/ambasciata_tegucigalpa; Av Enrique Tierno Galvan; 9-11:30am Mon-Thu)
Japan (Map p74; ☎ 236-6828; fax 236-6100; Calzada República de Paraguay btwn 4a & 5a Calles; 8:30am-noon Mon-Fri)
Mexico (☎ 232-0141, 232-4039; www.sre.gob.mx/honduras; Calle Eucalipto 1001; 9am-12:30pm Mon-Fri)
Netherlands (☎ 235-8090; cgnlhon@cablecolor.hn; 3a Av 2315; 9am-noon Mon-Fri)
Nicaragua (Map pp66-7; ☎ 232-7224; Bloque M-1, Col Lomas de Tepeyac; 8am-noon Mon-Fri)
Norway (☎ 236-5665; fax 236-8904; Av Los Próceres; 8am-5pm Mon-Fri)
Panama (Map p74; ☎ 239-5508; ephon@hondudata.com; Edif Palmira, 3rd fl, behind Hotel Honduras Maya; 8am-2pm Mon-Fri)
Spain (Map pp66-7; ☎ 236-6589; fax 236-8682; embesphn@correo.mae.es; Calle Santander 801; 9am-1pm Mon-Fri)
Sweden (Map pp66-7; ☎ 231-1812; ambassaden.tegucigalpa@sida.se; Centro Comercial El Dorado, 6th fl; Blvd Morazán; 8am-noon (1-5pm Mon-Fri)
Switzerland (☎ 236-8052; 6a Av 702, Col Lara; ☎ by appointment)
Taiwan (☎ 239-5837; fax 235-5662; Calle Eucalipto 3750; 8:30am-4:30pm Mon-Fri)
UK (☎ 237-6577, 237-6459; reforma@cascomark.com; Calle Principal 2402, Colonia La Reforma; 9am-noon Mon-Fri)
USA (Map p74; ☎ 236-9320; honduras.usembassy.gov; Av La Paz near 3a Av; walk-ins 8-11:30am Mon-Fri, telephone service 8am-5pm Mon-Fri)

SAN PEDRO SULA

Belize (☎ 551-6247; consuladobelice@yahoo.com; Edif Industrias Global, hwy to Puerto Cortés; 7-11am Mon)
Finland (☎ 553-1642; raymaalouf@ladylee.com; Megaplaza Mall; hwy to La Lima; 8am-5pm Mon-Fri)
Germany (Map p110; ☎ 553-1244; Circunvalación btwn 6 & Av NO, No 10; 9-11am Mon-Fri)
Nicaragua (Map p113; ☎ 550-0813; Hilanderas de Sula; 5a Av SO btwn 4a & 5a Calles; 10am-3pm Mon-Fri)
Taiwan (Map p110; ☎ 556-8490; fax 556-5802; sap@mofa.gov.tw; 24a Av btwn 11a & 12a Av SO; 8:30am-5:30pm Mon-Fri)
UK (Map p110; ☎ 550-2486, 550-2337; 2a Calle btwn 18a & 19a Avs NO; 8am-noon & 1-5pm Mon-Fri, 8am-noon Sat)

FESTIVALS & EVENTS

Just about every city, town and village in Honduras has a patron saint around which an annual festival or fair is celebrated. There are some big events, however, that attract crowds from far and wide

February

Feria de la Virgen de Suyapa (p43) This festival is held in honor of the tiny patron saint of Honduras, a 6cm wood statue who is believed to have performed thousands of miracles. Held in the town of Suyapa, on the outskirts of Tegucigalpa, the event kicks off on All-Saints Day (February 3) and continues for a week. Pilgrims from all over Honduras and Central America come to honor the Saint during this period.

March

Comayagua's Semana Santa (p160) Packed with impressive religious processions the week before Easter. The height of the celebration is on Friday morning, when the *Vía Crucis* procession walks over *alfombras* (intricate 'carpets' made of colored sawdust) on the city streets throughout the historical center.

April

Punta Gorda festival (p219) April 12 marks the arrival of the Garífuna in Honduras in 1797. Although it is celebrated in many Garífuna communities, Punta Gorda's festival is among the best attended. It lasts four days and includes a re-enactment of the Garífuna arrival on Roatán, the naming of a Queen, and plenty of music and dancing.

May

La Feria de San Isidro (p180) La Ceiba's patron-saint festival has morphed into one of the country's largest festivals. Also known as the Gran Carnival Nacional (Great National Carnival), the party culminates on the third Saturday in May, but crowds start arriving mid-week and 'mini-celebrations' in neighborhoods around town start even earlier. Over a quarter of a million people come for parades, street performances, floats and – after night falls – raucous partying at La Ceiba's nightclubs.

June

Feria Juniana (p112) San Pedro Sula's patron-saint festival and a party of national proportions. Held the last week of June, the celebration includes live music, street performances, and plenty of food and drink. The height of

STAYING HEALTHY

- Never drink unpurified water, even in mountain areas where locals do. Bottled water is cheap and easy to find, and canned and bottled drinks are a safe alternative. Fortunately, virtually all eateries and restaurants use purified water in their drinks and ice.
- Avoid uncooked, pre-cut fruit and vegetables. You have no way of knowing the cleanliness of the fruit, the cutting board, or the hands of the person who prepared it. Stick to fruits and vegetables that you can peel or wash in purified water yourself. Oranges, bananas, avocados and mangoes are all good. Remember to wipe the fruit down before peeling it so you don't end up with all the bad stuff on your hands.
- Skip the salad. Most *platos típicos* come with an enticing side salad, but grooves and ripples on salad leaves are notorious for retaining drops of water, which is unlikely to be purified.
- Travel with and use hand sanitizer. Public restrooms often do not have soap, and the water is unsafe.
- Stay hydrated by drinking lots of water or, on especially sweaty days, Gatorade. Dehydration and heat exhaustion will knock you out as quickly as a bad *baleada*.

the party is on June 29, when a huge parade makes its way down Avenida Circunvalación.

July

Garífuna Festival (p166) The largest of its kind, this festival is held from July 9 to 24 (usually) in the town of Baja Mar, east of Puerto Cortes. The party's peak is typically July 16, with an all-night dance competition.

August

Sun Jam (p229) Held in Utila on an uninhabited cay near the western end of the main island. DJs spin music for some 1500 people, who cram the islet for an all-day/all-night party. There's lots of food and drink, but buy your tickets in advance to be sure you get a spot.

FOOD

Honduras does not have an especially rich national cuisine, as any long-time traveler here can attest. Seafood figures prominently along the North Coast, of course. While chicken is the mainstay inland, pork and beef, especially *pinchos* (kebabs), are also popular.

Budget meals range from around L$50 to L$120. For this, you're getting a snack, like a *baleada*, or a set meal, which includes rice, beans and some type of meat. In the midrange (L$120 to L$250) you definitely get a bump in ambience, presentation, and food quality, with more international dishes on offer. Top-end restaurants, with meals starting at L$250, often feature beef or seafood dishes. They're not on-par with high-end restaurants in Europe or the US, generally, but you will get a good sip of elegance for the price.

See the Food & Drink chapter (p46) for more information.

GAY & LESBIAN TRAVELERS

Honduras is very much 'in the closet,' and open displays of affection between gay or lesbian couples are definitely frowned upon. Discreet homosexual behavior was more tolerated before the advent of HIV/AIDS in Honduras around 1985. Since then anti-gay incidents have increased, along with stricter legislation, so gays and lesbians must take extra care anywhere they are uncertain of prevailing attitudes. However, the AIDS crisis has also increased gay advocacy; organizations serving the gay, lesbian and transsexual/transgender communities, include **Grupo Prisma** (☎ 232-8342; prisma@sdnhon.org.hn), **Colectiva Violeta** (☎ 237-6398; alfredo@optinet.hn), and **Comunidad Gay San Pedrana** (☎ 550-6868). Check out www.globalgayz.com for the latest news.

HOLIDAYS

New Year's Day January 1
Day of the Americas April 14
Semana Santa (Holy Week) Thursday, Friday and Saturday before Easter Sunday
Labor Day May 1
Independence Day September 15
Francisco Morazán Day October 3
Día de la Raza (Columbus Day) October 12
Army Day October 21
Christmas Day December 25

INSURANCE

Travel insurance is always something worth considering, though relatively few tourists actually use it. Policies vary widely, but can include compensation for lost, damaged or stolen luggage, for cancelled or delayed trips (a concern mostly for cruise-ship passengers), and even for bad weather. Some include coverage for medical treatment or evacuation, or for car rental. Travel insurance makes the most sense for those spending a significant amount of money in one place, for example a week at a dive resort. Independent travelers may be interested in theft or damage insurance, and a plan with medical care and evacuation may be a good idea if you'll be doing any adventure activities.

INTERNET ACCESS

Virtually any city, town or village that travelers are likely to visit will have at least one internet café. Connections tend to be relatively fast, and cost L$15 (US$0.75) to L$20 (US$1) per hour. Many midrange and top-end hotels now have wi-fi connections.

LEGAL MATTERS

Police officers in Honduras tend to be friendly, but are not above squeezing tourists for a little extra cash now and then. This usually happens at road stops, where police will often tell you the plain truth: they need money to put gas in the patrol truck. You can politely say that you can't help, or you can hand over a couple of bucks and be on your way. A number of cities have tourist police, who are part of the same police force but are trained to deal with tourists (and wear simple khaki uniforms rather than camo); do not hesitate to contact them (or a regular police officer if that's easier) if you experience or witness a crime.

MAPS

Good maps are hard to find in Honduras. Tourist offices and visitors centers are the best places to get a decent one of Honduras or the region, department or city you happen to be in. Bookstores occasionally carry maps but don't count on it; they're often the same ones that the tourist office gives out for free (and in a bookshop, you're likely to drop L$100 on it).

The Instituto Geográfico Nacional in Tegucigalpa (ITM; p68) publishes high-quality maps of the various departments (states), both political and topographic. It sells a few city and municipal maps as well, though oddly enough, the Tegucigalpa one is unwieldy and expensive.

MONEY

The local currency is the lempira and it's considered to be relatively stable. For exchange rates see the inside front cover of this book. Also, consider checking out www.xe.com, a website that generates handy currency conversion cheat-sheets, which you can print out and keep in your wallet for easy conversions. For information on prices and the cost of traveling within Honduras, see p13.

ATMs

Cash machines are prevalent throughout the country, except in rural portions of Central Honduras and La Moskitia. ATMs operated by BAC/Credomatic, Banco Atlántida, HSBC and Unibanc are the most reliable, and most likely to accept out-of-country debit cards. Always be alert to your surroundings when withdrawing cash; whenever possible, take out money during the day, and at a machine that's in a lockable cabin (to get in, you typically have to swipe your ATM card at the door) or inside the bank itself. ATMs typically spit out 500-lempira bills, which can be a hassle to break – get in the habit of using big bills at hotels and larger restaurants, and saving the small bills for taxis, small eateries, street stands, etc.

Cash

Banks in larger cities usually exchange US dollars, and occasionally euros; bring your passport and go in the morning. Your hotel may let you pay in US dollars, or exchange them for you. In the Bay Islands, US dollars are the preferred currency.

Credit Cards

Visa and MasterCard are widely accepted, including at major supermarkets, retail stores, hotels and car rental agencies. Expect a 6% to 12% surcharge.

Cash advances on Visa cards are available at most banks, including BAC/Credomatic, Banco Atlántida and Banco de Occidente. BAC/Credomatic can usually process advances on MasterCard too. There's typically no transaction charge on the Honduran end for Visa or MasterCard cash advances, but of course the interest rates tend to be astronomical.

Moneychangers

Freelance moneychangers can be found – in fact, they'll find you – in the airports and in Parque Central in San Pedro Sula. It's not recommended you use them unless the banks are closed or the line is out the door (which is often the case). There are moneychangers at all border crossings, too; they are equally suspect, but using them is the best way to get rid of Guatemalan *quetzales* or Nicaraguan *córdobas* if you know you won't need them anymore (El Salvador uses the US dollar).

Tipping

A 10% tip is customary for tour guides and restaurant waiters, but not taxi drivers. At hotels, it is nice to tip someone for carrying your bags to your room, and the houseclean-ing staff – L$20 (US$1) to L$40 (US$2) per day is fair; you should pay more at higher-end hotels or for especially good service.

Traveler's Checks

American Express traveler's checks can be changed in all major towns; Banco Atlántida and BAC/Credomatic are the best banks to use. They will need your passport, and may charge a commission. Some banks only change traveler's checks and foreign cash in the morning.

Taxes & Surcharges

There is a hotel tax of 12% to 16% that is added at most larger hotels but often not charged at smaller hotels. In many cases, the tax is charged if you use a credit card, but not if you pay in cash.

PHOTOGRAPHY & VIDEO

The main concern for travelers when it comes to photography and video is downloading pictures from your camera once your memory card is full. Most internet cafés can download your pictures and burn them onto a CD for a couple of bucks. Definitely bring the USB cable specific to your camera, as most cafés won't have them. If you need an accessory or replacement part, try electronics stores in Tegucigalpa, San Pedro Sula or La Ceiba, especially in the malls.

POST

Post offices in most Honduran towns are typically open from Monday to Friday 8am to 5pm (often with a couple of hours off for lunch between noon and 2pm) and on Saturday from 8am to noon. Postcards/letters cost L$15/L$25 to the US, L$25/L$34 to Europe and L$34/L$40 to Australia. Delivery takes 10 to 14 days, longer for Australia (if your letter arrives at all).

You can theoretically receive mail by general delivery, known in Latin America as *lista de correos,* at any post office; have it directed to you at:

(Name),
Lista de Correos (town and department),
República de Honduras,
Central America.

For more secure delivery, try FedEx, DHL, Express Mail Service (EMS), or Urgent Express; all have offices in Tegucigalpa, San Pedro Sula and other major cities.

SHOPPING

Honduras doesn't have the myriad and varied folk art found in, say, Guatemala or Mexico, but a number of items are worth looking for. Around Copán Ruinas, replicas of Maya marks and glyphs, made of clay or stone, are great souvenirs; Lenca 'negative' pottery – recognizable for its black and white designs – is beautiful and affordable; and baskets from the Santa Bárbara region as well as tree-bark art *(tunu)* from La Moskitia make colorful, lightweight gifts. For a more modern selection, the malls in Tegucigalpa, San Pedro Sula and La Ceiba have stores of all sorts, including designer shoes and clothes.

As always, avoid buying items made from black coral or sea turtle shells. They do make for beautiful jewelry, but are protected species and buying such items only supports their destruction. The same goes for animal pelts, and jewelry or *artesanía* (handicrafts) made from exotic bird feathers, like macaws or quetzales (though such items are rare in Honduras).

Bargaining

Bargaining is expected in Honduras, though not to the degree or intensity that is common in Guatemala. Most merchants list their wares with reasonable prices, and have little room to go down and still make a profit. Avoid lowballing merchants too much, or haggling over every penny.

SOLO TRAVELERS

Honduras is a perfectly fine place to travel alone, assuming you take common-sense precautions for safety and security. Solo women should expect to get more stares and comments than they would if they were with a man or even another woman. In cities, solo men (and even twosomes) may get approached more frequently by prostitutes than if they were traveling with a woman.

Honduran hotels are divided in the way rooms are priced – some charge according to the number of beds, others by the number of people; the listings in this book indicate which rate each hotel uses. There are also a few hostels, mostly in popular destinations.

It's relatively easy to meet other travelers in Honduras, especially in destinations like Copán Ruinas and the Bay Islands where bars, hostels, guided excursions and, of course, dive classes serve as mixers. There is also a substantial foreign and expat community in many Honduran cities.

TELEPHONE & FAX

Many internet cafés offer a clear, inexpensive phone service using high-speed internet connections or VOIP services such as Skype. Calls to the US typically cost L$2 to L$5 per minute. Expect to pay a bit more to call Europe - L$5 to L$10 per minute.

Hondutel has call centers at its offices throughout the country. Rates to the US are competitive at just L$2 per minute. Calls to the rest of the world are higher. Call centers are usually open from 7am until around 9pm every day.

Some Hondutel offices and internet cafés with phone service have fax service. Prices vary widely, but are usually per page, as opposed to per minute. You can receive faxes as well, with a minimal per-page fee. Fax service typically has more limited hours, usually 8am to 4pm Monday to Friday.

Cell Phones

Honduran operators Tigo, Claro and Digicel use GSM 850 and 1900 protocols, which are used by North American carriers AT&T, T-Mobile and others, but will be incompatible with GSM 900/1800 phones common in Europe, Australia, New Zealand and many Asian countries. You can always switch out your chip, or buy a call-as-you-go phone from a cell-phone shop.

Phone Codes

Honduras' country code is ☎ 504. There are no area codes beyond the country code; when dialing Honduras from abroad simply dial the international access code plus the Honduran country code plus the local number. For domestic long distance calls within Honduras, there is no need to dial the area code. Some useful numbers:

Directory assistance for government telephone numbers ☎ 193
Domestic long-distance operator ☎ 191
International operator ☎ 197
Local directory assistance ☎ 192

A direct connection to an operator in the USA is available by dialing ☎ 800-0121 for Sprint, ☎ 800-0122 for MCI WorldCom and ☎ 800-0123 for AT&T.

Phonecards

Hondutel sells Telecards which have a code, and can be bought at most Hondutel offices. From any pay phone, simply follow the instructions on the back of the card to make a call.

TIME

Honduras is in one time zone, six hours behind Greenwich Mean Time (Mountain Standard Time in the USA). Honduras adopted daylight savings time in 2006, but many small towns around the country refused to implement it; when getting the time, always ask if it's *hora nueva* (new time) or *hora vieja* (old time). This is especially important for bus schedules.

TOILETS

Public toilets are few and far between in Honduras, so you should take 'rest breaks' at your hotel or at convenient restaurants. Western-style flush toilets are the norm in most places although toilet paper goes in the wastepaper basket, not down the hatch. The exception to the rule is La Moskitia, where running water is rare and latrines are typical.

TOURIST INFORMATION

The **Instituto Hondureño de Turismo** (IHT; ☎ 220-1600; www.letsgohonduras.com) is the national tourist office in Tegucigalpa. Around the country, tourist information offices are run by the municipal government and public agencies; these offices are listed in the Information section of each destination.

TRAVELERS WITH DISABILITIES

Disabled travelers will find few facilities designed for their convenience, other than in more expensive hotels and resorts. Wheelchair-bound visitors will find it difficult to get around major cities like Tegucigalpa and San Pedro Sula due to street congestion, and generally poor road or sidewalk surfaces. Even smaller villages are difficult to negotiate, since the road surfaces are either unpaved or made of cobblestones. Toilets for the disabled are virtually nonexistent, other than in four- or five-star hotels.

VISAS

Citizens of the United States, Canada, most European countries, Australia, Japan and New Zealand normally receive 90-day tourist cards when entering the country. A yellow slip of paper will be stapled or folded into your passport – don't lose this piece of paper, as you'll have to turn it in when you leave, or get it stamped if you extend your stay.

You can extend your stay once for another 90 days. After that, you'll be required to leave the country for at least three days. To extend your stay, take your passport to any immigration office and ask for a *prórroga* (visa extension); you'll have to fill out a form and pay L$400 (US$20).

Practically every large city and town in Honduras has an immigration office *(migración)* where you can do this.

VOLUNTEERING

A number of organizations offer volunteer opportunities in Honduras, on projects in many parts of the country and ranging from building homes to teaching English to involving school children in environmental programs. The website www.travel-to-honduras.com has a long list of groups that run volunteer programs in Honduras, from large operations like Casa Alianza and i-to-i, to smaller ones including the Cofradía Bilingual School and the Utila Iguana Conservation Project.

WOMEN TRAVELERS

Honduras is basically a good country for women travelers. As elsewhere, you'll probably attract less attention if you dress modestly. On the Bay Islands, where lots of beach-going foreigners tend to congregate, standards of modesty in dress are much more relaxed, though topless bathing is most definitely frowned upon.

Cases of rape of foreign tourists have been reported in a few places along the North Coast. As peaceful and idyllic as the coast looks – and usually is – be wary of going to isolated stretches of beach alone, and don't walk on the beach at night.

WORK

Most independent travelers who stay in (or come to) Honduras to work do so on the Bay Islands; dive instructors are almost exclusively foreigners, and many people completing divemaster training raise a little extra cash working as waiters or bartenders in West End, West Bay or Utila. Most do not have work permits and leave every three to six months to get a new tourist visa.

There are also a few opportunities to work in Copán Ruinas.

Transportation

CONTENTS

GETTING THERE & AWAY

ENTERING THE COUNTRY

Entering Honduras, whether by air, sea or land, is a relatively painless process. Arriving by air, you'll be given immigration and customs forms on the plane. After disembarking, you'll pass through immigration first; there's a line for residents and one for foreigners (*extranjeros*). There is no fee to enter, and tourists are typically issued 90-day tourist cards. You will be given a thin slip of paper – don't lose it, you'll need it when you exit the country. After passing through immigration, collect your bags and pass through customs. As in many Latin American countries, customs inspections are conducted at random. All passengers queue up to press a mechanical button; if the red light comes on you get inspected, if it's green you go through. Of course, customs officers may choose to inspect your bags anyway, so it's worth acting and dressing a bit sharp.

Most people entering by land do so at El Florido, Guatemala, near Copán Ruinas. Other busy crossings are Corinto, Guatemala, and El Amatillo or El Poy, El Salvador. A smaller number cross from Nicaragua. The drill is the same at all the crossings: go through the exit procedures for the country you're leaving, then present your passport at the Honduran office or window. There is no fee to enter the country, but some officers charge around L$60 (US$3) simply because they can.

You can extend your tourist visa once for another 90 days for L$400 (US$20) at almost any immigration office. In fact, the smaller offices tend to be faster and friendlier than the ones in Tegucigalpa or San Pedro Sula.

Passport

All foreign visitors must have a valid passport to enter Honduras. Be sure you have room for both an entry and exit stamp, and that your passport is valid for at least six months beyond your planned travel dates.

AIR

Frequent direct flights connect Honduras with all the Central American capitals and many destinations in North America, the Caribbean, South America and Europe. Most international flights arrive and depart from the airports at Tegucigalpa and San Pedro Sula; there are also direct flights between the USA and Roatán, coming from Houston, Miami and Atlanta.

Airports & Airlines

Honduras has three international airports: San Pedro Sula, Tegucigalpa and Roatán. Of the three, San Pedro Sula is the busiest. In addition, La Ceiba has a small domestic airport, and there are airstrips in Utila, Guanaja and throughout La Moskitia.

Aeropuerto Golosón (LCE; ☎ 443-3925) La Ceiba's airport, just west of town.

THINGS CHANGE...

The information in this chapter is particularly vulnerable to change. Check directly with the airline or a travel agent to make sure you understand how a fare (and ticket you may buy) works and be aware of the security requirements for international travel. Shop carefully. The details given in this chapter should be regarded as pointers and are not a substitute for your own careful, up-to-date research.

CLIMATE CHANGE & TRAVEL

Climate change is a serious threat to the ecosystems that humans rely upon, and air travel is the fastest-growing contributor to the problem. Lonely Planet regards travel, overall, as a global benefit, but believes we all have a responsibility to limit our personal impact on global warming.

Flying & Climate Change

Pretty much every form of motor travel generates CO_2 (the main cause of human-induced climate change) but planes are far and away the worst offenders, not just because of the sheer distances they allow us to travel, but because they release greenhouse gases high into the atmosphere. The statistics are frightening: two people taking a return flight between Europe and the US will contribute as much to climate change as an average household's gas and electricity consumption over a whole year.

Carbon Offset Schemes

Climatecare.org and other websites use 'carbon calculators' that allow jetsetters to offset the greenhouse gases they are responsible for with contributions to energy-saving projects and other climate-friendly initiatives in the developing world – including projects in India, Honduras, Kazakhstan and Uganda.

Lonely Planet, together with Rough Guides and other concerned partners in the travel industry, supports the carbon offset scheme run by climatecare.org. Lonely Planet offsets all of its staff and author travel.

For more information check out our website: lonelyplanet.com.

Aeropuerto Internacional Ramón Villeda Morales (SAP; ☎ 668-8880) San Pedro Sula's airport, located 15km east of town.

Aeropuerto Internacional Tocontín (TGU; ☎ 234-2702) Tegucigalpa's airport, located within the city limits.

Aeropuerto Juan Ramón Galvez (RTB) Roatán's airport, located just east of Coxen Hole.

Domestic and international carriers servicing Honduras include:

Aerolineas Sosa (NSO; www.aerolineasosa.com) Brus Laguna (☎ 433-8042); La Ceiba (☎ 440-0692); Puerto Lempira (☎ 433-6558); Roatán (☎ 445-1658); San Pedro Sula (☎ 550-6545); Tegucigalpa (Map p74; ☎ 233-4351)

Air France (AF; Map pp66-7; ☎ in Tegucigalpa 236-0029; www.airfrance.com)

American Airlines (AA; www.aa.com) San Pedro Sula (☎ 668-3244); Tegucigalpa (☎ 216-4800)

Continental/Copa Airlines (CO; www.continental.com) Roatán (☎ 445-0224); San Pedro Sula (☎ 550-7132); Tegucigalpa (☎ 220-0999)

Delta Air Lines (DL; ☎ 800-791-9000; www.delta.com)

Taca/Taca Regional (TA; www.taca.com) La Ceiba (☎ 441-3191); Roatán (☎ 552-9910); San Pedro Sula (☎ 668-3183); Tegucigalpa (Map p74; ☎ 236-8778)

SAMI Brus Laguna (☎ 433-8031); Puerto Lempira (☎ 433-6016)

Spirit Airlines (☎ 1-800-772-7117 in US; www.spiritair.com)

Tickets

It goes without saying that, for independent travelers, the internet has most of the best travel deals. Flying Monday to Thursday is generally cheaper.

Canada

Expedia (www.expedia.ca) Online bookings.

Travel Cuts (☎ 800-667-2887; www.travelcuts.com) Canada's national student travel agency.

Travelocity (www.travelocity.ca) Online bookings.

France

Anyway (☎ 08 92 89 38 92; www.anyway.fr)

Lastminute (☎ 08 92 70 50 00; www.lastminute.fr)

Nouvelles Frontières (☎ 08 25 00 07 47; www.nouvelles-frontieres.fr)

OTU Voyages (www.otu.fr) Specializes in student and youth travelers.

Voyageurs du Monde (☎ 01 40 15 11 15; www.vdm.com)

Germany

Expedia (www.expedia.de)

Just Travel (☎ 089 747 3330; www.justtravel.de)

Lastminute (☎ 01805 284 366; www.lastminute.de)

STA Travel (☎ 01805 456 422; www.statravel.de) For travelers under the age of 26.

Italy

CTS Viaggi (☎ 06 462 0431; www.cts.it) A recommended agent, specializing in student and youth travel.

Netherlands

Airfair (☎ 020 620 5121; www.airfair.nl)

Spain

Barcelo Viajes (☎ 902 116 226; www.barceloviajes.com)
Nouvelles Frontières (☎ 902 170 979; www.nouvelles-frontieres.es)

United Kingdom

Discount air travel is big business in London. Advertisements for many travel agencies appear in the travel pages of the weekend broadsheet newspapers, in *Time Out*, the *Evening Standard* and in the free online magazine *TNT* (www.tntmagazine.com).

Recommended travel agencies include:
Bridge the World (☎ 0870 444 7474; www.b-t-w.co.uk)
Flight Centre (☎ 0870 890 8099; flightcentre.co.uk)
Flightbookers (☎ 0870 814 4001; www.ebookers.com)
North-South Travel (☎ 01245 608 291; www.northsouthtravel.co.uk) North-South Travel donate part of their profit to projects in the developing world.
Quest Travel (☎ 0870 442 3542; www.questtravel.com)
STA Travel (☎ 0870 160 0599; www.statravel.co.uk) For travelers under the age of 26.
Trailfinders (www.trailfinders.co.uk)
Travel Bag (☎ 0870 890 1456; www.travelbag.co.uk)

United States

Discount travel agents in the US are known as consolidators (although you won't see a sign on the door saying 'consolidator').

The following agencies are recommended for online bookings:
American Express Travel (www.itn.net)
Cheap Tickets (www.cheaptickets.com)
Expedia (www.expedia.com)
Lowest Fare (www.lowestfare.com)
Orbitz (www.orbitz.com)
STA Travel (www.sta.com) For travelers under the age of 26.
Travelocity (www.travelocity.com)

LAND

Bus

Ordinary buses do not cross the border, which means you have to cross on foot and pick up another bus on the other side. However, several bus lines offer international service, including **Tica Bus** (www.ticabus.com), **Hedman Alas** (www.hedmanalas.com) **Fuente del Norte** (☎ 9843-0507), and **El Rey Express** (www.reyexpress.net). Between them, they offer services from Tegucigalpa and San Pedro Sula to San Salvador, Guatemala City, Antigua (Guatemala), Tapachula (Mexico), Managua (Nicaragua), San José (Costa Rica) and Panama City.

Car & Motorcycle

Most rental car agencies do not allow you to drive out of Honduras. Avis is the exception, though be sure that this is clear in your contract and that the vehicle remains covered by insurance.

El Salvador

The main crossings into El Salvador are at El Poy (see p138) and El Amatillo (see p90); there is a third crossing south of Marcala, but because of a longstanding border dispute, there is no Salvadoran immigration post there. There's no one to stop you, either, but entering here is technically illegal and you can be fined if your status is discovered. Some travelers have crossed into El Salvador as far as Perquín, Morazán, and returned to Honduras by the same crossing with no problem. Nevertheless, if you plan to go further or stay longer than a few days, it is best to use one of the official crossings.

BUS

From Tegucigalpa, Tica (L$500, 6½ hours) and **King Quality** (☎ 225-5415; L$500; 6-7hrs) offer direct service to San Salvador. Fuente del Norte also has a service from San Pedro Sula (L$500, six hours).

Guatemala

To Guatemala, the main crossings are at El Florido (see p267), Agua Caliente (see p138) and Corinto.

> **DEPARTURE TAX**
>
> Honduras levies a departure tax of L$646 (US$34) for people flying out of the country; it is payable in cash – US dollars or lempiras – after you've checked in but before you pass through security. For departures by land or sea, there is no departure tax.
>
> For domestic flights, there is a L$29 to L$32 (around US$1.50) departure tax, depending on the airport. It is payable in cash after you've checked in but before you pass the security checkpoint.

BORDER CROSSINGS

International borders in Central America tend to be busy, dirty and a bit dodgy. You're sure to be harangued by moneychangers when you arrive; if you need to change money, have it ready in a separate pocket and calculate ahead of time roughly what you expect to receive. Changers make a fair profit simply on mathematical trickery, believe it or not. You probably won't get a great rate, but don't be afraid to negotiate. Watch your bags at all times.

Some border officials are corrupt, though they tend not to bother travelers, preferring bigger fish such as truck drivers and importers. Crossing the border is supposed to be free, but you may be charged a fee to leave or enter Honduras; assuming it's a small amount – around L$60 (US$3) – it's best to just pay and move on. If it's a large amount, ask to see the regulation in writing, and say you want a receipt, either of which may discourage the agent from pursuing it.

Always be respectful and dress your best at the border; searches are very rare, but are most likely to occur if you have a disheveled appearance, which might encourage guards to stop and search.

BUS

From Tegucigalpa, King Quality has the most convenient service to Guatemala City, with just a two-hour layover in San Salvador (L$500 one way, 14 hours). Tica Bus has asimilar service but includes an overnight in San Salvador. From San Pedro Sula, you can take Fuente del Norte (L$500, 8½ hours). There are several shuttle services running between Copán Ruinas and Antigua, Guatemala (p124).

Nicaragua

There are three Nicaraguan border crossings in southern Honduras, at Las Manos, La Fraternidad/El Espino and Guasaule (see p90), and a fourth in La Moskitia, at Leimus (see p254).

BUS

All international buses to Managua pass through Tegucigalpa and use the Las Manos crossing via Danlí. Service is offered by Tica (L$600, eight hours) and King Quality (L$600, seven to eight hours). In La Moskitia, there are daily buses from Puerto Lempira to Leimus.

SEA

If you arrive or depart from Honduras by sea, be sure to clear your paperwork (visa, entry and exit stamps) immediately with the nearest immigration office.

Belize

The only regularly scheduled passenger boat service between Honduras and another country is a small boat operated by **Gulf Cruz** (☎ 9984-9544, 9982-6985). It runs twice weekly from Puerto Cortés to Dangriga (L$950, two hours). See p166 for details.

El Salvador

There is no regular boat service to El Salvador but it is possible to hire a fisherman in Amapala to take you across the Golfo de Fonseca to La Unión, El Salvador.

GETTING AROUND

AIR

Domestic flights are surprisingly affordable, and flying can be a good way to save some time if your schedule is tight. Of the airlines listed on p267, Aerolineas Sosa, Taca Regional and SAMI offer domestic services.

There are three (sometimes more) daily flights to Roatán, fewer to Utila and Guanaja; most originate in San Pedro with a stop in La Ceiba.

You can also fly to La Moskitia, and within the region once you get there. All flights go through La Ceiba; when we passed through, Sosa had daily flights to Puerto Lempira (p253) and three flights weekly to Brus Laguna.

SAMI has a semi-regular service at best – don't plan any tight schedules around its flights. Still, it is a convenient and affordable way to get around the vast Moskitia region; stops include Palacios, Brus Laguna, Ahuas, Wampusirpi and Puerto Lempira.

BICYCLE

Mountain biking around Honduras is not common, which is not to say it wouldn't be a great adventure as there are plenty of lightly trafficked dirt roads winding through beautiful terrain. Some of the highways in Olancho are known for roadside robberies – thieves may not know what to think of a cyclist, but better to play it safe and avoid those areas. Try Ruta Lenca and parts of the north coast, instead.

Bike rental is still uncommon in Honduras. There are rental outfits in Tela (p173), and mountain-biking tours and rentals in La Ceiba (p181). A few hotels also offer bicycles for guest use. Expect to pay around L$200 (US$10) to L$400 (US$20) per day.

BOAT

Ferry

Two comfortable, air-conditioned passenger ferries, the MV *Galaxy II* and the *Utila Princess,* serve Roatán (children 12 & under/economy/1st class L$284/524/624, one hour; see p203) and Utila (L$420, one hour; see p228) respectively. There is no scheduled service to or from Guanaja. Some travelers report you can hop Guanaja-bound ships from Trujillo for around L$600 (though you'll likely wait several days for a ship to leave).

Captain Vern (☎ 3346-2600, 9910-8040; vfine@hotmail.com) offers catamaran sailboat trips between Roatán's West End and Utila (daily, L$1038 one way, four to five hours).

Motorboat

In La Moskitia, almost all transportation is along the waterways, including the long ride up to Las Marías (p246) where a number of popular outings begin. You will also take motorized canoes from town to town in La Moskitia, and across one or more of the region's huge lagoons.

BUS

Buses are an easy and cheap way to get around in Honduras. Service usually starts very early in the morning – at 3am or 4am on some routes – but may end by early evening, or even late afternoon. Buses between Tegucigalpa and San Pedro Sula run later. *Microbuses* or *rapiditos* are smaller minivan-type buses that cover some routes, and tend to go faster and leave more frequently than regular buses.

Classes

On major bus routes, you'll often have a choice between taking a *directo* (direct) or *ordinario* (ordinary), also known as *parando* or *servicio a escala.* The *directo* is almost always worth the extra money, even on short trips. *Directos* can be twice as fast as *ordinario* buses, which stop frequently to let passengers on and off.

Deluxe buses offer even faster services between Tegucigalpa, San Pedro Sula, Copán Ruinas, La Ceiba and Trujillo, and use modern, air-conditioned buses (with service including movies and soft drinks). Fares on *ejecutivo* (executive) or *servicio de lujo* (luxury service) buses are often double those on *directos* (sometimes more), but can be a worthwhile splurge for long trips.

King Quality (☎ 225-5415) and **Hedman Alas** (www.hedmanalas.com) have 'super-deluxe' seats on international buses, with almost fully reclining seats and additional food and drink service, all in a special area below the main cabin.

Contrary to common wisdom, chicken buses (*ordinario*) are targeted for robbery more often than the direct or deluxe lines, mainly because there are more opportunities for ne'er-do-wells to board. You don't have to avoid chicken buses altogether – they're often your only option – but do try using direct and deluxe buses whenever possible.

Costs

Buses are very affordable. Some *directo* fares include L$120 Tegucigalpa–San Pedro Sula (4½ hours); L$110 San Pedro Sula–Copán Ruinas (three hours) and L$80 La Ceiba–Tela (1½ hours).

Reservations

Reservations aren't usually necessary and are rarely taken, even on *ejecutivo* buses. For travel during Semana Santa (Holy Week; the week preceding Easter), however, you should buy your ticket a day or two in advance, which assures you a spot and saves you the time and hassle of waiting in line in a jam-packed bus terminal.

CAR & MOTORCYCLE

Bring Your Own Vehicle

Bringing your own car into Honduras can be a headache, mostly due to all the fees and paperwork. Arriving at the border you'll be swarmed by *tramitadores,* young men who help you through the morass and are worth the expense. Travelers report widely different experiences and costs – from L$400 (US$20) to L$3000 (US$150) and from an hour to all day – depending mostly on the number and amount of bribe money it takes. Get to the border early and bring plenty of cash (though try not to pull out a huge wad, of course). As frustrating as the process can be, be patient and never insult a customs officer.

Driver's License

In general, foreign drivers can drive a car using their home driver's license for up to 30 days. Be sure your license is valid and won't expire while you're on the road. As with all important documents, make a copy of your license and stash it in a safe place.

Fuel & Spare Parts

Gas is expensive in Honduras, at least compared to the US. It costs around L$81 (US$4.30) per gallon, and is sold in diesel, unleaded or 'plus,' and the higher grade 'premium'. Annoyingly, many gas stations don't offer plus so you're forced to pay extra for premium. Luckily, there are many gas stations in both urban and rural areas.

Finding spare parts is not usually a problem, unless you're driving a very uncommon vehicle. Toyotas are extremely common in Honduras, so you'll have an easier time repairing them than any other brand.

Rental

Rental cars are available in all the major cities and on Roatán. Prices start at around L$567 (US$30) per day for an economy car and L$945 (US$50) for midsize cars or larger ones. Remember that renting at the airport typically costs 10% to 15% more than in town simply because of airport taxes. Rental agencies include:

Advance Rent A Car (www.advancerentacar.com) San Pedro Sula (☎ 552-2295); Tegucigalpa (☎ 235-9531)
Avis (www.avis.com.hn) Roatán (☎ 445-0122); San Pedro Sula (☎ 553-0888); Tegucigalpa (☎ 239-5712)
Best Car Rental (☎ in Roatán 445-2268; www.roatanbestcarrental.com)
Budget (www.budget.com) Roatán (☎ 445-2290); Tegucigalpa (☎ 235-9528)
Econo Rent-a-Car La Ceiba (☎ 442-1688, 442-8686); Tegucigalpa (☎ 235-8582)
Molinari Rent A Car (☎ in Tegucigalpa 237-5335; molinarirentacar@yahoo.com)
Union Rent A Car (☎ in La Ceiba 440-0439)
Thrifty (www.thrifty.com) La Ceiba (☎ 442-1532); Roatán (☎ 445-1729); San Pedro Sula (☎ 552-5498)

Insurance

Insurance is required on vehicles in Honduras; if you're renting, it will be included in the rate. A few companies will allow you to waive the collision damage insurance if you have coverage through your Visa or MasterCard. This can save you L$200 (US$10) per day or more. If you think you might rent a car in Honduras, take the time before you arrive to familiarize yourself with the terms of your credit-card coverage. Be sure to ask if the insurance covers dirt roads and pickup trucks.

Road Conditions

Honduras' main highways are paved and decently maintained. The busy CA-5, which connects San Pedro Sula and Tegucigalpa, is being widened and straightened, which might make a big difference if construction is ever finished. Away from the highways, road conditions range from excellent to disastrous. The rainy season can make traveling on dirt roads tough, since many develop deep mud holes. Always ask about road conditions before setting out, especially if you're using a secondary road.

Road Rules

Basic road rules here don't differ much from the US or most European countries. A few things to remember: it is illegal to turn right at a red stoplight, and seat belts are required for the driver and front-seat passenger at all times. Many towns and cities have a confusing system of one-way streets though, which are often unmarked.

There are a number of police checkpoints on the highways, which may look like military stops because Honduran police wear camouflage. If you're not waved down, keep rolling through. If you're stopped, you'll be asked for your driver's license and the vehicle registration card. Be polite and respectful at all times. Very rarely, you'll be asked for money; you are not obligated to give any, and you can usually get away with politely saying you can't. You can also give the officer L$50 to L$100 and be on your way. Mostly the money is used for gas for the police truck.

HITCHHIKING

Hitchhiking – *tomando un jalón,* or 'taking a hitch' – is never entirely safe in any country in the world, and we don't recommend it. However, it is very common in much of

Honduras, especially in rural areas like the Ruta Lenca and along the North Coast. Peace Corps volunteers, for example, do it frequently. Generally you just stand on the side of the road and wave down a pickup truck. You should offer the driver money, though many drivers will not accept it. Usually there are locations where people go to get *un jalón* – ask at your hotel.

LOCAL TRANSPORTATION

Boat

In La Moskitia, boats are the local transport of choice, as there are few roads and fewer bridges. On Roatán, water taxis are the best way to get from West End to West Bay, and around the town of Oakridge. *Lanchas* (motorboats) are also used to ferry passengers to and from Isla del Tigre, in southern Honduras.

Bus

It is highly recommended that travelers do not use city buses, especially in San Pedro Sula and Tegucigalpa. Not only is pick-pocketing and petty theft common, but public buses are occasionally targeted by area gangs for what amounts to a 'toll' for passing through certain neighborhoods. With taxi fares so low (and *colectivo* taxi fares even lower) buses just aren't worth the risk.

Moto-taxi

Small Thai-style three-wheeled moto-taxis have burst onto the Central American scene, going from unknown to ubiquitous in just a few years. Loud and slightly obnoxious, they are cheaper and more plentiful than taxis, making them a good option when you're lugging bags to or from the bus terminal on a hot day.

Taxi

Taxis don't have meters in Honduras, but in most towns there is a fixed one-ride fare, usually from L$10 (US$0.50) to L$20 (US$1) per person. You can expect longer journeys in a major city to cost around L$80 to L$100. In many cities, *colectivos* (shared taxis) ply a number of prescribed routes, costing around L$10 (US$0.50) per passenger. In all cases, confirm the price of the ride before you get into the cab. If it seems exorbitant, negotiate, or simply wait for another cab.

Health Dr David Goldberg

CONTENTS

Travelers to Honduras and the Bay Islands need to be concerned chiefly about food-borne diseases, though mosquito-borne infections can also be a problem. Most of these illnesses are not life threatening, but they can certainly have an impact on your trip or even ruin it. Besides getting the proper vaccinations, it's important that you bring along a good insect repellent and exercise great care in what you eat and drink.

BEFORE YOU GO

Since most vaccines don't produce immunity until at least two weeks after they're given, visit a physician four to eight weeks before departure. Ask your doctor for an International Certificate of Vaccination (otherwise known as the yellow booklet), which will list all the vaccinations you've received. This is mandatory for countries that require proof of yellow-fever vaccination upon entry, but it's a good idea to carry it wherever you travel.

Bring medications in their original containers, clearly labeled. A signed, dated letter from your physician describing all medical conditions and medications, including generic names, is also a good idea. If carrying syringes or needles, be sure to have a physician's letter documenting their medical necessity.

INSURANCE

Honduran medical treatment is generally inexpensive for common diseases and minor treatment, but public hospitals are extremely overcrowded and understaffed. If you suffer a serious medical problem or emergency, it is highly recommended you go to a private hospital or even fly home (if your condition allows it). Travel insurance can typically cover the costs. Some US health-insurance policies stay in effect (at least for a limited time) if you travel abroad, but it's worth checking exactly what you'll be covered for in Honduras. For people whose medical insurance or national health systems don't extend to Honduras – which includes most non-Americans – a travel policy is advisable. Check out the insurance section of www.lonelyplanet.com for more information.

You may prefer a policy that pays doctors or hospitals directly rather than one requiring you to pay on the spot and claim later. If you do have to claim later, keep all documentation. Some policies ask you to call collect to a center in your home country, where an immediate assessment of your problem is made. Check that the policy covers ambulances or an emergency flight home. Some policies offer lower and higher medical-expense options; the higher ones are chiefly for countries such as the US, which has extremely high medical costs. There is a wide variety of policies available, so be sure to check the small print.

MEDICAL CHECKLIST

It is a good idea to carry a medical and first-aid kit with you. Following is a list of items you should consider packing.

- acetaminophen/paracetamol (Tylenol) or aspirin
- adhesive or paper tape
- antibiotics
- antidiarrheal drugs (eg loperamide)
- antibacterial ointment (eg Bactroban) for cuts and abrasions
- anti-inflammatory drugs (eg ibuprofen)
- antihistamines (for hay fever and allergic reactions)
- bandages, gauze, gauze rolls
- iodine tablets or chlorine drops (for water purification)

- insect repellent containing DEET for the skin
- insect spray containing Permethrin for clothing, tents and bed nets
- oral rehydration salts
- pocket knife
- scissors, safety pins, tweezers
- steroid cream or cortisone (for poison ivy and other allergic rashes)
- sun block
- syringes and sterile needles
- thermometer

INTERNET RESOURCES

There is a wealth of travel-health advice on the internet; lonelyplanet.com is a good place to start. The World Health Organization publishes a superb book called *International Travel & Health,* which is revised annually and is available online at no cost at www.who.int/ith. Another website of general interest is www.mdtravelhealth.com, which provides complete travel health recommendations for every country, updated daily, also at no cost.

FURTHER READING

For further information, see *Healthy Travel Central & South America,* also from Lonely Planet. If you're traveling with children, Lonely Planet's *Travel with Children* may be useful. The *ABC of Healthy Travel,* by E Walker et al, and *Medicine for the Outdoors,* by Paul S Auerbach, are other valuable resources.

IN TRANSIT

DEEP VEIN THROMBOSIS (DVT)

Blood clots may form in the legs during plane flights, chiefly because of prolonged immobility. The longer the flight, the greater the risk. Though most blood clots are reabsorbed uneventfully, some may break off and travel through the blood vessels to the lungs, where they could cause life-threatening complications.

The chief symptom of DVT is swelling of, or pain in, the foot, ankle or calf, usually but not always on one side. When a blood clot travels to the lungs, it may cause chest pain and breathing difficulties. Travelers with any of these symptoms should immediately seek medical attention.

To prevent the development of DVT on long flights you should walk about the cabin, perform isometric compressions of the leg muscles (ie contract the leg muscles while sitting), drink plenty of fluids, and avoid alcohol.

JET LAG & MOTION SICKNESS

Jet lag is common when crossing more than five time zones, resulting in insomnia, fatigue, malaise or nausea. To avoid jet lag try drinking plenty of fluids (non-alcoholic) and eating light meals. Upon arrival, get exposure to natural sunlight and readjust your schedule (for meals, sleep etc) as soon as possible.

Antihistamines such as dimenhydrinate (Dramamine) and meclizine (Antivert, Bonine) are usually the first choice for treating motion sickness; their main side effect is drowsiness. A herbal alternative is ginger, which works like a charm for some people.

IN HONDURAS

AVAILABILITY & COST OF HEALTH CARE

There are a number of first-rate hospitals in Tegucigalpa (Honduras Medical Center, p68) and San Pedro Sula (Hospital Centro Mêdico Betesda, p111) In general, private facilities offer better care than public hospitals, though at greater cost.

Adequate medical care is available in other major cities, but facilities in rural areas may be limited.

Many doctors and hospitals expect payment in cash, regardless of whether you have travel-health insurance. If you develop a life-threatening medical problem, you'll probably want to be evacuated to a country with state-of-the-art medical care. Since this may cost tens of thousands of dollars, be sure you have insurance to cover this before you depart. You can find a list of medical evacuation and travel-insurance companies on the US State Department website (www.travel.state.gov).

Honduran pharmacies are identified by a green cross and a '*farmacia*' sign. Most are well supplied and the pharmacists well-trained. Some medications requiring a prescription in the US may be dispensed in Honduras without a prescription. To find an after-hours pharmacy, you can look in the local newspaper, ask your hotel concierge, or check the front door of a local pharmacy, which will often post the name of a nearby pharmacy that is open for the night.

INFECTIOUS DISEASES

Cholera

Cholera is an intestinal infection acquired through ingestion of contaminated food or water. The main symptom is profuse, watery diarrhea, which may be so severe that it causes life-threatening dehydration. The key treatment is drinking oral rehydration solution. Antibiotics are also given, usually tetracycline or doxycycline, though quinolone antibiotics such as ciprofloxacin and levofloxacin are also effective.

A handful of cholera outbreaks have been reported in Honduras over the last few years. The vaccine is no longer mandatory, though many health workers still recommend it.

Dengue Fever

Dengue fever is a viral infection found throughout Central America. It is most prevalent during the rainy season, which peaks from September to November on the North Coast. Wet weather is possible year-round, however, and outbreaks can occur at any time. Dengue is transmitted by Aedes mosquitoes, which bite preferentially during the day and are usually found close to human habitations, often indoors. They breed primarily in artificial water containers, such as jars, barrels, cans, cisterns, metal drums, plastic containers and discarded tires. As a result, dengue is especially common in densely populated, urban environments.

Dengue usually causes flu-like symptoms including fever, muscle aches, joint pains, headaches, nausea and vomiting, often followed by a rash. The body aches may be quite uncomfortable, but most cases are resolved uneventfully in a few days. Severe cases usually occur in children under 15 who are experiencing their second dengue infection.

There is no specific treatment for dengue fever except to take analgesics such as acetaminophen/paracetamol (Tylenol) and drink plenty of fluids. Severe cases may require hospitalization for intravenous fluids and supportive care. There is no vaccine. The cornerstone of prevention is insect protection measures.

Hepatitis A

Hepatitis A occurs throughout Central America. It's a viral infection of the liver usually acquired by ingestion of contaminated water, food or ice, though it may also be acquired by direct contact with infected persons. The illness occurs worldwide, but the incidence is higher in developing nations. Symptoms may include fever, malaise, jaundice, nausea, vomiting and abdominal pain. Most cases are resolved uneventfully, though hepatitis A occasionally causes severe liver damage. There is no treatment.

The vaccine for hepatitis A is extremely safe and highly effective. If you get a booster six to 12 months later, it lasts for at least 10 years. You really should get it before you go to Honduras or any other developing nation. Because the safety of the hepatitis A vaccine has not been established for pregnant women or children under two years, they should instead be given a gammaglobulin injection.

Hepatitis B

Like hepatitis A, hepatitis B is a liver infection that occurs worldwide but is more common in developing nations. Unlike hepatitis A, the disease is usually acquired by sexual contact or by exposure to infected blood, generally through blood transfusions or contaminated needles. The vaccine is recommended only for long-term travelers (on the road more than six months) who expect to live in rural areas or have close physical contact with the local population. Additionally, the vaccine is recommended for anyone who anticipates sexual contact with the local inhabitants or a possible need for medical, dental or other treatments while abroad, especially if a need for transfusions or injections is expected.

Hepatitis B vaccine is safe and highly effective. However, a total of three injections are necessary to establish full immunity. Several countries added hepatitis B vaccine to the list of routine childhood immunizations in the 1980s, so many young adults are already protected.

Malaria

Malaria occurs in every country in Central America, and is especially prevalent in Honduras' eastern coastal areas. It's transmitted by mosquito bites, which usually occur between dusk and dawn. The main symptom is high, spiking fevers, which may be accompanied by chills, sweats, headache, body aches, weakness, vomiting, or diarrhea. Severe cases may involve the central nervous system and lead to seizures, confusion, coma and death.

Taking malaria pills is strongly recommended when visiting lowland rural areas and in the departments of Gracias a Dios, Colón, Olancho, Yoro, Alántida, Cortés and the Bay Islands.

For Honduras, the first-choice malaria pill is chloroquine, taken once weekly in a dosage of 500mg (be sure to check that the amount of ingredient is in each pill, not just the size of the pill itself), starting one to two weeks before arrival and continuing through the trip and for four weeks after departure. Chloroquine is safe, inexpensive and highly effective. Side effects are typically mild and may include nausea, abdominal discomfort, headache, dizziness, blurred vision or itching. Severe reactions are uncommon.

Protecting yourself against mosquito bites (p278) is just as important as taking malaria pills, since no pills are 100% effective.

If you anticipate not having access to medical care while traveling, bring along additional pills for self-treatment, which you should undertake if you develop symptoms that suggest malaria, such as high fevers, and can't reach a doctor. One option is to take an anti-malarial (such as chloroquine). If you start self-medication, you should try to see a doctor at the earliest possible opportunity; also see a doctor if you are still developing the disease while taking an anti-malarial – it suggests resistance to the drug.

If you develop a fever after returning home, see a physician as malaria symptoms may not occur for months.

Typhoid Fever

Typhoid fever is caused by ingestion of food or water contaminated by a type of *Salmonella* known as *Salmonella typhi*. Fever occurs in virtually all cases. Other symptoms may include headache, malaise, muscle aches, dizziness, loss of appetite, nausea and abdominal pain. Either diarrhea or constipation may occur. Possible complications include intestinal perforation, intestinal bleeding, confusion, delirium or (rarely) coma.

Unless you expect to take all your meals in major hotels and restaurants, typhoid vaccination is a good idea. It's usually given orally, but is also available as an injection. Neither vaccine is approved for use in children under two years.

The drug of choice for typhoid fever is usually a quinolone antibiotic such as ciprofloxacin (Cipro) or levofloxacin (Levaquin), which many travelers carry for treatment of travelers' diarrhea. However, if you self-treat for typhoid fever, you may also need to self-treat for malaria, since the symptoms of the two diseases can be indistinguishable.

Yellow Fever

Yellow fever no longer occurs in Central America, but many Central American countries, including Honduras, require yellow-fever vaccination before entry if you're arriving from a country in Africa or South America where yellow fever occurs. If you're not arriving from a country with yellow fever, the vaccine is neither required nor recommended. Yellow-fever vaccine is given only in approved yellow-fever vaccination centers, which provide validated International Certificates of Vaccination (yellow booklets). The vaccine should be given at least 10 days before departure and remains effective for approximately 10 years. Reactions to the vaccine are generally mild and may include headaches, muscle aches, low-grade fevers or discomfort at the injection site. Severe, life-threatening reactions have been described but are extremely rare.

Other Infections

- **Brucellosis** This is an infection occurring in domestic and wild animals that may be transmitted to humans through direct animal contact or by consumption of unpasteurized dairy products from infected animals. Symptoms may include fever, malaise, depression, loss of appetite, headache, muscle aches and back pain. Complications can include arthritis, hepatitis, meningitis and endocarditis (heart valve infection).
- **Chagas' disease** This is a parasitic infection transmitted by triatomine insects (reduviid bugs), which inhabit crevices in the walls and roofs of substandard housing in South and Central America. In Honduras, most cases occur in lowland and coastal areas. The triatomine insect lays its feces on human skin as it bites, usually at night. A person becomes infected when they unknowingly rub the feces into the bite wound or any other open sore. Chagas' disease is extremely

rare in travelers. However, if you sleep in a poorly constructed house, especially one made of mud, adobe or thatch, you should be sure to protect yourself with a bed net and good insecticide.

- **Gnathostomiasis** This is a parasite acquired by eating raw or undercooked freshwater fish, perhaps in *ceviche* (a popular lime-marinated fish salad). The chief symptom is intermittent, migratory swellings under the skin, sometimes associated with joint pains, muscle pains or gastrointestinal problems. The symptoms may not begin until many months after exposure.
- **Histoplasmosis** Caused by a soil-based fungus, this is acquired by inhalation, often when soil has been disrupted. Initial symptoms may include fever, chills, dry cough, chest pain and headache, sometimes leading to pneumonia.
- **HIV/AIDS** Honduras has one of the highest infection rates in Central America. Be sure to use condoms for all sexual encounters.
- **Leishmaniasis** This occurs in the mountains and jungles of all Central American countries. The infection is transmitted by sand flies, which are about one-third the size of mosquitoes. Leishmaniasis may be limited to the skin, causing slow-growing ulcers over exposed parts of the body, or (less commonly) disseminate to the bone marrow, liver and spleen. The disease may be particularly severe in those with HIV. There is no vaccine for leishmaniasis. To protect yourself from sand flies, follow the same precautions as for mosquitoes (right), except that netting must be finer mesh (at least 18 holes to the linear inch).
- **Onchocerciasis** (river blindness): This is caused by a roundworm invading the eye, leading to blindness. The infection is transmitted by black flies, which breed along the banks of rapidly flowing rivers and streams.
- **Typhus** This may be transmitted by lice in scattered pockets of the country.

TRAVELERS' DIARRHEA

To prevent diarrhea, avoid tap water unless it has been boiled, filtered or chemically disinfected (iodine tablets or chlorine drops); only eat fresh fruits or vegetables if cooked or peeled; be wary of dairy products that might contain unpasteurized milk; and be highly selective when eating food from street vendors. See p262 for more tips.

If you develop diarrhea, be sure to drink plenty of fluids, preferably an oral rehydration solution containing lots of salt and sugar. A few loose stools don't require treatment, but if you start having more than four or five stools a day you should start taking an antibiotic (usually a quinolone drug) and an antidiarrheal agent (such as loperamide). If diarrhea is bloody or persists for more than 72 hours or is accompanied by fever, shaking chills or severe abdominal pain, you should seek medical attention.

ENVIRONMENTAL HAZARDS & TREATMENT

Animal Bites

Do not attempt to pet, handle or feed any animal, with the exception of domestic animals known to be free of any infectious disease. Most animal injuries are directly related to a person's attempt to touch or feed the animal.

Any bite or scratch by a mammal, including bats, should be promptly and thoroughly cleansed with large amounts of soap and water, followed by application of an antiseptic such as iodine or alcohol. Contact the local health authorities immediately for possible post-exposure treatment, whether or not you've been immunized against rabies. It may also be advisable to start an antibiotic, since wounds caused by animal bites and scratches frequently become infected. One of the newer quinolones, such as levofloxacin (Levaquin), which many travelers carry in case of diarrhea, is an appropriate choice.

Mosquito Bites

To prevent mosquito bites, wear long sleeves, long pants, hats and shoes (rather than sandals). Bring along insect repellent, preferably one containing DEET, which should be applied to exposed skin and clothing, but not to eyes, mouth, cuts, wounds or irritated skin. Products containing lower concentrations of DEET are as effective, but for shorter periods. In general, adults and children over 12 should use preparations containing 25% to 35% DEET, which usually lasts about six hours. Children between two and 12 years of age should use preparations containing no more than 10% DEET, applied sparingly, which should last about three hours. Neurological toxicity has been reported from DEET, especially in children, but appears to be extremely uncommon and generally related to overuse. Don't use DEET-containing compounds on children under two years.

Insect repellents containing certain botanical products, including oil of eucalyptus and soybean oil, are effective but last only 1½ to two hours. Where there is a high risk of malaria or yellow fever, use DEET-containing repellents. Products based on citronella are not effective.

For additional protection, apply permethrin to clothing, shoes, tents and bed nets. Permethrin treatments are safe and remain effective for at least two weeks, even when items are laundered. Permethrin should not be applied directly to skin.

Don't sleep with the window open unless there is a screen. If sleeping outdoors or in accommodation that allows entry of mosquitoes, use a bed net treated with permethrin, with edges tucked in under the mattress. The mesh size should be less than 1.5mm. Alternatively, use a mosquito coil, which will fill the room with insecticide through the night. Repellent-impregnated wristbands are not effective.

Snake & Scorpion Bites

Venomous snakes in Central America include the bushmaster, fer-de-lance (common lancehead), coral snake and various species of rattlesnakes. The fer-de-lance is the most lethal. It generally does not attack without provocation, but may bite humans who accidentally come too close as its lies camouflaged on the forest floor. The bushmaster is the world's largest pit viper, measuring up to 4m in length. Like all pit vipers, the bushmaster has a heat-sensing pit between the eye and nostril on each side of its head, which it uses to detect the presence of warm-blooded prey.

In the event of a venomous snake bite, place the victim at rest, keep the bitten area immobilized, and move them immediately to the nearest medical facility. Avoid tourniquets, which are no longer recommended.

Scorpions are a problem in many regions. If stung, you should immediately apply ice or cold packs, immobilize the affected body part and go to the nearest emergency room. To prevent scorpion stings, be sure to inspect and shake out clothing, shoes and sleeping bags before use, and wear gloves and protective clothing when working around piles of wood or leaves.

Sun

To protect yourself from excessive sun exposure, you should stay out of the midday sun, wear sunglasses and a wide-brimmed hat, and apply sunscreen with SPF 15 or higher, providing both UVA and UVB protection. Sunscreen should be generously applied to all exposed parts of the body approximately 30 minutes before sun exposure and be reapplied after swimming or vigorous activity. Drink plenty of fluids and avoid strenuous exercise when the temperature is high.

Tick Bites

To prevent tick bites, follow the same precautions as for mosquitoes; boots, with pants tucked in, are preferable to shoes and sandals. Perform a thorough tick check at the end of each day. You'll generally need the assistance of a friend or mirror for a full examination. Remove ticks with tweezers, grasping them firmly by the head. Insect repellents based on botanical products (described on left) have not been adequately studied for insects other than mosquitoes and cannot be recommended to prevent tick bites.

Water

Tap water in Honduras is generally not safe to drink. Vigorous boiling for one minute is the most effective means of water purification. At altitudes greater than 2000m, boil for three minutes. You can improve the taste of boiled water somewhat by pouring it back and forth between containers; it reoxygenates the water.

Another option is to disinfect water with iodine pills. Instructions are usually enclosed with the pills and should be carefully followed. Or you can add 2% tincture of iodine to 1L (quart) of water (five drops to clear water, 10 drops to cloudy water) and let stand for 30 minutes. If the water is cold, a longer time may be required. The taste of iodinated water can be improved by adding vitamin C (ascorbic acid). Don't consume iodinated water for more than a few weeks. Pregnant women, those with a history of thyroid disease and those allergic to iodine should not drink iodinated water. Chlorine is also an effective way to purify water, and may be easier to find in Honduras – ask for 'cloro'. Two drops per liter quart does the trick; there should be a slight swimming-pool smell. Always wait 10 minutes before drinking.

There are a number of water filters on the market. Those with smaller pores (reverse osmosis filters) provide the broadest protection, but they are relatively large and are readily plugged by debris. Those with somewhat larger pores (microstrainer filters) are ineffective against viruses, although they remove other organisms. Manufacturers' instructions must be carefully followed.

CHILDREN & PREGNANT WOMEN

In general, it's safe for children and pregnant women to go to Honduras. However, because some of the vaccines listed previously are not approved for use by children or pregnant women, these travelers should be particularly careful not to drink tap water or consume any questionable food or beverage. Also, when traveling with children, make sure they're up to date on all routine immunizations. It's sometimes appropriate to give children some of their vaccines a little early before visiting a developing nation. You should discuss this with your pediatrician. If pregnant, bear in mind that should a complication such as premature labor develop while abroad, the quality of medical care may not be comparable to that in your home country.

Since yellow-fever vaccine is not recommended for pregnant women or children younger than nine months old, obtain a waiver letter (if you are arriving from a country with yellow fever), preferably written on letterhead stationery and bearing the stamp used by official immunization centers to validate the International Certificate of Vaccination.

Language

CONTENTS

Spanish is the official language of Honduras and the main language the traveler will need. Every visitor to the country should attempt to learn some Spanish, the basic elements of which are easily acquired.

WHO SPEAKS WHAT WHERE?

Spanish is spoken throughout mainland Honduras, though it is a second language for some indigenous communities in La Moskitia and in Garífuna areas on the north coast. Miskitu (p287), Garífuna (p287) and English (in the Bay Islands and along the Caribbean Coast) are also used. While Bay Islanders traditionally speak English, an influx of mainlanders in search of construction jobs has begun to tip the balance toward Spanish, especially on Roatán.

SPANISH

A month-long language course taken before departure can go a long way toward facilitating communication and comfort on the road. Alternatively, language courses (see p259) are also available in Honduras. Even if classes are impractical, you should make the effort to learn a few basic words and phrases. Don't hesitate to practise your new skills – in general, Hondurans meet attempts to communicate in their languages with enthusiasm and appreciation.

For a more comprehensive guide to the Spanish of the region, get a copy of Lonely Planet's *Latin American Spanish Phrasebook*.

PRONUNCIATION

Spanish spelling is phonetically consistent, meaning that there's a clear and consistent relationship between what you see in writing and how it's pronounced. In addition, most Spanish sounds have English equivalents, so English speakers shouldn't have too much trouble being understood.

Vowels

a as in 'father'
e as in 'met'
i as in 'marine'
o as in 'or' (without the 'r' sound)
u as in 'rule'; the 'u' is not pronounced after **q** and in the letter combinations **gue** and **gui**, unless it's marked with a diaeresis (eg *argüir*), in which case it's pronounced as English 'w'
y at the end of a word or when it stands alone, it's pronounced as the Spanish **i** (eg *y* meaning 'and'); between vowels within a word it's as the 'y' in 'yes'

Consonants

As a rule, Spanish consonants resemble their English counterparts; the exceptions are listed below.

While the consonants **ch**, **ll** and **ñ** are generally considered distinct letters, **ch** and **ll** are now often listed alphabetically under **c** and **l** respectively in dictionaries. The letter **ñ** is still treated as a separate letter and comes after **n** in alphabetical listings.

b similar to English 'b'; referred to as 'b larga'
c as in 'celery' before **e** and **i**; otherwise as English 'k'
ch as in 'church'

d as in 'dog,' but between vowels and after **l** or **n**, the sound is closer to the 'th' in 'this'
g as the 'ch' in the Scottish *loch* before **e** and **i** (written as 'kh' in our guides to pronunciation); elsewhere, as in 'go'
h invariably silent, ie not pronounced; if your name begins with this letter, listen carefully if you're waiting for public officials to call you
j as the 'ch' in the Scottish *loch* (written as 'kh' in our pronunciation guides)
ll as the 'y' in 'yellow'
ñ as the 'ni' in 'onion'
r as in 'run', but strongly rolled, especially in words with **rr**
v similar to English 'b,' but softer; referred to as 'b corta'
x usually pronounced as **j** above; as in 'taxi' in other instances; note that in Mayan words **x** is pronounced like English 'sh'
z as the 's' in 'sun'

Word Stress

In general, words ending in vowels or the letters **n** or **s** have stress on the next-to-last syllable, while those with other endings have stress on the last syllable. Thus *vaca* (cow) and *caballos* (horses) both carry stress on the next-to-last syllable, while *ciudad* (city) and *infeliz* (unhappy) are both stressed on the last syllable.

Written accents will almost always appear in words that don't follow the rules above, eg *sótano* (basement), *América* and *porción* (portion).

In our pronunciation guides, the stressed syllables are in italics.

GENDER & PLURALS

In Spanish, nouns are either masculine or feminine, and there are rules to help determine gender (there are of course some exceptions). Feminine nouns generally end with -**a** or with the groups -**ción**, -**sión** or -**dad**. Other endings typically signify a masculine noun. Endings for adjectives also change to agree with the gender of the noun they modify (masculine/feminine -**o**/-**a**). Where both masculine and feminine forms are included in this language guide, they are separated by a slash, with the masculine form first, eg *perdido/a*.

If a noun or adjective ends in a vowel, the plural is formed by adding -**s** to the end. If it ends in a consonant, the plural is formed by adding -**es** to the end.

ACCOMMODATIONS

I'm looking for ...	*Estoy buscando ...*	es·*toy* boos·*kan*·do ...
Where is ...?	*¿Dónde hay ...?*	*don*·de ay ...
a guesthouse	*una casa de huéspedes*	*oo*·na *ka*·sa de *wes*·pe·des
a hotel	*un hotel*	oon o·*tel*
a youth hostel	*hostal*	os·*tal*

MAKING A RESERVATION

(for phone or written requests)

To ... /From ...	*A ... /De ...*
Date	*Fecha*
I'd like to book ...	*Quisiera reservar ...* (see the list under 'Accommodations' for bed and room options)
in the name of ...	*en nombre de ...*
for the nights of ...	*para las noches del ...*
credit card ...	*... de la tarjeta de crédito*
number	*número*
expiry date	*fecha de vencimiento*
Please confirm ...	*Puede confirmar ...?*
availability	*la disponibilidad*
price	*el precio*

I'd like a ... room.	*Quisiera una habitación ...*	kee·*sye*·ra *oo*·na a·bee·ta·*syon* ...
double	*doble*	*do*·ble
single	*sencilla*	sen·*see* ·ya
twin	*con dos camas*	kon dos *ka*·mas
How much is it per ...?	*¿Cuánto cuesta por ...?*	*kwan*·to *kwes*·ta por ...
night	*noche*	*no*·che
person	*persona*	per·*so*·na
week	*semana*	se·*ma*·na
full board	*pensión completa*	pen·*syon* kom·*ple*·ta
private/shared bathroom	*baño privado/ compartido*	*ba*·nyo pree·*va*·do/ kom·par·*tee*·do
cheaper	*más económico*	mas e·ko·*no*·mee·ko
discount	*descuento*	des·*kwen*·to
too expensive	*demasiado caro*	de·ma·*sya*·do *ka*·ro

Are there any rooms available?
¿Hay habitaciones libres? ay a·bee·ta·*syo*·nes *lee*·bres

Does it include breakfast?
¿Incluye el desayuno? een·*kloo*·ye el de·sa·*yoo*·no
May I see the room?
¿Puedo ver la habitación? *pwe*·do ver la a·bee·ta·*syon*
I don't like it.
No me gusta. no me *goos*·ta
It's fine. I'll take it.
Está bien. Lo tomo. es·*ta* byen lo *to*·mo
I'm leaving now.
Me voy ahora. me *voy* a·*o*·ra

CONVERSATION & ESSENTIALS

In their public behavior, Hondurans, like most Central Americans, are very conscious of civilities, sometimes to the point of ceremoniousness. Never approach a stranger for information without extending a greeting, and use only the polite form of address, especially with the police and public officials. Young people may be less likely to expect this, but it's best to stick to the polite form unless you're quite sure you won't offend by using the informal mode. The polite form is used in all cases in this guide; where options are given, the form is indicated by the abbreviations 'pol' and 'inf'.

Saying *por favor* (please) and *gracias* (thank you) are second nature to most Central Americans and are recommended tools for your travel kit. The three most common Spanish greetings are often shortened to simply *buenos* (for *buenos días*) and *buenas* (for *buenas tardes* and *buenas noches*).

Hello.	*Hola.*	*o*·la
Good morning.	*Buenos días.*	*bwe*·nos *dee*·as
Good afternoon.	*Buenas tardes.*	*bwe*·nas *tar*·des
Good evening/night.	*Buenas noches.*	*bwe*·nas *no*·ches
Goodbye.	*Adiós.*	a·*dyos* (rarely used)
Bye/See you soon.	*Hasta luego.*	*as*·ta *lwe*·go
Yes.	*Sí.*	see
No.	*No.*	no
Please.	*Por favor.*	por fa·*vor*
Thank you.	*Gracias.*	*gra*·syas
Many thanks.	*Muchas gracias.*	*moo*·chas *gra*·syas
You're welcome.	*De nada.*	de *na*·da
Pardon me.	*Perdón.*	per·*don*
Excuse me. (used when asking permission)	*Permiso.*	per·*mee*·so
Forgive me. (used when apologizing)	*Disculpe.*	dees·*kool*·pe

How are things?
¿Qué tal? ke tal
What's your name?
¿Cómo se llama? *ko*·mo se *ya*·ma (pol)
¿Cómo te llamas? *ko*·mo te *ya*·mas (inf)
My name is ...
Me llamo ... me *ya*·mo ...
It's a pleasure to meet you.
Mucho gusto. *moo*·cho *goos*·to
The pleasure is mine.
El gusto es mío. el *goos*·to es *mee*·o
Where are you from?
¿De dónde es/eres? de *don*·de es/*er*·es (pol/inf)
I'm from ...
Soy de ... soy de ...
Where are you staying?
¿Dónde está alojado? *don*·de es·*ta* a·lo·*kha*·do (pol)
¿Dónde estás alojado? *don*·de es·*tas* a·lo·*kha*·do (inf)
May I take a photo?
¿Puedo sacar una foto? *pwe*·do sa·*kar* *oo*·na *fo*·to

SIGNS

Entrada	Entrance
Salida	Exit
Información	Information
Abierto	Open
Cerrado	Closed
Prohibido	Prohibited
Policía (Turística)	(Tourist) Police Station
Servicios/Baños	Toilets
Hombres/Caballeros	Men
Mujeres/Damas	Women

DIRECTIONS

How do I get to ...?
¿Cómo puedo llegar a ...? *ko*·mo *pwe*·do ye·*gar* a ...
Is it far?
¿Está lejos? es·*ta* *le*·khos
Go straight ahead.
Siga/Vaya derecho. *see*·ga/*va*·ya de·*re*·cho
Turn left/right.
Doble a la izquierda/derecha. *do*·ble a la ees·*kyer*·da/de·*re*·cha
I'm lost.
Estoy perdido/a. es·*toy* per·*dee*·do/a
Can you show me (on the map)?
¿Me lo podría indicar (en el mapa)? me lo po·*dree*·a een·dee·*kar* (en el *ma*·pa)

north	*norte*	*nor*·te
south	*sur*	soor
east	*este/oriente*	*es*·te/o·*ryen*·te
west	*oeste/occidente*	o·*es*·te/ok·see·*den*·te

EMERGENCIES

Help!	*¡Socorro!*	so·*ko*·ro
Fire!	*¡Incendio!*	een·*sen*·dyo
I've been robbed.	*Me robaron.*	me ro·*ba*·ron
Go away!	*¡Déjeme!*	*de*·khe·me
Get lost!	*¡Váyase!*	*va*·ya·se

Call ...!	*¡Llame a ...!*	*ya*·me a ...
an ambulance	*una ambulancia*	*oo*·na am·boo·*lan*·sya
a doctor	*un médico*	oon *me*·dee·ko
the police	*la policía*	la po·lee·*see*·a

It's an emergency.
Es una emergencia. es *oo*·na e·mer·*khen*·sya
Could you help me, please?
¿Me puede ayudar, por favor? me *pwe*·de a·yoo·*dar* por fa·*vor*
I'm lost.
Estoy perdido/a. es·*toy* per·*dee*·do/a
Where are the toilets?
¿Dónde están los baños? *don*·de es·*tan* los *ba*·nyos

here	*aquí*	a·*kee*
there	*allí*	a·*yee*
avenue	*avenida*	a·ve·*nee*·da
block	*cuadra*	*kwa*·dra
street	*calle/paseo*	*ka*·ye/pa·*se*·o

HEALTH

I'm sick.
Estoy enfermo/a. es·*toy* en·*fer*·mo/a
I need a doctor.
Necesito un médico. ne·se·*see*·to oon *me*·dee·ko
Where's the hospital?
¿Dónde está el hospital? *don*·de es·*ta* el os·pee·*tal*
I'm pregnant.
Estoy embarazada. es·*toy* em·ba·ra·*sa*·da
It hurts here.
Me duele aquí. me *dwe*·le a·*kee*
I've been vaccinated.
Estoy vacunado/a. es·*toy* va·koo·*na*·do/a

I'm allergic to ...	*Soy alérgico/a ...*	soy a·*ler*·khee·ko/a ...
antibiotics	*a los antibióticos*	a los an·tee·*byo*·tee·kos
nuts	*a las nueces*	a las *nwe*·ses
peanuts	*a los maníes*	a los ma·*nee*·es
penicillin	*a la penicilina*	a la pe·nee·see·*lee*·na

I'm ...	*Soy ...*	soy ...
asthmatic	*asmático/a*	as·*ma*·tee·ko/a
diabetic	*diabético/a*	dya·*be*·tee·ko/a
epileptic	*epiléptico/a*	e·pee·*lep*·tee·ko/a

I have ...	*Tengo ...*	*ten*·go ...
a cough	*tos*	tos
diarrhea	*diarrea*	dya·*re*·a
a headache	*un dolor de cabeza*	oon do·*lor* de ka·*be*·sa
nausea	*náusea*	*now*·se·a

LANGUAGE DIFFICULTIES

Do you speak (English)?
¿Habla/Hablas (inglés)? *a*·bla/*a*·blas (een·*gles*) (pol/inf)
Does anyone here speak English?
¿Hay alguien que hable inglés? ay al·*gyen* ke *a*·ble een·*gles*
I (don't) understand.
Yo (no) entiendo. yo (no) en·*tyen*·do
How do you say ...?
¿Cómo se dice ...? *ko*·mo se *dee*·se ...
What does ... mean?
¿Qué quiere decir ...? ke *kye*·re de·*seer* ...

Could you please ...?	*¿Puede ..., por favor?*	*pwe*·de ... por *fa*·vor
repeat that	*repetirlo*	re·pe·*teer*·lo
speak more slowly	*hablar más despacio*	a·*blar* mas des·*pa*·syo
write it down	*escribirlo*	es·kree·*beer*·lo

NUMBERS

1	*uno*	*oo*·no
2	*dos*	dos
3	*tres*	tres
4	*cuatro*	*kwa*·tro
5	*cinco*	*seen*·ko
6	*seis*	says
7	*siete*	*sye*·te
8	*ocho*	*o*·cho
9	*nueve*	*nwe*·ve
10	*diez*	dyes
11	*once*	*on*·se
12	*doce*	*do*·se
13	*trece*	*tre*·se
14	*catorce*	ka·*tor*·se
15	*quince*	*keen*·se
16	*dieciséis*	dye·see·*says*
17	*diecisiete*	dye·see·*sye*·te
18	*dieciocho*	dye·see·*o*·cho
19	*diecinueve*	dye·see·*nwe*·ve
20	*veinte*	*vayn*·te
21	*veintiuno*	vayn·tee·*oo*·no
30	*treinta*	*trayn*·ta

31	*treinta y uno*	*trayn*·ta ee *oo*·no
40	*cuarenta*	kwa·*ren*·ta
50	*cincuenta*	seen·*kwen*·ta
60	*sesenta*	se·*sen*·ta
70	*setenta*	se·*ten*·ta
80	*ochenta*	o·*chen*·ta
90	*noventa*	no·*ven*·ta
100	*cien*	syen
101	*ciento uno*	syen·to *oo*·no
200	*doscientos*	do·*syen*·tos
1000	*mil*	meel
5000	*cinco mil*	*seen*·ko meel
10,000	*diez mil*	dyes meel
50,000	*cincuenta mil*	seen·*kwen*·ta meel

SHOPPING & SERVICES

I'd like to buy …
Quisiera comprar … kee·*sye*·ra kom·*prar* …
I'm just looking.
Sólo estoy mirando. *so*·lo es·*toy* mee·*ran*·do
May I look at it?
¿Puedo mirarlo/la? *pwe*·do mee·*rar*·lo/la
How much is it?
¿Cuánto cuesta? *kwan*·to *kwes*·ta
That's too expensive for me.
Es demasiado caro para mí. es de·ma·*sya*·do *ka*·ro *pa*·ra mee
Could you lower the price?
¿Podría bajar un poco el precio? po·*dree*·a ba·*khar* oon *po*·ko el *pre*·syo
I don't like it.
No me gusta. no me *goos*·ta
I'll take it.
Lo llevo. lo *ye*·vo

Do you accept …?	*¿Aceptan …?*	a·*sep*·tan …
American dollars	*dólares americanos*	*do*·la·res a·me·ree·*ka*·nos
credit cards	*tarjetas de crédito*	tar·*khe*·tas de *kre*·dee·to
traveler's checks	*cheques de viajero*	*che*·kes de vya·*khe*·ro

less	*menos*	*me*·nos
more	*más*	mas
large	*grande*	*gran*·de
small	*pequeño/a*	pe·*ke*·nyo/a

I'm looking for (the) …	*Estoy buscando …*	es·*toy* boos·*kan*·do …
ATM	*el cajero automático*	el ka·*khe*·ro ow·to·*ma*·tee·ko
bank	*el banco*	el *ban*·ko
bookstore	*la librería*	la lee·bre·*ree*·a
embassy	*la embajada*	la em·ba·*kha*·da
exchange house	*la casa de cambio*	la *ka*·sa de *kam*·byo
general store	*la tienda*	la *tyen*·da
laundry	*la lavandería*	la la·van·de·*ree*·a
market	*el mercado*	el mer·*ka*·do
pharmacy/chemist	*la farmacia/la droguería*	la far·*ma*·sya/la dro·ge·*ree*·a
post office	*el correo*	el ko·*re*·o
supermarket	*el supermercado*	el soo·per·mer·*ka*·do
tourist office	*la oficina de turismo*	la o·fee·*see*·na de too·*rees*·mo

What time does it open/close?
¿A qué hora abre/cierra? a ke *o*·ra *a*·bre/*sye*·ra
I want to change some money/traveler's checks.
Quiero cambiar dinero/cheques de viajero. *kye*·ro kam·*byar* dee·*ne*·ro/*che*·kes de vya·*khe*·ro
What is the exchange rate?
¿Cuál es el tipo de cambio? kwal es el *tee*·po de *kam*·byo
How many quetzals per dollar?
¿Cuántas lempiras por dólar? *kwan*·tas lem·*pee*·ras por *do*·lar
I want to call …
Quiero llamar a … *kye*·ro ya·*mar* a …

airmail	*correo aéreo*	ko·*re*·o a·e·re·o
letter	*carta*	*kar*·ta
registered mail	*certificado*	ser·tee·fee·*ka*·do
stamps	*estampillas*	es·tam·*pee*·yas

TIME & DATES

What time is it?	*¿Qué hora es?*	ke *o*·ra es
It's one o'clock.	*Es la una.*	es la *oo*·na
It's four o'clock.	*Son las cuatro.*	son las *kwa*·tro
half past two	*dos y media*	dos ee *me*·dya
midnight	*medianoche*	me·dya·*no*·che
noon	*mediodía*	me·dyo·*dee*·a

now	*ahora*	a·*o*·ra
today	*hoy*	oy
tonight	*esta noche*	*es*·ta *no*·che
tomorrow	*mañana*	ma·*nya*·na
yesterday	*ayer*	a·*yer*

Monday	*lunes*	*loo*·nes
Tuesday	*martes*	*mar*·tes
Wednesday	*miércoles*	*myer*·ko·les
Thursday	*jueves*	*khwe*·ves
Friday	*viernes*	*vyer*·nes
Saturday	*sábado*	*sa*·ba·do
Sunday	*domingo*	do·*meen*·go

January	*enero*	e·*ne*·ro
February	*febrero*	fe·*bre*·ro
March	*marzo*	*mar*·so
April	*abril*	a·*breel*
May	*mayo*	*ma*·yo
June	*junio*	*khoo*·nyo
July	*julio*	*khoo*·lyo
August	*agosto*	a·*gos*·to
September	*septiembre*	sep·*tyem*·bre
October	*octubre*	ok·*too*·bre
November	*noviembre*	no·*vyem*·bre
December	*diciembre*	dee·*syem*·bre

TRANSPORT

Public Transport

What time does ... leave/arrive?	*¿A qué hora ... sale/llega?*	a ke *o*·ra ... *sa*·le/*ye*·ga
the bus	*el autobús*	el ow·to·*boos*
the plane	*el avión*	el a·*vyon*
the ship	*el barco/buque*	el *bar*·ko/*boo*·ke

airport	*el aeropuerto*	el a·e·ro·*pwer*·to
bus station	*la estación de autobuses*	la es·ta·*syon* de ow·to·*boo*·ses
bus stop	*la parada de autobuses*	la pa·*ra*·da de ow·to·*boo*·ses
luggage check room	*guardería/ equipaje*	gwar·de·*ree*·a/ e·kee·*pa*·khe
ticket office	*la boletería*	la bo·le·te·*ree*·a

I'd like a ticket to ...
Quiero un boleto a ... — *kye*·ro oon bo·*le*·to a ...

What's the fare to ...?
¿Cuánto cuesta hasta ...? — kwan·to *kwes*·ta *as*·ta ...

student's	*de estudiante*	de es·too·*dyan*·te
1st class	*primera clase*	pree·*me*·ra *kla*·se
2nd class	*segunda clase*	se·*goon*·da *kla*·se
single/one-way	*ida*	*ee*·da
return/round trip	*ida y vuelta*	*ee*·da ee *vwel*·ta
taxi	*taxi*	*tak*·see

Private Transport

I'd like to hire a/an ...	*Quisiera alquilar ...*	kee·*sye*·ra al·kee·*lar* ...
bicycle	*una bicicleta*	*oo*·na bee·see·*kle*·ta
car	*un auto/ un coche*	oon *ow*·to/ oon *ko*·che
4WD	*un cuatro por cuatro*	oon *kwa*·tro por *kwa*·tro
motorbike	*una moto*	*oo*·na *mo*·to

ROAD SIGNS

Acceso	Entrance
Ceda el Paso	Give Way
Despacio	Slow
Dirección Única	One-Way
Estacionamiento	Parking
Mantenga Su Derecha	Keep to the Right
No Adelantar/ No Rebase	No Passing
No Estacionar	No Parking
Pare/Stop	Stop
Peaje	Toll
Peligro	Danger
Prohibido el Paso	No Entry
Salida de Autopista	Exit Freeway

pickup (truck)	*pickup*	*pee*·kop
truck	*camión*	ka·*myon*
to hitchhike	*pedir jalón*	pe·*deer* ja·*lon*

Is this the road to ...?
¿Se va a ... por esta carretera? — se va a ... por *es*·ta ka·re·*te*·ra

Where's a petrol station?
¿Dónde hay una gasolinera? — *don*·de ay *oo*·na *ga*·so·lee·*ne*·ra

Please fill it up.
Lleno, por favor. — *ye*·no por fa·*vor*

I'd like (10) gallons.
Quiero (diez) galones. — *kye*·ro (dyes) ga·*lo*·nes

diesel	*diésel*	*dye*·sel
gas (petrol)	*gasolina*	ga·so·*lee*·na

(How long) Can I park here?
¿(Por cuánto tiempo) Puedo estacionar aquí? — (por *kwan*·to *tyem*·po) *pwe*·do es·ta·syo·*nar* a·*kee*

Where do I pay?
¿Dónde se paga? — *don*·de se *pa*·ga

I need a mechanic.
Necesito un mecánico. — ne·se·*see*·to oon me·*ka*·nee·ko

The car has broken down (in ...).
El carro se ha averiado (en ...). — el *ka*·ro se a a·ve·*rya*·do (en ...)

The motorbike won't start.
No arranca la moto. — no a·*ran*·ka la *mo*·to

I have a flat tyre.
Tengo un pinchazo. — *ten*·go oon peen·*cha*·so

I've run out of petrol.
Me quedé sin gasolina. — me ke·*de* seen ga·so·*lee*·na

I've had an accident.
Tuve un accidente. — *too*·ve oon ak·see·*den*·te

HANDY MISKITU PHRASES

With more than 120,000 native speakers scattered along one of the Caribbean's most beautiful and untouched stretches of coastline, Miskitu isn't a bad language to know for the visitor to Honduras. Here are a few phrases to get you started.

Hello./Goodbye.	*Naksa./Aisabi.*
Yes./No.	*Ao./Apia.*
Please./Thank you.	*Pliskam./Tingki pali.*
How are you?	*Nakisma?*
good/fine	*pain*
bad/lousy	*saura*
friend	*pana*
Does anyone here speak Spanish?	*Upla nara ispail bila aisisa?*
How much is it?	*An mana atkisa?*
My name is (Jane).	*Yang nini (Jane).*
What's your name?	*Ninam dia?*
Could you tell me where a hotel is?	*Sip sma al wia hotel anira sapa?*
Excuse me, but could you help me?	*Ekskius al muns, ilp al muns, pliskam?*
I'm a vegetarian.	*Yang wina piras.*
I feel sick.	*Yan siknes sna.*
I'm allergic to mangos/peanuts.	*Pinda nani siknis al munisa mango/mani.*
Where is the bus station?	*Bus takaskaika, anira sa?*
What time does the bus/boat leave?	*Ani auwaska buska/butka swisa?*
How do I get to Bonanza?	*Nahka bonanzara waisna?*
Is it far/near?	*Wihka/naura sa!*
May I cross your property?	*Latam lua sip sna?*
Are there landmines?	*Tasba bombika bara sa?*
Where can I change dollars?	*Anira sip sna dalaska wlakaia?*
Can I smoke here?	*Sip sna puhbaia nara?*
Do you have a bathroom?	*Astabaika brisma?*

TRAVEL WITH CHILDREN

I need ...	*Necesito ...*	ne·se·*see*·to ...
Do you have ...?	*¿Hay ...?*	ay ...
a car baby seat	*un asiento de seguridad para bebés*	oon a·*syen*·to de se·goo·ree·*da* *pa*·ra be·*bes*
a child-minding service	*un servicio de cuidado de niños*	oon ser·*vee*·syo de kwee·*da*·do de *nee*·nyos
a children's menu	*una carta infantil*	*oo*·na *kar*·ta een·fan·*teel*
a creche	*una guardería*	*oo*·na gwar·de·*ree*·a
(disposable) diapers/nappies	*pañales (desechables)*	pa·*nya*·les (de·se·*cha*·bles)
an (English-speaking) babysitter	*una niñera (de habla inglesa)*	*oo*·na nee·*nye*·ra (de *a*·bla een·*gle*·sa)
formula (milk)	*fórmula infantil*	*for*·moo·la een·fan·*teel*
a highchair	*una silla para niños*	*oo*·na *see*·ya *pa*·ra *nee*·nyos
a potty	*una pelela*	*oo*·na pe·*le*·la
a stroller	*un cochecito*	oon ko·che·*see*·to

Do you mind if I breast-feed here?
¿Le molesta que dé el pecho aquí? — le mo·*les*·ta ke de el *pe*·cho a·*kee*

Are children allowed?
¿Se admiten niños? — se ad·*mee*·ten *nee*·nyos

GARÍFUNA

Until 1993 the Garífuna language had no standardized written form. The publication of the *People's Garífuna Dictionary* (National Garífuna Council of Belize) was part of an ongoing effort to preserve a language that has been slowly dying, as it is not generally taught in schools, and most Garinagu use Kriol or English as their first language.

It's not necessary to learn Garífuna – every Garífuna speaker will almost certainly have a better command of English than non-Garinagu will have of Garífuna – but we've included some handy phrases to use as ice-breakers or just to make a big impression on the locals.

The language itself is a mixture of Arawak, Yoruba, Swahili, Bantu, Spanish, English and French. For more information, look for the books *Garífuna History, Language and Culture of Belize, Central America and the Caribbean* (Cayetano, 1993) and the bilingual (English/Garífuna) *Marcella Our Legacy* (Lewis, 1994).

PRONUNCIATION

Consonants are pronounced as they are in English, and vowels are similar to those in Spanish (see Pronunciation on p281). Stress is usually placed on the first syllable of two-syllable words and the second syllable in longer words.

GREETINGS & CONVERSATION

Hello. *Mabuiga.*
Good morning. *Buiti binafi.*
Good afternoon. *Buiti amidi.*
Good evening. *Buiti raba weyu.*
Good night. *Buiti gunyon.*
How are you? *Ida biangi?*
I'm well. *Magadietina.*
How about you? *Angi buguya?*
Have a good day. *Buidi lamuga buweyuri.*
Thank you. *Seremein, nian bun.*
Thank you very much. *Owembu seremein na bun.*
What's your name? *Ka biri?*
My name is … *… niribei.*
Where do you come from? *Halia giendibu sa?*
I come from … *… giendina.*
I was born in America. *Meriga naguruwa.*
Where are you going? *Halion badibu?*
I'm going to … *Neibuga …*
I want to learn Garífuna. *Buseintina nafureinderu Garífuna.*
Teach me a little Garífuna. *Arufudahaba murusu Garífuna nu.*
What's this called in Garífuna? *Ka liri le lidan Garífuna.*
This is … in Garífuna. *… le lidan Garífuna.*
I don't understand. *Uwati gufaranda nanibu.*
Tell me again. *Arienga ya bei nu.*
Do you like it? *Hiseinti bun?*
I like it. *Hisienti nun.*
I don't like it. *Misienti.*
It's nice. *Semeti.*
It's not nice. *Mesemeti.*
It's good. *Buiti.*
It's bad. *Wuribati.*

Also available from Lonely Planet:
Latin American Spanish Phrasebook

Glossary

Here are some useful words you may come across during your time in Honduras. For definitions of some food and drink terms, see p49.

aguardiente – a clear, potent liquor made from sugarcane; also referred to as *caña*
alcaldía – city hall
alfombras – colorful, intricate carpets made of sawdust and seeds
artesanía – handicrafts
Av – abbreviation for *avenida* (avenue)

bahía – bay
barrio – district, neighborhood

cabaña – cabin or bungalow (also called cabina)
CAFTA-DR – Central America & Dominican Republic Free Trade Agreement
calle – street
calzada – causeway
campesino – peasant; farm laborer
carretera – highway
catedral – cathedral
catracho – slang for Honduran
cayo – cay; small island of sand or coral fragments
cayuco – a wood planked boat with an outboard motor
cerro – hill
ceviche – seafood marinated in lime juice, garlic and seasonings
champa – thatched, palm-leaf-roofed shelter with open sides; also called *palapa*
chicken bus – *ordinario* bus, stopping to pick up and drop off passengers
churrasco – Argentinean-style beef
cine – movie theater
ciudad – city
COHDEFOR – Honduran Corporation for Forest Development
colectivo – shared taxi, minibus or boat trip
colonia – a neighborhood within a city
comedor – a basic and cheap eatery, usually with a limited menu
Contras – counter-revolutionary military groups fighting against the Sandinista government in Nicaragua throughout the 1980s
costa – coast
criollo – Creole; born in Latin America of Spanish parentage; on the Caribbean coast it refers to someone of mixed African and European descent. See also mestizo and ladino.
cueva – cave

duppies – ghosts

edificio – building
entrada – entrance
expreso – express bus or express (private) boat

feria – a fair or festival
finca – farm, plantation, ranch

Garífuna – descendants of West African slaves and Carib Indians, brought to the Caribbean coast of Central America in the late 18th century from the island of St Vincent; also referred to as Black Caribs
golfo – gulf
gringo/a – mildly pejorative term used in Latin America to describe male/female foreigners, particularly those from the US; often applied to any visitor of European heritage
guancasco – an annual ceremony that confirms peace and friendship between neighboring communities
guifiti – A Garífuna drink of rum, herbs and spices.

hacienda – agricultural estate; plantation
hospedaje – guesthouse

iglesia – church
invierno – winter; the rainy season, which extends roughly from May through November
isla – island

jalón – to hitch a ride
junco – type of basket weaving

ladino – a person of mixed Indian and European parentage, often used to describe mestizos who speak Spanish; see also mestizo and *criollo*
lago – lake
laguna – lagoon or lake
lancha – boat, usually a small motorboat
lempira – Honduras' national currency
Lenca – indigenous group of southwestern Honduras.
licuado – fresh fruit drink, blended with milk or water

mar – sea
Maya-Chortí – Indigenous group living near the Guatemala border.
mercado – market
mestizo – person of mixed ancestry (usually Spanish and Indian); see also *criollo* and ladino
metate – flat stone on which corn is ground

migración – immigration; office of an immigration department
mirador – lookout point
Miskitu – indigenous group occupying coastal and inland areas in the state of Gracias a Dios and parts of Olancho; sometimes spelled Miskito
museo – museum

NAUI – National Association of Underwater Instructors
NGO – nongovernmental organization

ONG – Spanish for nongovernmental organization
ordinario – slow bus, stopping to pick up and drop off passengers; also known as chicken bus

PADI – Professional Association of Diving Instructors
palapa – thatched, palm-leaf-roofed shelter with open sides; also called *champa*
parque – park; also used to describe a plaza
parque central – the center of many cities and towns in Honduras
parque nacional – national park
Pech – a small indigenous group living along the interior rivers of La Moskitia.
pila – laundry station
pipante – flat-bottomed boat made from a single tree trunk
plato del día – plate (or meal) of the day
plato típico – a mixed plate of various foods typical for breakfast, lunch or dinner
playa – beach
pulpería – corner store, mini-mart
punta – point; traditional Garífuna dance involving much hip movement
pupusa – typical Honduran cornmeal stuffed with cheese or refried beans (or a mixture of both)

quetzal – Guatemala's national currency, named for the tropical bird

río – river

sacaguía – head guide
Semana Santa – Holy Week, the week preceding Easter
sendero – path or trail
sierra – mountain range; a saw
stela (s), **stelae** (p) – standing stone monument(s) of the ancient Maya, usually carved
supermercado – supermarket, from a corner store to a large, US-style supermarket

talavera – stylized ceramics or tiles, originating in Mexico
típica – basic Honduran fare
Tawahka – an indigenous group living mostly along the Río Patuca in La Moskitia.
Tolupanes – an indigenous group living in small villages in Yoro and Francisco Morazán; thought to be the oldest native community in Honduras.

verano – summer; Honduras' dry season, roughly from December to May

wanaragua – masked warrior dance of the Garífuna

Behind the Scenes

THIS BOOK

This 2nd edition of *Honduras & the Bay Islands* was researched and written by Greg Benchwick. Dr David Goldberg wrote the Health chapter. Special thanks go to Alejandra X Castañeda for reviewing the Language and Glossary chapters and the Eat Your Words boxed text; Kristin Landau for reviewing the history of the Copán archaeological site and the Rise & Fall of the Maya boxed text; and Mark Jamieson for reviewing the Miskitu Phrases boxed text. The 1st edition of *Honduras & the Bay Islands* was coordinated and written by Gary Chandler and Liza Prado. This guidebook was commissioned in Lonely Planet's Oakland office, and produced by the following:

Commissioning Editor Catherine Craddock-Carrillo
Coordinating Editor Dianne Schallmeiner
Coordinating Cartographer Ildiko Bogdanovits
Coordinating Layout Designer Kerrianne Southway
Managing Editors Sasha Baskett, Katie Lynch
Managing Cartographer Shahara Ahmed
Managing Layout Designers Sally Darmody
Assisting Editors Janice Bird, Jocelyn Harewood
Cover research Naomi Parker, lonelyplanetimages.com
Project Manager Craig Kilburn
Thanks to Amanda Jackson, Laura Crawford, Lisa Knights, Annelies Mertens, Emily K Wolman

THANKS

Greg Benchwick

As always, the biggest thanks of all goes to my wife, Alejandra. Your love and support make me a better man. My commissioning editor, Catherine Craddock, was amazing as always, as were the crack team of cartographers, editors and managers at Lonely Planet. Great job to all of you, and to Gary and Liza for blazing the way with the 1st edition.

A big shout out goes to the people that helped out along the way: Alberto for helping me explore a new trail in La Moskitia, Jenny Hepworth for filming me in Copán, Kristin Landau for her review of our Copán history, and of course, all the people who contributed their insiders' tips for our Ask a Local boxed texts.

Beyond that, I need to thank my friends and family. Mom and George, who supported me through years of struggling as a freelance writer; dad for continually challenging me; my sister and brother-in-law, who help me build fences and stay sane in an insane world; and of course my friends here in Denver – Squirrel, Heather, Julian, Cobin and Kori, Kessler, Liz, Brent, Goatie and Lara, Kris, the Hinds Boys, and the rest of the crew – your support and friendship mean so much to me.

THE LONELY PLANET STORY

Fresh from an epic journey across Europe, Asia and Australia in 1972, Tony and Maureen Wheeler sat at their kitchen table stapling together notes. The first Lonely Planet guidebook, *Across Asia on the Cheap,* was born.

Travelers snapped up the guides. Inspired by their success, the Wheelers began publishing books to Southeast Asia, India and beyond. Demand was prodigious, and the Wheelers expanded the business rapidly to keep up. Over the years, Lonely Planet extended its coverage to every country and into the virtual world via lonelyplanet.com and the Thorn Tree message board.

As Lonely Planet became a globally loved brand, Tony and Maureen received several offers for the company. But it wasn't until 2007 that they found a partner whom they trusted to remain true to the company's principles of travelling widely, treading lightly and giving sustainably. In October of that year, BBC Worldwide acquired a 75% share in the company, pledging to uphold Lonely Planet's commitment to independent travel, trustworthy advice and editorial independence.

Today, Lonely Planet has offices in Melbourne, London and Oakland, with over 500 staff members and 300 authors. Tony and Maureen are still actively involved with Lonely Planet. They're traveling more often than ever, and they're devoting their spare time to charitable projects. And the company is still driven by the philosophy of *Across Asia on the Cheap*: 'All you've got to do is decide to go and the hardest part is over. So go!'

CONTRIBUTING AUTHOR

David Goldberg MD wrote the Health chapter (p274). He completed his training in internal medicine and infectious diseases at Columbia-Presbyterian Medical Center in New York City, where he has also served as voluntary faculty. He is an infectious diseases specialist in Scarsdale, New York, and the editor-in-chief of the website MDTravelHealth.com.

OUR READERS

Many thanks to the travelers who used the last edition and wrote to us with helpful hints, useful advice and interesting anecdotes:

Rob Bell, Paul Boehlen, Richard Corbeil, Barbara Cordova, Richard Demeester, Greg Dupuy, Amy Escoto, Jodi Fertoli, Nicholas Harry, Sue Heydon, Sandra Leichtman, Diane Maes, Leon Megusar, Dennis Mogerman, Kat Monson, Nicole Notorangelo, Neil Orlando, Karlheinz Rieser, Howard Rosenzweig, Jackie S, Rebecca Sampson, Cynthia Seybolt, Jeroen Struik, Kate Suchomel, Cathy Tyndall, Shiri Yaniv

ACKNOWLEDGMENTS

Many thanks to the following for the use of their content:

Globe on title page ©Mountain High Maps 1993 Digital Wisdom, Inc.

SEND US YOUR FEEDBACK

We love to hear from travelers – your comments keep us on our toes and help make our books better. Our well-traveled team reads every word on what you loved or loathed about this book. Although we cannot reply individually to postal submissions, we always guarantee that your feedback goes straight to the appropriate authors, in time for the next edition. Each person who sends us information is thanked in the next edition and the most useful submissions are rewarded with a free book.

To send us your updates – and find out about Lonely Planet events, newsletters and travel news – visit our award-winning website: **lonelyplanet.com/contact**.

Note: we may edit, reproduce and incorporate your comments in Lonely Planet products such as guidebooks, websites and digital products, so let us know if you don't want your comments reproduced or your name acknowledged. For a copy of our privacy policy visit lonelyplanet.com/privacy.

Index

D

E

000 Map pages
000 Photograph pages

INDEX

000 Map pages
000 Photograph pages

GREENDEX

GOING GREEN

The following attractions, accommodations and restaurants have been selected by our Lonely Planet author because they demonstrate a commitment to sustainability. We've selected them for their support of local producers and sound environmental practices, and because they're involved in conservation or environmental education, or have been given an ecological award. We also highlight organizations and businesses that have demonstrated a proven commitment to bettering the life within their local communities. If you think we've omitted someone who should be listed, contact us at lonelyplanet.com/contact. For more information about sustainable tourism and Lonely Planet, see lonelyplanet.com/responsibletravel.

BAY ISLANDS

CENTRAL HONDURAS

LA MOSKITIA

NORTH COAST

TEGUCIGALPA & SOUTHERN HONDURAS

WESTERN HONDURAS